THE PROSE READER

Essays for Thinking, Reading, and Writing

SEVENTH EDITION

Kim Flachmann

Michael Flachmann

California State University
Bakersfield

PEARSON
Prentice
Hall

Upper Saddle River, New Jersey 07458

Library of Congress Cataloging-in-Publication Data

The prose reader : essays for thinking, reading, and writing / [compiled by] Kim Flachmann, Michael Flachmann.— 7th ed.

    p. cm.

    Includes index.

    ISBN 0-13-185016-4

    1. College readers. 2. English language—Rhetoric—Problems, exercises, etc. 3. Report writing—Problems, exercises, etc. I. Flachmann, Kim. II. Flachmann, Michael.

PE1417.P847 2005

808′.0427—dc22

2004000169

Senior Acquisitions Editor: Corey Good
Editor-in-Chief: Leah Jewell
Executive Marketing Manager: Brandy Dawson
Director of Marketing: Beth Mejia
Executive Managing Editor: Ann Marie McCarthy
Assistant Editor: Karen Schultz
Editorial Assistant: Steve Kyritz
Media Project Manager: Christy Schaack
Marketing Assistant: Allison Peck
Production Liaison: Fran Russello
Permissions Specialist: Mary Dalton-Hoffman
Manufacturing Buyer: Mary Ann Gloriande
Design Manager: Leslie Osher
Cover Design: Robert Farrar-Wagner
Cover Illustration/Photo: Klee, Paul (1879–1940) © ARS, NY. Florentine Villa District. 1926, Oil on board. Musee National d'Art Moderne, Centre Georges Pompidou, Paris, France © CNAC/MNAM/Dist. Reunion des Musees Nationaux/Art Resource, NY. Pixel Height 3352
Photo Researcher: Teri Stratford
Image Permission Coordinator: Charles Morris
Composition/Full-Service Project Management: Karen Berry/Pine Tree Composition
Printer/Binder: Courier Companies, Inc.
Cover Printer: The Lehigh Press, Inc.

For permission to use copyrighted material, grateful acknowledgment is made to the copyright holders on pages 678 to 681, which are hereby made part of this copyright page.

Pearson Education LTD., London
Pearson Education Singapore, Pte. Ltd
Pearson Education Canada, Ltd.
Pearson Education—Japan
Pearson Education Australia PTY, Limited

Pearson Education North Asia Ltd
Pearson Educación de Mexico, S.A. de C.V.
Pearson Education Malaysia, Pte. Ltd
Pearson Education, Upper Saddle River, New Jersey

10 9 8 7 6 5 4 3 2 1

Student ISBN: 0-13-1850164
AIE: 0-13-1850172

For Christopher and Laura,

who showed us how to teach

RHETORICAL TABLE OF CONTENTS

Thematic Table of Contents **xv**
Preface to the Instructor **xxiii**

INTRODUCTION: *Thinking, Reading, and Writing* **1**

Thinking Critically **3**
Reading Critically **5**
  Preparing to Read **5**
  Reading **9**
  Rereading **16**
  Reading Inventory **20**
Writing Critically **21**
  Preparing to Write **21**
  Writing **27**
  Rewriting **30**
  Writing Inventory **31**
Conclusion **35**

1 DESCRIPTION: *Exploring through the Senses* **36**

Defining Description **36**
Thinking Critically by Using Description **38**
Reading and Writing Descriptive Essays **40**
Student Essay: Description at Work **45**
Some Final Thoughts on Description **49**

RAY BRADBURY *Summer Rituals* **51**

The description of a simple, comforting ritual—the putting up of a front-porch swing in early summer—confirms the value of ceremony in the life of a small town.

KIMBERLY WOZENCRAFT *Notes from the Country Club* **58**

Have you ever wondered what being in prison is like? Kimberly Wozencraft takes us for a no-nonsense tour of the "correctional institution" in Kentucky that was her home for over a year.

JOHN McPHEE *The Pines* **72**

John McPhee's gift of richly detailed prose is captured in this compelling description of two very different natives of "The Pines," a wilderness area in the eastern United States.

MALCOLM COWLEY   *The View from 80*   **81**

In this humorous, touching, and ultimately optimistic essay, the author introduces us to the unfamiliar "country" of old age.

BERNARD COOPER   *Labyrinthine*   **94**

Bernard Cooper's brilliant analysis of his childhood obsession with mazes reminds us of how easily we all become "lost in the folds and bones" of our advancing years.

CHAPTER WRITING ASSIGNMENTS   **101**

---

2 NARRATION: *Telling a Story*   **102**

Defining Narration   **102**
Thinking Critically by Using Narration   **104**
Reading and Writing Narrative Essays   **105**
Student Essay: Narration at Work   **109**
Some Final Thoughts on Narration   **115**

LEWIS SAWAQUAT   *For My Indian Daughter*   **117**

A Native American responds to prejudice by searching for ethnic and cultural pride.

MAYA ANGELOU   *New Directions*   **124**

Deserted by her husband, a proud and determined Annie Johnson decides to "step off the road and cut . . . a new path" for herself.

RUSSELL BAKER   *The Saturday Evening Post*   **130**

In this autobiographical essay, Pulitzer Prize–winning author Russell Baker offers an unflinching look at his childhood days in the small town of Morrisonville, Virginia.

SANDRA CISNEROS   *Only daughter*   **141**

The only daughter in a large family, Sandra Cisneros feels overwhelming pride when her father praises her skill as a writer.

GARRISON KEILLOR   *How the Crab Apple Grew*   **148**

Humorist Garrison Keillor mixes a delightful literary stew out of marriage, mushrooms, a Piper Cub airplane, and an English assignment.

CHAPTER WRITING ASSIGNMENTS   **157**

---

3 EXAMPLE: *Illustrating Ideas*   **158**

Defining Examples   **158**
Thinking Critically by Using Example   **160**
Reading and Writing Essays That Use Examples   **162**

Student Essay: Examples at Work   **165**
Some Final Thoughts on Examples   **169**

BILL COSBY   *The Baffling Question*   171

Why do people have children? Comedian Bill Cosby presents several hilarious and ironic reasons in this truthful look at the effects kids have on our lives.

WILLIAM LEAST HEAT-MOON   *Red, White and Blue Highways*   177

In this perceptive meditation on "America's roads," William Least Heat-Moon explains how our nation's highways unite us all geographically and spiritually.

HAROLD KRENTS   *Darkness at Noon*   **184**

How should we treat the handicapped? Blind author Harold Krents gives us a few lessons in judging people on their abilities rather than their disabilities.

AMY TAN   *Mother Tongue*   **190**

In this provocative and intriguing essay, author Amy Tan examines the relationship between her mother's "fractured" English and her own talent as a writer.

BRENT STAPLES   *A Brother's Murder*   **200**

Brent Staples's horrifying description of his brother's inner city killing lays bare the decay of urban America and its effect on the young African-America men who are imprisoned there.

CHAPTER WRITING ASSIGNMENTS   **207**

4 PROCESS ANALYSIS: *Explaining Step by Step*   **208**
Defining Process Analysis   **208**
Thinking Critically by Using Process Analysis   **210**
Reading and Writing Process Analysis Essays   **212**
Student Essay: Process Analysis at Work   **216**
Some Final Thoughts on Process Analysis   **219**

EDWIN BLISS   *Managing Your Time*   **221**

Feeling frantic and disorganized? Time-management expert Edwin Bliss reveals secrets of organization that will make your life much easier.

JESSICA MITFORD   *Behind the Formaldehyde Curtain*   **229**

In this chilling and macabre essay, celebrated "muckraker" Jessica Mitford exposes the greed and hypocrisy of the American mortuary business.

JAY WEINER   *Sports Centered*   **241**

Had your fill of over-paid, pampered, prima donna professional athletes? Jay Weiner has just the solution in this impassioned plea to save sports from the greed of corporate America.

LINDA FORMICHELLI   *Engage in Word Play*   **248**

Do your participles dangle? Does your syntax sag? Is your rhetoric stuck in a rut? Check out Linda Formichelli's helpful suggestions for giving your prose some pizzazz.

JULIA BOURLAND   *Getting Out of Debt*
(and Staying Out)   **255**

Credit card bills getting you down? Author Julia Bourland suggests eight easy ways to pay off your balance and stay out of debt.

CHAPTER WRITING ASSIGNMENTS   **264**

---

5 DIVISION/CLASSIFICATION:
Finding Categories   **265**

Defining Division/Classification   **265**
Thinking Critically by Using Division/Classification   **267**
Reading and Writing Division/Classification Essays   **269**
Student Essay: Division/Classification at Work   **272**
Some Final Thoughts on Division/Classification   **275**

PHYLLIS SCHNEIDER   *Memory: Tips You'll Never*
Forget   **277**

Ever forget where you parked your car? Phyllis Schneider suggests how to perk up your aging memory.

K.C. COLE   *Calculated Risks*   **283**

Do you like to gamble? Have you ever put all your money on one spin of the roulette wheel? Or are you the type of person who prefers to play it safe? K. C. Cole examines the types of risks most of us are comfortable with and comes up with some very interesting conclusions.

JUDITH WALLERSTEIN AND SANDRA BLAKESLEE
Second Chances for Children of Divorce   **295**

Children of divorce often have a difficult time coping with their parents' separation, but they can return to a happy, well-adjusted life if they accomplish a series of important "tasks" identified in this fascinating essay.

FRANKLIN ZIMRING   *Confessions of an Ex-Smoker*   **305**

Are you a reformed smoker? Do you know someone who is? Franklin Zimring offers a witty classification of people who've kicked the habit.

JUDITH VIORST   *The Truth About Lying*   **312**

Do you always tell the truth? Judith Viorst classifies and evaluates several types of lies that are a part of our morally complex world.

CHAPTER WRITING ASSIGNMENTS   **321**

---

6 COMPARISON/CONTRAST: *Discovering Similarities and Differences*   **322**

Defining Comparison/Contrast   **323**
Thinking Critically by Using Comparison/Contrast   **324**
Reading and Writing Comparison/Contrast Essays   **325**
Student Essay: Comparison/Contrast at Work   **332**
Some Final Thoughts on Comparison/Contrast   **336**

BRUCE CATTON   *Grant and Lee: A Study in Contrasts*   **338**

Historian Bruce Catton vividly compares the backgrounds, personalities, and fighting qualities of two fascinating Civil War generals.

JIMMY SANTIAGO BACA   *Past Present*   **345**

When the author, formerly an inmate at San Quentin, returns to the prison as a free man to help film a movie he has written, the experience reawakens all the rage he felt while incarcerated and reminds him of the sweetness of freedom and the brutality of prison life.

WILLIAM OUCHI   *Japanese and American Workers: Two Casts of Mind*   **357**

The phrase "Made in Japan" will take on new meaning after you read this essay on "collective responsibility" in the Land of the Rising Sun.

GLORIA STEINEM   *The Politics of Muscle*   **367**

Feminist Gloria Steinem examines the muscle-bound world of women's bodybuilding and discovers that strength means sexual power.

SUCHENG CHAN   *You're Short, Besides!*   **376**

Blessed with an indomitable spirit, Sucheng Chan discusses the challenges, benefits, and cultural contrasts of being "non-white, female, handicapped . . . and short, besides."

CHAPTER WRITING ASSIGNMENTS   **388**

7 DEFINITION: *Limiting the Frame of Reference* 389

Defining Definition   389
Thinking Critically by Using Definition   390
Reading and Writing Definition Essays   392
Student Essay: Definition at Work   395
Some Final Thoughts on Definition   399

ERMA BOMBECK   *Grandma*   401

What's the difference between a mother and a grandmother? Light years, claims columnist Erma Bombeck! Grandmothers can "shed the yoke of responsibility, relax, and enjoy their grandchildren in a way that was not possible when they were raising their own children."

ROBERT RAMIREZ   *The Barrio*   409

Robert Ramirez lovingly describes the "feeling of family" in a typical inner-city barrio.

MARY PIPHER   *Beliefs About Families*   417

What is a "family"? Psychologist Mary Pipher attempts to answer this intriguing question by evaluating the effect that different categories of family members have on our ability to function in society as a whole.

WANG PING   *Ways to* Ai   426

In "Ways to *Ai*," author Wang Ping dissects the many different and often contradictory meanings of the word "love" in her native Chinese language, all of which converge at the human heart.

ELLEN GOODMAN   *A Working Community*   433

Been back to visit your old "neighborhood" lately? Pulitzer Prize–winning columnist Ellen Goodman gives new meaning to the term in her essay on the "communities" we all belong to.

CHAPTER WRITING ASSIGNMENTS   439

8 CAUSE/EFFECT: *Tracing Reasons and Results* 440

Defining Cause/Effect   441
Thinking Critically by Using Cause/Effect   444
Reading and Writing Cause/Effect Essays   445
Student Essay: Cause/Effect at Work   448
Some Final Thoughts on Cause/Effect   453

STEPHEN KING   *Why We Crave Horror Movies*   **455**

Seen any good horror movies lately? Best-selling author Stephen King explains why we are so fascinated by films that appeal to our darker instincts.

MICHAEL DORRIS   *The Broken Cord*   **462**

An angry and frustrated Michael Dorris describes the long-term damage done to his adopted son, Adam, by the ravages of fetal alcohol syndrome.

RICHARD RODRIGUEZ   *The Fear of Losing a Culture*   **470**

How can Hispanics "belong to America without betraying their past"? Richard Rodriguez offers some helpful insights on a complex cultural topic.

MARY ROACH   *Meet the Bickersons*   **477**

"Waddya Mean I never do the dishes?!" Mary Roach presents a light-hearted, but sensible view of arguing fairly within a relationship.

ALICE WALKER   *Beauty: When the Other Dancer Is the Self*   **483**

Looking back on an accident suffered many years ago, Alice Walker analyzes the connection between physical beauty and her own self-image.

CHAPTER WRITING ASSIGNMENTS   **495**

---

9 ARGUMENT AND PERSUASION: *Inciting People to Thought or Action*   **496**

Defining Argument and Persuasion   **497**
Thinking Critically by Using Argument and Persuasion   **499**
Reading and Writing Persuasive Essays   **501**
Student Essay: Argument and Persuasion at Work   **506**
Some Final Thoughts on Argument and Persuasion   **510**

bell hooks   *Justice: Childhood Love Lessons*   **512**

Do you believe children should be spanked when they misbehave? Author bell hooks examines the interrelated issues of love, discipline, and maturity in this interesting essay on "Childhood Love Lessons."

ROBERT HEILBRONER   *Don't Let Stereotypes Warp Your Judgment*   **524**

Whom would you rather date: Gloria or Bertha? Richard or Cuthbert? What specific images do these names conjure up in your mind? Robert Heilbroner invites us to avoid stereotypical thinking when we encounter the world around us—unless we are content with becoming a "stereo-type" ourselves!

DAVE GROSSMAN   *We Are Training Our Kids to Kill*   **531**

Retired Col. Dave Grossman questions the role models we are creating for our kids through the violence on TV. In this essay, he challenges us to regain control of child abuse, racism, and poverty in American society.

Opposing Viewpoints: *Media Coverage*   **544**

DAVID SHAW   *Embedded Reporters Make for Good Journalism*   **546**

JUSTIN EWERS   *Is the New News Good News?*   **550**

Should our armed forces overseas permit print and television journalists to be "embedded" in military units engaged in combat? David Shaw and Justin Ewers square off on this controversial and timely issue that illustrates our insatiable appetite for news.

Opposing Viewpoints: *Immigration*   **556**

MICHAEL SCOTT   *America Must Take Stronger Measures to Halt Illegal Immigration*   **558**

RICHARD RAYNOR   *Illegal Immigration Does Not Threaten America*   **564**

Is the United States "under year-round siege by hordes of illegal aliens," as Michael Scott claims, or is Richard Raynor correct when he argues that "America is an immigrant nation" that needs drive, generosity, and energy of people from other countries.

CHAPTER WRITING ASSIGNMENTS   **574**

---

10 DOCUMENTED ESSAYS: *Reading and Writing from Sources*   **575**

Defining Documented Essays   **575**
Reading and Writing Documented Essays   **577**
Student Essay: Documentation at Work   **584**
Some Final Thoughts on Documented Essays   **591**

BARBARA EHRENREICH   *The Ecstasy of War*   **593**

Do men and women possess a natural "warrior instinct" that enables them to kill their enemies during battle? Not so, claims Barbara

Ehrenreich, though many social and cultural rituals help transform ordinary people into effective soldiers.

JILL LESLIE ROSENBAUM AND MEDA CHESNEY-
LIND   *Appearance and Delinquency: A Research Note*   **603**

Criminologists Rosenbaum and Chesney-Lind offer some fascinating evidence about the relationship between the attractiveness of female offenders and the severity of their punishment.

CHAPTER WRITING ASSIGNMENTS   **617**

11 FURTHER THINKING, READING, AND WRITING   618

Essays

ROGER ROSENBLATT   *"I Am Writing Blindly"*   **620**

What is the basic, primal urge that drives us to communicate with each other? In this brief yet brilliant essay, Roger Rosenblatt examines the reasons why we write "blindly" to the world around us.

RITA MAE BROWN   *Writing as a Moral Act*   **622**

Novelist Rita Mae Brown argues persuasively that good writers should always tell the truth. "If you aren't reading books that challenge you, you're reading the wrong books," she claims.

Fiction

RICHARD WRIGHT   *The Library Card*   **629**

Set in the segregationist South, Wright's short story illustrates the triumph of one brave man's lust for learning over a society that seeks to keep him "in his place."

JESS ROW   *The Secrets of Bats*   **638**

In this enchanting narrative, an American instructor in a Hong Kong school learns the secrets of inter-cultural communication from one of his students.

Poetry

BILLY COLLINS   *Books*   **653**

"A choir of authors murmuring inside their books" calls to the author of this poem, inviting him to read about the universe around him.

ROBERT FRANCIS   *Catch* and *Glass*   **655**

These two poems depict poetry as a "ball" being thrown between two boys and as a "glass" through which life is seen most clearly.

Drama

NEENA BEBER   *Misreadings*   **657**

In this brief dramatic vignette about a teacher and her reluctant student, Neena Beber lays bare the distinctions between two entirely different world views of thinking, reading, and writing.

CHAPTER WRITING ASSIGNMENTS   **664**

Glossary of Useful Terms   **665**
Credits   **678**
Index of Authors and Titles   **682**

THEMATIC
TABLE OF CONTENTS

AFRICAN-AMERICAN STUDIES
Maya Angelou, *New Directions*   **124**
Brent Staples, *A Brother's Murder*   **200**
Alice Walker, *Beauty: When the Other Dancer Is the Self*   **483**
bell hooks, *Justice: Childhood Love Lessons*   **512**
Jill Leslie Rosenbaum and Meda Chesney-Lind, *Appearance
  and Delinquency: A Research Note*   **603**
Richard Wright, *The Library Card*   **629**

AGING
Malcolm Cowley, *The View from 80*   **81**
Bernard Cooper, *Labyrinthine*   **94**
Lewis Sawaquat, *For My Indian Daughter*   **117**
Sandra Cisneros, *Only daughter*   **141**
Jessica Mitford, *Behind the Formaldehyde Curtain*   **229**
Phyllis Schneider, *Memory: Tips You'll Never Forget*   **277**
Erma Bombeck, *Grandma*   **401**
Mary Pipher, *Beliefs About Families*   **417**

ART AND MEDIA
Bernard Cooper, *Labyrinthine*   **94**
Russell Baker, *The Saturday Evening Post*   **130**
Jay Weiner, *Sports Centered*   **241**
Stephen King, *Why We Crave Horror Movies*   **455**
Robert Heilbroner, *Don't Let Stereotypes Warp Your
  Judgment*   **524**
Dave Grossman, *We Are Training Our Kids to Kill*   **531**
David Shaw, *Media Coverage: Embedded Reporters Make for Good
  Journalism*   **546**
Justin Ewers, *Is the New News Good News?*   **550**

AUTOBIOGRAPHY
Ray Bradbury, *Summer Rituals*   **51**
Kimberly Wozencraft, *Notes from the Country Club*   **58**

John McPhee, *The Pines*   **72**
Malcolm Cowley, *The View from 80*   **81**
Bernard Cooper, *Labyrinthine*   **94**
Lewis Sawaquat, *For My Indian Daughter*   **117**
Maya Angelou, *New Directions*   **124**
Russell Baker, *The Saturday Evening Post*   **130**
Sandra Cisneros, *Only daughter*   **141**
Amy Tan, *Mother Tongue*   **190**
Brent Staples, *A Brother's Murder*   **200**
Jimmy Santiago Baca, *Past Present*   **345**
Sucheng Chan, *You're Short, Besides!*   **376**
Michael Dorris, *The Broken Cord*   **462**
Richard Rodriguez, *The Fear of Losing a Culture*   **470**
Alice Walker, *Beauty: When the Other Dancer Is the Self*   **483**

BEHAVIORAL SCIENCE

Kimberly Wozencraft, *Notes from the Country Club*   **58**
John McPhee, *The Pines*   **72**
Bill Cosby, *The Baffling Question*   **171**
Harold Krents, *Darkness at Noon*   **184**
Brent Staples, *A Brother's Murder*   **200**
Phyllis Schneider, *Memory: Tips You'll Never Forget*   **277**
K. C. Cole, *Calculated Risks*   **283**
Judith Wallerstein and Sandra Blakeslee, *Second Chances
    for Children of Divorce*   **295**
Franklin Zimring, *Confessions of an Ex-Smoker*   **305**
Judith Viorst, *The Truth About Lying*   **312**
Gloria Steinem, *The Politics of Muscle*   **367**
Sucheng Chan, *You're Short, Besides!*   **376**
Mary Pipher, *Beliefs About Families*   **417**
Ellen Goodman, *A Working Community*   **433**
Stephen King, *Why We Crave Horror Movies*   **455**
Michael Dorris, *The Broken Cord*   **462**
Richard Rodriguez, *The Fear of Losing a Culture*   **470**
Mary Roach, *Meet the Bickersons*   **477**
bell hooks, *Justice: Childhood Love Lessons*   **512**
Robert Heilbroner, *Don't Let Stereotypes Warp
    Your Judgment*   **524**
Dave Grossman, *We Are Training Our Kids to Kill*   **531**

Barbara Ehrenreich, *The Ecstasy of War*   **593**
Jill Leslie Rosenbaum and Meda Chesney-Lind, *Appearance and Delinquency: A Research Note*   **603**
Roger Rosenblatt, *"I Am Writing Blindly"*   **620**

BUSINESS
Maya Angelou, *New Directions*   **124**
Russell Baker, *The Saturday Evening Post*   **130**
Harold Krents, *Darkness at Noon*   **184**
Edwin Bliss, *Managing Your Time*   **221**
Jay Weiner, *Sports Centered*   **241**
Julia Bourland, *Getting Out of Debt (and Staying Out)*   **255**
K. C. Cole, *Calculated Risks*   **283**
William Ouchi, *Japanese and American Workers: Two Casts of Mind*   **357**
Ellen Goodman, *A Working Community*   **433**

CHICANO AND LATIN AMERICAN STUDIES
Sandra Cisneros, *Only daughter*   **141**
Jimmy Santiago Baca, *Past Present*   **345**
Robert Ramirez, *The Barrio*   **409**
Richard Rodriguez, *The Fear of Losing a Culture*   **470**
Michael Scott, *America Must Take Stronger Measures to Halt Illegal Immigration*   **558**
Richard Raynor, *Illegal Immigration Does Not Threaten America*   **564**

ECONOMICS
Edwin Bliss, *Managing Your Time*   **221**
Jay Weiner, *Sports Centered*   **241**
Julia Bourland, *Getting Out of Debt (and Staying Out)*   **255**
William Ouchi, *Japanese and American Workers: Two Casts of Mind*   **357**

EDUCATION
Garrison Keillor, *How the Crab Apple Grew*   **148**
Phyllis Schneider, *Memory: Tips You'll Never Forget*   **277**
Jimmy Santiago Baca, *Past Present*   **345**
Sucheng Chan, *You're Short, Besides!*   **376**

Dave Grossman, *We Are Training Our Kids to Kill*   **531**
Barbara Ehrenreich, *The Ecstasy of War*   **593**
Jill Leslie Rosenbaum and Meda Chesney-Lind, *Appearance and Delinquency: A Research Note*   **603**
Richard Wright, *The Library Card*   **629**
Neena Beber, *Misreadings*   **657**

HISTORY
Lewis Sawaquat, *For My Indian Daughter*   **117**
Russell Baker, *The Saturday Evening Post*   **130**
William Least Heat-Moon, *Red, White and Blue Highways*   **177**
Bruce Catton, *Grant and Lee: A Study in Contrasts*   **338**
William Ouchi, *Japanese and American Workers: Two Casts of Mind*   **357**
Barbara Ehrenreich, *The Ecstasy of War*   **593**
Roger Rosenblatt, *"I Am Writing Blindly"*   **620**
Richard Wright, *The Library Card*   **629**

LANGUAGE
Sandra Cisneros, *Only daughter*   **141**
Amy Tan, *Mother Tongue*   **190**
Linda Formichelli, *Engage in Word Play*   **248**
Judith Viorst, *The Truth About Lying*   **312**
Wang Ping, *Ways to Ai*   **426**
Robert Heilbroner, *Don't Let Stereotypes Warp Your Judgment*   **524**
Barbara Ehrenreich, *The Ecstasy of War*   **593**
Roger Rosenblatt, *"I Am Writing Blindly"*   **620**
Rita Mae Brown, *Writing as a Moral Act*   **622**

OTHER ETHNIC STUDIES
Lewis Sawaquat, *For My Indian Daughter*   **117**
William Least Heat-Moon, *Red, White and Blue Highways*   **177**
Amy Tan, *Mother Tongue*   **190**
William Ouchi, *Japanese and American Workers: Two Casts of Mind*   **357**

Sucheng Chan, *You're Short, Besides!* **376**
Wang Ping, *Ways to Ai* **426**
Jill Leslie Rosenbaum and Meda Chesney-Lind, *Appearance and Delinquency: A Research Note* **603**

PHILOSOPHY AND RELIGIOUS STUDIES
K. C. Cole, *Calculated Risks* **283**
Sucheng Chan, *You're Short, Besides!* **376**
Mary Pipher, *Beliefs About Families* **417**
Wang Ping, *Ways to Ai* **426**
Barbara Ehrenreich, *The Ecstasy of War* **593**
Rita Mae Brown, *Writing as a Moral Act* **622**

PHYSICAL EDUCATION
Jay Weiner, *Sports Centered* **241**
Phyllis Schneider, *Memory: Tips You'll Never Forget* **277**
Gloria Steinem, *The Politics of Muscle* **367**
Michael Dorris, *The Broken Cord* **462**
Dave Grossman, *We Are Training Our Kids to Kill* **531**
Barbara Ehrenreich, *The Ecstasy of War* **593**

POLITICAL SCIENCE
Bruce Catton, *Grant and Lee: A Study in Contrasts* **338**
Gloria Steinem, *The Politics of Muscle* **367**
Ellen Goodman, *A Working Community* **433**
Dave Grossman, *We Are Training Our Kids to Kill* **531**
Michael Scott, *America Must Take Stronger Measures to Halt Illegal Immigration* **558**
Richard Raynor, *Illegal Immigration Does Not Threaten America* **564**
Barbara Ehrenreich, *The Ecstasy of War* **593**
Jill Leslie Rosenbaum and Meda Chesney-Lind, *Appearance and Delinquency: A Research Note* **603**

PSYCHOLOGY
Maya Angelou, *New Directions* **124**
Harold Krents, *Darkness at Noon* **184**
Brent Staples, *A Brother's Murder* **200**
K. C. Cole, *Calculated Risks* **283**

Judith Wallerstein and Sandra Blakeslee, *Second Chances for Children of Divorce* **295**
Judith Viorst, *The Truth About Lying* **312**
Gloria Steinem, *The Politics of Muscle* **367**
Mary Pipher, *Beliefs About Families* **417**
Ellen Goodman, *A Working Community* **433**
Mary Roach, *Meet the Bickersons* **477**
Robert Heilbroner, *Don't Let Stereotypes Warp Your Judgment* **524**
Barbara Ehrenreich, *The Ecstasy of War* **593**
Roger Rosenblatt, *"I Am Writing Blindly"* **620**
Neena Beber, *Misreadings* **657**

READING
Russell Baker, *The Saturday Evening Post* **130**
Sandra Cisneros, *Only daughter* **141**
Linda Formichelli, *Engage in Word Play* **248**
Jimmy Santiago Baca, *Past Present* **345**
Sucheng Chan, *You're Short, Besides!* **376**
Wang Ping, *Ways to Ai* **426**
Roger Rosenblat, *"I Am Writing Blindly"* **620**
Rita Mae Brown, *Writing as a Moral Act* **622**
Richard Wright, *The Library Card* **629**

SCIENCE
Jessica Mitford, *Behind the Formaldehyde Curtain* **229**
Phyllis Schneider, *Memory: Tips You'll Never Forget* **277**
Michael Dorris, *The Broken Cord* **462**

SOCIOLOGY
Kimberly Wozencraft, *Notes from the Country Club* **58**
Malcolm Cowley, *The View from 80* **81**
Lewis Sawaquat, *For My Indian Daughter* **117**
Maya Angelou, *New Directions* **124**
Amy Tan, *Mother Tongue* **190**
Brent Staples, *A Brother's Murder* **200**
Jessica Mitford, *Behind the Formaldehyde Curtain* **229**
Judith Wallerstein and Sandra Blakeslee, *Second Chances for Children of Divorce* **295**

William Ouchi, *Japanese and American Workers: Two Casts of Mind*   **357**
Robert Ramirez, *The Barrio*   **409**
Mary Pipher, *Beliefs About Families*   **417**
Ellen Goodman, *A Working Community*   **433**
Richard Rodriguez, *The Fear of Losing a Culture*   **470**
Mary Roach, *Meet the Bickersons*   **477**
Dave Grossman, *We Are Training Our Kids to Kill*   **531**
Barbara Ehrenreich, *The Ecstasy of War*   **593**
Jill Leslie Rosenbaum and Meda Chesney-Lind, *Appearance and Delinquency: A Research Note*   **603**

WOMEN'S STUDIES
Maya Angelou, *New Directions*   **124**
Sandra Cisneros, *Only daughter*   **141**
Amy Tan, *Mother Tongue*   **190**
Judith Wallerstein and Sandra Blakeslee, *Second Chances for Children of Divorce*   **295**
William Ouchi, *Japanese and American Workers: Two Casts of Mind*   **357**
Gloria Steinem, *The Politics of Muscle*   **367**
Sucheng Chan, *You're Short, Besides!*   **376**
Erma Bombeck, *Grandma*   **401**
Mary Pipher, *Beliefs About Families*   **417**
Wang Ping, *Ways to Ai*   **426**
Alice Walker, *Beauty: When the Other Dancer Is the Self*   **483**
bell hooks, *Justice: Childhood Love Lessons*   **512**
Jill Leslie Rosenbaum and Meda Chesney-Lind, *Appearance and Delinquency: A Research Note*   **603**

WRITING
Sandra Cisneros, *Only daughter*   **141**
Garrison Keillor, *How the Crab Apple Grew*   **148**
Amy Tan, *Mother Tongue*   **190**
Linda Formichelli, *Engage in Word Play*   **248**
Jimmy Santiago Baca, *Past Present*   **345**
Wang Ping, *Ways to Ai*   **426**
David Shaw, *Media Coverage: Embedded Reporters Make for Good Journalism*   **546**

Justin Ewers, *Is the New News Good News?*   **550**
Roger Rosenblatt, *"I Am Writing Blindly"*   **620**
Rita Mae Brown, *Writing as a Moral Act*   **622**
Richard Wright, *The Library Card*   **629**

PREFACE TO THE INSTRUCTOR

The Prose Reader is based on the assumption that lucid writing follows lucid thinking, whereas poor written work is almost inevitably the product of foggy, irrational thought processes. As a result, our primary purpose in this book, as in the first six editions, is to help students *think* more clearly and logically—both in their minds and on paper.

Furthermore, we believe that college students should be able to think, read, and write on three increasingly difficult levels:

1. *Literal—characterized by a basic understanding of words and their meanings;*
2. *Interpretive—consisting of a knowledge of linear connections between ideas and an ability to make valid inferences based on those ideas; and*
3. *Critical—the highest level, distinguished by the systematic investigation of complex ideas and by the analysis of their relationship to the world around us.*

To demonstrate the vital interrelationship between reader and writer, our text provides students with prose models intended to inspire their own thinking and writing. Although studying rhetorical strategies is certainly not the only way to approach writing, it is a productive means of helping students become better writers. These essays are intended to encourage your students to improve their writing through a partnership with some of the best examples of professional prose available today. Just as musicians and athletes richly benefit from studying the techniques of the foremost people in their fields, your students will grow in spirit and language use from their collaborative work with the excellent writers in this collection.

HOW THE TEXT WORKS

Each chapter of *The Prose Reader* begins with an explanation of a single rhetorical technique. These explanations are divided into six sections that progress from the effect of this technique on our daily lives to its integral role in the writing process. Also in each introduction, we include a student paragraph and a student essay featuring each particular rhetorical strategy under discussion. The essay is highlighted by annotations and underlining to illustrate how to write that type of essay and to help bridge the gap between student writing and the professional selections that follow. After each essay, the student writer has drafted a personal note with some useful advice for other student writers.

The essays that follow each chapter introduction are selected from a wide variety of well-known contemporary authors. Needless to say, "pure" rhetorical types rarely exist, and when they do, the result often seems artificial. Therefore, although each essay in this collection focuses on a single rhetorical mode as its primary strategy, other strategies are always simultaneously at work. These selections concentrate on one primary technique at a time in much the same way a well-arranged photograph highlights a certain visual detail, though many other elements function in the background to make the picture an organic whole.

Before each reading selection, we offer some material to focus your students' attention on a particular writer and topic before they begin reading the essay. This "prereading" segment begins with biographical information about the author and ends with a number of questions to whet the reader's appetite for the essay that follows, including an Internet exercise with a companion writing assignment after the essay. This section is intended to help your students discover interesting relationships among ideas in their reading and then anticipate various ways of thinking about and analyzing the essay. The prereading questions forecast not only the content of the essay, but also the questions and writing assignments that follow.

The questions after each reading selection are designed as guides for thinking about the essay. These questions are at the heart of the relationship represented in this book among thinking, reading, and writing. They are divided into four interrelated sections that shepherd your students smoothly from a literal understanding of what they have just read, to interpretation, and finally to analysis.

After your students have studied the different techniques at work in a reading selection, specific essay assignments let them practice all these skills in unison and encourage them to discover even more secrets about the intricate and exciting details of effective communication. Four "Ideas for Discussion/Writing" topics (one based on the prereading Internet exercise) are preceded by "prewriting" questions to help your students generate new ideas. Most of these topics specify a purpose and an audience so that your students can focus their writing as precisely as possible. The word *essay* (which comes from the Old French *essai,* meaning a "try" or an "attempt") is an appropriate label for these writing assignments, because they all ask your students to wrestle with an idea or problem and then *attempt* to give shape to their conclusions in some effective manner. Such "exercises" can be equated with the development of athletic ability: The essay itself demonstrates that your students can put together all the various skills they have learned; it proves they can actually play the "sport" of writing.

WHAT REMAINS THE SAME?

▶ The Prose Reader *is still organized according to the belief that our mental abilities are logically sequential.*

In other words, students cannot read or write analytically before they are able to perform well on the literal and interpretive levels. Accordingly, the book progresses from selections that require predominantly literal skills (*Description, Narration,* and *Example*) through readings involving more interpretation (*Process Analysis, Division/Classification, Comparison/Contrast,* and *Definition*) to essays that demand a high degree of analytical thought (*Cause/ Effect* and *Argument/Persuasion*). Depending on your curriculum and the caliber of your students, these rhetorical modes can, of course, be studied in any order.

▶ The Prose Reader *provides two Tables of Contents.*

First, the book contains a Rhetorical Table of Contents, which includes a one- or two-sentence synopsis of each selection so you can peruse the list quickly and decide which essays to assign. An alternate Thematic Table of Contents lists selections by academic discipline.

▶ *The chapter introductions are filled with a variety of useful information about each rhetorical mode.*

Each of the nine rhetorical divisions in the text is introduced by an explanation of how to think, read, and write in that particular mode. Although each chapter focuses on one rhetorical strategy, students are continually encouraged to examine ways in which other modes help support each essay's main intentions.

▶ *Two separate student writing samples are featured in each chapter introduction.*

The chapter introductions contain a sample student paragraph and a complete student essay that illustrate each rhetorical pattern. After each essay, the student writer has provided a thorough analysis, explaining the most enjoyable, exasperating, or noteworthy aspects of writing that particular essay. We have found that this combination of student essays and commentaries makes the professional selections easier for students to read and more accessible as models of thinking and writing.

▶ *This edition still includes user-friendly checklists at the end of each chapter introduction.*

These checklists summarize the information in the chapter introduction and serve as references for the students in their own reading and writing tasks. Students should be directed to these lists as early in the course as possible.

▶ *We precede each reading selection with thorough biographical information on the author and provocative prereading questions on the subject of the essay.*

Because our own experience suggests that students often produce their best writing when they are personally involved in the topics of the essays they read and in the human drama surrounding the creation of those essays, the biographies explain the real experiences from which each essay emerged, and the prereading questions ("Preparing to Read") help students focus on the purpose, audience, and subject of the essay. The prereading material also foreshadows the questions and writing assignments that follow each selection. Personalizing this preliminary material encourages students to identify with both the author of an essay and its subject matter, thereby engaging the students' attention and energizing their responses to the selections they read.

▶ *The essays in* The Prose Reader *continue to represent a wide range of topics.*

As in the past, the essays in this edition were selected on the basis of five important criteria: (1) high interest level, (2) currency in the field, (3) moderate length, (4) readability, and (5) broad subject variety. Together, they portray the universality of human experience as expressed through the viewpoints of men and women, many different ethnic and racial groups, and a variety of ages and social classes. The essay topics in this volume include such provocative subjects as discrimination, ethnic identity, job opportunities, aging, war, the media, women's roles, prison life, time management, travel, risk-taking, sports, love, family values, immigration, physical handicaps, reading, and the writing process itself.

▶ *The Argument and Persuasion section (Chapter 9) includes three essays on a variety of topics and two sets of opposing-viewpoint essays.*

The essays in Chapter 9 are particularly useful for helping your students refine their critical thinking skills in preparation for longer, more sustained papers on a single topic. The first three essays in this chapter encourage students to grapple with provocative issues that make a crucial difference in how we all live. Then the two sets of opposing viewpoint essays help the students see coherent arguments at work from two different perspectives on a single issue. The argumentative essays cover such timely topics as discipline, stereotypes, and the relationship between television and violence; the opposing viewpoint essays are on media coverage and immigration.

▶ *"Documented Essays: Reading and Writing from Sources" (Chapter 10) features research papers throughout the college curriculum.*

These essays demonstrate the two most common documentation styles—Modern Language Association (MLA) and American Psychological Association (APA). By including documented essays, we intend to clarify some of the mysteries connected with research and documentation and to provide interesting material for creating longer and more elaborate writing assignments. These essays cover the history of war and the relationship between personal appearance and delinquency. We offer a full range of apparatus for these selections, and at the end of each selection we provide a list of Further Reading on each subject and suggested topics for longer, more sophisticated essays and research papers.

▶ *This edition offers four progressively more sophisticated types of questions at the end of each selection.*

These questions are designed to help students move sequentially from various literal-level responses to interpretation and analysis; they also help reveal both the form and content of the essays so your students can cultivate a similar balance in their own writing.

1. *Understanding Details—questions that test the students' literal and interpretive understanding of what they have read;*
2. *Analyzing Meaning—questions that require students to analyze various aspects of the essay;*
3. *Discovering Rhetorical Strategies—questions that investigate the author's rhetorical strategies in constructing the essay;*
4. *Making Connections—questions that ask students to find thematic and rhetorical connections among essays they have read.*

▶ *The writing assignments ("Ideas for Discussion/Writing") are preceded by Preparing to Write questions.*

These questions are designed to encourage students to express their feelings, thoughts, observations, and opinions on various topics. Questions about their own ideas and experiences help students produce writing that corresponds as closely as possible to the way they think.

▶ *The writing assignments after each essay seek to involve students in realistic situations.*

For instructors who like to use role-playing in their teaching, many writing assignments provide a specific purpose and audience for their essay topics. In this manner, student writers are drawn into rhetorical scenes that carefully focus their responses to a variety of questions or problems. These assignments are designed for use inside or outside the classroom.

▶ *We also offer a new set of writing assignments at the end of each chapter.*

These assignments are divided into two categories, offering (1) more practice in a specific rhetorical mode and (2) a focus on interesting contemporary topics regardless of rhetorical mode. In this way, you have a variety of prompts to choose from if you want your students to have further writing practice at any time.

▸ *The book concludes with a glossary of composition terms (along with examples and page references from the text) and an index of authors and titles.*

The glossary provides not only definitions of composition terms but also examples of these terms from essays in this book, including specific page numbers. The index lists the author and title of each essay in the book. Both the glossary and the index serve as excellent reference tools for your students as they progress through the material in the text.

WHAT IS NEW?

We have made several changes in the seventh edition of *The Prose Reader* that represent the responses of instructors from many different types of colleges and universities throughout the United States:

▸ *The seventh edition of* The Prose Reader *contains seventeen new essays and five selections of creative writing.*

We have updated some of the essays, added new authors, and introduced many new topics, such as maturing, travel, sports, writing, handling debts, taking risks, surviving prison, being handicapped, grandmothers, love, disciplining children, stereotypes, the relationship between children and violence in the media, media coverage of the war in Iran, and immigration.

▸ *This edition makes an even stronger commitment to cultural and gender diversity.*

Although multicultural and women's issues have always been well represented in *The Prose Reader,* this edition includes even more essays by women and ethnic-minority authors, among them William Least Heat-Moon, Linda Formichelli, Julia Bourland,

K.C. Cole, Jimmy Santiago Baca, Sucheng Chan, Erma Bombeck, Wang Ping, bell hooks, Richard Wright, and Neena Beber.

▶ *We have added photographs to the critical thinking section of each chapter introduction.*

Since most students have grown up accustomed to visual stimulation from television and video games, they often respond favorably to pictures. As a result, we have added one photograph to each chapter introduction with a guided assignment to help students learn how to think in that particular rhetorical mode. Finally, two additional critical-thinking assignments now appear in the margins of the book if your students need more practice in a particular mode.

▶ *We have added an Internet feature to this edition.*

The Prereading material before each essay now contains an Internet exercise that will allow your students to explore the topic at hand on the Internet before reading the essay. The exercises offer the students guidance in going to specific sites; these tasks then link with a writing assignment at the end of the essay.

▶ *We have completely renovated our popular "Thinking, Reading, and Writing" section (Chapter 11).*

This chapter now includes two essays, two short stories, two poems, and a brief play—all on the topics of thinking, reading, or writing. In addition to demonstrating all the rhetorical modes at work, these works provide a strong conclusion to the theoretical framework of this text by focusing intently on the interrelationships among thinking, reading, and writing.

WHAT SUPPLEMENTS ARE AVAILABLE?

Available with *The Prose Reader* is an extensive **Annotated Instructor's Edition** designed to help make your life in the classroom a little easier. We have filled the margins of the **AIE** with many different kinds of supplementary material, including instructor comments on teaching the different rhetorical modes, provocative quotations, background information about each essay, definitions of terms that may be unfamiliar to your students, a list of related readings from this text that can be taught together, innovative teaching ideas, detailed answers to the questions that follow each selection, additional essay topics, and various revising strategies.

In addition to the *Annotated Instructor's Edition,* we have also created the **Instructor's Resource Manual with Quiz Book.** In it, we identify and discuss some of the most widely used theoretical approaches to the teaching of composition; we then offer innovative options for organizing your course, specific suggestions for the first day of class, a summary of the advantages and disadvantages of using different teaching strategies, and several successful techniques for responding to student writing. Next, we provide two objective quizzes for each essay to help you monitor your students' mastery of the selection's vocabulary and content. This supplement ends with three additional professional essays (two opposing viewpoint essays and one documented essay), a series of student essays (one for each rhetorical strategy featured in the text) followed by the student writer's comments, and an annotated bibliography of books and articles about thinking, reading, and writing.

Also available with *The Prose Reader* is a Companion Website™ (**www.prenhall.com/flachmann**) that offers an extensive collection of additional resources for both the student and the instructor for every essay in the text. This Web site allows students to get additional reinforcement for the text material and provides an easy way for the instructors to integrate the World Wide Web into their courses. The site includes

► *author biographies with contextual links;*

► *online vocabulary comprehension quizzes for every selection, with instant scoring;*

► *pre-reading and post-reading assignments that foster critical thinking for every essay;*

► *dynamic Web links that provide a valuable source of additional information about the essay topics;*

► *communication tools such as chat rooms and message boards to facilitate online collaboration and communication;*

▶ *built-in routing that gives students the ability to forward essay responses and graded quizzes to their instructors; and*

▶ *a faculty module that includes an* Instructor's Resource Manual *with additional quizzes*

This entire instructional package, available to you free of charge, is intended to help your students discover what they want to say and to assist them in shaping their ideas into a coherent form, thereby encouraging their intelligent involvement in the complex and exciting world around them.

ACKNOWLEDGMENTS

We are pleased to acknowledge the kind assistance and support of a number of people who have helped us put together this seventh edition of *The Prose Reader*. For creative encouragement and editorial guidance at Prentice Hall, we thank Yolanda De Rooy, President of Humanities and Social Sciences; Leah Jewell, AVP/Editor in Chief; Corey Good, Senior Acquisitions Editor; Karen Schultz, Assistant Editor; Steven Kyritz, Editorial Assistant; Beth Mejia, AVP/Director of Marketing; Brandy Dawson, Executive Marketing Manager; Alison Peck, Marketing Assistant; Ann Marie McCarthy, Executive Managing Editor; Fran Russello, Project Manager; and Karen Berry, Production Editor.

For reviews of the manuscript at various stages of completion, we are grateful to Janice Jones, Kent State University, Kent, Ohio; Lyle W. Morgan II, Pittsburgh State University, Pittsburgh, Pennsylvania; Carolyn D. Coward, Shelby State Community College, Memphis, Tennessee; Teresa Purvis, Lansing Community College, Lansing, Michigan; Gena E. Christopher, Jacksonville State University, Jacksonville, Florida; Donnie Yeilding, Central Texas College, Killeen, Texas; Steve Katz, State Technical Institute, Memphis, Tennessee; Craig Howard White, University of Houston, Clear Lake, Houston, Texas; Judith Dan, Boston University, Boston, Massachusetts; Arlie R. Peck, University of Rio Grande, Rio Grande, Ohio; Barbara Smith, Iona College, New Rochelle, New York; Vermell Blanding, Hostos Community College, Bronx, New York; Nancy G. Wright, Austin Peay State University, Clarksville, Tennessee; Paula Miller, Azusa Pacific University, Azusa, California; Paul

Kistel, Pierce College, Tacoma, Washington; Christopher Belcher, Community College of Allegheny County, Pittsburgh, Pennsylvania; Helen F. Maxon, Southwestern Oklahoma State University, Oklahoma City, Oklahoma; Geoffrey C. Goodale, University of Massachusetts at Boston, Boston, Massachusetts; Martha Bergeron, Vance-Granville Community College, Henderson, North Carolina; Jan LaFever, Friends University, Wichita, Kansas; Virginia Leonard, West Liberty State College, Wichita, Kansas; Melissa A. Bruner, Southwestern Oklahoma State University, West Liberty, Virginia; James Zarzana, Southwest State University, Marshall, Minnesota; Terrence Burke, Cuyahoga Community College, Cleveland, Ohio; Ellen Dugan-Barrette, Brescia College, Owensboro, Kentucky; Lewis Emond, Dean Junior College, Franklin, Massachusetts; Jay Jernigan, Eastern Michigan University, Ypsilanti, Michigan; Nellie McCrory, Gaston College, Dallas, North Carolina; Leslie Shipp, Clark County Community College, Henderson, Nevada; William F. Sutlife, Community College of Allegheny County, Monroeville, Pennsylvania; Maureen Aitkn, University of Michigan; Mickie R. Braswell, Lenoir Community College; Judith Burnham, Tulsa Community College; Charles H. Cole, Carl Albert State College; Todd Lieber, Simpson College; Bill Marsh, National University; Felicia S. Pattison, Sterling College; Dianne Peich, Delaware County Community College; K. Siobhan Wright, Carroll Community College; Melody Ziff, Northern Virginia Community College Annandale; Robin Morris Hardin, Cape Fear Community College; Matthew Stiffler, Utah State University; Melanie Whitebread, Luzerne County Community College; June Farmer, Southern Union State Community College; Martha R. Bachman, Camden County College; Arnold Bradford, Northern Virginia Community College, Loudoun Campus; Nate Gordeon, Kiswaukee College; Alice Sink, High Point University; Bill Clemente, Peru State College; Stella Shepard, Henderson State University; Rosie Soy, Hudson County Community College; and Kevin Nebergall, Kirkwood Community College.

Several writing instructors across the United States have been kind enough to help shape *The Prose Reader* over the course of its development by responding to specific questions about their teaching experiences with the book: Charles Bordogna, Bergen

Community College, Paramus, New Jersey; Mary G. Marshall and Eileen M. Ward, College of DuPage, Glen Ellyn, Illinois; Michael J. Huntington and Judith C. Kohl, Dutchess Community College, Poughkeepsie, New York; Ted Johnston, El Paso County Community College, El Paso, Texas; Koala C. Hartnett, Rick James Mazza, and William H. Sherman, Fairmont State College, Fairmont, West Virginia; Miriam Dick and Betty Krasne, Mercy College, Dobbs Ferry, New York; Elvis Clark, Mineral Area College, Flat River, Missouri; Dayna Spencer, Pittsburg State University, Pittsburg, Kansas; James A. Zarzana, Southwest State University, Marshall, Minnesota; Susan Reinhart Schneling and Trudy Vanderback, Vincennes University, Vincennes, Indiana; Carmen Wong, Virginia Commonwealth University, Richmond, Virginia; John W. Hattman and Virginia E. Leonard, West Liberty State College, West Liberty, West Virginia; Jonathan Alexander, Widener University, Chester, Pennsylvania; Jo Ann Pevoto, College of the Mainland, Texas; Anita Pandey, University of Illinois at Urbana-Champaign, Illinois; Leaf Seligman, University of New Hampshire, Durham, New Hampshire; Arminta Baldwin, West Virginia Wesleyan College, Buckhannon, West Virginia; Joaquim Mendes, New York Institute of Technology, Old Westbury, New York; and Sandra R. Woods, Fairmont State College, Fairmont, West Virginia.

For student essays and writing samples, we thank Rosa Marie Augustine, Donel Crow, Dawn Dobie, Gloria Dumler, Jeff Hicks, Julie Anne Judd, Judi Koch, Dawn McKee, Paul Newberry, Joanne Silva-Newberry, JoAnn Slate, Peggy Stuckey, and Jan Titus.

We also want to thank two incredibly talented colleagues for helping us with some of the new features in this edition: Monica Bulger and Anne Elrod. We are grateful to two other colleagues who served as research assistants throughout the creation of this edition: Crystal Huddleston and Zee Stidham. We also greatly appreciate the keen insights of Brooke King. And for coordinating our department responsibilities in such a way that *The Prose Reader, seventh edition,* could become a reality, we thank our chair, Merry Pawlowski.

In preparing our *Annotated Instructor's Edition,* we owe special gratitude to Cheryl Smith, who revised and recast instructional material for this edition, and to the following writing instructors who have contributed their favorite techniques for teaching various rhetorical strategies: Mary P. Boyles, Pembroke State University; Terrence W. Burke, Cuyahoga Community College; Mary Lou Conlin, Cuyahoga Community College; Ellen Dugan-Barrette, Brescia College; Janet Eber, County College of Morris; Louis Emond, Dean Junior College; Peter Harris, West Virginia Institute of Technology, Montgomery; Jay Jernigan, Eastern Michigan University; Judith C. Kohl, Dutchess Community College; Joanne H. McCarthy, Tacoma Community College; Anthony McCrann, Peru State College; Nellie McCrory, Gaston College; Alan Price, Pennsylvania State University–Hazelton; Patricia A. Ross, Moorpark College; Leslie Shipp, Clark County Community College; Rodney Simard (deceased), California State University, San Bernardino; Elizabeth Wahlquist, Brigham Young University; John White, California State University, Fullerton; and Ted Wise, Porterville College.

This book also benefits from the amazing insights and consummate teaching of Kathryn Benander (Porterville College) and Cheryl Smith (California State University, Bakersfield), who served as editorial consultants throughout the entire project. Kathryn helped revise the margin notes of the *Annotated Instructor's Edition* and single-handedly revised the *Instructor's Resource Manual*. Their work and opinions were invaluable.

Our final and most important debt is to our children, Christopher and Laura, who have inspired us to be good teachers since the day they were born.

INTRODUCTION

Thinking, Reading, and Writing

Have you ever had trouble expressing your thoughts? If so, you're not alone. Many people have this difficulty—especially when they are asked to write their thoughts down. The good news is that this "ailment" can be cured. We've learned over the years that the more clearly students think about the world around them, the more easily they can express their ideas through written and spoken language. As a result, this textbook intends to improve your writing by helping you think clearly, logically, and critically about important ideas and issues that exist in our world today. You will learn to reason, read, and write about your environment in increasingly complex ways, moving steadily from a simple, literal understanding of topics to interpretation and analysis.

Part of becoming a better writer involves understanding that reading and writing are companion activities that engage people in the creation of thought and meaning—either as readers interpreting a text or as writers constructing one. Clear thinking, then, is the pivotal point that joins together these two efforts. Although studying the rhetorical strategies presented in *The Prose Reader* is certainly not the only way to approach writing, it does provide a productive

1

means of helping students improve their abilities to think, read, and write. Inspired by the well-crafted prose models in this text and guided by carefully worded questions, you can actually raise the level of your thinking skills while improving your reading and writing abilities on three progressively more difficult levels:

1. *The literal level* is the foundation of all human understanding; it entails knowing the meanings of words—individually and in relation to one another. In order for someone to comprehend the sentence "You must exercise your brain to reach your full mental potential" on the literal level, for example, that person would have to know the definitions of all the words in the sentence and understand the way those words work together to make meaning.

2. *Interpretation* requires the ability to make associations between details, draw inferences from pieces of information, and reach conclusions about the material. An interpretive understanding of the sample sentence in level 1 might be translated into the following thoughts: "Exercising the brain sounds a bit like exercising the body. I wonder if there's any correlation between the two. If the brain must be exercised, it is probably made up of muscles, much like the body is." None of these particular "thoughts" is made explicit in the sentence, but each is suggested in one way or another.

3. *Thinking, reading, and writing critically,* the most sophisticated form of rational abilities, involves a type of mental activity that is crucial for successful academic and professional work. A critical analysis of our sample sentence might proceed in the following way: "This sentence is talking to me. It actually addresses me with the word *you*. I wonder what *my* mental potential is. Will I be able to reach it? Will I know when I attain it? Will I be comfortable with it? I certainly want to reach this potential, whatever it is. Reaching it will undoubtedly help me succeed scholastically and professionally. The brain is obviously an important tool for helping me achieve my goals in life, so I want to take every opportunity I have to develop and maintain this part of my body." Students who can take an issue or idea apart in this fashion and understand its various components more thoroughly after reassembling them are rewarded intrinsically with a clearer knowledge of life's complexities and the ability to generate creative, useful ideas. They are also rewarded extrinsically with good grades

and are more likely to win responsible jobs with higher pay, because their understanding of the world around them is perceptive and they are able to apply this understanding effectively to their professional and personal lives.

In this textbook, you will learn to think critically by reading essays written by intelligent, interesting authors and by writing your own essays on a variety of topics. The next several pages offer guidelines for approaching the thinking, reading, and writing assignments in this book. These suggestions should also be useful to you in your other courses.

THINKING CRITICALLY

Recent psychological studies have shown that "thinking" and "feeling" are complementary operations. All of us have feelings that are automatic and instinctive. To feel pride after winning first place at a track meet, for example, or to feel anger at a spiteful friend is not behavior we have to study and master; such emotions come naturally to human beings. Thinking, on the other hand, is much less spontaneous than feeling; research suggests that study and practice are required for sustained mental development.

Thinking critically involves grappling with the ideas, issues, and problems that surround you in your immediate environment and in the world at large. It does not necessarily entail finding fault, which you might naturally associate with the word *critical,* but rather suggests continually questioning and analyzing the world around you. Thinking critically is the highest form of mental activity that human beings engage in; it is the source of success in college and in our professional and personal lives. Fortunately, all of us can learn how to think more critically.

Critical thinking means taking apart an issue, idea, or problem; examining its various parts; and reassembling the topic with a fuller understanding of its intricacies. Implied in this explanation is the ability to see the topic from one or more new perspectives. Using your mind in this way will help you find solutions to difficult problems, design creative plans of action, and ultimately live a life consistent with your opinions on important issues that we all must confront daily.

Since critical or analytical thinking is one of the highest forms of mental activity, it requires a great deal of concentration and practice. Once you have actually felt how your mind works and processes information at this level, however, re-creating the experience is somewhat like riding a bicycle: You will be able to do it naturally, easily, and skillfully whenever you want to.

Our initial goal, then, is to help you think critically when you are required to do so in school, on the job, or in any other area of your life. If this form of thinking becomes a part of your daily routine, you will quite naturally be able to call upon it whenever you need it.

Working with the rhetorical modes is an effective way to achieve this goal. With some guidance, each rhetorical pattern can provide you with a mental workout to prepare you for writing and critical thinking in the same way that physical exercises warm you up for various sports. Just as in the rest of the body, the more exercise the brain gets, the more flexible it becomes and the higher the levels of thought it can attain. Through these various guided thinking exercises, you can systematically strengthen your ability to think analytically.

As you move through the following chapters, we will ask you to isolate each rhetorical mode—much like isolating your abs, thighs, and biceps in a weight-lifting workout—so that you can concentrate on these thinking patterns one at a time. Each rhetorical pattern we study will suggest slightly different ways of seeing the world, processing information, and solving problems. Each offers important ways of thinking and making sense of our immediate environment and the larger world around us. Looking closely at rhetorical modes or specific patterns of thought helps us discover how our minds work. In the same fashion, becoming more intricately aware of our thought patterns lets us improve our basic thinking skills as well as our reading and writing abilities. Thinking critically helps us discover fresh insights into old ideas, generate new thoughts, and see connections between related issues. It is an energizing mental activity that puts us in control of our lives and our environment rather than leaving us at the mercy of our surroundings.

Each chapter introduction provides three exercises—one based on a photograph—specifically designed to help you focus in isolation on a particular pattern of thought. While you are attempting to learn what each pattern feels like in your head, use your imagination to play with these exercises on as many different levels as possible.

When you practice each of the rhetorical patterns of thought, you should be aware of building on your previous thinking skills. As the book progresses, the rhetorical modes become more complex and require a higher degree of concentration and effort. Throughout the book, therefore, you should keep in mind that ultimately you want to let these skills accumulate into a full-powered, well-developed ability to process the world around you—including reading, writing, seeing, and feeling—on the most advanced analytical level you can master.

READING CRITICALLY

Reading critically begins with developing a natural curiosity about an essay and nurturing that curiosity throughout the reading process. To learn as much as you can from an essay, you should first study any preliminary material you can find, then read the essay to get a general overview of its main ideas, and finally read the selection again to achieve a deeper understanding of its content. The three phases of the reading process explained next— preparing to read, reading, and rereading—will help you develop this "natural curiosity" so you can approach any reading assignment with an active, inquiring mind.

Preparing to Read

Focusing your attention is an important first stage in both the reading and the writing processes. In fact, learning as much as you can about an essay and its "context" (the circumstances surrounding its development) before you begin reading can help you move through the essay with an energetic, active mind and then reach some degree of analysis before writing on the assigned topics. In particular, knowing where an essay was first published, studying the writer's background, and doing some preliminary thinking on the subject of a reading selection will help you understand the writer's ideas and form some valid opinions of your own.

As you approach any essay, you should concentrate on four specific areas that will begin to give you an overview of the material you are about to read. We will use an essay by Lewis Thomas to demonstrate these techniques.

1. *Title.* A close look at the title will usually provide important clues about the author's attitude toward the topic, the author's

stand on an issue, or the mood of an essay. It can also furnish you with a sense of audience and purpose.

To Err Is Human

From this title, for example, we might infer that the author will discuss errors, human nature, and the extent to which mistakes influence human behavior. The title is half of a well-known proverbial quotation (Alexander Pope's "To err is human, to forgive, divine"), so we might speculate further that the author has written an essay intended for a well-read audience interested in the relationship between errors and humanity. After reading only four words of the essay—its title—you already have a good deal of information about the subject, its audience, and the author's attitude toward both.

  2. *Synopsis.* The Rhetorical Table of Contents in this text contains a synopsis of each essay, very much like the following, so that you can find out more specific details about its contents before you begin reading.

Physician Lewis Thomas explains how we can profit from our mistakes—especially if we trust human nature. Perhaps someday, he says, we can apply this same principle to the computer and magnify the advantages of these errors.

From this synopsis, we learn that Thomas's essay will be an analysis of human errors and of the way we can benefit from those errors. The synopsis also tells us the computer has the potential to magnify the value of our errors.

  3. *Biography.* Learning as much as you can about the author of an essay will generally stimulate your interest in the material and help you achieve a deeper understanding of the issues to be discussed. From the biographies in this book, you can learn, for example, whether a writer is young or old, conservative or liberal, open- or close-minded. You might also discover if the essay was written at the beginning, middle, or end of the author's career or how well versed the writer is on the topic. Such information will invariably help you reach a fuller, more thorough understanding of a selection's ideas, audience, and logical structure.

LEWIS THOMAS   (1913–1993)

Lewis Thomas was a physician who, until his death in 1993, was president emeritus of the Sloan-Kettering Cancer Center and scholar-in-residence at the Cornell University Medical Center in New York City. A graduate of Princeton University and Harvard Medical School, he was formerly head of pathology and dean of the New York University–Bellevue Medical Center and dean of the Yale Medical School. In addition to having written over two hundred scientific papers on virology and immunology, he authored many popular scientific essays, some of which have been collected in *Lives of a Cell* (1974), *The Medusa and the Snail* (1979), *Late Night Thoughts on Listening to Mahler's Ninth Symphony* (1983), *Etcetera, Etcetera* (1990), and *The Fragile Species* (1992). The memoirs of his distinguished career have been published in *The Youngest Science: Notes of a Medicine Watcher* (1983). Thomas liked to refer to his essays as "experiments in thought": "Although I usually think I know what I'm going to be writing about, what I'm going to say, most of the time it doesn't happen that way at all. At some point, I get misled down a garden path. I get surprised by an idea that I hadn't anticipated getting, which is a little bit like being in a laboratory."

As this information indicates, Thomas was a prominent physician who published widely on scientific topics. We know that he considered his essays "experiments in thought," which makes us expect a relaxed, spontaneous treatment of his subjects. From this biography, we can also infer that he was a leader in the medical world and that, because of the positions he has held, he was well respected in his professional life. Last, we can speculate that he had a clear sense of his audience because he was able to present difficult concepts in clear, everyday language.

    4. *Preparing to read.* One other type of preliminary material will broaden your overview of the topic and enable you to approach the essay with an active, thoughtful mind. The "Preparing to Read" sections following the biographies are intended to focus

your attention and stimulate your curiosity before you begin the essay. They will also get you ready to form your own opinions on the essay and its topic as you read. Keeping a journal to respond to these questions is an excellent idea, because you will then have a record of your thoughts on various topics related to the reading selection that follows.

Preparing to Read

The following essay, which originally appeared in the *New England Journal of Medicine* (January 1976), illustrates the clarity and ease with which Thomas explains complex scientific topics.

Exploring Experience: As you prepare to read this essay, take a few moments to think about the role mistakes play in our lives: What are some memorable mistakes you have made? Did you learn anything important from any of these errors? Do you make more or fewer mistakes than other people you know? Do you see any advantages to making mistakes? Any disadvantages?

Learning Online: Most computers have games included in their operating systems. Find a game on your computer, and play it for a while. Who won? What types of mistakes did the computer make? What types of mistakes did you make? Consider your experience while reading Thomas's essay.

Discovering where, why, and how an essay was first written will provide you with a context for the material you are about to read: Why did the author write this selection? Where was it first published? Who was the author's original audience? This type of information enables you to understand the circumstances surrounding the development of the selection and to identify any topical or historical references the author makes. All the selections in this textbook were published elsewhere first—in another book, a journal, or a magazine. The author's original audience, therefore, consisted of the readers of that particular publication.

From the sample "Preparing to Read" material, we learn that Thomas's essay "To Err Is Human" was originally published in the

New England Journal of Medicine, a prestigious periodical read principally by members of the scientific community. Written early in 1976, the article plays upon its audience's growing fascination with computers and with the limits of artificial intelligence—subjects just as timely today as they were in the mid-1970s.

The questions here prompt you to consider your own ideas, opinions, or experiences in order to help you generate thoughts on the topic of errors in our lives. These questions are, ideally, the last step in preparing yourself for the active role you should play as a reader.

At the end of the questions is an Internet exercise that helps you explore a specific topic on the Internet. These are enjoyable activities meant to stimulate your thinking and expand your knowledge on this and related subjects.

Reading

People read essays in books, newspapers, magazines, and journals for a great variety of reasons. One reader may want to be stimulated intellectually, whereas another seeks relaxation; one person reads to keep up with the latest developments in his or her profession, whereas the next wants to learn why a certain event happened or how something can be done; some people read in order to be challenged by new ideas, whereas others find comfort principally in printed material that supports their own moral, social, or political opinions. The essays in this textbook fulfill all these expectations in different ways. They have been chosen, however, not only for these reasons, but for an additional, broader purpose: Reading them can help make you a better writer.

Every time you read an essay in this book, you will also be preparing to write your own essay concentrating on the same rhetorical pattern. For this reason, as you read you should pay careful attention to both the content (subject matter) and the form (language, sentence structure, organization, and development of ideas) of each essay. You will also see how effectively experienced writers use particular rhetorical modes (or patterns of thought) to organize and communicate their ideas. Each essay in this collection features one dominant pattern that is generally supported by several others. In fact, the more aware you are of each author's writing techniques, the more rapidly your own writing process will mature and improve.

The questions before and after each essay teach you a way of reading that can help you discover the relationship of a writer's ideas to one another as well as to your own ideas. These questions can also help clarify for you the connection between the writer's topic, his or her style or manner of expression, and your own composing process. In other words, the questions are designed to help you understand and generate ideas, then discover various choices the writers make in composing their essays, and finally realize the freedom you have to make related choices in your own writing. Such an approach to the process of reading takes some of the mystery out of reading and writing and makes them manageable tasks at which anyone can become proficient.

Three general guidelines, each of which is explained below in detail, will help you develop your own system for reading and responding to what you have read:

1. Read the essay to get an overall sense of it.
2. Summarize the essay.
3. Read the questions and assignments that follow the essay.

Guideline 1. First, read the essay to get an overall sense of it in relation to its title, purpose, audience, author, and publication information.   Write (in the margins, on a separate piece of paper, or in a journal) your initial reactions, comments, and personal associations.

To illustrate, on the following pages is the Thomas essay with a student's comments in the margins, showing how the student reacted to the essay upon reading it for the first time.

LEWIS THOMAS   (1913–1993)

To Err Is Human

Boy is this true

Everyone must have had at least one per- 1
sonal experience with a computer error by
this time. Bank balances are suddenly
reported to have jumped from $379 into the
millions, appeals for charitable contributions
are mailed over and over to people with
crazy sounding names at your address,
<u>department stores send the wrong bills</u>, util- *Last spring this happened to me*
ity companies write that they're turning
everything off, that sort of thing. If you
manage to get in touch with someone and
complain, you then get instantaneously
typed, guilty letters from the same com- *exactly*
puter, saying, "Our computer was in error,
and an adjustment is being made in your
account."

These are supposed to be the sheerest, 2
blindest accidents. Mistakes are not believed
to be part of the normal behavior of a good
machine. If things go wrong, it must be a *How can this be?*
personal, human error, the result of finger-
ing, tampering, a button getting stuck,
someone hitting the wrong key. The computer, at its normal best, is infallible.

I wonder whether this can be true. After 3
all, the whole point of computers is that
they represent an extension of the human
brain, vastly improved upon but nonetheless
human, <u>superhuman</u> maybe. A good com- *In what way?*
puter can think clearly and quickly enough
to beat you at chess, and some of them have
even been programmed to write obscure
verse. They can do anything we can do, and *Can this be proven?*
more besides.

4

It is not yet known whether a computer has its own consciousness, and it would be hard to find out about this. When you walk into one of those great halls now built for the huge machines, and stand listening, it is easy to imagine that the faint, distant noises are the sound of thinking, and the turning of the spools gives them the look of wild creatures rolling their eyes in the effort to concentrate, choking with information. But real thinking, and dreaming, are other matters.

I expected this essay to be so much more stuffy than it is. I can even understand it.

In what way?

5

On the other hand, the evidences of something like an unconscious, equivalent to ours, are all around, in every mail. As extensions of the human brain, they have been constructed with the same property of error, spontaneous, uncontrolled, and rich in possibilities.

good, clear comparison for the general reader

6

Mistakes are at the very base of human thought, embedded there, feeding the structure like root nodules. If we were not provided with the knack of being wrong, we could never get anything useful done. We think our way along by choosing between right and wrong alternatives, and the wrong choices have to be made as frequently as the right ones. We get along in life this way. We are built to make mistakes, coded for error.

so true

great image

I don't understand this

I agree! This is how we learn

7   *??*

We learn, as we say, by "trial and error." Why do we always say that? Why not "trial and rightness" or "trial and triumph"? The old phrase puts it that way because that is, in real life, the way it is done.

8

A good laboratory, like a good bank or a corporation or government, has to run like a computer. Almost everything is done flawlessly, by the book, and all the numbers add up to the predicted sums. The days go

Another effective comparison for the general reader

by. And then, if it is a <u>lucky</u> day, and a <u>lucky</u> laboratory, somebody makes a mistake: the wrong buffer, something in one of the blanks, a decimal misplaced in reading counts, the warm room off by a degree and a half, a mouse out of his box, or just a misreading of the day's protocol. Whatever, when the results come in, something is obviously screwed up, and <u>then the action can begin</u>.

Isn't this a contradiction?

What?

The misreading is not the important error; <u>it opens the way</u>. The next step is the crucial one. If the investigator can bring himself to say, "But even so, look at that!" then the new finding, whatever it is, is ready for snatching. What is needed, for progress to be made, is <u>the move based on error</u>.

aha!

9

Whenever new kinds of thinking are about to be accomplished, or new varieties of music, there has to be an argument beforehand. With two sides debating in the same mind, haranguing, there is an amiable understanding that one is right and the other wrong. Sooner or later the thing is settled, but there can be no action at all if there are not the two sides, and the argument. <u>The hope is in the faculty of wrongness</u>, the tendency toward error. The capacity to leap across mountains of information and land lightly on the wrong side represents the highest of human endowments.

10

interesting idea

I believe Thomas here because of his background

It may be that this is a uniquely human gift, perhaps even stipulated in our genetic instructions. Other creatures do not seem to have DNA sequences for making mistakes as a routine part of daily living, certainly not for programmed error as a guide for action.

11

Could this be related to the human ability to think critically?

We are at our human finest, <u>dancing with our minds</u>, when there are more choices than two. Sometimes there are ten, even twenty different ways to go, all but one bound to be wrong, and the richness of selection in such situations can lift us onto totally new ground. This process is called exploration and is based on human fallibility. If we had only a single center in our brains, capable of responding only when a correct decision was to be made, instead of the jumble of different, credulous, easily conned clusters of neurons that provide for being flung off into blind alleys, up trees, down dead ends, out into blue sky, along wrong turnings, around bends, we could only stay the way we are today, stuck fast.

<u>The lower animals do not have this splendid freedom.</u> They are limited, most of them, to absolute infallibility. Cats, for all their good side, never make mistakes. <u>I have never seen a maladroit, clumsy, or blundering cat.</u> Dogs are sometimes fallible, occasionally able to make charming minor mistakes, but they get this way by trying to mimic their masters. <u>Fish are flawless in everything they do.</u> Individual cells in a tissue are mindless machines, perfect in their performance, as absolutely inhuman as bees.

We should have this in mind as we become dependent on more complex computers for the arrangement of our affairs. Give the computers their heads, I say; let them go their way. If we can learn to do this, turning our heads to one side and wincing while the work proceeds, the possibilities for the future of mankind, and computerkind, are limitless. <u>Your average good computer can make calculations in an</u>

Margin notes:

Yes, but this is so frustrating

I love the phrase "splendid freedom"

I never thought of mistakes this way

12
nice mental image

This is a great sentence— it has a lot of feeling

13
See ¶ 11

look up "maladroit"

I like this idea

14

so true

Thomas makes our technology sound really exciting

instant which would take a lifetime of slide rules for any of us. Think of what we could gain from the near infinity of precise, machine-made miscomputation which is now so easily within our grasp. We would begin the solving of some of our hardest problems. How, for instance, should we go about organizing ourselves for social living on a planetary scale, now that we have become, as a plain fact of life, a single community? We can assume, as a working hypothesis, that all the right ways of doing this are unworkable. What we need, then, for moving ahead, is a set of wrong alternatives much longer and more interesting than the short list of mistaken courses that any of us can think up right now. We need, in fact, an infinite list, and when it is printed out we need the computer to turn itself on and select, at random, the next way to go. If it is

Not a contradiction after all

a big enough mistake, we could find ourselves on a new level, stunned, out in the clear, ready to move again.

yes

We need to program computers to make deliberate mistakes so they can help our natural human tendency to learn thru error

So mistakes have value!

Guideline 2. After you have read the essay for the first time, summarize its main ideas in some fashion. The form of this task might be anything from a drawing of the main ideas as they connect with one another to a succinct written summary. You could draw a graph or map of the topics in the essay (in much the same way that a person would draw a map of an area for someone unfamiliar with a particular route); outline the ideas to get an overview of the piece; or summarize the ideas to check your understanding of the main points of the selection. Any of these tasks can be completed from your original notes and underlining. Each will give you a slightly more thorough understanding of what you have read.

Guideline 3. Next, read the questions and assignments following the essay to help focus your thinking for the second reading. Don't answer the questions at this time; just read them to make sure you are picking up the main ideas from the selection and thinking about relevant connections among those ideas.

Rereading

Following your initial reading, read the essay again, concentrating this time on how the author achieved his or her purpose. The temptation to skip this stage of the reading process is often powerful, but this second reading is crucial to your development as a critical reader in all of your courses. This second reading could be compared to seeing a good movie for the second time: The first viewing would provide you with a general understanding of the plot, the characters, the setting, and the overall artistic accomplishment of the director; during the second viewing, however, you would undoubtedly notice many more details and see their specific contributions to the artistic whole. Similarly, the second reading of an essay allows a much deeper understanding of the work under consideration and prepares you to analyze the writer's ideas.

You should also be prepared to do some detective work at this point and look closely at the assumptions the essay is based on: For example, how does the writer move from idea to idea in the essay? What hidden assertions lie behind these ideas? Do you agree or disagree with these assertions? Your assessment of these unspoken assumptions will often play a major role in your critical response to an essay. In the case of Thomas's essay, do you accept the unspoken connection he makes between the workings of the human brain and the computer? What parts of the essay hinge upon your acceptance of this connection? What other assumptions are fundamental to Thomas's reasoning? If you accept his thinking along the way, you are more likely to agree with the general flow of Thomas's essay. If you discover a flaw in his premises or assumptions, your acceptance of his argument will start to break down.

Next, answer the questions that follow the essay. The "Understanding Details" questions will help you understand and remember what you have read on both the literal and the interpretive levels. Some of the questions ask you to restate various important points the author makes (literal); others help you see relationships among the different ideas presented (interpretive).

Understanding Details

Literal   1. According to Thomas, in what ways are
                 computers and humans similar? How are they
                 different?

Lit/Interp   2. How do we learn by "trial and error"?
                 Why is this a useful way to learn?

Interpretive 3. What does Thomas mean by the statement,
                 "If we were not provided with the knack of
                 being wrong, we could never get anything use-
                 ful done" (paragraph 6)?

Interpretive 4. According to Thomas, in what important
                 ways do humans and "lower" animals differ?
                 What does this comparison have to do with
                 Thomas's main line of reasoning?

The "Analyzing Meaning" questions require you to analyze and
evaluate some of the writer's ideas in order to form valid opinions
of your own. These questions demand a higher level of thought
than the previous set and help you prepare more specifically for
the discussion/writing assignments that follow the questions.

Analyzing Meaning

Analytical   1. What is Thomas's main point in this essay?
                 How do the references to computers help him
                 make this point?

Analytical   2. In paragraph 10, Thomas explains that an
                 argument must precede the beginning of some-
                 thing new and different. Do you think this is
                 an accurate observation? Explain your answer.

Analytical   3. Why does Thomas perceive human error as
                 such a positive quality? What does "exploration"
                 have to do with this quality (paragraph 12)?

Analytical   4. What could we gain from "the near infin-
                 ity of precise, machine-made miscomputation"
                 (paragraph 14)? In what ways would our civi-
                 lization advance?

The "Discovering Rhetorical Strategies" questions ask you to look closely at what strategies the writer uses to develop his or her thesis and how those strategies work. The questions address important features of the writer's composing process, such as word choice, use of detail, transitions, statement of purpose, organization of ideas, sentence structure, and paragraph development. The intent of these questions is to raise various elements of the composing process to the conscious level so you can use them in creating your own essays. If you are able to understand and describe what choices a writer makes to create certain effects in his or her prose, you are more likely to be able to discover the range of choices available to you as you write, and you will also become more aware of your ability to control your readers' thoughts and feelings.

Discovering Rhetorical Strategies

1.   Thomas begins his essay with a list of experiences most of us have had at one time or another. Do you find this an effective beginning? Why or why not?
2.   Which main points in his essay does Thomas develop in most detail? Why do you think he chooses to develop these points so thoroughly?
3.   Explain the simile Thomas uses in paragraph 6: "Mistakes are at the very base of human thought, embedded there, feeding the structure like root nodules." Is this comparison between "mistakes" and "root nodules" useful in this context? Why or why not? Find another simile or metaphor in this essay, and explain how it works.
4.   What principal rhetorical strategies does Thomas use to make his point? Give examples of each from the essay.

A final set of questions, "Making Connections," asks you to consider the essay you have just read in reference to other essays in the book. Your instructor will assign these questions according to the essays you have read. The questions may have you compare the writers' treatment of an idea, the authors' style of writing, the difference in their opinions, or the similarities between their views of the world. Such questions will help you see connections in your own life—not only in your reading and your immediate environment, but also in the larger world around you. These questions, in particular, encourage you to move from specific references in the selections to a broader range of issues and circumstances that affect your daily life.

Making Connections

1. Kimberly Wozencraft ("Notes from the Country Club") and Judith Wallerstein and Sandra Blakeslee ("Second Chances for Children of Divorce") refer both directly and indirectly to learning from mistakes. Would Lewis Thomas agree with their approach to this topic? In what ways do these authors think alike about the benefits of making errors? In what ways do they differ on the topic? Explain your answer.
2. Lewis Thomas, Jessica Mitford ("Behind the Formaldehyde Curtain"), and Michael Dorris ("The Broken Cord") all write about the intersection of science and humanity. Which of these authors, in your opinion, is most intrigued by the human aspect of this equation? Why do you think this is true?
3. According to Thomas, humans are complex organisms with a great deal of untapped potential. Maya Angelou ("New Directions") and Barbara Ehrenreich ("The Ecstasy of War") also comment on the uniqueness of human beings. In what ways do these three writers agree or disagree with each other on the intelligence and resourcefulness of human beings? To what extent would each author argue that humans use their mental capacities wisely and completely? Explain your answer.

Because checklists can provide a helpful method of reviewing important information, we offer here a series of questions that represent the three stages of reading just discussed. All these guidelines can be generalized into a checklist for reading any academic assignment in any discipline.

Preparing to Read

Title

✓ What can I infer from the title of the essay?

✓ Who do I think is the author's audience? What is the principal purpose of the essay?

Synopsis

✓ What is the general subject of the essay?

✓ What is the author's approach to the subject?

Biography

✓ What do I know about the author's age, political stance, general beliefs?

✓ How qualified is the author to write on this subject?

✓ When did the author write the essay? Under what conditions? In what context?

✓ Where was the essay first published?

Content

✓ What would I like to learn about this topic?

✓ What are some of my opinions on this subject?

Reading

✓ What are my initial reactions to the ideas in this essay?

✓ What are the essay's main ideas?

✓ Did I read the questions and assignments following the essay?

Rereading

✓ How does the author achieve his or her purpose in this essay?

✓ What assumptions underlie the author's reasoning?

✓ Do I have a clear literal understanding of this essay? What words do I need to look up in a dictionary?

✓ Do I have a solid interpretive understanding of this essay? Do I understand the relationship among ideas? What conclusions can I draw from this essay?

✓ Do I have an accurate analytical understanding of this essay? Which ideas can I take apart, examine, and put back together again? What is my evaluation of this material?

✓ Do I understand the rhetorical strategies the writer uses and the way they work? Can I explain the effects of these strategies?

WRITING CRITICALLY

The last stage of responding to the reading selections in this text offers you various "Ideas for Discussion/Writing" that will allow you to demonstrate the different skills you have learned in each chapter. You will be most successful if you envision each writing experience as an organic process that follows a natural cycle of prewriting, writing, and rewriting.

Preparing to Write

The prewriting phase involves exploring a subject, generating ideas, selecting and narrowing a topic, analyzing an audience, and developing a purpose. Preceding the writing assignments are "Preparing to Write" questions you should respond to before trying to structure your thoughts into a coherent essay. These questions will assist you in generating new thoughts on the topics and may even stimulate new approaches to old ideas. Keeping a journal to respond to these questions is an excellent technique, because you will then have a record of your opinions on various topics related to the writing assignments that follow. No matter what format you use to answer these questions, the activity of prewriting generally continues in various forms throughout the writing process.

Responses to these questions can be prompted by a number of different "invention" techniques and carried out by you individually, with another student, in small groups, or as a class project. Invention strategies can help you generate responses to these questions and discover related ideas through the various stages of writing your papers. Because you will undoubtedly vary your approach to different assignments, you should be familiar with the following choices available to you:

Brainstorming. The basis of brainstorming is free association. Ideally, you should get a group of students together and bounce ideas, words, and thoughts off of one another until they begin to cluster around related topics. If you don't have a group of students handy, brainstorm by yourself or with a friend. In a group of students or with a friend, the exchange of thoughts usually starts orally but should transfer to paper when your ideas begin to fall into related categories. When you brainstorm by yourself, however, you should write down everything that comes to mind. The act of recording your ideas in this case becomes a catalyst for other thoughts; you are essentially setting up a dialogue with yourself on paper. Then, keep writing down words and phrases that occur to you until they begin to fall into logical subdivisions or until your new ideas come to an end.

Freewriting. Freewriting means writing to discover what you want to say. Set a time limit of about ten minutes, and just write by free association. Write about what you are seeing, feeling, touching, thinking; write about having nothing to say; recopy the sentence you just wrote—anything. Just keep writing on paper or on a computer. After you have generated some material, locate an idea that is central to your writing assignment, put it at the top of another page, and start freewriting again, letting your thoughts take shape around this central idea. This second type of preparation is called *focused freewriting* and is especially valuable when you already have a specific topic.

Journal Entries. Journal entries are much like freewriting, except you have some sense of an audience—probably either your instructor or yourself. In a journal, anything goes. You can respond to the "Preparing to Write" questions, jot down thoughts, paste up articles that spark your interest, write sections of dialogue, draft letters (the kind you never send), record dreams, or make lists. The possibilities are unlimited. An excellent way of practicing writing, the process of keeping a journal is also a wonderful means of dealing with new ideas—a way of fixing them in your mind and making them yours.

Direct Questions. This technique involves asking a series of questions useful in any writing situation to generate ideas, arrange thoughts, or revise prose. One example of this strategy is to use the inquiries journalists rely on to check the coverage in their articles:

Who:	*Who played the game?*
	Who won the game?
What:	*What kind of game was it?*
	What happened in the game?
Why:	*Why was the game played?*
Where:	*Where was the game played?*
When:	*When was the game played?*
How:	*How was the game played?*

If you ask yourself questions of this type on a specific topic, you will begin to produce thoughts and details that will undoubtedly be useful to you in the writing assignments that follow.

Clustering.   Clustering is a method of drawing or mapping your ideas as fast as they come into your mind. Put a word, phrase, or sentence in a circle in the center of a blank page. Then put every new idea that comes to you in a circle and show its relationship to a previous thought by drawing a line to the circle containing the original thought. You will probably reach a natural stopping point for this exercise in two to three minutes.

Although you can generate ideas in a number of different ways, the main principle behind the "Preparing to Write" questions in this text is to encourage you to do what is called *expressive writing* before you tackle any writing assignment. This is writing based on your feelings, thoughts, experiences, observations, and opinions. The process of answering questions about your own ideas and experiences makes you "think on paper," enabling you to surround yourself with your own thoughts and opinions. From this reservoir, you can then choose the ideas you want to develop into an essay and begin writing about them one at a time.

As you use various prewriting techniques to generate responses to the "Preparing to Write" questions, you should know that these responses can (and probably will) appear in many different forms. You can express yourself in lists, outlines, random notes, sentences and paragraphs, charts, graphs, or pictures—whatever keeps the thoughts flowing smoothly and productively. One of our students used a combination of brainstorming and clustering to generate the following thoughts in response to the prewriting exercise following the Thomas essay:

Brainstorming

Mistakes:

> *happen when I'm in a hurry*
> *make me feel stupid*
> *love*
> *relationships*
> *trip back East*
> *pride*
> *going in circles*
> *Bob*

learned a lot about people
people aren't what they seem
getting back on track
parents
corrections
learning from mistakes
I am a better person
my values are clear
mistakes help us change
painful
helpful
valuable

Clustering

From the free-flowing thoughts you generate, you need to decide what to write about and how to limit your subject to a manageable length. Our student writer chose topic 2 from the "Choosing a Topic" list after the essay (see page 27). Her initial responses to the prewriting questions helped her decide to write on "A Time I Got Lost." She then generated more focused ideas and opinions in the form of a journal entry. It is printed here just as she wrote it, errors and all.

Journal Entry

The craziest mistake I think I ever made was on a trip I took recently—I was heading to the east coast from California and reached Durham, North Carolina. I was so excited because I was going to get to see the Atlantic Ocean for the first time in my life and Durham was one of my last landmarks before I reached the sea. In Durham I was going to have to change from a northeast direction to due east.

When I got there the highway was under construction. I took the detour, but got all skrewed up till I realized that I had gone the wrong direction. By this time I was lost somewhere in downtown Durham and didn't know which way was east. I stoped and asked a guy at a gas station and he explained how to get back on the east-bound highway. The way was through the middle of town. By the time I got to where I was supposed to turn right I could only turn left. So I started left and then realized I couldn't turn back the other way! I made a couple of other stops after that, and one jerk told me I "just couldn't get there from here." Eventually I found a truck driver heading toward the same eastbound highway, and he told me to follow him. An hour and forty minutes after reaching Durham's city limits I finally managed to leave going east. I felt as if I had spent an entire month there!

The thing I learned from this was just how egocentric I am. I would not have made this error if I had not been so damn cocky about my sense of direction. My mistake was made worse because I got flustered and didn't listen to the directions clearly. I find that the reason I most often make a mistake is because I don't listen carefully to instructions. This has been a problem all my life.

After I got over feeling really dum I decided this kind of thing was not going to happen again. It was too much a waste of time and gas, so I was going to be more careful of road signs and directions.

This all turned out to be a positive experience though. I learned that there are lots of friendly, helpful people. It was kind of reassuring to know that other folks would help you if you just asked.

I feel this and other mistakes are crucial not only to my life but to my personal growth in general. It is the making of mistakes that helps people learn where they are misdirecting their energies. I think mistakes can help all of us learn to be more careful about some part of our lives. This is why mistakes are crucial. Otherwise, we would continue in the same old rut and never improve.

This entry served as the foundation upon which the student built her essay. Her next step was to consider *audience* and *purpose* (which are usually specified in the writing assignments in this text). The first of these features identifies the person or group of people you will address in your essay. The second is a declaration of your principal reason for writing the essay, which usually takes the form of a thesis statement (the statement of purpose or the controlling idea of an essay). Together these pieces of information consciously or subconsciously help you make most of the decisions you are faced with as you write: what words to choose, what sentence structures to use, what order to present ideas in, which topics to develop, and which to summarize. Without a doubt, the more you know about your audience (age, educational background, likes, dislikes, biases, political persuasion, and social status) and your purpose (to inform, persuade, and/or entertain), the easier the writing task will be. In the rough draft and final draft of the essay in the section that follows, the student knew she was writing to a senior English class at her old high school in order to convince them that mistakes can be positive factors in their lives. This clear sense of audience and purpose helped her realize she should use fairly advanced vocabulary, call upon a variety of sentence structures, and organize her ideas chronologically to make her point most effectively to her intended audience.

At this stage of the writing process, some people benefit from assembling their ideas in the form of an outline. Others use an outline as a check on their logic and organization after the first draft has been written. Whether your outlines are informal (a simple list) or more structured, they can help you visualize the logical relationship of your ideas to each other. We recommend using a rough outline throughout the prewriting and writing stages to ensure that your work will be carefully and tightly organized. Your outline, however, should be adjusted to your draft as it develops.

Writing

The writing stage asks you to draft an essay based on the prewriting material you have assembled. Because you have already made the important preliminary decisions regarding your topic, your audience, and your purpose, the task of actually writing the essay should follow naturally. (Notice we did not say this task should necessarily be easy—just natural.) At this stage, you should look upon your essay as a way of solving a problem or answering a question: The problem/question is posed in your writing assignment, and the solution/answer is your essay. The four "Choosing a Topic" assignments that follow the prewriting questions in the text invite you to consider issues related to the essay you just read. Although they typically ask you to focus on one rhetorical pattern, they draw on many rhetorical strategies (as do all writing assignments in the text) and require you to support your statements with concrete examples. These assignments refer to the Lewis Thomas essay and emphasize the use of example, his dominant rhetorical strategy.

Choosing a Topic

1. You have decided to write an editorial for your local newspaper concerning the impact of computers on our lives. Cite specific experiences you have had with computers to help make your main point.

2. You have been invited back to your high school to make a speech to a senior English class about how people can learn from their mistakes. Write your speech in the form of an essay explaining what you learned from a crucial mistake you have made. Use examples to show these students that mistakes can be positive factors in their lives.

3. In an essay for your writing class, explain one specific human quality. Use Thomas's essay as a model. Cite examples to support your explanation.

4. If you could repair a single mistake with an e-mail, what mistake would you fix? Who would you send the e-mail to? What would you say? Write an e-mail in which you reflect on this mistake and offer an explanation of its consequences and outcomes.

The following essay is our student's first-draft response to topic 2. After writing her journal entry, the student drafted a tentative thesis statement: "I know there are positive changes that can come from making a mistake because I recently had an opportunity to learn some valuable lessons from one of my errors." This statement helped the student writer further develop and organize her ideas as she focused finally on one well-chosen example to illustrate her thesis. At this point, the thesis is simply the controlling idea around which the other topics take shape; it is often revised several times before the final draft.

First Draft: A Time I Got Lost

Parents and teachers frequently pressure us to avoid committing errors. Meanwhile, our friends laugh at us when we make mistakes. With all these different messages, it is hard for us to think of mistakes as positive events. But if any of you take the time to think about what you have learned from mistakes, I bet you will realize all the good things that have come from these events. I know there are positive changes that can come from making a mistake because I recently had an opportunity to learn some valuable lessons in this way.

While traveling back east this last summer, I made the mistake of turning west on an interstate detour in order to reach the Atlantic Ocean. The adventure took me into the heart of Durham, North Carolina, where I got totally lost. I had to get directions several times until two hours later I was going in the right direction. As I was driving out of town, I realized that although I had made a dumb mistake, I had learned a great deal. Overall, the detour was actually a positive experience.

The first thing I remember thinking after I had gotten my wits together was that I had definitely learned something from making the mistake. I had the opportunity to see a new city, filled with new people—3,000 miles from my own hometown, but very much like it. I also became aware that the beach is not always toward the west, as it is in California. The entire experience was like getting a geography lesson firsthand.

As this pleasant feeling began to grow, I came to another realization. I was aware of how important other people can be in making a mistake into a positive experience. My first reaction was "Oh no, someone is going to know I made a mistake!" But the amazing part about this mistake was how supportive everyone was. The townspeople had been entirely willing to help someone they did not know. This mistake helped me learn that people tend to be nicer than I had imagined.

The final lesson I learned from getting lost in Durham was how to be more cautious about my actions so as not to repeat the same mistake. It was this internalization of all the information I gleaned from making the mistake that I see as the most positive part of the experience. I realized that in order to avoid such situations in the future I would have to be less egocentric in my decisions and more willing to listen to directions from other people. I needed to learn that my set way of doing things was not always the best way. If I had not made the mistake, I would not have been aware of my other options.

By making this mistake I learned that there is a more comprehensive manner of looking at the world. In the future, if we could all stop after making a mistake and ask ourselves, "What can I learn from this?" we would be less critical of ourselves and have a great many more positive experiences. If I were not able to make mistakes, I would probably not be able to expand my knowledge of my environment, my sense of others, and my understanding of myself.

Rewriting

The rewriting stage includes revising, editing, and proofreading. The first of these activities, **revising**, actually takes place during the entire writing process as you change words, recast sentences, and move whole paragraphs from one place to another. Making these linguistic and organizational choices means you will also be constantly adjusting your content to your purpose (what you want to accomplish) and your audience (the readers) in much the same way you alter your speech to communicate more effectively in response to the gestures, eye movements, or facial expressions of your listeners. Revising is literally the act of "reseeing" your essay, looking at it through your readers' eyes to determine whether or not it achieves its purpose. As you revise, you should consider matters of both content and form. *In content,* do you have an interesting, thought-provoking title for your essay? Do you think your thesis statement will be clear to your audience? Does your introduction capture the readers' attention? Is your treatment of your topic consistent throughout the essay? Do you support your assertions with specific examples? Does your conclusion sum up your main points? *In form,* is your essay organized effectively? Do you use a variety of rhetorical strategies? Are your sentence structure and vocabulary varied and interesting?

If you compose on a computer, you will certainly reap the benefits as you revise. Computers remove much of the drudgery of rewriting and retyping your drafts. In writing, you may not make as many major revisions as necessary because of the length of time needed to rewrite the material. Computers allow you to move paragraphs or whole sections of your paper from one position to another by pressing a few keys. Without the manual labor of cutting and pasting, you can immediately see if the new organization will improve the logic and coherence of your paper. You may then remove repetitions or insert words and sentences that will serve as the transitions between sections.

You should also consider the value of the graphic design options available on computer software, because the way you present your papers generally affects how your instructor evaluates them. If they are clearly laid out without coffee stains or paw prints from your dog, you have a better chance of being taken seriously than if they are sloppily done. A computer can help in this regard, giving you access to boldface type, italics, boxes, bullets, and graphs of all sorts and letting you make a new copy if you do have an unexpected encounter with a coffee cup or a frisky dog.

Editing entails correcting mistakes in your writing so that your final draft conforms to the conventions of standard written English. Correct punctuation, spelling, and mechanics will help you make your points and will encourage your readers to move smoothly through your essay from topic to topic. At this stage, you should be concerned about such matters as whether your sentences are complete, whether your punctuation is correct and effective, whether you have followed conventional rules for using mechanics, and whether the words in your essay are spelled correctly.

Proofreading involves reading over your entire essay, slowly and carefully, to make certain you have not allowed any errors to slip into your draft. (Most college instructors don't look upon errors as kindly as Thomas does.) In general, good writers try to let some time elapse between writing the final draft and proofreading it (at least a few hours, perhaps a day or so). Otherwise, they find themselves proofreading their thoughts rather than their words. Some writers even profit from proofreading their papers backward—a technique that allows them to focus on individual words and phrases rather than on entire sentences.

Because many writers work well with checklists, we present here a set of guidelines that will help you review the entire writing process.

WRITING INVENTORY

Preparing to Write

✓ Have I explored the prewriting questions through brainstorming, freewriting, journal entries, direct questions, or clustering?

✓ Do I understand my topic or assignment?

✓ Have I narrowed my topic adequately?

✓ Do I have a specific audience for my essay? Do I know their likes and dislikes? Their educational level? Their knowledge of the subject?

✓ Do I have a clear and precise purpose for my essay?

Writing

✓ Can I express my topic as a problem or question?

✓ Is my essay a solution or an answer to that problem or question?

Rewriting

Revising the Content

✓ Does my essay have a clear, interesting title?

✓ Will my statement of purpose (or thesis) be clear to my audience?

✓ Will the introduction make my audience want to read the rest of my essay?

✓ Have I included enough details to prove my main points?

✓ Does my conclusion sum up my central points?

✓ Will I accomplish my purpose with this audience?

Revising the Form

✓ Have I organized my ideas as effectively as possible for this audience?

✓ Do I use appropriate rhetorical strategies to support my main point?

✓ Is my sentence structure varied and interesting?

✓ Is my vocabulary appropriate for my topic, my purpose, and my audience?

✓ Do I present my essay as effectively as possible, including useful graphic design techniques on the computer, if appropriate?

Editing and Proofreading

✓ Have I written complete sentences throughout my essay?

✓ Have I used punctuation correctly and effectively (check especially the use of commas, apostrophes, colons, and semicolons)?

✓ Have I followed conventional rules for mechanics (capitalization, underlining or italics, abbreviations, and numbers)?

✓ Are all the words in my essay spelled correctly? (Use a dictionary or a spell-checker when in doubt.)

Following is the student's revised draft of her essay on making mistakes in life. The final draft of this typical freshman essay (written to high school seniors, as the assignment specifies) represents the entire writing process at work. We have made notes in the margin to highlight various effective elements in her essay, some of which we have underlined for emphasis.

Mistakes and Maturity

Catchy title; good change from first draft

Rapport with audience and point of view established

Parents and teachers frequently harp on us to correct our errors. Meanwhile, our friends laugh at us when we make mistakes. With all these negative messages, most of us have a hard time believing that problems can be positive experiences. But if we take the time to think about what we have learned from various blunders, we will realize all the good that has come from these events. <u>I know that making mistakes can have positive results because I recently learned several valuable lessons from one unforgettable experience.</u>

Clear, stimulating introduction for high school seniors

Revised thesis statement

<u>While I was traveling on the East Coast last summer</u>, I made the mistake of turning west on an interstate detour in an attempt to reach the Atlantic Ocean. This adventure took me into the center of Durham, North Carolina, where I became totally lost, bewildered, and angry at myself. I had to ask for directions several times until two hours later, when I finally found the correct highway toward the ocean. As I was driving out of town, I realized that although I had made a "dumb" mistake, I had actually learned a great deal. Overall, my adventure had been quite positive.

Good brief summary of complex experience (see notes from Preparing to Write)

Background information

Good details

First topic (topics are in chronological order)

The first insight I remember having after my wits returned was that <u>I had definitely learned more about United States geography from making this mistake</u>. I had become intimately acquainted with a town

3,000 miles from home that greatly resem- Adequate
bled my own city, and I had become aware number of
examples
that the beach is not always toward the west,
as it is in California. I had also met some
Nice close pleasant strangers. <u>Looking at my confusion</u>
to this <u>as a learning experience encouraged me to</u>
paragraph <u>have positive feelings about the mistake</u>.

As I relaxed and let this happy feeling
Second grow, I came to another realization. <u>I</u>
topic <u>became aware of how important other peo-</u>
<u>ple can be in turning a mistake into a posi-</u>
<u>tive event</u>. Although my first reaction had
been "Oh, no! Someone is going to know
I'm lost," I was amazed by how supportive Clear
other people were during my panic and explanation
with details
embarrassment. From an old man swinging
on his front porch to an elementary school
boy crossing the street with his bright blue
backpack, I found that the townspeople of
Durham were entirely willing to help some-
Good one they did not even know. <u>I realized that</u>
summary <u>people in general are nicer than I had previ-</u>
statement <u>ously thought</u>.

The final lesson I learned from making
this mistake was <u>how to be more cautious</u> Third topic
<u>about my future decisions</u>. This insight was,
in fact, the most positive part of the entire
experience. What I realized I must do to Specific
details
prevent similar errors in the future was to
relax, not be so bullheaded in my decisions,
and be more willing to listen to directions
from other people. <u>I might never have had</u> Good
<u>these positive realizations if I had not made</u> summary
statement
<u>this mistake</u>.

Clear Thus, <u>by driving in circles for two hours,</u>
transition <u>I developed a more comprehensive way of</u>
statement <u>looking at the world</u>. If I were unable to
make mistakes, I probably would not have
had this chance to <u>learn about my environ-</u> Good
summary of
<u>ment, improve my impressions of strangers,</u> three topics

and <u>reconsider the egocentric way in which</u> without being repetitive
<u>I act in certain situations</u>. Perhaps there's a
lesson here for all of us. Instead of criticizing
ourselves unduly, if each one of us could
pause after we make an error and ask, "How
Concluding statement applicable to all readers can I profit from this?," <u>we would realize</u> Nicely focused concluding remark
<u>that mistakes can often be turned into posi-</u>
<u>tive events that will help us become more</u>
<u>confident and mature.</u>

As these various drafts of the student paper indicate, the essay assignments in this book encourage you to transfer to your own writing your understanding of how form and content work together. If you use the short-answer questions after each reading selection as a guide, the writing assignments will help you learn how to give shape to your own ideas and to gain control of your readers' thoughts and feelings. In essence, they help you recognize the power you have through language over your life and your environment.

CONCLUSION

As you approach the essays in this text, remember that both reading and writing function most efficiently as processes of discovery. Through these skills, you educate and expand your own mind and the minds of your readers. They can provide a powerful means of discovering new information or clarifying what you already know. Reading and writing lead to understanding. And just as you can discover how to read through writing, so too can you become more aware of the details of the writing process through reading. We hope your time spent with this book is both pleasant and profitable as you refine your ability to discover and express effectively the good ideas within yourself.

1

DESCRIPTION
Exploring through the Senses

All of us use description in our daily lives. We might, for example, try to convey the horrors of a recent history exam to our parents, help a friend visualize someone we met on vacation, or describe an automobile accident for a police report. Whatever our specific purpose, description is a fundamental part of communication: We give and receive descriptions constantly, and our lives are continually affected by this simple yet important rhetorical technique.

DEFINING DESCRIPTION

Description may be defined as the act of capturing people, places, events, objects, and feelings in words so that a reader (or listener) can visualize and respond to them. Unlike narration, which traditionally presents events in a clear time sequence, description essentially suspends its objects in time, making them exempt from the limits of chronology. Narration tells a story, while pure description contains no action or time. Description is one of our primary forms of self-expression; it paints a verbal picture that helps the reader understand or share a sensory experience through the process of "showing" rather than "telling." *Telling* your friends, for example, that "the campgrounds were filled with friendly, happy activities" is not as engaging as *showing* them by saying, "The campgrounds were alive with the smell of spicy baked beans, the sound of high-pitched laughter, and the sight of happy families sharing the warmth of a fire." Showing your readers helps them understand your experience through as many senses as possible.

Descriptions fall somewhere between two extremes: (1) totally objective reports (with no trace of opinions or feelings), such as we might find in a dictionary or an encyclopedia; and (2) very subjective accounts, which focus almost exclusively on personal impressions. The same horse, for instance, might be described by one writer as "a large, solid-hoofed herbivorous mammal having a long mane and a tail" (objective) and by another as "a magnificent and spirited beast flaring its nostrils in search of adventure" (subjective). Most descriptive writing, however, falls somewhere between these two extremes: "a large, four-legged beast in search of adventure."

Objective description is principally characterized by its impartial, precise, and emotionless tone. Found most prominently in technical and scientific writing, such accounts might include a description of equipment to be used in a chemistry experiment, the results of a market survey for a particular consumer product, or a medical appraisal of a heart patient's physical symptoms. In situations like these, accurate, unbiased, and easily understandable accounts are of the utmost importance.

Subjective description, in contrast, is intentionally created to produce a particular response in the reader or listener. Focusing on feelings rather than on raw data, it tries to activate as many senses as possible, thereby leading the audience to a specific conclusion or state of mind. Examples of subjective descriptions are a parent's disapproving comments about one of your friends, a professor's glowing analysis of your most recent "A" paper, or a basketball coach's critique of the team's losing effort in last night's big game.

In most situations, the degree of subjectivity or objectivity in a descriptive passage depends to a large extent on the writer's purpose and intended audience. In the case of the heart patient mentioned above, the person's physician might present the case in a formal, scientific way to a group of medical colleagues; in a personal, sympathetic way to the invalid's spouse; and in financial terms to a number of potential contributors in order to solicit funds for heart disease research.

The following paragraph describes one student's fond memories of visiting "the farm." As you read it, notice the writer's use of subjective description to communicate to her readers the multitude of contradictory feelings she connects with this rural retreat.

The shrill scream of the alarm shatters a dream. This is the last day of my visit to the place I call "the farm," an old ramshackle house in the country owned by one of my aunts. I want to go out once more in the peace of the early morning, walk in the crisp and chilly fields, and breathe the sweet air. My body feels jarred as my feet hit the hard-packed clay dirt. I tune out my stiff muscles and cold arms and legs and instead focus on two herons playing hopscotch on the canal bank: Every few yards I walk toward them, they fly one over the other an almost equal distance away from me. A killdeer with its piercing crystalline cry dips its body as it flies low over the water, the tip of its wing leaving a ring to reverberate outward. The damp earth has a strong, rich, musky scent. To the east, dust rises, and for the first time I hear the clanking and straining of a tractor as it harrows smooth the soil before planting. A crop duster rises close by just as it cuts off its release of spray, the acrid taste of chemicals filtering down through the air. As the birds chatter and peck at the fields, I reluctantly return to my life in the city.

THINKING CRITICALLY BY USING DESCRIPTION

Each rhetorical mode in this book gives us new insights into the process of thinking by providing different options for arranging our thoughts and our experiences. The more we know about these options, the more conscious we become of how our minds operate and the better chance we have to improve and refine our communication skills.

As you examine description as a way of thinking, consider it in isolation for a moment—away from the other rhetorical modes. Think of it as a muscle you can isolate and strengthen on its own in a weight-training program before you ask it to perform together with other muscles. By isolating description, you will learn more readily what it entails and how it functions as a critical-thinking tool. In the process, you will also strengthen your knowledge of how to recognize and use description more effectively in your reading, in your writing, and in your daily life.

Just as you exercise to strengthen muscles, so too will you benefit from doing exercises to improve your skill in using descriptive techniques. As you have learned, description depends to a great extent on the keenness of your senses. So as you prepare to read and write descriptive essays, do the following tasks so that you can first learn what the process of description feels like in your own head. Really use your imagination to play with these exercises on as many different levels as possible. Also write when you are asked to do so. The combination of thinking and writing is often especially useful when you practice your thinking skills.

© Gerry Gavigan/Growbag.

1. Imagine what you might smell, taste, hear, feel, or see in the accompanying photograph taken by Gerry Gavigan. Then, using words that will create these sensory details, write a few sentences that might accompany this photograph if it were published in a newspaper or travel magazine.
2. Make a list of five descriptive words you would use to trigger each of the following senses: taste, sight, hearing, touch, and smell.
3. Choose an unusual object, and brainstorm about its physical characteristics. Then brainstorm about the emotions this object evokes. Why is this object so unusual or special? Compare your two brainstorming results, and draw some conclusions about their differences.

READING AND WRITING DESCRIPTIVE ESSAYS

All good descriptions share four fundamental qualities: (1) an accurate sense of audience (who the readers are) and purpose (why the essay was written), (2) a clear vision of the object being described, (3) a careful selection of details that help communicate the author's vision, and (4) a consistent point of view or perspective from which a writer composes. The dominant impression or main effect the writer wishes to leave with a specific audience dictates virtually all of the verbal choices in a descriptive essay. Although description is featured in this chapter, you should also pay close attention to how other rhetorical strategies (such as example, division/classification, and cause/effect) can best support an essay's dominant impression.

How to Read a Descriptive Essay

Preparing to Read.   As you approach the reading selections in this chapter, you should focus first on the author's title and try to make some initial assumptions about the essay that follows: Does Ray Bradbury reveal his attitude toward his subject in the title "Summer Rituals"? Can you guess what the general mood of Kimberly Wozencraft's "Notes from the Country Club" will be? Then scan the essay to discover its audience and purpose: What do you think John McPhee's purpose is in "The Pines"? Whom is Malcolm Cowley addressing in "The View from 80"? Why does Bernard Cooper write an essay about labyrinths? You should also read the synopsis of each essay in the Rhetorical Table of Contents (on pages v–xiv); these brief summaries will provide you with helpful information at this point in the reading process.

Next, learn as much as you can about the author and the conditions under which the essay was composed, information that is provided in the biographical statement before each essay. For a descriptive essay, the conditions under which the author wrote the essay, coupled with his or her purpose, can be very revealing: When and under what conditions did Kimberly Wozencraft write "Notes from the Country Club"? What was her intention in writing the essay? Can you determine when Malcolm Cowley's piece was written? Does it describe the author's life now or in the past? Learning where the essay was first published will also give you valuable information about its audience.

Last, before you begin to read, try to do some brainstorming on the essay's title. In this chapter, respond to the Preparing to Read questions before each essay, which ask you to begin thinking and writing about the topic under consideration. At the same time, take advantage of the Internet prompt to help you find more information on the topic you are about to consider. Then pose your own questions: What are some of the most important rituals in your life (Bradbury)? What would you like to learn from Cowley about the joys and frustrations of being eighty years old? What is one of your favorite hobbies (Cooper)?

Reading.   As you read each essay for the first time, jot down your initial reactions to it, and try to make connections and see relationships among the author's biography; the essay's title, purpose, and audience; and the synopsis. In this way, you will create a context or framework for your reading. See if you can figure out, for example, what Bradbury is implying about rituals in general in his essay "Summer Rituals" or why Wozencraft wrote an essay about her experiences in prison. Try to discover what the relationship is between purpose, audience, and publication information in Cowley's essay.

Also determine at this point if the author's treatment of his or her subject is predominantly objective (generally free of emotion) or subjective (heavily charged with emotion). Or perhaps the essay falls somewhere between these two extremes.

In addition, make sure you have a general sense of the dominant impression each author is trying to convey. Such an initial approach to reading these descriptive selections will give you a foundation upon which to analyze the material during your second, more in-depth reading.

Finally, at the end of your first reading, take a look at the questions after each essay to make certain you can answer them. This material will guide your rereading.

Rereading.   As you reread these descriptive essays, you should be discovering exactly what the essay's dominant impression is and how the author created it. Notice each author's careful selection of details and the way in which these details come together to leave you with this impression. Also try to determine how certain details add to and detract from that dominant impression and how the writer's point of view affects it: How does Cowley enable us to identify with his experiences if we have never been 80 years old? How does Cooper create a sense of mystery in "Labyrinthine"?

Try to find during this reading other rhetorical modes that support the description. Although the essays in this chapter describe various persons, places, or objects, all of the authors call upon other rhetorical strategies (especially example and comparison/contrast) to communicate their descriptions. How do these various rhetorical strategies work together in each essay to create a coherent whole? In addition, the authors all attempt to get your to see their view of the world.

Finally, answering the questions after each essay will check your understanding of the author's main points and help you think critically about the essay in preparing for the discussion/writing assignments that follow.

For an inventory of the reading process, you may want to review the checklists on page 20 of the Introduction.

How to Write a Descriptive Essay

Preparing to Write. Before you choose a writing assignment, use the prewriting questions that follow each essay to help you discover your own ideas and opinions about the general topic of the essay. Next, choose an assignment or read the one assigned to you. Then, just as you do when you read an essay, you should determine the audience and purpose for your description (if these are not specified for you in the assignment). To whom are you writing? And why? Will an impartial, objective report be appropriate, or should you present a more emotional, subjective account to accomplish your task? In assessing your audience, you need to determine what they do and do not know about your topic. This information will help you make decisions about what you are going to say and how you will say it. Your purpose will be defined by what you intend your audience to know, think, or believe after they have read your descriptive essay. Do you want them to make up their own minds about summer rituals or old age, for example, based on an objective presentation of data, or do you hope to sway their opinions through a more subjective display of information? Or perhaps you will decide to blend the two techniques, combining facts and opinions in order to achieve the impression of personal certainty based on objective evidence. What dominant impression do you want to leave with your audience? As you might suspect, decisions regarding audience and purpose are as important to writing descriptions as they are to reading descriptions and will shape your descriptive essay from start to finish.

The second quality of good description concerns the object of your analysis and the clarity with which you present it to the reader. Whenever possible, you should thoroughly investigate the person, place, moment, or feeling you wish to describe, paying particular attention to its effect upon each of your five senses. What can you see, smell, hear, taste, and touch as you examine it? If you want to describe your house, for example, begin by asking yourself a series of pertinent questions: How big is the house? What color is it? How many exterior doors does the house have? How many interior doors? Are any of the rooms wallpapered? If so, what are the colors and textures of that wallpaper? How many different shades of paint cover the walls? Which rooms have constant noises (from clocks and other mechanical devices)? Are the kitchen appliances hot or cold to the touch? What is the quietest room in the house? The noisiest? What smells do you notice in the laundry? In the kitchen? In the basement? Most important, do any of these sensory questions trigger particular childhood memories? Although you will probably not use all of these details in your descriptive essay, the process of generating and answering such detailed questions will help reacquaint you with the object of your description as it also assists you in designing and focusing your paper.

To help you generate some of these ideas, you may want to review the prewriting techniques introduced on pages 21–23.

Writing. As you write, you must select details for your description with great care and precision so that you leave your reader with a specific impression. If, for instance, you want your audience to feel the warmth and comfort of your home, you might concentrate on describing the plush carpets, the big upholstered chairs, the inviting scent of hot apple cider, and the crackling fire. If, on the other hand, you want to gain your audience's sympathy, you might prefer to focus on the sparse austerity of your home environment: the bare walls, the quietness, the lack of color and decoration, the dim lighting, and the frigid temperature. You also want to make sure you omit unrelated ideas, like a conversation between your parents you accidentally overheard. Your careful choice of details will help control your audience's reaction.

To make your impression even more vivid, you might use figurative language to fill out your descriptions. Using words "figuratively" means using them imaginatively rather than literally. The two most popular forms of figurative language are *simile* and *metaphor*. A *simile* is a comparison between two dissimilar objects or ideas introduced by *like* or *as:* "The rocking chairs sounded like crickets" (Bradbury). A *metaphor* is an implied comparison between two dissimilar objects or ideas that is not introduced by *like* or *as:* "Life for younger persons is still a battle royal of each against each" (Cowley). Besides enlivening your writing, figurative language helps your readers understand objects, feelings, and ideas that are complex or obscure by comparing them to those that are more familiar.

The last important quality of an effective descriptive essay is point of view, your physical perspective on your subject. Because the organization of your essay depends on your point of view, you need to choose a specific angle from which to approach your description. If you verbally jump around your home, referring first to a picture on the wall in your bedroom, next to the microwave in the kitchen, and then to the quilt on your bed, no reasonable audience will be able to follow your description. Nor will they want to. If, however, you move from room to room in some logical, sequential way, always focusing on the details you want your readers to know, you will be helping your audience form a clear, memorable impression of your home. Your vision will become their vision. In other words, your point of view plays a part in determining the organization of your description. Working spatially, you could move from side to side (from one wall to another in the rooms we have discussed), from top to bottom (from ceiling to floor), or from far to near (from the farthest to the closest point in a room), or you might progress from large to small objects, from uninteresting to interesting, or from funny to serious. Whatever plan you choose should help you accomplish your purpose with your particular audience.

Rewriting.   As you reread each of your descriptive essays, play the role of your audience and try to determine what dominant impression you receive by the end of your reading.

- Do you communicate the dominant impression you want to convey?
- Do you have a clear point of view on your subject?
- How does the essay make you feel?
- What does it make you think about?
- Which senses does it stimulate?
- Do you use similes or metaphors when appropriate?
- Are you *showing* rather than *telling* in your description?

For additional suggestions on the writing process, you may want to consult the checklists on pages 31–32 of the Introduction.

STUDENT ESSAY: DESCRIPTION AT WORK

In the following essay, a student relives some of her childhood memories through a subjective description of her grandmother's house. As you read it, pay particular attention to the different types of sensual details the student writer chooses to communicate her dominant impression of her grandmother's home. Notice also her use of carefully chosen details to *show* rather than *tell* us about her childhood reminiscences, especially her comparisons, which make the memory as vivid for the reader as it is for the writer.

Grandma's House

Writer's point of view or perspective

Dominant impression

Sight

Comparison (simile)

<u>My</u> <u>most vivid childhood memories</u> are set in my Grandma Goodlink's house, a curious blend of familiar and mysterious treasures. Grandma lived at the end of a dead-end street, in the same house she had lived in since the first day of her marriage. That was half a century and thirteen children ago. A set of crumbly steps made of concrete mixed with gravel led up to her front door. I remember a big gap between the house and the steps, <u>as if someone had not pushed them up close enough to the house.</u> Anyone who looked into the gap <u>could see old toys and books</u> that had fallen into the crack behind the steps and had remained there, forever irretrievable.

Comparison (simile)

Comparison (metaphor)

Sight

Sound

Smell

Smell

Sight

Sight

Sound

Sight

Sight

Sight

Smell

Sight

Touch
Sight

Taste

Comparison (Simile)

Sight

Only a hook-type lock on the front door protected Grandma's many beautiful antiques. Her living room was set up like a church or schoolroom, with an old purple velvet couch against the far wall and two chairs immediately in front of the couch facing the same direction. One-half of the couch was always buried in old clothes, magazines, and newspapers, and a lone shoe sat on top of the pile, a finishing touch to some bizarre modern sculpture. To one side was an aged and tuneless upright piano with yellowed keys. The ivory overlay was missing so that the wood underneath showed through, and many of the keys made only a muffled and frustrating thump, no matter how hard I pressed them. On the wall facing the piano was the room's only window, draped with yellowed lace curtains. Grandma always left that window open. I remember sitting near it, smelling the rain while the curtains tickled my face.

For no apparent reason, an old curtain hung in the door between the kitchen and the living room. In the kitchen, a large Formica-topped table always held at least a half-dozen varieties of homemade jelly, as well as a loaf of bread, gooseberry pies or cherry pies with the pits left in, boxes of cereal, and anything else not requiring refrigeration, as if the table served as a small, portable pantry. Grandma's kitchen always smelled of toast, and I often wondered—and still do—if she lived entirely on toast. A hole had eaten through the kitchen floor, not just the warped yellow linoleum, but all the way through the floor itself. My sisters and I never wanted to take a bath at Grandma's house, because we discovered that anyone who lay on the floor face down and put one

Sight eye to the hole <u>could see the bathtub</u>, which
was kept in the <u>musty</u> basement because the Smell
upstairs bathroom was too small.

The back bedroom was near the kitchen
and adjacent to the basement stairs. I once
heard one of my aunts call that room a fire-
trap, and indeed it was. The room was <u>wall-</u>
Sight <u>papered with the old newspapers</u> Grandma
liked to collect, and the bed was stacked
high with <u>my mother's and aunts' old</u> Sight
<u>clothes</u>. There was no space between the
furniture in that room, only a narrow path
against one wall leading to the bed. A sideboard was shoved against the opposite wall;
a sewing table was pushed up against the
sideboard; a short chest of drawers lay
against the sewing table; and so on. But no Sight
one could identify these pieces of forgotten
furniture without digging through the
sewing patterns, half-made dresses, dishes,
and books. Any outsider would just think
this was a part of the room where the floor
had been raised to about waist-level, so
thoroughly was the mass of furniture hidden.

Stepping off Grandma's sloping back
porch was <u>like stepping into an enchanted</u> Comparison
<u>forest</u>. The grass and weeds were hip-level, (simile)
with a tiny dirt path leading to nowhere, <u>as</u>
Comparison <u>if it had lost its way in the jungle.</u> <u>A fancy</u> Sight
(simile) <u>white fence</u>, courtesy of the neighbors, bordered the yard in back and vainly attempted
to hold in the <u>gooseberries, raspberries, and</u> Sight
<u>blackberries</u> that grew wildly along the side
of Grandma's yard. Huge <u>crabapple, cherry,</u>
Sight <u>and walnut trees</u> shaded the house and hid
the sky. I used to stand under them and look
up, pretending to be deep in a magic forest.
The ground was <u>cool and damp</u> under my Touch
bare feet, even in the middle of the day, and

Sound my head would fill with the <u>sweet fragrance</u> Smell <u>of mixed spring flowers</u> and <u>the throaty</u> <u>cooing of doves</u> I could never find but could always hear. But, before long, the wind would shift, and the <u>musty aroma of</u> Smell <u>petroleum</u> from a nearby refinery would jerk me back to reality.

Dominant impression rephrased Grandma's house is indeed a place of wonderful memories. Just as her decaying concrete steps store the treasures of many lost childhoods, <u>her house still stands,</u> <u>guarding the memories of generations of</u> <u>children and grandchildren.</u>

Student Writer's Comments

Writing this descriptive essay was easy and enjoyable for me—once I got started. I decided to write about my grandmother's house because I knew it so well, but I had trouble coming up with the impression I wanted to convey to my readers. I have so many recollections of this place I didn't know which set of memories would be most interesting to others. So I began by brainstorming, forcing myself to think of images from all five senses.

After I had accumulated plenty of images, which triggered other memories I had completely forgotten, I began to write. I organized my essay spatially as if I were walking through Grandma's house room by room. But I let my senses lead the way. Before I started writing, I had no idea how many paragraphs I would have, but as I meandered through the house recording my memories of sights, smells, sounds, tastes, and textures, I ended up writing one paragraph on each room, plus one for the yard. For this assignment, I wrote the three paragraphs about the inside of the house first; then, the introduction started to take shape in my head, so I got it down; and last, I wrote the paragraph on the backyard and my conclusion. Finally, my "dominant impression" came to me: This is a house that guards the memories of many generations. My grandmother has always lived in this house, and my mother has her own set of memories associated with this place too.

This focus for my paper made the revising process fairly easy, as I worked on the entire essay with a specific purpose in mind. Previously, my biggest problem had been that I had too many scattered memories and realized I had to be more selective. Once I had my dominant impression, I knew which images to keep and which to drop from my draft. Also, as I reworked my essay, I looked for ways to make my description more exciting and vivid for the reader—as if he or she were right there with me. To accomplish this, I explained some special features of my grandma's house by comparing them with items the reader would most likely be familiar with. I also worked, at this point, on making one paragraph flow into another by adding transitions that would move the reader smoothly from one group of ideas to the next. "Only a hook-type lock on the front door" got my readers into the living room. The old curtain between the kitchen and the living room moved my essay out of the living room and into the kitchen. I started my third paragraph about the indoors by saying "The back bedroom was near the kitchen and adjacent to the basement stairs" so my readers could get their bearings in relation to other parts of the house they had already been introduced to. Finally, I was satisfied that my essay was a clear, accurate description of my view of my grandma's house. My brother might have a completely different set of memories, but this was my version of a single generation of impressions organized, finally, into one coherent essay.

SOME FINAL THOUGHTS ON DESCRIPTION

Because description is one of the most basic forms of verbal communication, you will find descriptive passages in most of the reading selections throughout this textbook. Description provides us with the means to capture our audience's attention and clarify certain points in all of our writing. The examples chosen for the following section, however, are predominantly descriptive—the main purpose in each being to involve the readers' senses as vividly as possible. As you read through each of these essays, try to determine its intended audience and purpose, the object of the description, the extent to which details are included or excluded, and the author's point of view. Equipped with these four areas of reference, you can become an increasingly sophisticated reader and writer of descriptive prose.

DESCRIPTION IN REVIEW

Reading Descriptive Essays

Preparing to Read

✓ What assumptions can you make from the essay's title?

✓ Can you guess what the general mood of the essay is?

✓ What is the essay's purpose and audience?

✓ What does the synopsis tell you about the essay?

✓ What can you learn from the author's biography?

✓ Can you guess what the author's point of view toward the subject is?

✓ What are your responses to the "Preparing to Read" questions?

Reading

✓ Is the essay predominantly objective or subjective?

✓ What dominant impression is the author trying to convey?

✓ Did you preview the questions that follow the essay?

Rereading

✓ How does the author create the essay's dominant impression?

✓ What other rhetorical modes does the author use?

✓ What are your responses to the questions after the essay?

Writing Descriptive Essays

Preparing to Write

✓ What are your responses to the "Preparing to Write" questions?

✓ What is your purpose? Will you be primarily objective or subjective?

✓ Who is your audience?

✓ What is the dominant impression you want to convey?

Writing

✓ Do the details you are choosing support your dominant impression?

✓ Do you use words literally and figuratively?

✓ What is your point of view toward your subject?

✓ Do you *show* rather than *tell* your dominant impression?

Rewriting

✓ Do you communicate the dominant impression you want to convey?

✓ Do you have a clear point of view on your subject?

✓ Do you use similes or metaphors when appropriate?

RAY BRADBURY   (1920–   )

Summer Rituals

Ray Bradbury is one of America's best-known and most loved
writers of science fiction. His extensive publications include such
popular novels as *The Martian Chronicles* (1950), *The Illustrated
Man* (1951), *Fahrenheit 451* (1953), *Dandelion Wine* (1957), and
Something Wicked This Way Comes (1962). He has also written
dozens of short stories, poems, essays, plays, and radio and movie
scripts (including the screenplay of John Huston's film version of
Moby Dick). As a child, he escaped his strict Baptist upbringing
through a steady diet of Jules Verne, H. G. Wells, and Edgar
Rice Burroughs, along with Buck Rogers and Prince Valiant
comic books: "I was a sucker for lies, beautiful, fabulous lies,
which instruct us to better our lives as a result, but which don't
tell the truth." A frequent theme in his many novels is the impact
of science on humanity: "My stories are intended," he claims, "as
much to forecast how to prevent dooms, as to predict them."
Bradbury's more recent publications include *The Last Circus*
(1981), *The Complete Poems of Ray Bradbury* (1982), *The Love
Affair* (1983), *Dinosaur Tales* (1983), *A Memory for Murder* (1984),
Forever and the Earth (1984), *Death Is a Lonely Business* (1985), *The
Toynbee Convector* (1989), *A Day in the Life of Hollywood* (1992),
Quicker Than the Eye (1996), *Driving Blind* (1998), *From the Dust
Returned* (2000), and *Let's All Kill Constance* (2003). The author
lives in Cheviot Hills, California, where he enjoys painting and
making ceramics.

Preparing to Read

"Summer Rituals," an excerpt from *Dandelion Wine,* describes
the comfortable ceremony of putting up a front-porch swing in
early summer. Focusing on the perceptions of Douglas, a young
boy, the essay clearly sets forth the familiar yet deeply significant
rhythms of life in a small town.

Exploring Experience: Before you read this selection, take a few
moments to consider the value of ritual in your own life: Can you
think of any activities that you and your family have elevated to

the level of ceremonial importance? What about holidays? Birthdays? Sporting events? Spring cleaning? When do these activities take place? Do the same people participate in them every year? Why do you repeat these rituals? What purpose do they have for you? For others whom you know? For society in general?

Learning Online: Go to http://www.naturephotographs.com, and look at pictures in the "Summer" section. Find a picture that represents summer to you. Study the picture, and think about how you would describe the location or moment in time.

Yes, summer was rituals, each with its natural time   1 and place. The ritual of lemonade or ice-tea making, the ritual of wine, shoes, or no shoes, and at last, swiftly following the others, with quiet dignity, the ritual of the front-porch swing.

On the third day of summer in the late afternoon Grandfather   2 reappeared from the front door to gaze serenely at the two empty eye rings in the ceiling of the porch. Moving to the geranium-pot-lined rail like Ahab surveying the mild day and the mild-looking sky, he wet his finger to test the wind, and shucked his coat to see how shirt sleeves felt in the westering hours. He acknowledged the salutes of other captains on yet other flowered porches, out themselves to discern the gentle ground swell of weather, oblivious to their wives chirping or snapping like fuzzball hand dogs hidden behind black porch screens.

"All right, Douglas, let's set it up."   3

In the garage they found, dusted, and carried forth the howdah,   4 as it were, for the quiet summer-night festivals, the swing chair which Grandpa chained to the porch-ceiling eyelets.

Douglas, being lighter, was first to sit in the swing. Then, after   5 a moment, Grandfather gingerly settled his pontifical weight beside the boy. Thus they sat, smiling at each other, nodding, as they swung silently back and forth, back and forth.

Ten minutes later Grandma appeared with water buckets and   6 brooms to wash down and sweep off the porch. Other chairs, rockers and straight-backs, were summoned from the house.

"Always like to start sitting early in the season," said Grandpa,   7 "before the mosquitoes thicken."

About seven o'clock you could hear the chairs scraping back 8
from the tables, someone experimenting with a yellow-toothed
piano, if you stood outside the dining-room window and listened.
Matches being struck, the first dishes bubbling in the suds and tin-
kling on the wall racks, somewhere, faintly, a phonograph playing.
And then as the evening changed the hour, at house after house
on the twilight streets, under the immense oaks and elms, on shady
porches, people would begin to appear, like those figures who tell
good or bad weather in rain-or-shine clocks.

Uncle Bert, perhaps Grandfather, then Father, and some of the 9
cousins; the men all coming out first into the syrupy evening,
blowing smoke, leaving the women's voices behind in the cooling-
warm kitchen to set their universe aright. Then the first male
voices under the porch brim, the feet up, the boys fringed on the
worn steps or wooden rails where sometime during the evening
something, a boy or a geranium pot, would fall off.

At last, like ghosts hovering momentarily behind the door 10
screen, Grandma, Great-grandma, and Mother would appear, and
the men would shift, move, and offer seats. The women carried
varieties of fans with them, folded newspapers, bamboo whisks, or
perfumed kerchiefs, to start the air moving about their faces as they
talked.

What they talked of all evening long, no one remembered next 11
day. It wasn't important to anyone what the adults talked about; it
was only important that the sounds came and went over the delicate ferns that bordered the porch on three sides; it was only
important that the darkness filled the town like black water being
poured over the houses and that the cigars glowed and that the
conversations went on and on. The female gossip moved out, disturbing the first mosquitoes so they danced in frenzies on the air.
The male voices invaded the old house timbers; if you closed your
eyes and put your head down against the floor boards you could
hear the men's voices rumbling like a distant, political earthquake,
constant, unceasing, rising or falling a pitch.

Douglas sprawled back on the dry porch planks, completely 12
contented and reassured by these voices, which would speak on
through eternity, flow in a stream of murmurings over his body,
over his closed eyelids, into his drowsy ears, for all time. The rocking chairs sounded like crickets, the crickets sounded like rocking
chairs, and the moss-covered rain barrel by the dining-room

window produced another generation of mosquitoes to provide a topic of conversation through endless summers ahead.

Sitting on the summer-night porch was so good, so easy and so 13 reassuring that it could never be done away with. These were rituals that were right and lasting; the lighting of pipes, the pale hands that moved knitting needles in the dimness, the eating of foil-wrapped, chill Eskimo Pies, the coming and going of all the people. For at some time or other during the evening, everyone visited here; the neighbors down the way, the people across the street; Miss Fern and Miss Roberta humming by in their electric runabout, giving Tom or Douglas a ride around the block and then coming up to sit down and fan away the fever in their cheeks; or Mr. Jonas, the junkman, having left his horse and wagon hidden in the alley, and ripe to bursting with words, would come up the steps looking as fresh as if his talk had never been said before, and somehow it never had. And last of all, the children, who had been off squinting their way through a last hide-and-seek or kick-the-can, panting, glowing, would sickle quietly back like boomerangs along the soundless lawn, to sink beneath the talking talking talking of the porch voices which would weigh and gentle them down. . . .

Oh, the luxury of lying in the fern night and the grass night and 14 the night of susurrant, slumbrous voices weaving the dark together. The grownups had forgotten he was there, so still, so quiet Douglas lay, noting the plans they were making for his and their own futures. And the voices chanted, drifted, in moonlit clouds of cigarette smoke while the moths, like late appleblossoms come alive, tapped faintly about the far street lights, and the voices moved on into the coming years. . . .

UNDERSTANDING DETAILS

1. What are the main similarities and differences between Douglas and Grandfather in this essay? How are their views of the world the same? How are their views different?

2. From the scattered details you have read in this essay, describe Douglas's house. How large do you think the front porch is? What color is the house? How many trees and shrubs surround it? What part of your description is based on facts in the essay? What part comes from inferences you have made on your own?

3. How do the men differ from the women in this excerpt? Divide a piece of paper into two columns; then list as many qualities of each gender as you can find. (For example, the narrator hears the men's voices "rumbling" like an "earthquake"; in contrast, the women move like "ghosts," their gossip "disturbing the . . . mosquitoes.") What other descriptive differences can you find between the men and women? What conclusions can you draw from these differences?
4. How did the conversation blend with the surroundings in Bradbury's description?

ANALYZING MEANING

1. A "ritual" may be briefly defined as "a customarily repeated act that expresses a system of values." Using this definition, explain why the ritual of the front-porch swing is important to Douglas's family. What feelings or implicit values lie behind this particular ritual?
2. What other rituals are mentioned in this essay? How are they related to the front-porch swing? To summer? To Douglas and his family?
3. Bradbury helps us feel the comfort, warmth, and familiarity of the scene depicted in this essay through the use of a number of original descriptive details: for example, "summer-night festivals," "yellow-toothed piano," "rain-or-shine clocks," "syrupy evening," and "foil-wrapped, chill Eskimo Pies." Find at least five other descriptive words or phrases, and explain how each enables us to identify with the characters and situations in this story. Which of the five senses does each of these details arouse in the reader?
4. In what ways do you think Douglas was "completely contented and reassured" (paragraph 12) by the voices around him? Why did Douglas feel this contentment would last "for all time" (paragraph 12)?

DISCOVERING RHETORICAL STRATEGIES

1. Some of the author's sentences are very long and involved, whereas others are quite short. What effects do these changes in sentence length have on you as a reader? Give a specific

example of a shift in length from one sentence to another and explain its effect.

2. This descriptive essay is filled with many interesting similes (comparisons using the words *like* or *as*) and metaphors (comparisons without *like* or *as*). For example, Grandfather standing on the front porch looks *like* Ahab, the possessed sea captain from Herman Melville's epic novel *Moby Dick* (paragraph 2). Later, Bradbury uses a metaphor to focus his readers on "the night of susurrant, slumbrous voices weaving the dark together" (paragraph 14). Find at least one other comparison, either a simile or a metaphor, and explain how it works within the context of its sentence or paragraph. What type of comparison is being made (a simile or a metaphor)? What do we learn about the object being described (for example, Grandfather or the night) through its association with the other reference (Ahab or voices weaving the dark together)?

3. What is the point of view of the author in this selection? Would the essay be more effective if it were reported from the standpoint of Douglas? Of Grandfather? Of the women? Why or why not? How does the author's point of view help Bradbury organize his description? Should the fact that Bradbury's middle name is Douglas have any bearing on our interpretation of this story?

4. Although Bradbury draws mainly on description to write this essay, what other rhetorical strategies work together to help the reader grasp the full effect of "Summer Rituals"? Give examples of each strategy.

MAKING CONNECTIONS

1. For Douglas, hanging the porch swing was an important yearly ritual. What rituals can you find in the family backgrounds of Russell Baker ("The Saturday Evening Post") and/or Michael Dorris ("The Broken Cord")? What specific meanings did these rituals have within each author's family?

2. Compare and contrast Bradbury's neighborhood with that of Robert Ramirez ("The Barrio"). Which neighborhood would you feel most comfortable in? Why would you feel comfortable there?

3. Which author's relationship with his/her parents was most like your own: Ray Bradbury's, Russell Baker's ("The Saturday Evening Post"), or Sandra Cisneros's ("Only daughter")? How did each of these children relate differently to his or her parents?

IDEAS FOR DISCUSSION/WRITING

Preparing to Write

List some of the most important rituals in your life: How many times a year do these rituals occur? What purpose do they serve? How do rituals help create a strong social framework in your life? In your friends' lives? In society in general?

Choosing a Topic

1. Write a descriptive essay about a ritual that is significant in your life, addressing it to someone who has never experienced that particular activity. Include the people involved and the setting. Try to use all five senses in your description.
2. Choose a ritual that is part of your family life, and write an essay describing your feelings about this ceremonial event. Address it to someone outside your family. Use similes and metaphors to make your description as vivid as possible.
3. Explain to someone visiting the United States for the first time the value of a particular tradition in American society. Then help this person understand the importance of that tradition in your life.
4. Bradbury's descriptions develop his narrative by providing concrete and consistent details. Using either a photo that has special meaning for you or an interesting image from the Internet, write an essay describing a moment or place suspended in time.

Before beginning your essay, you might want to consult the checklists on page 50.

Notes from the Country Club

Kimberly Wozencraft grew up in Dallas, Texas, and dropped out of college when she was twenty-one to become a police officer. Her first assignment, prior to training at the police academy, was a street-level undercover narcotics investigation. Like many narcotics agents, Wozencraft became addicted to drugs, which impaired her judgment and resulted in a 1981 conviction for violating the civil rights of a reputed child pornographer. After serving an eighteen-month sentence in the Federal Correctional Institution at Lexington, Kentucky, she moved to New York City, where she has lived since her release. She holds a master of fine arts degree from Columbia University, and her essays, poems, and short stories have appeared in a variety of magazines, including *Northwest Review, Quarto, Big Wednesday,* and *Witness.* Her first novel, *Rush,* was made into a movie in 1992, and her most recent book, *The Catch,* was published by Doubleday in 1998.

Preparing to Read

Originally published in *Witness,* "Notes from the Country Club" was selected for inclusion in *The Best American Essays of 1988,* edited by Annie Dillard. Through carefully constructed prose, the author describes her prison environment and the anxiety caused by living for more than a year in such an alien, difficult place.

Exploring Experience: As you prepare to read this essay, take a moment to think about your own behavior in difficult situations: What kind of person do you become? How do you act toward other people? How is this behavior different from the way you usually act? How do you know when you're in a difficult situation? What do you generally do to relieve the tension?

Learning Online: Wozencraft's description of her experience as an undercover narcotics agent was made into a movie entitled *Rush.* To better understand her experience, go to http://www.mgm.com. Conduct a keyword search for "Rush." Click on the "multimedia" link to view photos or clips from the film.

They had the Haitians up the hill, in the "camp" section where they used to keep the minimum security cases. The authorities were concerned that some of the Haitians might be diseased, so they kept them isolated from the main coed prison population by lodging them in the big square brick building surrounded by eight-foot chain-link with concertina wire on top. We were not yet familiar with the acronym AIDS.

One or two of the Haitians had drums, and in the evenings when the rest of us were in the Big Yard, the drum rhythms carried over the bluegrass to where we were playing gin or tennis or softball or just hanging out waiting for dark. When they really got going some of them would dance and sing. Their music was rhythmic and beautiful, and it made me think of freedom.

There were Cubans loose in the population, spattering their guttural Spanish in streams around the rectangular courtyard, called Central Park, at the center of the prison compound. These were Castro's Boat People, guilty of no crime in this country, but requiring sponsors before they could walk the streets as free people.

Walking around the perimeter of Central Park was like taking a trip in microcosm across the United States. Moving leftward from the main entrance, strolling along under the archway that covers the wide sidewalk, you passed the doorway to the Women's Unit, where I lived, and it was how I imagined Harlem to be. There was a white face here and there, but by far most of them were black. Ghetto blasters thunked out rhythms in the sticky evening air, and folks leaned against the window sills, smoking, drinking Cokes, slinking, and nodding. Every once in a while a joint was passed around, and always there was somebody pinning, checking for hacks on patrol.

Past Women's Unit was the metal door to the Big Yard, the main recreation area of three or four acres, two sides blocked by the building, two sides fenced in the usual way—chain-link and concertina wire.

Past the Big Yard you entered the Blue Ridge Mountains, a sloping grassy area on the edge of Central Park, where the locals, people from Kentucky, Tennessee, and the surrounding environs, sat around playing guitars and singing, and every once in a while passing around a quart of hooch. They make it from grapefruit juice and a bit of yeast smuggled out of the kitchen. Some of the inmates who worked in Cable would bring out pieces of a black foam rubber substance and wrap it around empty Cremora jars to make thermos jugs of sorts. They would mix the grapefruit juice and yeast in the containers and stash them in some out-of-the-way spot for a few weeks until presto! you had hooch, bitter and tart and sweet all at once, only mildly alcoholic, but entirely suitable for evening cocktails in Central Park.

Next, at the corner, was the Commissary, a tiny store tucked 7 inside the entrance to Veritas, the second women's unit. It wasn't much more than a few shelves behind a wall of Plexiglas, with a constant line of inmates spilling out of the doorway. They sold packaged chips, cookies, pens and writing paper, toiletries, some fresh fruit, and the ever-popular ice cream, sold only in pints. You had to eat the entire pint as soon as you bought it, or else watch it melt, because there weren't any refrigerators. Inmates were assigned one shopping night per week, allowed to buy no more than seventy-five dollars' worth of goods per month, and were permitted to pick up a ten-dollar roll of quarters if they had enough money in their prison account. Quarters were the basic spending unit in the prison; possession of paper money was a shippable offense. There were vending machines stocked with junk food and soda, and they were supposedly what the quarters were to be used for. But we gambled, we bought salami or fried chicken sneaked out by the food service workers, and of course people sold booze and drugs. The beggars stood just outside the Commissary door. Mostly they were Cubans, saying, "Oyez! Mira! Mira! Hey, Poppy, one quarter for me. One cigarette for me, Poppy?"

There was one Cuban whom I was specially fond of. His name 8 was Shorty. The name said it. He was only about five-two, and he looked just like Mick Jagger. I met him in Segregation, an isolated section of tiny cells where prisoners were locked up for having violated some institutional rule or another. They tossed me in there the day I arrived; again the authorities were concerned, supposedly for my safety. I was a police woman before I became a convict, and they weren't too sure that the other inmates would like that. Shorty saved me a lot of grief when I went into Seg. It didn't matter if you were male or female there, you got stripped and handed a tee shirt, a pair of boxer shorts and a set of Peter Pans—green canvas shoes with thin rubber soles designed to prevent you from running away. As if you could get past three steel doors and a couple of hacks just to start with. When I was marched down the hall between the cells, the guys started whistling and hooting, and they didn't shut up even after I was locked down. They kept right on screaming until finally I yelled out, "Yo no comprendo!" and they all moaned and said, "Another . . . Cuban," and finally got quiet. Shorty was directly across from me, I could see his eyes through the rectangular slot in my cell door. He rattled off a paragraph or two of Spanish, all of which was lost on me, and I said quietly, "Yo no comprendo bien español. Yo soy de Texas, yo hablo inglés?" I could tell he was smiling by the squint of his eyes, and he just said, "Bueno." When the hacks came around to take us out for our mandatory hour of recreation, which consisted of standing around in the Rec area while two guys shot a game of pool on the balcony above the gym, Shorty slipped his hand into mine and smiled up at me until the hack told him to cut it out. He knew enough English to tell the others in Seg that I was not really Spanish, but he kept quiet about it, and they left me alone.

Beyond the Commissary, near the door to the dining hall, was 9 East St. Louis. The prison had a big portable stereo system which they rolled out a few times a week so that an inmate could play at being a disc jockey. They had a good-sized collection of albums, and there was usually some decent jazz blasting out of there. Sometimes people danced, unless there were uptight hacks on duty to tell them not to.

California was next. It was a laid back kind of corner near the 10 doors to two of the men's units. People stood around and smoked hash or grass or did whatever drugs happened to be available and there was sometimes a sort of slow-motion game of handball going on. If you wanted drugs, this was the place to come.

If you kept walking, you would arrive at the Power Station, the 11 other southern corner where the politicos-gone-wrong congregated. It might seem odd at first to see these middle-aged government mavens standing around in their Lacoste sport shirts and Sans-a-belt slacks, smoking pipes or cigars and waving their arms to emphasize some point or other. They kept pretty much to themselves and ate together at the big round tables in the cafeteria, sipping cherry Kool-Aid and pretending it was Cabernet Sauvignon.

That's something else you had to deal with—the food. It was 12 worse than elementary school steam table fare. By the time they

finished cooking it, it was tasteless, colorless, and nutritionless. The
first meal I took in the dining room was lunch. As I walked toward
the entry, a tubby fellow was walking out, staggering really, rolling
his eyes as though he were dizzy. He stopped and leaned over, and
I heard someone yell, "Watch out, he's gonna puke!" I ducked
inside so as to miss the spectacle. They were serving some rubbery,
faint pink slabs that were supposed to be ham, but I didn't even
bother to taste mine. I just slapped at it a few times to watch the
fork bounce off and then ate my potatoes and went back to the
unit.

Shortly after that I claimed that I was Jewish, having gotten the   13
word from a friendly New York lawyer who was in for faking
some of his clients' immigration papers. The kosher line was the
only way to get a decent meal in there. In fact, for a long time they
had a Jewish baker from Philadelphia locked up, and he made
some truly delicious cream puffs for dessert. They sold for seventy-
five cents on the black market, but once I had established myself
in the Jewish community, I got them as part of my regular fare.
They fed us a great deal of peanut butter on the kosher line; every
time the "goyim" got meat, we got peanut butter, but that was all
right with me. Eventually I was asked to light the candles at the
Friday evening services, since none of the real Jewish women
bothered to attend. I have to admit that most of the members of
our little prison congregation were *genuine alter kokers,* but some of
them were amusing. And I enjoyed learning first hand about
Judaism. The services were usually very quiet, and the music, the
ancient intoning songs, fortified me against the screeching pop-
rock vocal assaults that were a constant in the Women's Unit. I
learned to think of myself as the *shabot shiksa,* and before my time
was up, even the rabbi seemed to accept me.

I suppose it was quite natural that the Italians assembled just   14
"down the street" from the offending ex-senators, judges, and
power brokers. Just to the left of the main entrance. The first night
I made the tour, a guy came out of the shadows near the building
and whispered to me. "What do you need, sweetheart? What do
you want, I can get it. My friend Ahmad over there, he's very rich,
and he wants to buy you things. What'll it be, you want some
smoke, a few ludes, vodka, cigarettes, maybe some kosher salami
fresh from the kitchen? What would you like?" I just stared at him.
The only thing I wanted at that moment was out, and even

Ahmad's millions, if they existed at all, couldn't do that. The truth is, every guy I met in there claimed to be wealthy, to have been locked up for some major financial crime. Had I taken all of them up on their offers of limousines to pick me up at the front gate when I was released and take me to the airport for a ride home in a private Lear jet, I would have needed my own personal cop out front just to direct traffic.

Ahmad's Italian promoter eventually got popped for zinging the   15
cooking teacher one afternoon on the counter in the home economics classroom, right next to the new Cuisinart. The assistant warden walked in on the young lovebirds, and before the week was up, even the Cubans were walking around singing about it. They had a whole song down, to the tune of "Borracho Me Acosté a Noche."

At the end of the tour, you would find the jaded New Yorkers,   16
sitting at a picnic table or two in the middle of the park, playing gin or poker and bragging about their days on Madison Avenue and Wall Street, lamenting the scarcity of good deli, even on the kosher line, and planning where they would take their first real meal upon release.

If you think federal correctional institutions are about the busi-   17
ness of rehabilitation, drop by for an orientation session one day. There at the front of the classroom, confronting rows of mostly black faces, will be the warden, or the assistant warden, or the prison shrink, pacing back and forth in front of the blackboard and asking the class, "Why do you think you're here?" This gets a general grumble, a few short, choked laughs. Some well-meaning soul always says it—rehabilitation.

"Nonsense!" the lecturer will say. "There are several reasons for   18
locking people up. Number one is incapacitation. If you're in here, you can't be out there doing crime. Secondly, there is deterrence. Other people who are thinking about doing crime see that we lock people up for it and maybe they think twice. But the real reason you are here is to be punished. Plain and simple. You done wrong, now you got to pay for it. Rehabilitation ain't even part of the picture. So don't be looking to us to rehabilitate you. Only person can rehabilitate you is you. If you feel like it, go for it, but leave us out. We don't want to play that game."

So that's it. You're there to do time. I have no misgivings about   19
why I went to prison. I deserved it. I was a cop; I got strung out

on cocaine; I violated the rights of a pornographer. My own drug use as an undercover narcotics agent was a significant factor in my crime. But I did it, and I deserved to be punished. Most of the people I met in Lexington, though, were in for drugs, and the majority of them hadn't done anything more than sell an ounce of cocaine or a pound of pot to some apostle of the law.

It seems lately that almost every time I look at the *New York*   20
Times op-ed page, there is something about the drug problem. I have arrested people for drugs, and I have had a drug problem myself. I have seen how at least one federal correctional institution functions. It does not appear that the practice of locking people up for possession or distribution of an insignificant quantity of a controlled substance makes any difference at all in the amount of drug use that occurs in the United States. The drug laws are merely another convenient source of political rhetoric for aspiring officeholders. Politicians know that an antidrug stance is an easy way to get votes from parents who are terrified that their children might wind up as addicts. I do not advocate drug use. Yet, having seen the criminal justice system from several angles, as a police officer, a court bailiff, a defendant, and a prisoner, I am convinced that prison is not the answer to the drug problem, or for that matter to many other white-collar crimes. If the taxpayers knew how their dollars were being spent inside some prisons, they might actually scream out loud.

There were roughly 1,800 men and women locked up in Lex,   21
at a ratio of approximately three men to every woman, and it did get warm in the summertime. To keep us tranquil they devised some rather peculiar little amusements. One evening I heard a commotion on the steps at the edge of Central Park and looked over to see a rec specialist with three big cardboard boxes set up on the plaza, marked 1, 2, and 3. There were a couple of hundred inmates sitting at the bottom of the steps. Dennis, the rec specialist, was conducting his own version of the television game show *Let's Make a Deal!* Under one of the boxes was a case of soda, under another was a racquetball glove, and under the third was a fly swatter. The captive contestant picked door number 2, which turned out to contain the fly swatter, to my way of thinking the best prize there. Fly swatters were virtually impossible to get through approved channels, and therefore cost as much as two packs of cigarettes on the black market.

Then there was the Annual Fashion Show, where ten or twenty   22
inmates had special packages of clothing sent in, only for the one
evening, and modeled them on stage while the baddest drag queen
in the compound moderated and everyone else ooohed and
aahhed. They looked good up there on stage in Christian Dior and
Ralph Lauren instead of the usual fatigue pants and white tee
shirts. And if such activities did little to prepare inmates for a productive return to society, well, at least they contributed to the fan-
tasyland aura that made Lexington such an unusual place.

I worked in Landscape, exiting the rear gate of the compound   23
each weekday morning at about nine after getting a half-hearted
frisk from one of the hacks on duty. I would climb on my tractor to
drive to the staff apartment complex and pull weeds or mow the
lawn. Landscape had its prerogatives. We raided the gardens regularly and at least got to taste fresh vegetables from time to time. I had
never eaten raw corn before, but it could not have tasted better. We
also brought in a goodly supply of real vodka, and a bit of hash now
and then, for parties in our rooms after lights out. One guy strapped
a six-pack of Budweiser to his arms with masking tape and then put
on his prison-issue Army field jacket. When he got to the rear gate,
he raised his arms straight out at shoulder level, per instructions, and
the hack patted down his torso and legs, never bothering to check
his arms. The inmate had been counting on that. He smiled at the
hack and walked back to his room, a six-pack richer.

I was fortunate to be working Landscape at the same time as   24
Horace, a fellow who had actually lived in the city of Lexington
before he was locked up. His friends made regular deliveries of
assorted contraband, which they would stash near a huge elm tree
near the outer stone fence of the reservation. Horace would drive
his tractor over, make the pickup, and the rest of us would carry
it, concealed, through the back gate when we went back inside for
lunch or at the end of the day. "Contraband" included everything
from drugs to blue eye shadow. The assistant warden believed that
female inmates should wear no cosmetics other than what she herself used—a bit of mascara and a light shade of lipstick. I have
never been a plaything of Fashion, but I did what I could to help
the other women prisoners in their never-ending quest for that
Cover Girl look.

You could depend on the fact that most of the hacks would   25
rather have been somewhere else, and most of them really didn't

care *what* the inmates did, as long as it didn't cause any commotion. Of course, there were a few you had to look out for. The captain in charge of security was one of them. We tried a little experiment once, after having observed that any time he saw someone laughing, he took immediate steps to make the inmate and everyone around him acutely miserable. Whenever we saw him in the area, we immediately assumed expressions of intense unhappiness, even of despair. Seeing no chance to make anyone more miserable than they already appeared to be, the captain left us alone.

Almost all of the female hacks, and a good number of the males, had outrageously large derrières, a condition we inmates referred to as "the federal ass." This condition may have resulted from the fact that most of them appeared, as one inmate succinctly described it, simply to be "putting in their forty a week to stay on the government teat." Employment was not an easy thing to find in Kentucky. 26

Despite the fact that Lexington is known as a "country club" prison, I must admit that I counted days. From the first moment that I was in, I kept track of how many more times I would have to watch the sun sink behind eight feet of chain-link, of how many more days I would have to spend eating, working, playing, and sleeping according to the dictates of a "higher authority." I don't think I can claim that I was rehabilitated. If anything I underwent a process of dehabilitation. What I learned was what Jessica Mitford tried to tell people many years ago in her book *Kind and Usual Punishment*. Prison is a business, no different from manufacturing tires or selling real estate. It keeps people employed, and it provides cheap labor for NASA, the U.S. Postal Service, and other governmental or quasi-governmental agencies. For a short time, before I was employed in Landscape, I worked as a finisher of canvas mailbags, lacing white rope through metal eyelets around the top of the bags and attaching clamps to the ropes. I made one dollar and fourteen cents for every one hundred that I did. If I worked very hard, I could do almost two hundred a day. 27

It's not about justice. If you think it's about justice, look at the newspapers and notice who walks. Not the little guys, the guys doing a tiny bit of dealing or sniggling a little on their income tax, or the woman who pulls a stunt with welfare checks because her 28 husband has skipped out and she has no other way to feed her kids. I do not say that these things are right. But the process of selective prosecution, the "making" of cases by D.A.s and police departments, and the presence of some largely unenforceable statutes currently on the books (it is the reality of "compliance": no law can be forced on a public which chooses to ignore it; hence, selective prosecution) make for a criminal justice system which cannot realistically function in a fair and equitable manner. Criminal justice—I cannot decide if it is the ultimate oxymoron or a truly accurate description of the law enforcement process in America.

In my police undercover capacity, I have sat across the table   29
from an armed robber who said, "My philosophy of life is slit thy neighbor's throat and pimp his kids." I believe that the human animals who maim and kill people should be dealt with, as they say, swiftly and surely. But this business of locking people up, at enormous cost, for minor, nonviolent offenses does not truly or effectively serve the interest of the people. It serves only to promote the wasteful aspects of the federal prison system, a system that gulps down tax dollars and spews up *Let's Make a Deal!*

I think about Lexington almost daily. I will be walking up   30
Broadway to shop for groceries, or maybe riding my bike in the original Central Park, and suddenly I'm wondering who's in there now, at this very moment, and for what inane violations, and what they are doing. Is it chow time, is the Big Yard open, is some inmate on stage in the auditorium singing "As Time Goes By" in a talent show? It is not a fond reminiscence or a desire to be back in the Land of No Decisions. It is an awareness of the waste. The waste of tax dollars, yes, but taxpayers are used to that. It is the unnecessary trashing of lives that leaves me uneasy. The splitting of families, the enforced monotony, the programs which purport to prepare an inmate for re-entry into society but which actually succeed only in occupying a few more hours of the inmate's time behind the walls. The nonviolent offenders, such as small-time drug dealers and the economically deprived who were driven to crime out of desperation, could remain in society under less costly supervision, still undergoing "punishment" for their crime, but at least contributing to rather than draining the resources of society.

Horace, who was not a subtle sort of fellow, had some tee shirts   31
made up. They were delivered by our usual supplier out in

Landscape, and we wore them back in over our regular clothes. The hacks tilted their heads when they noticed, but said nothing. On the front of each shirt was an outline of the state of Kentucky, and above the northwest corner of the state were the words "Visit Beautiful Kentucky!" Inside the state boundary were:

- Free Accommodations
- Complimentary Meals
- Management Holds Calls
- Recreational Exercise

In small letters just outside the southwest corner of the state was: "Length of Stay Requirement." And in big letters across the bottom:

Take Time to Do Time

F.C.I. Lexington

I gave mine away on the day I finished my sentence. It is a   32
time-honored tradition to leave some of your belongings to friends who have to stay behind when you are released. But you must never leave shoes. Legend has it that if you do, you will come back to wear them again.

UNDERSTANDING DETAILS

1. Draw Lexington prison, and put the names on the sections of the facility. Then describe each section in your own words.
2. Why was walking around the outside of Central Park "like taking a trip in microcosm across the United States" (paragraph 4)? Give examples to explain your answer.
3. Why was Wozencraft especially fond of Shorty? What secret did they share at the beginning of the author's prison term?
4. Does the author feel she had been unfairly punished by being sent to prison? What had she done wrong?

ANALYZING MEANING

1. What was Wozencraft's attitude toward other people in Lexington prison? Why do you think she felt this way? What

types of relationships did she have with inmates and staff members?

2. Why does the author say, "If the taxpayers knew how their dollars were being spent inside some prisons, they might actually scream out loud" (paragraph 20)? What exactly is she referring to? What is she implying? Give some examples.

3. Why do you think Lexington is known as a "country club" prison? What features of the prison might have brought about its nickname?

4. Wozencraft feels strongly that people who perform minor, nonviolent crimes should not be put in prison. Why does she feel this way? Who should be locked up according to the author? From her point of view, how does rehabilitation take place?

DISCOVERING RHETORICAL STRATEGIES

1. This essay is organized predominantly as a clockwise tour of Lexington prison. How and when does Wozencraft introduce the facts about her own imprisonment and her opinions about the current American system of justice? Explain in as much detail as you can the effect of integrating the guided tour and the related facts and opinions.

2. Wozencraft uses specific prison jargon throughout this essay. In what way does this jargon add to or detract from the essay? What effect would the essay have without this jargon?

3. Wozencraft ends her essay with an explanation of "a time-honored tradition." Is this an effective ending for the piece? Why or why not?

4. Though spatial description is the dominant rhetorical strategy the author uses in this essay to accomplish her purpose, what other strategies help make the essay effective? Give examples of these strategies.

MAKING CONNECTIONS

1. If Kimberly Wozencraft, Ellen Goodman ("A Working Community"), and Richard Rodriguez ("The Fear of Losing a Culture") were discussing the importance of belonging to a "community," which author would argue most strongly that

community is a positive force in our lives? Explain your answer.

2. Malcolm Cowley ("The View from 80"), Harold Krents ("Darkness at Noon"), and Jimmy Santiago Baca ("Past Present") have all felt imprisoned in much the same way Wozencraft does in her essay. In what way is each of these authors "confined"? Have you ever felt imprisoned for any reason? Why? How did you escape?

3. What would Wozencraft, Ellen Goodman ("A Working Community"), and/or William Ouchi ("Japanese and American Workers: Two Casts of Mind") have to say about the importance of relying on other people to help endure difficult or challenging situations? How much do you rely on friends and relatives in your own life? How comfortable are you with these relationships?

IDEAS FOR DISCUSSION/WRITING

Preparing to Write

Write freely about your memories of a recent difficult or awkward situation in your life: What were the circumstances? What did you do? What did others do? How did you relate to others in this situation? Why was the situation so difficult? How did you get out of it?

Choosing a Topic

1. Write an essay describing for your peers a difficult or awkward situation you have been in recently. Why was it awkward? Explain the specific circumstances so that your classmates can clearly imagine the setting and the difficulty or problem. Then discuss your reaction to the situation.

2. A friend of yours has just been sentenced to prison for one year. Write a letter to this person describing what you think his or her biggest adjustments will be.

3. Wozencraft describes many problems within the prison system. With these problems in mind, write a letter to the editor of your local newspaper discussing whether prisons actually rehabilitate criminals. Use examples from Wozencraft's essay to help make your point.

4. Wozencraft develops a descriptive narrative from personal experience. She "shows" rather than "tells" her readers about Lexington prison's attitude toward rehabilitation. Compose an e-mail written to a friend not attending college that describes your current educational experience. Try to show, rather than tell your observations, achievements, frustrations, and unique experiences. Remember to organize your descriptions to convey a clear and consistent message.

Before beginning your essay, you might want to consult the checklists on page 50.

JOHN MCPHEE   (1931–   )

The Pines

The range of subjects investigated by author John McPhee is quite astounding. In his twenty books and numerous articles, he has written about sports, food, art, geology, geography, science, history, education, and a variety of other topics. One of the most famous of these "non-fictional, book-length narratives," as he calls them, is *A Sense of Where You Are* (1965), a study of former basketball great Bill Bradley; another is *Levels of the Game* (1969), a chronicle of the epic 1968 U.S. Open semifinal tennis match between Arthur Ashe and Clark Graebner. Most of McPhee's essays have appeared first in the *New Yorker,* a prestigious literary magazine for which he has been a staff writer since 1965. His more recent publications include *In Suspect Terrain* (1983), *La Place de la Concorde Suisse* (1984), *Table of Contents* (1985), *Rising from the Plains* (1986), *The Control of Nature* (1989), *Looking for a Ship* (1990), *Assembling California* (1993), *The Ransom of Russian Art* (1994), *The Second John McPhee Reader* (1996), *Irons in the Fire* (1997), *Annals of the Former World* (1998) (which was awarded the Pulitzer Prize in 1999), and *The Founding Fish* (2002). "What all these pieces of writing have in common," according to the author, "is that they are about real people and real places. All the different topics are just milieus in which to sketch people and places." McPhee lives in New Jersey near Princeton University, where he teaches a seminar entitled "The Literature of Fact." His hobbies include going on long bike rides, fishing for shad and pickerel, and skiing.

Preparing to Read

The following essay, "The Pines," is a small section from a longer piece called *The Pine Barrens* (1968), which describes a remote wilderness in southern New Jersey. Like many of McPhee's narrative essays, "The Pines" is structured around colorful characters—in this case, Fred Brown, a talkative backwoods native—and Bill Wasovwich, who speaks little, listens intently, and observes the world around him with great care. Both men worry openly about the encroaching civilization that threatens their unique way of life.

Exploring Experience: As you prepare to read this essay, think for a moment about the different types of people you know: Do you have talkative friends? Quiet friends? Which type of person is most appealing to you? Which type are you? Have you ever lived in the woods? What are the principal advantages of living in a rural environment rather than in a big city? What are the disadvantages?

Learning Online: Using Google's search engine (http://www.google.com), click on the "Images" tab to conduct a picture search for the term "cranberry bog." Take a few minutes to consider how you would describe this particular area. What is unique about this place, and what seems familiar?

Fred Brown's house is on an unpaved road that curves along the edge of a wide cranberry bog. What attracted me to it was the pump that stands in his yard. It was something of a wonder that I noticed the pump, because there were, among other things, eight automobiles in the yard, two of them on their sides and one of them upside down, all ten years old or older. Around the cars were old refrigerators, vacuum cleaners, partly dismantled radios, cathode-ray tubes, a short wooden ski, a large wooden mallet, dozens of cranberry picker's boxes, many tires, an orange crate dated 1946, a cord or so of firewood, mandolins, engine heads, and maybe a thousand other things. The house itself, two stories high, was covered with tarpaper that was peeling away in some places, revealing its original shingles, made of Atlantic white cedar from the stream courses of the surrounding forest. I called out to ask if anyone was home, and a voice inside called back, "Come in. Come in. Come on the hell in."

I walked through a vestibule that had a dirt floor, stepped up into a kitchen, and went on into another room that had several overstuffed chairs in it and a porcelain-topped table, where Fred Brown was seated, eating a pork chop. He was dressed in a white sleeveless shirt, ankle-top shoes, and undershorts. He gave me a cheerful greeting and, without asking why I had come or what I wanted, picked up a pair of khaki trousers that had been tossed onto one of the overstuffed chairs and asked me to sit down. He set the trousers on another chair, and he apologized for being in the middle of his breakfast, explaining that he seldom drank much but the night before he had had a few drinks and this had caused his day to start slowly. "I don't know what's the matter with me, but there's got to be something the matter with me, because drink don't agree with me anymore," he said. He had a raw onion in one hand, and while he talked he shaved slices from the onion and ate them between bites of the chop. He was a muscular and well-built man, with short, bristly white hair, and he had bright, fast-moving eyes in a wide-open face. His legs were trim and strong, with large muscles in the calves. I guessed that he was about sixty, and for a man of sixty he seemed to be in remarkably good shape. He was actually seventy-nine. "My rule is: Never eat except when you're hungry," he said, and he ate another slice of the onion.

In a straight-backed chair near the doorway to the kitchen sat a young man with long black hair, who wore a visored red leather cap that had darkened with age. His shirt was coarse-woven and had eyelets down a V neck that was laced with a thong. His trousers were made of canvas, and he was wearing gum boots. His arms were folded, his legs were stretched out, he had one ankle over the other, and as he sat there he appeared to be sighting carefully past his feet, as if his toes were the outer frame of a gunsight and he could see some sort of target in the floor. When I had entered, I had said hello to him, and he had nodded without looking up. He had a long, straight nose and high cheekbones, in a deeply tanned face that was, somehow, gaunt. I had no idea whether he was shy or hostile. Eventually, when I came to know him, I found him to be as shy a person as I have ever had a chance to know. His name is Bill Wasovwich, and he lives alone in a cabin about half a mile from Fred. First his father, then his mother left him when he was a young boy, and he grew up depending on the help of various people in the pines. One of them, a cranberry grower, employs him and has given him some acreage, in which Bill is building a small cranberry bog of his own, "turfing it out" by hand. When he is not working in the bogs, he goes roaming, as he puts it, setting out cross-country on long, looping journeys, hiking about thirty miles in a typical day, in search of what he calls "events"—surprising a buck, or a gray fox, or perhaps a poacher or a man with a still. Almost no one who is not native to the pines could do this, for the woods have an undulating sameness, and the understory—huckleberries, sheep laurel, sweet fern, high-bush blueberry—is often so dense that a wanderer can walk in a fairly tight circle and think that he is moving in a straight line. State forest rangers spend a good part of their time finding hikers and hunters, some of whom have vanished for days. In his long, pathless journeys, Bill always emerges from the woods near his cabin—and about when he plans to. In the fall, when thousands of hunters come into the pines, he sometimes works as a guide. In the evenings, or in the daytime when he is not working or roaming, he goes to Fred Brown's house and sits there for hours. The old man is a widower whose seven children are long since gone from Hog Wallow, and he is as expansively talkative and worldly as the young one is withdrawn and wild. Although there are fifty-three years between their ages, it is obviously fortunate for each of them to be the other's neighbor.

That first morning, while Bill went on looking at his outstretched toes, Fred got up from the table, put on his pants, and said he was going to cook me a pork chop, because I looked hungry and ought to eat something. It was about noon, and I was even hungrier than I may have looked, so I gratefully accepted his offer, which was a considerable one. There are two or three small general stores in the pines, but for anything as fragile as a fresh pork chop it is necessary to make a round trip from Fred's place of about fifty miles. Fred went into the kitchen and dropped a chop into a frying pan that was crackling with hot grease. He has a fairly new four-burner stove that uses bottled gas. He keeps water in a large bowl on a table in the kitchen and ladles some when he wants it. While he cooked the meat, he looked out a window through a stand of pitch pines and into the cranberry bog. "I saw a big buck out here last night with velvet on his horns," he said. "Them horns is soft when they're in velvet." On a nail high on one wall of the room that Bill and I were sitting in was a large meat cleaver. Next to it was a billy club. The wall itself was papered in a flower pattern, and the wallpaper continued out across the ceiling and down the three other walls, lending the room something of the appearance of the inside of a gift box. In some parts of the ceiling, the paper had come loose. "I didn't paper this year," Fred said. "For the last couple months, I've had sinus." The floor was covered with old rugs. They had been put down in random pieces, and in some places as many as six layers were stacked up. In winter, when the temperature approaches zero, the worst cold comes through the floor. The only source of heat in the house is a wood-burning stove in the main room. There were seven calendars on the walls, all current and none with pictures of nudes. Fading into pastel on one wall was a rotogravure photograph of President and Mrs. Eisenhower. A framed poem read:

> God hath not promised
> Sun without rain
> Joy without sorrow
> Peace without pain.

Noticing my interest in all this, Fred reached into a drawer and showed me what appeared to be a postcard. On it was a photograph of a woman, and Fred said with a straight face that she was his present girl, adding that he meets her regularly under a juniper tree on a road farther south in the pines. The woman, whose appearance suggested strongly that she had never been within a great many miles of the Pine Barrens, was wearing nothing at all. 5

I asked Fred what all those cars were doing in his yard, and he said that one of them was in running condition and the rest were its predecessors. The working vehicle was a 1956 Mercury. Each of the seven others had at one time or another been his best car, and each, in turn, had lain down like a sick animal and had died right there in the yard, unless it had been towed home after a mishap elsewhere in the pines. Fred recited, with affection, the history of each car. Of one old Ford, for example, he said, "I upset that up to Speedwell in the creek." And of an even older car, a station wagon, he said, "I busted that one up in the snow. I met a car on a little hill, and hit the brake, and hit a tree." One of the cars had met its end at a narrow bridge about four miles from Hog Wallow, where Fred had hit a state trooper, head on. 6

The pork was delicious and almost crisp. Fred gave me a potato with it and a pitcher of melted grease from the frying pan to pour over the potato. He also handed me a loaf of bread and a dish of margarine, saying, "Here's your bread. You can have one piece or two. Whatever you want." 7

Fred apologized for not having a phone, after I asked where I would have to go to make a call, later on. He said, "I don't have no phone because I don't have no electric. If I had electric, I 8 would have had a phone in here a long time ago." He uses a kerosene lamp, a propane lamp, and two flashlights.

He asked where I was going, and I said that I had no particular destination, explaining that I was in the pines because I found it hard to believe that so much unbroken forest could still exist so near the big Eastern cities, and I wanted to see it while it was still there. "Is that so?" he said, three times. Like many people in the pines, he often says things three times. "Is that so? Is that so?"   9

I asked him what he thought of a plan that has been developed by Burlington and Ocean Counties to create a supersonic jetport in the pines, connected by a spur of the Garden State Parkway to a new city of two hundred and fifty thousand people, also in the pines.   10

"They've been talking about that for three years, and they've never given up," Fred said.   11

"It'd be the end of these woods," Bill said. This was the first time I heard Bill speak. I had been there for an hour, and he had not said a word. Without looking up, he said again, "It'd be the end of these woods, I can tell you that."   12

Fred said, "They could build ten jetports around me. I wouldn't give a damn."   13

"You ain't going to be around very long," Bill said to him. "It would be the end of these woods."   14

Fred took that as a fact, and not as an insult. "Yes, it would be the end of these woods," he said. "But there'd be people here you could do business with."   15

Bill said, "There ain't no place like this left in the country, I don't believe—and I travelled around a little bit, too."   16

Eventually, I made the request I had intended to make when I walked in the door. "Could I have some water?" I said to Fred. "I have a jerry can, and I'd like to fill it at the pump."   17

"Hell, yes," he said. "That isn't my water. That's God's water. That right, Bill?"   18

"I *guess* so," Bill said, without looking up. "It's good water, I can tell you that."   19

"That's God's water," Fred said again. "Take all you want."   20

UNDERSTANDING DETAILS

1. What attracted McPhee to Fred Brown's house? In what ways is this object representative of Fred's yard? Of Fred's life?

2. What other things are in Fred's front yard? What does this collection of junk say about Fred and his lifestyle?
3. In paragraph 3, McPhee comments that, despite the wide difference in age between Fred and Bill, "it is obviously fortunate for each of them to be the other's neighbor." In what ways do the two characters need each other?
4. Describe in your own words the inside of Fred's house. Which details does McPhee stress in his description? Why does he focus on these and not on others?

ANALYZING MEANING

1. Why is McPhee visiting "the pines"? What do you think his opinion of "the pines" is? What specific references reveal his opinions?
2. Why does Bill go "roaming"? What do you think the purpose of these journeys is?
3. Why does Bill believe a jetport would be "the end of these woods" (paragraph 12)? Why do you think these were the first words Bill had spoken since the author arrived? Explain your answer.
4. Why do you think McPhee ends this piece with several references to God? How does the dialogue about "God's water" help us understand Fred and Bill even more specifically?

DISCOVERING RHETORICAL STRATEGIES

1. Which senses does McPhee concentrate on most in this description? Choose one paragraph to analyze. In one column, write down all the senses the description arouses; in another, record the words and phrases that activate these senses.
2. What "tone" or "mood" is McPhee trying to create in this excerpt? Is he successful? Explain your answer.
3. What is the author's point of view in this essay? How would the method of description change if the story were told from Fred's vantage point? From Bill's? How does this particular point of view help the author organize his description?
4. McPhee relies heavily on description to make his point. What other rhetorical modes support this narrative essay? Give examples of each of these modes from the essay.

MAKING CONNECTIONS

1. How does the friendship between Fred and Bill described in McPhee's essay differ from friendships in Kimberly Wozencraft's "Notes from the Country Club" and/or Robert Ramirez's "The Barrio"? Which friendships are stronger in your opinion? Explain your answer.
2. Compare and contrast McPhee's concern about preserving the environment with comparable feelings by William Least Heat-Moon ("Red, White and Blue Highways"). How are they similar? How are they different?
3. In McPhee's essay, how does Fred Brown feel about the uses and abuses of technology? Would Jessica Mitford ("Behind the Formaldehyde Curtain") or Dave Grossman ("We Are Training Our Kids to Kill") agree with him? Explain your answer.

IDEAS FOR DISCUSSION/WRITING

Preparing to Write

Write freely about someone you know who represents a specific personality "type": What distinguishes this type from other types you know? What do people of this type have in common? What are their looks, values, needs, desires, living conditions, and so on? What do you have in common with the type of person you have just described? How are you different?

Choosing a Topic

1. Give a name (either real or fictitious) to the person you have just described in the prewriting exercise, and write an essay depicting the house, apartment, or room in which this person lives. Try to make your description as vivid and as well organized as McPhee's portrait of Fred Brown. Imagine that the audience for your description is someone who has never met this person and has never seen where the person lives.
2. Write an essay describing for your classmates some of the "junk" you have collected over the years. Why are certain items junk to some people and treasures to others? What makes the things you are describing special to you?
3. Describe the inside of your house, apartment, or room, explaining to your class what the decorations say about you as

a person. If someone in your class were to see where you live, could he or she make any accurate deductions about your political, social, or moral values based on the contents and arrangement of the place you call "home"?

4. What is the dominant impression of McPhee's article? Using McPhee's example, write a description of a significant moment suspended in time. Use description to convey the significance of this moment to your reader. If you need inspiration, conduct an online image search.

Before beginning your essay, you might want to consult the checklists on page 50.

The View from 80

Malcolm Cowley had a long and distinguished career as a literary historian, critic, editor, and poet. After receiving his bachelor's degree at Harvard, he served in the American Ambulance Corps during World War I, then pursued graduate studies in literature at the University of Montpellier in France. In 1929, he became associate editor of *The New Republic,* presiding over the magazine's literary department for the next fifteen years. Perhaps his most important book of literary criticism is *Exile's Return* (1934), a study of the "lost generation" of expatriate Americans living in Paris in the 1920s, which included Ernest Hemingway, Ezra Pound, F. Scott Fitzgerald, and Hart Crane. Cowley returned to the same topic in 1973 with *A Second Flowering: Works and Days of the Lost Generation.* He also published editions of such authors as Hemingway, William Faulkner, Nathaniel Hawthorne, Walt Whitman, and Fitzgerald; two collections of his own poetry, *Blue Juniata* (1929) and *The Dry Season* (1941); and numerous other translations, editions, and books of criticism. His most recent publications include *The Flower and the Leaf: A Contemporary Record of American Writing Since 1941* (1985) and *Conversations with Malcolm Cowley* (1986). Asked the secret of his amazing productivity, Cowley replied: "Writers often speak of 'saving their energy,' as if each man were given a nickel's worth of it, which he is at liberty to spend. To me, the mind of the poet resembles Fortunatus' purse: The more spent, the more it supplies."

Preparing to Read

The following essay was originally commissioned by *Life* magazine (1978) for inclusion in a series of articles on aging. Cowley later converted the piece into the first chapter of a book with the same title: *The View from 80* (1980). Through a combination of vivid personal experience and well-researched documentation, the author crafted an essay that helps us experience what life is like for an eighty-year-old man.

Exploring Experience: As you prepare to read Cowley's description of "the country of age," take some time to think about age in general: How many people over the age of sixty do you know? Over the age of seventy? How do they behave? Do you think these older people see themselves in the same way you see them? Do you think they consider themselves "old"? What clues remind them of their advancing age? What events and attitudes remind you of your age? In what ways will you be different than you are now when you reach the age of eighty?

Learning Online: Visit the Web site of the American Association of Retired Persons (http://www.aarp.org), and read about some of the issues affecting the elderly. Keep these in mind while reading Cowley's descriptive observations about aging.

They gave me a party on my 80th birthday in August 1978. First there were cards, letters, telegrams, even a cable of congratulation or condolence; then there were gifts, mostly bottles; there was catered food and finally a big cake with, for some reason, two candles (had I gone back to very early childhood?). I blew the candles out a little unsteadily. Amid the applause and clatter I thought about a former custom of the Northern Ojibwas when they lived on the shores of Lake Winnipeg. They were kind to their old people, who remembered and enforced the ancient customs of the tribe, but when an old person became decrepit, it was time for him to go. Sometimes he was simply abandoned, with a little food, on an island in the lake. If he deserved special honor, they held a tribal feast for him. The old man sang a death song and danced, if he could. While he was still singing, his son came from behind and brained him with a tomahawk.

That was quick, it was dignified, and I wonder whether it was any more cruel, essentially, than some of our civilized customs or inadvertencies in disposing of the aged. I believe in rites and ceremonies. I believe in big parties for special occasions such as an 80th birthday. It is a sort of belated bar mitzvah, since the 80-year-old, like a Jewish adolescent, is entering a new stage of life; let him (or her) undergo a *rite de passage,* with toasts and a cantor. Seventy-year-olds, or septuas, have the illusion of being middle-aged, even if they have been pushed back on a shelf. The 80-year-old, the octo, looks at the double-dumpling figure and admits that he is old. The last act has begun, and it will be the test of the play.

To enter the country of age is a new experience, different from what you supposed it to be. Nobody, man or woman, knows the country until he has lived in it and has taken out his citizenship papers. Here is my own report, submitted as a road map and guide to some of the principal monuments.   3

The new octogenarian feels as strong as ever when he is sitting back in a comfortable chair. He ruminates, he dreams, he remembers. He doesn't want to be disturbed by others. It seems to him that old age is only a costume assumed for those others; the true, the essential self is ageless. In a moment he will rise and go for a ramble in the woods, taking a gun along, or a fishing rod, if it is spring. Then he creaks to his feet, bending forward to keep his balance, and realizes that he will do nothing of the sort. The body and its surroundings have their messages for him, or only one message: "You are old." Here are some of the occasions on which he receives the message: 4

- when it becomes an achievement to do thoughtfully, step by step, what he once did instinctively
- when his bones ache
- when there are more and more little bottles in the medicine cabinet, with instructions for taking four times a day
- when he fumbles and drops his toothbrush (butterfingers)
- when his face has bumps and wrinkles, so that he cuts himself while shaving (blood on the towel)
- when year by year his feet seem farther from his hands
- when he can't stand on one leg and has trouble pulling on his pants
- when he hesitates on the landing before walking down a flight of stairs
- when he spends more time looking for things misplaced than he spends using them after he (or more often his wife) has found them
- when he falls asleep in the afternoon
- when it becomes harder to bear in mind two things at once

- when a pretty girl passes him in the street and he doesn't turn his head
- when he forgets names, even of people he saw last month ("Now I'm beginning to forget nouns," the poet Conrad Aiken said at 80)
- when he listens hard to jokes and catches everything but the snapper
- when he decides not to drive at night anymore
- when everything takes longer to do—bathing, shaving, getting dressed or undressed—but when time passes quickly, as if he were gathering speed while coasting downhill. The year from 79 to 80 is like a week when he was a boy.

Those are some of the intimate messages. "Put cotton in your ears and pebbles in your shoes," said a gerontologist, a member of that new profession dedicated to alleviating all maladies of old people except the passage of years. "Pull on rubber gloves. Smear Vaseline over your glasses, and there you have it: instant aging." Not quite. His formula omits the messages from the social world, which are louder, in most cases, than those from within. We start by growing old in other people's eyes, then slowly we come to share their judgment.

I remember a morning many years ago when I was backing out of the parking lot near the railroad station in Brewster, New York. There was a near collision. The driver of the other car jumped out and started to abuse me; he had his fists ready. Then he looked hard at me and said, "Why, you're an old man." He got back into his car, slammed the door, and drove away, while I stood there fuming. "I'm only 65," I thought. "He wasn't driving carefully. I can still take care of myself in a car, or in a fight, for that matter."

My hair was whiter—it may have been in 1974—when a young woman rose and offered me her seat in a Madison Avenue bus. That message was kind and also devastating. "Can't I even stand up?" I thought as I thanked her and declined the seat. But the same thing happened twice the following year, and the second time I gratefully accepted the offer, though with a sense of having diminished myself. "People are right about me," I thought while wondering why all those kind gestures were made by women. Do men now regard themselves as the weaker sex, not called upon to show consideration? All the same it was a relief to sit down and relax.

A few days later I wrote a poem, "The Red Wagon," that 8 belongs in the record of aging:

> For his birthday they gave him a red express wagon
> with a driver's high seat and a handle that steered.
> His mother pulled him around the yard.
> "Giddyap," he said, but she laughed and went off
> to wash the breakfast dishes.
>
> "I wanta ride too," his sister said,
> and he pulled her to the edge of a hill.
> "Now, sister, go home and wait for me,
> but first give a push to the wagon."
> He climbed again to the high seat,
> this time grasping that handle-that-steered.
>
> The red wagon rolled slowly down the slope,
> then faster as it passed the schoolhouse
> and faster as it passed the store,
> the road still dropping away.
> Oh, it was fun.
> But would it ever stop?
> Would the road always go downhill?
> The red wagon rolled faster.
> Now it was in strange country.
> It passed a white house he must have dreamed about,
> deep woods he had never seen,
> a graveyard where, something told him, his sister
> was buried.
>
> Far below
> the sun was sinking into a broad plain.
>
> The red wagon rolled faster.
> Now he was clutching the seat, not even trying to steer.
> Sweat clouded his heavy spectacles.
> His white hair streamed in the wind.

Even before he or she is 80, the aging person may undergo 9 another identity crisis like that of adolescence. Perhaps there had also been a middle-aged crisis, the male or the female menopause, but the rest of adult life he had taken himself for granted, with his capabilities and failings. Now, when he looks in the mirror, he asks himself, "Is this really me?"—or he avoids the mirror out of distress at what it reveals, those bags and wrinkles. In his new makeup he is called upon to play a new role in a play that must be improvised. André Gide, that long-lived man of letters, wrote in his journal, "My heart has remained so young that I have the continual feeling of playing a part, the part of the 70-year-old that I certainly am; and the infirmities and weaknesses that remind me of my age act like a prompter, reminding me of my lines when I tend to stray. Then, like the good actor I want to be, I go back into my role, and I pride myself on playing it well."

In his new role the old person will find that he is tempted by   10
new vices, that he receives new compensations (not so widely known), and that he may possibly achieve new virtues. Chief among these is the heroic or merely obstinate refusal to surrender in the face of time. One admires the ships that go down with all flags flying and the captain on the bridge.

Among the vices of age are avarice, untidiness, and vanity,   11
which last takes the form of a craving to be loved or simply admired. Avarice is the worst of those three. Why do so many old persons, men and women alike, insist on hoarding money when they have no prospect of using it and even when they have no heirs? They eat the cheapest food, buy no clothes, and live in a single room when they could afford better lodging. It may be that they regard money as a form of power; there is a comfort in watching it accumulate while other powers are dwindling away. How often we read of an old person found dead in a hovel, on a mattress partly stuffed with bankbooks and stock certificates! The bankbook syndrome, we call it in our family, which has never succumbed.

Untidiness we call the Langley Collyer syndrome. To explain,   12
Langley Collyer was a former concert pianist who lived alone with his 70-year-old brother in a brownstone house on upper Fifth Avenue. The once fashionable neighborhood had become part of Harlem. Homer, the brother, had been an admiralty lawyer, but was now blind and partly paralyzed; Langley played for him and fed him on buns and oranges, which he thought would restore Homer's sight. He never threw away a daily paper because Homer, he said, might want to read them all. He saved other things as well and the house became filled with rubbish from roof to basement. The halls were lined on both sides with bundled

newspapers, leaving narrow passageways in which Langley had devised booby traps to catch intruders.

On March 21, 1947, some unnamed person telephoned the police to report that there was a dead body in the Collyer house. The police broke down the front door and found the hall impassable; then they hoisted a ladder to a second-story window. Behind it Homer was lying on the floor in a bathrobe; he had starved to death. Langley had disappeared. After some delay, the police broke into the basement, chopped a hole in the roof, and began throwing junk out of the house, top and bottom. It was 18 days before they found Langley's body, gnawed by rats. Caught in one of his own booby traps, he had died in a hallway just outside Homer's door. By that time the police had collected, and the Department of Sanitation had hauled away, 120 tons of rubbish, including, besides the newspapers, 14 grand pianos and the parts of a dismantled Model T Ford.   13

Why do so many old people accumulate junk, not on the scale of Langley Collyer, but still in a dismaying fashion? Their tables are piled high with it, their bureau drawers are stuffed with it, their closet rods bend with the weight of clothes not worn for years. I suppose that the piling up is partly from lethargy and partly from feeling that everything once useful, including their own bodies, should be preserved. Others, though not so many, have such a fear of becoming Langley Collyers that they strive to be painfully neat. Every tool they own is in its place, though it will never be used again; every scrap of paper is filed away in alphabetical order. At last their immoderate neatness becomes another vice of age, if a milder one.   14

The vanity of older people is an easier weakness to explain, and to condone. With less to look forward to, they yearn for recognition of what they have been: the reigning beauty, the athlete, the soldier, the scholar. It is the beauties who have the hardest time. A portrait of themselves at twenty hangs on the wall, and they try to resemble it by making an extravagant use of creams, powder, and dyes. Being young at heart, they think they are merely revealing their essential persons. The athletes find shelves for their silver trophies, which are polished once a year. Perhaps a letter sweater lies wrapped in a bureau drawer. I remember one evening when a no-longer athlete had guests for dinner and tried to find his sweater. "Oh, that old thing," his wife said. "The moths got into   15 it, and I threw it away." The athlete sulked, and his guests went home early.

But there are also pleasures of the body, or the mind, that are   16
enjoyed by a greater number of older persons. Those pleasures include some that younger people find hard to appreciate. One of them is simply sitting still, like a snake on a sunwarmed stone, with a delicious feeling of indolence that was seldom attained in earlier years. A leaf flutters down; a cloud moves by inches across the horizon. At such moments the older person, completely relaxed, has become a part of nature—and a living part, with blood coursing through his veins. The future does not exist for him. He thinks, if he thinks at all, that life for younger persons is still a battle royal of each against each, but that now he has nothing more to win or lose. He is not so much above as outside the battle, as if he had assumed the uniform of some small neutral country, perhaps Liechtenstein or Andorra. From a distance he notes that some of the combatants, men or women, are jostling ahead—but why do they fight so hard when the most they can hope for is a longer obituary? He can watch the scrounging and gouging, he can hear the shouts of exultation, the moans of the gravely wounded, and meanwhile he feels secure; nobody will attack him from ambush.

Age has other physical compensations besides the nirvana of   17
dozing in the sun. A few of the simplest needs become a pleasure to satisfy. When an old woman in a nursing home was asked what she really liked to do she answered in one word: "Eat." She might have been speaking for many of her fellows. Meals in a nursing home, however badly cooked, serve as climactic moments of the day. The physical essence of the pensioners is being renewed at an appointed hour; now they can go back to meditating or to watching TV while looking forward to the next meal. They can also look forward to sleep, which has become a definite pleasure, not the mere interruption it once had been.

Here I am thinking of old persons under nursing care. Others   18
ferociously guard their independence, and some of them suffer less than one might expect from being lonely and impoverished. They can be rejoiced by visits and meetings, but they also have company inside their heads. Some of them are busiest when their hands are still. What passes through the minds of many is a stream of persons, images, phrases, and familiar tunes. For some that stream has

continued since childhood, but now it is deeper; it is their present and their past combined. At times they conduct silent dialogues with a vanished friend, and these are less tiring—often more rewarding—than spoken conversations. If inner resources are lacking, old persons living alone may seek comfort and a kind of companionship in the bottle. I should judge from the gossip of various neighborhoods that the outer suburbs from Boston to San Diego are full of secretly alcoholic widows. One of those widows, an old friend, was moved from her apartment into a retirement home. She left behind her a closet in which the floor was covered wall to wall with whiskey bottles. "Oh, those empty bottles!" she explained. "They were left by a former tenant."

Not whiskey or cooking sherry but simply giving up is the   19 greatest temptation of age. It is something different from a stoical acceptance of infirmities, which is something to be admired.

The givers-up see no reason for working. Sometimes they lie in   20 bed all day when moving about would still be possible, if difficult. I had a friend, a distinguished poet, who surrendered in that fashion. The doctors tried to stir him to action, but he refused to leave his room. Another friend, once a successful artist, stopped painting when his eyes began to fail. His doctor made the mistake of telling him that he suffered from a fatal disease. He then lost interest in everything except the splendid Rolls-Royce, acquired in his prosperous days, that stood in the garage. Daily he wiped the dust from its hood. He couldn't drive it on the road any longer, but he used to sit in the driver's seat, start the motor, then back the Rolls out of the garage and drive it in again, back twenty feet and forward twenty feet; that was his only distraction.

I haven't the right to blame those who surrender, not being able   21 to put myself inside their minds or bodies. Often they must have compelling reasons, physical or moral. Not only do they suffer from a variety of ailments, but also they are made to feel that they no longer have a function in the community. Their families and neighbors don't ask them for advice, don't really listen when they speak, don't call on them for efforts. One notes that there are not a few recoveries from apparent senility when that situation changes. If it doesn't change, old persons may decide that efforts are useless. I sympathize with their problems, but the men and women I envy are those who accept old age as a series of challenges.

For such persons, every new infirmity is an enemy to be out-   22
witted, an obstacle to be overcome by force of will. They enjoy
each little victory over themselves, and sometimes they win a
major success. Renoir was one of them. He continued painting,
and magnificently, for years after he was crippled by arthritis; the
brush had to be strapped to his arm. "You don't need your hand
to paint," he said. Goya was another of the unvanquished. At 72
he retired as an official painter of the Spanish court and decided to
work only for himself. His later years were those of the famous
"black paintings" in which he let his imagination run (and also of
the lithographs, then a new technique). At 78 he escaped a reign
of terror in Spain by fleeing to Bordeaux. He was deaf, and his
eyes were failing; in order to work he had to wear several pairs of
spectacles, one over another, and then use a magnifying glass; but
he was producing splendid work in a totally new style. At 80 he
drew an ancient man propped on two sticks, with a mass of white
hair and beard hiding his face and with the inscription "I am still
learning."

"Eighty years old!" the great Catholic poet Paul Claudel wrote   23
in his journal. "No eyes left, no ears, no teeth, no legs, no wind!
And when all is said and done, how astonishingly well one does
without them!"

UNDERSTANDING DETAILS

1. Name five ways, according to Cowley, that people begin to
   realize they are "old." How did Cowley himself learn that he
   was old?
2. List three vices of old age, and explain them as Cowley sees
   them.
3. What are three compensations of advancing age? In what ways
   are these activities pleasurable?
4. What does Cowley mean in paragraph 15 by "the vanity of
   older people"? How do older people manifest this vanity?

ANALYZING MEANING

1. What does the wagon symbolize in the author's poem about
   aging (paragraph 8)? What purpose does this poem serve in the
   essay?

2. For older people, what is the value of the conversations, images, friends, relatives, and melodies that pass through their minds? How might the elderly use these distractions constructively?
3. According to this essay, what qualities characterize those people who "surrender" (paragraph 21) to old age and those who "accept old age as a series of challenges" (paragraph 21)? Why do you think Cowley has more respect for the latter group?
4. What is Cowley's general attitude toward "the country of age"? Why does he feel that way about this stage of life?

DISCOVERING RHETORICAL STRATEGIES

1. After reading this essay, try to summarize in a single word or phrase Cowley's impressions of old age. How does this dominant impression help the author organize the many different details presented in his essay?
2. Why did Cowley include the reference to the Ojibwas at the end of the first paragraph? What effect does that anecdote have on our sympathies as readers?
3. Cowley uses a number of distinct metaphors in describing old age. He equates being old, for example, with acting out a certain "role" in life. He also portrays aging as a "rite of passage," a "challenge," and an "unfamiliar country" through which we must travel. In what sense is each of these metaphors appropriate? How does each help us understand the process of growing old?
4. Cowley uses language to describe a state of being that most of us are not familiar with yet. What other rhetorical strategies does he call upon to make his descriptive essay effective? Give examples of each.

MAKING CONNECTIONS

1. What are the primary differences among the "ageism" recounted by Malcolm Cowley, the racism explained by Lewis Sawaquat ("For My Indian Daughter"), and/or the sexism described by Sandra Cisneros ("Only daughter")? Is one of these "isms" more dangerous than the others? Have you ever experienced any of these types of prejudice?

2. Compare and contrast the weaknesses of old age depicted in Cowley's essay with those portrayed by the grandfather in Ray Bradbury's "Summer Rituals" or by Fred Brown in John McPhee's "The Pines." Do you know anyone in his or her eighties? How does that person act? How do you think you will behave when you are that old?

3. How is Cowley's description of the "identity crisis" many older people go through similar to the identity crisis Lewis Sawaquat ("For My Indian Daughter") suffered when he discovered his Native American heritage and Richard Rodriguez ("The Fear of Losing a Culture") went through when he immigrated to America? Have you ever gone through an identity crisis? How did you resolve it? Was your crisis like those described by Cowley, Sawaquat, or Rodriguez in any way?

IDEAS FOR DISCUSSION/WRITING

Preparing to Write

Write freely about your impressions of one or more older people in your life: Who are they? What characteristics do they share? How are they different from each other? Different from you? Similar to you? How do you know they are "old"?

Choosing a Topic

1. Cowley explains at the outset of his essay that "the country of age is a new experience, different from what you supposed it to be. Nobody, man or woman, knows the country until he has lived in it and has taken out his citizenship papers" (paragraph 3). Interview an older person to discover his or her view of "the country of age." Then write an essay for your peers describing that person's opinions.

2. In his essay, Cowley describes the signals he receives from his body and his environment that tell him he is "old." What messages did you receive when you were young that indicated you were a "child"? What messages do you receive now that remind you of your present age? How are these messages different from those you received when you were a child? Describe these signals in a well-developed essay addressed to your classmates.

3. Do you think that Americans treat their aged with enough respect? Explain your answer in detail to an older person. Describe various situations that support your opinion.

4. In this essay, Cowley details many of the surprises and realities of aging. What "surprises and realities" have you encountered at your current age? Write an email to your future retired self, titled "The View from _____" [insert your age], describing these observations and experiences.

Before beginning your essay, you might want to consult the checklists on page 50.

BERNARD COOPER   (1951–   )

Labyrinthine

Bernard Cooper's two major publications serve as bookends to his intriguing career as an author, editor, and teacher. The first, *Maps to Anywhere* (1990), is a collection of over thirty autobiographical essays and poems that chronicle important milestones in his life, including the loss of his brother to leukemia, his father's aging, and his perceptions of life in the future. The second, *Guess Again* (2000), is a series of short stories about growing up gay, cruising, AIDS, and falling in love. Born in Hollywood, Cooper earned his M.F.A. at the California Institute of the Arts in 1979. After abandoning visual art for a career in writing, he supported himself as a shoe salesman while producing a wide range of short stories and poems. He has taught in the UCLA Writers Program and in the Creative Writing Program at Antioch University. His work has been published in *The Best American Essays* (1988, 1995, and 1997) and in *The Oxford Book of Literature on Aging* (2000). Among his many honors are the PEN/Ernest Hemingway Award (1991) and the prestigious O'Henry Prize (1995). In assessing the power of the written word, Cooper has argued that "a good piece of writing causes you to have a sense of identification, even if the experience . . . is remote from your own." He calls this transportation through language "one of the greatest pleasures literature can offer."

Preparing to Read

In the following selection, Bernard Cooper describes what he has learned from his life-long interest in mazes. Once he conquers the most complex mazes, he starts to see "labyrinthine" patterns in all aspects of life—even in his parents' faces.

Exploring Experience: As you prepare to read Cooper's description, take a few moments to think about a pastime from which you have learned important lessons. What is the pastime? What lessons did you learn? Could you have gained these insights in any other way? How valuable were these discoveries?

Learning Online: Visit the "Amazeingart" Web site (http://www.amazeingart.com) to discover the differences between mazes and labyrinths. Consider the many different types and sizes of mazes as you read Bernard Cooper's essay.

W hen I discovered my first maze among the pages of a coloring book, I dutifully guided the mouse in the margins toward his wedge of cheese at the center. I dragged my crayon through narrow alleys and around corners, backing out of dead ends, trying this direction instead of that. Often I had to stop and rethink my strategy, squinting until some unobstructed path became clear and I could start to move the crayon again.   1

I kept my sights on the small chamber in the middle of the page and knew that being lost would not be in vain; wrong turns only improved my chances, showed me that one true path toward my reward. Even when trapped in the hallways of the maze, I felt an embracing safety, as if I'd been zipped in a sleeping bag.   2

Reaching the cheese had about it a triumph and finality I'd never experienced after coloring a picture or connecting the dots. If only I'd known a word like "inevitable," since that's how it felt to finally slip into the innermost room. I gripped the crayon, savored the place.   3

The lines on the next maze in the coloring book curved and rippled like waves on water. The object of this maze was to lead a hungry dog to his bone. Mouse to cheese, dog to bone—the premise quickly ceased to matter. It was the tricky, halting travel I was after, forging a passage, finding my way.   4

Later that day, as I walked through our living room, a maze revealed itself to me in the mahogany coffee table. I sat on the floor, fingered the wood grain, and found a winding avenue through it. The fabric of my parents' blanket was a pattern of climbing ivy and, from one end of the bed to the other, I traced the air between the tendrils. Soon I didn't need to use a finger, mapping my path by sight. I moved through the veins of the marble heart, through the space between the paisleys on my mother's blouse. At the age of seven I changed forever, like the faithful who see Christ on the side of a barn or peering up from a corn tortilla. Everywhere I looked, a labyrinth meandered.   5

Soon the mazes in the coloring books, in the comic-strip sec-   6
tion of the Sunday paper, or on the placemats of coffee shops that
served "children's meals" became too easy. And so I began to
make my own. I drew them on the cardboard rectangles that my
father's dress shirts were folded around when they came back from
the cleaner's. My frugal mother, hoarder of jelly jars and rubber
bands, had saved a stack of them. She was happy to put the cardboard to use, if a bit mystified by my new obsession.

The best method was to start from the center and work out-   7
ward with a sharpened pencil, creating layers of complication. I
left a few gaps in every line, and after I'd gotten a feel for the
architecture of the whole, I'd close off openings, reinforce walls, a
slave sealing the pharaoh's tomb. My blind alleys were especially
treacherous; I constructed them so that, by the time one realized
he'd gotten stuck, turning back would be an exquisite ordeal.

My hobby required a twofold concentration: carefully planning   8
a maze while allowing myself the fresh pleasure of moving through
it. Alone in my bedroom, sitting at my desk, I sometimes spent the
better part of an afternoon on a single maze. I worked with the
patience of a redwood growing rings. Drawing myself into corners,
erasing a wall if all else failed, I fooled and baffled and freed myself.

Eventually I used shelf paper, tearing off larger and larger sheets   9
to accommodate my burgeoning ambition. Once I brought a huge
maze to my mother, who was drinking a cup of coffee in the
kitchen. It wafted behind me like an ostentatious cape. I draped it
over the table and challenged her to try it. She hadn't looked at it
for more than a second before she refused. "You've got to be kid-
ding," she said, blotting her lips with a paper napkin. "I'm lost
enough as it is." When my father returned from work that night,
he hefted his briefcase into the closet, his hat wet and drooping
from the rain. "Later," he said (his code word for "never") when
I waved the banner of my labyrinth before him.

It was inconceivable to me that someone wouldn't want to   10
enter a maze, wouldn't lapse into the trance it required, wouldn't
sacrifice the time to find a solution. But mazes had a strange effect
on my parents: they took one look at those tangled paths and
seemed to wilt.

I was a late child, a "big surprise" as my mother liked to say; by   11
the time I'd turned seven, my parents were trying to cut a swath
through the forest of middle age. Their mortgage ballooned. The

plumbing rusted. Old friends grew sick or moved away. The creases in their skin deepened, so complex a network of lines, my mazes paled by comparison. Father's hair receded, Mother's grayed. "When you've lived as long as we have . . . ," they'd say, which meant no surprises loomed in their future; it was repetition from here on out. The endless succession of burdens and concerns was enough to make anyone forgetful. Eggs were boiled until they turned brown, sprinklers left on till the lawn grew soggy, keys and glasses and watches misplaced. When I asked my parents about their past, they cocked their heads, stared into the distance, and often couldn't recall the details.

Thirty years later, I understand my parents' refusal. Why would 12 anyone choose to get mired in a maze when the days encase us, loopy and confusing? Remembered events merge together or fade away. Places and dates grow dubious, a jumble of guesswork and speculation. *What's-his-name* and *thingamajig* replace the bright particular. Recollecting the past becomes as unreliable as forecasting the future; you consult yourself with a certain trepidation and take your answer with a grain of salt. The friends you turn to for confirmation are just as muddled; they furrow their brows and look at you blankly. Of course, once in a while you find the tiny, pungent details poised on your tongue like caviar. But more often than not, you settle for sloppy approximations—"I was visiting Texas or Colorado, in 1971 or '72"—and the anecdote rambles on regardless. When the face of a friend from childhood suddenly comes back to me, it's sad to think that if a certain synapse hadn't fired just then, I may never have recalled that friend again. Sometimes I'm not sure if I've overheard a story in conversation, read it in a book, or if I'm the person to whom it happened; whose adventures, besides my own, are wedged in my memory? Then there are the things I've dreamed and mistaken as fact. When you've lived as long as I have, uncertainty is virtually indistinguishable from the truth, which as far as I know is never naked, but always wearing some disguise.

Mother, Father: I'm growing middle-aged, lost in the folds and 13 bones of my body. It gets harder to remember the days when you were here. I suppose it was inevitable that, gazing down at this piece of paper, I'd feel your weary expressions on my face. What have things been like since you've been gone? Labyrinthine. The very sound of that word sums it up—as slippery as thought, as perplexing as the truth, as long and convoluted as a life.

UNDERSTANDING DETAILS

1. Cooper calls his interest in mazes an "obsession" (paragraph 6), a "hobby" (paragraph 8), and a "burgeoning ambition" (paragraph 9). How would you describe his interest in mazes? Explain why you would use these particular words.
2. List at least three senses that the author refers to in this essay. How do these sensual details help the reader experience the author's hobby?
3. In what ways did the author change forever at 7 years old?
4. What is Cooper's dominant impression?

ANALYZING MEANING

1. What did working through mazes teach Cooper about life? Explain your answer.
2. Why do you think the author received such satisfaction from completing each maze?
3. In this essay, Cooper describes how he discovered mazes and complex patterns in many different aspects of life. Explain two of these discoveries.
4. What does Cooper mean when he says, "What have things been like since you've been gone? Labyrinthine." (paragraph 13)? Explain your answer.

DISCOVERING RHETORICAL STRATEGIES

1. What does Cooper realize 30 years later about his parents' refusal to work with mazes? Why do you think he waits to tell us this information until later in the essay?
2. Cooper makes several comparisons throughout his essay to bring his subject to life. One example is in paragraph 8 when he says, "I worked with the patience of a redwood, growing rings." Find two other examples of such vivid comparisons.
3. What is the tone of this essay? Use language taken from the essay to explain your answer.
4. Although this essay works predominantly through description, what other rhetorical modes support Cooper's dominant impression? Give examples of each of these modes in the essay.

MAKING CONNECTIONS

1. Compare and contrast Cooper's recollection of his childhood with those expressed by Ray Bradbury ("Summer Rituals"), Russell Baker ("The Saturday Evening Post"), and Alice Walker ("Beauty: When the Other Dancer is the Self").
2. In what ways is Cooper's analysis of life as a "maze" like similar attempts to cope with contradiction and confusion in Wang Ping's "Ways to Ai," Bill Cosby's "The Baffling Question," and Kimberly Wozencraft's "Notes from the Country Club"?
3. Compare Cooper's discoveries about the aging process with similar insights advanced by Malcolm Cowley ("The View from 80"), Phyllis Schneider ("Memory: Tips You'll Never Forget"), and Mary Pipher ("Beliefs About Families").

IDEAS FOR DISCUSSION/WRITING

Preparing to Write

Write freely for a few minutes about one of your most cherished hobbies or pastimes. What role did/does this hobby play in your life? Has it been a positive or negative influence on you? Did it ever turn into an obsession? What did it teach you about life? How did you make use of these important life lessons?

Choosing a Topic

1. Based on your memories, write a descriptive essay about a hobby of yours or someone else's. Decide on a dominant impression you want to communicate and a perspective that will help create that impression.
2. Describe for your classmates your favorite game. How many can play? What are the rules? When is the game most exciting? Why do you like this game?
3. Using your imagination, travel back in time to a particular moment or event in your past. Write an essay describing in detail what you saw, smelled, tasted, heard, and touched at that particular time in your life. Where were you? How old were you? What was happening at this moment in your past? What exactly were you doing? How did you feel while you were engaged in this activity? Who else was involved in the scene with you? Did you feel safe? Secure? Happy? Sad? Anxious to escape? Free?

4. If you were to create a Web site about your childhood games, what would it be called? Write an essay that would appear on the home page of your Web site. Describe your memories of a particular childhood game or hobby that you engaged in with other family members. Try to link this experience with your current life and describe how that game or pastime is reflective of your family relationships.

Before beginning your essay, you might want to consult the checklists on page 50.

CHAPTER WRITING ASSIGNMENTS
Practicing Description

1. Write a spatial description of your home by exploring its basic sections or rooms. What does your home reveal about you as a person? About your family?
2. Think about the extent to which influences such as family, education, and community have contributed to the person you are today. Describe the kind of person you are and the sources of a few of your most important qualities.
3. Consider the health of the environment in your immediate community (air, noise, landscape). Describe an environmental problem you have observed. Be sure to provide examples of the problem you are describing.

Exploring Ideas

1. Discuss a cultural icon (like a rock star or a prominent building) and what it represents about the culture you are describing. How did this person or object become an icon in its culture? What biases or ideals does it express? How do people outside this culture view it?
2. Think about the ways people's physical surroundings (office, weather, house, apartment) affect them. Discuss one important way these surroundings have influenced someone's behavior. Provide examples in your discussion that explore the relationship between various features in your surroundings and the manner in which people react to them.
3. In your opinion, how well are elderly people treated in America? Write an essay describing the level of respect older people get in American society. Use examples of people you know to support your ideas.

2

NARRATION
Telling a Story

A good story is a powerful method of getting someone's attention. The excitement that accompanies a suspenseful ghost story, a lively anecdote, or a vivid joke easily attests to this fact. In fact, narration is one of the earliest verbal skills we all learn as children, providing us with a convenient, logical, and easily understood means of sharing our thoughts with other people. Storytelling is powerful because it offers us a way of dramatizing our ideas so that others can identify with them.

DEFINING NARRATION

Narration involves telling a story that is often based on personal experience. Stories can be oral or written, real or imaginary, short or long. A good story, however, always has a point or purpose. Narration can be the dominant mode (as in a novel or short story), supported by other rhetorical strategies, or it can serve the purpose of another rhetorical mode (as in a persuasive essay, a historical survey, or a scientific report).

In its subordinate role, narration can provide examples or explain ideas. If asked why you are attending college, for instance, you might turn to narration to make your answer clear, beginning with a story about your family's hardships in the past. The purpose of telling such a story would be to show your listeners how important higher education is to you by encouraging them to understand and identify with your family history.

Unlike description, which generally portrays people, places, and objects in *space*, narration asks the reader to follow a series of actions through a particular *time* sequence. Description, however, often complements the movement of narration. People must be depicted, for instance, along with their relationships to one another, before their actions can have any real meaning for us; similarly, places must be described so that we can picture the setting and understand the activities in a specific scene. The organization of the action and the time spent on each episode in a story should be based principally on a writer's analysis of the interests and needs of his or her audience.

To be most effective, narration should prolong the exciting parts of a story and shorten the routine facts that simply move the reader from one episode to another. If you were robbed on your way to work, for example, a good narrative describing the incident would concentrate on the traumatic event itself rather than on such mundane and boring details as what you had for breakfast and what chroes you did prior to the attack. Finally, just like description, narration *shows* rather than *tells* its purpose to the audience. The factual statement "I was robbed this morning" could be made much more vivid and dramatic through the addition of some simple narration: "As I was walking to work at 7:30 A.M., a huge and angry-looking man ran up to me, thrust a gun into the middle of my stomach, and took my money, my new wristwatch, all my credit cards, and my pants—leaving me penniless and embarrassed."

The following paragraph written by a student recounts a recent parachuting experience. As you read this narrative, notice especially the writer's use of vivid detail to *show* rather than *tell* her message to the readers.

I have always needed occasional "fixes" of excitement in my life, so when I realized one spring day that I was more than ordinarily bored, I made up my mind to take more than ordinary steps to relieve that boredom. I decided to go parachuting. The next thing I knew, I was stuffed into a claustrophobically small plane with five other terrified people, rolling down a bumpy, rural runway, droning my way to

3,500 feet and an exhilarating experience. Once over the jump area, I waited my turn, stepped onto the strut, held my breath, and then kicked off into the cold, rushing air as my heart pounded heavily. All I could think was, "I hope this damn parachute opens!" The sensation of falling backward through space was unfamiliar and disconcerting till my chute opened with a loud "pop," momentarily pulling me upward toward the distant sky. After several minutes of floating downward, I landed rudely on the hard ground. Life, I remembered happily, could be awfully exciting, and a month later, when my tailbone had stopped throbbing, I still felt that way.

THINKING CRITICALLY BY USING NARRATION

Rhetorical modes offer us different ways of perceiving reality. Narration is an especially useful tool for sequencing or putting details and information in some kind of logical order, usually chronological. Practicing exercises in narrative techniques can help you see clear patterns in topics you are writing about.

Although narration is usually used in conjunction with other rhetorical modes, we are going to isolate it here so you can appreciate its specific mechanics separate from other mental activities. If you feel the process of narration in your head, you are more likely to understand exactly what it entails and thus to use it more effectively in reading essays and in organizing and writing your own essays.

For the best results, we will once again do some warm-up exercises to make your sequencing perceptions as accurate and successful as possible. In this way, you will actually learn to feel how your mind works in this particular mode and then be more aware of the thinking strategies available to you in your own reading and writing. As you become more conscious of the mechanics of the individual rhetorical modes, you will naturally become more adept at combining them to accomplish the specific purpose and the related effect you want to create.

The following exercises, which require a combination of thinking and writing skills, will help you practice this particular strategy in isolation. Just as in a physical workout, we will warm up your mental capabilities one by one as if they were muscles that can be developed individually before being used together in harmony.

1. Write or tell the story that goes with the accompanying Scott Alberts photo. Make this scene the beginning of your story, and then create the remainder of the plot.
2. Make a chronological list of the different activities you did yesterday, from waking in the morning to sleeping at night. Randomly pick two events from your day, and treat them as the highlights of your day. Now write freely for five minutes, explaining the story of your day and emphasizing the importance of these two highlights.
3. Recall an important event that happened to you between the ages of five and ten. Brainstorm about how this event made you feel at the time it happened. Then brainstorm about how this event makes you feel now. What changes have you discovered in your view of this event?

READING AND WRITING NARRATIVE ESSAYS

Making meaning in reading and writing is a fairly straightforward process with the narrative mode. To read a narrative essay most effectively, you should spend your time concentrating on the writer's main story line and use of details. Together, these tasks will help you make meaning as you read. To create an effective story, you have some important decisions to make before you write and certain variables to control as you actually draft your narrative. During the prewriting stage, you need to generate ideas and choose a point of view through which your story will be presented. Then, as you write, the preliminary decisions you have made regarding the selection and arrangement of your details (especially important in a narrative) will allow your story to flow more easily. Carefully controlled organization, along with appropriate timing and pacing, can influence your audience's reactions in very powerful ways.

How to Read a Narrative Essay

Preparing to Read.   As you prepare to read the narratives in this chapter, try to guess what each title tells you about its essay's topic and about the author's attitude toward that topic: Can you guess, for example, how Lewis Sawaquat feels about his daughter from his title "For My Indian Daughter" or what Maya Angelou's attitude is toward the events described in "New Directions"? Also, scan the essay and read its synopsis in the Rhetorical Table of Contents to help you anticipate as much as you can about the author's purpose and audience.

Next, the more you learn from the biography about the author and the circumstances surrounding the composition of a particular essay, the better prepared you will be to read the essay. For a narrative essay, the writer's point of view or perspective toward the story and its characters is especially significant. From the biographies, can you determine Maya Angelou's attitude toward Annie Johnson's energy and determination in "New Directions" or Russell Baker's opinion of his mother in "The Saturday Evening Post"? Also, what is Sandra Cisneros's reason for writing "Only daughter"?

Last, before you begin to read, answer the Preparing to Read questions, and then try to generate some of your own inquiries on the general subject of the essay: What do you want to know about being a Native American (Sawaquat)? What childhood experience greatly affected your life (Baker)? What do you think of children in general (Cisneros)?

Reading.   As you read a narrative essay for the first time, simply follow the story line, and try to get a general sense of the narrative and of the author's general purpose. Is Baker trying to encourage us all to be writers or simply to help us understand why he writes? Record your initial reactions to each essay as they occur to you. Is Keillor's purpose to make us feel sympathetic or antagonistic toward his childhood memories?

Based on the biographical information preceding the essay and on the essay's tone, purpose, and audience, try to create a context for the narrative as you read. How do such details help you understand your reading material more thoroughly? A first reading of this sort, along with a survey of the questions that follow the essay, will help prepare you for a critical understanding of the material when you read it for the second time.

Rereading. As you reread these narrative essays, notice the author's selection and arrangement of details. Why does Angelou organize her story one way and Cisneros another? What effect does their organization create?

Also, pay attention to the timing and the pacing of the story line. What do the long descriptions of Annie's plans add to Angelou's "New Directions"? What does the quick pace of Keillor's narrative communicate?

In addition, consider at this point what other rhetorical strategies the authors use to support their narratives. Which writers use examples to supplement their stories? Which use definitions? Which use comparisons? Why do they use these strategies?

Finally, when you answer the questions after each essay, you can check your understanding of the material on different levels before you tackle the discussion/writing topics that follow.

For a general checklist of reading guidelines, please see page 20 of the Introduction.

How to Write a Narrative Essay

Preparing to Write. First, you should answer the prewriting questions to help you generate thoughts on the subject at hand. Next, as in all writing, you should explore your subject matter and discover as many specific details as possible. (See pages 21–23 of the Introduction for a discussion of prewriting techniques.) Some writers rely on the familiar journalistic checklist of *who, what, when, where, why,* and *how* to make sure they cover all aspects of their narrative. If you were using the story of a basketball game at your college to demonstrate the team spirit of your school, for example, you might want to consider telling your readers *who* played in the game and/or *who* attended; *what* happened before, during, and after the game; *when* and *where* it took place; *why* it was being played (or *why* these particular teams were playing each other or *why* the game was especially important); and *how* the winning basket was shot. Freewriting or a combination of freewriting and the journalistic questions is another effective way of getting ideas and story details on paper for use in a first draft.

Once you have generated these ideas, you should always let your purpose and audience ultimately guide your selection of details, but the process of gathering such journalistic information gives you some material from which to choose. You will also need to decide whether to include dialogue in your narrative. Again, the difference here is between *showing* and *telling*: Will your audience benefit from reading what was actually said, word for word, during a discussion, or will a brief description of the conversation be sufficiently effective? In fact, all the choices you make at this stage of the composing process will give you material with which to create emphasis, suspense, conflict, and interest in your subject.

Next, you must decide upon the point of view that will most readily help you achieve your purpose with your specific audience. Point of view includes the (1) person, (2) vantage point, and (3) attitude of your narrator. *Person* refers to who will tell the story: an uninvolved observer, a character in the narrative, or an omniscient (all-seeing) narrator. This initial decision will guide your thoughts on *vantage point*, which is the frame of reference of the narrator: close to the action, far from the action, looking back on the past, or reporting on the present. Finally, your narrator will naturally have an *attitude*, or *personal feeling*, about the subject: accepting, hostile, sarcastic, indifferent, angry, pleased, or any number of similar emotions. Once you adopt a certain perspective in a story, you should follow it for the duration of the narrative. This consistency will bring focus and coherence to your essay.

Writing.   After you have explored your topic and adopted a particular point of view, you need to write a thesis statement and to select and arrange the details of your story coherently so that the narrative has a clear beginning, middle, and end. The most natural

way to organize the events of a narrative, of course, is chronologically. In your story about the school basketball game, you would
probably narrate the relevant details in the order they occurred
(i.e., sequentially, from the beginning of the game to its conclusion). More experienced writers may elect to use flashbacks: An
athlete might recall a significant event that happened during the
game, or a coach might recollect the contest's turning point. Your
most important consideration is that the elements of a narrative
essay follow some sort of time sequence, aided by the use of clear
and logical transitions (e.g., "then," "next," "at this point," "suddenly") that help the reader move smoothly from one event to the
next.

Rewriting.   As you reread the narrative you have written,
pretend you are a reader (instead of the writer) and make sure you
have told the story from the most effective point of view, considering both your purpose and your audience:

• Is your purpose (or thesis) clearly stated?

• Who is your audience?

• To what extent does this narrator help you achieve your purpose?

Further, as you reread, make certain you can follow the events
of the story as they are related:

• Does one event lead naturally to the next?

• Are all the events relevant to your purpose?

• Do you *show* rather than *tell* your message?

For more advice on writing and editing, see pages 27–31.

STUDENT ESSAY: NARRATION AT WORK

The following student essay characterizes the writer's mother
by telling a story about an unusual family vacation. As you read it,
notice that the student writer states her purpose clearly and succinctly in the first paragraph. She then becomes an integral part of
her story as she carefully selects examples and details that help convey her thesis.

A Vacation with My Mother

First-person narrator

<u>I</u> had an interesting childhood—not because of where I grew up and not because I ever did anything particularly adventuresome or thrilling. In fact, I don't think my life seemed especially interesting to me at the time. But now, telling friends about my supposedly ordinary childhood, I notice an array of responses ranging from astonishment to hilarity. <u>The source of their surprise and amusement is my mother</u>—gracious, charming, sweet, and totally out of synchronization with the rest of the world. <u>One strange family trip we took when I was eleven captures the essence of her zaniness.</u>

General subject

Specific subject

Thesis statement

My two sets of grandparents lived in Colorado and North Dakota, and my parents decided we would spend a few weeks driving to those states and seeing all the sights along the relaxed and rambling way. <u>My eight-year-old brother, David, and I had some serious reservations.</u> If Dad had ever had Mom drive him to school, we reasoned, he'd never even consider letting her help drive us anywhere out of town, let alone out of California. If we weren't paying attention, we were as likely to end up at her office or the golf course as we were to arrive at school. Sometimes she'd drop us off at a friend's house to play and then forget where she'd left us. The notion of going on a long trip with her was really unnerving.

Narrator's attitude

Examples

<u>How can I explain my mother to a stranger?</u> Have you ever watched reruns of the old *I Love Lucy* with Lucille Ball? I did as a child, and I thought Lucy Ricardo was normal. I lived with somebody a lot like her. Now, Mom wasn't a redhead (not usually, anyway), and Dad wasn't a Cuban

Transition

nightclub owner, but <u>at home we had the</u> <u>same situation of a loving but bemused hus-</u> <u>band trying to deal with the off-the-wall</u> <u>logic and enthusiasm of a frequently exas-</u> <u>perating wife.</u> <u>We all adored her, but we</u> <u>had to admit it: Mom was a flaky, absent-</u> <u>minded, genuine eccentric.</u>

Narrator's vantage point

<u>As the first day of our trip approached,</u> David and I reluctantly said good-bye to all of our friends. Who knew if we'd ever see any of them again? Finally, the moment of our departure arrived, and we loaded suit- cases, books, games, camping gear, and a tent into the car and bravely drove off. We bravely drove off again two hours later after we'd returned home to get the purse and traveler's checks that Mom had forgotten.

Transition

Careful selection of details

David and I were always a little nervous when using gas station bathrooms if Mom was driving while Dad napped: "You stand outside the door and play lookout while I go, and I'll stand outside the door and play lookout while you go." I had terrible visions: "Honey, where are the kids?" "What?! Oh, gosh . . . I thought they were being awfully quiet. Uh . . . Idaho?" We were never actually abandoned in a strange city, but we weren't about to take any chances.

Use of dialogue

Examples

<u>On the fourth or fifth night of the trip,</u> we had trouble finding a motel with a vacancy. After driving futilely for an hour, Mom suddenly had a great idea: Why didn't we find a house with a likely-looking back- yard and ask if we could pitch our tent there? To her, the scheme was eminently reasonable. Vowing quietly to each other to hide in the back seat if she did it, David and I groaned in anticipated mortification. To our profound relief, Dad vetoed the idea.

Transition

Passage of time

Example

Mom never could understand our objections. If a strange family showed up on her front doorstep, Mom would have been delighted. She thinks everyone in the world is as nice as she is. We finally found a vacancy in the next town. David and I were thrilled—the place featured bungalows in the shape of Native-American tepees.

Transition

The Native-American motif must have reminded my parents that we had not yet used the brand-new tent, Coleman stove, portable mattress, and other camping gear we had brought. We headed to a national park the next day and found a campsite by a lake. It took hours to figure out how to set

Chronological order

up the tent: It was one of those deluxe models with mosquito-net windows, canvas floors, and enough room for three large families to sleep in. It was after dark before we finally got it erected, and the night had turned quite cold. We fixed a hurried campfire dinner (chicken burned on the outside and raw in the middle) and prepared to go to sleep. That was when we realized that Mom had forgotten to bring along some important pieces of equipment—our sleeping bags. The four of us huddled together on our thin mattresses borrowed from our station-wagon floor. That ended our camping days. Give me a stucco tepee any time.

Careful selection of details

We drove through several states and saw lots of great sights along the way: the Grand Canyon, Carlsbad Caverns, caves, mountains, waterfalls, and even a haunted house. David and I were excited and amazed at all the wonders we found, and Mom was just as enthralled as we were. Her constant pleasure and sense of the world as a beautiful, magical place was infectious. I never realized until I grew up how really childlike—in the

Examples (spatial order)

best sense of the word—my mother actually is. She is innocent, optimistic, and always ready to be entertained.

Transition   <u>Looking back on that long-past family vacation, I now realize that my childhood</u>   Narrator's attitude
<u>was more special because I grew up with a</u>
<u>mother who wasn't afraid to try anything</u>
<u>and who taught me to look at the world as</u>
<u>a series of marvelous opportunities to be</u>
<u>explored.</u> What did it matter that she thought England was bordered by Germany? We were never going to try to drive   Examples
there. So what if she was always leaving her car keys in the refrigerator or some other equally inexplicable place? <u>In the end, we</u>
Concluding remark   <u>always got where we were going—and we</u>
<u>generally had a grand time along the way.</u>

Student Writer's Comments

I enjoyed writing about this childhood vacation because of all the memories it brought back. I knew I wanted to write a narrative to explain my mother, and the word *zany* immediately popped into my mind. So I knew what my focus was going to be from the outset. My prewriting started spontaneously as soon as I found this angle. So many thoughts and memories rushed into my head that I couldn't even get to a piece of paper to write them down before I lost some of them. But there were way too many to put into one essay. The hardest part of writing this narrative was trying to decide what material to use and what to leave out. Spending a little more time before writing my first draft proved to be a good investment in this case. I got a clean piece of paper and began freewriting, trying to mold some of my scattered ideas from brainstorming into a coherent, readable form. During this second stage of prewriting, I remembered one special vacation we took that I thought might capture the essence of my mother—and also of my family.

My first draft was about three times the length of this one. My point of view was the innocent participant/observer who came to know and love her mother or her absent-mindedness. I had really developed my thesis from the time I got this writing assignment. And I told my story chronologically except for looking back in the last paragraph when I attempted to analyze the entire experience. I had no trouble *showing* rather than *telling* because all of the details were so vivid to me—as if they had happened yesterday. But that was my downfall. I soon realized that I could not possibly include everything that was on the pages of my first draft.

The process of cranking out my rough draft made my point of view toward life with my mother very clear to me and helped me face the cutting that was ahead of me. I took the raw material of a very lengthy first draft and forced myself to choose the details and examples that best characterized my mother and what life was like growing up under the care of such a lovely but daffy individual. The sense of her being both "lovely" and "daffy" was the insight that helped me the most in revising the content of my essay. I made myself ruthlessly eliminate anything that interfered with the overall effect I was trying to create—from extraneous images and details to words and phrases that didn't contribute to this specific view of my mom.

The final result, according to my classmates, communicated my message clearly and efficiently. The main criticism I got from my class was that I might have cut too much from my first draft. But I think this focused picture with a few highlights conveys my meaning in the best possible way. I offered enough details to *show* rather than *tell* my readers what living with my mother was like, but not too many to bore them. I was also able to take the time in my essay to be humorous now and then ("David and I reluctantly said good-bye to all of our friends. Who knew if we'd ever see any of them again?" and "Give me a stucco tepee any time."), as well as pensive and serious ("I now realize that my childhood was more special because I grew up with a mother who wasn't afraid to try anything and who taught me to look at the world as a series of marvelous opportunities to be explored."). Even though in looking at the essay now I would tamper with a few things, I am generally happy with the final draft. It captures the essence of my mother from my point of view, and it also gave my class a few laughs. Aren't the readers' reactions the ultimate test of a good story?

SOME FINAL THOUGHTS ON NARRATION

Just as with other modes of writing, all decisions regarding narration should be made with a specific purpose and an intended audience constantly in mind. As you will see, each narrative in this section is directed at a clearly defined audience. Notice, as you read, how each writer manipulates the various features of narration so that the readers are simultaneously caught up in the plot and deeply moved to feel, act, think, and believe the writer's personal opinions.

NARRATION IN REVIEW

Reading Narrative Essays

Preparing to Read

✓ What assumptions can you make from the essay's title?
✓ Can you guess what the author's mood is?
✓ What is the essay's purpose and audience?
✓ What does the synopsis tell you about the essay?
✓ What can you learn from the author's biography?
✓ Can you guess what the author's point of view toward the subject is?
✓ What are your responses to the "Preparing to Read" questions?

Reading

✓ What is the essay's general story line?
✓ What is the author's purpose?
✓ Did you preview the questions that follow the essay?

Rereading

✓ What details did the author choose and how are they arranged?
✓ How does the author control the pace of the story?
✓ What other rhetorical modes does the author use?
✓ What are your responses to the questions after the essay?

Writing Narrative Essays

Preparing to Write

✓ What are your responses to the "Preparing to Write" questions?
✓ What is your purpose?
✓ Who is your audience?
✓ What is your narrator's point of view—including person, vantage point, and attitude toward the subject?

Writing

✓ What is your thesis?
✓ What details will best support this thesis?
✓ How can you arrange these details most effectively?
✓ Do you *show* rather than *tell* your story?
✓ Does your narrative essay follow a time sequence?

Rewriting

✓ Is your purpose (or thesis) clearly stated?
✓ Who is your audience?
✓ Does one event lead naturally to the next?
✓ Are all the events relevant to your purpose?

LEWIS SAWAQUAT   (1935–   )

For My Indian Daughter

Lewis Sawaquat is a Native American who is now retired from his thirty-year job as a surveyor for the Soil Conservation Service of the United States Department of Agriculture. He was born in Harbor Springs, Michigan, where his great-great-grandfather was the last official "chief" of the region. After finishing high school, Sawaquat entered the army, graduated from Army Survey School, and then completed a tour of duty in Korea. Upon returning to America, he enrolled in the Art Institute of Chicago to study commercial art. Sawaquat now lives in Peshawbestown, Michigan, where his hobbies include gardening, swimming, and walking in the woods. He serves as a pipe carrier and cultural/spiritual adviser to his Ottawa tribe. Recently, he started a consulting firm and travels around the country speaking on Native-American issues. He also hopes to write a book entitled *Dreams: The Universal Language*, which will investigate the Native-American approach to dream interpretation. His daughter, Gaia, who is described in the following essay, recently graduated from Yale University. His advice to students using *The Prose Reader* is to "pay attention to life; there's nothing more important to becoming a writer."

Preparing to Read

"For My Indian Daughter" originally appeared in the "My Turn" column of *Newsweek* magazine (September 5, 1983) under the author's former name, Lewis Johnson. In his article, the author speaks eloquently of prejudice, ethnic pride, and growing cultural awareness.

Exploring Experience: Before reading this selection, think for a few minutes about your own heritage: What is your ethnic identity? Are you content with this background? Have you ever gone through an identity crisis? Do you anticipate facing any problems because of your ancestry? If so, how will you handle these problems when they occur?

Learning Online: To understand the context in which Sawaquat is writing, visit the Smithsonian Web site (http:// www.si.edu), and type "American Indian Art and Design" into the search field. View the online exhibits of Native American culture, past and present.

My little girl is singing herself to sleep upstairs, her voice   1
mingling with the sounds of the birds outside in the old maple trees. She is two, and I am nearly 50, and I am very taken with her. She came along late in my life, unexpected and unbidden, a startling gift.

Today at the beach my chubby-legged, brown-skinned daugh-   2
ter ran laughing into the water as fast as she could. My wife and I laughed watching her, until we heard behind us a low guttural curse and then an unpleasant voice raised in an imitation war whoop.

I turned to see a fat man in a bathing suit, white and soft as a   3
grub, as he covered his mouth and prepared to make the Indian war cry again. He was middle-aged, younger than I, and had three little children lined up next to him, grinning foolishly. My wife suggested we leave the beach, and I agreed.

I knew the man was not unusual in his feelings against Indians.   4
His beach behavior might have been socially unacceptable to more civilized whites, but his basic view of Indians is expressed daily in our small town, frequently on the editorial pages of the county newspaper, as white people speak out against Indian fishing rights and land rights, saying in essence, "Those Indians are taking our fish, our land." It doesn't matter to them that we were here first, that the U.S. Supreme Court has ruled in our favor. It matters to them that we have something they want, and they hate us for it. Backlash is the common explanation of the attacks on Indians, the bumper stickers that say, "Spear an Indian, Save a Fish," but I know better. The hatred of Indians goes back to the beginning when white people came to this country. For me it goes back to my childhood in Harbor Springs, Mich.

Theft.   Harbor Springs is now a summer resort for the very   5
affluent, but a hundred years ago it was the Indian village of my Ottawa ancestors. My grandmother, Anna Showanessy, and other

Indians like her, had their land there taken by treaty, by fraud, by violence, by theft. They remembered how whites had burned down the village at Burt Lake in 1900 and pushed the Indians out. These were the stories in my family.

When I was a boy, my mother told me to walk down the alleys 6 in Harbor Springs and not to wear my orange football sweater out of the house. This way I would not stand out, not be noticed, and not be a target.

I wore my orange sweater anyway and deliberately avoided the 7 alleys. I was the biggest person I knew and wasn't really afraid. But I met my comeuppance when I enlisted in the U.S. Army. One night all the men in my barracks gathered together and, gang-fashion, pulled me into the shower and scrubbed me down with rough brushes used for floors, saying, "We won't have any dirty Indians in our outfit." It is a point of irony that I was cleaner than any of them. Later in Korea I learned how to kill, how to bully, how to hate Koreans. I came out of the war tougher than ever and, strangely, white.

I went to college, got married, lived in La Porte, Ind., worked 8 as a surveyor and raised three boys. I headed Boy Scout groups, never thinking it odd when the Scouts did imitation Indian dances, imitation Indian lore.

One day when I was 35 or thereabouts I heard about an Indian 9 powwow. My father used to attend them and so with great curios-ity and a strange joy at discovering a part of my heritage, I decided the thing to do to get ready for this big event was to have my friend make me a spear in his forge. The steel was fine and blue and iridescent. The feathers on the shaft were bright and proud.

In a dusty state fairground in southern Indiana, I found white 10 people dressed as Indians. I learned they were "hobbyists," that is, it was their hobby and leisure pastime to masquerade as Indians on weekends. I felt ridiculous with my spear, and I left.

It was years before I could tell anyone of the embarrassment of 11 this weekend and see any humor in it. But in a way it was that weekend, for all its silliness, that was my awakening. I realized I didn't know who I was. I didn't have an Indian name. I didn't speak the Indian language. I didn't know the Indian customs. Dimly I remembered the Ottawa word for dog, but it was a baby word, *kahgee*, not the full word, *muhkahgee*, which I was later to learn. Even more hazily I remembered a naming ceremony (my own). I remembered legs dancing around me, dust. Where had that been? Who had I been? "Sawaquat," my mother told me when I asked, "where the tree begins to grow."

That was 1968, and I was not the only Indian in the country   12
who was feeling the need to remember who he or she was. There were others. They had powwows, real ones, and eventually I found them. Together we researched our past, a search that for me culminated in the Longest Walk, a march on Washington in 1978. Maybe because I now know what it means to be Indian, it surprises me that others don't. Of course there aren't very many of us left. The chances of an average person knowing an average Indian in an average lifetime are pretty slim.

Circle.   Still, I was amused one day when my small, four-   13
year-old neighbor looked at me as I was hoeing in my garden and said, "You aren't a real Indian, are you?" Scotty is little, talkative, likable. Finally I said, "I'm a real Indian." He looked at me for a moment and then said, squinting into the sun, "Then where's your horse and feathers?" The child was simply a smaller, whiter version of my own ignorant self years before. We'd both seen too much TV, that's all. He was not to be blamed. And so, in a way, the moronic man on the beach today is blameless. We come full circle to realize other people are like ourselves, as discomfiting as that may be sometimes.

As I sit in my old chair on my porch, in a light that is fading so   14
the leaves are barely distinguishable against the sky, I can picture my girl asleep upstairs. I would like to prepare her for what's to come, take her each step of the way saying, there's a place to avoid, here's what I know about this, but much of what's before her she must go through alone. She must pass through pain and joy and solitude and community to discover her own inner self that is unlike any other and come through that passage to the place where she sees all people are one, and in so seeing may live her life in a brighter future.

UNDERSTANDING DETAILS

1. What is the principal point of this essay by Sawaquat? How many different stories does the author tell to make this point?
2. What does Sawaquat see as the origin of the hatred of Native Americans in the United States?

3. What does Sawaquat learn from his first powwow (paragraphs 9 and 10)?
4. How does Sawaquat discover his original identity? In what way does this knowledge change him?

ANALYZING MEANING

1. Why does Sawaquat begin this essay with the story about his daughter on the beach? How does the story make you feel?
2. Why do thoughts about his daughter prompt Sawaquat's memories of his own identity crisis? What does the author's identity have to do with his daughter?
3. The author calls paragraphs 5–12 "Theft" and paragraphs 13–14 "Circle." Explain these two subtitles from the author's point of view.
4. Why do you think Sawaquat says that his daughter "must pass through pain and joy and solitude and community to discover her own inner self" (paragraph 14)? To what extent do we all need to do this in our lives?

DISCOVERING RHETORICAL STRATEGIES

1. Sawaquat occasionally uses dialogue to help make his points. What does the dialogue add to the various narratives he cites here?
2. Describe as thoroughly as possible the point of view of Sawaquat's narrator. Include in your answer a discussion of person, vantage point, and attitude.
3. Why do you think Sawaquat divides his essay into three sections? Why do you think he spends most of his time on the second section?
4. Although Sawaquat uses primarily narration to advance his point of view, which other rhetorical strategies help support his essay? Give examples of each.

MAKING CONNECTIONS

1. Compare the concern Lewis Sawaquat has for his daughter with that displayed for Russell Baker ("The Saturday Evening Post") by his mother and/or that for Amy Tan ("Mother

Tongue") by her mother. Which parent do you think loves his or her child most? On what do you base this conclusion?

2. How strong is Sawaquat's attachment to his Native-American culture? Contrast the passion of his ethnic identity with that demonstrated by Richard Rodriguez ("The Fear of Losing a Culture"), Alice Walker ("Beauty: When the Other Dancer Is the Self"), or Sandra Cisneros ("Only daughter").

3. What responsibilities, according to Sawaquat, should parents accept regarding the eventual happiness of their children? Would Bill Cosby ("The Baffling Question") or Michael Dorris ("The Broken Cord") agree with him? Why or why not? To what extent do you agree with Sawaquat?

IDEAS FOR DISCUSSION/WRITING

Preparing to Write

Write freely about your own identity: What is your cultural heritage? How do you fit into your immediate environment? Has your attitude about yourself and your identity changed over the years? Do you know your own inner self? How do you plan to continue learning about yourself?

Choosing a Topic

1. Write a narrative essay that uses one or more stories from your past in order to describe to a group of friends the main features of your identity.

2. Explain to your children (whether real or imaginary) in narrative form some simple but important truths about your heritage. Take care to select your details well, choose an appropriate point of view, and arrange your essay logically so that you keep your readers' interest throughout the essay.

3. Have you recently experienced any social traumas in your life that you would like to prepare someone else for? Write a letter to the person you would like to warn. Use narration to explain the situation, and suggest ways to avoid the negative aspects you encountered.

4. Anyone can be an author on the Internet. If you owned a Web site that was a forum for your ideas, what topics would you want to write about and publish? How have you experienced ignorance? Perhaps you have suffered prejudice based on your

age, appearance, ethnicity, or abilities. Write a narrative for your personal website in which you share your experiences with prejudice. Using Sawaquat's essay as a model, describe specific incidents and they way they affected you.

Before beginning your essay, you might want to consult the checklists on page 116.

MAYA ANGELOU   (1928–   )

New Directions

Maya Angelou was born Marguerite Johnson on April 4, 1928, in St. Louis, Missouri. Nicknamed "Maya" by her brother, she moved with her family to California; then, at age three, she was sent to live with her grandmother in Stamps, Arkansas, where she spent the childhood years later recorded in her autobiographical novel *I Know Why the Caged Bird Sings* (1970). After a brief marriage, she embarked upon an amazingly prolific career in dance, drama, and writing. During the past forty years, Angelou has been at various times a nightclub performer specializing in calypso songs and dances, an actress, a playwright, a civil-rights activist, a newspaper editor, a television writer and producer, a poet, and a screenwriter. She has also written several television specials, including *Three Way Choice* (a five-part miniseries) and *Afro-Americans in the Arts*, both for PBS. Her most recent work has included a BBC-TV documentary entitled *Trying to Make It Home* (1988); a stage production of Errol John's *Moon on a Rainbow Shawl*, which she directed in London (1988); and five novels, *I Shall Not Be Moved* (1990), *Lessons in Living* (1993), *Wouldn't Take Nothing for My Journey Now* (1993), *A Brave and Startling Truth* (1995), and *Phenomenal Woman* (2000). More recently, she won the Presidential Medal of Arts in 2000, published *A Song Flung Up to Heaven* (2002), and was given a Grammy Award in 2003 for her recorded reading of the same book. A tall, graceful, and imposing woman, Angelou was once described as conveying "pride without arrogance, self-esteem without smugness."

Preparing to Read

Taken from Angelou's book *Wouldn't Take Nothing for My Journey Now*, the following essay describes how Annie Johnson, a strong and determined woman, found "a new path" in her life.

Exploring Experience: Before you read this essay, take a moment to think about a time you changed directions: What were the circumstances surrounding this change? Why did you make the change? What did you learn from the experience? What alterations would you make if you followed this path again?

Learning Online: Maya Angelou is a prolific poet and writer with some strong opinions on the topic of courage that she expressed in an interview with Oprah Winfrey. Listen to this interview to get a sense of Angelou's thoughts on this subject. Go to http://www.oprah.com/omagazine, and type "Oprah's cut with Maya Angelou" into the search field. Select the link titled "Oprah's Cut with Maya Angelou." Click the "watch" button. (You may elect to skip the introduction.) Watch the flash movie titled "Your life is defined by principles." As you read Angelou's article, consider how her attitudes toward courage and self-identity are evident in Annie Johnson's character.

In 1903 the late Mrs. Annie Johnson of Arkansas found herself   1
with two toddling sons, very little money, a slight ability to read and add simple numbers. To this picture add a disastrous marriage and the burdensome fact that Mrs. Johnson was a Negro.

When she told her husband, Mr. William Johnson, of her dis-   2
satisfaction with their marriage, he conceded that he too found it to be less than he expected and had been secretly hoping to leave and study religion. He added that he thought God was calling him not only to preach but to do so in Enid, Oklahoma. He did not tell her that he knew a minister in Enid with whom he could study and who had a friendly, unmarried daughter. They parted amicably, Annie keeping the one-room house and William taking most of the cash to carry himself to Oklahoma.

Annie, over six feet tall, big-boned, decided that she would not   3
go to work as a domestic and leave her "precious babes" to anyone else's care. There was no possibility of being hired at the town's cotton gin or lumber mill, but maybe there was a way to make the two factories work for her. In her words, "I looked up the road I was going and back the way I come, and since I wasn't satisfied, I decided to step off the road and cut me a new path." She told herself that she wasn't a fancy cook but that she could "mix groceries well enough to scare hunger away from a starving man."

She made her plans meticulously and in secret. One early   4
evening to see if she was ready, she placed stones in two five-

gallon pails and carried them three miles to the cotton gin. She rested a little, and then, discarding some rocks, she walked in the darkness to the saw mill five miles farther along the dirt road. On her way back to her little house and her babies, she dumped the remaining rocks along the path.

That same night she worked into the early hours boiling   5
chicken and frying ham. She made dough and filled the rolled-out pastry with meat. At last she went to sleep.

The next morning she left her house carrying the meat pies,   6
lard, an iron brazier, and coals for a fire. Just before lunch she appeared in an empty lot behind the cotton gin. As the dinner noon bell rang, she dropped the savors into boiling fat, and the aroma rose and floated over to the workers who spilled out of the gin, covered with white lint, looking like specters.

Most workers had brought their lunches of pinto beans and bis-   7
cuits or crackers, onions and cans of sardines, but they were tempted by the hot meat pies which Annie ladled out of the fat. She wrapped them in newspapers, which soaked up the grease, and offered them for sale at a nickel each. Although business was slow, those first days Annie was determined. She balanced her appearances between the two hours of activity.

So, on Monday if she offered hot fresh pies at the cotton gin   8
and sold the remaining cooled-down pies at the lumber mill for three cents, then on Tuesday she went first to the lumber mill pre-senting fresh, just-cooked pies as the lumbermen covered in saw-dust emerged from the mill.

For the next few years, on balmy spring days, blistering summer   9
noons, and cold, wet, and wintry middays, Annie never disap-pointed her customers, who could count on seeing the tall, brown-skin woman bent over her brazier, carefully turning the meat pies. When she felt certain that the workers had become dependent on her, she built a stall between the two hives of indus-try and let the men run to her for their lunchtime provisions.

She had indeed stepped from the road which seemed to have   10
been chosen for her and cut herself a brand-new path. In years that stall became a store where customers could buy cheese, meal, syrup, cookies, candy, writing tablets, pickles, canned goods, fresh fruit, soft drinks, coal, oil, and leather soles for worn-out shoes.

Each of us has the right and the responsibility to assess the roads   11
which lie ahead, and those over which we have traveled, and if the

future road looms ominous or unpromising, and the roads back uninviting, then we need to gather our resolve and, carrying only the necessary baggage, step off that road into another direction. If the new choice is also unpalatable, without embarrassment, we must be ready to change that as well.

UNDERSTANDING DETAILS

1. What path is Annie Johnson following that she dislikes? How does she change this path?
2. Describe Annie physically and mentally in your own words. Use as much detail as possible.
3. Why does Annie carry stones in two five-gallon pails for three miles? What is she trying to accomplish?
4. In what ways does Annie's business grow? How does Annie's personality make this growth possible?

ANALYZING MEANING

1. Why do you think Annie succeeds in her business? What are the main ingredients of her success?
2. In what ways are the details at the beginning of this narrative essay typical of the year 1903?
3. What does Angelou mean when she says, "Each of us has the right and the responsibility to assess the roads which lie ahead, and those over which we have traveled" (paragraph 11)? In what way is this message basic to an understanding of the essay?
4. Explain the title of the essay. Cite specific details from the essay in your explanation.

DISCOVERING RHETORICAL STRATEGIES

1. Angelou writes this narrative essay in a fairly formal style, using multisyllable words (*concede* rather than *yield* or *let*) and the characters' title and names (Mrs. Annie Johnson instead of Annie Johnson). Why do you think Angelou presents her essay in this way? Describe the tone she maintains throughout the essay.
2. The author uses the metaphor of taking a "new road" to describe Annie Johnson's decision. Is this metaphor effective in your opinion? Why or why not?

3. Over what period of time do you think this story took place? How does the author show her readers that time is passing in this narrative essay?

4. Angelou often ends her essays with lessons that she wants the readers to understand. How does her lesson in the last paragraph of this narrative essay affect the story? Does the story itself go with the lesson? How did you respond to having the author tell you what to think at the end of the story?

MAKING CONNECTIONS

1. In Angelou's essay, Annie Johnson cuts "a new path" for herself by selling food to factory workers. Contrast this sudden change in the direction of her life with similar "new paths" taken by Bill Cosby ("The Baffling Question"), by Brent Staples in "A Brother's Murder," or by female weightlifters in Gloria Steinem's "The Politics of Muscle." Who do you think had the most difficult transition to make? Explain your answer.

2. If Angelou, Russell Baker ("The Saturday Evening Post"), Sandra Cisneros ("Only daughter"), and Harold Krents ("Darkness at Noon") were discussing the value of persistence and determination in life, which author would argue most strongly for the importance of that quality? Why? Would you agree?

3. Food is an important ingredient not only in Angelou's essay, but also in those written by Ray Bradbury ("Summer Rituals"), Kimberly Wozencraft ("Notes From the Country Club"), and Garrison Keillor ("How the Crab Apple Grew"). Which of these most involves the topic of food? Which the least? Which authors use food as a structuring device in their essays?

IDEAS FOR DISCUSSION/WRITING

Preparing to Write

Write freely about all the major changes you have made in your life: Were most of these changes for the best? How did they benefit you? How did they benefit others? Did they hurt anyone? Do you think most people have trouble changing directions in their lives? Why or why not? How might we all improve our attitudes about change?

Choosing a Topic

1. The editor of your school newspaper has asked you to write a narrative essay about an important change you made in your life. The newspaper is running a series of essays about changing directions in life, and the staff has heard that you have a story to tell. Tell your story in essay form to be printed in the school newspaper.

2. Why are major changes so difficult for us to make? Write a narrative essay for your peers to respond to this question. Use characters to dramatize your answer.

3. Decide on an important truth about life, and then write a narrative essay to support that truth. Make the details as vivid as possible.

4. Go online and find an entrepreneur who inspires you. Possible examples include Shawn Fanning (Napster), Ben Cohen and Jerry Greenfield (Ben & Jerry's Ice Cream), Masaru Ibuka and Akio Morita (Sony), Walt Disney (Disneyland, Walt Disney Pictures), Anita Roddick (The Body Shop), Bill Gates (Microsoft), Oprah Winfrey (Oprah, O, HARPO), or Ted Turner (Cable News Network, Turner Network Television). Gather enough details about this person's life to write a narrative. Using Angelou's narrative style as a model, organize your story around a central theme or message.

Before beginning your essay, you might want to consult the checklists on page 116.

RUSSELL BAKER   (1925–   )

The Saturday Evening Post

Russell Baker is one of America's foremost satirists and humorists. Born in Virginia, he grew up in New Jersey and Maryland, graduated from Johns Hopkins University, and then served for two years as a pilot in the U.S. Navy. Following the service, he became a newspaper reporter for the *Baltimore Sun*, which sent him to England as its London correspondent. He subsequently joined the staff of the *New York Times* as a member of its Washington bureau. From 1962 to 1998, he wrote his widely syndicated "Observer" column in the *Times*, which blended wry humor, a keen interest in language, and biting social commentary about the Washington scene. His books include *An American in Washington* (1961), *No Cause for Panic* (1964), and *Poor Russell's Almanac* (1972), plus two collections of early essays, *So This Is Depravity* (1980) and *The Rescue of Miss Yaskell and Other Pipe Dreams* (1983). *Growing Up* (1982), a best-seller vividly recounting his own childhood, earned him the 1983 Pulitzer Prize for biography. His more recent publications include *The Good Times* (1989), which continues his life story from approximately age twenty until he began working for the *New York Times* in the early 1960s; *There's a Country in My Cellar: The Best of Russell Baker* (1990), a collection of his newspaper columns; *Inventing the Truth: The Art and Craft of Memoir* (1995, with William Zinsser), and *Looking Back*, a compilation of some of his articles written for *The New York Review of Books* (2002).

Preparing to Read

The following skillfully written essay is an excerpt from Baker's autobiography, *Growing Up*. In it, the author recalls enduring memories from his youth that clearly project the experiences and emotions of his coming of age in 1920s rural Virginia.

Exploring Experience: As you prepare to read this selection, think for a moment about some of your own childhood memories: What were your strengths as a child? Your weaknesses? Have these character traits changed as you've matured? How are you like or unlike various members of your family? How do you react to these similarities and/or differences? What are your main goals in life? How do your character traits affect these goals?

Learning Online: Explore the Norman Rockwell Museum Web site (http://www.nrm.org) to see online exhibits of *Saturday Evening Post* covers and other artistic representations of the 1930s and 1940s. These images represent the time period that Russell Baker describes. How do these pictures differ from your childhood images?

I began working in journalism when I was eight years old. It was 1 my mother's idea. She wanted me to "make something" of myself and, after a levelheaded appraisal of my strengths, decided I had better start young if I was to have any chance of keeping up with the competition.

The flaw in my character which she had already spotted was 2 lack of "gumption." My idea of a perfect afternoon was lying in front of the radio rereading my favorite Big Little Book, *Dick Tracy Meets Stooge Viller*. My mother despised inactivity. Seeing me having a good time in repose, she was powerless to hide her disgust. "You've got no more gumption than a bump on a log," she said. "Get out in the kitchen and help Doris do those dirty dishes."

My sister Doris, though two years younger than I, had enough 3 gumption for a dozen people. She positively enjoyed washing dishes, making beds, and cleaning the house. When she was only seven, she could carry a piece of short-weighted cheese back to the A&P, threaten the manager with legal action, and come back triumphantly with the full quarter-pound we'd paid for and a few ounces extra thrown in for forgiveness. Doris could have made something of herself if she hadn't been a girl. Because of this defect, however, the best she could hope for was a career as a nurse or schoolteacher, the only work that capable females were considered up to in those days.

This must have saddened my mother, this twist of fate that had 4 allocated all the gumption to the daughter and left her with a son who was content with Dick Tracy and Stooge Viller. If disappointed, though, she wasted no energy on self-pity. She would make me make something of myself whether I wanted to or not.

"The Lord helps those who help themselves," she said. That was the way her mind worked.

She was realistic about the difficulty. Having sized up the mate- 5 rial the Lord had given her to mold, she didn't overestimate what she could do with it. She didn't insist that I grow up to be President of the United States.

Fifty years ago parents still asked boys if they wanted to grow 6 up to be President, and asked it not jokingly but seriously. Many parents who were hardly more than paupers still believed their sons could do it. Abraham Lincoln had done it. We were only sixty-five years from Lincoln. Many a grandfather who walked among us could remember Lincoln's time. Men of grandfatherly age were the worst for asking if you wanted to grow up to be President. A surprising number of little boys said yes and meant it.

I was asked many times myself. No, I would say, I didn't want 7 to grow up to be President. My mother was present during one of these interrogations. An elderly uncle, having posed the usual question and exposed my lack of interest in the Presidency, asked, "Well, what *do* you want to be when you grow up?"

I loved to pick through trash piles and collect empty bottles, tin 8 cans with pretty labels, and discarded magazines. The most desirable job on earth sprang instantly to mind. "I want to be a garbage man," I said.

My uncle smiled, but my mother had seen the first distressing 9 evidence of a bump budding on a log. "Have a little gumption, Russell," she said. Her calling me Russell was a signal of unhappiness. When she approved of me, I was always "Buddy."

When I turned eight years old she decided that the job of start- 10 ing me on the road toward making something of myself could no longer be safely delayed. "Buddy," she said one day, "I want you to come home right after school this afternoon. Somebody's coming, and I want you to meet him."

When I burst in that afternoon, she was in conference in the 11 parlor with an executive of the Curtis Publishing Company. She introduced me. He bent low from the waist and shook my hand. Was it true as my mother had told him, he asked, that I longed for the opportunity to conquer the world of business?

My mother replied that I was blessed with a rare determination 12 to make something of myself.

"That's right," I whispered. 13

"But have you got the grit, the character, the never-say-quit 14
spirit it takes to succeed in business?"

My mother said I certainly did. 15

"That's right," I said. 16

He eyed me silently for a long pause, as though weighing 17
whether I could be trusted to keep his confidence, then spoke
man-to-man. Before taking a crucial step, he said, he wanted to
advise me that working for the Curtis Publishing Company placed
enormous responsibility on a young man. It was one of the great
companies of America. Perhaps the greatest publishing house in
the world. I had heard, no doubt, of the *Saturday Evening Post?*

Heard of it? My mother said that everyone in our house had 18
heard of the *Saturday Post* and that I, in fact, read it with religious
devotion.

Then doubtless, he said, we were also familiar with those two 19
monthly pillars of the magazine world, the *Ladies Home Journal* and
the *Country Gentleman.*

Indeed we were familiar with them, said my mother. 20

Representing the *Saturday Evening Post* was one of the weight- 21
iest honors that could be bestowed in the world of business,
he said. He was personally proud of being a part of the great
corporation.

My mother said he had every right to be. 22

Again he studied me as though debating whether I was worthy 23
of a knighthood. Finally: "Are you trustworthy?"

My mother said I was the soul of honesty. 24

"That's right," I said. 25

The caller smiled for the first time. He told me I was a lucky 26
young man. He admired my spunk. Too many young men
thought life was all play. Those young men would not go far in
this world. Only a young man willing to work and save and keep
his face washed and his hair neatly combed could hope to come
out on top in a world such as ours. Did I truly and sincerely
believe that I was such a young man?

"He certainly does," said my mother. 27

"That's right," I said. 28

He said he had been so impressed by what he had seen of me 29
that he was going to make me a representative of the Curtis
Publishing Company. On the following Tuesday, he said, thirty
freshly printed copies of the *Saturday Evening Post* would be

delivered at our door. I would place these magazines, still damp with the ink of the presses, in a handsome canvas bag, sling it over my shoulder, and set forth through the streets to bring the best in journalism, fiction, and cartoons to the American public.

He had brought the canvas bag with him. He presented it with   30
reverence fit for a chasuble. He showed me how to drape the sling over my left shoulder and across the chest so that the pouch lay easily accessible to my right hand, allowing the best in journalism, fiction, and cartoons to be swiftly extracted and sold to a citizenry whose happiness and security depended upon us soldiers of the free press.

The following Tuesday I raced home from school, put the can-   31
vas bag over my shoulder, dumped the magazines in, and, tilting to the left to balance their weight on my right hip, embarked on the highway of journalism.

We lived in Belleville, New Jersey, a commuter town at the   32
northern fringe of Newark. It was 1932, the bleakest year of the Depression. My father had died two years before, leaving us with a few pieces of Sears, Roebuck furniture and not much else, and my mother had taken Doris and me to live with one of her younger brothers. This was my Uncle Allen. Uncle Allen had made something of himself by 1932. As salesman for a soft-drink bottler in Newark, he had an income of $30 a week; wore pearl-gray spats, detachable collars, and a three-piece suit; was happily married; and took in threadbare relatives.

With my load of magazines I headed toward Belleville Avenue.   33
That's where the people were. There were two filling stations at the intersection with Union Avenue, as well as an A&P, a fruit stand, a bakery, a barber shop, Zuccarelli's drugstore, and a diner shaped like a railroad car. For several hours I made myself highly visible, shifting position now and then from corner to corner, from shop window to shop window, to make sure everyone could see the heavy black lettering on the canvas bag that said THE SAT-URDAY EVENING POST. When the angle of the light indicated it was suppertime, I walked back to the house.

"How many did you sell, Buddy?" my mother asked.   34
"None."   35
"Where did you go?"   36
"The corner of Belleville and Union Avenues."   37
"What did you do?"   38

"Stood on the corner waiting for somebody to buy a *Saturday*   39
Evening Post."

"You just stood there?"   40

"Didn't sell a single one."   41

"For God's sake, Russell!"   42

Uncle Allen intervened. "I've been thinking about it for some   43
time," he said, "and I've about decided to take the *Post* regularly.
Put me down as a regular customer." I handed him a magazine,
and he paid me a nickel. It was the first nickel I earned.

Afterwards my mother instructed me in salesmanship. I   44
would have to ring doorbells, address adults with charming self-
confidence, and break down resistance with a sales talk pointing
out that no one, no matter how poor, could afford to be without
the *Saturday Evening Post* in the home.

I told my mother I'd changed my mind about wanting to suc-   45
ceed in the magazine business.

"If you think I'm going to raise a good-for-nothing," she   46
replied, "you've got another think coming." She told me to hit
the streets with the canvas bag and start ringing doorbells the
instant school was out next day. When I objected that I didn't feel
any aptitude for salesmanship, she asked how I'd like to lend her
my leather belt so she could whack some sense into me. I bowed
to superior will and entered journalism with a heavy heart.

My mother and I had fought this battle almost as long as I could   47
remember. It probably started even before memory began, when
I was a country child in northern Virginia and my mother, dissat-
isfied with my father's plain workman's life, determined that I
would not grow up like him and his people, with calluses on their
hands, overalls on their backs, and fourth-grade educations in their
heads. She had fancier ideas of life's possibilities. Introducing me
to the *Saturday Evening Post*, she was trying to wean me as early as
possible from my father's world where men left with their lunch
pails at sunup, worked with their hands until the grime ate into the
pores, and died with a few sticks of mail-order furniture as their
legacy. In my mother's vision of the better life there were desks
and white collars, well-pressed suits, evenings of reading and lively
talk, and perhaps—if a man were very, very lucky and hit the jack-
pot, really made something important of himself—perhaps there
might be a fantastic salary of $5,000 a year to support a big house
and a Buick with a rumble seat and a vacation in Atlantic City.

And so I set forth with my sack of magazines. I was afraid of the   48
dogs that snarled behind the doors of potential buyers. I was timid
about ringing the doorbells of strangers, relieved when no one
came to the door, and scared when someone did. Despite my
mother's instructions, I could not deliver an engaging sales pitch.
When a door opened I simply asked, "Want to buy a *Saturday
Evening Post?*" In Belleville few persons did. It was a town of
30,000 people, and most weeks I rang a fair majority of its doorbells. But I rarely sold my thirty copies. Some weeks I canvassed
the entire town for six days and still had four or five unsold magazines on Monday evening; then I dreaded the coming of Tuesday
morning, when a batch of thirty fresh *Saturday Evening Posts* was
due at the front door.

"Better get out there and sell the rest of those magazines   49
tonight," my mother would say.

I usually posted myself then at a busy intersection where a traf-   50
fic light controlled commuter flow from Newark. When the light
turned red, I stood on the curb and shouted my sales pitch at the
motorists.

"Want to buy a *Saturday Evening Post?*"   51

One rainy night when car windows were sealed against me, I   52
came back soaked and with not a single sale to report. My mother
beckoned to Doris.

"Go back down there with Buddy and show him how to sell   53
these magazines," she said.

Brimming with zest, Doris, who was then seven years old,   54
returned with me to the corner. She took a magazine from the
bag, and when the light turned red, she strode to the nearest car
and banged her small fist against the closed window. The driver,
probably startled at what he took to be a midget assaulting his car,
lowered the window to stare, and Doris thrust a *Saturday Evening
Post* at him.

"You need this magazine," she piped, "and it only costs a   55
nickel."

Her salesmanship was irresistible. Before the light changed half   56
a dozen times, she disposed of the entire batch. I didn't feel humiliated. To the contrary. I was so happy I decided to give her a treat.
Leading her to the vegetable store on Belleville Avenue, I bought
three apples, which cost a nickel, and gave her one.

"You shouldn't waste money," she said.   57

"Eat your apple." I bit into mine.   58

"You shouldn't eat before supper," she said. "It'll spoil your   59
appetite."

Back at the house that evening, she dutifully reported me for   60
wasting a nickel. Instead of a scolding, I was rewarded with a pat
on the back for having the good sense to buy fruit instead of
candy. My mother reached into her bottomless supply of maxims
and told Doris, "An apple a day keeps the doctor away."

By the time I was ten I had learned all my mother's maxims by   61
heart. Asking to stay up past normal bedtime, I knew that a refusal
would be explained with, "Early to bed and early to rise, makes a
man healthy, wealthy, and wise." If I whimpered about having to
get up early in the morning, I could depend on her to say, "The
early bird gets the worm."

The one I most despised was, "If at first you don't succeed, try,   62
try again." This was the battle cry with which she constantly sent
me back into the hopeless struggle whenever I moaned that I had
rung every doorbell in town and knew there wasn't a single
potential buyer left in Belleville that week. After listening to my
explanation, she handed me the canvas bag and said, "If at first you
don't succeed. . . ."

Three years in that job, which I would gladly have quit after the   63
first day except for her insistence, produced at least one valuable
result. My mother finally concluded that I would never make
something of myself by pursuing a life in business and started considering careers that demanded less competitive zeal.

One evening when I was eleven, I brought home a short "com-   64
position" on my summer vacation which the teacher had graded
with an A. Reading it with her own schoolteacher's eye, my
mother agreed that it was top-drawer seventh grade prose and
complimented me. Nothing more was said about it immediately,
but a new idea had taken life in her mind. Halfway through supper she suddenly interrupted the conversation.

"Buddy," she said, "maybe you could be a writer."   65

I clasped the idea to my heart. I had never met a writer, had   66
shown no previous urge to write, and hadn't a notion how to
become a writer, but I loved stories and thought that making up
stories must surely be almost as much fun as reading them. Best of
all, though, and what really gladdened my heart, was the ease of
the writer's life. Writers did not have to trudge through the town

peddling from canvas bags, defending themselves against angry dogs, being rejected by surly strangers. Writers did not have to ring doorbells. So far as I could make out, what writers did couldn't even be classified as work.

I was enchanted. Writers didn't have to have any gumption at   67 all. I did not dare tell anybody for fear of being laughed at in the schoolyard, but secretly I decided that what I'd like to be when I grew up was a writer.

UNDERSTANDING DETAILS

1. How does Baker's ideal day differ from that of his sister?
2. According to the author's mother, what is the main flaw in his character? How does this flaw eventually affect his choice of a career?
3. Why does Baker feel he has no "aptitude for salesmanship" (paragraph 46)? What has led him to this conclusion?
4. Which of his mother's maxims does the author dislike the most? Explain his reaction.

ANALYZING MEANING

1. Why does Baker begin this selection with a comparison of his personality and his sister's? What does this comparison have to do with the rest of the essay?
2. Why does the author's mother insist that he work for the *Saturday Evening Post*? What does she think he will gain from the experience? What does he actually learn?
3. What "battle" (paragraph 47) have the author and his mother been fighting for as long as he can remember? Who finally wins this battle?
4. Why is Baker so delighted with the idea of becoming a writer when he grows up? How is this notion compatible with his personality?

DISCOVERING RHETORICAL STRATEGIES

1. How does Baker arrange the details in this excerpt? Why do you think he organizes them in this way? How would a different arrangement have changed the essay?

2. Who do you think is Baker's intended audience? Describe them in detail. How did you come to this conclusion?
3. What is the climax of Baker's narrative? How does he lead up to and develop this climactic moment? What stylistic traits tell us that this is the most exciting point in the story?
4. Besides narration, what other rhetorical strategies does Baker draw on to develop his thesis? Give examples of each of these strategies.

MAKING CONNECTIONS

1. Baker insists on the importance of dedicating oneself to a career. Compare and contrast his feelings on this subject with similar sentiments found in essays by Sandra Cisneros ("Only daughter"), William Ouchi ("Japanese and American Workers: Two Casts of Mind"), and Gloria Steinem ("The Politics of Muscle"). How dedicated do you intend to be to your own future career?
2. How is young Russell Baker's naive conception of a writer's "easy" life different from the views on writing expressed by Sandra Cisneros ("Only daughter"), Amy Tan ("Mother Tongue"), and Rita Mae Brown ("Writing as a Moral Act")? Which of these authors would argue most fervently that writing is "hard" work? How do you feel about the process of writing? Is it easy or hard for you? Explain your answer.
3. Russell Baker's mother had a strong influence over him as he grew up. Imagine a conversation among Baker, Bill Cosby ("The Baffling Question"), Judith Wallerstein and Sandra Blakeslee ("Second Chances for Children of Divorce"), and Mary Pipher ("Beliefs About Families") concerning the importance of proper parental guidance as a child matures. Which author would be most adamant about the importance of the role of parents in a child's upbringing? Explain your answer.

IDEAS FOR DISCUSSION/WRITING

Preparing to Write

Write freely about yourself in relation to your aspirations: What type of person are you? What do you think about? What are your ideals? Your hopes? Your dreams? Your fears? What do you enjoy doing in your spare time? How are you different from other members of your family? Is anyone in your family a model for you? How have members of your immediate family affected your daily life—past and present? Your career goals? How do you anticipate your family will affect your future?

Choosing a Topic

1. Write a narrative essay introducing yourself to your English class. To explain and define your identity, include descriptions of family members whenever appropriate.

2. Write a narrative that helps explain to a friend how you got involved in a current interest. To expand upon your narrative, refer whenever possible to your long-term goals and aspirations.

3. Ten years from now, your local newspaper decides to devote an entire section to people getting started in careers. You are asked to submit the story of how you got involved in your profession (whatever it may be). Write a narrative that might appear in your hometown newspaper ten years from now; be sure to give the article a catchy headline.

4. Reflect on your worst memory of working at a particular job or chore. Write a narrative e-mail to Baker in which you explain how an experience that seemed horrible at the time actually had positive results. Following Baker's example, establish a strong sense of time and place in your narrative.

Before beginning your essay, you might want to consult the checklists on page 116.

SANDRA CISNEROS   (1954–   )

Only daughter

Born in Chicago, Sandra Cisneros was the Only daughter raised in a family with six brothers. She moved frequently during her childhood, eventually earning a B.A. in English from Loyola University and an M.F.A. in creative writing from the University of Iowa, where she developed her unique voice of a strong and independent working-class, Mexican-American woman. Her first book, *The House on Mango Street* (1984), is a loosely structured series of vignettes focusing upon the isolation and cultural conflicts endured by Latina women in America. Later publications include *My Wicked, Wicked Ways* (1987), *Woman Hollering Creek* (1991), *The Future Is Mestizo: Life Where Cultures Meet* (2000), and *Caramelo* (2002). Critics have described her works of fiction as "poetic": "nearly every sentence contains an explosive sensory image. She gives us unforgettable characters that we want to lift off the page and hang out with for a while." Asked to analyze her writing style, Cisneros has explained that "I am a woman, and I am a Latina. Those are the things that make my writing distinctive. Those are the things that give my writing power. They are the things that give it *sabor* (flavor), that give it *picante* (spice)."

Preparing to Read

"Only daughter," an essay first published in *Glamour*, chronicles one of the author's most memorable experiences on a visit to her parents' home in Chicago. Full of family history, the story uses the reunion as a forum for Cisneros's observations about life in a Mexican family.

Exploring Experience: As you prepare to read this essay, take a few moments to consider the many social and cultural influences that shape your life: What is your family like? What activities do you enjoy? Have you ever felt that your family didn't accept these activities? Have you ever been angry at the extent to which social or cultural pressures have governed your life? How did you react to these forces? Can you think of a specific situation in which you overcame social or cultural differences? What was the result?

Learning Online: Explore the PBS "American Family" Web site (http://www.pbs.org/americanfamily) for a dynamic look into the Latino culture. While reading Cisneros' narrative, consider how her experience relates to the accounts on the Web site.

Once, several years ago, when I was just starting out my 1
writing career, I was asked to write my own contributor's note for an anthology. I wrote: "I am the only
daughter in a family of six sons. *That* explains everything."

Well, I've thought that ever since, and yes, it explains a lot to 2
me, but for the reader's sake I should have written: "I am the only
daughter in a *Mexican* family of six sons." Or even: "I am the only
daughter of a Mexican father and a Mexican-American mother."
Or: "I am the only daughter of a working-class family of nine."
All of these had everything to do with who I am today.

I was/am the only daughter and *only* a daughter. Being an only 3
daughter in a family of six sons forced me by circumstance to
spend a lot of time by myself because my brothers felt it beneath
them to play with a *girl* in public. But that aloneness, that loneliness, was good for a would-be writer—it allowed me time to
think and think, to imagine, to read and prepare myself.

Being only a daughter for my father meant my destiny would 4
lead me to become someone's wife. That's what he believed. But
when I was in the fifth grade and shared my plans for college with
him, I was sure he understood. I remember my father saying, *"Que
bueno, mi'ja,* that's good." That meant a lot to me, especially since
my brothers thought the idea hilarious. What I didn't realize was
that my father thought college was good for girls—good for finding a husband. After four years in college and two more in graduate school, and still no husband, my father shakes his head even
now and says I wasted all that education.

In retrospect, I'm lucky my father believed daughters were 5
meant for husbands. It meant it didn't matter if I majored in something silly like English. After all, I'd find a nice professional eventually, right? This allowed me the liberty to putter about

embroidering my little poems and stories without my father inter-rupting with so much as a "What's that you're writing?"

But the truth is, I wanted him to interrupt. I wanted my father 6
to understand what it was I was scribbling, to introduce me as "My only daughter, the writer." Not as "This is my only daughter. She teaches." *Es maestra*—teacher. Not even *profesora*.

In a sense, everything I have ever written has been for him, to 7
win his approval even though I know my father can't read English words, even though my father's only reading includes the brown-ink *Esto* sports magazines from Mexico City and the bloody *¡Alarma!* magazines that feature yet another sighting of *La Virgen de Guadalupe* on a tortilla or a wife's revenge on her philandering husband by bashing his skull in with a *molcajete* (a kitchen mortar made of volcanic rock). Or the *fotonovelas,* the little picture paper-backs with tragedy and trauma erupting from the characters' mouths in bubbles.

A father represents, then, the public majority. A public who is 8
disinterested in reading, and yet one whom I am writing about and for, and privately trying to woo.

When we were growing up in Chicago, we moved a lot 9
because of my father. He suffered bouts of nostalgia. Then we'd have to let go of our flat, store the furniture with mother's rela-tives, load the station wagon with baggage and bologna sand-wiches and head south. To Mexico City.

We came back, of course. To yet another Chicago flat, another 10
Chicago neighborhood, another Catholic school. Each time, my father would seek out the parish priest in order to get a tuition break, and complain or boast: "I have seven sons."

He meant *siete hijos,* seven children, but he translated it as 11
"sons." "I have seven sons." To anyone who would listen. The Sears Roebuck employee who sold us the washing machine. The short-order cook where my father ate his ham-and-eggs breakfasts. "I have seven sons." As if he deserved a medal from the state.

My papa. He didn't mean anything by the mistranslation, I'm 12
sure. But somehow I could feel myself being erased. I'd tug my father's sleeve and whisper: "Not seven sons. Six! and one *daughter.*"

When my oldest brother graduated from medical school, he ful-filled my father's dream that we study hard and use this—our 13
heads, instead of this—our hands. Even now my father's hands are

thick and yellow, stubbed by a history of hammer and nails and twine and coils and springs. "Use this," my father said, tapping his head, "and not this," showing us those hands. He always looked tired when he said it.

Wasn't college an investment? And hadn't I spent all those years   14
in college? And if I didn't marry, what was it all for? Why would anyone go to college and then choose to be poor? Especially someone who has always been poor.

Last year, after ten years of writing professionally, the financial   15
rewards started to trickle in. My second National Endowment for the Arts Fellowship. A guest professorship at the University of California, Berkeley. My book, which sold to a major New York publishing house.

At Christmas, I flew home to Chicago. The house was throb-   16
bing, same as always; hot *tamales* and sweet *tamales* hissing in my mother's pressure cooker, and everybody—my mother, six broth-ers, wives, babies, aunts, cousins—talking too loud and at the same time, like in a Fellini film, because that's just how we are.

I went upstairs to my father's room. One of my stories had just   17
been translated into Spanish and published in an anthology of Chicano writing, and I wanted to show it to him. Ever since he recovered from a stroke two years ago, my father likes to spend his leisure hours horizontally. And that's how I found him, watching a Pedro Infante movie on Galavision and eating rice pudding.

There was a glass filmed with milk on the bedside table. There   18
were several vials of pills and balled Kleenex. And on the floor, one black sock and a plastic urinal that I didn't want to look at but looked at anyway. Pedro Infante was about to burst into song, and my father was laughing.

I'm not sure if it was because my story was translated into   19
Spanish, or because it was published in Mexico, or perhaps because the story dealt with Tepeyac, the *colonia* my father was raised in and the house he grew up in, but at any rate, my father punched the mute button on his remote control and read my story.

I sat on the bed next to my father and waited. He read it very   20
slowly. As if he were reading each line over and over. He laughed at all the right places and read lines he liked out loud. He pointed and asked questions: "Is this So-and-so?" "Yes," I said. He kept reading.

When he was finally finished, after what seemed like hours, my   21
father looked up and asked: "Where can we get more copies of
this for the relatives?"

Of all the wonderful things that happened to me last year, that   22
was the most wonderful.

UNDERSTANDING DETAILS

1. How many children are in Cisneros's family? How many are
   boys?
2. Why does Cisneros's father always say he has seven sons? Why
   is this detail significant?
3. Why did Cisneros's father let her go to college? Explain your
   answer.
4. What are the differences in the way the author's father views
   his sons and his daughter?

ANALYZING MEANING

1. What does Cisneros mean when she says, "I am the only
   daughter and *only* a daughter" (paragraph 3)?
2. What does her cultural heritage have to do with the fact that
   she is the only daughter?
3. Why does Cisneros write for her father even though he can't
   read English?
4. Why was her father's reaction to her story published in Spanish
   "the most wonderful" (paragraph 22) thing that happened to
   her last year? Why is her father's opinion so important to her?

DISCOVERING RHETORICAL STRATEGIES

1. From what point of view does Cisneros write this narrative
   essay? How does this particular point of view help us understand her attitude toward the experience?
2. In writing this essay, Cisneros is making a comment about families in general and Mexican families in particular. What is her
   ultimate message? What details help you understand this message? Does the fact that she doesn't capitalize "daughter" in her
   title have anything to do with this message?
3. How does Cisneros organize the details of this narrative? Is this
   the most effective order for what she is trying to say?

4. Although Cisneros's essay is primarily narrative, what other rhetorical strategies does she use to make her point? Give examples of each.

MAKING CONNECTIONS

1. In "Only daughter," Sandra Cisneros describes the importance of her father's support of and appreciation for her writing career. Compare and contrast the theme of family support described by Sandra Cisneros, Russell Baker ("The Saturday Evening Post"), and Mary Pipher ("Beliefs about Families"). Which author would argue that support from one's family is most crucial to our development as a person? Why?
2. Both Sandra Cisneros and Amy Tan ("Mother Tongue") became extremely successful writers in English although they spoke another language at home as they grew up. Can you find any other common denominators in the experiences of these two authors that account for their current skill in using the English language?
3. Compare and contrast the use of examples in the essays by Sandra Cisneros, Harold Krentz ("Darkness at Noon"), and Brent Staples ("A Brother's Murder"). Which essay is most densely packed with examples? Which uses example most effectively? Which least effectively? Why?

IDEAS FOR DISCUSSION/WRITING

Preparing to Write

Write freely about a time in your life when you did not fit in with your own family: What were the circumstances? How did you feel? What were your alternatives? Did you take any action? What were the motivating forces for this action? Were you satisfied with the outcome? How do you feel about this experience now?

Choosing a Topic

1. Write a narrative essay telling your classmates about a time you did not fit in. Make a special effort to communicate your feelings regarding this experience. Remember to choose your details and point of view with an overall purpose in mind.

2. What is America's system of social classes? Where do you fit into the structure? Does our system allow for much mobility between classes? Write a narrative essay for your classmates explaining your understanding of the American class system. Use yourself and/or a friend as an example.

3. Explain in a coherent essay written for the general public why you think we are all sometimes motivated by cultural or personal influences beyond our control. Refer to the Cisneros essay or to experiences of your own to support your explanation.

4. Cisneros shares personal details about her family while recounting her struggle to gain recognition from her father. Consider a time when you attempted to receive recognition from a family member. Using Cisneros's narrative style as a model, write an essay describing your experience. Imagine that your article will be published as part of PBS's "American Family" online collection.

Before beginning your essay, you might want to consult the checklists on page 116.

GARRISON KEILLOR   (1942–   )

How the Crab Apple Grew

Best known for his creation of the Peabody Award-winning radio program *A Prairie Home Companion*, Garrison Keillor, a native of Anoka, Minnesota, began his career as a radio announcer and producer during his student days at the University of Minnesota. His show features an eclectic mix of traditional jazz and folk music, supplemented by Keillor's rambling, nostalgic, and often hilarious anecdotes about the zany inhabitants of the fictitious small town of Lake Wobegon, Minnesota. Chief among its residents are Father Emil, the local priest who blesses small animals on the lawn of Our Lady of Perpetual Responsibility Church; Dorothy, the garrulous owner of the Chatterbox Cafe; and Dr. Nute, a retired dentist who coaxes trout toward his fishing lure by intoning, "Open wide . . . this may sting a bit." Keillor—a tall, soft-spoken man who often performs in a tuxedo, high-top sneakers, red socks, and red suspenders—even has a pseudosponsor for the show: Powdermilk Biscuits, "a whole-wheat treat that gives shy people the strength to do what has to be done." Thus far, Keillor's monologues have spawned a number of short stories published in the *New Yorker* and several books, including *Happy to Be Here: Stories and Comic Pieces* (1982), *Lake Wobegon Days* (1985), *Leaving Home* (1987), *We Are Still Married* (1989), *WLT: A Radio Romance* (1992), *The Book of Guys* (1993), *Wobegon Boy* (1997), *Me: By Jimmy "Big Boy" Valente As Told to Garrison Keillor* (1999), *Lake Wobegon Summer 1956* (2001), and *Good Poems* (2002).

Preparing to Read

Taken from *Leaving Home*, this graceful and humorous story is a masterful demonstration by Keillor of how to write a narrative essay. In response to an English assignment, Keillor takes his main character through a series of memories that helps her understand her life a little better.

Exploring Experience: As you prepare to read this selection, take a few minutes to think about various items in your life (in your backyard, in your house, at school, at a friend's) that have special meaning to you: What are these items? Why is each of them significant? How do other people relate to these items? In what ways do your surroundings tell different stories about you? What items in your life bring complete stories to your mind? What are some of these stories?

Learning Online: Using Google's search engine (http://www. google.com), click on the "Images" tab to conduct a picture search for the term "crab apple tree." What stories come to mind when viewing these photos? Consider how you could develop a narrative around one of these images.

It has been a quiet week in Lake Wobegon. It was warm and sunny on Sunday, and on Monday the flowering crab in the Dieners' backyard burst into blossom. Suddenly, in the morning, when everyone turned their backs for a minute, the tree threw off its bathrobe and stood trembling, purple, naked, revealing all its innermost flowers. When you saw it standing where weeks before had been a bare stick stuck in the dirt, you had to stop; it made your head spin. 1

Becky Diener sat upstairs in her bedroom and looked at the tree. She was stuck on an assignment from Miss Melrose for English, a 750-word personal essay, "Describe your backyard as if you were seeing it for the first time." After an hour she had thirty-nine words, which she figured would mean she'd finish at 1:45 P.M. Tuesday, four hours late, and therefore would get an F even if the essay was great, which it certainly wasn't. 2

How can you describe your backyard as if you'd never seen it? If you'd never seen it, you'd have grown up someplace else, and wouldn't be yourself; you'd be someone else entirely, and how are you supposed to know what that person would think? 3

She imagined seeing the backyard in 1996, returning home from Hollywood. "Welcome Becky!" said the big white banner across McKinley Street as the pink convertible drove slowly along, everyone clapping and cheering as she cruised by, Becky Belafonte the movie star, and got off at her old house. "Here," she said to the reporters, "is where I sat as a child and dreamed my dreams, under this beautiful flowering crab. I dreamed I was a Chinese 4 princess." Then a reporter asked, "Which of your teachers was the most important to you, encouraging you and inspiring you?" And just then she saw an old woman's face in the crowd, Miss Melrose pleading, whispering, "Say me, oh please, say me," and Becky looked straight at her as she said, "Oh, there were so many, I couldn't pick out one, they were all about the same, you know. But perhaps Miss—Miss—oh, I can't remember her name—she taught English, I think—Miss Milross? She was one of them. But there were so many."

She looked at her essay. "In my backyard is a tree that has   5
always been extremely important to me since I was six years old when my dad came home one evening with this bag in the trunk and he said, 'Come here and help me plant this'—"

She crumpled the sheet of paper and started again.   6

"One evening when I was six years old, my father arrived home   7
as he customarily did around 5:30 or 6:00 P.M. except this evening he had a wonderful surprise for me, he said, as he led me toward the car.

"My father is not the sort of person who does surprising things   8
very often so naturally I was excited that evening when he said he had something for me in the car, having just come home from work where he had been. I was six years old at the time."

She took out a fresh sheet. "Six years old was a very special age   9
for me and one thing that made it special was when my dad and I planted a tree together in our backyard. Now it is grown and every spring it gives off large purple blossoms. . . ."

The tree was planted by her dad, Harold, in 1976, ten years   10
after he married her mother, Marlys. They grew up on Taft Street, across from each other, a block from the ballfield. They liked each other tremendously, and then they were in love, as much as you can be when you're so young. Thirteen and fourteen years old and sixteen and seventeen: they looked at each other a lot. She came and sat in his backyard to talk with his mother and help her shell peas but really to look at Harold as he mowed the lawn, and then he disappeared into the house and she sat waiting for him, and of course he was in the kitchen looking out at her. It's how we all began, when our parents looked at each other, as we say, "when you were just a gleam in your father's eye," or your mother's, depending on who saw who first.

Marlys was long-legged, lanky, had short black hair and sharp   11
eyes that didn't miss anything. She came over to visit the Dieners
every chance she got. Her father was a lost cause, like the
Confederacy, like the search for the Northwest Passage. He'd been
prayed for and suffered for and fought for and spoken for, by people who loved him dearly, and when all was said and done, he just
reached for the gin bottle and said, "I don't know what you're
talking about," and he didn't. He was a sore embarrassment to
Marlys, a clown, a joke, and she watched Harold for evidence that
he wasn't similar. One night she dropped in at the Dieners' and
came upon a party where Harold, now nineteen, and his friends
were drinking beer by the pail. Harold flopped down on his back
and put his legs in the air and a pal put a lit match up to Harold's
rear end and blue flame came out like a blowtorch, and Marlys
went home disgusted and didn't speak to him for two years.

Harold went crazy. She graduated from high school and started   12
attending dances with a geography teacher named Stu Jasperson,
who was tall and dark-haired, a subscriber to *Time* magazine, educated at Saint Cloud Normal School, and who flew a red Piper
Cub airplane. Lake Wobegon had no airstrip except for Tollerud's
pasture, so Stu kept his plane in Saint Cloud. When he was en
route to and from the plane was almost the only time Harold got
to see Marlys and try to talk sense into her. But she was crazy about
Stu the aviator, not Harold the hardware clerk, and in an hour Stu
came buzzing overhead doing loops and dives and dipping his
wings. Harold prayed for him to crash. Marlys thought Stu was the
sun and the moon; all Harold could do was sit and watch her, in
the backyard, staring up, her hand shielding her eyes, saying, "Oh,
isn't he marvelous?" as Stu performed aerial feats and then shut off
the throttle and glided overhead singing "Vaya con Dios" to her.
"Yes, he is marvelous," said Harold, thinking, "DIE DIE DIE."

That spring, Marlys was in charge of the Sweethearts Banquet   13
at the Lutheran church. Irene Holm had put on a fancy winter
Sweethearts Banquet with roast lamb, and Marlys wanted to top
her and serve roast beef with morel mushrooms, a first for a church
supper in Lake Wobegon. Once Irene had referred to Marlys's dad
as a lush.

Morel mushrooms are a great delicacy. They are found in the   14
wild by people who walk fifteen miles through the woods to get

ten of them and then never tell the location to a soul, not even on their deathbeds to a priest. So Marlys's serving them at the banquet would be like putting out emeralds for party favors. It would blow Irene Holm out of the water and show people that even if Marlys's dad was a lush, she was still someone to be reckoned with.

Two men felt the call to go and search for morels: Harold put 15 on his Red Wing boots and knapsack and headed out one evening with a flashlight. He was in the woods all night. Morels are found near the base of the trunk of a dead elm that's been dead three years, which you can see by the way moonlight doesn't shine on it, and he thought he knew where some were, but around midnight he spotted a bunch of flashlights behind him, a posse of morelists bobbing along on his trail, so he veered off and hiked five miles in the wrong direction to confuse them, and by then the sun was coming up so he went home to sleep. He woke at 2:00 P.M., hearing Stu flying overhead, and in an instant he knew. Dead elms! Of course! Stu could spot them from the air, send his ground crew to collect them for Marlys, and the Sweethearts Banquet would be their engagement dinner.

Stu might have done just that, but he wanted to put on a show 16 and land the Cub in Lake Wobegon. He circled around and around, and came in low to the west of town, disappearing behind the trees. "He's going to crash!" cried Marlys, and they all jumped in their cars and tore out, expecting to find the young hero lying bloody and torn in the dewy grass, with a dying poem on his lips. But there he was standing tall beside the craft, having landed successfully in a field of spring wheat. They all mobbed around him, and he told how he was going up to find the morels and bring them back for Marlys.

There were about forty people there. They seemed to enjoy it, 17 so he drew out his speech, talking about the lure of aviation and his boyhood and various things so serious that he didn't notice Harold behind him by the plane or notice the people who noticed what Harold was doing and laughed. Stu was too inspired to pay attention to the laughter. He talked about how he once wanted to fly to see the world but once you get up in the air you can see that Lake Wobegon is the most beautiful place of all, a lot of warm horse manure like that, and then he gave them a big manly smile and donned his flying cap and scarf and favored them with a second and third smile and a wave, and he turned and there was Harold to help him into the cockpit.

"Well, thanks," said Stu, "mighty kind, mighty kind." Harold 18 jumped to the propeller and threw it once and twice, and the third time the engine fired, and Stu adjusted the throttle, checked the gauges, flapped the flaps, fit his goggles, and never noticed the ground was wet and his wheels were sunk in. He'd parked in a wet spot, and then during his address someone had gone around and made it wetter, so when Stu pulled back on the throttle the Cub just sat, and he gave it more juice and she creaked a little, and he gave it more and the plane stood on its head with its tail in the air and dug in.

It pitched forward like the *Titanic*, and the propeller in the mud 19 sounded like he'd eaten too many green apples. The door opened and Stu climbed out, trying to look dignified and studious as he tilted eastward and spun, and Harold said, "Stu, we didn't say we wanted those mushrooms sliced."

Harold went out that afternoon and collected five hundred 20 morel mushrooms around one dead elm tree. Marlys made her mark at the Sweethearts dinner, amazing Irene Holm, who had thought Marlys was common. Harold also brought out of the woods a bouquet of flowering crab apple and asked her to marry him, and eventually she decided to.

The tree in the backyard came about a few years afterward. 21 They'd been married awhile, had two kids, and some of the gloss had worn off their life, and one afternoon, Harold, trying to impress his kids and make his wife laugh, jumped off the garage roof, pretending he could fly, and landed wrong, twisting his ankle. He lay in pain, his eyes full of tears, and his kids said, "Oh poor Daddy, poor Daddy," and Marlys said, "You're not funny, you're ridiculous."

He got up on his bum ankle and went in the woods and got her 22 a pint of morels and a branch from the flowering crab apple. He cut a root from another crab apple and planted the root in the ground. "Look, kids," he said. He sharpened the branch with his hatchet and split the root open and stuck the branch in and wrapped a cloth around it and said, "Now, there, that will be a tree." They said, "Daddy, will that really be a tree?" He said, "Yes." Marlys said, "Don't be ridiculous."

He watered it and tended it and, more than that, he came out   23
late at night and bent down and said, "GROW. GROW. GROW."
The graft held, it grew, and one year it was interesting, and the
next it was impressive and then wonderful, and finally it was magnificent. It's the most magnificent thing in the Dieners' backyard.
Becky finished writing 750 words late that night and lay down to
sleep. A backyard is a novel about us, and when we sit there on a
summer day, we hear the dialogue and see the characters.

UNDERSTANDING DETAILS

1. Where does this narrative essay take place? Describe this particular place in detail. What one word might characterize this setting?
2. Why is Becky worried about this particular assignment?
3. How many false starts does Becky make when she is trying to
   write this essay? What causes those false starts?
4. Explain the rivalry between Harold and Stu. What do they
   both want?

ANALYZING MEANING

1. How are the tree and Becky's writing assignment related?
2. Why does Marlys finally marry Harold?
3. What can you learn about writing from Becky's approach to
   this essay? How does she finally get started? How does she keep
   her essay going? How does she keep it focused? What truths
   from this experience can you apply to your own writing?
4. What does Keillor mean when he says, "A backyard is a novel
   about us, and when we sit there on a summer day, we hear the
   dialogue and see the characters" (paragraph 23)?

DISCOVERING RHETORICAL STRATEGIES

1. Keillor starts many of his narratives with "It has been a quiet
   week in Lake Wobegon." What effect does this beginning have
   on the rest of the essay?
2. What metaphor or comparison does Keillor use to explain in
   the beginning of his essay that the tree has bloomed? How
   effective is this opening? Explain your answer.
3. What does this particular crab apple symbolize? Explain your
   answer in detail.

4. How appropriate is the title of this essay? What are some other possible titles?

MAKING CONNECTIONS

1. Imagine that Mary Pipher ("Beliefs About Families") and Judith Wallerstein and Sandra Blakeslee ("Second Chances for Children of Divorce") have just read Keillor's essay about the courtship of Harold and Marlys Diener. According to these authors, how successful will the marriage between Harold and Marlys probably be?
2. Compare and contrast Keillor's technique of recalling the past in this essay with similar recollections in Ray Bradbury's "Summer Rituals," Russell Baker's "The Saturday Evening Post," and Phyllis Schneider's "Memory: Tips You'll Never Forget." Which author's technique of historical reporting seems most vivid and convincing to you? Explain why.
3. Throughout his essay, Keillor mentions a number of details that will strike most readers as funny. How is Keillor's use of humor different from that of Bill Cosby ("The Baffling Question"), Jessica Mitford ("Behind the Formaldehyde Curtain"), or Mary Roach ("Meet the Bickersons")? Which of these essays do you find most entertaining? Explain your answer.

IDEAS FOR DISCUSSION/WRITING

Preparing to Write

Write freely about various symbols in your life or your family's life: What are these symbols? What do they represent? Which of the symbols remind you of various relationships within your family? Which of these symbols are positive? Which are negative? Which symbols remind you of important stories about yourself or other family members? Why are these stories important? What makes specific family stories so important?

Choosing a Topic

1. Write a narrative essay introducing yourself to your English class through a special item in your life. To explain and define your identity, include your relationship to this item in your essay.

2. Write a narrative essay that explains how your parents met. What were the highlights of this meeting? Where did it lead? What is their relationship like now?

3. Your school newspaper is running a series of articles on symbols in our lives. You have been asked to submit a narrative essay on the item that best represents you as a student in college. What is this item? How does it represent you? Shape your answers to these questions into a narrative essay.

4. Return to Google's image search (http://www.google.com) and click on the "Images" tab. Enter "family" as your search term. Select a family photo from the listings and tell their story. Create a narrative that centers on an important event in this family's imagined life. Be sure to use specific details, as Keillor does, to provide a setting and purpose for your narrative.

Before beginning your essay, you might want to consult the checklists on page 116.

CHAPTER WRITING ASSIGNMENTS

Practicing Narration

1. Think of a story that is often repeated by your family members because of its special significance or its humor. Retell the story to an audience who does not know your family, and explain to your readers the story's significance.

2. What has been the most challenging and life-changing event in your life? Remember this event as clearly as you can by noting special details on scratch paper. Write an essay that describes what led up to this event, what happened, and how you reacted to the event. Explain why this experience was so challenging and/or life-changing.

3. Think of a time when you received a very special gift. Tell the story of how you received this gift, who gave it to you, and why it was memorable. For a more sophisticated approach, try to think of gifts that are not material or tangible objects, but rather intangible qualities or concepts (such as love, life, and happiness).

Exploring Ideas

1. Write an essay that identifies the most important qualities in a friend. Explain how each quality is important to a meaningful and fulfilling friendship.

2. Cut an advertisement out of a magazine or newspaper. Examine its "story" and the way the advertiser is selling the product. Write an essay that discusses the effect of advertising on individuals and on American society. How honest or believable should advertising be? What are our expectations for advertising?

3. Describe a time when you quit a job or hobby that others thought you should continue. Discuss the principal features of this activity, your frustration with them, and the main aspects of the job or hobby that others valued. In retrospect, do you think you made a wise decision?

3

EXAMPLE

Illustrating Ideas

Citing an example to help make a point is one of the most instinctive techniques we use in communication. If, for instance, you state that being an internationally ranked tennis player requires constant practice, a friend might challenge that assertion and ask what you mean by "constant practice." When you respond "at least three hours a day," your friend might ask for more specific proof. At this stage in the discussion, you could offer the following illustrations to support your statement: When not on tour, Kim Clijsters practices three hours per day; Andy Roddick, four hours; and Jennifer Capriati, five hours. Your friend's doubt will have been answered through your use of examples.

DEFINING EXAMPLES

Well-chosen examples and illustrations are an essay's building blocks. They are drawn from your experience, your observations, and your reading. They help you *show* rather than *tell* what you mean, usually by supplying concrete details (references to what we can see, smell, taste, hear, or touch) to support abstract ideas (such as faith, hope, understanding, and love), by providing specifics

Example   159

("I like chocolate") to explain generalizations ("I like sweets"), and by giving definite references ("Turn left at the second stoplight") to clarify vague statements ("Turn in a few blocks"). Though illustrations take many forms, writers often find themselves indebted to description or narration (or some combination of the two) in order to supply enough relevant examples to achieve their rhetorical intent.

As you might suspect, examples are important ingredients in producing exciting, vivid prose. Just as crucial is the fact that carefully chosen examples often encourage your readers to feel one way or another about an issue being discussed. If you tell your parents, for instance, that living in a college dormitory is not conducive to academic success, they may doubt your word, perhaps thinking that you are simply attempting to coerce money out of them for an apartment. You can help dispel this notion, however, by giving them specific examples of the chaotic nature of dorm life: the party down the hall that broke up at 2:00 A.M. when you had a chemistry exam that same morning at 8 o'clock; the stereo next door that seems to be stuck on its highest decibel level at all hours of the day and night; and the new "friend" you recently acquired who thinks you are the best listener in the world—especially when everyone else has the good sense to be asleep. After such a detailed and well-documented explanation, your parents could hardly deny the strain of this difficult environment on your studies. Examples can be very persuasive.

The following paragraphs written by a student use examples to explain how the writer reacts to boredom in his life. As you read this excerpt, notice how the writer shows rather than tells the readers how he copes with boredom by providing exciting details that are concrete, specific, and definite:

> *We all deal with boredom in our own ways. Unfortunately, most of us have to deal with it far too often. Some people actually seek boredom. Being bored means that they are not required to do anything; being boring means that no one wants anything from them. In short, these people equate boredom with peace and relaxation. But for the rest of us, boredom is not peaceful. It produces anxiety.*
>
> *Most people deal with boredom by trying to distract themselves from boring circumstances. Myself, I'm a reader. At the breakfast table*

over a boring bowl of cereal, I read the cereal box, the milk carton, the wrapper on the bread. (Have you ever noticed how many of those ingredients are unpronounceable?) Waiting in a doctor's office, I will gladly read weekly news magazines of three years ago, a book for five-year-olds, advertisements for drugs, and even the physician's odd-looking diplomas on the walls. Have you ever been so bored you were reduced to reading through all the business cards in your wallet? Searching for names similar to yours in the phone book? Browsing through the National Enquirer *while waiting in the grocery line? At any rate, that's my recipe for beating boredom. What's yours?*

THINKING CRITICALLY BY USING EXAMPLE

Working with examples gives you yet another powerful way of processing your immediate environment and the larger world around you. It involves a manner of thinking that is completely different from description and narration. Using examples to think critically means seeing a definite order in a series of specific, concrete illustrations related in some way that may or may not be immediately obvious to your readers.

Isolating this rhetorical mode involves playing with related details in such a way that they create various patterns that relay different messages to the reader. Often, the simple act of arranging examples helps both the reader and the writer make sense of an experience or idea. In fact, ordering examples and illustrations in a certain way may give one distinct impression, while ordering them in another way may send a completely different message. Each pattern creates a different meaning and, as a result, an entirely new effect.

With examples, more than with description and narration, patterns need to be discovered in the context of the topic, the writer's purpose, and the writer's ultimate message. Writers and readers of example essays must make a shift from chronological to logical thinking. A writer discussing variations in faces, for example, would be working with assorted memories of people, incidents, and age differences. All of these details will eventually take shape in some sort of statement about faces, but these observations would probably not follow a strictly chronological sequence.

The exercises here will help you experience the mental differences among the rhetorical modes we have studied so far and will

Example   161

also prepare you to make sense of details and examples through careful arrangement and rearrangement of them in your essay. In addition, these exercises will continue to give you more information about your mind's abilities and range.

1. In the photograph above by Naseeb Baroody, what kinds of examples do you see? Is this an example of simplicity or complexity? Good photography or bad photography? Make a list of at least five other ways this photograph could serve as an example.
2. For each sentence below, provide two to three examples that would illustrate the generalization:
    a. I really liked (disliked) some of the movies released this year.
    b. Many career opportunities await a college graduate.
    c. Some companies make large sums of money by selling products with the names of professional sports teams on them.
3. Jot down five examples of a single problem on campus that bothers you. First, arrange these examples in an order that would convince the president of your school that making some

changes in this area would create a more positive learning environment. Second, organize your five examples in such a way that they would convince your parents that the learning environment at your current school cannot be salvaged and you should immediately transfer to another school.

READING AND WRITING ESSAYS THAT USE EXAMPLES

A common criticism of college-level writers is that they often base their essays on unsupported generalizations, such as "All sports cars are unreliable." The guidelines discussed in this introduction will help you avoid this problem and use examples effectively to support your ideas.

As you read the essays in this chapter, take time to notice the degree of specificity the writers use to make various points. To a certain extent, the more examples you use in your essays, the clearer your ideas will be and the more your readers will understand and be interested in what you are saying.

Notice also that these writers know when to stop—when "more" becomes too much and boredom sets in for the reader. Most college students err by using too few examples, however, so we suggest that, when in doubt about whether or not to include another illustration, you should go ahead and add one.

How to Read an Essay that Uses Examples

Preparing to Read.   Before you begin reading the essays in this chapter, take some time to think about each author's title: What can you infer about Bill Cosby's attitude toward having children from his title "The Baffling Question"? What do you think is William Least Heat-Moon's view of America's highways? In addition, try to discover the writer's audience and purpose at this point in the reading process; scanning the essay and surveying its synopsis in the Rhetorical Table of Contents will provide you with useful information for this task.

Also important as you prepare to read is information about the author and about how a particular essay was written. Most of this material is furnished for you in the biography preceding each essay. From it, you might learn why Harold Krents is qualified to write about blindness or why Brent Staples published "A Brother's Murder."

Example   163

Finally, before you begin to read, take time to answer the Preparing to Read questions and to make some associations with the general subject of the essay: What do you know about traveling in the United States (William Least Heat-Moon)? What are some of your thoughts on bilingualism (Amy Tan)?

Reading.   As you first read these essays, record any ideas that come to mind. Make associations freely with the content of each essay, its purpose, its audience, and the facts about its publication. For example, try to learn why Cosby writes about having children or why Krents titles his essay "Darkness at Noon." At this point, you will probably be able to make some pretty accurate guesses about the audience each author is addressing. Creating a context for your reading—including the writer's qualifications; the essay's tone, purpose, and audience; and the publication data—is an important first step toward being able to analyze your reading material in any mode.

Finally, after you have read an essay in this section once, preview the questions after the selection before you read it again. Let these questions focus your attention for your second reading.

Rereading.   As you read the essays in this chapter for a second time, focus on the examples each writer uses to make his or her point: How relevant are these examples to the thesis and purpose of each essay? How many examples do the writers use? Do they vary the length of these examples to achieve different goals? Do the authors use examples their readers can easily identify with and understand? How are these examples organized in each case? Does this arrangement support each writer's purpose? For example, how relevant are Cosby's examples to his central idea? How many examples does Least Heat-Moon use to make each point? Does Krents vary the length of each of his examples to accomplish different purposes? How does Tan organize her examples? Does this arrangement help her accomplish her purpose? In what way? Does Staples use examples that everyone can identify with? How effective are his examples?

As you read, consider also how other rhetorical modes help each writer accomplish his or her purpose. What are these modes? How do they work along with examples to help create a coherent essay?

Last, answering the questions after each essay will help you check your grasp of its main points and will lead you from the literal to the analytical level in preparation for the discussion/writing assignments that follow.

For a thorough summary of reading tasks, you might want to consult the checklists on page 20 of the Introduction.

How to Write an Essay that Uses Examples

Preparing to Write.   Before you can use examples in an essay, you must first think of some. One good way to generate ideas is to use some of the prewriting techniques explained in the Introduction (pages 21–23) as you respond to the Preparing to Write questions that appear before the writing assignments for each essay. You should then consider these thoughts in conjunction with the purpose and audience specified in your chosen writing assignments. Out of these questions should come a number of good examples for your essay.

Writing.   In an example essay, a thesis statement or controlling idea will help you begin to organize your paper. (See page 28 for more information on thesis statements.) Examples become the primary method of organizing an essay when they actually guide the readers from point to point in reference to the writer's thesis statement. The examples you use should always be relevant to the thesis and purpose of your essay. If, for instance, the person talking about tennis players cited the practice schedules of only unknown players, her friend certainly would not be convinced of the truth of her statement about how hard internationally ranked athletes work at their game. To develop a topic principally with examples, you can use one extended example or several shorter examples, depending on the nature and purpose of your assertion. If you are attempting to prove that Americans are more health conscious now than they were twenty years ago, citing a few examples from your own neighborhood will not provide enough evidence to be convincing. If, however, you are simply commenting on a neighborhood health trend, you can legitimately refer to these local cases. Furthermore, always try to find examples with which your audience can identify so that they can follow your line of reasoning. If you want your parents to help finance an apartment, citing instances from the lives of current rock stars will probably not prove your point because your parents may not sympathize with these particular role models.

Example   165

The examples you choose must also be arranged as effectively as possible to encourage audience interest and identification. If you are using examples to explain the imaginative quality of Disneyland, for instance, the most logical approach would probably be to organize your essay by degrees (i.e., from least to most imaginative or most to least original). But if your essay uses examples to help readers visualize your bedroom, a spatial arrangement of the details (moving from one item to the next) might be easiest for your readers to follow. If the subject is a series of important events, like graduation weekend, the illustrations might most effectively be organized chronologically. As you will learn from reading the selections that follow, the careful organization of examples leads quite easily to unity and coherence in your essays. *Unity* is a sense of wholeness and interrelatedness that writers achieve by making sure all their sentences are related to the essay's main idea; *coherence* refers to logical development in an essay, with special attention to how well ideas grow out of one another as the essay develops. Unity and coherence produce good writing—and that, of course, helps foster confidence and accomplishment in school and in your professional life.

Rewriting.   As you reread your example essays, look closely at the choice and arrangement of details in relation to your purpose and audience:

- Have you included enough examples to develop each of your topics adequately?
- Are the examples you have chosen relevant to your thesis?
- Have you arranged these examples in a logical manner that your audience can follow?

For more detailed information on writing, see the checklists on pages 31–32 of the Introduction.

STUDENT ESSAY: EXAMPLES AT WORK

In the following essay, a student uses examples to explain and analyze her parents' behavior as they prepare for and enjoy their grandchildren during the Christmas holidays. As you read it, study the various examples the student writer uses to convince us that her parents truly undergo a transformation each winter.

Mom and Dad's Holiday Disappearing Act

General topic   Often during the winter holidays, people find surprises: Children discover the secret contents of brightly wrapped packages that have teased them for weeks; cooks are astonished by the wealth of smells and memories their busy kitchens can bring about; workaholics stumble upon the true joy of a few days' rest. My surprise over the past few winters has been the personality transformation my parents go through around mid-December as they change from Dad and Mom into Poppa and Granny. Yes, they become grandparents and are completely different from the people I know the other eleven and a half months of the year.

Details to capture holiday spirit

Background information

Thesis statement

The first sign of my parents' metamorphosis is the delight they take in visiting toy and children's clothing stores. These two people, who usually despise anything having to do with shopping malls, become crazed consumers. While they tell me to budget my money and shop wisely, they are buying every doll, dump truck, and velvet outfit in sight. And this is only the beginning of the holidays!

First point

Examples relevant to thesis

When my brother's children arrive, Poppa and Granny come into full form. First they throw out all ideas about a balanced diet for the grandkids. While we were raised in a house where everyone had to take two bites of broccoli, beets, or liver (foods that appeared quite often on our table despite constant groaning), the grandchildren never have to eat anything that does not appeal to them. Granny carries marshmallows in her pockets to bribe the littlest ones into following her around the house, while Poppa offers "surprises" of candy

Transition

Second point

Humorous examples (organized from particular to general)

Example   167

and cake to them all day long. Boxes of chocolate-covered cherries disappear while the bran muffins get hard and stale. The kids love all the sweets, and when the sugar revs up their energy levels, Granny and Poppa can always leave and do a bit more shopping or go to bed while my brother and sister-in-law try to deal with their supercharged, hyperactive kids.

Transition

Once the grandchildren have arrived, Granny and Poppa also seem to forget all of the responsibility lectures I so often hear in my daily life. If little Tommy throws a fit at a friend's house, he is "overwhelmed by the number of adults"; if Mickey screams at his sister during dinner, he is "developing his own personality"; if Nancy breaks Granny's vanity mirror (after being told twice to put it down), she is "just a curious child." But if I track mud into the house while helping to unload groceries, I become "careless"; if I scold one of the grandkids for tearing pages out of my calculus book, I am "impatient." If a grandchild talks back to her mother, Granny and Poppa chuckle at her spirit. If I mumble one word about all of this doting, Mom and Dad have a talk with me about petty jealousies.

Third point

Examples in the form of comparison

When my nieces and nephews first started appearing at our home for the holidays a few years ago, I probably was jealous, and I complained a lot. But now I spend more time simply sitting back and watching Mom and Dad change into what we call the "Incredible Huggers." They enjoy their time with these grandchildren so much that I easily forgive them their Granny and Poppa faults.

Transition to conclusion

Writer's attitude

I believe their personality change is due to the lack of responsibility they feel for the

Writer's analysis of situation

grandkids: In their role as grandparents, they don't have to worry about sugar causing cavities or temporary failures of self-discipline turning into lifetime faults. Those problems are up to my brother and sister-in-law. All Granny and Poppa have to do is enjoy and love their grandchildren. They have all the fun of being parents without any of the attendant obligations. And you know what? <u>I think they've earned the right</u>   Specific

Concluding   <u>to make this transformation—at least once a</u>   reference to

remark   <u>year.</u>   introduction

Student Writer's Comments

To begin this essay, I listed examples of my parents' antics during the Christmas holidays as parents and as grandparents and then tried to figure out how these examples illustrated patterns of behavior. Next, I scratched out an outline pairing my parents' actions with what I thought were the causes of those actions. But once I sat down to write, I was completely stumped. I had lots of isolated ideas and saw a few patterns, but I had no notion of where this essay was going.

I thought I might put the theory that writing is discovery to the ultimate test and sit down to write out a very rough first draft. I wanted the introduction to be humorous, but I also wanted to maintain a dignified tone (so I wouldn't sound like a whiny kid!). I was really having trouble getting started. I decided to write down *anything* and then come back to the beginning later on. All of the examples and anecdotes were swimming around in my head wanting to be committed to paper. But I couldn't make sense of many of them, and I still couldn't see where I was headed. I found I needed my thesaurus and dictionary from the very beginning; they helped take the pressure off me to come up with the perfect word every time I was stuck. As I neared the middle of the paper, the introduction popped into my head, so I jotted down my thoughts and continued with the flow of ideas I needed for the body of my essay.

Example   169

Writing my conclusion forced me to put my experiences with my parents into perspective and gave me an angle for revising the body of my essay. But my focus didn't come to me until I began to revise my entire paper. At that point, I realized I had never really tried to analyze how I felt toward my parents' actions or why they acted as they do during the Christmas holidays. I opened the conclusion with "I believe their [my parents'] personality change is due to" and sat in one place until I finished the statement with a reason that made sense out of all these years of frustration. It finally came to me: They act the way they do during the holidays because they don't have primary responsibility for their grandkids. It's a role they have never played before, and they are loving it. (Never mind how it is affecting me!) This basic realization led me to new insights about the major changes they go through during the holidays and ended up giving me a renewed appreciation of their behavior. I couldn't believe the sentence I wrote to close the essay: "I think they've earned the right to make this transformation—at least once a year." Holy cow! Writing this essay actually brought me to a new understanding of my parents.

Revising was a breeze. I felt as if I had just been through a completely draining therapy session, but I now knew what I thought of this topic and where my essay was headed. I dropped irrelevant examples, reorganized other details, and tightened up some of the explanations so they set up my conclusion more clearly. Both my parents and I were delighted with the results.

SOME FINAL THOUGHTS ON EXAMPLES

Although examples are often used to supplement and support other methods of development—such as cause/effect, comparison/contrast, and process analysis—the essays in this section focus principally on examples. A main idea is expressed in the introduction of each, and the rest of the essay provides examples to bolster that contention. As you read these essays, pay close attention to each author's choice and arrangement of examples; then try to determine which organizational techniques are most persuasive for each specific audience.

EXAMPLE IN REVIEW

Reading Example Essays

Preparing to Read

- ✓ What assumptions can you make from the essay's title?
- ✓ Can you guess what the general mood of the essay is?
- ✓ What is the essay's purpose and audience?
- ✓ What does the synopsis tell you about the essay?
- ✓ What can you learn from the author's biography?
- ✓ Can you guess what the author's point of view toward the subject is?
- ✓ What are your responses to the "Preparing to Read" questions?

Reading

- ✓ What general message is the author trying to convey?
- ✓ Did you preview the questions that follow the essay?

Rereading

- ✓ What examples help the author communicate the essay's message?
- ✓ How are these examples organized?
- ✓ What other rhetorical modes does the author use?
- ✓ What are your responses to the questions after the essay?

Writing Example Essays

Preparing to Write

- ✓ What are your responses to the "Preparing to Write" questions?
- ✓ What is your purpose?
- ✓ Who is your audience?
- ✓ What is the message you want to convey?

Writing

- ✓ What is your thesis or controlling idea?
- ✓ Do the examples you are choosing support this thesis?
- ✓ Are these examples arranged as effectively as possible?
- ✓ What is your point of view toward your subject?
- ✓ How do you achieve unity and coherence in your essay?

Rewriting

- ✓ Have you included enough examples to develop each of your topics adequately?
- ✓ Are the examples you have chosen relevant to your thesis?
- ✓ Have you arranged these examples in a logical manner that your audience can follow?

BILL COSBY   (1937–   )

The Baffling Question

Comedian, actor, recording artist, and author Bill Cosby is undoubtedly one of America's best-loved entertainers. From his beginnings on the *I Spy* television series through his *Fat Albert* years and his work on *Sesame Street*, his eight Grammy awards for comedy albums, his commercials for everything from Kodak film to Jell-O pudding, his portrayal of the affable obstetrician Cliff Huxtable on his immensely popular *Cosby Show*, and his latest role in *Kids Say the Darndest Things*, he has retained his public persona of an honest and trustworthy storyteller intrigued by the ironies in our everyday lives. "When I was a kid," he has explained, "I always used to pay attention to things that other people didn't even think about. I'd remember funny happenings, just little trivial things, and then tell stories about them later. I found I could make people laugh, and I enjoyed doing it because it gave me a sense of security. I thought that if people laughed at what you said, that meant they liked you." After a series of hit movies in the 1970s, Cosby returned to prime-time television in 1984 because of his concern about his family's viewing habits: "I got tired of seeing TV shows that consisted of a car crash, a gunman, and a hooker talking to a Black pimp. It was cheaper to do a series than to throw out my family's six television sets." At the peak of its success, *The Cosby Show* was seen weekly by over sixty million viewers. Cosby's publications include *You Are Somebody Special* (1978), *Fatherhood* (1986), *Time Flies* (1988), *Love and Marriage* (1989), and a children's book entitled *Friends of a Feather* (illustrated by his daughter, Erika Cosby, 2003). He lives with his wife, Camille, in Los Angeles, where he relaxes by playing an occasional game of tennis.

Preparing to Read

The following selection is from one of Cosby's six books, *Fatherhood,* which details the joys and frustrations of raising children. In this essay, he puts a comic spin on several serious issues connected with parenthood.

Exploring Experience: Before reading this piece, pause to consider the effect parenthood has had or might have on your life:
How did/would you make the decision whether to have children?
What variables were/would be involved in this decision? What
are/would be some of the difficulties involved in raising children?
Some of the joys? How did your parents react to you when you
were a child? What memories do you have of your own childhood?

Learning Online: Cosby uses personal examples to develop his
essay. Visit the United States Department of Health and Human
Safety Web site located at http://www.hhs.gov, and select an article related to children or new parents. What types of examples do
the writers use to support their main claims? While reading "The
Baffling Question," consider how these examples differ from the
types of examples used by Bill Cosby.

So you've decided to have a child. You've decided to give up   1
quiet evenings with good books and lazy weekends with
good music, intimate meals during which you finish whole
sentences, sweet private times when you've savored the thought
that just the two of you and your love are all you will ever need.
You've decided to turn your sofas into trampolines and to abandon the joys of leisurely contemplating reproductions of great art
for the joys of frantically coping with reproductions of yourselves.

Why?   2

Poets have said the reason to have children is to give yourself   3
immortality; and I must admit I did ask God to give me a son
because I wanted someone to carry on the family name. Well,
God did just that, and I now confess that there have been times
when I've told my son not to reveal who he is.

"You make up a name," I've said. "Just don't tell anybody who   4
you are."

Immortality? Now that I have had five children, my only hope   5
is that they all are out of the house before I die.

No, immortality was not the reason why my wife and I pro-   6
duced these beloved sources of dirty laundry and ceaseless noise.
And we also did not have them because we thought it would be
fun to see one of them sit in a chair and stick out his leg so that
another one of them running by was launched like Explorer I.

After which I said to the child who was the launching pad, "Why did you do that?"

"Do what?" he replied.   7

"Stick out your leg."   8

"Dad, I didn't know my leg was going out. My leg, it does that   9
a lot."

If you cannot function in a world where things like this are said, 10
then you better forget about raising children and go for daffodils.

My wife and I also did not have children so they could yell at   11
each other all over the house, moving me to say, "What's the
problem?"

"She's waving her foot in my room," my daughter replied.   12

"And something like that *bothers* you?"   13

"Yes, I don't *want* her foot in my room."   14

"Well," I said, dipping into my storehouse of paternal wisdom,   15
"why don't you just close the door?"

"Then I can't see what she's doing!"   16

Furthermore, we did not have the children because we thought   17
it would be rewarding to watch them do things that should be
studied by the Menninger Clinic.

"Okay," I said to all five one day, "go get into the car."   18

All five then ran to the same car door, grabbed the same han-   19
dle, and spent the next few minutes beating each other up. Not
one of them had the intelligence to say, "Hey, *look*. There are
three more doors." The dog, however, was already inside.

And we did not have the children to help my wife develop new   20
lines for her face or because she had always had a desire to talk out
loud to herself: "Don't tell *me* you're *not* going to do something
when I tell you to move!" And we didn't have children so I could
always be saying to someone, "Where's my change?"

Like so many young couples, my wife and I simply were unable   21
to project. In restaurants we did not see the small children who
were casting their bread on the water in the glasses the waiter had
brought; and we did not see the mother who was fasting because
she was both cutting the food for one child while pulling another
from the floor to a chair that he would use for slipping to the floor
again. And we did not project beyond those lovely Saturdays of
buying precious little things after leisurely brunches together. We
did not see that *other* precious little things would be coming along
to destroy the first batch.

UNDERSTANDING DETAILS

1. According to Cosby, exactly what is "the baffling question"? Why is this question "baffling"?
2. If everyone felt as Cosby does about raising children, what kinds of people would have children?
3. List three important issues that Cosby believes couples should consider before they have children.
4. From Cosby's point of view, in what important ways do children change a couple's life?

ANALYZING MEANING

1. Why do you think Cosby focuses on the problems children create in a couple's life? What effect does this approach have on his main point?
2. What does Cosby mean when he says, "You've decided . . . to abandon the joys of leisurely contemplating reproductions of great art for the joys of frantically coping with reproductions of yourselves" (paragraph 1)? Whom is he addressing?
3. Following Cosby's logic, why did he and his wife have children? What examples lead you to this conclusion?
4. In what way is the last sentence in this essay a good summary statement? What specific thoughts does it summarize?

DISCOVERING RHETORICAL STRATEGIES

1. How does the first paragraph set the tone for the rest of the essay?
2. Cosby's primary strategy in this essay is irony. That is, he suggests reasons for having children by listing reasons *not* to have children. What effect is this approach likely to have on his readers?
3. How does Cosby use specific examples to create humor? Is his humor effective? Explain your answer.
4. Cosby is a master of choosing vivid examples to make his point. What other rhetorical strategies does Cosby use to develop his essay? Give examples of each.

MAKING CONNECTIONS

1. Compare Bill Cosby's comments about raising children with those made about films by Stephen King in "Why We Crave

Horror Movies." To what extent do these authors see our need for children and horror flicks as a kind of self-affirming masochism?

2. How seriously does Cosby intend his readers to take his "advice" about not having children? Do you see any connection between his point of view and that expressed by Jessica Mitford in "Behind the Formaldehyde Curtain"? How do both of these essays work through the rhetorical device of irony (saying the opposite of what we really mean)? Which essay is more effective? Explain your answer.

3. Contrast Cosby's rapport with his children with the parent–child relationships depicted in Lewis Sawaquat's "For My Indian Daughter," Sandra Cisneros's "Only daughter," or Michael Dorris's "The Broken Cord." Which parents do you think love their children most? Why do you believe this is true?

IDEAS FOR DISCUSSION/WRITING

Preparing to Write

Write freely about the art of parenthood: From your observations or experience, what are some of the principal problems and joys of parenthood? How is being a parent different from babysitting? What pleasant baby-sitting experiences have you had? What unpleasant experiences? What kind of child were you? What specific memories led you to this conclusion?

Choosing a Topic

1. Write an essay for the general public explaining one particular problem or joy of parenthood. In your essay, mimic Cosby's humorous approach to the topic. Use several specific examples to make your point.

2. Write an editorial for your local newspaper on your own foolproof techniques for doing one of the following: (a) babysitting, (b) raising children, or (c) becoming a model child. Use specific examples to explain your approach.

3. Interview one or two relatives who are older than you; ask them about the type of child you were. Have them recall some particularly memorable details that characterized your behavior. Then write an essay explaining their predominant impressions of you. Use examples to support these impressions.

4. What is an area in which you are an expert? Select an area in which you feel you have a great deal of expertise. This could be a sport, such as basketball or surfing, or a skill, such as drawing or cooking. Identify your own "baffling question" surrounding the topic, and write an essay that develops this problem. In organizing your essay, consider the types of examples you decide to use. Find facts and/or statistics about your topic online, and determine whether they would serve as effective examples.

Before beginning your essay, you might want to consult the checklists on page 170.

WILLIAM LEAST HEAT-MOON
(1939–   )

Red, White, and Blue Highways

Born William Lewis Trogdon in Kansas City, Missouri, the author inherited the name "Heat-Moon" from his father's Osage heritage and adopted the given-name "Least" because he was his family's youngest son. He attended the University of Missouri at Columbia, where he earned four degrees: a B. A., an M. A., and a Ph.D. in literature and a B.A. in photojournalism. After a stint teaching English at Stephens College in Columbia, Heat-Moon became restless and set out on a journey across America with $450 cash in a Ford Econoline Van which he called "Ghost Dancer." The result was a remarkable odyssey through the back roads of the United States following the small, blue lines on highway maps, which resulted in a brilliant and highly acclaimed book titled *Blue Highways: A Journey Into America* (1983). His next "road novel" was *PrairyErth (a deep map)*, an exploration of the grasslands of Chase County, Kansas (1991). This was followed by *River Horse: A Voyage Across America* (1999), which chronicled his excussion through the United States on its many waterways, where he experienced the land just as our early explorers must have. For each of these seminal works, the author not only wrote the narrative describing his journeys, but he also took the many enchanting photographs that illustrate each book. Heat-Moon still lives near Columbia on an old tobacco farm not far from the bluffs overlooking the Missouri River, where he enjoys walking in the open spaces so beautifully described in his many publications.

Preparing to Read

"Red, White, and Blue Highways," which originally appeared in the national magazine for American Automobile Association (AAA) members (July/August 2002), discusses ways we are linked together in our mobile American society. The writer refers to both physical and cultural connections we can enjoy as Americans.

Exploring Experience: As you prepare to read this essay, take a few moments to consider your own feelings and reactions to traveling: Do you like to travel? Why do you travel? What was your favorite trip? Do you feel a connection with others when you travel? Do you travel mostly by car, train, or plane? Why do you usually travel this way? How often do you travel? Are you looking forward to your next trip? Why or why not? Where do you plan to go next?

Learning Online: Take a brief journey using an online map Web site (for example, Rand McNally, http://www. randmcnally.com). Find the area surrounding the Mississippi River, and trace the distance from Kansas City, Missouri, to Baton Rouge, Louisiana. Keep this area in mind while reading William Least Heat-Moon's essay.

Because of a certain ice cream soda, it's possible that I've ended up where and what I am. The ingredients—vanilla ice cream, chocolate syrup, carbonated water—were not the cause, unless you figure in how they often drew me to Murphy's Drugstore in Kansas City, Missouri. My favorite seat was at the soda fountain on the spin-top stool closest to a large plate glass window that allowed me to watch the happenings at the intersection of 75th Street and Troost Avenue.

On one particular October afternoon in 1949, the streets were empty, as they rarely are now. In the face of such emptiness, I found myself staring at the pavement of Troost, which at that location was also U.S. Highway 71, the route from Rainy Lake on the Minnesota–Canada border to the swamps of southern Louisiana. In a week, I was to leave with my father on my first long road trip and would serve as navigator. Having learned to read maps soon after I learned to read words, I considered myself qualified. In the midst of imagining our destination at New Orleans, I realized that those twin concrete slabs of avenue were like a frozen river. They extended in a continuous, if unmoving, flow from where I sat all the way to the ferry landing on the Mississippi River at Baton Rouge, about an hour northwest of New Orleans.

For a 10-year-old to unexpectedly comprehend that Murphy's soda fountain belonged to a distant world of alligators—unseen but nevertheless there, like a great-uncle I'd never met or a book not yet read—was to reformulate my perception of American geography. Education and maturity, like civilization itself, are the business of making connections. I then understood that alligators lay outside that drugstore window just as my own bedroom did, never mind the distance.

In those days, it wasn't so easy to see a Louisiana alligator, and 4
my lone disappointment of our journey was not spotting a single one. But I did discover another ancient creature of our waters: a fresh oyster, shucked before my eyes and set out on the counter in front of me at a French Quarter oyster house. With a boldness enabled by the maximum amount of ketchup and horseradish such a slippery thing can hold, I nipped into one of those fruits of the Gulf and was no longer just a boy from Kansas City—I was on my way to becoming a citizen of America, for it was there I began a lifetime of conjoining places and cultures, accents and aromas, ice cream sodas and oysters.

Murphy's window, edged with gold letters promising sundries 5
and prescriptions, was a window, if not on the world, then at least on a nation linked by a federal highway where one could find watery worlds of walleye at one end and oysters at the other. The next year, at my urging, my father and I tied into a couple of the fish in upper Minnesota. Traveling the thousand miles between Murphy's and walleyes to the north or oysters to the south put in me a love of the American open road and its landscapes that eventually turned me from a traveler into a writer of travels.

Last summer, I retraced a fair portion of another highway pass- 6
ing near my childhood home. U.S. 40, still known east of the Mississippi as the Old National Road, runs out of Atlantic City to St. Louis, and from there west, under the newer name of Highway 40. At Salt Lake City, the road now connects with Interstate 80 and heads into San Francisco. The Boardwalk at one end and the Golden Gate at the other: I was a boy living between two exotic places. To see myself then so longitudinally and latitudinally linked with the country gave me a sense of belonging that has held me in thrall ever since, and from it came my wish to visit every American county, all 3,000 and some of them, a quest that took me 50 years to complete. So I decided to follow the Old National Road to see how it was faring and to freshen my memories of its terrains.

When I reached the halfway point, at Zanesville, Ohio, I   7
remembered reading about an inn once there called the National
Hotel. The highway reached that place in 1831, and the propri-
etor, Colonel Henry Orndorff, saw an opportunity. Up to that
time, common fare in roadhouses included pickled oysters eaten
with buttered bread or crackers and, perhaps, accompanied by a
side of pickled pigs' feet. Pickling, of course, was a substitute for
refrigeration. The new highway, the Colonel reasoned, could
make it possible for Chesapeake oysters fresh from the bay to reach
Ohio without pickling. He soon came up with enough wagons to
haul the mollusks from Baltimore to Zanesville—and later on to
towns farther west—in such abundance that the transport company became known as the Oyster Line.

I submit that few things—perhaps none other—have served   8
more to unite us than our roads. They allow us to feel in some
small way that eating shell-fish in Zanesville helps us share a piece
of national destiny with oyster tongers out on the Chesapeake.
Perhaps I'm thinking this because three days after I stopped for
gasoline along U.S. 40 in Somerset County, Pennsylvania, the
fourth hijacked plane of September 11, the one that didn't reach
its terrorist destination, came down in a field only a few miles
away. My passage through there linked me forever with that dark
history in a way that televised pictures or printed words never
could.

The pavement of our highways is more than just concrete—it   9
is also the cement of our national culture. We have common weal
because we can meet face-to-face: the Texans sitting across the
table (Pass the hot sauce, please) from the Washingtonian introducing them to Willapa Bay oysters; the Arizonan (May I stand
you another round?) explaining to Michiganders the dry bed of
the Salt River. When such interchanges occur, we continue our
forging of nationhood, and—through the wonder of topographi-
cal transport—we transform political theory and history itself into
food and fact, tales and truths; we become Americans linked into
union not just gustatorily, but also spiritually and emotionally.

Many Americans are aware of the significance of the Lewis and   10
Clark Expedition, which Thomas Jefferson employed to help
unite the western half of the United States with the eastern. But
another Jeffersonian action perhaps even more practically brought
the nation together. The first published account by a participant in

the Lewis and Clark Expedition had been out only a year when the president's secretary of the treasury sent a report to Congress. Speaking of the national necessity for good roads, Albert Gallatin in 1808 said, "No other single operation, within the power of Government, can more effectively tend to strengthen and perpetuate that Union which secures external independence, domestic peace, and internal liberty."

It's a commonplace to say no one can interpret America without understanding our use of automobiles, but what we mean is that one can't comprehend America without taking into account our mobility, and preeminently that means roadways. We are a widely dispersed, numerous people bound together by nearly three million miles of concrete, macadam, and yellow stripes. We invented neither the highway nor the automobile, yet within living memories of our eldest citizens, those paired pieces of engineering have put their mark on us, for better and for worse, more than on any other nation. They remade us as soon as we made them and began to use them to find our way onto our land, into our selves, and unto each other. After all, beyond everyone's street, no matter how distant and unseen, lie oysters of the Chesapeake, the Gulf, and Willapa Bay, but most of all, there reside our fellow citizens of those shores.

11

UNDERSTANDING DETAILS

1. How did "a certain ice cream soda" (paragraph 1) make William Least Heat-Moon what he is today?
2. How did the author become "a citizen of America" (paragraph 4)? What did this change mean to him?
3. How did the highway and the automobile "remake us" (paragraph 11). Explain your answer in detail.
4. How did the Oyster Line come about? What is its significance?

ANALYZING MEANING

1. According to the author, how are education and maturity related to civilization?
2. Why did Least Heat-Moon want to visit every American county?
3. In what ways is the author linked to 9/11?

4. What does the author mean when he says, "The pavement of our highways is more than just concrete—it is also the cement of our national culture" (paragraph 9)?

DISCOVERING RHETORICAL STRATEGIES

1. List the author's main points in this essay. Why does he choose to deal with these topics in this particular order?
2. What examples does Least Heat-Moon use to support each of his main ideas?
3. Describe Least Heat-Moon's intended audience in as much detail as possible. Why do you think he has aimed his essay at this particular group?
4. Besides examples, what other rhetorical strategies does the author draw on to make his statement about American mobility? List one example of each.

MAKING CONNECTIONS

1. Compare and contrast Heat-Moon's spiritual devotion to America's "Blue Highways" with the fascination Bernard Cooper ("Labyrinthine") has with mazes. How does each author use geography as a metaphor for finding oneself?
2. How does Heat-Moon use examples differently than Harold Krents ("Darkness at Noon") and Amy Tan ("Mother Tongue"). Which author's use of examples is most persuasive within its own context? Explain your answer.
3. Examine the sense of "community" reflected in "Red, White, and Blue Highways" (Heat-Moon), "The Pines" (John McPhee), "A Brother's Murder" (Brent Staples), and "A Working Community" (Ellen Goodman). Which of the communities described by these authors is the largest geographically? Which is the smallest? Which is the most metaphoric?

IDEAS FOR DISCUSSION/WRITING

Preparing to Write

Write freely about your own sense of mobility: Do you feel a connection with roads and automobiles in America? In what ways do you value your freedom to travel? Why is it important to you?

How would you exist if someone took away your primary means of transportation? Would this change affect your identity in any way? Explain your answer.

Choosing a Topic

1. Using many well-chosen examples to support his argument, Least Heat-Moon claims in his essay that mobility is at a premium in American society. From your point of view, write an example essay explaining to your friends another quality in American society that is also very important in our culture.

2. As a college student, you see many events that link students across the United States, maybe even across the world. Write an essay for your school newspaper explaining a common social or cultural trend that connects students pursuing higher education.

3. Travel for Americans has declined since the terrorist attacks of 9/11. How do you feel about traveling these days? Write an essay using examples to support your current thoughts about travel safety.

4. William Least Heat-Moon describes the ways roads unite him with the world around him. How does the Internet connect you to the outside world? Write an essay describing your experiences with the Internet. Following Heat-Moon's example, use details that progress from being personally significant to having a global impact.

Before beginning your essay, you might want to consult the checklists on page 170.

Darkness at Noon

Raised in New York City, Harold Krents earned a B.A. and a law degree at Harvard, studied at Oxford University, worked as a partner in a Washington, D.C., law firm, was the subject of a long-running Broadway play, and wrote a popular television movie—all despite the fact that he was born blind. His "1-A" classification by a local draft board, which doubted the severity of his handicap, brought about the 1969 Broadway hit play *Butterflies Are Free* by Leonard Gershe. Krents once explained that he was merely the "prototype" for the central character: "I gave the story its inspiration—the play's plot is not my story; its spirit is." In 1972, Krents wrote *To Race the Wind*, which was made into a CBS-TV movie in 1980. During his career as a lawyer, Krents worked hard to expand legal protection for the handicapped and fought to secure their right to equal opportunity in the business world. He died in 1987 of a brain tumor.

Preparing to Read

In the following article, originally published in *The New York Times* in 1976, the author gives examples of different kinds of discrimination he has suffered because of his blindness.

Exploring Experience: As you prepare to read this essay, take a few minutes to think about disabilities or handicaps in general: Do you have a disability? If so, how are you treated by others? How do you feel others respond to your handicap? Do you know someone else who has a disability? How do you respond to that person? How do you think he or she wants to be treated? To what extent do you think disabilities should affect a person's job opportunities? What can be done to improve society's prejudices against the disabled?

Learning Online: In this essay, Harold Krents describes his frustrations at people's misconceptions about his disability. To gain a better perspective on his experience, go to http://www. nfb.org/futref.htm, the National Federation of the Blind's Web site for parents and teachers of blind children. The bottom of the page contains links to its magazine, *Future Reflections*. Select the most current issue, and pick a topic that sounds interesting. Consider the experiences mentioned on the Web site as you read Krents's account.

B lind from birth, I have never had the opportunity to see 1
myself and have been completely dependent on the image
I create in the eye of the observer. To date it has not been narcissistic.

There are those who assume that since I can't see, I obviously 2 also cannot hear. Very often people will converse with me at the top of their lungs, enunciating each word very carefully. Conversely, people will also often whisper, assuming that since my eyes don't work, my ears don't either.

For example, when I go to the airport and ask the ticket agent 3 for assistance to the plane, he or she will invariably pick up the phone, call a ground hostess and whisper: "Hi, Jane, we've got a 76 here." I have concluded that the word "blind" is not used for one of two reasons: Either they fear that if the dread word is spoken, the ticket agent's retina will immediately detach, or they are reluctant to inform me of my condition of which I may not have been previously aware.

On the other hand, others know that of course I can hear, but 4 believe that I can't talk. Often, therefore, when my wife and I go out to dinner, a waiter or waitress will ask Kit if "*he* would like a drink" to which I respond that "indeed *he* would."

This point was graphically driven home to me while we were 5 in England. I had been given a year's leave of absence from my Washington law firm to study for a diploma in law degree at Oxford University. During the year I became ill and was hospitalized. Immediately after admission, I was wheeled down to the X-ray room. Just at the door sat an elderly woman—elderly I would judge from the sound of her voice. "What is his name?" the woman asked the orderly who had been wheeling me.

"What's your name?" the orderly repeated to me. 6

"Harold Krents," I replied. 7

"Harold Krents," he repeated. 8

"When was he born?" 9

"When were you born?" 10

"November 5, 1944," I responded. 11

"November 5, 1944," the orderly intoned.   12

This procedure continued for approximately five minutes at   13
which point even my saint-like disposition deserted me. "Look,"
I finally blurted out, "this is absolutely ridiculous. Okay, granted I
can't see, but it's got to have become pretty clear to both of you
that I don't need an interpreter."

"He says he doesn't need an interpreter," the orderly reported   14
to the woman.

The toughest misconception of all is the view that because I   15
can't see, I can't work. I was turned down by over forty law firms
because of my blindness, even though my qualifications included
a cum laude degree from Harvard College and a good ranking in
my Harvard Law School class.

The attempt to find employment, the continuous frustration of   16
being told that it was impossible for a blind person to practice law,
the rejection letters, not based on my lack of ability but rather on
my disability, will always remain one of the most disillusioning
experiences of my life.

I therefore look forward to the day, with the expectation that it   17
is certain to come, when employers will view their handicapped
workers as a little child did me years ago when my family still lived
in Scarsdale.

I was playing basketball with my father in our backyard accord-   18
ing to procedures we had developed. My father would stand
beneath the hoop, shout, and I would shoot over his head at the
basket attached to our garage. Our next-door neighbor, aged five,
wandered over into our yard with a playmate. "He's blind," our
neighbor whispered to her friend in a voice that could be heard
distinctly by Dad and me. Dad shot and missed; I did the same.
Dad hit the rim; I missed entirely; Dad shot and missed the garage
entirely. "Which one is blind?" whispered back the little friend.

I would hope that in the near future when a plant manager is   19
touring the factory with the foreman and comes upon a handicapped and nonhandicapped person working together, his comment after watching them work will be, "Which one is disabled?"

UNDERSTANDING DETAILS

1. According to Krents, what are three common misconceptions
   about blind people?

2. What important details did you learn about Krents's life from this essay? How does he introduce this information?
3. In what ways was Krents frustrated in his search for employment? Was he qualified for the jobs he sought? Why or why not?
4. What attitude toward the handicapped does Krents look forward to in the future?

ANALYZING MEANING

1. What does Krents mean when he says that his self-image gained through the eyes of others "has not been narcissistic" (paragraph 1)? Why do you think this is the case?
2. What is Krents's attitude toward his handicap? What parts of his essay reveal that attitude?
3. How do you account for the reactions to his blindness that Krents tells about in this essay? Are you aware of such behavior in yourself? In others?
4. Do you think we will ever arrive at the point in the working world that Krents describes in the last paragraph? How can we get there? What advantages or disadvantages might accompany such a change?

DISCOVERING RHETORICAL STRATEGIES

1. How does Krents organize the three main points in his essay? Why does he put them in this order? What is the benefit of discussing employment last?
2. Krents often offers specific examples in the form of dialogue or spoken statements. Are these effective ways to develop his main points? Explain your answer.
3. Krents establishes a fairly fast pace in this essay as he discusses several related ideas in a small amount of space. How does he create this sense of speed? What effect does this pace have on his essay as a whole?
4. Although the author's dominant rhetorical mode is example in this essay, what other strategies does he use to develop his ideas? Give examples of each of these strategies.

MAKING CONNECTIONS

1. Compare the employment discrimination faced by Krents because of his blindness with the racial and social discrimination

suffered by Lewis Sawaquat ("For My Indian Daughter") and Franklin Zimring ("Confessions of an Ex-Smoker"). Which person has been treated most unfairly by society? Explain your answer.

2. How similar is Krents's use of humor to that of Russell Baker ("The Saturday Evening Post") and Bill Cosby ("The Baffling Question")? Which author do you find most amusing? Why? Is humor used in a different way in Krents's essay than it is in the Cosby essay? If so, how?

3. How many examples does Krents use in his essay? Does Krents use more or fewer examples per page than Bill Cosby ("The Baffling Question") or Brent Staples ("A Brother's Murder")? How does the number of examples affect the believability of each author's argument?

IDEAS FOR DISCUSSION/WRITING

Preparing to Write

Write freely about disabilities: If you are disabled, what is your response to the world? Why do you respond the way you do? How does society respond to you? Are you pleased or not with your relationship to society in general? If you are not disabled, what do you think your attitude would be if you were disabled? How do you respond to disabled people? To what extent does your response depend upon the disability? Are you satisfied with your reaction to other people's disabilities? Are you prejudiced in any way against people with disabilities? Do you think our society as a whole demonstrates any prejudices toward the disabled? If so, how can we correct these biases?

Choosing a Topic

1. As a reporter for your campus newspaper, you have been assigned to study and write about the status of services for the disabled on your campus. Is your school equipped with parking for the handicapped? A sufficient number of ramps for wheelchairs? Transportation for the handicapped? Other special services for the handicapped? Interview some disabled students to get their views on these services. Write an example essay for the newspaper, explaining the situation.

2. With your eyes closed, take a walk through a place that you know well. How does it feel to be nearly sightless? What senses begin to compensate for your loss of vision? Write an essay for your classmates detailing your reactions. Use specific examples to communicate your feelings.

3. Do you have any phobias or irrational fears that handicap you in any way? Write a letter to a friend explaining one of these "handicaps" and your method of coping with it.

4. Select three of your favorite Web sites, and spend a few minutes visiting each one. Now return to them and consider how you would use the site if you were either blind or deaf. What accommodations, if any, have the Web sites made to accommodate differently abled users? Using Krents's article and your experiences with these Web sites as examples, write an essay evaluating the accessibility of the Internet for those who are disabled. Following Krents' writing style, consider the effect of differentways of organizing your examples.

Before beginning your essay, you might want to consult the checklists on page 170.

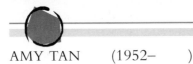

AMY TAN   (1952–   )

Mother Tongue

In a very short time, Amy Tan has established herself as one of the foremost Chinese-American writers. Her first novel, *The Joy Luck Club* (1989), which was praised as "brilliant . . . a jewel of a book" by *The New York Times Book Review*, focuses on the lives of four Chinese women in pre-1949 China and their American-born daughters in modern-day California. Through a series of vignettes, Tan weaves together the dreams and sorrows of these mothers and daughters as they confront oppression in China and equally difficult cultural challenges in the new world of the United States. Like the protagonists in *The Joy Luck Club*, Tan's parents, a Baptist minister and a licensed vocational nurse, emigrated to America shortly before Tan's birth. She showed an early talent for writing when, at age eight, she won an essay contest (and a transistor radio) with a paper entitled "Why I Love the Library." Following the tremendous success of her first novel, Tan apparently had great difficulty writing her second book, *The Kitchen God's Wife* (1991). As she was working on it, she began grinding her teeth, which resulted in two broken molars and a sizable dental bill. "I am glad that I shall never again have to write a second book," the author has confessed. "Actually, I cannot recall any writer—with or without a splashy debut—who said the second book came easily." Successful film and stage adaptations of *The Joy Luck Club* in 1993 were followed by *The Chinese Siamese Cat* (1994), *The Hundred Secret Senses* (1995), *The Year of No Flood* (1996), *The Bonesetter's Daughter* (2001), and *The Opposite of Fate: A Book of Musings* (2003).

Preparing to Read

In the following essay, originally published in *The Threepenny Review*, Amy Tan explains the different "Englishes" she learned to use in her youth. These had a significant effect on her as she grew up to be a successful writer.

Exploring Experience: As you prepare to read this essay, take a few minutes to think about the different varieties of English that you use: How do you change your use of English when you relay the same message to different people? Why do you make these changes? Do you feel as if you do well in English class? On English tests? Do your test scores represent your true abilities in English? In Math? How could you become an even better writer and speaker of English than you already are?

Learning Online: Tan often refers to her childhood and family in her writing. To better understand the cultural context to which she is referring, conduct an Internet search on the experience of Chinese immigrants in the United States. Pay special attention to the Chinese-American women's experience after 1950. To start your search, you may want to visit "Becoming an American: The Chinese Experience" located at http://www.pbs.org/becomingamerican. In reading "Mother Tongue," consider the many unique social pressures affecting Tan's use of her "different Englishes."

I am not a scholar of English or literature. I cannot give you   1
much more than personal opinions on the English language and its variations in this country or others.

I am a writer. And by that definition, I am someone who has   2
always loved language. I am fascinated by language in daily life. I spend a great deal of my time thinking about the power of language—the way it can evoke an emotion, a visual image, a complex idea, or a simple truth. Language is the tool of my trade. And I use them all—all the Englishes I grew up with.

Recently, I was made keenly aware of the different Englishes I   3
do use. I was giving a talk to a large group of people, the same talk I had already given to half a dozen other groups. The nature of the talk was about my writing, my life, and my book, *The Joy Luck Club*. The talk was going along well enough, until I remembered one major difference that made the whole talk sound wrong. My mother was in the room. And it was perhaps the first time she had heard me give a lengthy speech, using the kind of English I have never used with her. I was saying things like, "The intersection of memory upon imagination" and "There is an aspect of my fiction that relates to thus-and-thus"—a speech filled with carefully wrought grammatical phrases, burdened, it suddenly seemed to

me, with nominalized forms, past perfect tenses, conditional phrases, all the forms of standard English that I had learned in school and through books, the forms of English I did not use at home with my mother.

Just last week, I was walking down the street with my mother,   4 and I again found myself conscious of the English I was using, the English I do use with her. We were talking about the price of new and used furniture and I heard myself saying this: "Not waste money that way." My husband was with us as well, and he didn't notice any switch in my English. And then I realized why. It's because over the twenty years we've been together I've often used the same kind of English with him, and sometimes he even uses it with me. It has become our language of intimacy, a different sort of English that relates to family talk, the language I grew up with.

So you'll have some idea of what this family talk I heard sounds   5 like, I'll quote what my mother said during a recent conversation which I videotaped and then transcribed. During this conversation, my mother was talking about a political gangster in Shanghai who had the same last name as her family's, Du, and how the gangster in his early years wanted to be adopted by her family, which was rich by comparison. Later, the gangster became more powerful, far richer than my mother's family, and one day showed up at my mother's wedding to pay his respects. Here's what she said in part:

"Du Yusong having business like fruit stand. Like of the street   6 kind. He is Du like Du Zong—but not Tsung-ming Island people. The local people call *putong,* the river east side, he belong to that side local people. That man want to ask Du Zong father take him in like become own family. Du Zong father wasn't look down on him, but didn't take seriously, until that man big like become a mafia. Now important person, very hard to inviting him. Chinese way, came only to show respect, don't stay for dinner. Respect for making big celebration, he shows up. Mean gives lots of respect. Chinese custom. Chinese social life that way. If too important won't have to stay too long. He come to my wedding. I didn't see, I heard it. I gone to boy's side, they have YMCA dinner, Chinese age I was nineteen."

You should know that my mother's expressive command of   7 English belies how much she actually understands. She reads the *Forbes* report, listens to *Wall Street Week,* converses daily with her stockbroker, reads all of Shirley MacLaine's books with ease—all kinds of things I can't begin to understand. Yet some of my friends tell me they understand 50 percent of what my mother says. Some say they understand 80 to 90 percent. Some say they understand none of it, as if she were speaking pure Chinese. But to me, my mother's English is perfectly clear, perfectly natural. It's my mother tongue. Her language, as I hear it, is vivid, direct full of observation and imagery. That was the language that helped shape the way I saw things, expressed things, made sense of the world.

Lately, I've been giving more thought to the kind of English 8 my mother speaks. Like others, I have described it to people as "broken" or "fractured" English. But I wince when I say that. It has always bothered me that I can think of no way to describe it other than "broken," as if it were damaged and needed to be fixed, as if it lacked a certain wholeness and soundness. I've heard other terms used, "limited English," for example. But they seem just as bad, as if everything is limited, including people's perceptions of the limited English speaker.

I know this for a fact, because when I was growing up, my 9 mother's "limited" English limited *my* perception of her. I was ashamed of her English. I believed that her English reflected the quality of what she had to say. That is, because she expressed them imperfectly, her thoughts were imperfect. And I had plenty of empirical evidence to support me: the fact that people in department stores, at banks, and at restaurants did not take her seriously, did not give her good advice, pretended not to understand her, or even acted as if they did not hear her.

My mother has long realized the limitations of her English as 10 well. When I was fifteen, she used to have me call people on the phone and pretend I was she. In this guise, I was forced to ask for information or even to complain and yell at people who had been rude to her. One time it was a call to her stockbroker in New York. She had cashed out her small portfolio, and it just so happened we were going to go to New York the next week, our very first trip outside California. I had to get on the phone and say in an adolescent voice that was not very convincing, "This is Mrs. Tan."

And my mother was standing in the back whispering loudly, 11 "Why he don't send me check, already two weeks late. So mad he lie to me, losing my money."

And then I said in perfect English, "Yes, I'm getting rather con-   12
cerned. You had agreed to send the check two weeks ago, but it
hasn't arrived."

Then she began to talk more loudly. "What he want, I come to   13
New York tell him front of his boss, you cheating me?" And I was
trying to calm her down, make her be quiet, while telling the
stockbroker, "I can't tolerate any more excuses. If I don't receive
the check immediately, I am going to have to speak to your manager when I'm in New York next week." And sure enough, the
following week there we were in front of this astonished stockbroker, and I was sitting there red-faced and quiet, and my mother, the real Mrs. Tan, was shouting at his boss in her impeccable
broken English.

We used a similar routine just five days ago, for a situation that   14
was far less humorous. My mother had gone to the hospital for an
appointment, to find out about a benign brain tumor a CAT scan
had revealed a month ago. She said she had spoken very good
English, her best English, no mistakes. Still, she said, the hospital
did not apologize when they said they had lost the CAT scan and
she had come for nothing. She said they did not seem to have any
sympathy when she told them she was anxious to know the exact
diagnosis, since her husband and son had both died of brain
tumors. She said they would not give her any more information
until the next time and she would have to make another appointment for that. So she said she would not leave until the doctor
called her daughter. She wouldn't budge. And when the doctor
finally called her daughter, me, who spoke in perfect English—lo
and behold—we had assurances the CAT scan would be found,
promises that a conference call on Monday would be held, and
apologies for any suffering my mother had gone through for a
most regrettable mistake.

I think my mother's English almost had an effect on limiting my   15
possibilities in life as well. Sociologists and linguists probably will
tell you that a person's developing language skills are more influenced by peers. But I do think that the language spoken in the
family, especially in immigrant families which are more insular,
plays a large role in shaping the language of the child. And I
believe that it affected my results on achievement tests, IQ tests,
and the SAT. While my English skills were never judged as poor,
compared to math, English could not be considered my strong

suit. In grade school I did moderately well, getting perhaps B's, sometimes B-pluses, in English and scoring perhaps in the sixtieth or seventieth percentile on achievement tests. But those scores were not good enough to override the opinion that my true abilities lay in math and science, because in those areas I achieved A's and scored in the ninetieth percentile or higher.

This was understandable. Math is precise; there is only one correct answer. Whereas, for me at least, the answers on English tests were always a judgment call, a matter of opinion and personal experience. Those tests were constructed around items like fill-in-the-blank sentence completion, such as "Even though Tom was _____, Mary thought he was _____." And the correct answer always seemed to be the most bland combinations of thoughts, for example, "Even though Tom was shy, Mary thought he was charming," with the grammatical structure "even though" limiting the correct answer to some sort of semantic opposites, so you wouldn't get answers like, "Even though Tom was foolish, Mary thought he was ridiculous." Well, according to my mother, there were very few limitations as to what Tom could have been and what Mary might have thought of him. So I never did well on tests like that.

The same was true with word analogies, pairs of words in which you were supposed to find some sort of logical, semantic relationship—for example, "Sunset is to nightfall as _____ is to _____." And here you would be presented with a list of four possible pairs, one of which showed the same kind of relationship: *red* is to *stoplight, bus* is to *arrival, chills* is to *fever, yawn* is to *boring.* Well, I could never think that way. I knew what the tests were asking, but I could not block out of my mind the images already created by the first pair, "*sunset is to night-fall*"—and I would see a burst of colors against a darkening sky, the moon rising, the lowering of a curtain of stars. And all the other pairs of words—red, bus, stoplight, boring—just threw up a mass of confusing images, making it impossible for me to sort out something as logical as saying: "A sunset precedes nightfall" is the same as "a chill precedes a fever." The only way I would have gotten that answer right would have been to imagine an associative situation, for example, my being disobedient and staying out past sunset, catching a chill at night, which turns into feverish pneumonia as punishment, which indeed did happen to me.

16

17

I have been thinking about all this lately, about my mother's   18
English, about achievement tests. Because lately I've been asked,
as a writer, why there are not more Asian Americans represented
in American literature. Why are there few Asian Americans
enrolled in creative writing programs? Why do so many Chinese
students go into engineering? Well, these are broad sociological
questions I can't begin to answer. But I have noticed in surveys—
in fact, just last week—that Asian students, as a whole, always do
significantly better on math achievement tests than in English. And
this makes me think that there are other Asian-American students
whose English spoken in the home might also be described as
"broken" or "limited." And perhaps they also have teachers who
are steering them away from writing and into math and science,
which is what happened to me.

Fortunately, I happen to be rebellious in nature and enjoy the   19
challenge of disproving assumptions made about me. I became an
English major my first year in college, after being enrolled as pre-
med. I started writing nonfiction as a freelancer the week after I
was told by my former boss that writing was my worst skill and I
should hone my talents toward account management.

But it wasn't until 1985 that I finally began to write fiction. And   20
at first I wrote using what I thought to be wittily crafted sentences,
sentences that would prove I had mastery over the English language. Here's an example from the first draft of a story that later
made its way into *The Joy Luck Club,* but without this line: "That
was my mental quandary in its nascent state." A terrible line,
which I can barely pronounce.

Fortunately, for reasons I won't get into today, I later decided   21
I should envision a reader for the stories I would write. And the
reader I decided upon was my mother, because these were stories
about mothers. So with this reader in mind—and in fact she did
read my early drafts—I began to write stories using all the
Englishes I grew up with: the English I spoke to my mother,
which for lack of a better term might be described as "simple"; the
English she used with me, which for lack of a better term might
be described as "broken"; my translation of her Chinese, which
could certainly be described as "watered down"; and what I imagined to be her translation of her Chinese if she could speak in perfect English, her internal language, and for that I sought to preserve the essence, but neither an English nor a Chinese structure.

I wanted to capture what language ability tests can never reveal: her intent, her passion, her imagery, the rhythms of her speech, and the nature of her thoughts.

Apart from what any critic had to say about my writing, I knew   22
I had succeeded where it counted when my mother finished reading my book and gave me her verdict: "So easy to read."

UNDERSTANDING DETAILS

1. What do you think is Tan's main reason for writing this essay?
2. What are the four "Englishes" that Tan grew up with? Explain each in your own words.
3. What is Tan referring to when she uses the term "mother tongue"?
4. How did Tan feel about her mother's "limited English" in the past?

ANALYZING MEANING

1. How did Amy Tan become a writer? In what way did her rebellious nature help her make this decision?
2. How do all the Englishes Tan grew up with help her as a writer? Explain your answer.
3. What relationship does Tan see between achievement test scores and actual abilities?
4. Why did Tan choose her mother as the audience she envisions when she writes?

DISCOVERING RHETORICAL STRATEGIES

1. Why does Tan actually quote some of her mother's language early in her essay? What effect does this example have on you as a reader?
2. List Tan's main points in this essay. Why do you think she deals with these topics in this particular order?
3. Describe Tan's intended audience in as much detail as possible. Why do you think she aims her essay at this particular group?
4. What other rhetorical strategies does Tan use to help make her point? Give examples of each of these strategies.

MAKING CONNECTIONS

1. Compare and contrast Amy Tan's relationship with her mother and the parent–child relationships examined in the following essays: Lewis Sawaquat's "For My Indian Daughter," Russell Baker's "The Saturday Evening Post," Bill Cosby's "The Baffling Question," and Wallerstein and Blakeslee's "Second Chances for Children of Divorce."

2. In her essay, Tan describes her love of English and her avocation as a writer despite her relatively weak performance on English achievement tests as a child. Examine the manner in which other people exceeded the expectations placed on them as expressed in Maya Angelou's "New Directions," Russell Baker's "The Saturday Evening Post," Harold Krents's "Darkness at Noon," and Alice Walker's "Beauty: When the Other Dancer Is the Self."

3. Discuss the theme of "the limitations of language" as it appears in the following essays: Amy Tan's "Mother Tongue," Judith Viorst's "The Truth About Lying," Mary Roach's "Meet the Bickersons," and Rita Mae Brown's "Writing as a Moral Act."

IDEAS FOR DISCUSSION/WRITING

Preparing to Write

Write freely about your own abilities in English: Do you feel you use more than one version of English? How does your oral English differ from your written English? Is English your first language? What do you think of yourself as a writer? As a reader? How well do you perform on English achievement tests?

Choosing a Topic

1. As a college student, you see different people approaching their writing assignments in different ways every day. Some students get right down to work. Others procrastinate until the last minute. Some write in spurts until they have finished the task. Write an essay for your school newspaper explaining your observations about the different ways people write. Use carefully chosen examples to illustrate your observations. You might even want to interview some of your peers about their writing rituals.

2. You have been asked to respond to a national survey on the role of education in our lives. The organization conducting the survey wants to know the extent to which education has helped or hindered you in achieving your goals. In a well-developed essay written for a general audience, explain the benefits and liabilities of education in your life at present. Use specific examples to develop your essay.

3. In her essay, Tan refers to the fact that her teachers steered her "away from writing and into math and science" (paragraph 18) primarily because of her test scores. But she believes her test scores were not an accurate measurement of her ability in English because of her background in the language. Do you think test scores are ever used inappropriately to advise students? Or do you think these scores are the best way we currently have to measure ability and aptitude? Direct your comments to the general public, and use several specific examples to support your opinion.

4. Tan refers to the ways in which family, culture, and education affect how she speaks and writes. Using recent e-mails you have written, examine the "different Englishes" and other languages you use when communicating with diverse audiences. For example, what words do you use when writing to your friends, your family, or your teachers? How do your language choices differ in each instance? What social pressures affect your use of "different Englishes"? Write an essay that examines your different uses of English and/or other languages. Consider your reasons for using various words when communicating with different people. Use specific examples from your e-mails to support and develop your essay.

Before beginning your essay, you might want to consult the checklists on page 170.

BRENT STAPLES   (1951–   )

A Brother's Murder

Brent Staples was the first of nine children born to a truck driver and a housewife in Chester, Pennsylvania, a factory town fifteen miles south of Philadelphia. He was educated at the Philadelphia Military College and Penn Moton College, eventually graduating from Widener College with honors. A prestigious Danforth Fellowship took him to the University of Chicago, where he earned a Ph. D. in Psychology. His brilliant memoir, *Parallel Time: Growing Up in Black and White* (published by Pantheon Books in 1994), was a finalist for the *Los Angeles Times* Book Award and a winner of the Annisfield Wolff Award, which had previously been won by such luminaries as James Baldwin, Ralph Ellison, and Zora Neale Hurston. A past editor of the *New York Times* Book Review section and an assistant metropolitan editor, Staples currently writes on politics and culture for the *Times* editorial page. He is an avid gardener and is especially fond of roses. He advises college writers that "ninety percent of writing is rewriting. The simple declarative sentence is your best friend in the world."

Preparing to Read

"A Brother's Murder" was first published in an anthology of African-American writing entitled *Bearing Witness*. In this emotional account of his brother's death, Staples realizes many important truths about the role of violence among African-American men.

Exploring Experience: Before reading this essay, think for a few moments about violence in general: From your observations, which kinds of people are most violent? Why do these people use violence? What do you think is the cause of most violent acts? In your opinion, why is the crime rate so high in American society today? Can we do anything to reduce this crime rate? What are some of your constructive suggestions for controlling violence today?

Learning Online: Brent Staples uses personal examples to explore the causes and effects of youth violence in his hometown. Visit the "Building Blocks for Youth" Web site located at: http://www.buildingblocksforyouth.org/. Click on the "Research" button, and read one of their online articles about violence in African-American communities. Consider the use of examples, such as statistics and dates, in the article as you read Staples's essay.

It has been more than two years since my telephone rang with the news that my younger brother Blake—just 22 years old—had been murdered. The young man who killed him was only 24. Wearing a ski mask, he emerged from a car, fired six times at close range with a massive .44 Magnum, then fled. The two had once been inseparable friends. A senseless rivalry—beginning, I think, with an argument over a girlfriend—escalated from posturing, to threats, to violence, to murder. The way the two were living, death could have come to either of them from anywhere. In fact, the assailant had already survived multiple gunshot wounds from an incident much like the one in which my brother lost his life. 1

As I wept for Blake, I felt wrenched backward into events and circumstances that had seemed light-years gone. Though a decade apart, we both were raised in Chester, Pennsylvania, an angry, heavily black, heavily poor, industrial city southwest of Philadelphia. There, in the 1960s, I was introduced to mortality, not by the old and failing, but by beautiful young men who lay wrecked after sudden explosions of violence. The first, I remember from my 14th year—Johnny, brash lover of fast cars, stabbed to death two doors from my house in a fight over a pool game. The next year, my teenage cousin, Wesley, whom I loved very much, was shot dead. The summers blur. Milton, an angry young neighbor, shot a crosstown rival, wounding him badly. William, another teen-age neighbor, took a shotgun blast to the shoulder in some urban drama and displayed his bandages proudly. His brother, Leonard, severely beaten, lost an eye and donned a black patch. It went on. 2

I recall not long before I left for college, two local Vietnam veterans—one from the Marines, one from the Army—arguing fiercely, nearly at blows about which outfit had done the most in 3 the war. The most killing, they meant. Not much later, I read in a magazine article that set that dispute in a context. In the story, a noncommissioned officer—a sergeant, I believe—said he would pass up any number of affluent, suburban-born recruits to get hardcore soldiers from the inner city. They jumped into the rice paddies with "their manhood on their sleeves," I believe he said. These two items—the veterans arguing and the sergeant's words—still characterize for me the circumstances under which black men in their teens and 20's kill one another with such frequency. With a touchy paranoia born of living battered lives, they are desperate to be *real* men. Killing is only *machismo* taken to the extreme. Incursions to be punished by death were many and minor, and they remain so: they include stepping on the wrong toe, literally; cheating in a drug deal; simply saying "I dare you" to someone holding a gun; crossing territorial lines in a gang dispute. My brother grew up to wear his manhood on his sleeve. And when he died, he was in that group—black, male, and in its teens and early 20's—that is far and away the most likely to murder or be murdered.

I left the East Coast after college, spent the mid- and late-1970's   4
in Chicago as a graduate student, taught for a time, then became a journalist. Within 10 years of leaving my hometown, I was over-educated and "upwardly mobile," ensconced on a quiet, tree-lined street where voices raised in anger were scarcely ever heard. The telephone, like some grim umbilical, kept me connected to the old world with news of deaths, imprisonings, and misfortune. I felt emotionally beaten up. Perhaps to protect my self, I added a psychological dimension to the physical distance I had already achieved. I rarely visited my hometown. I shut it out.

As I fled the past, so Blake embraced it. On Christmas of 1983,   5
I traveled from Chicago to a black section of Roanoke, Virginia, where he then lived. The desolate public housing projects, the hopeless, idle young men crashing against one another—these reminded me of the embittered town we'd grown up in. It was a place where once I would have been comfortable, or at least sure of myself. Now, hearing of my brother's forays into crime, his scrapes with police and street thugs, I was scared, unsteady on foreign terrain.

I saw Blake's romance with the street life, and the hustler image   6
had flowered dangerously. One evening that late December, standing in some Roanoke dive among drug dealers and grim,

hair-trigger losers, I told him I feared for his life. He had affected the image of the tough he wanted to be. But behind the dark glasses and the swagger, I glimpsed the baby-faced toddler I'd once watched over. I nearly wept. I wanted desperately for him to live. The young think themselves immortal, and a dangerous light shone in his eyes as he spoke laughingly of making fools of the policemen who had raided his apartment looking for drugs. He cried out as I took his right hand. A line of stitches lay between the thumb and index finger. Kickback from a shotgun, he explained, nothing serious. Gunplay had become part of his life.

I lacked the language simply to say: Thousands have lived this   7
for you and died. I fought the urge to lift him bodily and shake him. This place and the way you are living smells of death to me, I said. Take some time away, I said. Let's go downtown tomorrow and buy a plane ticket anywhere, take a bus trip, anything to get away and cool things off. He took my alarm casually. We arranged to meet the following night—an appointment he would not keep. We embraced as though through glass. I drove away.

As I stood in my apartment in Chicago holding the receiver that   8
evening in February 1984, I felt as though part of my soul had been cut away. I questioned myself then, and I still do. Did I not reach back soon or earnestly enough for him? For weeks I awoke crying from a recurrent dream in which I chased him, urgently trying to get him to read a document I had, as though reading it would protect him from what had happened in waking life. His eyes shining like black diamonds, he smiled and danced just out of my grasp. When I reached for him, I caught only the space where he had been.

UNDERSTANDING DETAILS

1. What does Staples mean when he refers to his brother's death by saying, "The way the two were living, death could have come to either of them from anywhere" (paragraph 1)?
2. What stages did Staples's brother and his murderer go through before Blake was killed?
3. Why do you think Staples wrote this essay? What is his main point?
4. What did Staples learn about African-American males by examining his brother's life?

ANALYZING MEANING

1. In what ways does Brent Staples's brother represent an important segment of the African-American male population?
2. Why did Staples create a distance between his present life and his past?
3. What examples does Staples use to prove his theory that "killing is only *machismo* taken to the extreme" (paragraph 3)? Do you agree with this conclusion? Can you think of any examples that demonstrate the opposite position?
4. What was "Blake's romance with the street life" (paragraph 6)?

DISCOVERING RHETORICAL STRATEGIES

1. Describe in as much detail as possible Staples's intended audience. Why do you think he aims his essay at this particular group?
2. In what way does Staples's recurring dream (paragraph 8) symbolize the author's relationship with his brother? How does this final paragraph sum up Staples's feelings about the plight of African-American males in American society today?
3. In paragraph 7, Staples uses a simile (a special comparison between two unlike items, using "like" or "as"): "We embraced as though through glass." This image adds an extra dimension to Staples's description. Find another simile in this essay, and explain its effect on you.
4. This essay progresses most obviously through the use of examples. What other rhetorical strategies support this dominant mode? In what ways do they add to Staples's main point?

MAKING CONNECTIONS

1. Through hard work and a college education, Brent Staples was able to rise above the violent environment that contributed to his brother's death. Examine each of the following essays, and explain how the central characters escaped their own difficult environments: Maya Angelou's "New Directions," Harold Krents's "Darkness at Noon," and Wallerstein and Blakeslee's "Second Chances for Children of Divorce."
2. Compare and contrast Staples's comments about violence with opinions on the topic voiced by Kimberly Wozencraft's "Notes

from the Country Club," Bruce Catton's "Grant and Lee: A
Study in Contrasts," Stephen King's "Why We Crave Horror
Movies," Dave Grossman's "We Are Training Our Kids to
Kill," and Barbara Ehrenreich's "The Ecstasy of War."

3. How do Brent Staples's insights about the community in which
his brother lived differ from the sense of "community" in the
following essays: William Ouchi's "Japanese and American
Workers: Two Casts of Mind," Robert Ramirez's "The
Barrio," and Ellen Goodman's "A Working Community"?

IDEAS FOR DISCUSSION/WRITING

Preparing to Write

Write freely about your view of violence in American society
today: What is the source of most of this violence? How can we
control violence in American society? Why do you think violence
is increasing? How else might we channel our innate violent reactions? What other suggestions do you have for reducing violent
crimes today?

Choosing Your Topic

1. Write an essay for a college-educated audience based on one of
the following statements: "Current pressure in contemporary
society causes most of the violence today" or "People's natural
instincts cause most of the violence in contemporary society."

2. Interview some people about how they manage their anger:
What do they do when they get mad? How do they control
their reactions? Have they ever become violent? Then write an
essay for the students in your English class explaining your
findings.

3. According to Staples, the military frame of mind—the urge to
kill—is at the heart of "the circumstances under which black
men in their teens and 20's kill one another with such frequency" (paragraph 3). Do you agree or disagree with this
statement? Write a well-developed essay, using examples from
your experience, to support your opinion.

4. Staples relates his painful experience to help explain the perva-
siveness of youth violence. He selects personal examples rather
than statistics or news stories to present his argument. Choose
an issue about which you feel strongly, and write an essay in

which you argue your position using carefully selected relevant examples. Try to clarify general concepts by using specific details as Staples does. Use the Internet to find statistics or case studies, if necessary, to support your argument.

Before beginning your essay, you might want to consult the checklists on page 170.

CHAPTER WRITING ASSIGNMENTS

Practicing Example

1. Think about some qualities that irritate you in other people's behavior (such as how someone drives, how someone talks on the phone, or how someone laughs). In an essay, use examples to explain a behavior that irritates you and the reason it bothers you so much.

2. Think about all the different roles people play, such as father, teacher, big brother, or sister. Who in your experience provides the best example of how this "role" should be performed? Write an essay that explains why this person is the best example of this role.

3. What do you do best as a writer? Which parts of the writing process do you seem to deal with most successfully? Taking examples from your own writing, compose an essay that discusses your strengths as a writer.

Exploring Ideas

1. Should America as a country promote the use of a single national language, or should we instead acknowledge and encourage the use of multiple languages? Write an essay that explores the advantages and/or disadvantages of either single or multiple languages in American society. As you write, use specific examples to support your position.

2. In what ways do all forms of the media use stereotypes? Choose a specific "type" (such as liberal, conservative, radical, athlete), and, using as many specific examples as possible, explain how the media help or hinder our understanding of a certain personality or issue.

3. Discuss a time when someone embarrassed you publicly. Describe what happened and how it affected you. What, if anything, did you learn from the experience?

4

PROCESS ANALYSIS
Explaining Step by Step

Human nature is characterized by the perpetual desire to understand and analyze the process of living well. The bestseller list is always crowded with books on how to know yourself better, how to be assertive, how to become famous, how to survive a natural disaster, or how to be rich and happy—all explained in three easy lessons. Open almost any popular magazine, and you will find numerous articles on how to lose weight, how elections are run in this country, how to dress for success, how a political rally evolved, how to gain power, or how to hit a successful topspin backhand. People naturally gravitate toward material that tells them how something is done, how something happened, or how something works, especially if they think the information will help them improve their lives in a significant way.

DEFINING PROCESS ANALYSIS

A *process* is a procedure that follows a series of steps or stages; *analysis* involves taking a subject apart and explaining its components in order to better understand the whole. Process analysis, then, explains an action, a mechanism, or an event from beginning to end. It concentrates on either a mental or a physical operation:

how to solve a chemistry problem, how to tune up your car, how John F. Kennedy was shot, how the telephone system works. In fact, the explanation of the writing process beginning on page 21 of this book is a good case in point: It divides writing into three interrelated verbal activities and explains how they each work—separately and together.

A process analysis can take one of two forms: (1) It can give directions, thereby explaining how to do something (directive), or (2) it can give information about how something happened or how something works (informative). The first type of analysis gives directions for a task the reader may wish to attempt in the future. Examples include how to make jelly, how to lose weight, how to drive to Los Angeles, how to assemble stereo equipment, how to make money, how to use a microscope, how to knit, how to resuscitate a dying relationship, how to win friends, how to discipline your child, and how to backpack.

The second type of analysis furnishes information about what actually occurred in specific situations or how something works. Examples include how Hiroshima was bombed, how certain Hollywood stars live, how the tax system works, how the movie *Chicago* was filmed, how Babe Ruth earned a place in the Baseball Hall of Fame, how gold was first discovered in California, how computers work, how a kibbutz functions, and how the Gulf War began. These subjects and others like them respond to a certain fascination we all have with mastering some processes and understanding the intricate details of others. They all provide us with opportunities to raise our own standard of living, either by helping us directly apply certain processes to our own lives or by increasing our understanding of how our complex world functions.

The following student paragraph analyzes the process of constructing a garden compost pit. Written primarily for people who might wish to make such a pit, this piece is directive rather than informative. Notice in particular the amount of detail the student calls upon to explain each stage of the process and the clear transitions she uses to guide us through her analysis.

No garden is complete without a functioning compost pit. Here's a simple, inexpensive way to make your garbage work for you! To begin with, make a pen out of hog wire or chicken wire, four feet long by eight feet wide by four feet high, splitting it down the middle with another piece of wire so that you end up with a structure that looks like a capital "E" on its side. This is a compost duplex. In the first pen, place a layer of soda ash, just sprinkled on the surface of the dirt. Then pile an inch or so of leaves, grass clippings, or sawdust on top of the soda ash. You're now ready for the exciting part. Start throwing in all the organic refuse from your kitchen (no meat, bones, or grease, please). After the food is a foot or so deep, throw in a shovelful of steer manure, and cover the entire mess with a thin layer of dirt. Then water it down. Continue this layering process until the pile is three to three-and-a-half feet high. Allow the pile to sit until it decomposes (from one month in warm climates to six months in colder weather). Next, take your pitchfork and start slinging the contents of pen one into pen two (which will land in reverse order, of course, with the top on the bottom and the bottom on the top). This ensures that everything will decompose evenly. Water this down and begin making a new pile in pen one. That's all there is to it! You now have a ready supply of fertilizer for your garden.

THINKING CRITICALLY BY USING PROCESS ANALYSIS

Process analysis embodies clear, careful, step-by-step thinking that takes one of three different forms: chronological, simultaneous, or cyclical. The first follows a time sequence from "first this" to "then that." The second forces you to deal with activities or events that happen or happened at the same time, such as people quietly studying or just getting home from work when the major 1994 earthquake hit Los Angeles. And the third requires you to process information that is continuous, like the rising and setting of the sun. No other thinking pattern will force you to slow down as much as process analysis because the process you are explaining probably won't make any sense if you leave out even the slightest detail.

Good process analysis can truly help your reader see an event in a totally new light. An observer looks at a product already assembled or at a completed event and has no way of knowing without the help of a good process analysis how it got to this final stage. Such an analysis gives the writer or speaker as well as the observer a completely new way of "seeing" the subject in question. Separating process analysis from the other rhetorical modes lets you practice this method of thinking so that you will have a better understanding of the various mental procedures going on in your head. Exercising this possibility in isolation will help you feel its range and its intricacies so that you can become more adept at using it, fully developed, in combination with other modes of thought.

© Rick Doyle/CORBIS.

1. In the accompanying picture, the photographer manipulates our view by using a particular lens and by positioning the photo so that the man on the surfboard is almost in the middle of the scene. What are other ways we manipulate or influence people's views? Brainstorm about how you influence the views or ideas of people around you? What are your most effective techniques? Explain to someone else in class how you effectively influence people you know, or explain how to avoid unfairly manipulating or influencing others.

2. List as many examples of each type of process (chronological, simultaneous, and cyclical) that you can think of. Share your list with the class.

3. Write a paragraph telling how *not* to do something. Practice your use of humor as a technique for creating interest in the essay by emphasizing the "wrong" way, for example, to wash a car or feed a dog.

READING AND WRITING PROCESS ANALYSIS ESSAYS

Your approach to a process analysis essay should be fairly straightforward. As a reader, you should be sure you understand the author's statement of purpose and then try to visualize each step as you go along. As a writer, you need to adapt the mechanics of the way you normally write to the demands of a process analysis paper, beginning with an interesting topic and a number of clearly explained ideas or stages. As usual, the intended audience determines the choice of words and the degree of detail.

How to Read a Process Analysis Essay

Preparing to Read.   Preparing to read a process analysis essay is as uncomplicated as the essay itself. The title of Edwin Bliss's essay in this chapter, "Managing Your Time," tells us exactly what we are going to learn about. Julia Bourland's title, "Getting Out of Debt (and Staying Out)," also lets us know what we are going to get. Scanning each selection to assess the author's audience will give you an even better idea of what to expect in these essays, while the synopsis of each in the Rhetorical Table of Contents will help focus your attention on its subject.

Also important as you prepare to read these essays are the qualifications of each author to write on their subject: Has he or she performed the task, worked with the mechanism, or seen the event? Is the writer's experience firsthand? When Edwin Bliss discusses "Managing Your Time," is he writing from his personal experience? What is Jessica Mitford's experience with mortuaries? How does she know what goes on "Behind the Formaldehyde Curtain"? The biography preceding each essay will help you uncover this information and find out other publication details that will encourage you to focus on the material you are about to read.

Finally, before you begin reading, answer the prereading questions, and then do some brainstorming on the subject of the essay: What do you want to know about sports heroes (Jay Weiner)?

How adept are you at using words, and what do you think you can learn about the subject from Linda Formichelli?

Reading.   When you read the essays in this chapter for the first time, record your initial reactions to them. Consider the preliminary information you have been studying in order to create a context for each author's composition: What circumstances prompted Mitford's "Behind the Formaldehyde Curtain"? Why did Jay Weiner write "Sports Centered"? Who do you think is Bourland's target audience in "Getting Out of Debt (and Staying Out)"?

Also determine at this point whether the essay you are reading is *directive* (explaining how to do something) or *informative* (giving information about how something happened or how something works). This fundamental understanding of the author's intentions, along with a reading of the questions following the essay, will prepare you to approach the contents of each selection critically when you read it a second time.

Rereading.   As you reread these process analysis essays, look for an overview of the process at the beginning of the essay so you know where each writer is headed. The body of each essay, then, is generally a discussion of the stages of the process.

This central portion of the essay is often organized *chronologically* (as in Mitford's essay), with clear transitions so that readers can easily follow the writer's train of thought. Other methods of organization are *cyclical* (such as the Formichelli essay on writing and the Bourland essay on debt), describing a process that has no clear beginning or end, and *simultaneous* (such as the essays by Bliss on organizing one's time and by Weiner on writing an sports), in which many activities occur at the same time with a clear beginning and end. Most of these essays discuss the process as a whole at some point. During this second reading, you will also benefit from discovering what rhetorical modes each writer uses to support his or her process analysis and why these rhetorical modes work effectively. What does Bliss's cause/effect reasoning add to his essay on time management? And how do the descriptions in Mitford's essay on mortuaries heighten the horror of the American mortuary business? Do the examples that Formichelli gives help explain how to get your writing out of a rut? How do all the rhetorical modes in each essay help create a coherent whole? After reading each essay for a second time, answer the questions that follow the selection to see if you are understanding your reading material on the literal, interpretive, and analytical levels before you take on the discussion/writing assignments.

For an overview of the entire reading process, you might consult the checklists on page 20 of the Introduction.

How to Write a Process Analysis Essay

Prewriting.   As you begin a process analysis assignment, you first need to become as familiar as you can with the action, mechanism, or event you are going to describe. If possible, try to go through the process yourself at least once or twice. If you can't actually carry out the procedure, going through the process mentally and taking notes is a good alternative. Then, try to read something about the process. After all this preparation (and careful consideration of your audience and purpose), you should be ready to brainstorm, freewrite, cluster, or use your favorite prewriting technique (see pages 21-23 of the Introduction) in response to the prewriting questions before you start composing your paper.

Writing.   The essay should begin with an overview of the process or event to be analyzed. This initial section should introduce the subject, divide it into a number of recognizable steps, and describe the result once the process is complete. Your thesis in a process essay is usually a purpose statement that clearly and briefly explains your approach to the procedure you will discuss: "Building model airplanes can be divided into four basic steps" or "The American courts follow three stages in prosecuting a criminal case."

Next, a directive or informative essay should proceed logically through the various stages of the process, from beginning to end. The parts of a process usually fall nicely into chronological order, supported by such transitions as "at first," "in the beginning," "next," "then," "after that," and "finally." Some processes, however, are either simultaneous, forcing the writer to choose a more complex logical order for the essay (such as classification), or cyclical, requiring the writer to choose a starting point and then explain the cycle stage by stage. Playing the guitar, for example, involves two separate and simultaneous components that must work together: holding the strings against the frets with the fingers of one hand and strumming with the other hand. In analyzing this procedure, you would probably want to describe both parts of the process and then explain how the hands work together to produce music. An example of a cyclical process would be the changing of the seasons. To explain this concept to a reader, you would need to pick a starting point, such as spring, and describe the entire cycle, stage by stage, from that point onward.

In a process paper, you need to be especially sensitive to your intended audience, or they will not be able to follow your explanation. The amount of information, the number of examples and illustrations, and the terms to be defined all depend on the prior knowledge and background of your readers. A writer explaining to a group of amateur cooks how to prepare a soufflé would take an entirely different approach to the subject than he or she would if the audience were a group of bona fide chefs hoping to land jobs in elegant French restaurants. The professional chefs would need more sophisticated and precise explanations than their recreational counterparts, who would probably find such an approach tedious and complicated because of the extraneous details.

The last section of a process analysis paper should consider the process as a whole. If, for example, the writer is giving directions on how to build a model airplane, the essay might end with a good description or drawing of the plane. The informative essay on our legal system might offer a summary of the stages of judging and sentencing a criminal. And the essay on cooking a soufflé might finish with a photograph of the mouth-watering dish.

Rewriting.   In order to revise a process analysis essay, first make sure your main purpose is apparent throughout your paper:

- Have you written a directive or an informative essay?
- Is your purpose statement clear?

Next, you need to determine if your paper is aimed at the proper audience:

- Have you given your readers an overview of the process you are going to discuss?
- Do you go through the process you are explaining step by step?
- At the end of the essay, do you help your readers see the process as a complete entity?

The checklists on pages 31–32 will give you further guidelines for writing, revising, and proofreading.

STUDENT ESSAY: PROCESS ANALYSIS AT WORK

The student essay that follows analyzes the process of using a "home permanent" kit. Notice that, once the student gives an overview of the process, she discusses the steps one at a time, being careful to follow a logical order (in this case, chronological) and to use clear transitions. Then, see how the end of the essay shows the process as a whole.

Follow the Simple Directions

Although fickle hairstylists in Paris and Hollywood decide what is currently "in," many romanticists disregard fashion and *Purpose* yearn for a mane of delicate tendrils. Sharing *statement* this urge but resenting the cost, I opted for *for* *informative* a "home perm" kit. Any literate person with *process* normal dexterity could follow illustrated *analysis* directions, I reasoned, and the eight easy steps would energize my limp locks in less *Overview* than two hours. "Before" and "after" photos of flawless models showed the metamorphosis one might achieve. Confidently, I assembled towels, rollers, hair clips, waving lotion, neutralizer, end papers, and a plastic *First step,* cap. While shampooing, I chortled about *(chronolog-* *ical order)* my ingenuity and economy.

Transition   After towel-drying my hair, I applied the *Second step* gooey, acidic waving lotion thoroughly. Then I wrapped an end paper around a *Third step* parted section and rolled the first curl ("securely but not too tightly"). Despite the reassuring click of the fastened rollers, as I sectioned each new curl the previous one developed its own volition and slowly unrolled itself. Resolutely, I reapplied waving lotion and rewound—and rewound— *Transition* each curl. Since my hair was already saturated, I regarded the next direction skepti-

cally: "<u>Apply waving lotion to each curl</u>."   Fourth step
Faithfully, however, I complied with the
Transition instructions. <u>Ignoring the fragile state of the
fastened rollers, I then feigned assurance and</u> Fifth step
<u>enclosed my entire head in a plastic cap</u>. In
forty minutes, chemical magic would occur.

    Restless with anticipation, I puttered
about the house; while absorbed in small
chores, I felt the first few drops of lotion
escape from the plastic tent. Stuffing wads of
cotton around the cap's edges did not help,
and the small drops soon became rivulets
that left red streaks on my neck and face and
splattered on the floor. (Had I overdone the
waving lotion?) Ammonia fumes so permeated each room that I was soon asked to
leave. Retreating to the bathroom, I opened
the window and dreamed of frivolous new
hairstyles.

Transition   <u>Finally, the waving time had elapsed;
neutralizing was next</u>. I removed my plastic Sixth step
cap, carefully heeding the caution: "Do not
disturb curlers as you rinse waving lotion
from hair." With their usual impudence,
however, all the curlers soon bobbed in the
sink; undaunted, I continued. "This next
step is critical," warned the instructions.
Thinking half-hearted curls were better than
no curls at all, I poured the entire bottle of
Transition neutralizer on my hair. <u>After a drippy ten-</u>
Seventh <u>minute wait, I read the next step</u>: "<u>Carefully</u>
step <u>remove rollers</u>." <u>As this advice was superflu-</u> Transition
<u>ous, I moved anxiously to the finale</u>: "<u>Rinse</u> Eighth step
<u>all solution from your hair, and enjoy your</u>
<u>curls</u>."

Final   Lifting my head from the sink and
product expecting visions of Aphrodite, I saw
instead Medusa's image in the mirror. Limp
question–mark spirals fell over my eyes, and
each "curl" ended in an explosion of steel-

wool frizz. Reflecting on my ineptitude, I knew why the direction page was illustrated only with drawings. After washing a large load of ammonia-scented towels, I took two aspirin and called my hairdresser. <u>Some</u> <u>repair services are cheap at any price.</u>

Concluding remark

Student Writer's Comments

Any person with normal dexterity can probably do a successful perm, but I sure had trouble! I decided I wanted to communicate that trouble in my process analysis essay. When I was given this writing assignment, I knew immediately that I wanted to explain how to do a perm. But I didn't know how to handle the humor that had resulted from my misguided attempt to administer a perm to myself. Part of my response to this assignment resides deep within my personality (I'm a closet comedian), but part of it simply has to do with the relationship between me and permanents (actually, anything having to do with cosmetics). But as I started out on this project, I had no idea if I could mold the comedy into a step-by-step analysis of a process.

First, I went to the store and bought a brand-new home perm, so I could review the guidelines step by step. On a piece of paper, I listed the procedures for giving myself a perm. On another sheet of paper, I wrote down any stories or associations I had with each stage of the process. Some of the notes on the second sheet of paper took the form of full paragraphs, others a list of words and phrases, and still others a combination of lists and full sentences. I found myself laughing aloud at some of the memories the home perm directions triggered.

I knew I was writing a directive essay for someone who might actually want to try a home perm. After making my preliminary lists of ideas, I just let my natural sense of humor direct my writing. My overview and purpose statement came easily. Next, I went through the directions one by one, laughing at myself and the process along the way. Before I knew it, I found myself writing, "After washing a large load of ammonia-scented towels, I took two aspirin and called my hairdresser"—the perfect end, or so I thought, to my comedy of errors. I had written the whole first draft from start to finish without once surfacing for air.

When I reread my draft, I realized that the approach I had taken to this process analysis assignment was a satirical one. It allowed me to go through the proper procedure of giving myself a home perm while simultaneously poking fun at myself along the way. As I revised my essay, I tried to exaggerate some of the humorous sections that demonstrated my ineptness or my failure to follow the directions correctly, hoping they would communicate the true ridiculousness of this entire situation. After omitting some details and embellishing others, I came up with the current last sentence of the essay: "Some repair services are cheap at any price." This new concluding remark took the edge off the whiny tone of the previous sentence and brought the essay to an even lighter close than before. I ended up liking the way the humor worked in the essay, because besides accurately capturing my most recent process analysis experience, it made a potentially dull essay topic rather entertaining. My only problem now is that I'm still not sure I got all the frizz out of my hair!

SOME FINAL THOUGHTS ON PROCESS ANALYSIS

In this chapter, a single process dictates the development and organization of each of the essays that follow. Both directional and informational methods are represented here. Notice in particular the clear purpose statements that set the focus of the essays in each case, as well as the other rhetorical modes (such as narration, comparison/contrast, and definition) that are used to help support the writers' explanations.

PROCESS ANALYSIS IN REVIEW

Reading Process Analysis Essays

Preparing to Read

✓ What assumptions can you make from the essay's title?
✓ Can you guess what the general mood of the essay is?
✓ What is the essay's purpose and audience?
✓ What does the synopsis tell you about the essay?
✓ What can you learn from the author's biography?
✓ Can you guess what the author's point of view toward the subject is?
✓ What are your responses to the "Preparing to Read" questions?

Reading

✓ Is the essay *directive* (explaining how to do something) or *informative* (giving information about how something happened)?
✓ What general message is the author trying to convey?
✓ Did you preview the questions that follow the essay?

Rereading

✓ Does the author furnish an overview of the process?
✓ How is the essay organized—chronologically, cyclically, or simultaneously?
✓ What other rhetorical modes does the author use?
✓ What are your responses to the questions after the essay?

Writing Process Analysis Essays

Preparing to Write

✓ What are your responses to the "Preparing to Write" questions?
✓ What is your purpose?
✓ Who is your audience?

Writing

✓ Do you provide an overview of the process at the beginning?
✓ Does your first paragraph introduce your subject, divide it into steps, describe the result of the process, and include a purpose statement?
✓ Is your process analysis essay either directive or informative?
✓ Are the essay's details organized chronologically, simultaneously, or cyclically?

Rewriting

✓ Is your purpose statement clear?
✓ Have you given your readers an overview of the process you are going to discuss?
✓ Do you go through the process step by step?
✓ At the end, do you help your readers see the process as a whole?

EDWIN BLISS   (1923–   )

Managing Your Time

An internationally known consultant on time-management techniques, Edwin Bliss earned his B.S. and M.S. degrees at the University of Utah, worked as a reporter for the *Columbus Dispatch,* taught journalism at a variety of schools, and was a lobbyist for the National Industrial Council and the U.S. Chamber of Commerce. Not until he became a member of the Washington staff of Senator Wallace F. Bennett, however, did he begin to understand the importance of time management. Since then, Bliss has put his management techniques to work as a consultant for a number of businesses in America and abroad through public seminars sponsored by a company called CareerTrack. "Organizing your time properly is especially important for college students," he claims; "a knowledge of time-management skills can help you avoid writers' block so that you turn your papers in on time." His first book, *Getting Things Done: The ABC's of Time Management,* was published in 1976 (updated and reissued in 1991); his second, *Doing It Now: A Twelve-Step Program for Overcoming Procrastination,* came out in 1983; and his third, *Are Your Employees Stealing You Blind?* (coauthored with Isamu Aoki), appeared in 1993. Bliss currently lives in central California, where he is writing a book on how to operate a small business.

Preparing to Read

In the following essay, which is taken from *Getting Things Done: The ABC's of Time Management,* Bliss offers a number of specific suggestions to help you organize your time more efficiently.

Exploring Experience: Before reading his essay, take a few minutes to think about how you arrange your days: How carefully do you schedule your time? Do you make lists of things you want to do every day? Do you usually accomplish more or less than you wanted to in a typical day? How well do you concentrate on a single activity? Are you able to say *no* to events you don't want to participate in? How much do you procrastinate? Are all aspects of your life in a healthy balance (e.g., work, recreation, school, and family)? If not, what could you do to create a more balanced life for yourself?

Learning Online: Conduct an Internet search on the phrase "time management," and visit two or more websites that appear in the results list. Is time management described as a process on these pages? If so, how do you know it is a process? If not, how is it described? Consider different techniques for presenting time management while reading Bliss's article.

I first became interested in the effective use of time when I was   1
an assistant to a U.S. Senator. Members of Congress are faced
with urgent and conflicting demands on their time—for committee work, floor votes, speeches, interviews, briefings, correspondence, investigations, constituents' problems, and the need to be informed on a wide range of subjects. The more successful Congressmen develop techniques for getting maximum benefit from minimum investments of time. If they don't, they don't return.

Realizing that I was not one of those who use time effectively,   2
I began to apply in my own life some of the techniques I had observed. Here are ten I have found most helpful.

Plan.   You need a game plan for your day. Otherwise, you'll   3
allocate your time according to whatever happens to land on your desk. And you will find yourself making the fatal mistake of dealing primarily with problems rather than opportunities. Start each day by making a general schedule, with particular emphasis on the two or three major things you would like to accomplish—including things that will achieve long-term goals. Remember, studies prove what common sense tells us: The more time we spend planning a project, the less total time is required for it. Don't let today's busywork crowd planning-time out of your schedule.

Concentrate.   Of all the principles of time management, none   4
is more basic than concentration. People who have serious time-management problems invariably are trying to do too many things at once. The amount of time spent on a project is not what counts: It's the amount of *uninterrupted* time. Few problems can resist an all-out attack; few can be solved piecemeal.

Take Breaks.   To work for long periods without taking a 5
break is not an effective use of time. Energy decreases, boredom
sets in, and physical stress and tension accumulate. Switching for a
few minutes from a mental task to something physical—isometric
exercises, walking around the office, even changing from a sitting
position to a standing position for a while—can provide relief.
Merely resting, however, is often the best course, and you 6
should not think of a "rest" break as poor use of time. Not only
will being refreshed increase your efficiency, but relieving tension
will benefit your health. Anything that contributes to health is
good time management.

Avoid Clutter.   Some people have a constant swirl of papers 7
on their desks and assume that somehow the most important matters will float to the top. In most cases, however, clutter hinders
concentration and can create tension and frustration—a feeling of
being "snowed under."
Whenever you find your desk becoming chaotic, take time out 8
to reorganize. Go through all your papers (making generous use of
the wastebasket) and divide them into categories: (1) Immediate
action, (2) Low priority, (3) Pending, (4) Reading material. Put
the highest priority item from your first pile in the center of your
desk, then put everything else out of sight. Remember, you can
think of only one thing at a time, and you can work on only one
task at a time, so focus all your attention on the most important
one. A final point: Clearing the desk completely, or at least organizing it, each evening should be standard practice. It gets the next
day off to a good start.

Don't Be a Perfectionist.   There is a difference between 9
striving for excellence and striving for perfection. The first is
attainable, gratifying, and healthy. The second is often unattain-
able, frustrating, and neurotic. It's also a terrible waste of time. The
stenographer who retypes a lengthy letter because of a trivial error,
or the boss who demands such retyping, might profit from examining the Declaration of Independence. When the inscriber of that
document made two errors of omission, he inserted the missing
letters between the lines. If this is acceptable in the document that
gave birth to American freedom, surely it would be acceptable in
a letter that will be briefly glanced at en route to someone's file
cabinet or wastebasket.

Don't Be Afraid to Say No. Of all the time-saving tech-   10
niques ever developed, perhaps the most effective is frequent use
of the word *no*. Learn to decline, tactfully but firmly, every request
that does not contribute to your goals. If you point out that your
motivation is not to get out of work but to save your time to do
a better job on the really important things, you'll have a good
chance of avoiding unproductive tasks. Remember, many people
who worry about offending others wind up living according to
other people's priorities.

Don't Procrastinate. Procrastination is usually a deeply   11
rooted habit. But we can change our habits provided we use the
right system. William James, the father of American psychology,
discussed such a system in his famous *Principles of Psychology*, published in 1890. It works as follows:

1. Decide to start changing as soon as you finish reading this article, while you
   are motivated. Taking that first step promptly is important.
2. Don't try to do too much too quickly. Just force yourself right now to do one
   thing you have been putting off. Then, beginning tomorrow morning, start
   each day by doing the most unpleasant thing on your schedule. Often it will
   be a small matter: an overdue apology; a confrontation with a fellow worker;
   an annoying chore you know you should tackle. Whatever it is, do it before
   you begin your usual morning routine. This simple procedure can well set the
   tone for your day. You will get a feeling of exhilaration from knowing that
   although the day is only 15 minutes old, you have already accomplished the
   most unpleasant thing you have to do all day.

There is one caution: Do not permit any exceptions. William   12
James compared it to rolling up a ball of string; a single slip can
undo more than many turns can wind up. Be tough with yourself,
for the first few minutes of each day, for the next two weeks, and
I promise you a new habit of priceless value.

Apply Radical Surgery. Time-wasting activities are like   13
cancers. They drain off vitality and have a tendency to grow. The
only cure is radical surgery. If you are wasting your time in activities that bore you, divert you from your real goals, and sap your
energy, cut them out, once and for all.

The principle applies to personal habits, routines, and activities   14
as much as to ones associated with your work. Check your
appointment calendar, your extracurricular activities, your reading

list, your television viewing habits, and ax everything that doesn't give you a feeling of accomplishment or satisfaction.

Delegate. An early example of failure to delegate is found in   15
the Bible. Moses, having led his people out of Egypt, was so impressed with his own knowledge and authority that he insisted on ruling personally on every controversy that arose in Israel. His wise father-in-law, Jethro, recognizing that this was poor use of a leader's time, recommended a two-phase approach: First, educate the people concerning the laws; second, select capable leaders and give them full authority over routine matters, freeing Moses to concentrate on major decisions. The advice is still sound.

You don't have to be a national leader or a corporate executive   16
to delegate, either. Parents who don't delegate household chores are doing a disservice to themselves and their children. Running a Boy Scout troop can be as time-consuming as running General Motors if you try to do everything yourself. One caution: Giving subordinates jobs that neither you nor anyone else wants to do isn't delegating, it's assigning. Learn to delegate the challenging and rewarding tasks, along with sufficient authority to make necessary decisions. It can help to free your time.

Don't Be a "Workaholic." Most successful executives I   17
know work long hours, but they don't let work interfere with the really important things in life, such as friends, family, and fly fishing. This differentiates them from the workaholic who becomes addicted to work just as people become addicted to alcohol. Symptoms of work addiction include refusal to take a vacation, inability to put the office out of your mind on weekends, a bulging briefcase, and a spouse, son, or daughter who is practically a stranger.

Counseling can help people cope with such problems. But for   18
starters, do a bit of self-counseling. Ask yourself whether the midnight oil you are burning is adversely affecting your health. Ask where your family comes in your list of priorities, whether you are giving enough of yourself to your children and spouse, and whether you are deceiving yourself by pretending that the sacrifices you are making are really for them.

Above all else, good time management involves an aware-   19
ness that today is all we ever have to work with. The past is

irretrievably gone; the future is only a concept. British art critic John Ruskin had the word "TODAY" carved into a small marble block that he kept on his desk as a constant reminder to "Do It Now." But my favorite quotation is by an anonymous philosopher:

> Yesterday is a canceled check.
> Tomorrow is a promissory note.
> Today is ready cash. Use it!

UNDERSTANDING DETAILS

1. What are the ten techniques for managing time that Bliss learned from observing successful members of Congress at work? Explain each in your own words.
2. According to Bliss, what is the difference between "delegating" and "assigning" chores (paragraph 16)?
3. What is a "workaholic" (paragraph 17)? What characteristics identify this type of person?
4. Explain Bliss's favorite quotation:

> Yesterday is a canceled check.
> Tomorrow is a promissory note.
> Today is ready cash. Use It!

What does this saying have to do with time management?

ANALYZING MEANING

1. Why is concentration such an important part of time management? Have you found this to be true in your own experience? Explain your answer.
2. Which of Bliss's guidelines for managing time could you benefit from most? How could it help you? Why do you have trouble in this area?
3. Why does Bliss advise us not to be workaholics? Does this advice conflict with the other guidelines Bliss lists in this essay? Why or why not?
4. In what parts of the essay does Bliss refer to our personal lives? According to the author, how can we balance our personal and professional lives? How realistic are these ideas?

DISCOVERING RHETORICAL STRATEGIES

1. Bliss introduces each new suggestion for managing time as a command and then fully explains each command. How effective is this approach? What effect would headings beginning with present participles have on the essay (e.g., planning, taking breaks, avoiding clutter)?
2. How does Bliss organize his techniques for managing time? Is this order successful? Explain your answer.
3. What is Bliss's general attitude toward time management? In your opinion, is this an efficient attitude toward the subject?
4. What other rhetorical modes does Bliss use to support this process analysis essay? Give examples of each of these modes.

MAKING CONNECTIONS

1. How would William Ouchi ("Japanese and American Workers: Two Casts of Mind") respond to Bliss's essay? Would he agree or disagree with the author's recommendations and conclusions? Do Bliss's suggestions about time management sound more "Japanese" or "American," according to Ouchi's definition of each society's business practices?
2. Bliss's essay analyzing the process of managing our time and Jessica Mitford's essay ("Behind the Formaldehyde Curtain") analyzing funeral customs both try to persuade us to adopt a certain opinion as they describe a process. Which essay is more convincing to you? Explain your answer in detail.
3. Pretend that you are Edwin Bliss giving advice to young Russell Baker ("The Saturday Evening Post"), who wants to become a good salesperson. Which of Bliss's suggestions should Baker follow most earnestly? Why? Which of these suggestions would be most helpful in your own life?

IDEAS FOR DISCUSSION/WRITING

Preparing to Write

Write freely about various aspects of time management: Do you manage time well from day to day? What benefits can you receive from managing your time better? Can you identify any disadvantages that could result from managing your time better? How can you avoid these problems? Are you a workaholic, or do you strike a good balance between the various aspects of your life? What is the relationship between time management and quality of life?

Choosing a Topic

1. You have been asked by the editor of your campus newspaper to adapt Bliss's suggestions to the life of a student. Write a process analysis essay adjusting Bliss's ten guidelines to a college environment.
2. Interview someone in your class about his or her ability to use time wisely. Use Bliss's guidelines to establish whether the person manages time well. Then, direct a process analysis essay to this person, briefly evaluating his or her time-management skills and then offering suggestions for improvement.
3. At times, Bliss's approach to time management (do all you can in a day) seems to conflict with the fundamental tenets for leading a quality life (relax and enjoy yourself). Do you think these two aspects of life are incompatible, or are there ways to reconcile the two? Write an essay for your classmates detailing a solution to this dilemma.
4. Along with two of your classmates, write a process for using a computer program on the Internet. You can describe how to use email, how to attach a file, or how to create a table in Microsoft Word, for example. You could also describe how to conduct Internet research or create a Power Point presentation. Consider whether your essay will be informative or directive and whether you will use the chronological, simultaneous, or cyclical approach.

Before beginning your essay, you might want to consult the checklists on page 220.

Behind the Formaldehyde Curtain

Once called "Queen of the Muckrakers" in a *Time* magazine review, Jessica Mitford has written scathing exposés of the Famous Writers' School, American funeral directors, television executives, prisons, a "fat farm" for wealthy women, and many other venerable social institutions. She was born in England into the gentry, immigrated to the United States, and later became a naturalized American citizen. After working at a series of jobs, she achieved literary fame at age forty-six with the publication of *The American Way of Death* (1963), which relentlessly shatters the image of funeral directors as "compassionate, reverent family-friends-in-need." Her other major works include *Kind and Unusual Punishment: The Prison Business* (1973); *Poison Penmanship: The Gentle Art of Muckraking* (1979), an anthology of Mitford's articles in the *Atlantic, Harper's*, and other periodicals covering a twenty-two-year time span; two volumes of autobiography, *Daughters and Rebels* (1960) and *A Fine Old Madness* (1977); *Faces of Philip: A Memoir of Philip Toynbee* (1984); *Grace Had an English Heart: The Story of Grace Darling, Heroine and Victorian Superstar* (1988); and *The American Way of Birth* (1992). Superbly skilled in the techniques of investigative reporting, satire, and black humor, Mitford was described in a *Washington Post* article as "an older, more even-tempered, better-read Jane Fonda who has maintained her activism long past middle age."

Preparing to Read

The following essay, taken from *The American Way of Death,* clearly illustrates the ruthless manner in which Mitford exposes the greed and hypocrisy of the American mortuary business.

Exploring Experience: As you prepare to read this article, think for a few minutes about funeral customs in our society: Have you attended a funeral service recently? Which rituals seemed particularly vivid to you? What purpose did these symbolic actions serve? What other interesting customs are you aware of in American society? What purpose do these customs serve? What public images do these customs have? Are these images accurate? Do you generally approve or disapprove of these customs?

Learning Online: In this controversial essay, Jessica Mitford graphically describes the embalming process. Before reading her article, familiarize yourself with some technical mortuary terms by visiting HBO's "Six Feet Under" Web site (http://www. hbo.com/sixfeetunder). Select "Video" from the menu options to view farcical commercials that poke fun at the funeral industry.

The drama begins to unfold with the arrival of the corpse at the mortuary.   1

Alas, poor Yorick! How surprised he would be to see   2
how his counterpart of today is whisked off to a funeral parlor and is in short order sprayed, sliced, pierced, pickled, trussed, trimmed, creamed, waxed, painted, rouged, and neatly dressed—transformed from a common corpse into a Beautiful Memory Picture. This process is known in the trade as embalming and restorative art and is so universally employed in the United States and Canada that the funeral director does it routinely, without consulting corpse or kin. He regards as eccentric those few who are hardy enough to suggest that it might be dispensed with. Yet no law requires embalming, no religious doctrine commends it, nor is it dictated by considerations of health, sanitation, or even of personal daintiness. In no part of the world but in Northern America is it widely used. The purpose of embalming is to make the corpse presentable for viewing in a suitably costly container; and here too the funeral director routinely, without first consulting the family, prepares the body for public display.

Is all this legal? The processes to which a dead body may be   3
subjected are after all to some extent circumscribed by law. In most states, for instance, the signature of next of kin must be obtained before an autopsy may be performed, before the deceased may be cremated, before the body may be turned over to a medical school for research purposes; or such provision must be made in the decedent's will. In the case of embalming, no such permission is required nor is it ever sought. A textbook, *The Principles and Practices of Embalming*, comments on this: "There is some question

regarding the legality of much that is done within the preparation room." The author points out that it would be most unusual for a responsible member of a bereaved family to instruct the mortician, in so many words, to "*embalm*" the body of a deceased relative. The very term "embalming" is so seldom used that the mortician must rely upon custom in the matter. The author concludes that unless the family specifies otherwise, the act of entrusting the body to the care of a funeral establishment carries with it an implied permission to go ahead and embalm.

Embalming is indeed a most extraordinary procedure, and one 4 must wonder at the docility of Americans who each year pay hundreds of millions of dollars for its perpetuation, blissfully ignorant of what it is all about, what is done, how it is done. Not one in ten thousand has any idea of what actually takes place. Books on the subject are extremely hard to come by. They are not to be found in most libraries or bookshops.

In an era when huge television audiences watch surgical opera- 5 tions in the comfort of their living rooms, when, thanks to the animated cartoon, the geography of the digestive system has become familiar territory even to the nursery school set, in a land where the satisfaction of curiosity about almost all matters is a national pastime, the secrecy surrounding embalming can, surely, hardly be attributed to the inherent gruesomeness of the subject. Custom in this regard has within this century suffered a complete reversal. In the early days of American embalming, when it was performed in the home of the deceased, it was almost mandatory for some relative to stay by the embalmer's side and witness the procedure. Today, family members who might wish to be in attendance would certainly be dissuaded by the funeral director. All others, except apprentices, are excluded by law from the preparation room.

A close look at what does actually take place may explain in 6 large measure the undertaker's intractable reticence concerning a procedure that has become his major *raison d'être.* Is it possible he fears that public information about embalming might lead patrons to wonder if they really want this service? If the funeral men are loath to discuss the subject outside the trade, the reader may, understandably, be equally loath to go on reading at this point. For those who have the stomach for it, let us part the formaldehyde curtain. . . .

The body is first laid out in the undertaker's morgue—or   7
rather, Mr. Jones is reposing in the preparation room—to be read-
ied to bid the world farewell.

The preparation room in any of the better funeral establish-   8
ments has the tiled and sterile look of a surgery, and indeed the
embalmer-restorative artist who does his chores there is beginning
to adopt the term "dermasurgeon" (appropriately corrupted by
some mortician-writers as "demisurgeon") to describe his calling.
His equipment, consisting of scalpels, scissors, augers, forceps,
clamps, needles, pumps, tubes, bowls, and basins, is crudely imita-
tive of the surgeon's, as is his technique, acquired in a nine- or
twelve-month post-high-school course in an embalming school.
He is supplied by an advanced chemical industry with a bewilder-
ing array of fluids, sprays, pastes, oils, powders, creams, to fix or
soften tissue, shrink or distend it as needed, dry it here, restore the
moisture there. There are cosmetics, waxes and paints to fill and
cover features, even plaster of Paris to replace entire limbs. There
are ingenious aids to prop and stabilize the cadaver: A Vari-Pose
Head Rest, the Edwards Arm and Hand Positioner, the Repose
Block (to support the shoulders during the embalming), and the
Throop Foot Positioner, which resembles an old-fashioned stocks.

Mr. John H. Eckels, president of the Eckels College of   9
Mortuary Science, thus describes the first part of the embalming
procedure: "In the hands of a skilled practitioner, this work may
be done in a comparatively short time and without mutilating the
body other than by slight incision—so slight that it scarcely would
cause serious inconvenience if made upon a living person. It is
necessary to remove the blood, and doing this not only helps in
the disinfecting, but removes the principal cause of disfigurements
due to discoloration."

Another textbook discusses the all-important time element: 10
"The earlier this is done, the better, for every hour that elapses
between death and embalming will add to the problems and com-
plications encountered. . . ." Just how soon should one get going
on the embalming? The author tells us, "On the basis of such scanty
information made available to this profession through its rudimentary and haphazard system of technical research, we must conclude
that the best results are to be obtained if the subject is embalmed
before life is completely extinct—that is, before cellular death has
occurred. In the average case, this would mean within an hour after

somatic death." For those who feel that there is something a little rudimentary, not to say haphazard, about this advice, a comforting thought is offered by another writer. Speaking of fears entertained in early days of premature burial, he points out, "One of the effects of embalming by chemical injection, however, has been to dispel fears of live burial." How true; once the blood is removed, chances of live burial are indeed remote.

To return to Mr. Jones, the blood is drained out through the veins and replaced by embalming fluid pumped in through the arteries. As noted in *The Principles and Practices of Embalming,* "every operator has a favorite injection and drainage point—a fact which becomes a handicap only if he fails or refuses to forsake his favorites when conditions demand it." Typical favorites are the carotid artery, femoral artery, jugular vein, subclavian vein. There are various choices of embalming fluid. If Flextone is used, it will produce a "mild, flexible rigidity. The skin retains a velvety softness, the tissues are rubbery and pliable. Ideal for women and children." It may be blended with B. and G. Products Company's Lyf-Lyk tint, which is guaranteed to reproduce "nature's own skin texture . . . the velvety appearance of living tissue." Suntone comes in three separate tints: Suntan; Special Cosmetic Tint, a pink shade "especially indicated for young female subjects"; and Regular Cosmetic Tint, moderately pink.

About three to six gallons of a dyed and perfumed solution of formaldehyde, glycerin, borax, phenol, alcohol, and water is soon circulating through Mr. Jones, whose mouth has been sewn together with a "needle directed upward between the upper lip and gum and brought out through the left nostril," with the corners raised slightly "for a more pleasant expression." If he should be bucktoothed, his teeth are cleaned with Bon Ami and coated with colorless nail polish. His eyes, meanwhile, are closed with flesh-tinted eye caps and eye cement.

The next step is to have at Mr. Jones with a thing called a trocar. This is a long, hollow needle attached to a tube. It is jabbed into the abdomen, poked around the entrails and chest cavity, the contents of which are pumped out and replaced with "cavity fluid." This done, and the hole in the abdomen sewn up, Mr. Jones's face is heavily creamed (to protect the skin from burns which may be caused by leakage of the chemicals), and he is covered with a sheet and left unmolested for a while. But not for long—there is more, much more, in store for him. He has been embalmed, but not yet restored, and the best time to start the restorative work is eight to ten hours after embalming, when the tissues have become firm and dry.

The object of all this attention to the corpse, it must be remem-   14
bered, is to make it presentable for viewing in an attitude of healthy repose. "Our customs require the presentation of our dead in the semblance of normality . . . unmarred by the ravages of illness, disease, or mutilation," says Mr. J. Sheridan Mayer in his *Restorative Art.* This is rather a large order since few people die in the full bloom of health, unravaged by illness and unmarked by some disfigurement. The funeral industry is equal to the challenge: "In some cases the gruesome appearance of a mutilated or disease-ridden subject may be quite discouraging. The task of restoration may seem impossible and shake the confidence of the embalmer. This is the time for intestinal fortitude and determination. Once the formative work is begun and affected tissues are cleaned or removed, all doubts of success vanish. It is surprising and gratifying to discover the results which may be obtained."

The embalmer, having allowed an appropriate interval to   15
elapse, returns to the attack, but now he brings into play the skill and equipment of sculptor and cosmetician. Is a hand missing? Casting one in plaster of Paris is a simple matter. "For replacement purposes, only a cast of the back of the hand is necessary; this is within the ability of the average operator and is quite adequate." If a lip or two, a nose or an ear should be missing, the embalmer has at hand a variety of restorative waxes with which to model replacements. Pores and skin texture are simulated by stippling with a little brush, and over this cosmetics are laid on. Head off? Decapitation cases are rather routinely handled. Ragged edges are trimmed, and head joined to torso with a series of splints, wires, and sutures. It is a good idea to have a little something at the neck—a scarf or a high collar—when time for viewing comes. Swollen mouth: Cut out tissue as needed from inside the lips. If too much is removed, the surface contour can easily be restored by padding with cotton. Swollen necks and cheeks are reduced by removing tissue through vertical incisions made down each side of the neck. "When the deceased is casketed, the pillow will hide the suture incisions. . . . As an extra precaution against leakage, the suture may be painted with liquid sealer."

The opposite condition is more likely to present itself—that of   16
emaciation. His hypodermic syringe now loaded with massage
cream, the embalmer seeks out and fills the hollowed and sunken
areas by injection. In this procedure the backs of the hands and fingers and the under-chin area should not be neglected.

Positioning the lips is a problem that recurrently challenges the   17
ingenuity of the embalmer. Closed too tightly, they tend to give a
stern, even disapproving expression. Ideally, embalmers feel, the
lips should give the impression of being ever so slightly parted, the
upper lip protruding slightly for a more youthful appearance. This
takes some engineering, however, as the lips tend to drift apart.
Lip drift can sometimes be remedied by pushing one or two
straight pins through the inner margin of the lower lip and then
inserting them between the two front upper teeth. If Mr. Jones
happens to have no teeth, the pins can just as easily be anchored
in his Armstrong Face Former and Denture Replacer. Another
method to maintain lip closure is to dislocate the lower jaw, which
is then held in its new position by a wire run through holes which
have been drilled through the upper and lower jaws at the mid-
line. As the French are fond of saying, *il faut souffrir pour être belle.*

If Mr. Jones had died of jaundice, the embalming fluid will very   18
likely turn him green. Does this deter the embalmer? Not if he has
intestinal fortitude. Masking pastes and cosmetics are heavily laid
on, burial garments and casket interiors are color-correlated with
particular care, and Jones is displayed beneath rose-colored lights.
Friends will say "How *well* he looks." Death by carbon monoxide,
on the other hand, can be rather a good thing from the embalmer's
viewpoint: "One advantage is the fact that this type of discoloration is an exaggerated form of a natural pink coloration." This
is nice because the healthy glow is already present and needs but
little attention.

The patching and filling completed, Mr. Jones is now shaved,   19
washed, and dressed. Cream-based cosmetic, available in pink,
flesh, suntan, brunette, and blond, is applied to his hands and face,
his hair is shampooed and combed (and, in the case of Mrs. Jones,
set), his hands manicured. For the horny-handed son of toil special care must be taken; cream should be applied to remove
ingrained grime, and the nails cleaned. "If he were not in the habit
of having them manicured in life, trimming and shaping is advised
for appearance—never questioned by kin."

Jones is now ready for casketing (this is the present participle of   20
the verb "to casket"). In this operation his right shoulder should
be depressed slightly "to turn the body a bit to the right and soften
the appearance of lying flat on the back." Positioning the hands is
a matter of importance, and special rubber positioning blocks may
be used. The hands should be cupped slightly for a more lifelike,
relaxed appearance. Proper placement of the body requires a delicate sense of balance. It should lie as high as possible in the casket,
yet not so high that the lid, when lowered, will hit the nose. On
the other hand, we are cautioned, placing the body too low "creates the impression that the body is in a box."

Jones is next wheeled into the appointed slumber room where a   21
few last touches may be added—his favorite pipe placed in his hand
or, if he was a great reader, a book propped into position. (In the
case of little Master Jones a Teddy bear may be clutched.) Here he
will hold open house for a few days, visiting hours 10 A.M. to 9 P.M.

All now being in readiness, the funeral director calls a staff con-   22
ference to make sure that each assistant knows his precise duties.
Mr. Wilber Kriege writes "This makes your staff feel that they are
a part of the team, with a definite assignment that must be properly carried out if the whole plan is to succeed. You never heard
of a football coach who failed to talk to his entire team before they
go on the field. They have drilled on the plays they are to execute
for hours and days, and yet the successful coach knows the importance of making even the bench-warming third-string substitute
feel that he is important if the game is to be won." The winning
of *this* game is predicated upon glass-smooth handling of the logistics. The funeral director has notified the pallbearers whose names
were furnished by the family, has arranged for the presence of
clergyman, organist, and soloist, has provided transportation for
everybody, has organized and listed the flowers sent by friends. In
Psychology of Funeral Service, Mr. Edward A. Martin points out:
"He may not always do as much as the family thinks he is doing,
but it is his helpful guidance that they appreciate in knowing they
are proceeding as they should. . . . The important thing is how
well his services can be used to make the family believe they are
giving unlimited expression to their own sentiment."

The religious service may be held in a church or in the chapel   23
of the funeral home; the funeral director vastly prefers the latter
arrangement, for not only is it more convenient for him but it

affords him the opportunity to show off his beautiful facilities to the gathered mourners. After the clergyman has had his say, the mourners queue up to file past the casket for a last look at the deceased. The family is *never* asked whether they want an open-casket ceremony; in the absence of their instruction to the contrary, this is taken for granted. Consequently, well over 90 percent of all American funerals feature the open casket—a custom unknown in other parts of the world. Foreigners are astonished by it. An English woman living in San Francisco described her reaction in a letter to the writer:

> I myself have attended only one funeral here—that of an elderly fellow worker of mine. After the service I could not understand why everyone was walking towards the coffin (sorry, I mean casket), but thought I had better follow the crowd. It shook me rigid to get there and find the casket open and poor old Oscar lying there in his brown tweed suit, wearing a suntan makeup and just the wrong shade of lipstick. If I had not been extremely fond of the old boy, I have a horrible feeling that I might have giggled. Then and there I decided that I could never face another American funeral—even dead.

The casket (which has been resting throughout the service on a   24
Classic Beauty Ultra Metal Casket Bier) is now transferred by a hydraulically operated device called Porto-Lift to a balloon-tired, Glide Easy casket carriage which will wheel it to yet another conveyance, the Cadillac Funeral Coach. This may be lavender, cream, light green—anything but black. Interiors, of course, are color-correlated, "for the man who cannot stop short of perfection."

At graveside, the casket is lowered into the earth. This office,   25
once the prerogative of friends of the deceased, is now performed by a patented mechanical lowering device. A "Life-time Green" artificial grass mat is at the ready to conceal the sere earth, and overhead, to conceal the sky, is a portable Steril Chapel Tent ("resists the intense heat and humidity of summer and the terrific storms of winter . . . available in Silver Grey, Rose, or Evergreen"). Now is the time for the ritual scattering of earth over the coffin, as the solemn words "earth to earth, ashes to ashes, dust to dust" are pronounced by the officiating cleric. This can today be accomplished "with a mere flick of the wrist with the Gordon Leak-Proof Earth Dispenser. No grasping of a handful of dirt, no soiled fingers. Simple, dignified, beautiful, reverent! The modern way!" The Golden Earth Dispenser (at $5) is of nickel-plated brass

construction. It is not only "attractive to the eye and long wearing"; it is also "one of the 'tools' for building better public relations" if presented as "an appropriate non-commercial gift" to the clergyman. It is shaped something like a saltshaker.

Untouched by human hand, the coffin and the earth are now   26
united.

It is in the function of directing the participants through the   27
maze of gadgetry that the funeral director has assigned to himself his relatively new role of "grief therapist." He has relieved the family of every detail, he has revamped the corpse to look like a living doll, he has arranged for it to nap for a few days in a slumber room, he has put on a well-oiled performance in which the concept of *death* has played no part whatsoever—unless it was inconsiderately mentioned by the clergyman who conducted the religious service. He has done everything in his power to make the funeral a real pleasure for everybody concerned. He and his team have given their all to score an upset victory over death.

UNDERSTANDING DETAILS

1. List the major steps of the embalming process that the author reveals in this essay.
2. Why, according to Mitford, do funeral directors not want to make public the details of embalming? To what extent do you think their desire for secrecy is warranted?
3. Why isn't the permission of a family member needed for embalming? From Mitford's perspective, what does this custom reveal about Americans?
4. In what ways has embalming become the undertaker's *raison d'être*? How do American funeral customs encourage this procedure?

ANALYZING MEANING

1. What is Mitford's primary purpose in this essay? Why do you think she has analyzed this particular process in such detail?
2. Explain the title of this essay.
3. Do you think the author knows how gruesome her essay is? How can you tell? What makes the essay so horrifying? How does such close attention to macabre detail help Mitford accomplish her purpose?

4. What does Mitford mean when she argues that the funeral director and his team "have given their all to score an upset victory over death" (paragraph 27)? Who or what is "the team"? Why does Mitford believe death plays no part in American burial customs?

DISCOVERING RHETORICAL STRATEGIES

1. Why does Mitford begin her essay with a one-sentence paragraph? Is it effective? Why or why not?
2. A euphemism is a deceptively pleasant term used in place of a straightforward, less pleasant one. In what way is "Beautiful Memory Picture" (paragraph 2) a euphemism? How are we reminded of this phrase throughout the essay? What other euphemisms can you find in this selection?
3. What tone does Mitford establish in the essay? What is her reason for creating this particular tone? What is your reaction to it?
4. What other rhetorical strategies does Mitford use besides gruesome examples and illustrations to make her point? Give examples of each of these different strategies.

MAKING CONNECTIONS

1. Imagine that Stephen King ("Why We Crave Horror Movies") has just read Mitford's essay on funeral customs. According to King, what would be the source of our fascination with these macabre practices? Why do essays like Mitford's both intrigue and repulse us at the same time?
2. Compare and contrast Mitford's use of examples with those used by Harold Krents ("Darkness at Noon") or Amy Tan ("Mother Tongue"). How often does each author use examples? What is the relationship between the frequency of examples in each essay and the extent to which you are convinced by the author's argument?
3. In this essay, Mitford lifts the curtain on certain bizarre funeral practices in much the same way that Judith Wallerstein and Sandra Blakeslee expose the trauma of divorce ("Second Chances for Children of Divorce"), Jay Weiner ("Sports Centered") uncover corporate greed in athletics, and Barbara Ehrenreich discloses the pleasures of combat ("The Ecstasy of

War"). Which of these "exposés" seems most complete and devastating to you? Explain your answer.

IDEAS FOR DISCUSSION/WRITING

Preparing to Write

Write freely about a particularly interesting custom in America or in another country: Why does this custom exist? What role does it play in the society? What value does it have? What are the details of this custom? In what way is this custom a part of your life? Your family's life? What purpose does it serve for you? Is it worth continuing? Why or why not?

Choosing a Topic

1. In a process analysis essay directed to your classmates, explain a custom you do not approve of. Decide on your tone and purpose before you begin to write.
2. In a process analysis essay directed to your classmates, explain a custom you approve of. Select a specific tone and purpose before you begin to write.
3. You have been asked to address a group of students at a college of mortuary science. In this role, you have an opportunity to influence the opinion of these students concerning the practice of embalming. Write a well-reasoned lecture to this group arguing either for or against the process of embalming.
4. Not all process descriptions are as explicit as Mitford's article. Why do you think she felt it was necessary to provide such disturbing descriptions in her process analysis? Consider a task you find unpleasant. How can you connect this unpleasant task with an important issue? For example, perhaps you dislike writing papers for class assignments. Perhaps you could connect the unpleasant task of writing papers with the actual volume of paper you use and/or throw away. This could lead to a paper about either tree conservation or the need to recycle in order to avoid negatively affecting landfills. Write a process analysis with a purpose. Using Mitford's style as a guideline, incorporate relevant issues into your process analysis and offer specific solutions.

Before beginning your essay, you might want to consult the checklists on page 220.

JAY WEINER   (1954–   )

Sports Centered

A sports writer for the *Minneapolis Star Tribune,* Jay Weiner was born in Philadelphia and educated at Temple University, where he earned an interdisciplinary degree in Sports Studies. He has been a sports journalist for the past twenty-five years, specializing in off-the-field articles that relate to business and social issues. His most recent book, *Stadium Games: Fifty Years of Big League Greed and Bush League Boondoggles* (2000), is an analysis of professional sports facilities in Minnesota. He has, in addition, published articles on sports in the *New York Times, Business Week, TV Guide, Newsweek.com,* the *Utne Reader,* and many other newspapers and periodicals, and he is a frequent contributor to Minnesota Public Radio on the topic of athletics. In his spare time, he runs, rides a bicycle, and admits to watching "a lot of ESPN." His advice to students using *The Prose Reader* is to "read and write a great deal." Although "the very best writers seem to have God-given talents, the rest of us can steadily improve the way we write through constant practice." He counsels students who want to go into journalism to "read as many newspapers each day as you can, which will help you learn your craft."

Preparing to Read

The following essay from the *Utne Reader* discusses ways to bridge the gap that the author believes has developed between sports and the public. He reminisces about sports heroes and suggests some new approaches to professional sports in the future.

Exploring Experience: As you prepare to read this article, pause for a moment to consider your own interest in sports: Do you participate in any sports? If so, which ones? Do you like athletics? Why or why not? What role do sports play in American society? Why do you think they have become such a big business in this country? Have you gotten more or less involved in spectator sports over the past few years? What is the primary reason for this change?

Learning Online: Choose the name of a famous athlete who still actively competes in his or her sport. Conduct an Internet search on the athlete's name. What types of links appear? Do the Web sites bearing the name of your chosen athlete focus on athletic ability and recent performance, or do the sites concentrate more on physical appearance, advertising, or social gossip? Consider your findings while reading Weiner's article.

---

ow far back must we go to remember that sports matter? How deeply into our personal and national pasts must we travel to recall that we once cared?   1

Do we have to return to 1936? Adolf Hitler tried to make the Olympics into a propaganda machine for anti-Semitism and racism. In that case, American track star Jesse Owens, demonstrating that the master race could be mastered at racing, stole Hitler's ideological show. Were not sports a vehicle of significant political substance then?   2

Or should we return to 1947 and Jackie Robinson? A baseball player integrated our "national pastime" a year before the U.S. Army considered African Americans equal. Robinson's barrier-break may have been largely based on ticket-selling economics for the Brooklyn Dodgers' owners, but didn't sports do something good?   3

Their fists raised, their dignity palpable, track stars Tommie Smith and John Carlos spread the American black power and student protest movements to the world when they stood on the victory stand at the 1968 Olympics in Mexico City. Politics and sports mixed beautifully then.   4

Remember when tennis feminist Billie Jean King took on an old fart named Bobby Riggs in 1973, boldly bringing the women's movement to the playing fields? That moment of sports theater stirred up sexual politics as much as any Betty Friedan essay or Miss America bra burning could ever do.   5

Sports had meaning. And sports were accessible.   6

Remember when your grandfather or your uncle—maybe your mother—took you to a game when you were a little kid? The hot dog was the best. The crowd was mesmerizing. The colors were bright. The crack of the bat under the summer sun or the autumn chill wrapped around that touchdown run was unforgettable. Back then, some nobody became your favorite player, somebody named Johnny Callison or Hal Greer or Clarence Peaks or Vic   7

Hadfield, someone who sold cars in the off-season and once signed autographs for your father's men's club for a $50 appearance fee. Those "heroes" were working-class stiffs, just like us.

Now you read the sports pages—or, more exactly, the business 8 and crime pages—and you realize you've disconnected from the institution and it from you. Sports is distant. It reeks of greed. Its politics glorify not the majestic drama of pure competition, but a drunken, gambling masculinity epitomized by sports-talk radio, a venue for obnoxious boys on car phones.

How can we reconcile our detachment from corporatized pro 9 sports, professionalized college sports—even out-of-control kids' sports—with our appreciation for athleticism, with our memories? And how, after we sort it all out, can we take sports back?

Part of the problem is that we want sports to be mythological 10 when, in our hearts, we know they aren't. So reclaiming sports requires that we come to grips with our own role in the myth-making. Owens, Robinson, Smith, Carlos, and King played to our highest ideals and so have been enshrined in our sports pantheon. But we've also made heroes of some whose legacies are much less clear-cut. Take Joe Namath, the 1960s quarterback who represented sexual freedom, or Bill Walton, the 1970s basketball hippie who symbolized the alienated white suburban Grateful Dead sports antihero. Neither deserves the reverence accorded Owens or Robinson or even King, but both captured the essence of their era. Or how about relief pitcher Steve Howe, who symbolized the evils of drug addiction in the '80s, or Mike Tyson, who currently plays the archetypal angry black male? No less than Tommie Smith and John Carlos, these anti-icons were emblematic of their age.

It may be discomfiting, but it's true: The power of sports and 11 sports heroes to mirror our own aspirations have also contributed to the sorry state of the institution today. The women's sports movement Billie Jean King helped create proved a great leap forward for female athletes, but it also created a generation of fitness *consumers,* whose appetite for Nikes and Reeboks created a new generation of Asian sweatshops.

Fans applauded the courage of renegade Curt Flood, the St. 12 Louis Cardinals outfielder who in 1969 refused to be traded, arguing that baseball players should be free to play where they want to play. We cheered—all the way to the Supreme Court—his challenge to the cigar-smoking owners' hold on their pinstripeknickered chattel. Now players can sell their services to the highest bidder, but their astronomical salaries—deserved or not—alienate us from the games as much as the owners' greed.

The greed isn't new, of course. The corporate betrayal of the   13
fan is as traditional as the seventh-inning stretch. The Boston Braves moved to Milwaukee in 1953, and the Dodgers and New York Giants fled to California in 1958, for money, subsidized facilities, and better TV contracts. But what has always been a regrettable by-product of sports has suddenly become its dominant ethos. Our worship of sports and our worship of the buck have now become one and the same. So it shouldn't surprise us that we get the heroes we expect—and maybe deserve.

So how do we as a society reclaim sports from the corporate   14
entertainment behemoth that now controls it? Some modest proposals:

- **Deprofessionalize college and high school sports.**   15

Let's ban college athletic scholarships in favor of financial aid based on need, as for any other student. And let's keep high school athletics in perspective. Why should local news coverage of high school sports exceed coverage given to the band, debating society, or science fair? Sports stars are introduced to the culture of athletic privilege at a very young age.

- **Allow some form of public ownership of professional**   16
  sports teams.

Leagues and owners ask us to pay for the depreciating asset of a stadium but give us no share of the appreciating asset of a franchise. Lease agreements between teams and publicly financed stadiums should also include enforceable community-involvement clauses.

- **Make sports affordable again.**   17

Sports owners call their games "family entertainment." For whose family? Bill Gates'? Owners whose teams get corporate subsidies should set aside 20 percent of their tickets at prices no higher than a movie admission. And, like any other business feeding at the public trough, they should be required to pay livable wages even to the average schmoes who sell hot dogs.

- **Be conscious of the messages sport is sending.**   18

Alcohol-related advertising should be banned from sports broadcasting. Any male athlete convicted of assaulting a woman should be banned from college and pro sports. Fighting in a sports event should be at least a misdemeanor and maybe a felony, rather than a five-minute stay in the penalty box.

Let's take the sports establishment by its lapels and shake it back   19
toward us. Because even with all the maddening messages of male dominance, black servility, homophobia, corporate power, commercialism, and brawn over brains, sports still play an important role in many lives. When we watch a game, we are surrounded by friends and family. There are snacks and beverages. We sit in awe of the players' remarkable skills. We can't do what they do. They extend our youth. The tension of the competition is legitimate. The drama is high.

And therein lies the essence of modern American sport. It's a   20
good show, albeit bread and circuses. And we just can't give it up. So why not take it back for ourselves as best we can, looking for ways to humanize an institution that mirrors our culture, understanding that those who own sport won't give it up without a fight, knowing that we like it too much to ever just walk away.

UNDERSTANDING DETAILS

1. In what ways do sports reflect our culture? Explain your answer in detail.
2. Why does Weiner think sports have drifted away from the American public?
3. According to Weiner, how can we "take sports back"? Summarize the author's suggestions.
4. What does the author believe is the main purpose of modern American sports?

ANALYZING MEANING

1. What is the principal purpose of this essay? To what extent do you think it accomplishes its goals? Explain your answer.

2. Why do you think Weiner says we want to mythologize our love of sports?

3. How have "our worship of sports and our worship of the buck . . . become one and the same" (paragraph 12)? Explain your answer.

4. What does Weiner mean when he says, "The corporate betrayal of the fan is as traditional as the seventh inning stretch" (paragraph 12)?

DISCOVERING RHETORICAL STRATEGIES

1. How does Weiner organize the ideas in his essay? Why does he choose this particular order? Is it effective in achieving his purpose? Why or why not?

2. Describe in detail Weiner's intended audience. How did you come to this conclusion?

3. Analyze Weiner's use of examples throughout this essay. How does he raise our awareness regarding the relationship between sports and culture?

4. Weiner uses examples to set up his essay. What other rhetorical strategies does he use to make his point about sports? Give an example of each of these strategies.

MAKING CONNECTIONS

1. Imagine that Jay Weiner, Gloria Steinem ("The Politics of Muscle"), and Robert Heilbroner ("Don't Let Stereotypes Warp Your Judgment") were having a discussion about the role of sports in America. To what extent would each say that stereotypes about male athletic figures help contribute to the moral and ethical decay of our country?

2. What advice would Julia Bourland ("Getting Out of Debt (and Staying Out)") give to Weiner about coping with the corporate takeover of American professional sports?

3. Compare and contrast the growing inaccessibility of professional sports decried in Weiner's article with the loss of our wilderness areas in John McPhee's "The Pines," the loss of cultural heritage in Richard Rodriguez's "The Fear of Losing a Culture," and the loss of control over our country's borders debated by Michael Scott's and Richard Rayner's opposing-viewpoints articles on immigration controls. Which "loss" will

be most detrimental to the United States in the long run? Why do you think this is so?

IDEAS FOR DISCUSSION/WRITING

Preparing to Write

Write freely about your impressions of sports today: Do you enjoy participating in sports? Do you like watching sports? What specific pleasures do you derive from watching or participating in sports? What role do sports play in American society? How did they get so much influence over our lives? Are sports mostly a positive or negative influence on our younger generation?

Choosing a Topic

1. One of your friends who is still in high school has asked you for information about social activities in college. Write to this friend, using process analysis to explain how to survive college while having a life full of outside activities. Decide on a purpose and a point of view before you begin to write.

2. Greed is evident throughout American society. Where else, in addition to sports, do you see examples of greed? How does greed become the motivating force behind an organization? Write an essay suggesting how a company or organization can avoid greed and still remain focused and successful.

3. Take one of Weiner's suggestions and develop it into an essay explaining how to accomplish this particular recommendation. Flesh out the essay with as many details as possible.

4. Weiner uses process analysis to suggest a method through which society can "reclaim sports from the corporate entertainment behemoth that now controls it" (paragraph 13). Using the information you gained from an Internet search on a famous athlete, write a process analysis outlining the athlete's rise to fame. How did your chosen athlete rise from the ranks of amateur to professional? Use your process description to either support or refute Weiner's claims. Did your athlete benefit from athletic scholarships, competitive salaries, and/or prize money? Do you feel that similar athletes will excel in the future if Weiner's recommendations are adopted?

Before beginning your essay, you might want to consult the checklists on page 220.

LINDA FORMICHELLI   (1969–   )

Engage in Word Play

Linda Formichelli was born in Poughkeepsie, New York, and educated at SUNY Albany, where she earned a B.A. in Russian language in 1991, and at UC Berkeley, from which she graduated in 1995 with an M.A. in Slavic Linguistics. After working in retail sales for several years "wandering from mall job to mall job," she served as a marketing assistant in San Francisco and Utrecht, the Netherlands, for five years before making the leap to full-time freelance writing. Since that time, she has written articles for more than one hundred magazines, including *Woman's Day, Men's Fitness, Family Circle, Psychology Today, Wired, Writer's Digest,* and many other popular journals. Her first book, *The Renegade Writer: A Totally Unconventional Guide to Freelance Writing Success* (co-authored with Diana Burrell), was published by Marion Street Press in 2003. Her hobbies include Okinawan Kenpo Karate, to which she has been "frantically devoted" since 2001. She and her husband, who is also a freelance magazine writer, recently founded BadAds.org, a popular Web site that tracks intrusive advertising. Her advice to aspiring writers is "not to let rejection get you down." "So many writers," she claims, "are paralyzed by rejection that it keeps them from getting their work out the door. It took me three years and dozens of rejections before I was able to break into newsstand magazines like *Family Circle* and *Woman's Day.*"

Preparing to Read

Taken from *Writer's Digest* (February 2003), the following essay addresses the advantages and disadvantages of living our lives according to a routine. Keeping your life on schedule but also being creative in your job can be a difficult mission.

Exploring Experience: Before reading this essay, think for a few minutes about your own daily schedule: Is your routine each day stimulating or boring? Do you ever get into a rut? Do these ruts sometimes serve a purpose in your life? In what ways? How do they affect your school work? How do they affect your study habits? What suggestions do you have for getting out of a rut?

Learning Online: All writers must face the blank page. Visit the *Writer's Digest* Web site (http://www.writersdigest.com), and click on the "Write Better" or "Get Creative" tab. Look for helpful tips for overcoming writer's block. Do you find this Web site helpful? Compare the ways in which the Web designers and writers present their information.

The business article came out great, but I was stuck for an ending. Finally, I hit upon the conclusion: "Follow these tips and boost your bottom line." Perfect! Snappy, fun, alliterative, Just one problem—I had used that same phrase to end my last five business articles. 1

My sense of wordplay wasn't the only thing stuck in a rut—even my article ideas were getting frayed from overuse. I was querying the same business and career ideas over and over: how to succeed at a trade show, how to find a job online, how to market on a budget. My ideas for health and women's magazines were getting pretty stale, too: 10 Ways to Do X, 15 Reasons to Do Y. I'd written on those topics so many times that I could do them without cracking a book or even revving up my modem. Heck, I realized, I could pound out one of those articles using only 10 percent of my brain capacity, while the other 90 percent was busy watching *Iron Chef*. 2

Not that reusing ideas is inherently bad. As a professional writer for the last five years, I've come to realize that it's wise, economically, to make the most bucks from the fewest ideas. And because I've developed a few specialties in the writing world—business, career, women's interest and health—it's a good thing to be able to whip out articles on trade shows or fad diets or timesaving cleaning tips with minimum brainpower. 3

But what's good for the pocket-book isn't necessarily good for the soul. When I'm churning out my fourth article on how to ace a job interview, freelancing starts to feel less like an adventure and more like a tedious 9-to-5 job. The freedom of having a five-second commute to my office at 11 a.m. is overshadowed by the drudgery of interviewing the same people, asking the same questions, writing the same words. And my writing suffers when I fall into the groove of starting every article with an anecdote, ending every article with a cliché and lacing every article with alliterative subheads. 4

Hoping to leap out of my writer's rut, I started checking around   5
for advice. And talk about overused ideas—every article on the
topic advises the writer to "Take a walk" or "Brush your teeth
with your non-dominant hand" (a sure recipe for cavities, not creativity). These musty tips just weren't doing it for me, so I had to
discover my own ways of keeping my writing from becoming as
stale as yesterday's bagels.

Play Games with Words

Two other writers and I came up with a game to rev up the   6
idea-generating process. One of us would throw out a word, then
we'd all try to think up ideas related to that word. "Green," Diana
challenged at our last session. "An inside look at how money is
made," Eric offered. "Tips from golf course owners on how to
care for your lawn," I suggested. "How to deal with friends who
are green with envy over your successes," said Diana.

The word "tea" inspired ideas such as 10 things to do with tea   7
(antique linens, add shine to dark hair), how to brew the perfect
pot, and a look at teapots and the people who collect them.

Read Outside the Box

Another way I break out of writing ruts is to check out maga-   8
zines that I don't usually read. Browsing through *Aeronautics
Monthly* or *Modern Ferret* not only helps me find fresh ideas that I
can reslant for other markets, it introduces me to a whole new
world of writers and writing styles. And I can do this anytime I
want, gratis, by going to my local bookstore/cafe, gathering arm-
loads of magazines from sections I rarely peruse and reading them
over a cup of java.

Take on a New Pursuit

I'm a freelance writer. That means I get up at 11, sit in front of   9
a computer all day and spend my spare time in bookstores and
cafes with other writers who get up at 11 and sit in front of computers all day. The problem is, a humdrum life leads to humdrum
writing.

So one day, I surprised myself—and gave my writing a shot of   10
adrenaline—by signing up for karate classes. Soon I was spending

four evenings a week kicking, punching and yelling, which is pretty much the opposite of researching, interviewing, and stringing nouns and verbs. What a wake-up call! I've met kindergarten teachers, sound system engineers and people who work with gibbons at the zoo—all with fascinating stories to tell. And one of the most blessed benefits is having four hours per week when I'm too absorbed in something to worry about deadlines.

On top of all that, my new diversion got the idea wheels churning, and I ended up selling an article on the benefits of martial arts to a women's fitness mag.   11

For me karate was the answer, but for other writers it may be bowling, in-line skating, the local softball league—anything that gets the heart pumping and the mind off writing. Or, come to think of it, any class, from flower arranging to American history, can shake up a writer's life.   12

Take Time Off

Sometimes you have to empty your mind of all the junk that's bouncing around to make room for new, fresh ideas—and what better way than to take a break? Last year, I was hit with a writer's block the size of Montana; everything I wrote was stale, boring, lame. So I cleared a couple of days on my schedule, packed my bags, and headed to New Hampshire for some R&R at a B&B. Soaking in a hot tub and drinking port in front of a roaring fire certainly helped me forget about writing for a little while—and when I got back to the office, my writing once again had that spark of originality.   13

Taking a break doesn't always require a lot of free time and cash. Even one day of reading on the couch instead of staring frustrated at a computer screen can bring an infusion of creativity. I used to work through the weekends in a fit of Type A pique but realized I can face Mondays with much more creative energy if I give myself the weekend to read, explore the town, and hang out with my friends.   14

Enjoy It All

If I let writing turn into a burden-some, repetitive task, I pay for it in stilted prose. That's why the tactics I use to climb out of a writing rut—playing games, doing karate, reading, taking time   15 off—are all about having fun. A relaxed mind is an open mind, and an open mind is prepared to accept new and creative ideas. So above all other writing tips, I remind myself to enjoy the craft—no matter what.

I'm tempted to tell you that these tips will "boost your bottom line"—so that's my cue to stop writing and call a friend for a few laughs.   16

UNDERSTANDING DETAILS

1. What is the main idea in this essay?
2. Formichelli says that her writing tends to get "stuck in a rut" (paragraph 2) occasionally. Why is getting out of a rut important to her?
3. What advice does the author have for escaping her "writer's rut" (paragraph 5)? Summarize each of her suggestions.
4. What does the author mean when she says, "A relaxed mind is an open mind, and an open mind is prepared to accept new and creative ideas" (paragraph 15)? Explain your answer in detail.

ANALYZING MEANING

1. Which of Formichelli's suggestions could you use in your own writing? Explain your answer.
2. How could you apply Formichelli's suggestions to other aspects of your life?
3. To what extent do you identify with the author of this essay? Explain your answer.
4. Do you agree with Formichelli that "having fun" (paragraph 15) in our chosen profession is important to our success?

DISCOVERING RHETORICAL STRATEGIES

1. Who do you think is Formichelli's primary audience? On what information do you base your answer?
2. How does the author organize her ideas in this essay? Is this order effective? Why or why not?
3. Formichelli refers to her "bottom line" phrase at the beginning and the end of her essay. How effective is this reference?
4. Explain the title of this essay.

MAKING CONNECTIONS

1. Imagine that Linda Formichelli, Russell Baker ("The Saturday Evening Post"), Sandra Cisneros ("Only daughter"), Amy Tan ("Mother Tongue"), and Rita Mae Brown ("Writing as a Moral Act") were having a round-table discussion about the top ten qualities every good writer must have to be successful. Which particular qualities would each author argue for? Would your own top ten be the same as those suggested by these writers? Why or why not?

2. If Formichelli ranked essays in *The Prose Reader* on the basis of which were written in the most "lively" manner, which three or four would be her favorites? Would you agree or disagree with these choices? Why?

3. If Formichelli, who is a martial arts enthusiast, and Gloria Steinem ("The Politics of Muscle") were discussing women and sports, would they agree or disagree? Why? What is your own opinion about female athletes?

IDEAS FOR DISCUSSION/WRITING

Preparing to Write

Write freely about your daily schedule: Do you occasionally get into a "rut"? How does this rut affect your energy and motivation? Do you think getting out of ruts is important? Or should we just let them run their course? How do you escape your own ruts? Explain your answer.

Choosing a Topic

1. A popular magazine has asked you to describe the details of a good routine for a college student. For the magazine, write a process analysis essay explaining your formula for an effective and efficient daily routine. The explanation should be aimed at people who are interested in going to college. Gather any information you need before you begin to write.

2. In order to get a laugh, explain a funny example of a rut you have been in. What did you learn from this experience.

3. Prepare for your English class a two- or three-minute talk on one of the following topics:

How to Get into a Rut
How to Get out of a Rut
How to Study for a Test
How to Manage Your Time as a Student
How to Survive the College Experience

4. Do you have a creative solution for approaching a boring task? Using Formichelli's narrative style, write a procedure for your creative way to make a stale or repetitive task fulfilling. Check out www.about.com or www.ehow.com for ideas.

Before beginning your essay, you might want to consult the checklists on page 220.

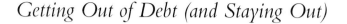

JULIA BOURLAND   (1970–   )

Getting Out of Debt (and Staying Out)

Born and raised in Dallas, Texas, Julia Bourland moved to California in 1989, where she graduated from Mills College with a B.A. in Political Science. A full-time writer, she is the author of two extremely popular books—*The Go-Girl Guide: Surviving Your 20's with Savvy, Soul, and Style* (2000) and *Hitched: The Go-Girl Guide to the First Year of Marriage* (2003)—along with numerous articles in such periodicals as *Bride's Magazine, Shape, 7 × 7, Parenting,* and many others. Her past positions include senior producer of the Relationships Channel at *Women.com* and associate editor of *Parenting* magazine. Recently married, she enjoys hiking, cycling, running, and practicing yoga. Her advice to students using *The Prose Reader* is to "allow yourself time every day just for unedited, free-flowing writing. Twenty minutes in the morning or evening can really open up any blockage you may be experiencing, especially knowing that this writing doesn't 'count.' By that, I mean that no one ever has to see it. Don't get out of the habit. It's like going to the gym—you've got to do it every day, or else you start mentally resisting it. Also, read other good writers for inspiration." Bourland currently lives near San Francisco, where she is working on her third book.

Preparing to Read

The following essay, from a book called *The Go-Girl Guide: Surviving Your 20s with Savvy, Soul, and Style,* offers extremely helpful advice for getting and staying out of debt. Everyone can use a little help in this area.

Exploring Experience: As you prepare to read this essay, take a few minutes to think about money in general: Which do you enjoy more: making or spending money? Do you work? If so, do you feel you are paid fairly? Are you comfortable spending money? Do you ever buy on credit? Do you have trouble limiting your spending to the money you earn? How much difficulty do you have controlling your spending?

Learning Online: Visit the Motley Fool Web site (http://www.fool.com/ccc/debt/debt01.htm), or go to your campus financial aid Web site. Read a few paragraphs describing ways to get out of debt or methods for paying student loans. How do the techniques suggested in these Web sites differ from Bourland's advice?

I'm going to make the bold assumption that you have incurred a little debt during your great entrance into adulthood, from either student loans, devilish credit cards, or that car loan you recently signed with its 36 easy installment payments. If you haven't tasted debt, you are abnormally perfect and un-American and can just skip on down to the next section on retirement planning and chill out until the rest of us catch up with you.

Some debt, such as student loans, is money well borrowed and an investment in your future. Because of their relatively low interest rates, manageable (though seemingly eternal) repayment plans, and reasonable deferment options, student loans should not be the source of midnight panic attacks during your second semester of senior year, even if you've incurred thousands and thousands of dollars to fund your education and still don't have a job that suggests that all the debt was worth it. If you haven't graduated yet, toward the end of your final semester, your college student loan officer will give you all the dirty details of your repayment schedule (hopefully armed with ample tissue for the tears that are certain to flood your contacts), as well as tell you how to defer paying back your loans if you aren't employed by the time your repayment grace period is up, as was my case. The cheery thing I discovered about deferring repayment is that the groovy government actually paid the interest I owed during my six-month deferment. That's not the case with all student loans, but you'll find that out when you start reading the fine print.

If you're like me, you may have several loans to repay. Again, you probably got (or will get) the skinny from your financial aid administrator at college, but in case he or she is on drugs, I'll summarize. There are a few consolidation plans that can make the whole process of paying back your loans less horrifying. Consolidating means that you will be able to merge all of your loans into one giant superloan that offers a low interest rate, as well as various options for shortening or lengthening your repayment schedule (which will increase or decrease the amount you owe each month, thereby increasing or decreasing the amount of interest you ultimately end up paying). But the best reason to consolidate your loans is that you will receive only one bill every month, which means you have to think and stress about all the student loan money you owe only once every 30 days! I highly recommend consolidation, if only for that.

If you have several loans from one financial institution, contact your lender directly about its consolidation options, or try these two programs: Federal Direct Consolidation Loan Program (800-557-7392; www.ed.gov/directloan) and Student Loan Marketing Association (a.k.a. Sallie Mae) Smart Loan Account (800-524-9100; www.salliemae.com).   4

Student loans are much less threatening and guilt-provoking than credit card debt, to which we 20-somethings are painfully vulnerable. There are so many things we want and need. Credit card companies seize upon our vulnerability, especially during college, sending us application after application with such enticing incentives as a *free water bottle, a two-pound bag of M & Ms, a 10% discount* on first purchases, *free checks* to spend anywhere we please, our very own *head shot* on the card, a *4.9% introductory interest rate,* and *bonus airline miles.* My first advice on the whole matter of credit card debt is to avoid it like the devil! I know many honest, smart girls who've become submerged in debt through the seductive power of plastic.   5

Our society once thrived without credit, so it *is* possible to stay out of debt as we begin our adult lives. But since you will probably experiment with credit despite the danger, memorize these eight guidelines compliments of those who've battled the plastic demons: 6

#1: No Department Store Credit Cards

In-store credit usually carries a much higher interest rate than credit cards issued by banks. If you don't pay your debt back right away, what you buy is going to cost you much more than you bargained for. The only exception is if you have money to pay off your debt as soon as the bill arrives, and signing up for a card gives you a substantial discount on your first purchase. In these cases, get   7 the card (and discount), pay your bill in full, and immediately cancel the card and shred it into a million pieces, lest you be tempted to use it again without the discount and money to pay for it. Note: If the discount isn't more than $10 or 20, don't even bother, because when you sign on, you'll probably get put on some annoying direct-mail list that will be sold to a bunch of trashy companies who will send you junk mail every single day.

#2: One Card Only

The fewer little plastic rectangles you have, the less you'll be   8
tempted to live beyond your meager means (and the fewer hysteria-provoking bills you'll receive). Ideally, you should use your card only for items that you know you can pay off with your next paycheck or for unavoidable emergencies, like getting new brakes for your clunker or fillings for your insatiable sweet tooth. The ideal cards have fixed annual percentage rates ranging from 9 to 12 percent, or less if you can find them, no annual fee, and a grace period that doesn't start charging interest on what you buy until the bill's due date. If you are a conscientious customer, you will be inundated with appealing offers for new cards boasting Platinum status and $25,000 credit lines. When you receive these, gingerly toss them into the recycling bin. Opening them will only lead you into trouble. There is one exception to this rule, but I'll get to that when we talk about transferring balances. First, a few more basic tips.

#3: Use Your ATM Credit/Debit Card Instead

If you're diligent about balancing your checkbook, there's no   9
reason to fear the credit card capabilities of your ATM card, which most banks are offering these days. Keep the receipt for whatever you purchase with your card as you would had you withdrawn money from the bank, and record the amount in your checkbook ledger as you would a check. Your debit card is just as convenient as a credit card, but your purchase won't accrue interest, which will save you money. Definitely use your debit card instead of a real credit card when grocery shopping or buying little things at the pharmacy, unless you like the idea of paying 18 percent interest on cereal and tampons. Trust your elders: the interest on all the little things makes them as costly as a raging girls' night out.

#4: Pay Back as Much as You Can, as Soon as You Can

If we take the *minimum* payment request on our monthly state-   10
ments to heart, we may not pay off our account in full until we
qualify for social security. That's because interest continues to
accrue on our balance each month. If we don't pay off everything
we owe, the remainder plus the interest we've amassed will be
charged interest the following month and the month after that,
which means our balance continues to grow at the speed of our
card's annual percentage rate (APR) despite the fact that we pay
our minimum due every month and have hidden our credit card
in the closet under five shoe boxes. That's how credit card companies make so much money and why we should avoid getting
into debt in every humanly possible (but legal) way.

If you have debt from several sources, pay back whatever has   11
higher interest rates first—usually your credit cards—then tackle
the typically lower-rated student loan and car loan debts. If your
credit card debt is spiraling out of control, you could refinance
your student or car loans so that you will owe less on them each
month, using the extra money to pay off your credit cards. Then,
when your costlier debts have been paid off (and cards dumped in
the nearest incinerator), you can designate all your funds to paying back your temporarily neglected student and car loans as
quickly as you can.

#5: Trash Those Credit Card Checks That Come with Your Statement, and Shun Cash Advances from the ATM

Both checks and cash advances will cost you dearly, since many   12
card companies tack on an additional finance charge to your bill
when you use them, plus impose an interest rate for the amount
you borrow that's much higher than the rate you have for normal
purchases. That means that if you withdraw $100 from your card
at a bank or ATM or use one of those checks for your rent, you'll
be paying back your credit card company a lot more than the
amount you borrowed.

6: Switch to a Card with a Lower Interest Rate

I said earlier that you should throw away offers for additional   13
credit cards, and that is a good rule unless you are carrying a

balance on a card (or cards) with an outrageous interest rate, say more than 12 percent. In that case, it's a good financial move to transfer your balance(s) to one card with the lowest rate you can find. Some offer temporary introductory interest rates as low as 2.9 percent on all transferred balances; when you apply, make sure you note the expiration date for those low rates on your calendar, and have another card offer lined up and ready to take on the load when the time comes. I know this sounds tedious, but careful organization and diligence will save you money as you attempt to pay the whole balance off.

If you play credit card musical chairs, keep three things in mind.   14
First, some balance transfer offers have associated fees or finance charges that aren't exactly highlighted in their promotions. Always inquire about transfer fees, and try to talk them out of it; many issuers are willing to waive the fees upon request. Second, even after you transfer your balance in full, the account remains open. To close it, you must officially cancel. The issuing bank won't automatically cancel a zero-balance account, so if you don't, your access to that credit line will remain on your credit report. That could be problematic later on when you're applying for a mortgage and have thousands of dollars worth of potential debt in your financial profile—something that makes lenders skittish. The other reason to cancel is to avoid the temptation to start using that clean slate of credit that your old card suddenly presents. And the third caveat: when you transfer your balance, do not use this new card to purchase new things. Declare it a debt repayment card only, and stick that shiny piece of plastic in the file where you keep your monthly statements. Here's why:

When you charge new items on a card that has adopted old   15
debt, many card issuers apply a different (and uber-exorbitant) interest rate to those new purchases. The higher interest rate will remain on the amount of your new purchases until your entire debt has been repaid. Therefore, when you are trying to pay off a large debt, you should try to have two credit cards—one with a very low balance-transfer interest rate for your main debt and another with a reasonable interest rate on new purchases that you will use for emergencies only, since you are, after all, trying to get out of the hole, not rack up new debt. A good resource for finding low-rate, no-fee cards is a company called CardWeb.com, Inc., which publishes a newsletter called CardTrak that lists these

desirable cards. You can access the newsletter and other credit card consumer information on its website (www.cardweb.com) or by calling (800) 344-7714.

#7: Apply for a Secured Credit Card if Your Credit Is Screwed

If you have damaged your credit rating by defaulting on a loan or debt, your main priority (besides coming up with a repayment plan that suits all your creditors) is to rebuild your credit. Secured credit cards can help. You give the issuer a certain sum of money up front, which is kept in an account for you as a security deposit. Depending on the terms of your agreement, you can then charge a specified amount on that card. Once you've proved that you can repay your debts in this secured way, you may be offered a new card with real credit that doesn't require you to put up money ahead of time. CardWeb.com, Inc. (cited in the previous entry) can provide a list of secured credit cards as well as low-rate, no-fee cards.

If you are in a bad situation and creditors are calling you about monster debt that you can't currently pay off, don't pack up and move to North Dakota, thinking creditors won't be able to find you—they will. A couple of nonprofit credit counseling organizations can help with debt-repayment planning assistance: Consumer Credit Counseling Services, associated with the National Foundation for Consumer Credit (800-388-2227; www.nfcc.org), and Debt Counselors of America (800-698-3782 www.dca.org).

#8: Check Your Credit Report

I've already expounded on why a clean credit report is so important, so I won't beat that dead horse, but I will add that it's wise to check up on your report every now and then to make sure there are no surprises (or mistakes) that need mending. There are three agencies that compile credit reports, and they all get their information separately, so what one company says is part of your credit history may differ from what another company includes. You can get copies of your credit report from each company for $8 or less, depending on your state of residence. If you have had bad credit in the past but believe you've been exonerated (usually after seven years), you should make sure all three companies are showing you in the proper light.

The three agencies keeping tabs are Experian (formerly TRW)   19
(888-397-3742; www.experian.com/ecommerce/consumercredit.
html); Equifax (800-685-1111; www.econsumer.equifax.com);
and Trans Union (800-888-4213; www.transunion.com/Personal/
PersonalSolutions.jsp).

UNDERSTANDING DETAILS

1. According to Bourland, what types of debts are worthwhile?
2. What does "consolidating loans" (paragraph 3) mean? What are the benefits of consolidating loans?
3. What are Bourland's eight guidelines for avoiding credit card debt? Summarize each guideline.
4. How can you check your credit rating?

ANALYZING MEANING

1. Have you incurred any debts in your life so far? Explain your answer by giving specifics.
2. Why does Bourland think debts are a normal part of life?
3. Why are young adults especially vulnerable to credit card debt?
4. Which of Bourland's guidelines are most likely to help you now and in the future? Explain your answer.

DISCOVERING RHETORICAL STRATEGIES

1. How would you characterize the tone of this essay? What specific details bring you to this conclusion?
2. Who do you think is Bourland's primary audience in this essay? On what do you base your answer?
3. What method does Bourland use to organize her advice in this essay?
4. What other rhetorical strategies, besides process analysis, does Bourland use to strengthen her argument about handling debt? Give an example of each of these strategies.

MAKING CONNECTIONS

1. Compare and contrast the advice Julia Bourland provides about managing your money with similar suggestions by Edwin Bliss about managing your time. Which type of advice will be most useful to you in the future? Why do you think so?

2. How is Bourland's description of the process of staying out of debt similar to the process of embalming dead bodies described by Jessica Mitford in "Behind the Formaldehyde Curtain"? Which process seems most difficult to you? Explain your answer.

3. What advice would K. C. Cole ("Calculated Risks") give to Julia Bourland about the risks of money management? Which of these two authors would be more likely to make a big financial gamble in her life? Explain your answer.

IDEAS FOR DISCUSSION/WRITING

Preparing to Write

Write freely about your spending habits: Do you spend money wisely? Do you usually spend more than you make? How do you establish limits for your spending? Do you follow these limits? Have you built up a lot of debt? How do you plan to pay off this debt?

Choosing a Topic

1. Debt is widespread in contemporary American society, especially among college students. As a result, your college newspaper is running a special series of articles focusing on debt in college. Find out as much as you can about this problem, its causes, and its solutions, and write an article for your campus newspaper on the various causes of student debt and some ways to avoid it.

2. Most people hope to find a job that fulfills and interests them as their lives progress. But they generally don't start out with the job of their dreams. Write a letter to a high school student offering realistic advice on securing a good job during college.

3. Using Hansen's advice, explain what characterizes successful money management in your opinion. Direct your essay to college students.

4. Do you have a creative solution for approaching a boring task? Using Bourland's style, write a procedure for your creative way to make a stale or repetitive task fulfilling. Check out www.about.com or www.ehow.com for ideas.

Before beginning your essay, you might want to consult the checklists on page 220.

CHAPTER WRITING ASSIGNMENTS

Practicing Process Analysis

1. Make a list of some of the activities you do well. Choose one activity, and think about exactly what you must do to perform this skill. Write an essay that describes to another person the process of doing this activity well. Be as specific and clear in your directions as you can.

2. Identify a task or responsibility that seems impossible for you to do well. What keeps you from performing this task with skill or efficiency? Write an essay that describes how to fail at this activity. Describe this method for failure in a humorous or sarcastic manner.

3. What is your best method for solving major life problems? Think of times in your life when you have had to solve a problem or make an important decision. Write an essay that explains to a person looking for problem-solving ideas the method you rely on when faced with important problems that need to be solved.

Exploring Ideas

1. How do you think your ability to manage money affects your daily life? Do you think this ability has mostly positive or negative effects on your lifestyle? Use specific examples to support your opinion.

2. Find a recent advertisement on television, in the newspaper, on a billboard, or on the radio that you think is especially successful. Examine this ad, and write an essay explaining its success. What makes it good? Whom does it reach? How effectively does it address its target population?

3. Should we "force" students to stay in school until the age of sixteen, or should we allow students who do not choose to go to school the right to drop out before they finish high school? Respond to these questions in an organized essay.

5

DIVISION/CLASSIFICATION
Finding Categories

Both division and classification play important roles in our everyday lives: Bureau drawers separate one type of clothing from another; kitchen cabinets and drawers organize food, dishes, and utensils into groups; grocery stores shelve similar items together so shoppers can easily locate what they want to buy; school notebooks with tabs help students divide up their academic lives; newspapers classify local and national events in order to organize a great deal of daily information for the general public; and our own personal classification systems assist us in separating what we like from what we don't so that we can have access to our favorite foods, our favorite cars, our favorite entertainment, our favorite people. The two processes of division and classification are so natural to us, in fact, that we sometimes aren't even aware that we are using them.

DEFINING DIVISION/CLASSIFICATION

Division and classification are actually mirror images of each other. Division is the basic feature of process analysis, which we studied in the last chapter; it moves from a general concept to subdivisions of that concept or from a single category to multiple subcategories. Classification works in the opposite direction, moving from specifics to a group with common traits or from multiple subgroups to a single, larger, and more inclusive category. These techniques work together in many ways: A college, for example, is *divided* into departments (single to multiple), whereas courses are *classified* by department (multiple to single); the medical field is *divided* into specialties, whereas doctors are *classified* by a single specialty; a cookbook is *divided* into chapters, whereas recipes are *classified* according to type; and athletics is *divided* into specific sports, whereas athletes are *classified* by the sport in which they participate. Division is the separation of an idea or an item into its basic parts, such as a home into rooms, a course into assignments, or a job into various duties or responsibilities; classification is the organization of items with similar features into a group or groups, such as finding all green-eyed people in a large group, omitting all carbohydrates from your diet, or watching only the track and field events during the Olympics.

Classification is an organizational system for presenting a large amount of material to a reader or listener. This process helps us make sense of the complex world we live in by letting us work with smaller, more understandable units of that world. Classification must be governed by some clear, logical purpose (such as focusing on all lower-division course requirements), which will then dictate the system of categories to be used. The plan of organization that results should be as flexible as possible, and it should illustrate the specific relationship to each other of items in a group and of the groups themselves to one another.

As you already know, many different ways of classifying the same elements are possible. If you consider the examples at the outset of this chapter, you will realize that bureau drawers vary from house to house and even from person to person; that no one's kitchen is set up exactly the same way as someone else's; and that grocery stores have similar but not identical systems of classification. (Think, for instance, of the many different schemes for organizing dairy products, meats, foreign foods, etc.) In addition, your friends probably use a method different from yours to organize their school notebooks; different newspapers vary their presentation of the news; and two professors will probably teach the same course material in separate ways. We all have distinct and uniquely logical methods of classifying the elements in our own lives.

The following student paragraph about friends illustrates both division and classification. As you read it, notice how the student writer moves back and forth smoothly from general to specific and from multiple to single:

> *The word* friend *can refer to many different types of relationships. Close friends are "friends" at their very best: people for whom we feel respect, esteem, and, quite possibly, even love. We regard these people and their well-being with kindness, interest, and goodwill; we trust them and will go out of our way to help them. Needless to say, we could all use at least one close friend. Next come "casual friends," people with whom we share a particular interest or activity. The investment of a great amount of time and energy in developing this type of friendship is usually not required, though casual friends often become close friends with the passage of time. The last division of "friend" is most general and is composed of all those individuals whose acquaintance we have made and who feel no hostility toward us. When one is counting friends, this group should certainly be included, since such friendships often develop into "casual" or "close" relationships. Knowing people in all three groups is necessary, however, because all types of friends undoubtedly help us live healthier, happier lives.*

THINKING CRITICALLY BY USING DIVISION/CLASSIFICATION

The thinking strategies of division and classification are the flip sides of each other: Your textbook is *divided* into chapters (one item divided into many), but chapters are *classified* (grouped) into sections or units. Your brain performs these mental acrobatics constantly, but to be as proficient at this method of thinking as possible, you need to be aware of the cognitive activities you go through. Focusing on these two companion patterns of thought will develop your skill in dealing with these complex schemes as it simultaneously increases your overall mental capabilities.

You might think of division/classification as a driving pattern that goes forward and then doubles back on itself in reverse. Division is a movement from a single concept to multiple categories, while classification involves gathering multiple concepts into a single group. Dividing and/or classifying helps us make sense of our subject by using categories to highlight similarities and differences. In the case of division, you are trying to find what differences break the items into separate groups, while, with classification, you let the similarities among the items help you put the material into meaningful categories. Processing your material in this way helps your readers see your particular subject in a new way and often brings renewed insights to both reader and writer.

Experimenting with division and classification is important to your growth as a critical thinker. It will help you process complex information so you can understand more fully your options for dealing with material in all subject areas. Practicing division and classification separate from other rhetorical modes makes you concentrate on improving this particular pattern of thinking before adding it to your expanding arsenal of critical thinking skills.

1. Describe the people, windows, and doors in this photograph by Bill Carden. How could they be divided and classified into groups? What do you learn by looking at the photograph in this way?

2. Study the table of contents of a magazine that interests you. Into what sections is the magazine divided? What distinguishing fea-

tures does each section have? Now study the various advertisements in the same magazine. What different categories would you use to classify these ads? List the ads in each category.
3. Make a chart classifying the English instructors at your school. Explain your classification system to the class.

READING AND WRITING DIVISION/ CLASSIFICATION ESSAYS

Though writers of division/classification essays will probably use both division and classification in their essays, they should decide if they are primarily going to break down a topic into many separate parts or group together similar items into one coherent category; a writer's purpose will, of course, guide him or her in this decision. Readers must likewise recognize and understand which of these two parallel operations an author is using to structure an essay. Another important identifying feature of division/ classification essays is an explanation (explicit or implicit) of the significance of a particular system of organization.

How to Read a Division/Classification Essay

Preparing to Read.   As you approach the selections in this chapter, you should study all the material that precedes each essay so you can prepare yourself for your reading. First of all, what hints does the title give you about what you are going to read? To what extent does K. C. Cole reveal his attitude toward risks? Who do you think Judith Wallerstein and Sandra Blakeslee's audience is in "Second Chances for Children of Divorce"? Does Judith Viorst's title give us any indication about her point of view in "The Truth About Lying"? Then see what you can learn from scanning each essay and reading its synopsis in the Rhetorical Table of Contents.

Also important as you prepare to read the essays in this chapter is your knowledge about each author and the conditions under which each essay was written: What does the biographical material tell you about Phyllis Schneider's "Memory: Tips You'll Never Forget"? About Franklin Zimring's "Confessions of an Ex-Smoker"? Knowing where these essays were first published will give you even more information about each author's purpose and audience.

Finally, before you begin to read, answer the Preparing to Read questions, and then think freely for a few minutes about the general topic: What do you want to know about children of divorce from Wallerstein and Blakeslee? What are some different types of lies you have told (Viorst)?

Reading.   As you read each essay for the first time, write down your initial reactions to the topic itself, to the preliminary material, to the mood the writer sets, or to a specific incident in the essay. Make associations between the essay and your own experiences.

In addition, create a context for each essay by drawing on the preliminary material you just read about the essay: What is Schneider implying about the relationship between remembering and forgetting, and why does she care about this relationship? What is significant about Zimring's point of view in "Confessions of an Ex-Smoker"? According to Viorst, why are some lies permissible?

Also in this first reading, notice when the writers divided (split up) or classified (gathered together) their material to make their point. Finally, read the questions after each essay, and let them guide your second reading of the selection.

Rereading.   When you read these division/classification essays a second time, notice how the authors carefully match their dominant rhetorical approach (in this case, division or classification) to their purpose in a clear thesis. What, for example, is Cole's dominant rhetorical approach to his subject? How does this approach further his purpose? What other rhetorical strategies support his thesis? Then see how these writers logically present their division or classification systems to their readers, defining new categories as their essays progress. Finally, notice how each writer either implicitly or explicitly explains the significance or value of his or her division/classification system. How do Wallerstein and Blakeslee explain their system of organization? And how does Viorst give her organizing principle significance? Now answer the questions after each essay to check your understanding and to help you analyze your reading in preparation for the discussion/writing topics that follow.

For a more complete survey of reading guidelines, you may want to consult the checklists on page 20 of the Introduction.

How to Write a Division/Classification Essay

Preparing to Write.   You should approach a division/classification essay in the same way you have begun all your other writing assignments—with some kind of prewriting activity that will help you generate ideas, such as the Preparing to Write questions featured in this chapter. The prewriting techniques outlined in the Introduction on pages 21–23 can help you approach these questions imaginatively. Before you even consider the selection and arrangement of details, you need to explore your subject, choose a topic, and decide on a specific purpose and audience. The best way to explore your subject is to think about it, read about it, and then write about it. Look at it from all possible angles, and see what patterns and relationships emerge. To choose a specific topic, you might begin by listing any groups, patterns, or combinations you discover within your subject matter. Your purpose should take shape as you form your thesis, and your audience is probably dictated by the assignment. Making these decisions before you write will make the rest of your task much easier.

Writing. As you begin to write, certain guidelines will help you structure your ideas for a division/classification essay:

1. First, declare an overall purpose for your division/classification.
2. Then divide the item or concept you are dealing with into categories.
3. Arrange these categories into a logical sequence.
4. Define each category, explaining the difference between your categories and demonstrating that difference through examples.
5. Explain the significance of your classification system (Why is it worth reading? What will your audience learn from it?).

All discussion in such an essay should reinforce the purpose stated at the beginning of your paper. Other rhetorical modes— such as narration, example, and comparison/contrast—will naturally be used to supplement your classification.

To make your division/classification as workable as possible, take special care that your categories do not overlap and that all topics fall into their proper places. If, for example, you were dividing/classifying all the jobs performed by students in your writing class, the categories of (1) indoor work and (2) outdoor work would probably be inadequate because some jobs fit into both categories. At a pizza parlor, a florist, or a gift shop, for example, a delivery person's time would be split between indoor and outdoor work. So you would need to alter the classification system to avoid this problem. The categories of (1) indoor work, (2) outdoor work, and (3) a combination of indoor and outdoor work would be much more useful for this task. Making sure your categories don't overlap will help make your classification essays more readable and more accurate.

Rewriting.   As you rewrite your division/classification essays, consider carefully the probable reactions of your readers to the form and content of your paper:

- Does your thesis communicate your purpose clearly?
- Have you divided your topic into separate and understandable categories?
- Are these categories arranged logically?
- Do you explain the significance of your particular classification system?

More guidelines for writing and rewriting are available on pages 31–32 of the Introduction.

STUDENT ESSAY: DIVISION/CLASSIFICATION AT WORK

The following student essay divides skiers into interesting categories based on their physical abilities. As you read it, notice how the student writer weaves the significance of his study into his opening statement of purpose. Also, pay particular attention to his logical method of organization and clear explanation of categories as he moves with ease from multiple to single and back to multiple again throughout the essay.

People on the Slopes

<u>When I first learned to ski,</u> I was amazed   Subject
by the shapes who whizzed by me and
slipped down trails marked only by a black
diamond signifying "most difficult," while
others careened awkwardly down the
Thesis   "bunny slopes." <u>These skiers, I discovered,</u>
statement   <u>could be divided into distinct categories—</u>
<u>for my own entertainment and for the pur-</u>   Overall
<u>pose of finding appropriate skiing partners.</u>   purpose

First
category First are the "poetic skiers." They glide down the mountainside silently with what seems like no effort at all.

Definition They float from side to side on the intermediate slopes, their knees bent perfectly above parallel skis, while their sharp skills allow them to bypass slower skiers with safely executed turns at remarkable speeds.

Supporting details

Second
category The "crazy skiers" also get down the mountain quickly, but with a lot more noise attending their descent. At every hill, they

Definition yell a loud "Yahoo!" and slam their skis into the snow. These go-for-broke athletes always whiz by faster than everyone else, and they especially seem to love the crowded runs where they can slide over the backs of other people's skis. I often find crazy skiers in mangled messes at the bottoms of steep hills, where they are yelling loudly, but not the famous "Yahoo!"

Supporting details (with humor)

After being overwhelmed by the crazy skiers, I am always glad to find other skiers

Transition

Third like myself: "the average ones." We are
category polite on the slopes, concentrate on improving our technique with every run, and ski the beginner slopes only at the beginning of

Definition the day to warm up. We go over the moguls (small hills) much more cautiously than the crazy or poetic skiers, but we still seek adventure with a little jump or two each day. We remain a silent majority on the mountain.

Supporting details (comparative)

Below us in talent, but much more evident on the mountainside, are what I call

Transition

Fourth the "eternal beginners." These skiers stick to
category the same beginner slope almost every run of

Definition every day during their vacation. Should they venture onto an intermediate slope, they quickly assume the snowplow position (a pigeon-toed stance) and never leave it.

Eternal beginners weave from one side of the run to the other and hardly ever fall, because they proceed so slowly; however, they do yell quite a bit at the crazies who like to run over the backs of their skis.

Supporting details

Transition

Having always enjoyed people-watching, I have fun each time I am on the slopes observing the myriad of skiers around me. I use these observations to pick out possible ski partners for myself and others. Since my mother is an eternal beginner, she has more fun skiing with someone who shares her interests than with my dad, who is a poetic skier with solitude on his mind. After taking care of Mom, I am free to find a partner I'll enjoy. My sister, the crazy skier of the family, just heads for the rowdiest group she can find! As the years go by and my talents grow, I am trusting my perceptions of skier types to help me find the right partner for life on and off the slopes. No doubt watching my fellow skiers will always remain an enjoyable pastime.

Significance of classification system

Concluding remarks

Student Writer's Comments

To begin this paper—the topic of which occurred to me as I flew over snow-capped mountains on a trip—I brainstormed. I jotted down the general groups of skiers I believed existed on the slopes and recorded characteristics of each group as they came to me. The ideas flowed quite freely at this point, and I enjoyed imagining the people I was describing. This prewriting stage brought back some great memories from the slopes that cluttered my thinking at times, but in most cases one useless memory triggered two or three other details or skiing stories that helped me make sense of my division/classification system.

I then felt ready to write a first draft but was having a lot of trouble coming up with a sensible order for my categories. So I just began to write. My categories were now clear to me, even though I wanted to work a little more on their labels. And the definitions of each category came quite naturally as I wrote. In fact, the ease with which they surfaced made me believe that I really had discovered some ultimate truth about types of skiers. I also had tons of details and anecdotes to work with from my brainstorming session. When I finished the body of my first draft (it had no introduction or conclusion yet), I realized that every paragraph worked nicely by itself—four separate category paragraphs. But these paragraphs didn't work together yet at all.

As I reworked the essay, I knew my major job was to reorganize my categories in some logical way and then smooth out the prose with transitions that would make the essay work as a unified whole. To accomplish this, I wrote more drafts of this single paper than I can remember writing for any other assignment. But I feel that the order and the transitions finally work now. The essay moves logically from type to type, and I think my transitions justify my arrangement along the way. My overall purpose came to me as I was reorganizing my categories, at which point I was able to write my introduction and conclusion. After I had put my purpose into words, the significance of my division/classification system became clear. I saved it, however, for the conclusion.

The most exciting part of this paper was realizing how often I had used these mental groupings in pairing my family and friends with other skiers. I had just never labeled, defined, or organized the categories I had created. Writing this paper helped me verbalize these categories and ended up being a lot of fun (especially when it was finished).

SOME FINAL THOUGHTS ON DIVISION/CLASSIFICATION

The essays collected in this chapter use division and/or classification as their primary organizing principle. All of these essays show both techniques at work to varying degrees. As you read these essays, you might also want to be aware of the other rhetorical modes that support these division/classification essays, such as description and definition. Finally, pay special attention to how these authors bring significance to their systems of classification and, as a result, to their essays themselves.

DIVISION/CLASSIFICATION IN REVIEW

Reading Division/Classification Essays

Preparing to Read

✓ What assumptions can you make from the essay's title?
✓ Can you guess what the general mood of the essay is?
✓ What is the essay's purpose and audience?
✓ What does the synopsis tell you about the essay?
✓ What can you learn from the author's biography?
✓ Can you guess what the author's point of view toward the subject is?
✓ What are your responses to the "Preparing to Read" questions?

Reading

✓ What do you think the context of the essay is?
✓ Did the author use division or classification most often?
✓ Did you preview the questions that follow the essay?

Rereading

✓ How does division or classification help the author accomplish his/her purpose?
✓ What other rhetorical strategies does the author use?
✓ How does the writer explain the significance of his/her approach?
✓ What are your responses to the questions after the essay?

Writing Division/Classification Essays

Preparing to Write

✓ What are your responses to the "Preparing to Write" questions?
✓ What is your purpose?
✓ Who is your audience?

Writing

✓ Do you declare an overall purpose for your essay?
✓ Do you divide your subject into distinct categories?
✓ Do you arrange these categories into a logical sequence?
✓ Do you define each category?
✓ Do you explain the significance of your approach?

Rewriting

✓ Does your thesis communicate your purpose clearly?
✓ Have you divided your topic into separate categories?
✓ Are these categories arranged logically?
✓ Do you explain the significance of your classification system?

Memory: Tips You'll Never Forget

Born in Seattle, Washington, Phyllis Schneider received her B.A. in English at Pacific Lutheran University and her M.A. in Advanced Writing at the University of Washington. She has been articles editor at *Seventeen* magazine, founding editor of *YM* magazine, and managing editor of *Weight Watchers* magazine. She currently works for Consumers Union, the publisher of *Consumer Reports,* for whom she has written a fundraising newsletter and various promotional materials. She has also published articles in *Working Woman, Redbook, Woman's Day, New Choices, Parents* magazine, and many other periodicals, and she writes health-care career supplements for the Greater New York Hospital Association and *The New York Times.* A lover of animals (she has a mixed-breed dog named "Jenny"), she also enjoys making jewelry in her spare time and serving as an associate at an Episcopal convent. Her advice to students using *The Prose Reader* is to "learn grammar." "Many young people have the enthusiasm to write well," she explains, "but not the proper skills."

Preparing to Read

The following essay, originally published in *New Choices,* offers us some important insights into the strengths and weaknesses of our memories in an attempt to classify some of the typical memory lapses we all experience on a daily basis.

Exploring Experience: Prior to reading this essay, consider the strengths and weaknesses of your own memory. What information do you remember best? What do you have trouble remembering? Do you have any minor problems with your memory on a daily basis? Do your memory lapses fall into any particular categories? What are these categories?

Learning Online: How do you organize your life? Look at files on your computer hard drive or e-mail "Inbox," and consider the techniques you use for remembering where you store important information.

When my husband, Ted, started "losing" our car, I began   1
to worry. In his 30s and 40s, he'd leave a store or a theater and head straight for our vehicle—no problem.
But shortly after his 50th birthday, Ted walked into a mall parking garage and stopped short. Scratching his head, he asked,
"Where did we park?"

In the ensuing months, there were times when Ted would for-   2
get where he put his glasses, his keys, his wallet. And walking by a
restaurant one day, he remarked, "Remember what a great dinner
we had there"? I'd never been in that restaurant and said so. But he
insisted: he'd ordered the sole, and I'd had the salmon; we had both
agreed it was one of the best restaurants we'd ever been to.

Though I found Ted's memory lapses troublesome, most   3
experts would say that such forgetfulness doesn't necessarily signal
trouble. "You needn't worry about these lapses unless you experience a noticeable and consistent decline in memory or you aren't
able to function at work," says psychologist Daniel L. Schacter of
Harvard University. At that point, of course, you should see a
doctor.

For most people, such lapses are just a normal—if annoying—   4
part of life. Mild deficits in memory do begin in the 40s and 50s
and increase in later years, but stress, fatigue, and a mere lack of
attention all can trigger temporary memory glitches in people of
all ages.

Here are some common types and strategies for minimizing   5
difficulties.

"It's on the Tip of My Tongue."   You start to introduce an   6
old friend to someone, and suddenly you can't remember that
someone's name—even though you sense it just beyond the grasp
of your memory. Or you can't quite retrieve the name of a movie
you just saw. Such tip-of-the-tongue—or TOT—incidents happen to most everyone, notes Deborah Burke, a psychologist at
Pomona College in Claremont, Calif.

These lapses have nothing to do with remembering the mean-   7
ing of a word, but rather with its sound, "Often, the sound of a
word is arbitrary and senseless," says Burke. This sheer arbitrariness
sometimes can make word retrieval challenging.

The best way to prevent the problem is to use the name of a   8
person or object as frequently as possible. "I tell clients to do what
salespeople often do—repeat people's names several times just

before you plan to see them," says psychologist Liz Zelinski of the University of Southern California in Los Angeles.

A TOT experience can seem worse when a similar-sounding, but incorrect, word pops into your head and stays there. Burke tells the story of a student who was trying to remember the name of a particular recreational vehicle. The student wanted the word *Winnebago,* but she could only come up with *rutabaga.* When this happens shift your focus to something else, suggests Burke. "If you stop fretting about it, the correct word eventually will come to you."   9

"Where Did I Put My Keys?"   Most episodes of absent-mindedness—forgetting where you left something or wondering why you just entered a room—are caused by a simple lack of attention, says Harvard's Schacter. "You're supposed to remember something, but you haven't encoded it deeply."   10

Encoding, Schacter explains, is a special way of paying attention to an event that has a major impact on recalling it later. Failure to encode properly can create annoying situations. If you put your cell phone in a pocket, for example, and don't pay attention to what you did because you're involved in a conversation, you'll probably forget that the phone is in the jacket now hanging in your closet. "Your memory per se isn't failing you," says Schacter. "Rather, you didn't give your memory system the information it needed."   11

Lack of interest can also lead to absent-mindedness. "A man who can recite baseball scores from 30 years ago," says Zelinski, "may not remember to drop a letter in the mailbox." Women have slightly better memories than men, possibly because they pay more attention to their environment, and memory relies on just that.   12

Visual cues can help prevent absent-mindedness, says Schacter. "But be sure the cue is clear and available," he cautions. If you want to remember to take a medication with lunch, put the pill bottle on the kitchen table—don't leave it in the medicine chest and write yourself a note that you tuck in a pocket.   13

Another common episode of absent-mindedness: walking into a room and wondering why you're there. Most likely, you were thinking about something else. "Everyone does this from time to time," says Zelinski. The best thing to do is to return to where you were before entering the room, and you'll likely remember.   14

"That's Not the Way I Remember It."   Most of us occasionally experience a memory error called "misattribution." You   15 correctly remember something that happened but attribute it to the wrong source. For example, you share a story with a friend and credit it to your mutual acquaintance Jim. Although the incident actually happened to John—from whom you heard of it in the first place—you remain convinced that it originated with Jim.

In a similar way, people often come up with ideas that were   16 someone else's to begin with—a phenomenon known as unintentional plagiarism. At dinner one night, a friend related "her" recent experience at a store: Seeing a mother carrying her baby in a backpack, she remarked on the cute toy clutched in the infant's fist. "Oh, no—that's not hers!" the mother exclaimed. "She must have grabbed it from a shelf."

Then my friend's daughter piped up: "Mom, that happened to   17 me. I told you about it last month."

False memory, another trick the mind can play, is closely related   18 to misattribution. You may "remember" that you fell off the pier when your father took you fishing, though in reality you only witnessed such a scene in a movie many years ago.

As annoying as these kinds of memory lapses can be, there's a   19 positive side, says Schacter. If our brains did store all that we saw, heard, or read, we'd be overwhelmed. Our ability to splice together bits of necessary information and throw out the rest is essential for sound thinking.

I find this theory reassuring. Now when my husband forgets   20 where the car is, I tell myself that he's busy selecting and storing information that is really important to him—like ordering tickets to a sporting event—instead of concentrating on trivial stuff. And when we pass the restaurant that he insists we dined at years ago, I just smile and let him savor his memory of a delectable—and obviously unforgettable—dinner.

UNDERSTANDING DETAILS

1. What exactly is Schneider classifying in this essay? Explain her three categories.
2. What is the positive side of memory lapses, according to Schneider?
3. Which of these memory problems have you experienced? How did you solve the problem?
4. What are some of the main causes of memory lapses?

ANALYZING MEANING

1. Are you surprised to know that experts agree that lapses in memory don't "necessarily signal trouble" (paragraph 3)? Explain your answer.
2. Which of Schneider's categories do you suppose is most common among students?
3. Why do you think Schneider cited so many experts in this essay? What do these authoritative voices add to her essay?
4. What do all the solutions Schneider proposes for each type of memory lapse have in common?

DISCOVERING RHETORICAL STRATEGIES

1. In what ways does Schneider use division and classification in this essay? How does she give significance or value to her system of organization? What other rhetorical techniques does she use to accomplish her purpose?
2. What types of memory lapses do you experience in a typical day? How would you classify these lapses?
3. What is Schneider's point of view toward forgetfulness in general?
4. Why do you think Schneider opened and closed her essay with references to her husband? Are her beginning and ending effective? Explain your answer.

MAKING CONNECTIONS

1. Examine the tricks memory plays on us by contrasting Schneider's essay with Malcolm Cowley's "The View from 80," Russell Baker's "The Saturday Evening Post," Robert Ramirez's "The Barrio," and Michael Dorris's "The Broken Cord."
2. Compare and contrast the way Schneider organizes her advice with the organizational techniques of Edwin Bliss's "Managing Your Time," K. C. Cole's "Calculated Risks," and Judith Viorst's "The Truth About Lying."
3. Schneider defines *encoding* as "a special way of paying attention to an event that has a major impact on recalling it later." What advice do you think the following authors would give us about "encoding" important events in life: Ray Bradbury ("Summer Rituals"), Russell Baker ("The Saturday Evening Post"), and Roger Rosenblatt ("I Am Writing Blindly")?

IDEAS FOR DISCUSSION/WRITING

Preparing to Write

Write freely about various memory lapses you have experienced. What activities do they involve? Are they easily classified? Do they occur frequently in your life? When do they happen?

Choosing a Topic

1. Your English teacher has asked about the accuracy of your memory. Respond to this question by classifying for this teacher all the different types of memory work you do in a typical day. Remember that each memory task you do should fit into a specific category. Decide on a point of view before you begin to write.

2. Speculate about the memory of a close friend or relative by analyzing that person's behavior and preferences. Remember that analysis is based on the process of division. Divide this person's behavior and preferences into logical parts; then study those parts so that you can better understand the person's reasoning techniques. Decide on a purpose and audience before you begin to write.

3. If the mental activities we perform say something important about us, analyze yourself by writing an essay that classifies the different mental activities you have carried out in the last week. Discuss your choices as you proceed.

4. Pretend that you are writing a "how-to" Web site. Select a topic such as time management, exercise, or organization, and divide your topic into clear and separate categories. Write an article for online publication that provides an overview of your topic, describes the challenges associated with it, and classifies your method into clear categories.

Before beginning your essay, you might want to consult the checklists on page 276.

K.C. COLE   (1946–   )

Calculated Risks

K. C. Cole spent her early childhood in Rio de Janeiro, then grew up in Port Washington, New York, and Shaker Heights, Ohio. After graduating from Barnard College with a B.A. in political science, she worked for Radio Free Europe as an editor and subsequently lived in Czechoslovakia, the Soviet Union, and Hungary. While working as a writer and editor at the *Saturday Review* in San Francisco, she developed a love for physics and started writing about science. In the 1970s, she became an editor at *Newsday,* for which she wrote personal essays on politics, humor, and women's issues. Her first book, *What Only a Mother Can Tell You,* was published in 1982; a collection of essays titled *Between the Lines* came out two years later. She has also written *Sympathetic Vibrations: Reflections on Physics as a Way of Life* (1985, with an introduction by Frank Oppenheimer), *The Universe and the Teacup* (1998), and *The Hole in the Universe* (2001). Since 1994, she has covered physical science for *The Los Angeles Times,* where she also writes the column "Mind Over Matter." Her recreational activities include rollerblading, hiking, listening to Bach, and watching *Six Feet Under* and *Sex in the City.* Her advice to students using *The Prose Reader* is "to be passionate. There's no point in writing if you don't really care about what you say. And don't be afraid to make mistakes. If you don't make mistakes, you aren't taking enough risks."

Preparing to Read

The following essay first appeared in K. C. Cole's book entitled *The Universe and the Teacup: The Mathematics of Truth and Beauty* (1998). It suggests that the way we calculate risks in our lives doesn't make much sense.

Exploring Experience: As you prepare to read this article, take a few moments to think about how you analyze potential risks in your life: What constitutes a "risk" for you? What risks do you take every day? Do you take these risks readily and willingly? Give some examples. When do you avoid risks? Is taking risks a positive or negative force in your life? In what ways does taking risks influence your life? How does taking risks energize or diminish your actions?

Learning Online: K. C. Cole explains that "Risk assessment is rarely based on purely rational considerations." Before reading her essay, read a humorous approach to fear and evaluating risk. Go to Michael Moore's "Bowling for Columbine" Web site (http://www.bowlingforcolumbine.com), and select "Film Clips and Soundtracks." In the "Film Clips" category, choose "A Brief History of America." Consider how this presentation of risk assessment relates to Cole's theories.

Newsweek magazine plunged American women into a state   1
of near panic some years ago when it announced that the chances of a college-educated thirty-five-year-old woman finding a husband was less than her chance of being killed by a terrorist. Although Susan Faludi made mincemeat of this so-called statistic in her book *Backlash*, the notion that we can precisely quantify risk has a strong hold on the Western psyche. Scientists, statisticians, and policy makers attach numbers to the risk of getting breast cancer or AIDS, to flying and food additives, to getting hit by lightning or falling in the bathtub.

Yet despite (or perhaps because of) all the numbers floating   2
around, most people are quite properly confused about risk. I know people who live happily on the San Andreas Fault and yet are afraid to ride the New York subways (and vice versa). I've known smokers who can't stand to be in the same room with a fatty steak and women afraid of the side effects of birth control pills who have unprotected sex with strangers. Risk assessment is rarely based on purely rational considerations—even if people could agree on what those considerations were. We worry about negligible quantities of Alar in apples, yet shrug off the much higher probability of dying from smoking. We worry about flying, but not driving. We worry about getting brain cancer from cellular phones, although the link is quite tenuous. In fact, it's easy to make a statistical argument—albeit a fallacious one—that cellular phones prevent cancer, because the proportion of people with brain tumors is smaller among cell phone users than among the general population.

Even simple pleasures such as eating and breathing have   3
become suspect. Love has always been risky, and AIDS has made
intimacy more perilous than ever. On the other hand, not having
relationships may be riskier still. According to at least one study,
the average male faces three times the threat of early death associated with not being married as he does from cancer.

Of course, risk isn't all bad. Without knowingly taking risks, no   4
one would ever walk out the door, much less go to school, drive
a car, have a baby, submit a proposal for a research grant, fall in
love, or swim in the ocean. It's hard to have any fun, accomplish
anything productive, or experience life without taking on risks—
sometimes substantial ones. Life, after all, is a fatal disease, and the
mortality rate for humans, at the end of the day, is 100 percent.

Yet, people are notoriously bad at risk assessment. I couldn't get   5
over this feeling watching the aftermath of the crash of TWA
Flight 800 and the horror it spread about flying, with the long lines
at airports, the increased security measures, the stories about grieving families day after day in the newspaper, the ongoing attempt
to figure out why and who and what could be done to prevent
such a tragedy from happening again.

Meanwhile, tens of thousands of children die every day around   6
the world from common causes such as malnutrition and disease.
That's roughly the same as a hundred exploding jumbo jets full of
children every single day. People who care more about the victims
of Flight 800 aren't callous or ignorant. It's just the way our minds
work. Certain kinds of tragedies make an impact; others don't.
Our perceptual apparatus is geared toward threats that are exotic,
personal, erratic, and dramatic. This doesn't mean we're ignorant,
just human.

This skewed perception of risk has serious social consequences,   7
however. We aim our resources at phantoms, while real hazards
are ignored. Parents, for example, tend to rate drug abuse and
abduction by strangers as the greatest threats to their children. Yet
hundreds of times more children die each year from choking,
burns, falls, drowning, and other accidents that public safety efforts
generally ignore. . . .

Even in terms of simple dollars, our policies don't make any   8
sense. It's well known, for example, that prenatal care for pregnant
women saves enormous amounts of money—in terms of care

infants need in the first year of life—and costs a pittance. Yet millions of low-income women don't get it.

Numbers are clearly not enough to make sense of risk assessment. Context counts, too. Take cancer statistics. It's always frightening to hear that cancer is on the rise. However, at least one reason for the increase is simply that people are living longer—long enough to get the disease. 9

What you consider risky, after all, depends somewhat on the circumstances of your life and lifestyle. People who don't have enough to eat don't worry about apples contaminated with Alar. People who face daily violence at their front door don't worry about hijackings on flights to the Bahamas. Attitudes toward risk evolve in cultural contexts and are influenced by everything from psychology to ethics to beliefs about personal responsibility. 10

In addition to context, another factor needed to see through the maze of conflicting messages about risk is human psychology. For example, imminent risks strike much more fear in our hearts than distant ones; it's much harder to get a teenager than an older person to take long-term dangers like smoking seriously. 11

Smoking is also a habit people believe they can control, which makes the risk far more acceptable. (People seem to get more upset about the effects of passive smoking than smoking itself—at least in part because smokers get to choose, and breathers don't.) 12

As a general principle, people tend to grossly exaggerate the risk of any danger perceived to be beyond their control, while shrugging off risks they think they can manage. Thus, we go skiing and skydiving, but fear asbestos. We resent and fear the idea that anonymous chemical companies are putting additives into our food; yet the additives we load onto our own food—salt, sugar, butter—are millions of times more dangerous. 13

This is one reason that airline accidents seem so unacceptable— because strapped into our seats in the cabin, what happens is completely beyond our control. In a poll taken soon after the TWA Flight 800 crash, an overwhelming majority of people said they'd be willing to pay up to fifty dollars more for a round-trip ticket if it increased airline safety. Yet the same people resist moves to improve automobile safety, for example, especially if it costs money. 14

The idea that we can control what happens also influences who we blame when things go wrong. Most people don't like to pay 15 the costs for treating people injured by cigarettes or riding motorcycles because we think they brought these things on themselves. Some people also hold these attitudes toward victims of AIDS or mental illness, because they think the illness results from lack of character or personal morals.

In another curious perceptual twist, risks associated with losing   16
something and gaining something appear to be calculated in our minds according to quite different scales. In a now-classic series of studies, Stanford psychologist Amos Tversky and colleague Daniel Kahneman concluded that most people will bend over backward to avoid small risks, even if that means sacrificing great potential rewards. "The threat of a loss has a greater impact on a decision than the possibility of an equivalent gain," they concluded.

In one of their tests, Tversky and Kahneman asked physicians to   17
choose between two strategies for combating a rare disease, expected to kill 600 people. Strategy A promised to save 200 people (the rest would die), while Strategy B offered a one-third probability that everyone would be saved, and a two-thirds probability that no one would be saved. Betting on a sure thing, the physicians choose A. But presented with the identical choice, stated differently, they choose B. The difference in language was simply this: Instead of stating that Strategy A would guarantee 200 out of 600 saved lives, it stated that Strategy A would mean 400 sure deaths.

People will risk a lot to prevent a loss, in other words, but risk   18
very little for possible gain. Running into a burning house to save a pet or fighting back when a mugger asks for your wallet are both high-risk gambles that people take repeatedly in order to hang on to something they care about. The same people might not risk the hassle of, say, fastening a seat belt in a car even though the potential gain might be much higher.

The bird in the hand always seems more attractive than the two   19
in the bush. Even if holding on to the one in your hand comes at a higher risk and the two in the bush are gold-plated.

The reverse situation comes into play when we judge risks of   20
commission versus risks of omission. A risk that you assume by actually doing something seems far more risky than a risk you take by not doing something, even though the risk of doing nothing may be greater.

Deaths from natural causes, like cancer, are more readily accept-   21
able than deaths from accidents or murder. That's probably one

reason it's so much easier to accept thousands of starving children than the death of one in a drive-by shooting. The former is an act of omission—a failure to step in and help, send food or medicine. The latter is the commission of a crime—somebody pulled the trigger.

In the same way, the Food and Drug Administration is far more   22
likely to withhold a drug that might help a great number of people if it threatens to harm a few; better to hurt a lot of people by failing to do something than act with the deliberate knowledge that some people will be hurt. Or as the doctors' credo puts it: First do no harm.

For obvious reasons, dramatic or exotic risks seem far more   23
dangerous than more familiar ones. Plane crashes and AIDS are risks associated with ambulances and flashing lights, sex and drugs. While red dye #2 strikes terror in our hearts, that great glob of butter melting into our baked potato is accepted as an old friend. "A woman drives down the street with her child romping around in the front seat," says John Allen Paulos. "Then they arrive at the shopping mall, and she grabs the child's hand so hard it hurts, because she's afraid he'll be kidnapped."

Children who are kidnapped are far more likely to be whisked   24
away by relatives than strangers, just as most people are murdered by people they know.

Familiar risks creep up on us like age and are often difficult to   25
see until it's too late to take action. Mathematician Sam C. Saunders of Washington State University reminds us that a frog placed in hot water will struggle to escape, but the same frog placed in cool water that's slowly warmed up will sit peacefully until it's cooked. "One cannot anticipate what one does not perceive," he says, which is why gradual accumulations of risk due to lifestyle choices (like smoking or eating) are so often ignored. We're in hot water, but it's gotten hot so slowly that no one notices.

To bring home his point, Saunders asks us to imagine that cig-   26
arettes are not harmful—with the exception of an occasional one that has been packed with explosives instead of tobacco. These dynamite-stuffed cigarettes look just like normal ones. There's only one hidden away in every 18,250 packs—not a grave risk, you might say. The only catch is, if you smoke one of those explosive cigarettes, it might blow your head off.

The mathematician speculates, I think correctly, that given such   27
a situation, cigarettes would surely be banned outright. After all, if
30 million packs of cigarettes are sold each day, an average of
1,600 people a day would die in gruesome explosions. Yet the
number of deaths is the same to be expected from normal smoking. "The total expected loss of life or health to smokers using
dynamite-loaded (but otherwise harmless) cigarettes over forty
years would not be as great as with ordinary filtered cigarettes,"
says Saunders.

We can accept getting cooked like a frog, in other words, but   28
not getting blown up like a firecracker.

It won't come as a great surprise to anyone that ego also plays   29
a role in the way we assess risks. Psychological self-protection leads
us to draw consistently wrong conclusions. In general, we overestimate the risks of bad things happening to others, while vastly
underrating the possibility that they will happen to ourselves.
Indeed, the lengths people go to minimize their own perceived
risks can be downright "ingenious," according to Rutgers psychologist Neil Weinstein. For example, people asked about the
risk of finding radon in their houses always rate their risk as
"low" or "average," never "high." "If you ask them why," says
Weinstein, "they take anything and twist it around in a way that
reassures them. Some say their risk is low because the house is
new; others, because the house is old. Some will say their risk is
low because their house is at the top of a hill; others, because it's
at the bottom of a hill."

Whatever the evidence to the contrary, we think, "It won't   30
happen to me." Weinstein and others speculate that this has something to do with preservation of self-esteem. We don't like to see
ourselves as vulnerable. We like to think we've got some magical
edge over the others. Ego gets involved especially in cases where
being vulnerable to risk implies personal failure—for example, the
risk of depression, suicide, alcoholism, drug addiction. "If you
admit you're at risk," says Weinstein, "you're admitting that you
can't handle stress. You're not as strong as the next person."

Average people, studies have shown, believe that they will   31
enjoy longer lives, healthier lives, and longer marriages than the
"average" person. Despite the obvious fact that they themselves
are, well, average people too. According to a recent poll, 3 out of

4 baby boomers (those born between 1946 and 1964) think they look younger than their peers, and 4 out of 5 say they have fewer wrinkles than other people their age—a statistical impossibility.

Kahneman and Tversky studied this phenomenon as well and   32 found that people think they'll beat the odds because they're special. This is no doubt a necessary psychological defense mechanism, or no one would ever get married again without thinking seriously about the potential for divorce. A clear view of personal vulnerability, however, could go a long way toward preventing activities like drunken driving. But then again, most people think they are better than average drivers—even when intoxicated.

We also seem to believe it won't happen to us if it hasn't hap-   33 pened yet. That is, we extrapolate from the past to the future. "I've been taking that highway at eighty miles per hour for ten years and I haven't crashed yet," we tell ourselves. This is rather like reasoning that flipping a coin ten times that comes up heads guarantees that heads will continue to come up indefinitely.

Curiously, one advertising campaign against drunken driving   34 that was quite successful featured the faces of children killed by drunken drivers. These children looked real to us. We could identify with them in the same way as we could identify with the people on TWA Flight 800. It's much easier to empathize with someone who has a name and a face than a statistic.

That explains in part why we go to great expense to rescue   35 children who fall down mine shafts, but not children dying from preventable diseases. Economists call this the "rule of rescue." If you know that someone is in danger and you know that you can help, you have a moral obligation to do so. If you don't know about it, however, you have no obligation. Columnist Roger Simon speculates that's one reason the National Rifle Association lobbied successfully to eliminate the program at the Centers for Disease Control that keeps track of gun deaths. If we don't have to face what's happening, we won't feel obligated to do anything about it.

Even without the complication of all these psychological fac-   36 tors, however, calculating risks can be tricky because not everything is known about every situation. "We have to concede that a single neglected or unrecognized risk can invalidate all the reliability calculations, which are based on known risk," writes Ivar

Ekeland. There is always a risk, in other words, that the risk assessment itself is wrong.

Genetic screening, like tests for HIV infection, has a certain   37
probability of being wrong. If your results come back positive, how much should you worry? If they come back negative, how safe should you feel?

The more factors involved, the more complicated the risk   38
assessment becomes. When you get to truly complex systems like nationwide telephone networks and power grids, worldwide computer networks and hugely complex machines like space shuttles, the risk of disaster becomes infinitely harder to pin down. No one knows when a minor glitch will set off a chain reaction of events that will culminate in disaster. Potential risk in complex systems, in other words, are subject to . . . exponential amplification. . . .

Needless to say, the way a society assesses risk is very different   39
from the way an individual views the same choices. Whether or not you wish to ride a motorcycle is your own business. Whether society pays the bills for the thousands of people maimed by cycle accidents, however, is everybody's business. Any one of us might view our own survival on a transatlantic flight as more important than the needs of the nation's children. Governments, one presumes, ought to have a somewhat different agenda.

But how far does society want to go in strictly numerical   40
accounting? It certainly hasn't helped much in the all-important issue of health care, where an ounce of prevention has been proven again and again to be worth many pounds of cures. Most experts agree that we should be spending much more money preventing common diseases and accidents, especially in children. But no one wants to take health dollars away from precarious newborns or the elderly—where most of it goes. These are decisions that ultimately will not be made by numbers alone. Calculating risks only helps us to see more clearly what exactly is going on.

According to anthropologist Melvin Konner, author of *Why the*   41
Reckless Survive, our poor judgment about potential risks may well be the legacy of evolution. Early peoples lived at constant risk from predators, disease, accidents. They died young. And in evolutionary terms, "winning" means not longevity, but merely sticking around long enough to pass on your genes to the next generation. Taking risks was therefore a "winning" strategy, especially if it meant a chance to mate before dying. Besides, decisions had to

be made quickly. If going for a meal of ripe berries meant risking an attack from a saber-toothed tiger, you dove for the berries. For a half-starved cave dweller, this was a relatively simple choice. Perhaps our brains are simply not wired, speculates Konner, for the careful calculations presented by the risks of modern life. . . .

UNDERSTANDING DETAILS

1. Why does Cole claim that people are basically confused about risk assessment (paragraph 2)?
2. What role does "context" play in our assessment of risks?
3. What three psychological factors affect people's perceptions of risk? Explain each in your own words.
4. In what ways does an individual calculate risk differently from the way society calculates risk?

ANALYZING MEANING

1. What is the overall purpose of Cole's essay? How do you know? What clues make this purpose clear?
2. Why are faces and names more persuasive to us than statistics when considering risks in our own lives?
3. According to Cole, how do we form our own personal attitudes about risks? What does our lifestyle have to do with these attitudes?
4. Why does Cole think risk assessment is such a complex and difficult process?

DISCOVERING RHETORICAL STRATEGIES

1. Where in this essay does the author use division? Where does she use classification? Give specific examples. What other rhetorical modes does Cole use in her essay?
2. List the topics of each section of the body of this essay (paragraphs 9–40) (i.e., list one topic for each section). What advantages does this order have over other possible arrangements of the same ideas? How would the effect have been altered if Cole had changed the order of these ideas?
3. Why does Cole quote Melvin Kooner at the end of the essay: "Perhaps our brains are simply not wired, speculates Kooner,

for the careful calcuations peresented by the risks of modern life" (paragraph 41). What does this quote mean in the context of this essay?

4. What point of view does Cole take in her article? What tone results from this point of view?

MAKING CONNECTIONS

1. If K. C. Cole were having a round-table discussion with Brent Staples ("A Brother's Murder"), Julia Bourland ("Getting Out of Debt (and Staying Out)"), and Michael Dorris ("The Broken Cord"), which of the four would speak most forcefully for the value and necessity of taking risks in life? Explain your answer.

2. What would Judith Viorst ("The Truth About Lying") say about the kinds of lies we tell ourselves every day concerning the many risks we take? To what extent do you think K. C. Cole would agree with her?

3. Compare and contrast the way K. C. Cole divides and classifies types of risks with similar techniques of division and classification used by Franklin Zimring ("Confessions of an Ex-Smoker") and Phyllis Schneider ("Memory: Tips You'll Never Forget").

IDEAS FOR DISCUSSION/WRITING

Preparing to Write

Write freely about the risks you take: What criteria do you use to decide whether or not to take a particular risk? What risks do you confront on a daily basis? What risks have you taken beyond your daily routine? Why do you take these risks? How often do you seek out risks? Which risks do you avoid most aggressively? Why? What do risks add or detract from your life?

Choosing a Topic

1. Use division/classification to explain the types of risks you deal with in your life. Divide the risks you face into categories, and then discuss those categories in an essay written for your English class. Make sure you decide on a purpose and a point of view before you begin to write.

2. How do you make decisions? Use division/classification to explain how you approach a decision and make up your mind.

Decide on a purpose and pont of view before you begin to write.

3. Write an essay for your classmates in which you convince them to take a specific risk that you have taken. This might be anything from riding a roller coaster to filling out a job application. Be creative in your essay.

4. Visit your favorite online news source. What are today's most important headlines? How do they fit into K. C. Cole's categories of risk taking? Select a current event, and write an essay in which you analyze its actual risk using K. C. Cole's method of classification.

Before beginning your essay, you might want to consult the checklists on page 276.

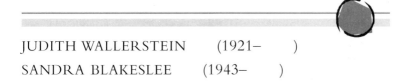

JUDITH WALLERSTEIN   (1921–   )

SANDRA BLAKESLEE   (1943–   )

Second Chances for Children of Divorce

Judith Wallerstein grew up in New York City, earned her Ph.D. at Lund University in Sweden, and now lives and works in Marin County, California, where she serves as director of the Center for the Family in Transition. Since 1965, she has taught psychology at the University of California at Berkeley, where she specializes in divorce and its effect on family members. Her first book, *Surviving the Breakup* (coauthored by Joan Kelly, 1980), analyzes the impact of divorce on young children in the family. Her next, *Second Chances: Men, Women, and Children a Decade After Divorce* (1989), is a study of the long-term effects of divorce on teenagers and young adults. Her most recent book, *The Unexpected Legacy of Divorce* (2000), is a study of the effects of divorce on children twenty-five years after their parents' breakup. Now hard at work on a study of happy marriages, Wallerstein is very concerned about what is happening to the American family. "There's a lot of anger in relationships between men and women today," she explains. "It's always easier to express anger than love." An avid reader, she collects ideas the way "other people collect recipes." She advises college students to read as much as possible: "The first prerequisite a writer must have is a love of reading." Her coauthor on *Second Chances*, Sandra Blakeslee, was born in Flushing, New York, and earned her B.S. degree at Berkeley, where her specialty was neurobiology. She is currently the West Coast science and medicine correspondent for the *New York Times*. A former Peace Corps volunteer in Borneo, she advises students using *The Prose Reader* to travel as much as possible: "You need a wide range of experiences to be a good writer." Blakeslee goes mountain biking and running in her spare time. She and Wallerstein recently collaborated on a new book entitled *What About the Kids? Raising Your Children Before, During, and After Divorce* (2003).

Preparing to Read

In the following essay from *Second Chances,* Wallerstein and Blakeslee classify the psychological tasks children who have suffered through the divorce of their parents must complete to free themselves from the past.

Exploring Experience: As you prepare to read this article, take a few minutes to think about the effects of divorce on yourself or someone you know: How close have you been to a divorce experience? How were people directly associated with the experience affected? What differences did you notice in the way adults and children responded to the same situation? What feelings were most common among the adults? Among the children? Why do you think the divorce rate has been so high during the last fifty years? Do you think this trend will continue, or will it taper off in the next few years?

Learning Online: Conduct an Internet search using the term *divorce statistics.* Keep in mind your findings when reading Wallerstein and Blakeslee's description of the different ways in which children are affected by divorce.

At each stage in the life cycle, children and adults face pre-   1 dictable and particular issues that represent the coming together of the demands of society and a biological and psychological timetable. Just as we physically learn to sit, crawl, walk, and run, we follow an equivalent progression in our psychological and social development. Each stage presents us with a sequence of tasks we must confront. We can succeed or fail in mastering them, to varying degrees, but everyone encounters the tasks. They begin at birth and end at death.

Children move upward along a common developmental lad-   2 der, although each goes it alone at his or her own pace. Gradually, as they pass through the various stages, children consolidate a sense of self. They develop coping skills, conscience, and the capacity to give and receive love.

Children take one step at a time, negotiating the rung they   3 are on before they can move up to the next. They may—and often do—falter in this effort. The climb is not steady under the best of circumstances, and most children briefly stand still in their ascent. They may even at times move backward. Such regressions are not a cause for alarm; rather, they may represent an appropriate response to life's stresses. Children who fail one task are not stalled forever; they will go on to the next stage, although they may be weakened in their climb. Earlier failures will not necessarily imperil their capacity as adults to trust a relationship, make a commitment, hold an appropriate job, or be a parent—to make use of their second chances at each stage of development.

I propose that children who experience divorce face an additional set of tasks specific to divorce in addition to the normal developmental tasks of growing up. Growing up is inevitably harder for children of divorce because they must deal with psychological issues that children from well-functioning intact families do not have to face.   4

The psychological tasks of children begin as difficulties, escalate between the parents during the marriage, and continue through the separation and divorce and throughout the postdivorce years.   5

TASK: *Understanding the Divorce*

The first and most basic task at the time of separation is for the children to understand realistically what the divorce means in their family and what its concrete consequences will be. Children, especially very young children, are thrown back on frightening and vivid fantasies of being abandoned, being placed in foster care, or never seeing a departed parent again, or macabre fantasies such as a mother being destroyed in an earthquake or a father being destroyed by a vengeful mother. All of these fantasies and the feelings that accompany them can be undone only as the children, with the parents' continuing help, begin to understand the reality and begin to adjust to the actual changes that the divorce brings.   6

The more mature task of understanding what led to the marital failure awaits the perspective of the adolescent and young adult. Early on, most children regard divorce as a serious error, but by adolescence most feel that their parents never should have married. The task of understanding occurs in two stages. The first involves accurately perceiving the immediate changes that divorce brings and differentiating fantasy fears from reality. The second occurs later, when children are able at greater distance and with more mature understanding to evaluate their parents' actions and can draw useful lessons for their own lives.   7

TASK: Strategic Withdrawal

Children and adolescents need to get on with their own   8
lives as soon as possible after the divorce, to resume their normal
activities at school and at play, to get back physically and emotionally to the normal tasks of growing up. Especially for adolescents who may have been beginning to spread their wings, the
divorce pulls them back into the family orbit, where they may
become consumed with care for siblings or a troubled parent. It
also intrudes on their academic and social life, causing them to
spend class time preoccupied with worry and to pass up social
activities because of demands at home. This is not to say that
children should ignore the divorce. Their task is to acknowledge
their concern and to provide appropriate help to their parents
and siblings, but they should strive to remove the divorce from
the center of their own thoughts so that they can get back to
their own interests, pleasures, problems, and peer relationships.
To achieve this task, children need encouragement from their
parents to *remain* children.

TASK: Dealing with Loss

In the years following divorce, children experience two pro-   9
found losses. One is the loss of the intact family together with the
symbolic and real protection it has provided. The second is the loss
of the presence of one parent, usually the father, from their daily
lives.

In dealing with these losses, children fall back on many fan-   10
tasies to mask their unhappiness. As we have seen, they may ide-
alize the father as representative of all that is lacking in their current lives, thinking that if only he were present, everything would
be better.

The task of absorbing loss is perhaps the single most difficult   11
task imposed by divorce. At its core, the task requires children to
overcome the profound sense of rejection, humiliation, unlovabil-
ity, and powerlessness they feel with the departure of one parent.
When the parent leaves, children of all ages blame themselves.
They say, "He left me because I was not lovable. I was not worthy." They conclude that had they been more lovable, worthy, or
different, the parent would have stayed. In this way, the loss of the
parent and lowered self-esteem become intertwined.

To stave off these intensely painful feelings of rejection, chil-   12
dren continually try to undo the divorce scenario, to bring their
parents back together, or to somehow win back the affection of
the absent parent. The explanation "Had he loved me, he would
not have left the family" turns into a new concern. "If he loved
me, he would visit more often. He would spend more time with
me." With this in mind, the children not only are pained at the
outset but remain vulnerable, sometimes increasingly, over the
years. Many reach out during adolescence to increase contact with
the parent who left, again to undo the sad scenario and to rebuild
their self-esteem as well.

This task is easier if parents and children have a good rela-   13
tionship, within the framework of a good visiting or joint custody
arrangement.

Some children are able to use a good, close relationship with   14
the visiting parent to promote their growth within the divorced
family. Others are able to acknowledge and accept that the visiting parent could never become the kind of parent they need, and
they are able to turn away from blaming themselves. Still others
are able to reject, on their own, a rejecting parent or to reject a
role model that they see as flawed. In so doing, these youngsters
are able to effectively master the loss and get on with their lives.

TASK: Dealing with Anger

Divorce, unlike death, is always a voluntary decision for at   15
least one of the partners in a marriage. Everyone involved knows
this. The child understands that divorce is not a natural disaster like
an earthquake or tornado; it is caused by the decision of one or
both of the parents to separate. Its true cause lies in the parents'
failure to maintain the marriage, and someone is culpable.

Given this knowledge, children face a terrible dilemma. They   16
know that their unhappiness has been caused by the very people
charged with their protection and care—their parents are the
agents of their distress. Furthermore, the parents undertook this
role voluntarily. This realization puts children in a dreadful bind
because they know something that they dare not express—out of
fear, out of anxiety, out of a wish to protect their parents.

Children get angry at their parents, experiencing divorce   17
as indifference to their needs and perceiving parents sometimes

realistically as self-centered and uncaring, as preaching a corrupt morality, and as weak and unable to deal with problems except by running away.

At the same time, children are aware of their parents' neediness, weaknesses, and anxiety about life's difficulties. Although children have little understanding of divorce, except when the fighting has been open and violent, they fully recognize how unhappy and disorganized their parents become, and this frightens them very much. Caught in a combination of anger and love, the children are frightened and guilty about their anger because they love their parents and perceive them as unhappy people who are trying to improve their lives in the face of severe obstacles. Their concern makes it difficult even to acknowledge their anger.

A major task, then, for children is to work through this anger, to recognize their parents as human beings capable of making mistakes, and to respect them for their real efforts and their real courage.

Cooling of anger and the task of forgiveness go hand in hand with children's growing emotional maturity and capacity to appreciate the various needs of the different family members. As anger diminishes, young people are better able to put the divorce behind them and experience relief. As children forgive their parents, they forgive themselves for feeling anger and guilt and for failing to restore the marriage. In this way, children can free themselves from identification with the angry or violent parent or with the victim.

TASK: Working Out Guilt

Young children often feel responsible for divorce, thinking that their misbehavior may have caused one parent to leave. Or, in a more complicated way, they may feel that their fantasy wish to drive a wedge between their mother and father has been magically granted. Many guilty feelings arise at the time of divorce but dissipate naturally as children mature. Others persist, usually with roots in a profound continuing sense of having caused the unthinkable—getting rid of one parent so as to be closer to the other.

Other feelings of guilt are rooted in children's realization that they were indeed a cause of marital difficulty. Many divorces occur after the birth of a child, and the child correctly comprehends that he or she really did drive a wedge between the adults.

We see another kind of guilt in girls who, in identifying with their troubled mothers, become afraid to surpass their mothers.

These young women have trouble separating from their mothers, whom they love and feel sorry for, and establishing their own successful relationships with suitable young men. The children of divorce need to separate from guilty ties that bind them too closely to a troubled parent and to go on with their lives with compassion and love.

TASK: Accepting the Permanence of the Divorce

At first, children feel a strong and understandable need to deny the divorce. Such early denial may be a first step in the coping process. Like a screen that is alternately lowered and raised, the denial helps children confront the full reality of the divorce, bit by bit. They cannot take it in all at once.   24

Nevertheless, we have learned that five and even ten years after divorce, some children and adolescents refuse to accept the divorce as a permanent state of affairs. They continue to hope, consciously or unconsciously, that the marriage will be restored, finding omens of reconciliation even in a harmless handshake or a simple friendly nod.   25

In accepting permanence, the children of divorce face a more difficult task than children of bereavement. Death cannot be undone, but divorce happens between living people who can change their minds. A reconciliation fantasy taps deep into children's psyches. Children need to feel that their parents will still be happy together. They may not overcome this fantasy of reconciliation until they themselves finally separate from their parents and leave home.   26

TASK: Taking a Chance on Love

This is perhaps the most important task for growing children and for society. Despite what life has dealt them, despite lingering fears and anxieties, the children of divorce must grow, become open to the possibility of success or failure, and take a chance on love. They must hold on to a realistic vision that they can both love and be loved.   27

This is the central task for youngsters during adolescence and at entry into young adulthood. And as we have seen, it is the task on which so many children tragically flounder. Children who lose a parent through death must take a chance on loving with the   28 knowledge that all people eventually die and that death can take away our loved ones at any time. Children who lose the intact family through divorce must also take a chance on love, knowing realistically that divorce is always possible but being willing nevertheless to remain open to love, commitment, marriage, and fidelity.

More than the ideology of hoping to fall in love and find   29
commitment, this task involves being able to turn away from the model of parents who could not stay committed to each other. While all the young people in our study were in search of romantic love, a large number of them lived with such a high degree of anxiety over fears of betrayal or of not finding love that they were entirely unable to take the kind of chances necessary for them to move emotionally into successful young adulthood.

This last task, taking a chance on love, involves being able to   30
venture, not just thinking about it, and not thinking one way and behaving another. It involves accepting a morality that truly guides behavior. This is the task that occupies children of divorce throughout their adolescence. It is what makes adolescence such a critical and difficult time for them. The resolution of life's tasks is a relative process that never ends, but this last task, which is built on successfully negotiating all the others, leads to psychological freedom from the past. This is the essence of second chances for children of divorce.

UNDERSTANDING DETAILS

1. Name the seven categories into which Wallerstein and Blakeslee divide the psychological growth of the children of divorce. How long will it take most children to go through these stages?
2. Choose one of these tasks and explain it in your own words.
3. According to Wallerstein and Blakeslee, what is probably the most difficult task that results from divorce? Why do the authors believe this stage is so painful?
4. What did Wallerstein and Blakeslee find out about their subjects' ability to deal with love in their lives?

ANALYZING MEANING

1. In your opinion, which of the emotional tasks that Wallerstein and Blakeslee describe is likely to be most traumatic in a child's life after a divorce? On what do you base your conclusion?

2. What is the relationship suggested in this essay between the parents' divorce and a child's sense of rejection?
3. In what ways does dealing with all facets of their anger create a problem for children of divorce? Do you know anyone who has worked through such a problem? Explain your answer in detail.
4. How might an understanding of the seven tasks discussed in this essay help people deal more effectively with children affected by divorce?

DISCOVERING RHETORICAL STRATEGIES

1. How do Wallerstein and Blakeslee organize their categories in this essay? Why do they place these tasks in this particular order?
2. What is the authors' general attitude toward divorce? What references in the essay reveal this point of view?
3. Describe the authors' intended audience. What makes you think they are directing their comments to this group?
4. What other rhetorical modes do Wallerstein and Blakeslee use in this essay besides division and classification? How do these other modes support the authors' division/classification system?

MAKING CONNECTIONS

1. Compare and contrast the love and support needed by children of divorce with the love and support provided naturally by the different types of families described in Mary Pipher's "Beliefs About Families."
2. What are the principal differences between Wallerstein and Blakeslee's prescriptions for how a child can best cope with the death of his or her parents' relationship and the way in which funeral directors in Jessica Mitford's "Behind the Formaldehyde Curtain" try to help us endure the death of a friend or relative? Which coping mechanisms are the same? Which are different?
3. Wallerstein and Blakeslee divide their essay into seven "tasks" that must be accomplished by children of divorce. Find a division/classification essay in this section of *The Prose Reader* that has more subdivisions. Then, find one that has fewer. How does the number of subdivisions in a division/classification essay affect your ability to understand the author's entire

argument? Which of these essays is the easiest to follow? Which is the most difficult? Why?

IDEAS FOR DISCUSSION/WRITING

Preparing to Write

Write freely about your thoughts on divorce and the effects of divorce on others: Do you know anyone who has gone through a divorce? How did the experience affect the couple getting divorced? How did it affect their friends, their relatives, and their children? How do you think the high divorce rate is affecting Americans in general? Why is America's national divorce rate so high? What changes could we make to lower the divorce rate?

Choosing a Topic

1. Assume that you are an expert on the variety and scope of college relationships. In an essay written for your classmates, divide your observations on different types of relationships into categories that will show students the full range of these associations in a college setting.

2. Because you have been involved with divorce in some way, you have been asked to submit to your college newspaper an editorial classifying the various ways in which different types of people react to divorce (husbands, wives, children, friends, and so on). You have been told to pay particular attention to the reactions of college students whose parents are going through or have gone through a divorce.

3. In an essay written for the general public, speculate about the reasons for the high national divorce rate. Use your own experience, interview others, or consult sources in the library to investigate the reasons for this trend. Suggest how we could solve this problem in America.

4. What other important issues affect children? Visit the United Nations Children's Fund Web site (http://www.unicef.org), and explore issues affecting children internationally. Write an essay in which you either select a single issue and divide it into subsections or you classify several different topics into a thematic order.

Before beginning your essay, you might want to consult the checklists on page 276.

FRANKLIN ZIMRING   (1942–   )

Confessions of an Ex-Smoker

Born in Los Angeles, Franklin Zimring earned his B.A. at
Wayne State University and his law degree at the University of
Chicago and then served for ten years as the director of the
Center for Studies in Criminal Justice at the University of
Chicago before moving to his present post as director of the Earl
Warren Legal Institute at the University of California at
Berkeley. A specialist in legal policy, he has published a number
of books on a wide variety of topics, many of which were
coauthored with colleague Gordon Hawkins, including *The
Citizen's Guide to Gun Control* (1987), *The Scale of Imprisonment*
(1991), *The Search for Rational Drug Control* (1992), *Incapacitation:
Penal Confinement and the Restraint of Crime* (1995), *Crime Is Not
the Problem: Lethal Violence in America* (1997), *American Youth
Violence* (1998), *Punishment and Democracy: Three Strikes and
You're Out* (2000), and *The Contradictions of Capital Punishment*
(2003). His advice to students using *The Prose Reader* is to "listen
to your own internal prompter as you write." A great believer in
E. M. Forster's famous question "How do I know what I think
till I see what I say?," Zimring counsels students to "relax and
decide what you really think about a topic, and then express it as
clearly and concisely as possible." The author's own relaxation
comes from the sport of swimming, to which he confesses a
"religious devotion."

Preparing to Read

Originally published in *Newsweek* magazine (April 20, 1987),
the following article is one in a series of "Mid-Life Memoranda"
that Zimring has been writing since 1985. It offers a witty classification of ex-smokers into four distinct groups: zealots, evangelists,
the elect, and the serene.

Exploring Experience: As you prepare to read this essay, think
for a few moments about your own addictions: Have you ever had
any addictions? Were they good addictions or bad? Are any of
these addictions still with you? Why are these addictions part of

your life? Do you want to change the status of these addictions? Why or why not? What do you think causes people to be addicted to certain substances or behavior? How can we break away from addictions successfully?

Learning Online: Using Google's search engine (http://www.google.com), click on the "Images" tab to conduct a picture search for the term *cigarette ads.* Consider how smokers are portrayed in the past and present.

Americans can be divided into three groups—smokers, non-   1 smokers, and that expanding pack of us who have quit. Those who have never smoked don't know what they're missing, but former smokers, ex-smokers, reformed smokers can never forget. We are veterans of a personal war, linked by that watershed experience of ceasing to smoke and by the temptation to have just one more cigarette. For almost all of us ex-smokers, smoking continues to play an important part in our lives. And now that it is being restricted in restaurants around the country and will be banned in almost all indoor public places in New York State, it is vital that everyone understand the different emotional states cessation of smoking can cause. I have observed four of them; and in the interest of science I have classified them as those of the zealot, the evangelist, the elect, and the serene. Each day, each category gains new recruits.

Not all antitobacco zealots are former smokers, but a substan-   2 tial number of fire-and-brimstone opponents do come from the ranks of the reformed. Zealots believe that those who continue to smoke are degenerates who deserve scorn not pity and the penalties that will deter offensive behavior in public as well. Relations between these people and those who continue to smoke are strained.

One explanation for the zealot's fervor in seeking to outlaw   3 tobacco consumption is his own tenuous hold on abstaining from smoking. But I think part of the emotional force arises from sheer envy as he watches and identifies with each lung-filling puff. By making smoking in public a crime, the zealot seeks reassurance that he will not revert to bad habits; give him strong social penalties, and he won't become a recidivist.

No systematic survey has been done yet, but anecdotal evi- 4
dence suggests that a disproportionate number of doctors who
have quit smoking can be found among the fanatics. Just as the
most enthusiastic revolutionary tends to make the most enthusiastic counterrevolutionary, many of today's vitriolic zealots include
those who had been deeply committed to tobacco habits.

By contrast, the antismoking evangelist does not condemn 5
smokers. Unlike the zealot, he regards smoking as an easily curable
condition, as a social disease, and not a sin. The evangelist spends
an enormous amount of time seeking and preaching to the uncon-
verted. He argues that kicking the habit is not *that* difficult. After
all, *he* did it; moreover, as he describes it, the benefits of quitting
are beyond measure and the disadvantages are nil.

The hallmark of the evangelist is his insistence that he never 6
misses tobacco. Though he is less hostile to smokers than the
zealot, he is resented more. Friends and loved ones who have been
the targets of his preachments frequently greet the resumption of
smoking by the evangelist as an occasion for unmitigated glee.

Among former smokers, the distinctions between the evange- 7
list and the elect are much the same as the differences between
proselytizing and nonproselytizing religious sects. While the evangelists preach the ease and desirability of abstinence, the elect do
not attempt to convert their friends. They think that virtue is its
own reward and subscribe to the Puritan theory of predestination.
Since they have proved themselves capable of abstaining from
tobacco, they are therefore different from friends and relatives who
continue to smoke. They feel superior, secure that their salvation
was foreordained. These ex-smokers rarely give personal testimony on their conversion. They rarely speak about their tobacco
habits, while evangelists talk about little else. Of course, active
smokers find such blue-nosed behavior far less offensive than that
of the evangelist or the zealot, yet they resent the elect simply
because they are smug. Their air of self-satisfaction rarely escapes
the notice of those lighting up. For active smokers, life with a
member of the ex-smoking elect is less stormy than with a zealot
or evangelist, but it is subtly oppressive nonetheless.

I have labeled my final category of former smokers the serene. 8
This classification is meant to encourage those who find the other
psychic styles of ex-smokers disagreeable. Serenity is quieter than
zealotry and evangelism, and those who qualify are not as self-

righteous as the elect. The serene ex-smoker accepts himself and also accepts those around him who continue to smoke. This kind of serenity does not come easily nor does it seem to be an immediate option for those who have stopped. Rather it is a goal, an end stage in a process of development during which some former smokers progress through one or more of the less-than-positive psychological points en route. For former smokers, serenity is thus a positive possibility that exists at the end of the rainbow. But all former smokers cannot reach that promised land.

What is it that permits some former smokers to become serene?   9
I think the key is self-acceptance and gratitude. The fully mature former smoker knows he has the soul of an addict and is grateful for the knowledge. He doesn't regret that he quit smoking, nor any of his previous adventures with tobacco. As a former smoker, he is grateful for the experience and memory of craving a cigarette.

Serenity comes from accepting the lessons of one's life. And   10
ex-smokers who have reached this point in their world view have much to be grateful for. They have learned about the potential and limits of change. In becoming the right kind of former smoker, they developed a healthy sense of self. This former smoker, for one, believes that it is better to crave (one hopes only occasionally) and not to smoke than never to have craved at all. And by accepting that fact, the reformed smoker does not need to excoriate, envy, or disassociate himself from those who continue to smoke.

UNDERSTANDING DETAILS

1. What are the four categories of reformed smokers that Zimring has observed? What characterizes each type?
2. What is the difference between the "elect" and the "serene" ex-smokers according to the author?
3. What is the general purpose of this division/classification essay?
4. How are becoming "the right kind of former smoker" and "a healthy sense of self" (paragraph 10) related? How do they affect one another?

ANALYZING MEANING

1. How does Zimring portray smokers in this essay? What effect does this attitude have on the rest of the essay?

2. What type of ex-smoker do you think would be most difficult to live with and why?
3. Why do you think many doctors who stop smoking become zealots?
4. Do you agree with Zimring that the key to being a "serene" ex-smoker is "self-acceptance and gratitude" (paragraph 9)? Are these positive qualities in an ex-smoker? Explain your answer in detail.

DISCOVERING RHETORICAL STRATEGIES

1. Who do you think is Zimring's specific audience for this essay? Explain your answer.
2. What do you think is Zimring's purpose in writing this essay? How did you come to this conclusion?
3. Zimring discusses these types of reformed smokers in a specific order. Explain this progression and discuss whether it is effective in achieving Zimring's overall purpose.
4. What rhetorical modes support the author's division/classification? Give examples of each.

MAKING CONNECTIONS

1. Compare Zimring's description of the addictive nature of tobacco with Michael Dorris's account of alcohol addiction in "The Broken Cord." Which substance do you think is most addictive? Explain your answer.
2. Use Zimring's definition of a "zealot" to help analyze essays by Gloria Steinem ("The Politics of Muscle"), Dave Grossman ("We Are Training Our Kids to Kill"), and Barbara Ehrenreich ("The Ecstasy of War"). To what extent are these authors zealots in support of their cause? Which author is most passionate in his or her opinion? Which is the least? Are you zealous about any particular issue? If so, which one?
3. Examine Jessica Mitford's "Behind the Formaldehyde Curtain," Jimmy Santiago Baca's "Past Present," and Wang Ping's "Ways to *Ai*" in order to determine whether any of these authors has reached Zimring's level of "serenity" in life. Which of these writers would you characterize as "zealots"? Which as "evangelists"? Which as "the elect"? What are the principal differences in the approaches of these three authors?

IDEAS FOR DISCUSSION/WRITING

Preparing to Write

Write freely about the role addiction plays in our lives in America: What do you know about addiction in general? What different substances and activities can people be addicted to? How can they break an addiction? What addictions are most dominant in American society? In what ways have you avoided addiction? In what ways are you addicted? What are your worst addictions? What are some of your friends' addictions? What do your addictions say about your personality? What do your friends' addictions say about them? What are some of America's major addictions? How could we alleviate these problems?

Choosing a Topic

1. Your high school graduating class has decided to put together a brochure about substance abuse and addiction for students starting high school. You have been asked to explain addiction and its consequences to this audience. Make your essay as vivid as possible.

2. Pretend that your college newspaper is running a special issue distinguishing between different generations of students. In a coherent essay written for the readers of this newspaper, classify the students of your generation in some logical, interesting fashion. Remember that classification is a rhetorical movement from "many" to "one." Group the members of your generation by some meaningful guidelines or general characteristics that you establish. Be sure to decide on a purpose and a point of view before you begin to write.

3. You have had many different types of friends over the years. Discuss one type of friend by dividing into logical categories the actual behavior of that type of person. Discuss each part of your division, giving examples as frequently as possible. Decide on a purpose and a point of view before you begin to write.

4. Zimring uses humor to classify former smokers that he observes. Spend some time watching the way people use one of the following: computers, the Internet, or e-mail. You may do this by reading through your e-mails or spending time in a campus computer lab, library, or coffee shop. How do people differ in their use of this technological equipment? Write a

humorous essay in which you divide the users you observe into specific groups. Use concrete details to support your categories.

Before beginning your essay, you might want to consult the checklists on page 276.

JUDITH VIORST   (1931–   )

The Truth About Lying

A poet, journalist, writer of children's books, and contributing editor of *Redbook* magazine, Judith Viorst reached the top of *The New York Times* best-seller list with *Necessary Losses* (1986), a detailed examination of "the loves, illusions, dependencies, and impossible expectations that all of us have to give up in order to grow." She earned her B.A. at Rutgers University in 1952 and began writing poetry. These early efforts, she claims, were "terrible poems about dead dogs, mostly . . . the meaning of life, death, pain, lust, and suicide." Her first complete book of poetry, however, entitled *The Village Square* (1965), was quite successful, as were such subsequent volumes as *People and Other Aggravations* (1971), *How Did I Get to Be Forty and Other Atrocities* (1976), *Love and Guilt and the Meaning of Life* (1984), and *Forever Fifty and Other Negotiations* (1989). Additional publications include *The Washington, D.C. Underground Gourmet* (1970), *Yes, Married: A Saga of Love and Complaint* (1972), *Love and Guilt and the Meaning of Life, Etc.* (1979), *The Good-bye Book* (1988), *Earrings!* (1990), *Murdering Mr. Monti: A Merry Tale of Sex and Violence* (1994), *Imperfect Control* (2000), *Grown-Up Marriage: What We Know, Wish We Had Known, and Still Need to Know About Being Married* (2002), and several books for children. The author lives in Washington with her husband, Milton Viorst (a syndicated political columnist).

Preparing to Read

"The Truth About Lying," originally published in the March 1981 issue of *Redbook* magazine, classifies and describes the different categories of lies we all experience at some point in our lives.

Exploring Experience: As you prepare to read this essay, take a few moments to consider various lies you have told: Under what conditions are you tempted to lie? When have you actually lied? Why did you do so? Can you generalize about the types of lies you habitually tell? Are you irritated when people lie to you?

Why or why not? In what circumstances might lying be acceptable? Why?

Learning Online: Reflect on past e-mails that friends have forwarded to you. How many of them tell some sort of unbelievable story of redemption or suffering? Would you classify these types of e-mail stories as "lies"? Consider the ways you define and classify lies as you read Viorst's essay.

I've been wanting to write on a subject that intrigues and challenges me: the subject of lying. I've found it very difficult to do. Everyone I've talked to has a quite intense and personal but often rather intolerant point of view about what we can—and can never *never*—tell lies about. I've finally reached the conclusion that I can't present any ultimate conclusions, for too many people would promptly disagree. Instead, I'd like to present a series of moral puzzles, all concerned with lying. I'll tell you what I think about them. Do you agree?

Social Lies

Most of the people I've talked with say that they find social lying acceptable and necessary. They think it's the civilized way for folks to behave. Without these little white lies, they say, our relationships would be short and brutish and nasty. It's arrogant, they say, to insist on being so incorruptible and so brave that you cause other people unnecessary embarrassment or pain by compulsively assailing them with your honesty. I basically agree. What about you?

Will you say to people, when it simply isn't true, "I like your new hairdo," "You're looking much better," "It's so nice to see you," "I had a wonderful time"?

Will you praise hideous presents and homely kids?

Will you decline invitations with "We're busy that night—so sorry we can't come," when the truth is you'd rather stay home than dine with the So-and-sos?

And even though, as I do, you may prefer the polite evasion of "You really cooked up a storm" instead of "The soup"—which tastes like warmed-over coffee—"is wonderful," will you, if you must, proclaim it wonderful?

There's one man I know who absolutely refuses to tell social 7
lies. "I can't play that game," he says; "I'm simply not made that
way." And his answer to the argument that saying nice things to
someone doesn't cost anything is, "Yes, it does—it destroys your
credibility." Now, he won't, unsolicited, offer his views on the
painting you just bought, but you don't ask his frank opinion
unless you want *frank*, and his silence at those moments when the
rest of us liars are muttering, "Isn't it lovely?" is, for the most part,
eloquent enough. My friend does not indulge in what he calls
"flattery, false praise, and mellifluous comments." When others tell
fibs, he will not go along. He says that social lying is lying, that little white lies are still lies. And he feels that telling lies is morally
wrong. What about you?

Peace-Keeping Lies

Many people tell peace-keeping lies; lies designed to avoid 8
irritation or argument; lies designed to shelter the liar from possible blame or pain; lies (or so it is rationalized) designed to keep
trouble at bay without hurting anyone.

I tell these lies at times, and yet I always feel they're wrong. I 9
understand why we tell them, but still they feel wrong. And
whenever I lie so that someone won't disapprove of me or think
less of me or holler at me, I feel I'm a bit of a coward, I feel I'm
dodging responsibility, I feel . . . guilty. What about you?

Do you, when you're late for a date because you overslept, say 10
that you're late because you got caught in a traffic jam?

Do you, when you forget to call a friend, say that you called 11
several times but the line was busy?

Do you, when you didn't remember that it was your father's 12
birthday, say that his present must be delayed in the mail?

And when you're planning a weekend in New York City and 13
you're not in the mood to visit your mother, who lives there, do
you conceal—with a lie, if you must—the fact that you'll be in
New York? Or do you have the courage—or is it the cruelty?—to
say, "I'll be in New York, but sorry—I don't plan on seeing you"?

(Dave and his wife Elaine have two quite different points of 14
view on this very subject. He calls her a coward. She says she's
being wise. He says she must assert her right to visit New York
sometimes and not see her mother. To which she always patiently

replies: "Why should we have useless fights? My mother's too old to change. We get along much better when I lie to her.")

Finally, do you keep the peace by telling your husband lies on the subject of money? Do you reduce what you really paid for your shoes? And in general do you find yourself ready, willing, and able to lie to him when you make absurd mistakes or lose or break things? 15

"I used to have a romantic idea that part of intimacy was confessing every dumb thing that you did to your husband. But after a couple of years of that," says Laura, "have I changed my mind!" 16

And having changed her mind, she finds herself telling peace-keeping lies. And yes, I tell them too. What about you? 17

Protective Lies

Protective lies are lies folks tell—often quite serious lies—because they're convinced that the truth would be too damaging. They lie because they feel there are certain human values that supersede the wrong of having lied. They lie, not for personal gain, but because they believe it's for the good of the person they're lying to. They lie to those they love, to those who trust them most of all, on the grounds that breaking this trust is justified. 18

They may lie to their children on money or marital matters. 19

They may lie to the dying about the state of their health. 20

They may lie about adultery, and not—or so they insist—to save their own hide, but to save the heart and the pride of the men they are married to. 21

They may lie to their closest friend because the truth about her talents or son or psyche would be—or so they insist—utterly devastating. 22

I sometimes tell such lies, but I'm aware that it's quite presumptuous to claim I know what's best for others to know. That's called playing God. That's called manipulation and control. And we never can be sure, once we start to juggle lies, just where they'll land, exactly where they'll roll. 23

And furthermore, we may find ourselves lying in order to back up the lies that are backing up the lie we initially told. 24

And furthermore—let's be honest—if conditions were reversed, we certainly wouldn't want anyone lying to us. 25

Yet, having said all that, I still believe that there are times   26
when protective lies must nonetheless be told. What about you?

If your Dad had a very bad heart and you had to tell him some   27
bad family news, which would you choose: to tell him the truth
or lie?

If your former husband failed to send his monthly childsup-   28
port check and in other ways behaved like a total rat, would you
allow your children—who believed he was simply wonderful—to
continue to believe that he was wonderful?

If your dearly beloved brother selected a wife whom you   29
deeply disliked, would you reveal your feelings or would you
fake it?

And if you were asked, after making love, "And how was that   30
for you?" would you reply, if it wasn't too good, "Not too good"?

Now, some would call a sex lie unimportant, little more than   31
social lying, a simple act of courtesy that makes all human intercourse run smoothly. And some would say all sex lies are bad news
and unacceptably protective. Because, says Ruth, "a man with an
ego that fragile doesn't need your lies—he needs a psychiatrist."
Still others feel that sex lies are indeed protective lies, more serious than simple social lying, and yet at times they tell them on the
grounds that when it comes to matters sexual, everybody's ego is
somewhat fragile.

"If most of the time things go well in sex," says Sue, "I think   32
you're allowed to dissemble when they don't. I can't believe it's
good to say, 'Last night was four stars, darling, but tonight's performance rates only a half.'"

I'm inclined to agree with Sue. What about you?   33

Trust-Keeping Lies

Another group of lies are trust-keeping lies, lies that involve tri-   34
angulation, with *A* (that's you) telling lies to *B* on behalf of *C*
(whose trust you'd promised to keep). Most people concede that
once you've agreed not to betray a friend's confidence, you can't
betray it, even if you must lie. But I've talked with people who
don't want you telling them anything that they might be called on
to lie about.

"I don't tell lies for myself," says Fran, "and I don't want to   35
have to tell them for other people." Which means, she agrees, that

if her best friend is having an affair, she absolutely doesn't want to know about it.

"Are you saying," her best friend asks, "that if I went off with a lover and I asked you to tell my husband I'd been with you, that you wouldn't lie for me, that you'd betray me?"   36

Fran is very pained but very adamant. "I wouldn't want to betray you, so . . . don't ask me."   37

Fran's best friend is shocked. What about you?   38

Do you believe you can have close friends if you're not prepared to receive their deepest secrets?   39

Do you believe you must always lie for your friends?   40

Do you believe, if your friend tells a secret that turns out to be quite immoral or illegal, that once you've promised to keep it, you must keep it?   41

And what if your friend were your boss—if you were perhaps one of the President's men—would you betray or lie for him over, say, Watergate?   42

As you can see, these issues get terribly sticky.   43

It's my belief that once we've promised to keep a trust, we must tell lies to keep it. I also believe that we can't tell Watergate lies. And if these two statements strike you as quite contradictory, you're right—they're quite contradictory. But for now they're the best I can do. What about you?   44

Some say that truth will out and thus you might as well tell the truth. Some say you can't regain the trust that lies lose. Some say that even though the truth may never be revealed, our lies pervert and damage our relationships. Some say . . . well, here's what some of them have to say.   45

"I'm a coward," says Grace, "about telling close people important, difficult truths. I find that I'm unable to carry it off. And so if something is bothering me, it keeps building up inside till I end up just not seeing them any more."   46

"I lie to my husband on sexual things, but I'm furious," says Joyce, "that he's too insensitive to know I'm lying."   47

"I suffer most from the misconception that children can't take the truth," says Emily. "But I'm starting to see that what's harder and more damaging for them is being told lies, is *not* being told the truth."   48

"I'm afraid," says Joan, "that we often wind up feeling a bit of contempt for the people we lie to."   49

And then there are those who have no talent for lying.   50

"Over the years, I tried to lie," a friend of mine explained,   51
"but I always got found out and I always got punished. I guess I
gave myself away because I feel guilty about any kind of lying. It
looks as if I'm stuck with telling the truth."

For those of us, however, who are good at telling lies, for   52
those of us who lie and don't get caught, the question of whether
or not to lie can be a hard and serious moral problem. I liked the
remark of a friend of mine who said, "I'm willing to lie. But just
as a last resort—the truth's always better."

"Because," he explained, "though others may completely   53
accept the lie I'm telling, I don't."

I tend to feel that way too.   54

What about you?   55

UNDERSTANDING DETAILS

1. Viorst discusses four types of lies in this essay. Explain each in
   your own words.
2. What types of lies are most serious? What does the author mean
   by "serious"?
3. What does Viorst mean by "Watergate lies" in paragraph 44?
   What is your feeling about this level of trust-keeping lies?
4. According to Viorst, what is the relationship between lying and
   her self-image?

ANALYZING MEANING

1. In what ways is lying a moral problem?
2. Why do people respond in so many different ways to the issue
   of lying?
3. In your opinion or experience, what are the principal consequences of lying? Do the negative consequences outweigh the
   positive, or is the reverse true? Explain your answer in as much
   detail as possible.
4. How do you feel about lying? Does your opinion vary according to the type of lie you tell? Why? Explain your answer in
   detail.

DISCOVERING RHETORICAL STRATEGIES

1. In this essay, Viorst works with both division and classification as she arranges lies into several distinct categories. Write down the main subdivisions of her classification system; then, list under each category the examples she cites. How has she organized these categories? Do all her examples support the appropriate classification? How does she give significance or value to this system of classification?
2. Who do you think is Viorst's intended audience? What specific verbal clues in the essay help you reach this conclusion?
3. Notice that the author repeats the question "What about you?" several times. What effect does this repetition have on your response to the essay?
4. What other rhetorical modes besides division/classification does Viorst use to make her point in the essay? Give specific examples to support your answers.

MAKING CONNECTIONS

1. Judith Viorst categorizes several different types of lies as "a series of moral puzzles" (paragraph 1). To what extent do Bernard Cooper ("Labyrinthine"), Brent Staples ("A Brother's Murder"), and Barbara Ehrenreich ("The Ecstasy of War") all deal with "moral puzzles" in their essays? Which of these "puzzles" is most easily solved? Which is most difficult? Why?
2. In "Behind the Formaldehyde Curtain," Jessica Mitford exposes the "lies" surrounding funeral homes. Would Viorst agree with Mitford that funeral directors lie to us? If so, why do they do so? And why do we continue to allow them to lie to us?
3. How separate and exclusive are Viorst's categories of lies? Could some lies fit within two categories at the same time? Examine Phyllis Schneider's "Memory: Tips You'll Never Forget" and/or Franklin Zimring's "Confessions of an Ex-Smoker" to determine if these authors' categories overlap in the same way that Viorst's do. Do division/classification essays work better if there is little or no overlap between categories? If so, why?

IDEAS FOR DISCUSSION/WRITING

Preparing to Write

Write freely about various lies you have told in the past: When did you lie? When did you consider lying but told the truth? In what types of situations do you most often resort to lying? Why do you lie in these circumstances? How does lying make you feel? How does telling the truth make you feel? Do you have a general philosophy about lying that you try to follow? If so, what is it?

Choosing a Topic

1. At some time in our lives, we all tell or receive lies as Viorst defines them. Choose a particularly memorable lie (one you either told or received), and classify all your feelings connected with the experience. What did you learn from the situation?

2. You have decided that your future roommate/spouse deserves an honest profile of your personality before you begin living together. Analyze for him or her some fundamental truths about your character by classifying your reactions to the information in one of the categories in Viorst's essay.

3. Being in school presents a number of potential opportunities for lying. Answers to such questions as "Why is your homework late?" "Why can't you go out this weekend?" and "Why did you miss class yesterday?" can get people *into* or *out of* all sorts of trouble. For a friend of yours still in high school, write an essay offering advice on handling situations such as these. Devise a useful classification system for these school-related dilemmas; then, explain what your experiences have taught you in each case about lying.

4. Select another moral issue, such as stealing or cheating. Conduct an Internet search on your topic, using credible Web sites to gather expert opinions. Following Viorst's model, classify and evaluate the varying degrees of morality associated with your issue. Integrate quotes from your Internet search into your essay.

Before beginning your essay, you might want to consult the checklists on page 276.

CHAPTER WRITING ASSIGNMENTS
Practicing Division/Classification

1. Do you think public schools should teach students ethics and personal values? If so, which values should schools teach in order to produce "good citizens"? Classify these values in an essay, and explain how these categories would have fit into your high school curriculum.

2. What problems are most destructive to a healthy relationship? Choose a specific type of relationship (friend, spouse, parent-child), and write an essay discussing various categories of problems that can cause the most trouble in this type of relationship. Explain why the qualities you identify would be destructive in the kind of relationship you describe.

3. Think about the ideal _____ (fill in the blank with one of the many roles we play every day [for example, wife, husband, teacher, student, friend, or cousin]). List the qualities that person needs. What categories do these qualities fall into? Why are these characteristics ideal? Write an essay explaining the categories you have developed for the role you chose to discuss.

Exploring Ideas

1. We all have bad habits, but few people know how to break them. What advice do you have for people who want to change their behavior in some important way or break a bad habit? How do you know your method works?

2. Explain a cultural tradition we are in danger of losing in society today. Discuss the value of the tradition itself and the ways this tradition is changing, along with the value and effects of this change. Make sure you discuss this topic in an unbiased way.

3. How do a person's cultural views and beliefs affect the educational process? In what ways does our current system of education acknowledge, hinder, or ignore our diverse cultural backgrounds? In a well-developed essay, discuss how our educational system successfully or unsuccessfully deals with our various cultural differences. Are the categories in your essay distinct from one another? What rhetorical strategies support your essay?

6

COMPARISON/CONTRAST

Discovering Similarities and Differences

Making comparisons is such a natural and necessary part of our everyday lives that we often do so without conscious effort. When we were children, we compared our toys with those of our friends, we contrasted our height and physical development to other children's, and we constantly evaluated our happiness in comparison with that evidenced by our parents and childhood companions. As we grew older, we habitually compared our dates, teachers, parents, friends, cars, and physical attributes. In college, we learn about anthropology by writing essays on the similarities and differences between two African tribes, about political science by contrasting the Republican and Democratic platforms, about business by comparing annual production rates, and about literature by comparing Shakespeare with Marlowe or Browning with Tennyson. Comparing and contrasting various elements in our lives helps us make decisions, such as which course to take or which house to buy, and it justifies preferences that we already hold, such as liking one city more than another or loving one person more than the next. In these ways and in many others, the skillful use of comparison and contrast is clearly essential to our social and professional lives.

DEFINING COMPARISON/CONTRAST

Comparison and contrast allow us to understand one subject by putting it next to another. Comparing involves discovering likenesses or similarities, whereas contrasting is based on finding differences. Like division and classification, comparison and contrast are generally considered part of the same process, because we usually have no reason for comparing unless some contrast is also involved. Each technique implies the existence of the other. For this reason, the word *compare* is often used to mean both techniques.

Comparison and contrast are most profitably applied to two items that have something in common, such as cats and dogs or cars and motorcycles. A discussion of cats and motorcycles, for example, would probably not be very rewarding or stimulating, because they do not have much in common. If more than two items are compared in an essay, they are still most profitably discussed in pairs: for instance, motorcycles and cars, cars and bicycles, or bicycles and motorcycles.

An analogy is an extended, sustained comparison. Often used to explain unfamiliar, abstract, or complicated thoughts, this rhetorical technique adds energy and vividness to a wide variety of college-level writing. The process of analogy differs slightly from comparison/contrast in three important ways: Comparison/contrast begins with subjects from the same class and places equal weight on both of them. In addition, it addresses both the similarities and the differences of these subjects. Analogy, conversely, seldom explores subjects from the same class and focuses principally on one familiar subject in an attempt to explain another, more complex one. Furthermore, it deals only with similarities, not with contrasts. A comparison/contrast essay, for example, might study two veterans' ways of coping with the trauma of the War in Iraq by pointing out the differences in their methods as well as the similarities. An analogy essay might use the familiar notion of a fireworks display to reveal the chilling horror of the lonely hours after dark during this war: "Nights in Bagdad were similar to a loud, unending fireworks display. We had no idea when the next blast was coming, how loud it would be, or how close. We cringed in terror after dark, hoping the next surprise would not be our own death." In this example, rather than simply hearing about an event, we participate in it through this highly refined form of comparison.

The following student paragraph compares and contrasts married and single life. As you read it, notice how the author compares similar social states and, in the process, justifies her current lifestyle:

> Recently I saw a bumper sticker that read, "It used to be wine, women, and song, and now it's beer, the old lady, and TV." Much truth may be found in this comparison of single and married lifestyles. When my husband and I used to date, for example, we'd go out for dinner and drinks and then maybe see a play or concert. Our discussions were intelligent, often ranging over global politics, science, literature, and other lofty topics. He would open doors for me, buy me flowers, and make sure I was comfortable and happy. Now, three years later, after marriage and a child, the baby bottle has replaced the wine bottle, the smell of diapers wipes out the scent of roses, and our nights on the town are infrequent, cherished events. But that's all right. A little bit of the excitement and mystery may be gone, but these intangible qualities have given way to a sturdy, dependable trust in each other and a quiet confidence about our future together.

THINKING CRITICALLY BY USING COMPARISON/CONTRAST

Comparison and contrast are basic to a number of different thought processes. We compare and contrast quite naturally on a daily basis, but all of us would benefit greatly from being more aware of these companion strategies in our own writing. They help us not only in perceiving our environment but also in understanding and organizing large amounts of information.

The basic skill of finding similarities and differences will enhance your ability to create accurate descriptions, to cite appropriate examples, to present a full process analysis, and, of course, to classify and label subjects. It is a pattern of thought that is essential to more complex thinking strategies, so perfecting the ability to use it is an important step in your efforts to improve your critical thinking.

Once again, we are going to practice this strategy in isolation to get a strong sense of its mechanics before we combine it with other rhetorical modes. Isolating this mode will make your reading and writing even stronger than they are now, because the individual parts of the thinking process will be more vigorous and effective, thus making your academic performance more powerful than ever.

© Zach Gold/CORBIS.

1. Make a list of similarities and differences for the photograph above. What messages or ideas do you think the photographer is able to communicate through this photograph?
2. Find magazine ads that use comparison/contrast to make a point or sell a product. What is the basis of each comparison? How effective or ineffective is each comparison?
3. Have you ever been to the same place twice? Think for a moment about how the first and second visits to this place differed. How were they similar? What were the primary reasons for the similarities and differences in your perceptions of these visits?

READING AND WRITING COMPARISON/ CONTRAST ESSAYS

Many established guidelines regulate the development of a comparison/contrast essay and should be taken into account from both the reading and the writing perspectives. All good comparative studies serve a specific purpose. They attempt either to examine their subjects separately or to demonstrate the superiority of one over the other. In evaluating two different types of cars, for example, a writer might point out the amazing gas mileage of one model and the smooth handling qualities of the other or the superiority of one car's gas mileage over that of another. Whatever the intent, comparison/contrast essays need to be clear and logical and have a precise purpose.

How to Read a Comparison/Contrast Essay

Preparing to Read.   As you begin reading this chapter, pull together as much preliminary material as possible for each essay so you can focus your attention and have the benefit of prior knowledge before you start to read. In particular, you should try to discover what is being compared or contrasted and why. From the title of his essay, can you tell what Bruce Catton is comparing in "Grant and Lee: A Study in Contrasts"? What does William Ouchi's title ("Japanese and American Workers: Two Casts of Mind") suggest to you? From glancing at the essay itself and reading the synopsis in the Rhetorical Table of Contents, what do you think Sucheng Chan's essay will try to accomplish?

Also, before you begin to read these essays, try to discover information about the author and about the conditions under which each essay was written. What is Gloria Steinem's stand on women's bodybuilding? To what extent do you expect her opinions on this topic to color her comparison of women's past and present physical strength? Why is Ouchi qualified to write about Japanese and American workers? How does he reveal his background in his essay?

Finally, just before you begin to read, answer the Preparing to Read questions, and then make some free associations with the general topic of each essay: For example, what do you think are some of the main similarities and differences in the past and present of an ex-convict (Jimmy Santiago Baca)? What is your general view on women's bodybuilding (Gloria Steinem)?

Reading.   As you read each comparison/contrast essay for the first time, be sure to record your own feelings and opinions. Some of the issues presented in this chapter are highly controversial. You will often have strong reactions to them, which you should try to write down as soon as possible.

In addition, you may want to comment on the relationship between the preliminary essay material, the author's stance in the essay, and the content of the essay itself. For example, what motivated Baca to write "Past Present"? Who is his primary audience? What is Chan's tone in "You're Short, Besides!," and how does it advance her purpose? Answers to questions such as these will provide you with a context for your first reading of these essays and will assist you in preparing to analyze the essays in more depth on your second reading.

At this point in the chapter, you should make certain you understand each author's thesis and then take a close look at his or her principal method of organization: Is the essay arranged (1) point by point, (2) subject by subject, (3) as a combination of these two, or (4) as separate discussions of similarities and differences between two subjects? (See the chart on page 330 for an illustration of these options.) Last, preview the questions that follow the essay before you read it again.

Rereading.   When you read these essays a second time, you should look at the comparison or contrast much more closely than you have up to now. First, look in detail at the writer's method of organization (see the chart on page 330). How effective is it in advancing the writer's thesis?

Next, you should consider whether each essay is fully developed and balanced: Does Catton compare similar items? Does Baca discuss the same elements of his subjects? Does Ouchi deal with all aspects of the comparison between Japanese and American workers? Is Steinem's treatment of her subjects well balanced? And does Chan give her audience enough specific details to clarify the extent of her comparison? Do all the writers in this chapter use well-chosen transitions so you can move smoothly from one point to the next? Also, what other rhetorical modes support each comparison/contrast in this chapter?

Finally, the answers to the questions after each selection will let you evaluate your understanding of the essay and help you analyze its contents in preparation for the discussion/writing topics that follow.

For a more thorough inventory of the reading process, you should turn to page 20 in the Introduction.

How to Write a Comparison/Contrast Essay

Preparing to Write. As you consider various topics for a comparison/contrast essay, you should answer the Preparing to Write questions that precede the assignments and then use the prewriting techniques explained in the Introduction (pp. 21–23) to generate even more ideas on these topics.

As you focus your attention on a particular topic, keep the following suggestions in mind:

1. Always compare/contrast items in the same category (e.g., compare two professors, but not a professor and a swimming pool).
2. Have a specific purpose or reason for writing your essay.
3. Discuss the same qualities of each subject (if you evaluate the teaching techniques of one professor, do so for the other professor as well).
4. Use as many pertinent details as possible to expand your comparison/contrast and to accomplish your stated purpose.
5. Deal with all aspects of the comparison that are relevant to the purpose.
6. Balance the treatment of the different subjects of your comparison (i.e., don't spend more time on one than on another).
7. Determine your audience's background and knowledge so that you will know how much of your comparison should be explained in detail and how much can be skimmed over.

Next, in preparation for a comparison/contrast project, you might list all the elements of both subjects that you want to compare. This list can then help you give your essay structure as well as substance. At this stage in the writing process, the task may seem similar to pure description, but a discussion of two subjects in relation to one another rapidly changes the assignment from description to comparison.

Writing. The introduction of your comparison/contrast essay should (1) clearly identify your subjects, (2) explain the basis of your comparison/contrast, and (3) state your purpose and the overall limits of your particular study. Identifying your subject is, of course, a necessary and important task in any essay. Similarly, justifying the elements you will be comparing and contrasting creates interest and gives your audience some specifics to look for in the essay. Finally, your statement of purpose or thesis (for example, to prove that one professor is superior to another) should include the boundaries of your discussion. You cannot cover all the reasons for your preference in one short essay, so you must limit your consideration to three or four basic categories (perhaps teaching techniques, the clarity of the assignments given, classroom attitude, and grading standards). The introduction is the place to make all these limits known.

You can organize the body of your paper in one of four ways: (1) a point-by-point, or alternating, comparison; (2) a subject-by-subject, or divided, comparison; (3) a combination of these two methods; or (4) a division between the similarities and differences.

The point-by-point comparison evaluates both subjects in terms of each category. If the issue, for example, is which of two cars to buy, you might discuss both models' gasoline mileage first; then, their horsepower; next, their ease in handling; and, finally, their standard equipment. Following the second method of organization, subject by subject, you would discuss the gasoline mileage, horsepower, ease in handling, and standard equipment of car A first and then follow the same format for car B. The third option would allow you to introduce, say, the standard equipment of each car point by point (or car by car) and then to explain the other features in your comparison (miles per gallon, horsepower, and ease in handling) subject by subject. To use the last method of organization, you might discuss the similarities between the two models first and the differences second (or vice versa). If the cars you are comparing have similar miles-per-gallon (MPG) ratings but completely different horsepower, steering systems, and optional equipment, you could discuss the gasoline mileage and then emphasize the differences by mentioning them later in the essay. If, instead, you are trying to emphasize the fact that the MPG ratings of these models remain consistent despite their differences, then reverse the order of your essay.

When confronted with the task of choosing a method of organization for a comparison/contrast essay, you need to find the pattern that best suits your purpose. If you want single items to

Methods of Organization

Point by Point*

MPG, car A
MPG, car B

Horsepower, car A
Horsepower, car B

Handling, car A
Handling, car B

Equipment, car A
Equipment, car B

*Emphasizes individual points. Is best for long essays. Helpful hint: Use transitions to avoid lists.

Subject by Subject+

MPG, car A
Horsepower, car A
Handling, car A
Equipment, car A

MPG, car B
Horsepower, car B
Handling, car B
Equipment, car B

+Emphasizes each subject. Is best for short essays. Helpful hint: Use transitions to avoid two separate essays.

Combination

Equipment, car A
Equipment, car B

————

MPG, car A
Horsepower, car A
Handling, car A

MPG, car B
Horsepower, car B
Handling, car B

Similarities/Differences

Similarities:
    MPG, cars A & B

Differences:
    Horsepower, cars A & B
    Handling, cars A & B
    Equipment, cars A & B

stand out in a discussion, for instance, the best choice will be the point-by-point system; it is especially appropriate for long essays but has a tendency to turn into an exercise in listing if you don't pay careful attention to your transitions. If, however, the subjects themselves (rather than the itemized points) are the most interesting feature of your essay, you should use the subject-by-subject comparison; this system is particularly good for short essays in which the readers can retain what was said about one subject while they read about a second subject. Through this second method of organization, each subject becomes a unified whole, an approach to an essay that is generally effective unless the theme becomes awkwardly divided into two separate parts. You must also remember, if you choose this second method of organization, that the second (or last) subject is in the most emphatic position because that is what your readers will have seen most recently. The final two options for organizing a comparison/contrast essay give you some built-in flexibility so that you can create emphasis and attempt to manipulate reader opinion simply by the structure of your essay.

Using logical transitions in your comparison/contrast essays will establish clear relationships between the items in your comparisons and will also move your readers smoothly from one topic to the next. If you wish to indicate comparisons, use such words as *like, as, also, in like manner, similarly,* and *in addition;* to signal contrasts, try *but, in contrast to, unlike, whereas,* and *on the one hand/on the other hand.*

The conclusion of a comparison/contrast essay summarizes the main points and states the deductions drawn from those points. As you choose your method of organization, remember not to get locked into a formulaic approach to your subjects, which will adversely affect the readability of your essay. To avoid making your reader feel like a spectator at a verbal table tennis match, be straightforward, honest, and patient as you discover and recount the details of your comparison.

Rewriting.   When you review the draft of your comparison/contrast essay, you need once again to make sure that you communicate your purpose as effectively as possible to your intended audience. Two guidelines previously mentioned should help you accomplish this goal:

- Do you identify your subjects clearly?
- Does your thesis clearly state the purpose and overall limits of your particular study?

You will also need to pay close attention to the following in the development of your essay:

- Are you attempting to compare/contrast items from the same general category?
- Do you discuss the same qualities of each subject?
- Do you balance the treatment of the different subjects of your essay?
- Do you organize your topic as effectively as possible?
- Does your conclusion contain a summary and analysis of your main points?

For further information on writing and revising your comparison/contrast essays, consult the checklists on pages 31–32 of the Introduction.

STUDENT ESSAY: COMPARISON/CONTRAST AT WORK

The following student essay compares the advantages and disadvantages of macaroni and cheese versus tacos in the life of a harried college freshman. As you read it, notice that the writer states his intention in the first paragraph and then expands his discussion with appropriate details to produce a balanced essay. Also, try to determine what effect he creates by using two methods of organization: first subject by subject, then point by point.

Dormitory Chef

To this day, I will not eat either macaroni and cheese or tacos. No, it's not because of any allergy; it's because during my freshman year at college, I prepared one or the other of these scrumptious dishes more times than I care to remember. However, my choice of which culinary delight to cook on any given night was not as simple a decision as one might imagine.

Topics

Basis of comparison

Thesis statement: Purpose and limits of comparison

Macaroni and cheese has numerous advantages for the dormitory chef. First of all, it is inexpensive. No matter how poor one may be, there's probably enough change under the couch cushion to buy a box at the market. All that starch for only $5.29. What a bargain! Second, it can be

Paragraph on Subject A: Macaroni and cheese

Point 1 (Price)

Point 2 (Preparation)

<u>prepared in just one pan</u>. This is especially important given the meager resources of the average dorm kitchen. <u>Third, and perhaps most important, macaroni and cheese is odorless</u>. By odorless, I mean that no one else can smell it. It is a well-known fact that dorm residents hate to cook and that they love nothing better than to wander dejectedly around the kitchen with big, sad eyes after someone else has been cooking. But with macaroni and cheese, no enticing aromas are going to find their way into the nose of any would-be mooch.

Point 3 (Odor) appears in the left margin.

Tacos, <u>on the other hand</u>, are a different matter altogether. For the dorm cook, <u>the most significant difference is obviously the price</u>. To enjoy tacos for dinner, the adventurous dorm gourmet must purchase no fewer than five ingredients from the market: corn tortillas, beef, lettuce, tomatoes, and cheese. Needless to say, this is a major expenditure. <u>Second, the chef must adroitly shuffle these ingredients back and forth among his or her very limited supply of pans and bowls</u>. <u>And finally, tacos smell great</u>. That wouldn't be a problem if the tacos didn't also smell great to about twenty of the cook's newest—if not closest—friends, who appear with those same pathetic, starving eyes mentioned earlier. When this happens, the cook will be lucky to get more than two of his own creations.

Paragraph on Subject B: Tacos / *Transition* / *Point 1 (Price)* / *Point 2 (Preparation)* / *Point 3 (Odor)* appear in the margins.

<u>Tacos, then</u>, wouldn't stand much of a chance if they didn't outdo <u>macaroni and cheese</u> in one area: taste. Taste is almost—but not quite—an optional requirement in the opinion of a frugal dormitory hash-slinger. Taste is just important enough so that tacos are occasionally prepared, despite their disadvantages.

Subject B / *Transition* / *Subject A* / *Paragraph on Point 4: Taste* appear in the margins.

Transition	But tacos have other advantages besides	Subject B
Paragraph on Point 5: Color	their taste. With their enticing, colorful ingredients, they even look good. The only thing that can be said about the color of macaroni and cheese is that it's a color not found in nature.	Subject A
Transition	On the other hand, macaroni and cheese is quick. It can be prepared in about ten	Subject A
Paragraph on Point 6: Time	minutes, while tacos take more than twice as long. And there are occasions—such as final exam week—when time is a scarce and precious resource.	Subject B
Transition	As you can see, quite a bit of thinking went into my choice of food in my younger years. These two dishes essentially got me	Summary
Analysis	through my freshman year and indirectly taught me how to make important decisions (like what to eat). But I still feel a certain revulsion when I hear their names today.	Concluding statement

Student Writer's Comments

I compare and contrast so many times during a typical day that I took this rhetorical technique for granted. In fact, I had overlooked it completely. The most difficult part of writing this essay was finding two appropriate subjects to compare. Ideally, I knew they should be united by a similarity. So I brainstormed to come up with some possible topics. Then, working from this list of potential subjects, I began to freewrite to see if I could come up with two topics in the same category on which I could write a balanced comparison. Out of my freewriting came this reasoning: Macaroni and cheese and tacos, in reality, are two very different kinds of food from the same category. Proving this fact is easy and might even result in an interesting essay. Their similar property of being popular dorm foods unites the two despite their differences and also gives me two important reasons for writing the comparison: to discover why they are both popular dorm delicacies and to determine which one has more advantages for my particular purposes. In proportion to writing and revising, I spent most of my time choosing my topic, brainstorming, freewriting, and rebrainstorming to make sure I could develop every aspect of my comparison adequately. Most of my prewriting work took the form of two columns, in which I recorded my opinions on the choice between macaroni and cheese versus tacos.

Sitting down to mold my lists into an essay posed an entirely new set of problems. From the copious notes I had taken, I easily wrote the introductory paragraph, identifying my topics, explaining the basis of my comparison/contrast, and stating the purpose and limits of my study (my thesis statement). But now that I faced the body of the essay, I needed to find the best way to organize my opinions on these two dorm foods: point by point, subject by subject, a combination of these two, or a discussion of similarities and differences?

I wrote my first draft discussing my topics point by point. Even with an occasional joke and a few snide comments interjected, the essay reminded me of a boring game of ping pong with only a few attempts at changing the pace. I started over completely with my second draft and worked through my topics subject by subject. I felt this approach was better, but not quite right for my particular purpose and audience. I set out to do some heavy-handed revising.

Discussing my first three points (price, preparation, and odor) subject by subject seemed to work quite well. I was actually satisfied with the first half of my discussion of these two subjects. But the essay really started to get sluggish when I brought up the fourth point: taste. So I broke off my discussion there and rewrote the second half of my essay point by point, dealing with taste, color, and time each in its own paragraph. This change gave my essay the new direction it needed to keep the readers' attention and also offered me some new insights into my comparison. Then I returned to the beginning of my essay and revised it for readability, adding transitions and making sure the paper now moved smoothly from one point or subject to the next. Finally, I added my final paragraph including a brief summary of my main points and an explanation of the deductions I had made. My concluding remark ("But I still feel a certain revulsion when I hear their names today.") came to me as I was putting the final touches on this draft.

What I learned from writing this particular essay is that comparison/contrast thinking, more than thinking in other rhetorical modes, is much like a puzzle. I really had to spend an enormous amount of time thinking through, mapping out, and rethinking my comparison before I could start to put my thoughts in essay form. The results are rewarding, but I sure wore out a piece of linoleum on the den floor on the way to my final draft.

SOME FINAL THOUGHTS ON COMPARISON/CONTRAST

The essays in this section demonstrate various methods of organization as well as a number of distinct stylistic approaches to writing a comparison/contrast essay. As you read these selections, pay particular attention to the clear, well-focused introductions; the different logical methods of organization; and the smooth transitions between sentences and paragraphs.

COMPARISON/CONTRAST IN REVIEW

Reading Comparison/Contrast Essays

Preparing to Read

✓ What assumptions can you make from the essay's title?
✓ Can you guess what the general mood of the essay is?
✓ What is the essay's purpose and audience?
✓ What does the synopsis tell you about the essay?
✓ What can you learn from the author's biography?
✓ Can you guess what the author's point of view toward the subject is?
✓ What are your responses to the "Preparing to Read" questions?

Reading

✓ What is the author's thesis?
✓ How is the essay organized?
✓ Did you preview the questions that follow the essay?

Rereading

✓ Is the writer's method of organization effective?
✓ Is the essay fully developed?
✓ What other rhetorical strategies does the author use?
✓ What are your responses to the questions after the essay?

Writing Comparison/Contrast Essays

Preparing to Write

✓ What are your responses to the "Preparing to Write" questions?
✓ What is your purpose?
✓ Have you generated as many pertinent details as possible?

Writing

✓ Does your introduction (1) identify your subjects, (2) explain the basis of your comparison, and (3) state the purpose and limits of your study?
✓ Does your thesis include the boundaries of your discussion?
✓ Is your paper organized point by point, subject by subject, as a combination of the two, or as a discussion of similarities and differences?

Rewriting

✓ Does your thesis state the purpose and limits of your study?
✓ Do you compare items in the same general category?
✓ Do you discuss the same qualities of each subject?
✓ Do you balance the treatment of your topics?
✓ Does your conclusion summarize and analyze your main points?

BRUCE CATTON   (1899–1978)

Grant and Lee: A Study in Contrasts

Bruce Catton was a much-loved and respected historian of the U.S. Civil War, whose many books and articles have brought an "eyewitness" vividness to this crucial period in American development. Believing that history "ought to be a good yarn," Catton saw himself as more of a reporter than a historian, stripping away the romantic glamour of war to reveal with vigor and clarity the reality of this important historical era. A native of Benzonia, Michigan, the author was fascinated during his childhood by stories told by the many Civil War veterans who had returned to his small town. Catton attended Oberlin College, worked for a time as a newspaper reporter, and then turned his attention principally to researching and writing about the Civil War. His most popular and influential book was *A Stillness at Appomattox* (the third part of his *Army of the Potomac* trilogy), which won both the Pulitzer Prize and the National Book Award for history in 1954. Among his many other books are *This Hallowed Ground* (1956), *The Coming Fury* (1961), *Terrible Swift Sword* (1963), *Grant Takes Command* (1969), and *Michigan: A Bicentennial History* (1976). For the last twenty-four years of his life, Catton was also editor of *American Heritage* magazine.

Preparing to Read

The following essay is taken from *The American Story* (1956), a collection of essays by distinguished historians; it examines the similarities and differences between Generals Grant and Lee at the conclusion of the Civil War.

Exploring Experience: As you prepare to read this article, take a few moments to consider heroes in your life: What special qualities turn people into heroic figures? Why do you think some heroes are admired more than others? What historical events bring forth heroes? How does American society act in general toward these people? Why do most of us seem to need heroic figures in our lives?

Learning Online: In this essay, Catton describes the historic meeting between Grant and Lee at the Appomattox Courthouse.

To view a photo and brief history of the courthouse, go to the National Park Service Web site (http://www.nps.gov/apco).

W hen Ulysses S. Grant and Robert E. Lee met in the parlor of a modest house at Appomattox Court House, Virginia, on April 9, 1865, to work out the terms for the surrender of Lee's Army of Northern Virginia, a great chapter in American life came to a close, and a great new chapter began.   1

These men were bringing the Civil War to its virtual finish. To be sure, other armies had yet to surrender, and for a few days the fugitive Confederate government would struggle desperately and vainly, trying to find some way to go on living now that its chief support was gone. But in effect it was all over when Grant and Lee signed the papers. And the little room where they wrote out the terms was the scene of one of the poignant, dramatic contrasts in American history.   2

They were two strong men, these oddly different generals, and they represented the strengths of two conflicting currents that, through them, had come into final collision.   3

Back of Robert E. Lee was the notion that the old aristocratic concept might somehow survive and be dominant in American life.   4

Lee was tidewater Virginia, and in his background were family, culture, and tradition . . . the age of chivalry transplanted to a New World which was making its own legends and its own myths. He embodied a way of life that had come down through the age of knighthood and the English country squire. America was a land that was beginning all over again, dedicated to nothing much more complicated than the rather hazy belief that all men had equal rights and should have an equal chance in the world. In such a land Lee stood for the feeling that it was somehow of advantage to human society to have a pronounced inequality in the social structure. There should be a leisure class, backed by ownership of land; in turn, society itself should be keyed to the land as the chief source of wealth and influence. It would bring forth (according to this ideal) a class of men with a strong sense of obligation to the community; men who lived not to gain advantage for themselves, but to meet the solemn obligations which had been laid on them by the very fact that they were privileged. From them the country would get its leadership; to them it could look   5

for the higher values—of thought, of conduct, of personal deport-
ment—to give it strength and virtue.

Lee embodied the noblest elements of this aristocratic ideal.   6
Through him, the landed nobility justified itself. For four years,
the Southern states had fought a desperate war to uphold the ideals
for which Lee stood. In the end, it almost seemed as if the
Confederacy fought for Lee; as if he himself was the Confederacy . . . the best thing that the way of life for which the
Confederacy stood could ever have to offer. He had passed into
legend before Appomattox. Thousands of tired, underfed, poorly
clothed Confederate soldiers, long since past the simple enthusiasm of the early days of the struggle, somehow considered Lee the
symbol of everything for which they had been willing to die. But
they could not quite put this feeling into words. If the Lost Cause,
sanctified by so much heroism and so many deaths, had a living
justification, its justification was General Lee.

Grant, the son of a tanner on the Western frontier, was every-   7
thing Lee was not. He had come up the hard way and embodied
nothing in particular except the eternal toughness and sinewy fiber
of the men who grew up beyond the mountains. He was one of a
body of men who owed reverence and obeisance to no one, who
were self-reliant to a fault, who cared hardly anything for the past
but who had a sharp eye for the future.

These frontier men were the precise opposites of the tidewater   8
aristocrats. Back of them, in the great surge that had taken people
over the Alleghenies and into the opening Western country, there
was a deep, implicit dissatisfaction with a past that had settled into
grooves. They stood for democracy, not from any reasoned conclusion about the proper ordering of human society, but simply
because they had grown up in the middle of democracy and knew
how it worked. Their society might have privileges, but they would
be privileges each man had won for himself. Forms and patterns
meant nothing. No man was born to anything, except perhaps to a
chance to show how far he could rise. Life was competition.

Yet along with this feeling had come a deep sense of belong-   9
ing to a national community. The Westerner who developed a
farm, opened a shop, or set up in business as a trader could hope
to prosper only as his own community prospered—and his community ran from the Atlantic to the Pacific and from Canada
down to Mexico. If the land was settled, with towns and highways

and accessible markets, he could better himself. He saw his fate in terms of the nation's own destiny. As its horizons expanded, so did his. He had, in other words, an acute dollars-and-cents stake in the continued growth and development of his country.

And that, perhaps, is where the contrast between Grant and 10 Lee becomes most striking. The Virginia aristocrat, inevitably, saw himself in relation to his own region. He lived in a static society which could endure almost anything except change. Instinctively, his first loyalty would go to the locality in which that society existed. He would fight to the limit of endurance to defend it, because in defending it he was defending everything that gave his own life its deepest meaning.

The Westerner, on the other hand, would fight with an equal 11 tenacity for the broader concept of society. He fought so because everything he lived by was tied to growth, expansion, and a constantly widening horizon. What he lived by would survive or fall with the nation itself. He could not possibly stand by unmoved in the face of an attempt to destroy the Union. He would combat it with everything he had, because he could only see it as an effort to cut the ground out from under his feet.

So Grant and Lee were in complete contrast, representing two 12 diametrically opposed elements in American life. Grant was the modern man emerging; beyond him, ready to come on the stage, was the great age of steel and machinery, of crowded cities and a restless burgeoning vitality. Lee might have ridden down from the old age of chivalry, lance in hand, silken banner fluttering over his head. Each man was the perfect champion of his cause, drawing both his strengths and his weaknesses from the people he led.

Yet it was not all contrast, after all. Different as they were— 13 in background, in personality, in underlying aspiration—these two great soldiers had much in common. Under everything else, they were marvelous fighters. Furthermore, their fighting qualities were really very much alike.

Each man had, to begin with, the great virtue of utter tenacity 14 and fidelity. Grant fought his way down the Mississippi Valley in spite of acute personal discouragement and profound military handicaps. Lee hung on in the trenches at Petersburg after hope itself had died. In each man there was an indomitable quality. . . . the born fighter's refusal to give up as long as he can still remain on his feet and lift his two fists.

Daring and resourcefulness they had, too; the ability to think   15
faster and move faster than the enemy. These were the qualities
which gave Lee the dazzling campaigns of Second Manassas and
Chancellorsville and won Vicksburg for Grant.

Lastly, and perhaps greatest of all, there was the ability, at the   16
end, to turn quickly from war to peace once the fighting was over.
Out of the way these two men behaved at Appomattox came the
possibility of a peace of reconciliation. It was a possibility not
wholly realized, in the years to come, but which did, in the end,
help the two sections to become one nation again . . . after a war
whose bitterness might have seemed to make such a reunion
wholly impossible. No part of either man's life became him more
than the part he played in this brief meeting in the McLean house
at Appomattox. Their behavior there put all succeeding generations of Americans in their debt. Two great Americans, Grant and
Lee—very different, yet under everything very much alike. Their
encounter at Appomattox was one of the great moments of
American history.

UNDERSTANDING DETAILS

1. What two conflicting views of American life does the author
   believe these two generals represented?
2. What special qualities of Grant and Lee does Catton contrast to
   achieve his purpose? What qualities does he compare?
3. How did both Grant and Lee respond to progress and change
   in general? Explain your answer in detail.
4. What does Catton imply about the behavior of these two generals at Appomattox Court House? According to this essay,
   why was the encounter of Grant and Lee at Appomattox "one
   of the great moments of American history" (paragraph 16)?

ANALYZING MEANING

1. What is Catton's purpose in this essay? What truths, according
   to the author, needed to be made clear about these two great
   Civil War generals? Why did Catton study similarities as well as
   differences in these two men?
2. What does Catton mean when he says, "Life was competition"
   (paragraph 8) in Grant's philosophy? What aspects of this philosophy do you see in today's society?

3. In what ways were Lee and Grant emblems of the past and the future, respectively?

4. About the actions of these men at Appomattox, Catton says, "Their behavior there put all succeeding generations of Americans in their debt" (paragraph 16). What does he mean by this statement? What influences of these two men can we still see in our culture today?

DISCOVERING RHETORICAL STRATEGIES

1. Which of the four main methods of organizing a comparison/contrast essay does Catton use? How many paragraphs does the author spend on each part of his comparison? Why do you think he spends this amount of time on each?

2. What transitional words or phrases does the author use to move from one part of this essay to the next? Give at least three specific examples. Do these devices hold the essay together effectively? Explain your answer.

3. In what ways does the last paragraph of this essay echo the first paragraph? Why is this echoing technique an effective way to end the essay?

4. What other rhetorical strategies besides comparison and contrast does Catton use to achieve his purpose in this essay? Give examples of each strategy.

MAKING CONNECTIONS

1. Like Bruce Catton, Alice Walker ("Beauty: When the Other Dancer Is the Self") describes one particular moment in time when life was changed forever. What similarities can you find between the two important events described by each of these authors?

2. First, Catton contrasts Grant and Lee, and then he compares them. How is this structural approach different from the comparison/contrast essays written by Sucheng Chan ("You're Short, Besides!") and William Ouchi ("Japanese and American Workers: Two Casts of Mind")? Which organizational technique do you find most effective? Explain your answer.

3. According to Catton, Grant and Lee each represented "the strengths of two conflicting currents that, through them, had

come into final collision" (paragraph 3). Along the same lines, how do "mazes" signify complexity in life for Bernard Cooper in "Labyrinthine," and how does an "unfamiliar country" symbolize old age for Malcolm Cowley in "The View from 80"? In other words, how do these three authors use symbols to give significance to everyday events?

IDEAS FOR DISCUSSION/WRITING

Preparing to Write

Write freely about heroes and heroines in American society: Name some public figures you respect. Why do you admire them? What qualifies someone as a heroic figure in your opinion? What do most of the heroes and heroines you admire have in common? How are they different? How are history and heroic figures related in your mind?

Choosing a Topic

1. In an essay written for your classmates, compare and/or contrast two famous people in history. As Catton did, try to explain what forces in society these figures represent. Decide on a clear focus and point of view before you begin.
2. Choose two people who have had a significant influence on your life. Then, compare and/or contrast how they have affected you.
3. America has had many new beginnings throughout its history. The time at the end of the Civil War, discussed in this essay, was one of them. Explain to your classmates another new beginning for America. What were the details of this new start? Who were the heroes? Where, when, how, and why did it take place?
4. Visit your favorite online news source. Who is in the headlines? Select a person in today's news. Following Catton's example, compare this person with someone who may share some character traits but seems diametrically opposed in every other way. Write an essay in which you use Catton's method of presenting each person, while comparing and contrasting their backgrounds and actions.

Before beginning your essay, you might want to consult the checklists on page 337.

JIMMY SANTIAGO BACA   (1952–   )

Past Present

Born in Santa Fe, New Mexico, Jimmy Santiago Baca describes himself as "a mestizo of Apache and Yaqui descent; half of my family are Apaches, on my father's side, and on my mother's side everybody is Hispanic or European . . . so I think that we are deeply mixed bloods." Abandoned by his parents as a semi-literate youngster, he spent his early years in orphanages and later became a violent drug user and criminal, for which he was sent to prison for five years (four of them in solitary confinement). During this time, he began reading voraciously and eventually became a writer, publishing several poems while still incarcerated. Between earning a B. A. in English (1984) and a Ph.D. in Literature at the University of New Mexico (2003), Baca has published nearly twenty books of poetry—including *Immigrants in Our Own Land* (1979), *Black Mesa Poems* (1989), *In the Way of the Sun* (1997), and *Winter Poems Along the Rio Grande* (2004)—along with several plays and screenplays. His many honors and awards include the American Book Award for Poetry (1988), the National Hispanic Heritage Award (1989), and a Wallace Stevens Poetry Fellowship at Yale University. For recreation, he loves mountain running, swimming, and fishing. His advice to students using *The Prose Reader* is to "read, read, read. That's the key to becoming a good writer."

Preparing to Read

In the following essay, taken from H. Bruce Franklin's *Prison Writing in 20th Century America* (1998), Jimmy Baca compares his past and present by looking closely at imprisonment and freedom. He actually has a very difficult time psychologically separating his past imprisonment from his current freedom.

Exploring Experience: As you prepare to read this essay, take a few moments to think about freedom in general: Is your personal freedom important to you? Why or why not? Do you take your freedom for granted? What do you value most about your freedom? Would you be willing to risk your life for your freedom?

Name some countries that do not enjoy freedom? What do you know about these societies? Have you ever been to a country where personal freedom was restricted? What was your experience there?

Learning Online: Jimmy Santiago Baca's essay focuses on a description of San Quentin prison, its inmates, and his experience within its walls. To contextualize Baca's experience, visit the San Quentin Web site. Conduct an Internet search on the term *San Quentin,* and select the State of California's official Web site for San Quentin. Consider the numbers provided on this site: pay attention especially to the number of inmates and staff and the types of programs offered.

W hen I finished my last prison term twelve years ago, I   1
never dreamed I would go back. But not long ago I found myself looking up at the famous San Quentin tower as I followed an escort guard through the main gates. I should have been overjoyed since this time I was a free man, the writer of a film which required a month of location-shooting there. But being there had a disquieting effect on me. I was confused. I knew that I would be able to leave every night after filming, but the enclosing walls, the barbed wire, and the guards in the towers shouldering their carbines made old feelings erupt in me. While my mind told me I was free, my spirit snarled as if I were a prisoner again, and I couldn't shake the feeling. Emotionally, I could not convince myself that I was not going to be subjected once more to horrible indignities, that I would not have to live through it all again. Each morning when the guards checked my shoulder bag and clanked shut the iron door behind me, the old convict in me rose up full of hatred and rage for the guards, the walls, the terrible indecency of the place. I was still the same man who had entered there freely, a man full of love for his family and his life. But another self from the past reawakened, an imprisoned self, seething with the desire for vengeance on all things not imprisoned.

As I followed the guard, passing with the crew and the actors   2
from one compound to another, a hollow feeling of disbelief possessed me, and I was struck dumb. The grounds were impeccably

planted and groomed, serene as a cemetery. Streamlined circles of flowers and swatches of smooth lawn rolled to trimmed green margins of pruned shrubbery, perfectly laid out against the limestone and red brick cellblocks. But I knew that when you penetrated beyond this pretty landscaping, past the offices, also with their bouquets of flowers, past the cellblock's thick walls, there thrived America's worst nightmare. There the green, concealing surface lifted from the bubbling swamp, a monster about to rise from its dark depths. There writhed scaly demons, their claws and fangs primed for secret and unspeakable brutalities.

Even within those walls, the free man that I am eventually   3
found himself able to forgive the sufferings of the past. But the convict in me was inflamed by everything I saw. It was all so familiar, so full of bitter memory: the milk-paned windows and linoleum tiles of the offices; the flyers thumbtacked to cork boards on the walls; the vast lower yard and the great upper yard with its corrugated shed pocked with light-pierced, jagged bullet holes; the looming limestone cellblocks. The thought of the thousands of human beings whose souls were murdered here in the last hundred years made my blood run cold. The faintly humming body energy of six thousand imprisoned human beings bored a smoking hole in my brain. And through that hole, as if through a prison-door peephole, I saw all the free people going about their lives on the other side, while my place was again with the convicts. Anyone opening that door from the other side must die or be taken hostage and forced to understand our hatred, made to experience the insane brutality that is the convict's daily lot, and that makes him, in turn, brutal and insane.

Since I was acting in the film, I had to dress out daily in   4
banaroos, prison-issue blue denims. I was made up to look younger than I am, as I might have looked in 1973. After this outer transformation, I seemed more and more to become the person I had left behind twelve years ago, until finally that former self began to consume the poet and husband and father who had taken his place. I didn't know what was happening to me.

Dragged back into dangerous backwaters, I encountered my old   5
demons. The crew seemed to sense this and gave me a wide berth. The familiar despair and rage of the prisoners was like a current sucking me down into the sadness of their wasted lives. The guards who paced the cellblocks now were no different from the guards

who had leered and spit at me, beaten and insulted me. Even though I knew that now I wouldn't have to take their shit and that now I could speak up for the cons who had to hold their tongues, part of me was still caught in this time warp of displacement.

When we went to the recreational building, where I was to   6
choose some of the convicts to act as extras, I was surprised by how young they were. I realized I was now the old man among them. In my prison days, the convicts had always seemed to be grizzled older guys, but now, for the most part, they were young kids in their twenties. After I selected the group of extras, I explained to them that the movie was about three kids from East L.A., one of whom goes to prison. As I spoke, my convict stance and manners came back to me, and the old slang rolled off my tongue as if I had never left. Memories of my own imprisonment assailed me, dissolving the barrier between us.

Although technically I was free, that first week I used my free-   7
dom in a strange way, venting hatred on anyone who looked at me, the cons included, because they, too, in the prison world, are joined in their own hierarchy of brutality.

One day a documentary crew came to where we were filming   8
in the weight pit and asked to interview me. Prisoners of every race were present. I looked around me and was filled with contempt for every living soul there. After repeatedly refusing to speak, while microphones were shoved in my face, I suddenly decided to answer their questions.

How did I feel about returning to a prison to help film and act   9
in this movie I had written? Was I proud and pleased? I sat on a bench-press seat curling about thirty pounds as I spoke.

I said I hated being back and that no movie could begin to   10
show the injustices practiced here. I said that fame was nothing weighed against the suffering and brutality of prison life. I told them that these cons should tear the . . . walls down and allow no one to dehumanize them in this way. What were my feelings about being here?

I said that I hated everyone and just wanted to be left alone. . . .   11
Just leave me alone!

I got up and walked away. There was a terrible tearing wound   12
in my heart that I thought no one could see. But Gina, the associate producer, came up to me weeping, pleading for me to come back to myself, to be again the man she knew. She hugged me.

One of the actors also approached and talked to me quietly. In spite of their attempts to comfort me, I felt helplessly encaged by powers I couldn't vanquish or control. I was ensnared in a net of memories. When the few convicts who had been hanging with me started to put some distance between us, I felt as if no one could see me or hear me. I was disoriented, as if I had smashed full force into some invisible barrier.

After a couple of days, I came out of it, dazed and bewildered, 13 shocked and weak as if after major surgery. People I previously couldn't bring myself to speak to, I spoke with now. I felt that sense of wonder one feels after a narrow escape from death.

As I continued to live my double life, I became a keen observer 14 of both worlds. On the streets people could cry freely, but in prison tears led to challenges and deep, embittered stares. In prison no one shakes hands, that common gesture of friendship and trust. The talk never varies from the subjects of freedom and imprisonment; the stories and the laughs are about con jobs and scams. Outside everything is always changing; there are surprises, and you talk about that. But in prison the only news is old news. It is a dead land, filled with threat, where there is no appeal from the death sentence meted out for infractions of the convict code. Imagine being hunted through the jungles of Nam day after day for twenty years, and that will tell you a little of what prison is about.

The days went by. When we finished filming, late in the 15 evenings, I would go back to my trailer, change into my street clothes, and walk alone across the lower yard. The dead exercise pit, where many of the men spend a lot of time buffing themselves out, looked forlorn. It was very late as I crossed the lower yard to a waiting van, but the lights around the lower yard, huge, looming, twenty-eyed klieg lights, made it seem like daytime. Everything about prison life distorts reality, starting with the basic assumption that imprisonment can alter criminal behavior, when the truth is that it entrenches it more firmly. Confinement perverts and destroys every skill a man needs to live productively in society.

As I walked on, my mind full of these thoughts, buses from all 16 over California pulled up in the eerie yellow light, disgorging new inmates who were lined up to get their prison clothes before being marched off to the cellblocks. A van was waiting to take me back to my corporate-paid condo, where there was fresh food waiting for me, where I could relax and phone my wife, turn on some soft

music and write a little, read a little, in the silence; walk to the
window and smell the cool night air and look across the bay to
the Golden Gate Bridge and beyond to San Francisco, a city as
angelic at night as any heavenly sanctum conjured up in medieval
tapestries.

But all of these anticipated pleasures only intensified my anguish   17
for those I was leaving behind, for those imprisoned who have—
nothing. The cells in San Quentin's Carson block are so small that
a man cannot bend or stretch without bruising himself against
some obstacle. And two men share each cell. The cellblocks stink
of mildew and drying feces. The noise is a dull, constant, numb-
ing beating against the brain. Had I really inhabited such a cell for
seven years? It didn't happen; it couldn't have happened. How did
I survive? Who was that kid that lived through this horror? It was
me. Since that time I had grown, changed; but I was still afraid to
touch that reality with my mind, that unspeakable pain.

On those lonely night walks into freedom, the tremendous grief   18
and iron rage of the convict revived in me. The empty yard, with
its watchful glare, mercilessly mirrored the cold, soul-eaten bar-
renness of those confined within. In the world outside, convicts
have mothers and wives and children, but here, in this world, they
have nothing but the speed of their fists. They have only this one
weapon of protest against the oppression of brain-dead keepers
who represent a society whose judicial standards are so disparate
for rich and poor.

When a man leaves prison, he cannot look into the mirror for   19
fear of seeing what he has become. In the truest sense, he no
longer knows himself. Treated like a child by the guards, forced to
relinquish every vestige of dignity, searched at whim, cursed,
beaten, stripped, deprived of all privacy, he has lived for years in
fear; and this takes a terrible toll. The saddest and most unforgiv-
able thing of all is that most first-time felons could be rehabilitated,
if anyone cared or tried. But society opts for the quickest and least
expensive alternative—stark confinement, with no attempt at
help—that in the future will come to haunt it.

Each day that we filmed at San Quentin, where I was sur-   20
rounded by men whose sensibilities were being progressively
eroded by prison society, the urge grew in me to foment a revolt:
tear down the walls, herd the guards into the bay, burn down
everything until nothing was left but a smoldering heap of black-

ened bricks and molten iron. And I was filled with a yearning to escape, to go home and live the new life I had fought so hard to make. The two worlds I inhabited then were so far apart I could find no bridge between them, no balance in myself. My disorientation was radical.

My days were spent in this prison, among men who had been 21 stripped of everything, who had no future; and of an evening I might find myself in the affluence of Mill Valley, attending a ballet with my visiting wife and two sons, my wife's cousin's daughter dancing on stage in a mist of soft lights. . . .

As the weeks passed I realized I had gone through changes that 22 left me incapable of recognizing my own life. What was most shocking to me was not that I had survived prison, but that the prisons still stood, that the cruelty of that life was still going on, that in San Quentin six thousand men endured it daily, and that the system was growing stronger day by day. I realized that America is two countries: a country of the poor and deprived and a country of those who had a chance to make something of their lives. Two societies, two ways of living, going on side by side every hour of every day. And in every aspect of life, from opportunities to manners and morals, the two societies stand in absolute opposition. Most Americans remain ignorant of this, of the fact that they live in a country that holds hostage behind bars another populous country of their fellow citizens.

I do not advocate the liberation of murderers, rapists, and 23 sociopaths. But what of the vast majority of convicts, imprisoned for petty crimes that have more to do with wrong judgment than serious criminal intent or character defect? They are not yet confirmed in criminality, but the system makes them criminals. Society must protect itself against those who are truly dangerous. But they comprise only a small proportion of our prison population.

One day, late in the afternoon after we had shot a riot scene, 24 the cellblock was in disarray: burning mattresses, men screaming, hundreds of cons shaking the bars with such force that the whole concrete and iron cellblock groaned and creaked with their rage. The cons were not acting. The scene had triggered an outrage waiting to be expressed. Finally, all that was left were a few wisps of black smoke, the tiers dripped water, and hundreds of pounds of soaked, charred newspapers were heaped on the concrete.

Clothing and bed sheets, shredded to rags, dangled from the concertina wire surrounding the catwalks.

Quiet fell, the kind of dead quiet that comes after hundreds of   25
men have been venting their wrath for hours, cursing and flailing
and threatening. The smoldering trash on the cellblock floor testi-
fied to a fury that now withdrew, expressing itself only in their
eyes. One of the convicts walked over to me through the silence.
He told me that another convict wanted to speak with me and led
me to a cell that was in total darkness, where he spoke my name.
A voice from the top bunk replied. I heard the man jump from the
bunk to the floor and come to the bars. He was a tall, young
Chicano with a crew cut, whose eyes were white orbs. He lived
in the absolute darkness of the blind, in this small cell no bigger
than a phone booth. In a soft voice he told me he had a story to
tell and asked my advice. He wanted his story to go out into the
world, in print or on film.

Never has a man evoked from me such sympathy and tender-   26
ness as this blind warrior. It was plain to me that he had suffered
terribly in this man-made hell and that, somehow, his spirit had
survived. I knew that his courage and his heart were mountains
compared to the sand grains of my heart and courage. From
behind the bars, this tall, lean brown kid with blind eyes told me
how, after the guards had fired random warning shots into a group
of convicts, he found himself blinded for life. I looked at him and
saw the beautiful face of a young Spanish aristocrat who might be
standing on a white balcony overlooking a garden of roses and
lilies at dawn. I could also see in him the warrior. How softly he
spoke and how he listened, so attentive to the currents of sound.

Blind Chicano brother of mine, these words are for you, and   27
my work must henceforth be a frail attempt to translate your heart
for the world, your courage and *carnalismo*. While the world
blindly grabs at and gorges on cheap titillations, you go on in your
darkness, in your dark cell, year after year, groping in your imagination for illumination that will help you make sense of your life
and your terrible fate. I couldn't understand you. I could only look
at you humbly, young Chicano warrior. You spoke to me, spoke
to me with the words and in the spirit in which I have written my
poems. Looking at you, I reaffirmed my vow to never give up
struggling for my people's right to live with dignity. From you I
take the power to go on fighting until my last breath for our right

to live in freedom, secure from the brutality in which you are imprisoned. From your blind eyes, I reimagined my vision and my quest to find words that can cut through steel. You asked me to tell your story. I promised I would.

Today, as I was writing these words, a sociologist consulting on 28 the movie led me to a viewing screen to see the eclipse: July 11th, 1991, 11:00 A.M. I looked through the shade glass and saw the sun and moon meet. I thought of you, my blind brother, and how our eyes met, yours and mine, dark moons and white suns that touched for a moment in our own eclipse, exchanging light and lives before we parted: I to tell my people's stories as truly as I can, you to live on in your vision-illuminated darkness. And I thought how the Mayans, at the time of eclipse, would rekindle with their torches the altar flame, bringing the temples to new light; how their great cities and pyramids came out of darkness and they journeyed to the sun in their hearts, prepared to live for another age with new hope and love, forgiveness and courage. The darkness again gave way to the light, and I thought of you in your darkness, and of myself, living in what light I can make or find; and of our meeting each in our own eclipse and lighting the altar flame in each other's hearts, before passing on in our journeys to give light to our people's future.

Copies of my books that I had ordered from New York arrived 29 in San Quentin on the last day of filming. I signed them and handed them out to the convicts who had helped us. As they accepted these books of my poems, I saw respect in their eyes. To me, I was still one of them; for them, I was someone who had made it into a free and successful life. This sojourn in prison had confused me, reawakening the old consuming dragons of hatred and fear. But I had faced them, finally, and perhaps I will be a better poet for it. Time will tell.

The next morning, I woke up early and packed my bags. Then 30 I went back to San Quentin for the last time. The production company vans and trailers, the mountains of gear, the crew and the actors, were gone. I made my way across the sad and vacant yard to make my last farewells. This final visit was a purposeful one: I would probably never set foot in a prison again. I was struck with pity for those who had to stay and with simple compassion, too, for myself: for the pain I had endured in this month and for that eighteen-year-old kid I once was, who had been confined behind walls like these and had survived, but who would never entirely be free of the demons he met behind bars. This last pilgrimage was for him, who is the better part of me and the foundation for the man I am today, still working in the dark to create for my people our own unique light.

UNDERSTANDING DETAILS

1. What caused "hatred and rage" (paragraph 1) to flare up in Baca?
2. What "indignities" (paragraph 1) did Baca suffer during his time in prison?
3. What made Baca feel disoriented during the filming of his movie?
4. According to Baca, in what ways does prison life distort reality? Explain your answer in detail.

ANALYZING MEANING

1. What is Baca actually comparing in this essay? Summarize the four main points of his comparison.
2. What are the "scaly demons" Baca refers to in paragraph 2?
3. In what ways were Baca's mind and spirit separate during the filming of his movie?
4. What does Baca mean at the end of the essay by "our own unique light" (paragraph 30)?

DISCOVERING RHETORICAL STRATEGIES

1. Why do you think Baca wrote this essay?
2. Baca uses similes (comparisons using "like" or "as") and metaphors (comparisons not using "like" or "as") throughout this essay. One example is "I was ensnared in a net of memories" (paragraph 12), a metaphor in which his memories are the net that entangles him. Find four other similes or metaphors, and explain what the author is comparing in each.
3. Why do you think Baca includes the story of the "blind warrior" (paragraph 26) in this essay? What purpose does it serve? How effective is it?
4. Explain the title of Baca's essay.

MAKING CONNECTIONS

1. Compare and contrast the images of prison life presented by Jimmy Santiago Baca and Kimberly Wozencraft ("Notes From the Country Club"). If you had to live in one of these two prisons for six months, which one would you choose? Why?
2. Imagine that Baca, Brent Staples ("A Brother's Murder"), Dave Grossman ("We Are Training Our Kids to Kill"), and Barbara Ehrenreich ("The Ecstasy of War") are having a round-table discussion about mankind's inbred violent instincts. Which author would see men and women as most naturally vicious? Why?
3. Several other essays in *The Prose Reader* deal with people who undergo radical changes from one way of life to another. Compare the life changes described by Baca, Maya Angelou ("New Directions"), Jessica Mitford ("Behind the Formaldehyde Curtain"), Judith Wallerstein and Sandra Blakeslee ("Second Chances for Children of Divorce"), and Michael Dorris ("The Broken Cord"). Which of these changes is most severe? Which is the least? Which is most like a change you have gone through in your own life?

IDEAS FOR DISCUSSION/WRITING

Preparing to Write

Write freely about what the term "freedom" means to you: Do you think consciously about your freedom? Have you ever been confined in any way—either with limitations, rules, or physical boundaries? Do you sense the difference between freedom and confinement even if you have never been in prison? What exactly does freedom mean to you? Why does it have this significance for you?

Choosing a Topic

1. For your college sociology class, compare two aspects of your current lifestyle (for example, school and work, academics and athletics, friends and family), discussing the principal qualities of each.
2. As objectively as possible, consider the implications of confinement and freedom in American society today. What do these terms mean? What do they imply? What negative and positive connotations do you associate with each word?

3. You have been asked to make a prediction about the future of American prisons for *The Sociological Quarterly*. The readers of this journal are especially interested in whether prisons will be changed radically in the next hundred years or will stay relatively the same as they are now. Offer your prediction, and explain your reasoning in a comparison/contrast essay to be published in this periodical.

4. Most of us have not spent time in prison like Jimmy Santiago Baca, but we do have memories or insecurities that imprison us. Consider a past experience that has significantly changed you. Compose an e-mail in which you compare your present self to your past self. Offer advice to a fictional person who may be struggling with a similar experience. Use point-by-point comparisons to organize your essay.

Before beginning your essay, you might want to consult the checklists on page 337.

WILLIAM OUCHI (1943–   )

Japanese and American Workers: Two Casts of Mind

Born in Honolulu, Hawaii, William Ouchi is an internationally known expert on business management—particularly on the relationship between American and Japanese corporations. Ouchi was educated at Williams College, Stanford University, and the University of Chicago; since then, he has taught in business programs at several major American universities, most recently at the Anderson Graduate School of Management at UCLA, where he is vice dean and faculty director of the Executive Education Program. The author has also served as associate study director for the National Opinion Research Center and as a business consultant for many of America's most successful companies. He has written three books on organization and management: *Theory Z: How American Business Can Meet the Japanese Challenge* (1981) is a thorough analysis of the differences between American and Japanese industrial productivity; *The M-Form Society: How American Teamwork Can Recapture the Competitive Edge* (1984) is the result of a three-year study by a team of sixteen researchers led by Ouchi; and *Organizational Economics* (1986) is a textbook coedited with Jay Barney. His latest book is titled *Making Schools Work: A Revolutionary Plan to Get Your Children the Education They Need* (2003). He advises students using *The Prose Reader* to spend plenty of time revising their material. "No one writes a good first draft," he explains. "You must continue to revise your work till you understand exactly what you want to say and you have constructed a group of sentences that say it clearly." Ouchi lives with his wife and three children in Santa Monica, California, where he enjoys playing golf as frequently as his busy schedule allows.

Preparing to Read

The following essay, excerpted from *Theory Z,* compares and contrasts Japan's collective work ethic with the American spirit of individualism. Ouchi's analysis highlights many of the most important cultural similarities and differences between the two countries.

Exploring Experience: As you prepare to read this essay, think about your own work ethic: When you study, for example, do you prefer working alone or with a group of people? What kinds of jobs have you held during your life? Did they stress individual or collective behavior? Were you often rewarded for individual achievement, or did you work mostly within a homogeneous group? In what sort of work environment are you most productive? Most satisfied?

Learning Online: Select an industry such as cars or electronics. Find Web sites for an American company and a Japanese company in your chosen industry. Try to access the companies' mission statements, and think about ways in which their company philosophies are both similar and different.

Perhaps the most difficult aspect of the Japanese for Westerners to comprehend is the strong orientation to collective values, particularly a collective sense of responsibility. Let me illustrate with an anecdote about a visit to a new factory in Japan owned and operated by an American electronics company. The American company, a particularly creative firm, frequently attracts attention within the business community for its novel approaches to planning, organizational design, and management systems. As a consequence of this corporate style, the parent company determined to make a thorough study of Japanese workers and to design a plant that would combine the best of East and West. In their study they discovered that Japanese firms almost never make use of individual work incentives, such as piecework or even individual performance appraisal tied to salary increases. They concluded that rewarding individual achievement and individual ability is always a good thing.

In the final assembly area of their new plant long lines of young Japanese women wired together electronic products on a piece-rate system: The more you wired, the more you got paid. About two months after opening, the head foreladies approached the plant manager. "Honorable plant manager," they said humbly as they bowed, "we are embarrassed to be so forward, but we must speak to you because all of the girls have threatened to quit work this Friday." (To have this happen, of course, would be a great disaster for all concerned.) "Why," they wanted to know, "can't our plant have the same compensation system as other Japanese companies? When you hire a new girl, her starting wage should be fixed by her age. An eighteen-year-old should be paid more than a sixteen-year-old. Every year on her birthday, she should receive an automatic increase in pay. The idea that any one of us can be more productive than another must be wrong, because none of us in final assembly could make a thing unless all of the other people in the plant had done their jobs right first. To single one person out as being more productive is wrong and is also personally humiliating to us." The company changed its compensation system to the Japanese model.

Another American company in Japan had installed a suggestion system much as we have in the United States. Individual workers were encouraged to place suggestions to improve productivity into special boxes. For an accepted idea the individual received a bonus amounting to some fraction of the productivity savings realized from his or her suggestion. After a period of six months, not a single suggestion had been submitted. The American managers were puzzled. They had heard many stories of the inventiveness, the commitment, and the loyalty of Japanese workers, yet not one suggestion to improve productivity had appeared. 3

The managers approached some of the workers and asked why the suggestion system had not been used. The answer: "No one can come up with a work improvement idea alone. We work together, and any ideas that one of us may have are actually developed by watching others and talking to others. If one of us was singled out for being responsible for such an idea, it would embarrass all of us." The company changed to a group suggestion system, in which workers collectively submitted suggestions. Bonuses were paid to groups which would save bonus money until the end of the year for a party at a restaurant or, if there was enough money, for family vacations together. The suggestions and productivity improvements rained down on the plant. 4

One can interpret these examples in two quite different ways. 5 Perhaps the Japanese commitment to collective values is an anachronism that does not fit with modern industrialism but brings economic success despite that collectivism. Collectivism seems to be inimical to the kind of maverick creativity exemplified in Benjamin Franklin, Thomas Edison, and John D. Rockefeller. Collectivism does not seem to provide the individual incentive to excel which has made a great success of American enterprise. Entirely apart from its economic effects, collectivism implies a loss of individuality, a loss of the freedom to be different, to hold fundamentally different values from others.

The second interpretation of the examples is that the Japanese collectivism is economically efficient. It causes people to work well together and to encourage one another to better efforts. Industrial life requires interdependence of one person on another. But a less obvious but far-reaching implication of the Japanese collectivism for economic performance has to do with accountability.

In the Japanese mind, collectivism is neither a corporate or individual goal to strive for nor a slogan to pursue. Rather, the nature of things operates so that nothing of consequence occurs as a result of individual effort. Everything important in life happens as a result of teamwork or collective effort. Therefore, to attempt to assign individual credit or blame to results is unfounded. A Japanese professor of accounting, a brilliant scholar trained at Carnegie-Mellon University who teaches now in Tokyo, remarked that the status of accounting systems in Japanese industry is primitive compared to those in the United States. Profit centers, transfer prices, and computerized information systems are barely known even in the largest Japanese companies, whereas they are commonplace in even small United States organizations. Though not at all surprised at the difference in accounting systems, I was not at all sure that the Japanese were primitive. In fact, I thought their system a good deal more efficient than ours.

Most American companies have basically two accounting systems. One system summarizes the overall financial state to inform stockholders, bankers, and other outsiders. That system is not of interest here. The other system, called the managerial or cost accounting system, exists for an entirely different reason. It measures in detail all of the particulars of transactions between departments, divisions, and key individuals in the organization, for the purpose of untangling the interdependencies between people.

When, for example, two departments share one truck for deliveries, the cost accounting system charges each department for part of the cost of maintaining the truck and driver, so that at the end of the year, the performance of each department can be individually assessed, and the better department's manager can receive a larger raise. Of course, all of this information processing costs money, and furthermore may lead to arguments between the departments over whether the costs charged to each are fair.

In a Japanese company a short-run assessment of individual   9
performance is not wanted, so the company can save the considerable expense of collecting and processing all of that information. Companies still keep track of which department uses a truck how often and for what purposes, but like-minded people can interpret some simple numbers for themselves and adjust their behavior accordingly. Those insisting upon clear and precise measurement for the purpose of advancing individual interests must have an elaborate information system. Industrial life, however, is essentially integrated and interdependent. No one builds an automobile alone, no one carries through a banking transaction alone. In a sense the Japanese value of collectivism fits naturally into an industrial setting, whereas the Western individualism provides constant conflicts. The image that comes to mind is of Chaplin's silent film *Modern Times* in which the apparently insignificant hero played by Chaplin successfully fights against the unfeeling machinery of industry. Modern industrial life can be aggravating, even hostile, or natural: All depends on the fit between our culture and our technology.

The *shinkansen* or "bullet train" speeds across the rural areas of   10
Japan giving a quick view of cluster after cluster of farmhouses surrounded by rice paddies. This particular pattern did not develop purely by chance, but as a consequence of the technology peculiar to the growing of rice, the staple of the Japanese diet. The growing of rice requires construction and maintenance of an irrigation system, something that takes many hands to build. More importantly, the planting and the harvesting of rice can only be done efficiently with the cooperation of twenty or more people. The "bottom line" is that a single family working alone cannot produce enough rice to survive, but a dozen families working together can produce a surplus. Thus the Japanese have had to develop the capacity to work together in harmony, no matter

what the forces of disagreement or social disintegration, in order to survive.

Japan is a nation built entirely on the tips of giant, suboceanic 11
volcanoes. Little of the land is flat and suitable for agriculture. Terraced hillsides make use of every available square foot of arable land. Small homes built very close together further conserve the land. Japan also suffers from natural disasters such as earthquakes and hurricanes. Traditionally homes are made of light construction materials, so a house falling down during a disaster will not crush its occupants and also could be quickly and inexpensively rebuilt. During the feudal period until the Meiji restoration of 1868, each feudal lord sought to restrain his subjects from moving from one village to the next for fear that a neighboring lord might amass enough peasants with which to produce a large agricultural surplus, hire an army, and pose a threat. Apparently bridges were not commonly built across rivers and streams until the late nineteenth century, since bridges increased mobility between villages.

Taken all together, this characteristic style of living paints the 12
picture of a nation of people who are homogeneous with respect to race, history, language, religion, and culture. For centuries and generations these people have lived in the same village next door to the same neighbors. Living in close proximity and in dwellings which gave very little privacy, the Japanese survived through their capacity to work together in harmony. In this situation, it was inevitable that the one most central social value which emerged, the one value without which the society could not continue, was that an individual does not matter.

To the Western soul this is a chilling picture of society. 13
Subordinating individual tastes to the harmony of the group and knowing that individual needs can never take precedence over the interests of all is repellent to the Western citizen. But a frequent theme of Western philosophers and sociologists is that individual freedom exists only when people willingly subordinate their self-interests to the social interest. A society composed entirely of self-interested individuals is a society in which each person is at war with the other, a society which has no freedom. This issue, constantly at the heart of understanding society, comes up in every century, and in every society, whether the writer be Plato, Hobbes, or B. F. Skinner. The question of understanding which

contemporary institutions lie at the heart of the conflict between automatism and totalitarianism remains. In some ages, the kinship group, the central social institution, mediated between these opposing forces to preserve the balance in which freedom was realized; in other times the church or the government was most critical. Perhaps our present age puts the work organization as the central institution.

In order to complete the comparison of Japanese and   14 American living situations, consider a flight over the United States. Looking out of the window high over the state of Kansas, we see a pattern of a single farmhouse surrounded by fields, followed by another single homestead surrounded by fields. In the early 1800s in the state of Kansas there were no automobiles. Your nearest neighbor was perhaps two miles distant; the winters were long, and the snow was deep. Inevitably, the central social values were self-reliance and independence. Those were the realities of that place and age that children had to learn to value.

The key to the industrial revolution was discovering that non-   15 human forms of energy substituted for human forms could increase the wealth of a nation beyond anyone's wildest dreams. But there was a catch. To realize this great wealth, non-human energy needed huge complexes called factories with hundreds, even thousands of workers collected into one factory. Moreover, several factories in one central place made the generation of energy more efficient. Almost overnight, the Western world was transformed from a rural and agricultural country to an urban and industrial state. Our technological advance seems to no longer fit our social structure: In a sense, the Japanese can better cope with modern industrialism. While Americans still busily protect our rather extreme form of individualism, the Japanese hold their individualism in check and emphasize cooperation.

UNDERSTANDING DETAILS

1. Describe in your own words the two different philosophies Ouchi is comparing in this essay.
2. What is Ouchi's main point in this essay? Where does he introduce his purpose?
3. According to the author, what is the most difficult aspect of the Japanese business ethic for Westerners to understand?

4. Why does "collectivism" work better for the Japanese than for the Americans? What is its history in Japan? How is it different from Western "individualism"?

ANALYZING MEANING

1. What is Ouchi's personal opinion of the two value systems he is comparing? At what points does he reveal his preference?
2. Why does the author introduce the origins of American and Japanese living conditions?
3. Which set of business values do you prefer after reading Ouchi's comparison? Explain the reasons for your preference.
4. In what ways is the "work organization" the middle ground between automatism and totalitarianism today? Give examples of this observation from your own experience.

DISCOVERING RHETORICAL STRATEGIES

1. How does Ouchi organize this essay? Outline the main points he covers for each subject.
2. Why do you think the author introduces the two anecdotes at the outset of this essay? How do these stories help Ouchi achieve his purpose?
3. Who do you think is the author's intended audience? How much knowledge about these two subjects does he assume they have? What evidence can you give to support your answer?
4. What other rhetorical strategies besides comparison and contrast does Ouchi use to achieve his purpose in this essay? Give examples of each strategy.

MAKING CONNECTIONS

1. Ouchi argues persuasively that geography has played a major role in Japan's orientation toward "collective" values. Scarcity of land and crowded conditions have forced Japanese citizens to work together harmoniously in ways that seem alien to our concept of self-reliance and independence born on the wide-open American frontier. In what similar ways does geography play a part in the essays by John McPhee ("The Pines"), William Least Heat-Moon ("Red, White and Blue High-

ways"), Bruce Catton ("Grant and Lee: A Study in Contrasts"), and Richard Rodriguez ("The Fear of Losing a Culture")?

2. Imagine that Ouchi, Robert Ramirez ("The Barrio"), and Ellen Goodman ("A Working Community") are having a conversation about the importance of cooperation among people who live close together. What would these authors say are the principal difficulties of achieving such necessary cooperation? What would they say are the main rewards? How "cooperative" is the neighborhood in which you live? Do you wish it were more so? Why or why not?

3. Compare the suggestions made by Ouchi and Edwin Bliss ("Managing Your Time") concerning how American businesses could work more effectively and efficiently. What ideas would you like to share with our business leaders to help make American industry more productive?

IDEAS FOR DISCUSSION/WRITING

Preparing to Write

Write freely about the work ethic that characterizes your immediate environment—at school, at home, or on the job: How do the people in each of these environments feel about one another? How do you feel about them? When are you most productive in these environments? What are the circumstances? Do you work better individually or collectively? Why?

Choosing a Topic

1. Would you prefer to live your social life individually or collectively (as Ouchi defines the two methods)? Explain your preference to a friend, comparing the advantages and disadvantages of both situations. What implications does your preference have? Be sure to make your purpose as clear as possible.

2. Would you rather work in a factory that follows the Japanese or the American method of organization outlined by Ouchi? Explain your preference to your best friend or your immediate supervisor at work. Compare the advantages and disadvantages of both situations. What implications does your preference have? Be sure to make your purpose as clear as possible.

3. *Leisure* magazine has asked you to compare work and leisure from a college student's point of view. Consider the advantages

and disadvantages of each. Be sure to decide on a purpose before you begin to write your comparison.

4. Ouchi explores "Two Casts of Mind" in the business world. Have you observed differences in perspective based on age, gender, or culture outside the business arena? How do these differences in perspective affect individual or collective behavior? Select an online magazine whose audience would be interested in your observations. Using Ouchi's technique of alternating comparisons, prepare an article that compares and contrasts these differences in perspective and analyzes their effect on individual and/or collective behavior.

Before beginning your essay, you might want to consult the checklists on page 337.

GLORIA STEINEM   (1934–   )

The Politics of Muscle

Once described as a writer with "unpretentious clarity and forceful expression," Gloria Steinem is one of the foremost organizers and champions of the modern women's movement. She was born in Toledo, Ohio, earned a B.A. at Smith College, and pursued graduate work in political science at the universities of Delhi and Calcutta in India before returning to America to begin a freelance career in journalism. One of her earliest and best-known articles, "I Was a Playboy Bunny," was a witty exposé of the entire Playboy operation written in 1963 after she had worked undercover for two weeks in the New York City Playboy Club. In 1968 she and Clay Felker founded *New York* magazine; then, in 1972, they started *Ms.* magazine, which sold out its entire 300,000-copy run in eight days. Steinem's subsequent publications have included *Outrageous Acts and Everyday Rebellions* (1983), *Marilyn: Norma Jean* (1986), *Bedside Book of Self-Esteem* (1989), and *Moving Beyond Words* (1994). She has also written several television scripts and is a frequent contributor to such periodicals as *Esquire, Vogue, Cosmopolitan, Seventeen,* and *Life.* An articulate and passionate spokesperson for feminist causes, Steinem has been honored nine times by the *World Almanac* as one of the twenty-five most influential women in America.

Preparing to Read

Taken from the author's newest book, *Moving Beyond Words,* "The Politics of Muscle" is actually an introduction to a longer essay entitled "The Strongest Woman in the World," which celebrates the virtues of women's bodybuilding champion Bev Francis. In this introductory essay, Steinem examines the sexual politics of women's weightlifting and the extent to which a "new beauty standard" has begun to evolve because of pioneers in the sport like Francis.

Exploring Experience: As you prepare to read this essay, examine for a few minutes your own thoughts about the associations

Americans make with weakness and strength in both men and women: Which sex do you think of as stronger? In America, what does strength have to do with accomplishment? With failure? Do these associations vary for men and women? What does weakness suggest in American culture? Do these suggestions vary for men and women? What are the positive values Americans associate with muscles and strength? With helplessness and weakness? What are the negative values Americans associate with muscles and strength? With helplessness and weakness? What connections have you made from your experience between physical strength and gender roles?

Learning Online: Read expert opinions about Gloria Steinem by conducting an Internet search using the terms "Perspectives of Gloria Steinem." As you read these perspectives, consider the ways Steinem uses her writing for social and political activism.

I come from a generation of women who didn't do sports. Being a cheerleader or a drum majorette was as far as our imaginations or role models could take us. Oh yes, there was also being a strutter—one of a group of girls (and we were girls then) who marched and danced and turned cartwheels in front of the high school band at football games. Did you know that big football universities actually gave strutting scholarships? That shouldn't sound any more bizarre than football scholarships, yet somehow it does. Gender politics strikes again.

But even winning one of those rare positions, the stuff that dreams were made of, was more about body display than about the considerable skill they required. You could forget about trying out for them if you didn't have the right face and figure, and my high school was full of girls who had learned to do back flips and twirl flaming batons, all to no avail. Winning wasn't about being the best in an objective competition or achieving a personal best, or even about becoming healthy or fit. It was about *being chosen.*

That's one of many reasons why I and other women of my generation grew up believing—as many girls still do—that the most important thing about a female body is not what it does but how it looks. The power lies not within us but in the gaze of the observer. In retrospect, I feel sorry for the protofeminist gym teachers who tried so hard to interest us in half-court basketball and other team sports thought suitable for girls in my high school, while we worried about the hairdo we'd slept on rollers all night to achieve. Gym was just a stupid requirement you tried to get out of, with ugly gym suits whose very freedom felt odd on bodies accustomed to being constricted for viewing. My blue-collar neighborhood didn't help much either, for it convinced me that sports like tennis or golf were as remote as the country clubs where they were played—mostly by men anyway. That left tap dancing and ballet as my only exercise, and though my dancing school farmed us out to supermarket openings and local nightclubs, where we danced our hearts out in homemade costumes, those events were about display too, about smiling and pleasing and, even during the rigors of ballet, about looking ethereal and hiding any muscles or strength.

My sports avoidance continued into college, where I went   4 through shock about class and wrongly assumed athletics were only for well-to-do prep school girls like those who brought their own lacrosse sticks and riding horses to school. With no sports training to carry over from childhood—and no place to become childlike, as we must when we belatedly learn basic skills—I clung to my familiar limits. Even at the casual softball games where *Ms.* played the staffs of other magazines, I confined myself to cheering. As the *Ms.* No Stars, we prided ourselves on keeping the same lineup, win or lose, and otherwise disobeying the rules of the jockocracy, so I contented myself with upsetting the men on the opposing team by cheering for their female team members. It's amazing how upset those accustomed to conventional divisions can become when others refuse to be divided by them.

In my case, an interest in the politics of strength had come not   5 from my own experience but from observing the mysterious changes in many women around me. Several of my unathletic friends had deserted me by joining gyms, becoming joggers, or discovering the pleasure of learning to yell and kick in self-defense class. Others who had young daughters described the unexpected thrill of seeing them learn to throw a ball or run with a freedom that hadn't been part of our lives in conscious memory. On campuses, I listened to formerly anorexic young women who said their obsession with dieting had diminished when they discovered strength as a third alternative to the usual fat-versus-thin dichotomy. Suddenly, a skinny, androgynous, "boyish" body was no longer the only way to escape the soft, female, "victim" bodies they associated with their mothers' fates. Added together, these examples of before-and-after-strength changes were so dramatic that the only male analogues I could find were Vietnam amputees whose confidence was bolstered when they entered marathons in wheelchairs or on artificial legs, or paralyzed accident survivors whose sense of themselves was changed when they learned to play wheelchair basketball. Compared to their handicapped female counterparts, however, even those men seemed to be less transformed. Within each category, women had been less encouraged to develop whatever muscle and skills we had.

Since my old habits of ignoring my body and living inside my head weren't that easy to break, it was difficult to change my nonathletic ways. Instead, I continued to learn secondhand from watching my friends, from reading about female strength in other cultures, and from asking questions wherever I traveled.   6

Though cultural differences were many, there were political similarities in the way women's bodies were treated that went as deep as patriarchy itself. Whether achieved through law and social policy, as in this and other industrialized countries, or by way of tribal practice and religious ritual, as in older cultures, an individual woman's body was far more subject to other people's rules than was that of her male counterpart. Women always seemed to be owned to some degree as the means of reproduction. And as possessions, women's bodies then became symbols of men's status, with a value that was often determined by what was rare. Thus, rich cultures valued thin women, and poor cultures valued fat women. Yet all patriarchal cultures valued weakness in women. How else could male dominance survive? In my own country, for example, women who "belong" to rich white men are often thinner (as in "You can never be too rich or too thin") than those who "belong" to poor men of color; yet those very different groups of males tend to come together in their belief that women are supposed to be weaker than men; that muscles and strength aren't "feminine."   7

If I had any doubts about the psychological importance of cultural emphasis on male/female strength difference, listening to arguments about equality put them to rest. Sooner or later, even the most intellectual discussion came down to men's supposedly   8 superior strength as a justification for inequality, whether the person arguing regretted or celebrated it. What no one seemed to explore, however, was the inadequacy of physical strength as a way of explaining oppression in other cases. Men of European origin hadn't ruled in South Africa because they were stronger than African men, and blacks hadn't been kept in slavery or bad jobs in the United States because whites had more muscles. On the contrary, males of the "wrong" class or color were often confined to laboring positions precisely because of their supposedly greater strength, just as the lower pay females received was often rationalized by their supposedly lesser strength. Oppression has no logic— just a self-fulfilling prophecy, justified by a self-perpetuating system.

The more I learned, the more I realized that belief in great   9 strength differences between women and men was itself part of the gender mind-game. In fact, we can't really know what those differences might be, because they are so enshrined, perpetuated, and exaggerated by culture. They seem to be greatest during the childbearing years (when men as a group have more speed and upper-body strength, and women have better balance, endurance, and flexibility) but only marginal during early childhood and old age (when females and males seem to have about the same degree of physical strength). Even during those middle years, the range of difference *among* men and *among* women is far greater than the generalized difference *between* males and females as groups. In multiracial societies like ours, where males of some races are smaller than females of others, judgments based on sex make even less sense. Yet we go right on assuming and praising female weakness and male strength.

But there is a problem about keeping women weak, even in a   10 patriarchy. Women are workers, as well as the means of reproduction. Lower-class women are especially likely to do hard physical labor. So the problem becomes: How to make sure female strength is used for work but not for rebellion? The answer is: Make women ashamed of it. Though hard work requires lower-class women to be stronger than their upper-class sisters, for example, those strong women are made to envy and imitate the weakness of women who "belong" to, and are the means of reproduction for, upper-class men—and so must be kept even *more* physically restricted if the lines of race and inheritance are to be kept "pure." That's why restrictive dress, from the chadors, or full-body veils, of the Middle East to metal ankle and neck rings in Africa, from nineteenth-century hoop skirts in Europe to corsets and high heels here, started among upper-class women and then sifted downward as poor women were encouraged to envy or imitate them. So did such bodily restrictions as bound feet in China, or clitoridectomies and infibulations in much of the Middle East and Africa, both of which practices began with women whose bodies were the means of reproduction for the powerful, and gradually became generalized symbols of feminity. In this country, the self-starvation known as anorexia nervosa is mostly a white, upper-middle-class, young-female phenomenon, but all women are encouraged to envy a white and impossibly thin ideal.

Sexual politics are also reflected through differing emphases on   11
the reproductive parts of women's bodies. Whenever a patriarchy wants females to populate a new territory or replenish an old one, big breasts and hips become admirable. Think of the bosomy ideal of this country's frontier days, or the *zaftig,* Marilyn Monroe–type figure that became popular after the population losses of World War II. As soon as increased population wasn't desirable or necessary, hips and breasts were deemphasized. Think of the Twiggy look that arrived in the 1960s.

But whether bosomy or flat, *zaftig* or thin, the female ideal   12
remains weak, and it stays that way unless women ourselves organize to change it. Suffragists shed the unhealthy corsets that produced such a tiny-waisted, big-breasted look that fainting and smelling salts became routine. Instead, they brought in bloomers and bicycling. Feminists of today are struggling against social pressures that exalt siliconed breasts but otherwise stick-thin silhouettes. Introducing health and fitness has already led to a fashion industry effort to reintroduce weakness with the waif look, but at least it's being protested. The point is: Only when women rebel against patriarchal standards does female muscle become more accepted.

For these very political reasons, I've gradually come to believe   13
that society's acceptance of muscular women may be one of the most intimate, visceral measures of change. Yes, we need progress everywhere, but an increase in our physical strength could have more impact on the everyday lives of most women than the occasional role model in the boardroom or in the White House.

UNDERSTANDING DETAILS

1. According to Steinem, what is "gender politics" (paragraph 1)?
2. In what ways does Steinem equate "winning" with "being chosen" (paragraph 2)? Why is this an important premise for her essay?
3. What does Steinem mean when she says, "Oppression has no logic" (paragraph 8)? Explain your answer in detail.
4. In what ways does "power" lie with the observer rather than within the female?

ANALYZING MEANING

1. Why does Steinem call the female body a "victim" body (paragraph 5)? What did girls' mothers have to do with this association?
2. Do you agree with the author that a woman's body is "far more subject to other people's rules than that of her male counterpart" (paragraph 7)? Explain your answer, giving examples from your own experience.
3. What is Steinem implying about the political overtones connected with female weakness and male strength? According to Steinem, why are these judgments so ingrained in American social and cultural mores?
4. What are Steinem's reasons for saying that "society's acceptance of muscular women may be one of the most intimate, visceral measures of change" (paragraph 13)? Do you agree with this statement or not? Explain your reaction in detail.

DISCOVERING RHETORICAL STRATEGIES

1. Who do you think is Steinem's intended audience for this essay? On what do you base your answer?
2. In your opinion, what is Steinem's primary purpose in this essay? Explain your answer in detail.
3. How appropriate is the title of this essay? What would be some possible alternate titles?
4. What rhetorical modes support the author's comparison/contrast? Give examples of each.

MAKING CONNECTIONS

1. To what extent would Erma Bombeck ("Grandma"), Mary Pipher ("Beliefs About Families"), and Barbara Ehrenreich ("The Ecstasy of War") agree with Gloria Steinem's assertion that "the most important thing about a female body is not what it does but how it looks" (paragraph 3)? Do you agree or disagree with this assertion? Give at least three reasons for your opinion.

2. If Steinem is correct that American women have not traditionally found power in their muscles, where have they found it? If you were able to ask Sandra Cisneros ("Only daughter"), Linda Formichelli ("Engage in Word Play!"), or Wang Ping ("Ways to *Ai*") this same question, what do you think their responses would be? With whom would you agree most? Explain your answer?

3. How would Jill Leslie Rosenbaum and Meda Chesney-Lind ("Appearance and Delinquency: A Research Note") feel about the revolution Steinem describes in women's bodybuilding that is bringing renewed power and strength to women of all ages. To what extent might they see this trend as an antidote to the epidemic of sex crimes against women?

IDEAS FOR DISCUSSION/WRITING

Preparing to Write

Write freely about the definition and role of strength and weakness in American society: What does strength generally mean in American society? What does weakness mean? What associations do you have with both modes of behavior? Where do these associations come from? What are the political implications of these associations? The social implications? In what ways are strength and weakness basic to the value system in American culture?

Choosing a Topic

1. Compare two different approaches to the process of succeeding in a specific job or activity. Develop your own guidelines for making the comparison; then, write an essay for your fellow students about the similarities and differences you have

observed between these two different approaches. Be sure to decide on a purpose and a point of view before you begin to write.

2. Interview your mother and your father about their views on physical strength in their separate family backgrounds. If you have grandparents or stepparents, interview them as well. Then compare and contrast these various influences in your life. Which of them are alike? Which are different? How have you personally dealt with these similarities and differences? Be sure to decide on a purpose and a point of view before you begin to write.

3. In her essay, Steinem argues that "an increase in our [women's] physical strength could have more impact on the everyday lives of most women than the occasional role model in the board-room or in the White House" (paragraph 13). Do you agree with the author? Write an essay to be published in your home-town newspaper explaining your views on this issue.

4. Gloria Steinem organizes her comparison of males and females around the issue of "muscle." What other comparisons can be made between men and women? Visit both an online men's magazine and an online women's magazine, and examine the headlines. Find an issue that is explored in both magazines, and write an essay that analyzes their similarities and differences. Following Steinem's example, organize your analysis around single issue, and include your own perspective where appropriate.

Before beginning your essay, you might want to consult the checklists on page 337.

SUCHENG CHAN   (1941–   )

You're Short, Besides!

Sucheng Chan was born in the Peoples' Republic of China and emigrated to the United States in 1957 at the age of sixteen. Following a B.A. at Swarthmore College, an M.A. from the University of Hawaii, and a Ph.D. at the University of California, Berkeley, she held a number of prestigious academic positions, including Assistant Professor of History at Sonoma State University; Professor of History and Provost of Oakes College at the University of California, Santa Cruz; and Professor of Global Studies and Chair of Asian Studies at the University of California, Santa Barbara, where she is now a distinguished professor emeritus. Among her many influential books are *This Bittersweet Soil* (1986), *Asian Americans: An Interpretive History* (1990), *Entry Denied: Exclusion and the Chinese Community in America* (1991), *Peoples of Color in the American West* (1994), and *Not Just Victims: Conversations With Cambodian Community Leaders in the United States* (2003). Her advice to students using *The Prose Reader* is to "read as much good writing as you can, and be sure to read different genres of writing. That will help you pick up (often subconsciously) the sounds and rhythms of felicitous prose. Of course, writing classes also help." Chan currently lives in Santa Barbara, where she continues to publish books and articles in the field of Asian Studies.

Preparing to Read

The following essay, from *Making Space, Making Soul: Creative Perspectives by Women of Color,* edited by Gloria Anzalvúa (1990), gives us many valuable insights into the life of a handicapped person. In it, the author presents a resilient self-concept that had to be adjusted several times to cope with new circumstances.

Exploring Experience: As you prepare to read this essay, examine for a few minutes your own ideas about the handicapped: If you are handicapped, how would your life be different as an able-bodied person? If you are able-bodied, how would your life be different as a handicapped person? How physically independent could you be in either situation? Is physical independence important to you? In what ways? How dependent are you on others in your daily life? Does this dependence bother you in any way? To what extent are your goals in life influenced by your dependence on other people?

Learning Online: Visit the "Americans with Disabilities" Web site (http://www.ada.gov), and spend a few moments exploring some of the frequent issues people with disabilities face. When reading Sucheng Chan's article, consider the way she presents her experience and how she compares the differences in Asian and American perspectives.

When asked to write about being a physically handi- 1
capped Asian-American woman, I considered it an
insult. After all, my accomplishments are many, yet I was not asked to write about any of them. Is being handicapped the most salient feature about me? The fact that it might be in the eyes of others made me decide to write the essay as requested. I realized that the way I think about myself may differ considerably from the way others perceive me. And maybe that's what being physically handicapped is all about.

I was stricken simultaneously with pneumonia and polio at the 2
age of four. Uncertain whether I had polio of the lungs, seven of the eight doctors who attended me—all practitioners of Western medicine—told my parents they should not feel optimistic about my survival. A Chinese fortune teller my mother consulted also gave a grim prognosis, but for an entirely different reason: I had been stricken because my name was offensive to the gods. My grandmother had named me "grandchild of wisdom," a name that the fortune teller said was too presumptuous for a girl. So he advised my parents to change my name to "chaste virgin." All these pessimistic predictions notwithstanding, I hung onto life, if only by a thread. For three years, my body was periodically pierced with electric shocks as the muscles of my legs atrophied. Before my illness, I had been an active, rambunctious, precocious, and very curious child. Being confined to bed was thus a mental agony as great as my physical pain. Living in war-torn China, I received little medical attention; physical therapy was unheard of.

But I was determined to walk. So one day, when I was six or seven, I instructed my mother to set up two rows of chairs to face each other so that I could use them as I would parallel bars. I attempted to walk by holding my body up and moving it forward with my arms while dragging my legs along behind. Each time I fell, my mother gasped, but I badgered her until she let me try again. After four nonambulatory years, I finally walked once more by pressing my hands against my thighs so my knees wouldn't buckle.

My father had been away from home during most of those years   3 because of the war. When he returned, I had to confront the guilt he felt about my condition. In many East Asian cultures, there is a strong folk belief that a person's physical state in this life is a reflection of how morally or sinfully he or she lived in previous lives. Furthermore, because of the tendency to view the family as a single unit, it is believed that the fate of one member can be caused by the behavior of another. Some of my father's relatives told him that my illness had doubtless been caused by the wild carousing he did in his youth. A well-meaning but somewhat simple man, my father believed them.

Throughout my childhood, he sometimes apologized to me for   4 having to suffer retribution for his former bad behavior. This upset me; it was bad enough that I had to deal with the anguish of not being able to walk, but to have to assuage his guilt as well was a real burden! In other ways, my father was very good to me. He took me out often, carrying me on his shoulders or back, to give me fresh air and sunshine. He did this until I was too large and heavy for him to carry. And ever since I can remember, he has told me that I am pretty.

After getting over her anxieties about my constant falls, my   5 mother decided to send me to school. I had already learned to read some words of Chinese at the age of three by asking my parents to teach me the sounds and meaning of various characters in the daily newspaper. But between the ages of four and eight, I received no education since just staying alive was a full-time job. Much to her chagrin, my mother found no school in Shanghai, where we lived at the time, which would accept me as a student. Finally, as a last resort, she approached the American School, which agreed to enroll me only if my family kept an *amah* (a servant who takes care of children) by my side at all times. The tuition at the school was twenty U.S. dollars per month—a huge sum of money during those years of runaway inflation in China—and payable only in U.S. dollars. My family afforded the high cost of tuition and the expense of employing a full-time *amah* for less than a year.

We left China as the Communist forces swept across the coun- 6 try in victory. We found an apartment in Hong Kong across the street from a school run by Seventh-Day Adventists. By that time I could walk a little, so the principal was persuaded to accept me. An *amah* now had to take care of me only during recess when my classmates might easily knock me over as they ran about the playground.

After a year and a half in Hong Kong, we moved to Malaysia, 7 where my father's family had lived for four generations. There I learned to swim in the lovely warm waters of the tropics and fell in love with the sea. On land I was a cripple; in the ocean I could move with the grace of a fish. I liked the freedom of being in the water so much that many years later, when I was a graduate student in Hawaii, I became greatly enamored with a man just because he called me a "Polynesian water nymph."

As my overall health improved, my mother became less anxious 8 about all aspects of my life. She did everything possible to enable me to lead as normal a life as possible. I remember how once some of her colleagues in the high school where she taught criticized her for letting me wear short skirts. They felt my legs should not be exposed to public view. My mother's response was, "All girls her age wear short skirts, so why shouldn't she?"

The years in Malaysia were the happiest of my childhood, even 9 though I was constantly fending off children who ran after me calling, *"Baikah! Baikah!"* ("Cripple! Cripple!" in the Hokkien dialect commonly spoken in Malaysia). The taunts of children mattered little because I was a star pupil. I won one award after another for general scholarship as well as for art and public speaking. Whenever the school had important visitors, my teacher always called on me to recite in front of the class.

A significant event that marked me indelibly occurred when I 10 was twelve. That year my school held a music recital, and I was one of the students chosen to play the piano. I managed to get up the steps to the stage without any problem, but as I walked across the stage, I fell. Out of the audience, a voice said loudly and clearly, "Ayah! A *baikah* shouldn't be allowed to perform in public." I got up before anyone could get on stage to help me and, with tears streaming uncontrollably down my face, I rushed to the piano and began to play. Beethoven's "Für Elise" had never been played so fiendishly fast before or since, but I managed to finish the whole piece. That I managed to do so made me feel really strong. I never again feared ridicule.

In later years I was reminded of this experience from time 11
to time. During my fourth year as an assistant professor at the University of California at Berkeley, I won a distinguished teaching award. Some weeks later I ran into a former professor who congratulated me enthusiastically. But I said to him, "You know what? I became a distinguished teacher by *limping* across the stage of Dwinelle 155!" (Dwinelle 155 is a large, cold classroom that most colleagues of mine hate to teach in.) I was rude not because I lacked graciousness but because this man, who had told me that my dissertation was the finest piece of work he had read in fifteen years, had nevertheless advised me to eschew a teaching career.

"Why?" I asked.   12

"Your leg . . ." he responded.   13

"What about my leg?" I said, puzzled.   14

"Well, how would you feel standing in front of a large lecture 15
class?"

"If it makes any difference, I want you to know I've won a 16
number of speech contests in my life, and I am not the least bit self-conscious about speaking in front of large audiences. . . . Look, why don't you write me a letter of recommendation to tell people how brilliant I am and let *me* worry about my leg!"

This incident is worth recounting only because it illustrates a 17
dilemma that handicapped persons face frequently: those who care about us sometimes get so protective that they unwittingly limit our growth. This former professor of mine had been one of my greatest supporters for two decades. Time after time, he had written glowing letters of recommendation on my behalf. He had spoken as he did because he thought he had my best interests at heart; he thought that if I got a desk job rather than one that required me to be a visible, public person, I would be spared the misery of being stared at.

Americans, for the most part, do not believe as Asians do that 18
physically handicapped persons are morally flawed. But they are equally inept at interacting with those of us who are not able-

bodied. Cultural differences in the perception and treatment of handicapped people are most clearly expressed by adults. Children, regardless of where they are, tend to be openly curious about people who do not look "normal." Adults in Asia have no hesitation in asking visibly handicapped people what is wrong with them, often expressing their sympathy with looks of pity, whereas adults in the United States try desperately to be polite by pretending not to notice.

One interesting response I often elicited from people in Asia 19 but have never encountered in America is the attempt to link my physical condition to the state of my soul. Many a time while living and traveling in Asia people would ask me what religion I belonged to. I would tell them that my mother is a devout Buddhist, that my father was baptized a Catholic but has never practiced Catholicism, and that I am an agnostic. Upon hearing this, people would try strenuously to convert me to their religion so that whichever God they believed in could bless me. If I would only attend this church or that temple regularly, they urged, I would surely get cured. Catholics and Buddhists alike have pressed religious medallions into my palm, telling me if I would wear these, the relevant deity or saint would make me well. Once while visiting the tomb of Muhammad Ali Jinnah in Karachi, Pakistan, an old Muslim, after finishing his evening prayers, spotted me, gestured toward my legs, raised his arms heavenward, and began a new round of prayers, apparently on my behalf.

In the United States adults who try to act "civilized" toward 20 handicapped people by pretending they don't notice anything unusual sometimes end up ignoring handicapped people completely. In the first few months I lived in this country, I was struck by the fact that whenever children asked me what was the matter with my leg, their adult companions would hurriedly shush them up, furtively look at me, mumble apologies, and rush their children away. After a few months of such encounters, I decided it was my responsibility to educate these people. So I would say to the flustered adults, "It's okay, let the kid ask." Turning to the child, I would say, "When I was a little girl, no bigger than you are, I became sick with something called polio. The muscles of my leg shrank up and I couldn't walk very well. You're much luckier than I am because now you can get a vaccine to make sure you never get my disease. So don't cry when your mommy takes you to get a polio vaccine, okay?" Some adults and their little companions I talked to this way were glad to be rescued from embarrassment; others thought I was strange.

Americans have another way of covering up their uneasiness: 21 they become jovially patronizing. Sometimes when people spot my crutch, they ask if I've had a skiing accident. When I answer that unfortunately it is something less glamorous than that they say, "I bet you *could* ski if you put your mind to it!" Alternately, at parties where people dance, men who ask me to dance with them get almost belligerent when I decline their invitation. They say, "Of course you can dance if you *want* to!" Some have given me pep talks about how if I would only develop the right mental attitude, I would have more fun in life.

Different cultural attitudes toward handicapped persons came 22 out clearly during my wedding. My father-in-law, as solid a representative of middle America as could be found, had no qualms about objecting to the marriage on racial grounds, but he could bring himself to comment on my handicap only indirectly. He wondered why his son, who had dated numerous high school and college beauty queens, couldn't marry one of them instead of me. My mother-in-law, a devout Christian, did not share her husband's prejudices, but she worried aloud about whether I could have children. Some Chinese friends of my parents, on the other hand, said that I was lucky to have found such a noble man, one who would marry me despite my handicap. I, for my part, appeared in church in a white lace wedding dress I had designed and made myself—a miniskirt!

How Asian Americans treat me with respect to my handicap 23 tells me a great deal about their degree of acculturation. Recent immigrants behave just like Asians in Asia; those who have been here longer or who grew up in the United States behave more like their white counterparts. I have not encountered any distinctly Asian American pattern of response. What makes the experience of Asian American handicapped people unique is the duality of responses we elicit.

Regardless of racial or cultural background, most handicapped 24 people have to learn to find a balance between the desire to attain physical independence and the need to take care of ourselves by not overtaxing our bodies. In my case. I've had to learn to accept the fact that leading an active life has its price. Between the ages of eight and eighteen. I walked without using crutches or braces, but the effort caused my right leg to become badly misaligned. Soon after I came to the United States, I had a series of operations to straighten out the bones of my right leg; afterwards, though my leg looked straighter and presumably better, I could no longer walk on my own. Initially my doctors fitted me with a brace, but I found wearing one cumbersome and soon gave it up. I could move around much more easily—and more important, faster—by using one crutch. One orthopedist after another warned me that using a single crutch was a bad practice. They were right. Over the years my spine developed a double-S curve, and for the last twenty years I have suffered from severe, chronic back pains, which neither conventional physical therapy nor a lighter work load can eliminate.

The only thing that helps my backaches is a good massage, but the soothing effect lasts no more than a day or two. Massages are expensive, especially when one needs them three times a week. So I found a job that pays better, but at which I have to work longer hours, consequently increasing the physical strain on my body—a sort of vicious circle. When I was in my thirties, my doctors told me that if I kept leading the strenuous life I did, I would be in a wheelchair by the time I was forty. They were right on target: I bought myself a wheelchair when I was forty-one. But being the incorrigible character that I am, I use it only when I am *not* in a hurry! 25

It is a good thing, however, that I am too busy to think much about my handicap or my backaches because pain can physically debilitate as well as cause depression. And there are days when my spirits get rather low. What has helped me is realizing that being handicapped is akin to growing old at an accelerated rate. The contradiction I experience is that often my mind races along as though I'm only twenty while my body feels about sixty. But fifteen or twenty years hence, unlike my peers who will have to cope with aging for the first time, I shall be full of cheer because I will have already fought, and I hope won, that battle long ago. 26

Beyond learning how to be physically independent and, for some of us, living with chronic pain or other kinds of discomfort, the most difficult thing a handicapped person has to deal with, especially during puberty and early adulthood, is relating to potential sexual partners. Because American culture places so much emphasis on physical attractiveness, a person with a shriveled limb, 27 or a tilt to the head, or the inability to speak clearly, experiences great uncertainty—indeed trauma—when interacting with someone to whom he or she is attracted. My problem was that I was not only physically handicapped, small, and short, but worse, I also wore glasses and was smarter than all the boys I knew! Alas, an insurmountable combination. Yet somehow I have managed to have intimate relationships, all of them with extraordinary men. Not surprisingly, there have also been countless men who broke my heart—men who enjoyed my company "as a friend," but who never found the courage to date or make love with me, although I am sure my experience in this regard is no different from that of many able-bodied persons.

The day came when my backaches got in the way of having 28 an active sex life. Surprisingly, that development was liberating because I stopped worrying about being attractive to men. No matter how headstrong I had been, I, like most women of my generation, had had the desire to be alluring to men ingrained into me. And that longing had always worked like a brake on my behavior. When what men think of me ceased to be compelling, I gained greater freedom to be myself.

I've often wondered if I would have been a different person had 29 I not been physically handicapped. I really don't know, though there is no question that being handicapped has marked me. But at the same time I usually do not *feel* handicapped—and consequently, I do not *act* handicapped. People are therefore less likely to treat me as a handicapped person. There is no doubt, however, that the lives of my parents, sister, husband, other family members, and some close friends have been affected by my physical condition. They have had to learn not to hide me away at home, not to feel embarrassed by how I look or react to people who say silly things to me, and not to resent me for the extra demands my condition makes on them. Perhaps the hardest thing for those who live with handicapped people is to know when and how to offer help. There are no guidelines applicable to all situations. My advice is, when in doubt, ask, but ask in a way that does not smack of pity or embarrassment. Most important, please don't talk to us as though we are children.

So, has being physically handicapped been a handicap? It all 30 depends on one's attitude. Some years ago, I told a friend that I had once said to an affirmative action compliance officer (somewhat sardonically, since I do not believe in the head count approach to affirmative action) that the institution which employs me is triply lucky because it can count me as non-white, female and handicapped. He responded, "Why don't you tell them to count you four times? . . . Remember, you're short, besides!"

UNDERSTANDING DETAILS

1. What "folk belief" (paragraph 3) did Chan's family think might be the cause of her condition?
2. How was Chan finally able to walk after four years of not walking?
3. What specific event enabled the author to tolerate ridicule without fear?
4. In what ways have Chan's friends and family had to adjust to her condition?

ANALYZING MEANING

1. What is Chan comparing in this essay? Explain three topics that she discusses in her comparison.
2. According to Chan, why do most handicapped people need to "find a balance between the desire to attain physical independence and the need to take care of ourselves by not overtaxing our bodies" (paragraph 24)? Explain your answer.
3. How does Chan plan to win the battle against aging before her peers take it on?
4. Why was giving up on sex a liberating experience for Chan? Explain your answer.

DISCOVERING RHETORICAL STRATEGIES

1. In what way does the background information Chan gives us in the first paragraph set up the entire essay? Explain your answer.
2. Who do you think is Chan's intended audience? On what evidence do you base your answer?
3. What is the author's attitude toward her subject in this essay? What details in the essay reveal this point of view?
4. Which rhetorical modes does Chan use to support her comparison? How effective are these in fulfilling her purpose?

MAKING CONNECTIONS

1. Imagine that Chan, Harold Krents ("Darkness at Noon"), and Alice Walker ("Beauty: When the Other Dancer is the Self") are having a discussion about whether their physical disability has been a "handicap" to them. Which of these authors do you think would feel least handicapped by his or her disability? Why?

2. Chan, Amy Tan ("Mother Tongue"), William Ouchi ("Japanese and American Workers: Two Casts of Mind"), and Wang Ping ("Ways to *Ai*") all exhibit distinctive Oriental views of life. In what ways do these authors share similar philosophies? How are they different?

3. How do Chan's comparison/contrast techniques differ from those used by Jimmy Santiago Baca ("Past Present") and Gloria Steinem ("The Politics of Muscle")?

IDEAS FOR DISCUSSION/WRITING

Preparing to Write

Write freely about your own physical independence: If you are handicapped, how "independent" do you feel? If you are able bodied, are you aware of your physical independence? How much do you value your independence? In what ways is it a part of your identity? What would happen if your independence were threatened or taken away? How is physical independence related to your identity?

Choosing a Topic

1. In a magazine popular with your peers, explain some specific elements in your ideal life by comparing and contrasting them to those aspects in other people's lives. Is your ideal based on anyone's life in particular? In what way is he or she a role model for you? Does this person play an active role in helping you achieve your ideal existence?

2. Write a comparison essay explaining your attraction to the types of people you date or have married. Why do you like these people? What do your feelings about this type of person tell other people about you?

3. Discuss the concepts of independence and dependence by comparing these ideas to one another. Give examples to support your main points.

4. Select two Web sites that address either a specific disability or disabilities in general. First, identify their commonalities, and then compare the ways in which they are different. Write an essay comparing the two Web sites' approaches and perspectives toward disability. Following Chan's example, integrate your perspective into your examples.

Before beginning your essay, you might want to consult the checklists on page 337.

CHAPTER WRITING ASSIGNMENTS

Practicing Comparison/Contrast

1. Compare one feature of your culture to the same aspect of someone else's culture. Make sure you are not making random or biased judgments, but are exploring similarities, differences, and their significance.

2. Compare the styles of two different writers in *The Prose Reader*. First, identify the major features of each writer's style. Then narrow your ideas to a few points of comparison. For example, perhaps one writer is serious and another funny; one writer may write long, complex sentences, while another writes mostly simple sentences. Discuss the effects each essay has on its readers based on these specific differences in style.

3. Discuss the major differences between two views of a political issue or between two political candidates. Identify the main sources of the differences, and then defend the point of view you believe is most reasonable.

Exploring a Theme

1. What does being "an individual" mean? How important is individualism to you personally? When might being an individual clash with the needs of society? Identify and discuss a situation in which individualism and the needs of society might conflict. If such a conflict occurs, which needs should prevail and why?

2. Identify a disturbing trend that you see in American society. Describe this trend in an essay, providing examples from your observations and experiences.

3. Think about a business or organization that is not what it appears to be. Then write an essay explaining the differences between the image this business or organization projects and the way it actually functions. Include specific examples to illustrate the differences between its image and the reality experienced by its customers or clients.

7

DEFINITION

Limiting the Frame of Reference

Definitions help us function smoothly in a complex world. All effective communication, in fact, is continuously dependent on our unique human ability to understand and employ accurate definitions of a wide range of words, phrases, and abstract ideas. If we did not work from a set of shared definitions, we would not be able to carry on coherent conversations, write comprehensible letters, or respond to even the simplest radio and television programs. Definitions help us understand basic concrete terms (such as automobiles, laser beams, and the gross national product), discuss various events in our lives (such as snowboarding, legal proceedings, and a Cinco de Mayo celebration), and grasp difficult abstract ideas (such as democracy, ambition, and resentment). The ability to comprehend definitions and use them effectively helps us keep our oral and written level of communication accurate and accessible to a wide variety of people.

DEFINING DEFINITION

Definition is the process of explaining a word, object, or idea in such a way that the reader (or listener) knows as precisely as possible what we mean. A good definition sets up intellectual boundaries by focusing on the special qualities of a word or phrase that set it apart from other similar words or phrases. Clear definitions always give the writer and the reader a mutual starting point on the sometimes bumpy road to successful communication.

Definitions vary from short, dictionary-length summaries to longer, "extended" accounts that determine the form of an entire essay. Words or ideas that require expanded definitions are usually abstract, complex, or unavoidably controversial; they generally bear many related meanings or many shades of meaning. Definitions can be *objective* (technically precise and generally dry) or *subjective* (colored with personal opinion), and they can be used to instruct, to entertain, or to accomplish a combination of these two fundamental rhetorical goals.

In the following paragraph, a student defines "childhood" by putting it into perspective with other important stages of life. Though mostly entertaining, the paragraph is also instructive as the student objectively captures the essence of this phase of human development:

> *Childhood is a stage of growth somewhere between infancy and adolescence. Just as each developmental period in our lives brings new changes and concerns, childhood serves as the threshold to puberty—the time we learn to discriminate between good and bad, right and wrong, love and lust. Childhood is neither a time of irresponsible infancy nor responsible adulthood. Rather, it is marked by duties that we don't really want, challenges that excite us, feelings that puzzle and frighten us, and limitless opportunities that help us explore the world around us. Childhood is a time when we solidify our personalities in spite of pressures to be someone else.*

THINKING CRITICALLY BY USING DEFINITION

Definitions are building blocks in communication that help us make certain we are functioning from the same understanding of terms and ideas. They give us a foundation to work from in both reading and writing. Definitions force us to think about meanings and word associations that make other logical strategies stronger and easier to work with.

The process of thinking through our definitions forces us to come to some understanding about a particular term or concept we are mentally wrestling with. Articulating that definition helps us move to other modes of thought and higher levels of understanding. Practicing definitions in isolation to get a feel for them is much like separating the skill of pedaling from the process of riding a bike. The better you get at pedaling, the more natural the rest of the cycling process becomes. The following exercises ask you to practice definitions in a number of different ways. Being more conscious of what definition entails will make it more useful to you in both your reading and your writing.

1. What does the ring in this photograph mean? Identify at least three ways in which people could define this ring. Write your definitions as precisely as possible, and share one with your class.

2. Define in one or two sentences one of the concrete words and one of the abstract words listed here.

    Concrete: *cattle, book, ranch, water, gum*

    Abstract: *freedom, progress, equality, fairness, boredom*

What were some of the differences between the process you went through to explain the concrete word and the abstract word? What can you conclude from this brief exercise about the differences in defining abstract and concrete words?

3. Define the word *grammar*. Consult a dictionary, several handbooks, and maybe even some friends to get their views on the word's meaning. Then write a humorous definition of *grammar* that consolidates all these views into a single definition.

READING AND WRITING DEFINITION ESSAYS

Extended definitions, which may range from two or three paragraphs to an entire essay, seldom follow a set pattern of development or organization. Instead, as you will see from the examples in this chapter, they draw on a number of different techniques to help explain a word, object, term, concept, or phenomenon.

How to Read a Definition Essay

Preparing to Read.   As you begin to read each of the definition essays in this chapter, take some time to consider the author's title and the synopsis of the essay in the Rhetorical Table of Contents: What do you sense is the general mood of Mary Pipher's "Beliefs About Families"? What do you think Wang Ping's attitude is in "Ways to *Ai*"? How much can you learn about Ellen Goodman's topic from her title, "A Working Community"?

Equally important as you prepare to read is scanning an essay and finding information from its prefatory material about the author and the circumstances surrounding the composition of the essay. What can you learn about Erma Bombeck and the role of grandmothers in our lives? And what do you think is Robert Ramirez's purpose in his definition of the barrio?

Last, as you prepare to read these essays, answer the prereading questions before each essay, and then spend a few minutes thinking freely about the general subject of the essay at hand: What do you want to know from Pipher about families? What role does love play in your life (Ping)? What interests you about communities (Goodman)?

Reading.   As you read a definition essay, as with all essays, be sure to record your initial reactions to your reading material. What are some of your thoughts or associations in relation to each essay?

As you get more involved in the essay, reconsider the preliminary material so you can create a context within which to analyze what the writer is saying: What is Bombeck's purpose in writing "Grandma"? Does her tone effectively support that purpose? Who do you think is Ramirez's primary audience? Do you think his essay will effectively reach that group of people? In what ways is Ping qualified to write about the Chinese word for love (*ai*)?

Also, determine at this point whether the author's treatment of his or her subject is predominantly objective or subjective. Then, make sure you understand the main points of the essay on the literal, interpretive, and analytical levels by reading the questions that follow.

Rereading.   When you read these definition essays for a second time, check to see how each writer actually sets forth his or her definition: Does the writer put each item in a specific category with clear boundaries? Do you understand how the item being defined is different from other items in the same category? Did the author name the various components of the item, explain its etymology (linguistic origin and history), discuss what it is not, or perform a combination of these tasks?

To evaluate the effectiveness of a definition essay, you need to reconsider the essay's primary purpose and audience. If Bombeck is trying to get the general reader to understand the vital role of a grandmother in a typical family, how effective is she? In like manner, is Pipher successful in communicating to the same audience the value of the family unit?

Especially applicable is the question of what other rhetorical strategies help the author communicate this purpose. What other modes does Ramirez use to help him define the barrio? Through what other modes does Goodman define a working community?

For an inventory of the reading process, you can review the guidelines on page 20 of the Introduction.

How to Write a Definition Essay

Preparing to Write.   As with other essays, you should begin the task of writing a definition essay by answering the prewriting questions featured in this text and then by exploring your subject and generating other ideas. (See the explanation of various prewriting techniques on pages 21–23 of the Introduction.) Be sure you know what you are going to define and how you will approach your definition. You should then focus on a specific audience and purpose as you approach your writing assignment.

Writing. The next step toward developing a definition essay is usually to describe the general category to which the word belongs and then to contrast the word with all other words in that group. To define *exposition,* for example, you might say that it is a type of writing. Then, to differentiate it from other types of writing, you could go on to say that its main purpose is to "expose," or present information, as opposed to rhetorical modes such as description and narration, which describe and tell stories. In addition, you might want to cite some expository methods, such as example, process analysis, division/classification, and comparison/contrast.

Yet another way to begin a definition essay is to provide a term's etymology. Tracing a word's origin often illuminates its current meaning and usage as well. *Exposition,* for example, comes from the Latin *exponere,* meaning "to put forth, set forth, display, declare, or publish" (*ex* = out; *ponere* = to put or place). This information can generally be found in any good dictionary or encyclopedia.

Another approach to defining a term is to explain what it does *not* mean. For example, *exposition* is not creative writing. By limiting the readers' frame of reference in these various ways, you are helping to establish a working definition for the term under consideration.

Finally, rhetorical methods that we have already studied, such as description, narration, example, process analysis, division/classification, and comparison/contrast, are particularly useful to writers in expanding their definitions. To clarify the term *exposition,* you might **describe** the details of an expository theme, **narrate** a story about the wide use of the term in today's classroom, or **give examples** of assignments that would produce good expository writing. In other situations, you could **analyze** various writing assignments and discuss the **process** of producing an expository essay, **classify** exposition apart from creative writing and then **divide** it into categories similar to the headings of this book, or **compare** and **contrast** it with creative writing. Writers also use definition quite often to support other rhetorical modes.

Rewriting.   Reviewing and revising a definition essay is a relatively straightforward task:

- Have you chosen an effective beginning for your paper?
- Did you create a reasonable context for your definition?
- Have you used appropriate rhetorical strategies to develop your ideas?
- Have you achieved your overall purpose as effectively as possible?

Other guidelines to direct your writing and revising appear on pages 31–32 of the Introduction.

STUDENT ESSAY: DEFINITION AT WORK

In the following essay, a student defines "the perfect yuppie." Notice how the writer puts this term in a category and then explains the limits of that category and the uniqueness of this term within the category. To further inform her audience about the features of "yuppiedom," the student calls on the word's etymology, its dictionary definition, an itemization of the term's basic characteristics, a number of examples that explain those characteristics, and, finally, a general discussion of causes and effects that regulate a yuppie's behavior.

The Perfect Yuppie

Many people already know that <u>the letters YUP stand for "young urban professional.</u>" *Young* in this context is understood to mean fortyish; *urban* often means suburban; and *professional* means most definitely college-educated. Double the *P* and add an *I* and an *E* at the end, and you get <u>yuppie</u>—that 1980s' bourgeois, the marketers' darling, and the 1960s' inheritance. But let's not generalize. <u>Not every forty-year-old suburban college graduate qualifies as a yuppie. Nor is every yuppie in his or her forties.</u> True yuppiness involves much more than the words that make up the acronym. Being

Margin annotations:
- Etymology/ dictionary definition
- Subject
- Limitations set
- General category of word being defined
- Why the dictionary definition is inadequate

Writer's credibility the little sister of a couple of yups, I am in an especially good position to define the perfect yuppie. I watched two develop.

The essence of yuppiness is generally <u>new money</u>. In the yuppie's defense, I will admit that most yuppies have worked hard for their money and social status. Moreover, the **Cause/ Effect** baby boom of which they are a part has caused a glut of job seekers in their age bracket, forcing them to be competitive if they want all the nice things retailers have designed for them. But with new money **General charac- teristic** comes <u>an interesting combination of wealth, naiveté, and pretentiousness.</u> **General characteristic**

For example, most yuppies worthy of the **Specific example** title have long ago <u>traded in their fringed suede jackets for fancy fur coats</u>. Although they were animal rights activists in the **Cause/ Effect** 1960s, they will not notice the irony of this change. In fact, they may be shameless enough to <u>parade in their fur coats— fashion-show style—for friends and family.</u> **Specific example** Because of their "innocence," yuppies generally will not see the vulgarity of their actions.

Because they are often quite wealthy, **General charac- teristic** yuppies <u>tend to have a lot of "things."</u> They are simply over-whelmed by the responsibility of spending all that money. For example, <u>one yup I know has fourteen pairs of sunglasses and seven watches</u>. She, her husband, and their three children own at least <u>twenty collections of everything from comic books to Civil War memorabilia.</u> **Specific example** Most yuppies have so much money that I often wonder why the word "yuppie" does not have a dollar sign in it somewhere.

Perhaps in an effort to rid themselves of **Cause/ Effect** **General charac- teristic** this financial burden, <u>all good yuppies go to Europe</u> as soon as possible. Not Germany or

France or Portugal, mind you, but Europe. They do not know what they are doing there and thus generally spend much more money than they need to—but, after all, no yuppie ever claimed to be frugal. Most important, they bring home slides of Europe and show them to everyone they know. A really good yuppie will forget and show you his or her slides more than once. Incidentally, when everyone has seen the slides of Europe twice, the yuppie's next stop is Australia.

Cause/ Effect

General charac- teristic

A favorite pastime of yuppies is having wine-tasting parties for their yuppie friends. At these parties, they must make a great to- do about tasting the wine, cupping their faces over the glass with their palms (as if they were having a facial), and even sniffing the cork, for goodness sake. I once knew a yuppie who did not understand that a bottle of wine could not be rejected simply because he found he "did not like that kind." Another enjoyed making a show of having his wife choose and taste the wine occasionally, which they both thought was adorable.

General charac- teristic

Specific example

Specific example

Specific example

Some yuppie wanna-bes drive red or black BMWs, but don't let them fool you. A genuine, hard-core yuppie will usually own a gold or silver Volvo station wagon. In this yuppie-mobile, the yuppie wife will chauffeur her young yupettes to and from their modeling classes, track meets, ballet, the manicurist, and boy scouts, for the young yuppie is generally as competitive and socially active as his or her parents. On the same topic, one particularly annoying trait of yuppie parents is bragging about their yupettes. You will know yuppies by the fact that they have the smartest, most

What it is not

General charac- teristic

Specific examples

Cause/ Effect

General talented children in the world. They will
charac- show you their kids' report cards, making
teristic sure you notice any improvements from last   Specific
quarter.   example

    Perhaps I have been harsh in my portrayal
of the perfect yuppie, and, certainly, I will
be accused by some of stereotyping. But
Division/ consider this: I never classify people as yup-
Classifi- pies who do not so classify themselves. The   General
cation ultimate criterion for being yuppies is that   character-
they will always proudly label themselves as   istic and
such.   concluding
                                                 statement

Student Writer's Comments

The most difficult part about writing this definition essay was choosing a topic. I knew it had to be a word or phrase with different shades of meaning, but it also had to be either something I knew more about than the average person or something I had an unusual perspective on. I figured *yuppie* was a good word, not only because it has different meanings for different people, but also because it is an acronym, and acronyms tend to be greater than the sum of their parts.

I started by looking the word up in the dictionary and writing down its etymology (which I later referred to in my opening sentence). I then used freewriting to record the various meanings and natural associations I have with the word *yuppie,* which helped me discover relationships between these meanings and associations. I felt my mind wandering freely over all aspects of this word as I filled up pages and pages of freewriting. I then felt as if I had enough material to work with, so I began to write a draft of my essay.

I started writing the essay from the beginning, a process that was a real novelty for me. After citing the etymology of my word and placing it in a general category, I explained why the dictionary definition was inadequate. Then, I let the general characteristics I associate with the word take me step by step through the essay. As I wrote, I found myself mentally reorganizing my prewriting notes so that I could stay slightly ahead of my actual writing. I kept looping back and forth into my notes, looking for the next best characters to introduce, then writing, then going back to my notes again. I generated my entire first draft this way and revised the order only slightly in my final draft.

As I reworked my essay before handing it in, I added some humor from my own experience with my older sisters and looked closely at other rhetorical modes I had used to support my definition. Naturally, I had scattered examples throughout my essay and had discussed causes and effects quite openly. I revised my paper to make some of the connections I had in mind clearer by either adding transitions or explaining the relationships in other words. I found that this process lengthened my essay quite a bit as I revised. I also worked on the essay at this point to bring out a secondary point I had in mind, which is that some yuppies have lost the 1960s values they once had but often don't even realize it.

I spent the remainder of my time on my conclusion, which I rewrote from scratch four times. I finally ended up directly addressing the classification of yuppies, at which point I stumbled on the ultimate criterion for being a yuppy: "They will always proudly label themselves as such." When I reached this insight, I knew my paper was finished, and I was content with the results. I also realized that rewriting the conclusion so many times had given me a headache, but the pain was worth it.

SOME FINAL THOUGHTS ON DEFINITION

The following selections feature extended definitions whose main purpose is to explain a specific term or idea to their readers. Each essay in its own way helps its audience identify with various parts of the definitions, and each successfully communicates the unique qualities of the term or idea in question. Notice what approaches to definition each writer takes and how these approaches limit the readers' frame of reference in the process of effective communication.

DEFINITION IN REVIEW

Reading Definition Essays

Preparing to Read

✓ What assumptions can you make from the essay's title?
✓ Can you guess what the general mood of the essay is?
✓ What is the essay's purpose and audience?
✓ What does the synopsis tell you about the essay?
✓ What can you learn from the author's biography?
✓ Can you guess what the author's point of view toward the subject is?
✓ What are your responses to the "Preparing to Read" questions?

Reading

✓ Have you recorded your reactions to the essay?
✓ Is the author's treatment of the subject predominantly subjective or objective?
✓ Did you preview the questions that follow the essay?

Rereading

✓ How does the author lay out the definition?
✓ What is the essay's main purpose and audience?
✓ What other rhetorical strategies does the author use?
✓ What are your responses to the questions after the essay?

Writing Definition Essays

Preparing to Write

✓ What are your responses to the "Preparing to Write" questions?
✓ Do you know what you are going to define and how you will approach your topic?
✓ Who is your audience?

Writing

✓ Does the beginning of your essay suit your purpose?
✓ Do you use effective strategies to define your word or concept effectively?
✓ What rhetorical strategies do you use to expand your definition essay?

Rewriting

✓ Have you chosen an effective beginning for your paper?
✓ Did you create a reasonable context for your definition?
✓ Have you used appropriate rhetorical strategies to develop your ideas?
✓ Have you achieved your overall purpose as effectively as possible?

ERMA BOMBECK   (1927–1996)

Grandma

One of our country's best-loved humorists, Erma Bombeck made a brilliant career out of satirizing the trials of the American housewife. Born in Dayton, Ohio, she was intrigued by journalism at an early age, working part-time for the *Dayton Journal Herald* while she was in high school and college. After graduating from the University of Dayton with a degree in English, she became a full-time staff writer for the newspaper. Bombeck then took off twelve years to raise her three children, returning to journalism in 1965 to write a humorous column for homemakers, for which she was originally paid three dollars per column. Later syndicated under the title "At Wit's End," it was carried by over seven-hundred newspapers prior to her death in 1996 from kidney disease. Most of her books are extensions of her column, including such classics as *Just Wait Till You Have Children of Your Own* (1971), *I Lost Everything in the Post-Nasal Depression* (1973), *The Grass Is Always Greener Over the Septic Tank* (1976), *If Life Is a Bowl of Cherries, What Am I Doing in the Pits* (1978), *Motherhood: The Second Oldest Profession* (1983), and *Family: The Ties That Bind . . . and Gag!* (1987). For over three decades, she did all her columns on an old IBM Selectric. "I tried to write on a computer for a while," she explained, "but it didn't write funny. Maybe you have to pay more." *Forever, Erma* (1996), released eight months after the author's death, is a collection of two hundred of her most-loved columns.

Preparing to Read

The following nostalgic essay, originally published in *At Wit's End*, attempts to define grandmothers. Bombeck supports her definition with stories, examples, comparisons, and a discussion of causes and effects that helps us understand the valuable role of grandmothers in our lives.

Exploring Experience: As you prepare to read this essay, pause a few moments to think about any associations you make with the word *grandmother:* Do you have a good relationship with your grandmothers? What special qualities characterize those relation-ships? How close are you to your grandparents? How did you develop your relationship with them? What have you learned about your parents from them? What do you think your kids will learn about you from your parents? If you have children, what have they already learned about you from your parents?

Learning Online: Visit the Erma Bombeck Museum online to become acquainted with the life of Erma Bombeck (http://www.ermamuseum.org).

---

grandma (grand/ma), n. The mother of one's father or mother.

The role of a grandmother has never been really defined. Some sit in rockers, some sky dive, some have careers. Others clean ovens. Some have white hair. Others wear wigs. Some see their grandchildren once a day (and it's not enough). Others, once a year (and that's too much).   1

Once I conducted an interesting survey among a group of eight-year-olds on grandmas. I asked them three questions. One, what is a grandmother? Two, what does she do? And three, what is the difference between a grandmother and a mother?   2

To the first question, the answers were rather predictable. "She's old (about eighty), helps around the house, is nice and kind, and is Mother's mother or Father's mother, depending on the one who is around the most."   3

To the second question, the answers again were rather obvious. Most of them noted grandmothers knit, do dishes, clean the bath-room, make good pies; and a goodly number reveled in the fact that Grandma polished their shoes for them.   4

It was the third question that stimulated the most reaction from them. Here is their composite of the differences between a mother and a grandmother. "Grandma has gray hair, lives alone, takes me places, and lets me go into her attic. She can't swim. Grandma doesn't spank you and stops Mother when she does. Mothers scold better and more. Mothers are married. Grandmas aren't.   5

"Grandma goes to work and my mother doesn't do anything. Mom gives me shots, but Grandma gives me frogs. Grandma lives far away. A mother you're born from. A grandmother gets mar-ried to a grandfather first, a mother to a father last.   6

"Grandma always says, 'Stay in, it's cold outside,' and my   7
mother says, 'Go out, it's good for you.'"

And here's the clincher. Out of thirty-nine children queried, a   8
total of thirty-three associated the word "love" with Grandma.
One summed up the total very well with, "Grandma loves me all
the time."

Actually this doesn't surprise me one small bit. On rare occa-   9
sions when I have had my mother baby-sit for me, it often takes a
snake whip and a chair to restore discipline when I get them
home.

"Grandma sure is a neat sitter," they yawn openly at the break-   10
fast table. "We had pizza and cola and caramel popcorn. Then we
watched Lola Brooklynbridgida on the late show. After that we
played Monopoly till you came home. She said when you were a
kid you never went to bed. One night you even heard them play
'The Star-Spangled Banner' before the station went off."

"Did Grandma tell you I was twenty-eight at the time?" I   11
snapped.

"Grandma said twenty-five cents a week isn't very much   12
money for an allowance. She said we could make more by running away and joining the Peace Corps. She said you used to blow
that much a week on jawbreakers."

"Well, actually," I said grimacing, "Grandma's memory isn't as   13
good as it used to be. She was quite strict, and as I recall my
income was more like ten cents a week, and I bought all my own
school clothes with it."

"Grandma sure is neat all right. She told us you hid our skate-   14
board behind the hats in your closet. She said that was dirty pool.
What's dirty pool, Mama?"

"It's Grandma telling her grandchildren where their mother hid   15
the skateboard."

"Mama, did you really give a live chicken to one of your teach-   16
ers on class day? And did you really play barbershop once and cut
off Aunt Thelma's hair for real? Boy, you're neat!" They looked
at me in a way I had never seen before.

Naturally I brought Mother to task for her indiscretion.   17
"Grandma," I said, "you have a forked tongue and a rotten memory. You've got my kids believing I'm 'neat.' Now I ask you,
what kind of an image is that for a mother?"

"The same image your grandmother gave me," she said.   18

Then I remembered Grandma. What a character.   19

In fact, I never see a Japanese war picture depicting kamikaze   20
pilots standing erect in their helmets and goggles, their white scarfs
flying behind them, toasting their last hour on earth with a glass of
sake, that I don't think of riding to town with my grandma on
Saturdays.

We would climb into her red and yellow Chevy coupe and jerk   21
in first gear over to the streetcar loop, where Grandma would take
her place in line between the trolley cars. Due to the rigorous concentration it took to stay on the tracks and the innumerable stops
we had to make, conversation was kept to a minimum. A few
times a rattled shopper would tap on the window for entrance, to
which Grandma would shout angrily, "If I wanted passengers, I'd
dingle a bell!"

Once, when I dared to ask why we didn't travel in the same   22
flow of traffic as the other cars, Grandma shot back, "Laws, child,
you could get killed out there." Our first stop in town was always
a tire center. I could never figure this out. We'd park in the "For
Customers Only" lot, and Grandma would walk through the cool
building. She'd kick a few tires, but she never purchased one. One
day she explained, "The day I gain a new tire is the day I lose the
best free parking spot a woman ever had."

I don't have Grandma's guts in the traffic or her cunning. But   23
I thought about her the other day as I sat bumper to bumper in
the hot downtown traffic. "Hey, lady," yelled a voice from the
next car, "wanta get in our pool? Only cost a quarter. We're
putting odds on the exact minute your radiator is going to blow.
You can have your choice of two minutes or fifteen seconds."
Boy, Grandma would have shut his sassy mouth in a hurry.

We had an understanding, Grandma and I. She didn't treat me   24
like a child, and I didn't treat her like a mother. We played the
game by rules. If I didn't slam her doors and sass, then she didn't
spank and lecture me. Grandma treated me like a person already
grown up.

She let me bake cookies with dirty hands . . . pound on the   25
piano just because I wanted to . . . pick the tomatoes when they
were green . . . use her clothespins to dig in the yard . . . pick her
flowers to make a necklace chain. Grandma lived in a "fun" house.
The rooms were so big you could skate in them. There were a
hundred thousand steps to play upon, a big eave that invited cool

summer breezes and where you could remain "lost" for hours. And around it all was a black, iron fence.

I liked Grandma the best, though, when she told me about my mama, because it was a part of Mama I had never seen or been close to. I didn't know that when Mama was a little girl a photographer came one day to take a picture of her and her sister in a pony cart. I couldn't imagine they had to bribe them into good behavior by giving them each a coin. In the picture Mama is crying and biting her coin in half. It was a dime, and she wanted the bigger coin—the nickel—given to her sister. Somehow, I thought Mama was born knowing the difference between a nickel and a dime. 26

Grandma told me Mama was once caught by the principal for writing in the front of her book, "In Case of Fire, Throw This in First." I had never had so much respect for Mama as the day I heard this. 27

From Grandma I learned that Mama had been a child and had traveled the same route I was traveling now. I thought Mom was "neat." (And what kind of an image is that for a mother?) 28

If I had it to do all over again, I would never return to Grandma's house after she had left it. No one should. For that grand, spacious house tended to shrink with the years. Those wonderful steps that I played upon for hours were broken down and rather pathetic. There was a sadness to the tangled vines, the peeling paint, and the iron fence that listed under the burden of time. The big eave was an architectural "elephant" and would mercifully crumble under the ax of urban renewal. 29

Grandmas defy description. They really do. They occupy such a unique place in the life of a child. They can shed the yoke of responsibility, relax, and enjoy their grandchildren in a way that was not possible when they were raising their own children. And they can glow in the realization that here is their seed of life that will harvest generations to come. 30

UNDERSTANDING DETAILS

1. What three questions did Bombeck ask on her survey about grandmothers?
2. Summarize the answers she received to the first two questions on the survey.

406   CHAPTER 7 ~ *Definition*

3. Analyze the answers to question 3 in Bombeck's survey, and explain the main difference in the answers between mothers and grandmothers.
4. How does each generation in Bombeck's family learn that their mothers were actually normal kids when growing up?

ANALYZING MEANING

1. Why do you think one child from the survey said, "Grandma loves me all the time" (paragraph 8)?
2. How did the stories Bombeck's mother told her children make the kids believe their mom was really "neat"? How did they develop a new appreciation for her?
3. Why was returning to Grandma's house not a good idea for Bombeck?
4. What does Bombeck mean when she says, "Grandmas defy description" (paragraph 30)?

DISCOVERING RHETORICAL STRATEGIES

1. Several details in this essay give us clues about when it was written. What specific information helps you guess the approximate date of this essay? What do you think that date is?
2. How does Bombeck organize her essay? How does she introduce each new generation?
3. What is the tone of this essay? What details bring you to this decision?
4. What rhetorical strategies, besides definition, does Bombeck use in this essay? Give examples of each strategy.

MAKING CONNECTIONS

1. Compare and contrast the view of older people offered by Bombeck, Malcolm Cowley ("The View from 80"), Sandra Cisneros ("Only daughter"), and Amy Tan ("Mother Tongue"). Which of these authors seems to depict seniors in the most favorable way? Which the least? How do you account for this difference in perspectives?
2. How do Bombeck, Mary Pipher ("Beliefs About Families"), and Ellen Goodman ("A Working Community") differ in the

ways they define the subject of their essays. Which definition seems most clear to you? Why?

3. Imagine that Bombeck, Judith Viorst ("The Truth About Lying"), Gloria Steinem ("The Politics of Muscle"), and Mary Roach ("Meet the Bickersons") were having a discussion about the role of women in today's society. Which author would probably adopt the most traditional view? Which the most *avant-garde?* With which of these writers would you most likely agree? Explain your answer.

IDEAS FOR DISCUSSION/WRITING

Preparing to Write

Write freely about the different relationships in your family: What special qualities characterize each of these family members? Whom do you like the best? How many different roles do you play in your family (i.e., father/mother, son/daughter, brother/sister, husband/wife)? Which of these roles do you like best? Why? What makes some of your relationships with family members better than others? To what extent are you able to control these relationships?

Choosing a Topic

1. In a humorous and coherent essay written for your classmates, define a relative other than a grandmother. What special qualities characterize this relative in most families? Why are these qualities prominent in this particular relative?

2. You play many roles in relation to the members of your family. You are a son or daughter, and also perhaps an aunt, uncle, cousin, parent, or nephew. What is your favorite role in your family? Why is it your favorite? Do you think your opinion about this role will change over time? Why or why not?

3. Choose one of the definitional techniques explained in the introduction to this chapter, and define the word *family* in a well-developed, logically organized essay written for the general public. Introduce your main topic at the beginning of your essay; then explain and illustrate it clearly as your essay progresses. You may use other definition techniques in addition to your main choice.

4. Write an e-mail to a family member, mentor, or close friend. Define the crucial role the person plays or has played in your life. Using Bombeck's style, start with a general definition/ description of the role, and then shift to a more personal definition of the person's importance in your life. Strengthen your definition by using descriptive examples.

Before beginning your essay, you might want to consult the checklists on page 400

ROBERT RAMIREZ   (1949–   )

The Barrio

Robert Ramirez was born and raised in Edinburg, a southern Texas town near the Mexican border in an area that has been home to his family for almost two hundred years. After graduating from the University of Texas–Pan American, he taught freshman composition and worked for a while as a photographer. For the next several years, he was a salesman, reporter, and announcer/anchor for the CBS affiliate station KGBT-TV in Harlingen, Texas. His current job has brought him full circle, back to the University of Texas–Pan American, where he serves as a development officer responsible for alumni fund-raising. He loves baseball and once considered a professional career, but he now contents himself with bike riding, swimming, and playing tennis. A conversion to the Baha'i faith in the 1970s has brought him much spiritual happiness. When asked to give advice to students using *The Prose Reader,* Ramirez responded, "The best writing, like anything else of value, requires a great deal of effort. Rewriting is 90 percent of the process. Sometimes, if you are fortunate, your work can take on a life of its own, and you end up writing something important that astounds and humbles you. This is what happened with 'The Barrio,' which is much better than the essay I originally intended. There's an element of the divine in it, as there is in all good writing."

Preparing to Read

First titled "The Woolen Sarape," Ramirez's essay was written while he was a student at the University of Texas–Pan American. His professor, Edward Simmens, published it in an anthology entitled *Pain and Promise: The Chicano Today* (1972). In it, the author defines the exciting, colorful, and close-knit atmosphere typical of many Hispanic barrios or communities.

Exploring Experience: As you prepare to read this essay, take a few moments to think about a place that is very special to you: What are its physical characteristics? What memories are connected to this place for you? What kinds of people live there?

What is the relationship of these people to each other? To people in other places? Why is this place so special to you? Is it special to anyone else?

Learning Online: Gain a stronger perspective on Robert Ramirez's definition of home by visiting the Web site for the PBS series "American Family" (http://www.pbs.org/americanfamily/). Click on the link for "Cisco's Journal" to see an artistic interpretation of life in the *barrio*.

The train, its metal wheels squealing as they spin along the silvery tracks, rolls slower now. Through the gaps between the cars blinks a streetlamp, and this pulsing light on a barrio street corner beats slower, like a weary heartbeat, until the train shudders to a halt, the light goes out, and the barrio is deep asleep.   1

Throughout Aztlán (the Nahuatl term meaning "land to the north"), trains grumble along the edges of a sleeping people. From Lower California, through the blistering Southwest, down the Rio Grande to the muddy Gulf, the darkness and mystery of dreams engulf communities fenced off by railroads, canals, and expressways. Paradoxical communities, isolated from the rest of the town by concrete columned monuments of progress, and yet stranded in the past. They are surrounded by change. It eludes their reach, in their own backyards, and the people, unable and unwilling to see the future, or even touch the present, perpetuate the past.   2

Leaning from the expressway or jolting across the tracks, one enters a different physical world permeated by a different attitude. The physical dimensions are impressive. It is a large section of town which extends for fifteen blocks north and south along the tracks, and then advances eastward, thinning into nothingness beyond the city limits. Within the invisible (yet sensible) walls of the barrio are many, many people living in too few houses. The homes, however, are much more numerous than on the outside.   3

Members of the barrio describe the entire area as their home. It is a home, but it is more than this. The barrio is a refuge from the harshness and the coldness of the Anglo world. It is a forced refuge. The leprous people are isolated from the rest of the community and contained in their section of town. The stoical pariahs   4

of the barrio accept their fate, and from the angry seeds of rejection grow the flowers of closeness between outcasts, not the thorns
of bitterness and the mad desire to flee. There is no want to escape,
for the feeling of the barrio is known only to its inhabitants, and
the material needs of life can also be found here.

The *tortillería* fires up its machinery three times a day, produc-   5
ing steaming, round, flat slices of barrio bread. In the winter, the
warmth of the tortilla factory is a wool sarape in the chilly morning hours, but in the summer, it unbearably toasts every noontime
customer.

The *panadería* sends its sweet messenger aroma down the dimly   6
lit street, announcing the arrival of fresh, hot, sugary *pan dulce*.

The small corner grocery serves the meal-to-meal needs of cus-   7
tomers, and the owner, a part of the neighborhood, willingly gives
credit to people unable to pay cash for foodstuffs.

The barbershop is a living room with hydraulic chairs, radio,   8
and television, where old friends meet and speak of life as their
salted hair falls aimlessly about them.

The pool hall is a junior level country club where 'chucos,   9
strangers in their own land, get together to shoot pool and rap,
while veterans, unaware of the cracking, popping balls on the
green felt, complacently play dominoes beneath rudely hung
Playboy foldouts.

The *cantina* is the night spot of the barrio. It is the country club   10
and the den where the rites of puberty are enacted. Here the
young become men. It is in the taverns that a young dude shows
his *machismo* through the quantity of beer he can hold, the stories
of *rucas* he has had, and his willingness and ability to defend his
image against hardened and scarred old lions.

No, there is no frantic wish to flee. It would be absurd to leave   11
the familiar and nervously step into the strange and cold Anglo
community when the needs of the Chicano can be met in the
barrio.

The barrio is closeness. From the family living unit, familial   12
relationships stretch out to immediate neighbors, down the block,
around the corner, and to all parts of the barrio. The feeling of
family, a rare and treasurable sentiment, pervades and accounts for
the inability of the people to leave. The barrio is this attitude manifested on the countenances of the people, on the faces of their
homes, and in the gaiety of their gardens.

The color-splashed homes arrest your eyes, arouse your curios- 13
ity, and make you wonder what life scenes are being played out in
them. The flimsy, brightly colored, wood-frame houses ignore no
neon-brilliant color. Houses trimmed in orange, chartreuse, lime
green, yellow, and mixtures of these and other hues beckon the
beholder to reflect on the peculiarity of each home. Passing
through this land is refreshing like Brubeck, not narcoticizing like
revolting rows of similar houses, which neither offend nor please.

In the evenings, the porches and front yards are occupied with 14
men calmly talking over the noise of children playing baseball in
the unpaved extension of the living room, while the women cook
supper or gossip with female neighbors as they water the *jardines*.
The gardens mutely echo the expressive verses of the colorful
houses. The denseness of multicolored plants and trees gives the
house the appearance of an oasis or a tropical isand hideaway, shel-
tered from the rest of the world.

Fences are common in the barrio, but they are fences and not 15
the walls of the Anglo community. On the western side of town,
the high wooden fences between houses are thick, impenetrable
walls, built to keep the neighbors at bay. In the barrio, the fences
may be rusty, wire contraptions or thick green shrubs. In either
case you can see through them and feel no sense of intrusion when
you cross them.

Many lower-income families of the barrio manage to maintain 16
a comfortable standard of living through the communal action of
family members who contribute their wages to the head of the
family. Economic need creates interdependence and closeness.
Small barefooted boys sell papers on cool, dark Sunday mornings,
deny themselves pleasantries, and give their earnings to *mamá*. The
older the child, the greater the responsibility to help the head of
the household provide for the rest of the family.

There are those, too, who for a number of reasons have not 17
achieved a relative sense of financial security. Perhaps it results
from too many children too soon, but it is the homes of these people and their situation that numbs rather than charms. Their
houses, aged and bent, oozing children, are fissures in the horn of
plenty. Their wooden homes may have brick-pattern asbestos tile
on the outer walls, but the tile is not convincing.

Unable to pay city taxes or incapable of influencing the city to 18
live up to its duty to serve all the citizens, the poorer barrio families

remain trapped in the nineteenth century and survive as best they can. The backyards have well-worn paths to the outhouses, which sit near the alley. Running water is considered a luxury in some parts of the barrio. Decent drainage is usually unknown, and when it rains, the water stands for days, an incubator of health hazards and an avoidable nuisance. Streets, costly to pave, remain rough, rocky trails. Tires do not last long, and the constant rattling and shaking grind away a car's life and spread dust through screen windows.

The houses and their *jardines,* the jollity of the people in an   19
adverse world, the brightly feathered alarm clock pecking away at supper and cautiously eyeing the children playing nearby, produce a mystifying sensation at finding the noble savage alive in the twentieth century. It is easy to look at the positive qualities of life in the barrio and look at them with a distantly envious feeling. One wishes to experience the feelings of the barrio and not the hardships. Remembering the illness, the hunger, the feeling of time running out on you, the walls, both real and imagined, reflecting on living in the past, one finds his envy becoming more elusive, until it has vanished altogether.

Back now beyond the tracks, the train creaks and groans, the   20
cars jostle each other down the track, and as the light begins its pulsing, the barrio, with all its meanings, greets a new dawn with yawns and restless stretchings.

UNDERSTANDING DETAILS

1. Define the barrio in your own words.
2. What is the difference between fences in the barrio and in the Anglo community?
3. In Ramirez's view, what creates "interdependence and closeness" (paragraph 16)? How does this phenomenon work in the barrio?
4. According to Ramirez, why are the houses in the barrio so colorful? What do you think is the relationship between color and happiness in the barrio?

ANALYZING MEANING

1. Why does Ramirez call the people in the barrio "leprous" (paragraph 4)?

CHAPTER 7 ~ Definition

2. What does the author mean when he says, "The barrio is closeness" (paragraph 12)? How does this statement compare with the way you feel about your neighborhood? Why can't people leave the barrio?
3. Why might people look at the barrio with "a distantly envious feeling" (paragraph 19)? What other feelings may alter or even erase this sense of envy?
4. In what ways does the barrio resemble the communal living of various social groups in the 1960s?

DISCOVERING RHETORICAL STRATEGIES

1. How does Ramirez use the train to help him define the barrio? In what ways would the essay be different without the references to the train?
2. Ramirez uses metaphors masterfully throughout this essay to help us understand the internal workings of the barrio. He relies on this technique especially in paragraphs 4 through 10. For example, a metaphor that explains how relationships develop in the barrio is "The stoical pariahs of the barrio accept their fate, and from the angry seeds of rejection grow the flowers of closeness between outcasts, not the thorns of bitterness and the mad desire to flee" (paragraph 4). In this garden metaphor, "rejection" is likened to "angry seeds," "closeness between outcasts" to "flowers," and "bitterness" to "thorns." Find four other metaphors in these paragraphs, and explain how the comparisons work. What are the familiar and less familiar items in each comparison?
3. What tone does Ramirez establish in this essay? How does he create this tone?
4. The dominant method the author uses to organize his essay is definition. What other rhetorical strategies does Ramirez use to support his definition?

MAKING CONNECTIONS

1. Compare and contrast the "feeling of family" described by Ramirez with that depicted by Sandra Cisneros ("Only daughter") and Mary Pipher ("Beliefs About Families").
2. Ramirez does a wonderful job of creating a sensual experience in his essay as he chronicles the vivid sights, sounds, smells,

tastes, and textures of life in the barrio. In the same way, Ray Bradbury ("Summer Rituals") and John McPhee ("The Pines") appeal to our senses in their descriptive essays. Which author's prose style do you find most sensual? Explain your answer.

3. While Ramirez defines the "barrio" through description, Ellen Goodman ("A Working Community") defines her principal topic in a different fashion. How do the two authors differ in constructing their definitions? Which technique do you find most persuasive? Explain your answer.

IDEAS FOR DISCUSSION/WRITING

Preparing to Write

Write freely about a place that is special to you: Describe this place from your perspective. Is this place special to anyone else? Describe this place from someone else's perspective. How do these descriptions differ? What characteristics differentiate this place from other places? What makes this place special to you?

Use some metaphors to relay to your readers your feelings about certain features of this place. Do you think this place will always be special to you? Why or why not?

Choosing a Topic

1. Ramirez's definition of the barrio demonstrates a difference between an insider's view and an outsider's view of the same location. In an essay for your classmates, define your special place from both the inside and the outside. Then discuss the similarities and differences between these two points of view.

2. In essay form, define the relationships among the people who are your extended family. These could be people from your neighborhood, your school, your job, or a combination of places. How did these relationships come about? Why are you close to these people? Why are these people close to you? To each other?

3. What primary cultural or social traditions have made you what you are today? In an essay written to a close friend, define the two or three most important traditions you practiced as a child, and explain what effects they had on you.

4. Ramirez defines *barrio* by using rich description. What does the term *home* mean to you? Create a virtual tour of a place you

have lived. Feel free to describe each room, the neighborhood, or the region. Develop your definition of *home* so that the reader can walk with you through each detail.

Before beginning your essay, you might want to consult the checklists on page 400.

MARY PIPHER   (1947–   )

Beliefs About Families

The oldest of seven children, Mary Pipher was born in Springfield, Missouri. She earned her B.A. in cultural anthropology at the University of California, Berkeley, and her Ph.D. in clinical psychology at the University of Nebraska. Currently a professor in the graduate clinical training program at the University of Nebraska, Lincoln, she became a writer only after her children had been raised, declaring that "Writing has been the great gift of my middle years. It is my reason to wake up in the morning." Her first book, *Hunger Pains: The Modern Woman's Tragic Quest for Thinness* (1987), was followed by *Reviving Ophelia: Saving the Selves of Adolescent Girls* (1994), an enormously influential study of the world of teenage girls. Her most recent books are *The Shelter of Each Other: Rebuilding Our Families* (1996), which examines family relationships in America today; *Another Country: Navigating the Emotional Terrain of Our Elders* (1999), an analysis of how the United States isolates and misunderstands its senior citizens; *The Middle of Everywhere: The World's Refugees Come to Our Town* (2002); and *Letters to a Young Therapist: The Art of Mentoring* (2003). An avid outdoorswoman who loves hiking, backpacking, and watching sunsets, Pipher has the following advice for students using *The Prose Reader:* "What all writers have in common is a yearning to communicate. That yearning is what makes it impossible not to write. The important thing for all writers is to care enough about the quality of the writing to keep working."

Preparing to Read

The following essay from *The Shelter of Each Other: Rebuilding Our Families* attempts to define the notion of "family" in contemporary society.

Exploring Experience: As you prepare to read this essay, take a few moments to think about the role family plays in your life: Are you close to your biological family? Are you a part of any other groups that function like a family? How do they work? Are you aware of your roles in these various groups? What is the relationship betwen your role in your immediate family and your personal goals? Does your family provide support for you and what you want to accomplish?

Learning Online: To gain a perspective on the varied media representations of "family," go to the TV Land Web site (http://www.tvland.com). Choose "shows" from the menu, and then select the "Leave it to Beaver" link from the alphabetized list. Peruse the episode descriptions, sound bytes, and photos from the sitcom. Contrast this family with the one portrayed in "American Beauty." Visit the Internet Movie Database Web site (http://www.imdb.com), enter "American Beauty" into the search field, and view the movie trailer. Consider how these "families" relate to Pipher's definition as you read her essay.

When I speak of families, I usually mean biological families. There is a power in blood ties that cannot be denied. But in our fragmented, chaotic culture, many people don't have biological families nearby. For many people, friends become family. Family is a collection of people who pool resources and help each other over the long haul. Families love one another even when that requires sacrifice. Family means that if you disagree, you still stay together. 1

Families are the people for whom it matters if you have a cold, are feuding with your mate or training a new puppy. Family members use magnets to fasten the newspaper clippings about your bowling team on the refrigerator door. They save your drawings and homemade pottery. They like to hear stories about when you were young. They'll help you can tomatoes or change the oil in your car. They're the people who will come visit you in the hospital, will talk to you when you call with "a dark night of the soul" and will loan you money to pay the rent if you lose your job. Whether or not they are biologically related to each other, the people who do these things are family. 2

If you are very lucky, family is the group you were born into. But some are not that lucky. When Janet was in college, her parents were killed in a car wreck. In her early twenties she married, but three years later she lost her husband to leukemia. She has one 3 sister, who calls mainly when she's suicidal or needs money. Janet is a congresswoman in a western state, a hard worker and an idealist. Her family consists of the men, women, and children she's grown to depend on in the twenty-five years she's lived in her community. Except for her beloved dog, nobody lives with her. But she brings the cinnamon rolls to one family's Thanksgiving dinner and has a Mexican fiesta for families at her house on New Year's Eve. She attends Bar Mitzvahs, weddings, school concerts, and soccer matches. She told me with great pride, "When I sprained my ankle skiing last year, three families brought me meals."

I think of Morgan, a jazz musician who long ago left his small   4
town and rigid, judgmental family. He had many memories of his father whipping him with a belt or making him sleep in the cold. Once he said to me, "I was eighteen years old before anyone ever told me I had something to offer." Indeed he does. He plays the violin beautifully. He teaches improvisation and jazz violin and organizes jazz events for his town. His family is the family of musicians and music lovers that he has built around him over the years.

If you are very unlucky, you come from a nuclear family that   5
didn't care for you. Curtis, who as a boy was regularly beaten by his father, lied about his age so that he could join the Navy at sixteen. Years later he wrote his parents and asked if he could return home for Christmas. They didn't answer his letter. When I saw him in therapy, I encouraged him to look for a new family, among his cousins and friends from the Navy. Sometimes cutoffs, tragic as they are, are unavoidable.

I think of Anita, who never knew her father and whose mother   6
abandoned her when she was seven. Anita was raised by an aunt and uncle, whom she loved very much. As an adult she tracked down her mother and tried to establish a relationship, but her mother wasn't interested. At least Anita was able to find other family members to love her. She had a family in her aunt and uncle.

Family need not be traditional or biological. But what family   7
offers is not easily replicated. Let me share a Sioux word, *tiospaye,* which means the people with whom one lives. The *tiospaye* is probably closer to a kibbutz than to any other Western institution. The *tiospaye* gives children multiple parents, aunts, uncles and grandparents. It offers children a corrective factor for problems in

their nuclear families. If parents are difficult, there are other adults around to soften and diffuse the situation. Until the 1930s, when the *tiospaye* began to fall apart with sale of land, migration and alcoholism, there was not much mental illness among the Sioux. When all adults were responsible for all children, people grew up healthy.

What *tiospaye* offers and what biological family offers is a place   8 that all members can belong to regardless of merit. Everyone is included regardless of health, likability or prestige. What's most valuable about such institutions is that people are in by virtue of being born into the group. People are in even if they've committed a crime, been a difficult person, become physically or mentally disabled or are unemployed and broke. That ascribed status was what Robert Frost valued when he wrote that home "was something you somehow hadn't to deserve."

Many people do not have access to either a supportive biolog-   9 ical family or a *tiospaye*. They make do with a "formed family." Others simply prefer a community of friends to their biological families. The problem with formed families is they often have less staying power. They might not take you in, give you money if you lose a job or visit you in a rest home if you are paralyzed in a car crash. My father had a stroke and lost most of his sight and speech. Family members were the people who invited him to visit and helped him through the long tough years after his stroke. Of course, there are formed families who do this. With the AIDS crisis, many gays have supported their friends through terrible times. Often immigrants will help each other in this new country. And there are families who don't stick together in crisis. But generally blood is thicker than water. Families come through when they must.

Another problem with formed families is that not everyone has   10 the skills to be included in that kind of family. Friendship isn't a product that can be obtained for cash. People need friends today more than ever, but friends are harder to make in a world where people are busy, moving, and isolated. Some people don't have the skills. They are shy, abrasive, or dull. Crack babies have a hard time making friends, as do people with Alzheimer's. Formed families can leave many people out.

From my point of view the issue isn't biology. Rather the issues   11 are commitment and inclusiveness. I don't think for most of us it has to be either/or. A person can have both a strong network of friends and a strong family. It is important to define family broadly so that all kinds of families, such as single-parent families, multi-generational families, foster families and the families of gays are included. But I agree with David Blankenberg's conclusion in his book *Rebuilding the Nest:* "Even with all the problems of nuclear families, I will support it as an institution until something better comes along."

Americans hold two parallel versions of the family—the ideal-   12 ized version and the dysfunctional version. The idealized version portrays families as wellsprings of love and happiness, loyal, whole-some, and true. This is the version we see in *Leave It to Beaver* or *Father Knows Best*. The dysfunctional version depicts families as disturbed and disturbing, and suggests that salvation lies in extricating oneself from all the ties that bind. Both versions have had their eras. In the 1950s the idealized version was at its zenith. Extolling family was in response to the Depression and war, which separated families. People who had been wrenched away from home missed their families and thought of them with great long-ing. They idealized how close and warm they had been.

In the 1990s the dysfunctional version of family seems the most   13 influential. This belief system goes along with the culture of nar-cissism, which sells people the idea that families get in the way of individual fulfillment. Currently, many Americans are deeply mis-trustful of their own and other people's families. Pop psychology presents families as pathology-producing. Talk shows make fami-lies look like hotbeds of sin and sickness. Day after day people tes-tify about the diverse forms of emotional abuse that they suffered in their families. Movies and television often portray families as useless impediments.

In our culture, after a certain age, children no longer have per-   14 mission to love their parents. We define adulthood as breaking away, disagreeing and making up new rules. Just when teenagers most need their parents, they are encouraged to distance them-selves from them. A friend told me of walking with her son in a shopping mall. They passed some of his friends, and she noticed that suddenly he was ten feet behind, trying hard not to be seen with her. She said, "I felt like I was drooling and wearing purple plaid polyester." Later her son told her that he enjoyed being with her, but that his friends all hated their parents and he would be teased if anyone knew he loved her. He said, "I'm confused about this. Am I supposed to hate you?"

This socialized antipathy toward families is unusual. Most cultures revere and respect family. In Vietnam, for example, the tender word for lover is "sibling." In the Kuma tribe of Papua New Guinea, family members are valued above all others. Siblings are seen as alter egos, essential parts of the self. The Kuma believe that mates can be replaced, but not family members. Many Native American tribes regard family members as connected to the self. To be without family is to be dead. 15

From the Greeks, to Descartes, to Freud and Ayn Rand, Westerners have valued the independent ego. But Americans are the most extreme. Our founders were rebels who couldn't tolerate oppression. When they formed a new government they emphasized rights and freedoms. Laws protected private property and individual rights. Responsibility for the common good was not mandated. 16

American values concerning independence may have worked better when we lived in small communities surrounded by endless space. But we have run out of space and our outlaws live among us. At one time the outlaw mentality was mitigated by a strong sense of community. Now the values of community have been superseded by other values. 17

We have pushed the concept of individual rights to the limits. Our laws let adults sell children harmful products. But laws are not our main problem. People have always been governed more by community values than by laws. Ethics, rather than laws, determine most of our behavior. Unwritten rules of civility—for taking turns, not cutting in lines, holding doors open for others and lowering our voices in theaters—organize civic life. Unfortunately, those rules of civility seem to be crumbling in America. We are becoming a nation of people who get angry when anyone gets in our way. 18

Rudeness is everywhere in our culture. Howard Stern, G. Gordon Liddy, and Newt Gingrich are rude. It's not surprising our children copy them. Phil Donahue and Jay Leno interrupt, and children learn to interrupt. A young man I know was recently injured on a volleyball court. The player who hurt him didn't apologize or offer to help him get to an emergency room. An official told him to get off the floor because he was messing it up with his blood and holding up the game. I recently saw an old man hes- 19 itate at a busy intersection. Behind him drivers swore and honked. He looked scared and confused as he turned into traffic and almost wrecked his car. At a festival a man stood in front of the stage, refusing to sit down when people yelled out that they couldn't see. Finally another man wrestled him to the ground. All around were the omnipresent calls of "Fuck You." Over coffee a local politician told me she would no longer attend town meetings. She said, "People get out of control and insult me and each other. There's no dialogue, it's all insults and accusations."

We have a crisis in meaning in our culture. The crisis comes   20
from our isolation from each other, from the values we learn in a culture of consumption and from the fuzzy, self-help message that the only commitment is to the self and the only important question is—Am I happy? We learn that we are number one and that our own immediate needs are the most important ones. The crisis comes from the message that products satisfy and that happiness can be purchased.

We live in a money-driven culture. But the bottom line is not   21
the only line, or even the best line for us to hold. A culture organized around profits instead of people is not user friendly to families. We all suffer from existential flu, as we search for meaning in a culture that values money, not meaning. Everyone I know wants to do good work. But right now we have an enormous gap between doing what's meaningful and doing what is reimbursed.

UNDERSTANDING DETAILS

1. How does Pipher define *families?* What particular activities characterize a "family" member?
2. What do "commitment and inclusiveness" (paragraph 11) have to do with being in a family?
3. According to Pipher, what are the two parallel versions of the family and when were they dominant?
4. According to Pipher, what poses the biggest problem to the integrity of the family as a unit?

ANALYZING MEANING

1. In what way does the Sioux word *tiospaye* (paragraph 7) describe the traits of a family?

2. According to Pipher, why do "people need friends today more than ever" (paragraph 10)?
3. What is difficult about "formed families" (paragraph 10)?
4. Do you agree with Pipher that we have "a crisis of meaning in our culture" (paragraph 20)? Explain your answer in detail.

DISCOVERING RHETORICAL STRATEGIES

1. Why does the author introduce the stories of Janet, Morgan, Curtis, and Anita?
2. What do you think Pipher's purpose is in this essay?
3. Pipher approaches her definition from many different angles before suggesting that the American culture is facing a crisis in understanding and agreeing upon what a family is. How do her various definitions support her statement about a crisis? Explain your answer.
4. What rhetorical modes support the author's definition? Give examples of each.

MAKING CONNECTIONS

1. Which parts of Mary Pipher's definition of "family" would Judith Wallerstein and Sandra Blakeslee ("Second Chances for Children of Divorce"), Robert Ramirez ("The Barrio"), and Ellen Goodman ("A Working Community") most agree with? Why?
2. Imagine that Russell Baker ("The Saturday Evening Post"), Mary Roach ("Meet the Bickersons"), and Mary Pipher are discussing the extent to which people in a family have to compromise. Which author would you probably agree with and why?
3. Compare and contrast the ways in which Erma Bombeck ("Grandma"), Robert Ramirez ("The Barrio"), and Mary Pipher begin their definition essays.

IDEAS FOR DISCUSSION/WRITING

Preparing to Write

Write freely about the qualities that constitute a good family member: How do you recognize a good family member? What characterizes him or her? Do you personally appreciate your biological family? Are you a part of other families? If so, what are the characteristics of these families? Why is some type of family important to our well-being? What role does the notion of family play in your self-definition?

Choosing a Topic

1. Write an essay for your classmates defining "a family" that you belong to.
2. In a well-organized essay, use examples to define the dysfunctional family as it exists today. Be as specific as possible.
3. The relationship between family and individual has changed since your parents were in school. Explain to them the current relationship between you and your family. What are the connections between your personal goals and your role in your immediate family?
4. Conduct Internet research on international representations of "family." Start with the United Nations Children's Fund (UNICEF) Web site (http://www.unicef.org). Use terms such as *family practices* to begin your search. Write an essay in which you expand Pipher's definition of *family* to include at least three detailed examples of global family practices. Use Pipher's developed example of Sioux customs as a model for your expanded descriptions.

Before beginning your essay, you might want to consult the checklists on page 400.

WANG PING   (1957–   )

Ways to Ai 爱

Wang Ping is a Professor of English at Macalester College in St. Paul, Minnesota, where she specializes in teaching poetry and creative writing. A native of China, she emmigrated to the United States in 1985 after earning a B.A. in English Literature from Beijing University. Her degrees also include an M.A. in English from Long Island University and a Ph.D. in Comparative Literature from New York University. Her most recent publications are *American Visa* (1994), a book of short stories; *Foreign Devil* (1996), a novel; *New Generation* (1999), a translation of modern Chinese poetry; *Aching for Beauty* (2000), a cultural study of the ancient art of footbinding in China (later published in paperback by Random House, 2002); and *The Magic Whip* (2003), a collection of poems. She is the recipient of may honors and awards, most recently fellowships from the National Endowment for the Arts, the New York Foundation for the Arts, and the Minnesota Arts Board. She admits to a passion for shaoling martial arts, yoga, flamenco, and gardening. Her advice to students using *The Prose Reader* is "to experience life as much as possible—even if it means going through hardship, bitterness, disappointment, and pain—because all of these will become invaluable source materials for a writer and will help connect you to readers at different levels."

Preparing to Read

The following essay, taken from a collection of essays called *Speakeasy,* attempts to define the abstract notion of love. In it, the author looks at the word *love* from a number of different perspectives.

Exploring Experience: As you prepare to read Wang Ping's essay, take a few moments to think about your own experiences with love: Have you encountered many different types of love during your life? What are some types of love you have experienced? How many people do you love? How many people love you? What are the essential qualities of love? Is your love for different people limitless or limited? In what ways do you express your love? How are your expressions of love different for different types of love?

Learning Online: Using online dictionaries, conduct an Internet search on the definition of the word *love*. Find three sources, and compare the differences and similarities of their definitions.

L ove? Can love buy you a decent meal with rice and meat? 1 Can it keep you warm in snow? Safe in a storm?" my grandma would answer whenever I asked about her arranged marriage, her long widowed life.

"Don't even think about 'talking love' before you turn 25, 2 before you join the Communist Party and have made something of life!" my father warned when I left home at 15.

"There's no such thing as love without a reason, just as there is 3 no such thing as hate without a reason." We chanted Mao's words as we spat and kicked at the teachers we had once adored, broke windows, burnt books, beat up Red Guards from a different faction who were once our best friends.

My grandma's favorite dinner story is about a widow who cut 4 chunks of flesh from her arms and thighs to make broth for her dying mother-in-law. Such a filial deed moved the gods so much that they let the old woman revive and live another ten years. As the story proceeded, my mother would bang her chopsticks and rice bowl louder and louder on the table and finally stomp out. "Have you heard a better love story than that?" my grandma would ask, her cheeks sunk deep in a toothless mouth.

"This is for the burnt rice," my mother said as she whipped us 5 with her bamboo stick. "And this is for the bowl you broke, the corner you didn't sweep, the dirty words that slipped out of your mouth." She aimed at our thighs, where the meat was the thickest, the pain unforgettable. "A filial son comes from under a rod. I want you to remember this, with your flesh. You'll be grateful when you grow up, and you'll pass it on to your children, and next, and next. And this is the best love a mother can give you, kiddos."

I've never written a love poem, nor said the word love—*ai*— 6 in Chinese. When pressed by my Chinese boyfriend, I'd say it in

English and French only. (He found it cute in the beginning, but later used it as an excuse to dump me.) The word sounds like bad luck, too much like a sigh—*ai*. It makes me feel like an old man bent with heavy loads. We say *teng ai* (pain love) to our children, *eng ai* (gratitude love) or *ai qing* (love emotion) between husband and wife, *lian ai* (pity love) to a mistress or a child. Love is conditioned, heavily.

I trace the word on paper. First is the hand, then the roof of a house. This makes sense. You want to keep a firm hand on your shelter, your safety, before you can even start talking about love. Is that why my father warned me over and over again not to "talk love" before I've established myself? Then comes the part "friend." I open my biggest dictionary, *Ocean of Words*. Seventeen years away from China, and I'm losing my mother tongue. It's a complicated system, each word made with two, three, even six different components. No, I'm not wrong, the word does end with a friend, a friend holding up the roof of a house with an assuring hand. So what does it have to do with love? I look back into the dictionary again. It says "love among brothers." Ok, brotherly love, love of the same sex before it extends to the other. Then it says "love = adultery." I squirm in my chair. That explains why I've been so reluctant to say "I love you" in my mother tongue. The third item: "love = penny-pinch = greed." 7

My palms get clammy with cold sweat. The definitions of love in my Chinese dictionary don't seem friendly, and I can't discard them as rubbish, for they are all backed up by Confucius' writing, history, famous poets, and politicians. All of them seem to say: love is a wild animal. Control it or it will tear you apart, drag you into the abyss. 8

"Don't talk love before you turn 25." How the father knows! 9

And the companion words—*gratitude, respect, duty, pain, pity, addiction, treasure,* and many, many others—that go side by side with the taboo word *ai*. Are they meant to tame this beast deep in our hearts? Does it mean we Chinese can't love for the sake of love? And if we do, we must love with all the pain, all the duties, all the consequences? Is this how my grandmas, my ancestors, women of my race, find their happiness, though they never met their men before wedding nights, though their husbands may beat them up, sell them to redeem a debt, take in as many concubines as they could afford, whenever they wanted? 10

Does it mean I'm hopeless?   11

"Love?" poofed my mother. "Love is puffed rice. It satisfies you   12
for five minutes. That's all. And men. You can't believe a word
they say; they're like commercials. So when you choose a husband, no need to look at his face or crotch, just look into his
checking account."

"Love is a wild deer in the forest. It won't return no matter   13
how you call it," my twice-divorced sister said on the phone.

When pressed to remarry, she replied, "Men are like parking   14
lots. All the good ones are taken, and the rest are handicapped."

"It's possible to bear fruit before blossom," my grandma in-   15
sisted. "Children first, then respect, then love."

I suppose, I suppose, I mutter to myself as my index finger goes   16
up and down the dictionary. Security, responsibility, control, all
wise and sound. But something is missing. Suddenly my eyes pop
wide. At the bottom is the traditional version of the character *ai:*
a hand, a roof, a friend, the usual stuff. Then in the middle,
between the friend and roof, stands a heart. It was taken out by the
government in the 50s to make Chinese words easier to use.

"That's it!" I shout out loud. That's what's been missing, the   17
heart—心—*xin.*

Dot by dot, I try out the newly found character, adding the   18
heart. Memories rush to me from all sides: first crush, first fight,
first betrayal, the whipping, the cursing, my mother and grandmas
barking their stories to my ears, my ancestors, their ways of love,
of hatred, cunning and twisted, with its own wisdom and truth. I
thought I'd buried them, to make my life easier, more modern,
more western, but they've been living with me, all these years,
waiting to come out.

爱—the hand comes first, then the roof, then the heart—心.   19
Its three dots spurt and drip like blood over a standing leg. For
decades, the heart has been erased from books, papers, magazines. But its pulse has never stopped. It's been pulsing in my
grandmas' stories, my sister's waiting for the reunion with her
long lost daughter, in the shafts of sunlight, moon rise, fallen
leaves, in the whip my mother carefully placed behind the bedroom door.

"*Ai,*" I sigh as I complete the last stroke. The heart looks a bit   20
squashed between the house and people, a bit fragile under the
weight of the roof. But it's there, beating with its own rhythm, its

own rules of law. Someday, when the heart takes root again, I'll learn how to say the word, in my native tongue, a sound that can also mean a sigh, an obstacle, a sound soaked with pain and joy.

UNDERSTANDING DETAILS

1. Restate Wang Ping's definition of *love* in your own words.
2. What caused the author to lose confidence in her Chinese language skills?
3. What was the missing element the author discovered in the Chinese word for love?
4. What are the "companion words" (paragraph 10) to the Chinese word for love? How are they all related to *ai?*

ANALYZING MEANING

1. Why does Ping spend so much time researching the background of the word *love* in Chinese?
2. Why has Ping never said the Chinese word for love? Discuss both her stated and implied reasons.
3. What does Wang Ping mean when she says, "Love is a wild animal. Control it or it will tear you apart, drag you into the abyss" (paragraph 8)?
4. How accurately does Ping capture the essence of love in her essay? Which details communicate this message most effectively?

DISCOVERING RHETORICAL STRATEGIES

1. In your opinion, what is Ping's primary purpose in this essay? Explain your answer in detail.
2. How does Ping organize her definition? Is this the most effective arrangement for her ideas? Why or why not?
3. Ping uses similes and metaphors (comparisons of two unlike items) to help explain the concept of love. In paragraph 13, for example, "love" is described as "a wild deer in the forest." Explain this comparison, and find one other example of this same figurative technique.
4. What additional rhetorical strategies support the author's definition? Give examples of each.

MAKING CONNECTIONS

1. Wang Ping's essay works through the correspondence between a single Chinese word (*ai*) and the graphic linguistic symbol that represents it. In what ways are the definition essays by Robert Ramirez ("The Barrio") and Mary Pipher ("Beliefs About Families") organized?
2. In what ways would Wang and Amy Tan ("Mother Tongue") agree that insights into ancient Chinese culture and linguistics can help us decipher life in modern-day America?
3. How do each of the following authors use the concept of anatomy in their essays to create symbols: Wang, Harold Krents ("Darkness at Noon"), Sucheng Chan ("You're Short, Besides!"), and Alice Walker ("Beauty: When the Other Dancer is the Self")? Do you have any physical characteristic that has achieved metaphoric status? If so, what is it?

IDEAS FOR DISCUSSION/WRITING

Preparing to Write

Write freely about your views on love: How many different forms does love come in? Do you enjoy all these types of love in your life? Do you have a good understanding of all the aspects of the word *love*? What does love in its broadest sense mean to you? What aspects of love are missing from your life? Why are they missing? What can you do to remedy this situation?

Choosing a Topic

1. You have been asked to speak at freshman orientation at your college. Your assigned topic is "The Role of Love in a College Student's Life." Using Wang Ping's article as a resource, define love from a student's perspective. (Remember to cite your source whenever necessary.) Supplement your definition with examples from your own experience and observations.
2. For a group of people your own age, define the word *friendship*. How is friendship different from love? Are they both equally important parts of life, or is one more important than the other?
3. Write a letter to one of your past lovers explaining why the relationship didn't work. This could focus on his or her inadequacies as a partner or perhaps on the reasons the two of

you weren't compatible. Give examples to support your main points.

4. Wang Ping's article focuses on the various definitions of the word *love*. Select a term that is equally difficult to define. Using online dictionaries, conduct an Internet search of your chosen word's definition. Find three sources of definitions, and compare their differences and similarities. Following Wang Ping's example, write an essay in which you develop the meaning of the word by analyzing it through the lens of your personal experience.

Before beginning your essay, you might want to consult the checklists on page 400.

ELLEN GOODMAN   (1941–   )

A Working Community

Ellen Goodman is a nationally syndicated columnist and associate editor of the *Boston Globe,* who frequently pens newspaper columns on such topics as feminism, child rearing, divorce, alternative lifestyles, and gardening. Although Goodman once appealed principally to women, her essays now interest readers of both sexes who are, in the words of *New York Times* critic John Leonard, "full of gratitude for having been introduced to a witty and civilized human being in a vulgar and self-pitying decade." Born in Newton, Massachusetts, and educated at Radcliffe College, Goodman began her career in journalism as a researcher and reporter at *Newsweek* magazine, then moved to the *Detroit Free Press* as a feature writer. In 1967, she was hired as a feature writer and "At Large" columnist by the *Boston Globe.* Her first book was *Turning Points* (1979), which examines how men and women have reacted to the changes brought on by the feminist movement. Other publications include five collections of her best newspaper columns: *Close to Home* (1979), *At Large* (1981), *Keeping in Touch* (1985), *Making Sense* (1989), and *Value Judgments* (1993). She is also coauthor with Patricia O'Brien of *I Know Just What You Mean: The Power of Friendship in Women's Lives* (2000). In 1980, Goodman's reputation as a first-rate journalist was confirmed when she was awarded the Pulitzer Prize for distinguished commentary. Syndicated now in more than 300 newspapers throughout the country, Goodman lives in Brookline, Massachusetts.

Preparing to Read

The following essay, originally written for the *Washington Post,* proposes a new definition of "community."

Exploring Experience: Before you read this essay, take a few moments to consider your views on the concept of community: What does *community* mean to you? Are different communities a part of your life? What roles do you play in these communities? Why do you play these roles? How do these different communities contribute to who you are? Which communities are your favorites? Which are your least favorite? Explain your answer.

Learning Online: Visit an online community, and spend a few moments on Ebay's online auction Web site (www.ebay.com). What types of communication methods do members use? What common traits do users of this site seem to share? Consider whether this "community" fits Goodman's definition.

I have a friend who is a member of the medical comunity. It does not say that, of course, on the stationery that bears her home address. This membership comes from her hospital work.   1

I have another friend who is a member of the computer community. This is a fairly new subdivision of our economy, and yet he finds his sense of place in it.   2

Other friends and acquaintances of mine are members of the academic community, or the business community, or the journalistic community.   3

Though you cannot find these on any map, we know where we belong.   4

None of us, mind you, was born into these communities. Nor did we move into them, U-Hauling our possessions along with us. None has papers to prove we are card-carrying members of one such group or another. Yet it seems that more and more of us are identified by work these days, rater than by street.   5

In the past, most Amerians lived in neighborhoods. We were members of precincts or parishes or school districts. My dictionary still defines community, first of all in geographic terms, as "a body of people who live in one place."   6

But today fewer of us do our living in that one place; more of us just use it for sleeping. Now we call our towns "bedroom suburbs," and many of us, without small children as icebreakers, would have trouble naming all the people on our street.   7

It's not that we are more isolated today. It's that many of us   8 have transferred a chunk of our friendships, a major portion of our everyday social lives, from home to office. As more of our neighbors work away from home, the workplace becomes our neighborhood.

The kaffeeklatsch of the fifties is the coffee break of the eight-   9
ies. The water cooler, the hall, the elevator, and the parking lot are the back fences of these neighborhoods. The people we have lunch with day after day are those who know the running saga of our mother's operations, our child's math grades, our frozen pipes, and faulty transmissions.

We may be strangers at the supermarket that replaced the cor-   10
ner grocer, but we are known at the coffee shop in the lobby. We share with each other a cast of characters from the boss in the corner office to the crazy lady in Shipping, to the lovers in Marketing. It's not surprising that when researchers ask Americans what they like best about work, they say it is "the shmoose factor." When they ask young mothers at home what they miss most about work, it is the people.

Not all the neighborhoods are empty, nor is every workplace a   11
friendly playground. Most of us have had mixed experiences in these environments. Yet as one woman told me recently, she knows more about the people she passes on the way to her desk than on her way around the block. Our new sense of community hasn't just moved from house to office building. The labels that we wear connect us with members from distant companies, cities, and states. We assume that we have something "in common" with other teachers, nurses, city planners.

It's not unlike the experience of our immigrant grandparents.   12
Many who came to this country still identified themselves as members of the Italian community, the Irish community, the Polish community. They sought out and assumed connections with people from the old country. Many of us have updated that experience. We have replaced ethnic identity with professional identity, the way we replaced neighborhoods with the workplace.

This whole realignment of community is surely most obvious   13
among the mobile professions. People who move from city to city seem to put roots down into their professions. In an age of specialists, they may have to search harder to find people who speak the same language.

I don't think that there is anything massively disruptive about this   14
shifting sense of community. The continuing search for connection and shared enterprise is very human. But I do feel uncomfortable

with our shifting identity. The balance has tipped, and we seem increasingly dependent on work for our sense of self.

If our offices are our new neighborhoods, if our professional 15 titles are our new ethnic tags, then how do we separate our selves from our jobs? Self-worth isn't just something to measure in the marketplace. But in these new communities, it becomes harder to tell who we are without saying what we do.

UNDERSTANDING DETAILS

1. What does Goodman mean when she says, "The kaffeklatsch of the fifties is the coffee break of the eighties" (paragraph 9)?
2. According to Goodman, how has our sense of community changed during the past few years?
3. How is a sense of community related to a sense of belonging?
4. Explain Goodman's statement about self-worth at the end of her essay: "Self-worth isn't just something to measure in the marketplace" (paragraph 15).

ANALYZING MEANING

1. Why are our towns called "bedroom suburbs" (paragraph 7)?
2. Why do you think Americans generally say they like "the shmoose factor" (paragraph 10) best about work?
3. Do you feel you have something in common with students around the world? Explain your answer.
4. According to Goodman, in what way is our identity as humans changing? Explain your answer.

DISCOVERING RHETORICAL STRATEGIES

1. Goodman starts her essay off with four very short paragraphs. What effect does this technique have on the essay as a whole?
2. Goodman's essay is made up to a large extent of items in a series and independent clauses that present her ideas as equivalent and balanced with one another. Find two examples of each of these techniques, and explain how they help Goodman make her point.
3. Goodman asks only one question in this essay. What is that question? Where does it appear in the essay? And what effect does it have on the essay as a whole?

4. What other rhetorical strategies, besides definition, does Goodman use in this essay? Give examples of each.

MAKING CONNECTIONS

1. Imagine that Goodman, William Ouchi ("Japanese and American Workers: Two Casts of Mind"), and Robert Ramirez ("The Barrio") were discussing the relationships between "identity" and "community." How would each explain this connection? Who would you most likely agree with? Explain your answer.
2. Compare and contrast the ways in which Goodman, Robert Ramirez ("The Barrio"), and Barbara Ehrenreich ("The Ecstasy of War") describe the relative difficulty of joining various "communities." Which community mentioned by these authors would be most difficult to belong to? Which would be least difficult? Why?
3. To what extent would Goodman and Mary Pipher ("Beliefs About Families") agree that a family is a "community"? Compare and contrast the way each of these authors defines her central term ("communities" and "families"). Which definition seems most complete and convincing to you? Why?

IDEAS FOR DISCUSSION/WRITING

Preparing to Write

Write freely about your current response to the idea of "community": What role does our sense of community play in American society today? In what ways are communities important to a society? What communities do you belong to? What role do communities play in your life? Why do you belong to these communities? What do you have in common with other "members" of these communities? Has your sense of community changed as you grew older? In what ways?

Choosing a Topic

1. Choose a "community" to which you belong and define your role in that group.
2. For your college newspaper, define the term *students* or *faculty* as communities in the academic world. Determine an audience and focus before you begin to write.

3. Write an essay in which you agree or disagree with the last line of Goodman's essay: "But in these new communities, it becomes harder and harder to tell who we are without saying what we do" (paragraph 15). Make sure you support your opinion with enough evidence.

4. Do you belong to any online communities? Perhaps you participate in forum discussions, receive weekly newsletters, or frequently purchase items from the same Web site. On the other hand, your online community may simply consist of a group of friends to whom you regularly send emails. Write an essay that defines and describes an online community in which you participate. Use Goodman's style of building a definition through concrete examples.

Before beginning your essay, you might want to consult the checklists on page 400.

CHAPTER WRITING ASSIGNMENTS
Practicing Definition

1. Identify a term people use to describe you (for example, *trustworthy, sloppy,* or *athletic*). In a well-developed essay, define this term as clearly as you can, and discuss whether or not it accurately represents you. Support your claim with carefully chosen details.

2. In what ways do our families define us? How do our families shape who we are and who we have become? In an essay, define the concept of family by explaining how your family members relate to each other.

3. Think of an object you value greatly. For example, a ring might represent a special relationship. Then, in essay form, explain what this object says about you. Why is it your favorite? What does it mean to you?

Exploring Ideas

1. Have you ever felt jealous? What do you think are the most common sources of jealousy? Do you think that jealousy is mostly a productive or unproductive emotion? Write an essay discussing the main qualities of jealousy. What do most people need to know about this feeling?

2. Think of all the "communities" to which you belong (for example, school, church, neighborhood, friends). Choose one that is really important to you, and, in an essay, identify the major features of this community. What makes this community so important in your life?

3. In essay form, describe an ugly part of your campus or city, and explore some important ways this place could be improved or changed. What effects do you think these changes might have on your community or campus? How did you come to this conclusion?

8

CAUSE/EFFECT
Tracing Reasons and Results

Wanting to know why things happen is one of our earliest, most basic instincts: Why can't I go out, Mommy? Why are you laughing? Why won't the dog stop barking? Why can't I swim faster than my big brother? These questions, and many more like them, reflect the innately inquisitive nature that dwells within each of us. Closely related to this desire to understand *why* is our corresponding interest in *what* will happen in the future as a result of some particular action: What will I feel like tomorrow if I stay up late tonight? How will I perform in the track meet Saturday if I practice all week? What will be the result if I mix together these two potent chemicals? What will happen if I turn in my next English assignment two days early?

A daily awareness of this intimate relationship between causes and effects allows us to begin to understand the complex and inter-related series of events that make up our lives and the lives of others. For example, trying to understand the various causes of the conflict between Palestine and Israel teaches us about international relations; knowing our biological reactions to certain foods helps us make decisions about what to eat; understanding the interrelated reasons for the outbreak of World War II offers us insight into historical trends and human nature; knowing the effects of sunshine on various parts of our bodies helps us make decisions about how much ultraviolet exposure we can tolerate and what suntan lotion to use; and understanding the causes of America's most recent recession will help us respond appropriately to the next economic crisis we encounter. More than anything else, tracing causes and effects teaches us how to think clearly and react intelligently to our multifaceted environment.

In college, you will often be asked to use this natural interest in causes and effects to analyze particular situations and to discern general principles. For example, you might be asked some of the following questions on essay exams in different courses:

Anthropology: Why did the Mayan culture disintegrate?

Psychology: Why do humans respond to fear in different ways?

Biology: How do lab rats react to caffeine?

History: What were the positive effects of the Spanish–American War?

Business: Why did so many computer manufacturing companies go bankrupt in the early 1980s?

Your ability to answer such questions will depend in large part on your skill at understanding cause/effect relationships.

DEFINING CAUSE/EFFECT

Cause/effect analysis requires the ability to look for connections between different elements and to analyze the reasons for those connections. As the name implies, this rhetorical mode has two separate components: cause and effect. A particular essay might concentrate on cause (Why do you live in a dorm?), on effect (What are the resulting advantages and disadvantages of living in a dorm?), or on some combination of the two. In working with causes, we are searching for any circumstances from the past that may have caused a single event; in looking for effects, we seek occurrences that took place after a particular event and resulted from that event. Like process analysis, cause/effect makes use of our intellectual ability to analyze. Process analysis addresses *how* something happens, whereas causal analysis discusses *why* it happened and *what* the result was. A process analysis paper, for example, might explain how to advertise more effectively to increase sales, whereas a cause/effect study would discover that three specific elements contributed to an increase in sales: effective advertising, personal service, and selective discounts. The study of causes and effects, therefore, provides many different and helpful ways for humans to make sense of and clarify their views of the world.

Looking for causes and effects requires an advanced form of thinking. It is more complex than most rhetorical strategies we have studied because it can exist on a number of different and progressively more difficult levels. The most accurate and effective causal analysis accrues from digging for the real or ultimate causes or effects, as opposed to those that are merely superficial or immediate. Actress Angela Lansbury would have been out of work on an episode of the television show *Murder, She Wrote*, for example, if her character had stopped her investigation at the immediate cause of death (slipping in the bathtub) rather than searching diligently for the *real* cause (an overdose of cocaine administered by an angry companion, which resulted in the slip in the tub). Similarly, voters would be easy to manipulate if they considered only the immediate effects of a tax increase (a slightly higher tax bill) rather than the ultimate benefits that would result (the many years of improved education that our children would receive because of the specialized programs created by such an increase). Only the discovery of the actual reasons for an event or an idea will lead to the logical and accurate analysis of causes and effects important to a basic understanding of various aspects of our lives.

Faulty reasoning assigns causes to a sequence of actions without adequate justification. One such logical fallacy is called *post hoc, ergo propter hoc* ("after this, therefore because of this"): The fact that someone lost a job after walking under a ladder does not mean that the two events are causally related; by the same token, if we get up every morning at 5:30 A.M., just before the sun rises, we cannot therefore conclude that the sun rises *because* we get up (no matter how self-centered we are!). Faulty reasoning also occurs when we oversimplify a particular situation. Most events are connected to a multitude of causes and effects. Sometimes one effect has many causes: A student may fail a history exam because she's been working two part-time jobs, she was sick, she didn't study hard enough, and she found the instructor very boring. One cause may also have many effects. If a house burns down, the people who lived in it will be out of a home. If we look at such a tragic scene more closely, however, we may also note that the fire traumatized a child who lived there, helped the family learn what good friends they had, encouraged the family to double their future fire insurance, and provided the happy stimulus that they needed to make a long-dreamed-of move to another city. One event has thus resulted in many interrelated effects. Building an argument on insecure foundations or oversimplifying the causes or effects connected with an event will seriously hinder the construction of a rational essay. No matter what the nature of the cause/effect analysis, it must always be based on clear observation, accurate facts, and rigorous logic.

In the following paragraph, a student writer analyzes some of the causes and effects connected with the controversial issue of euthanasia. Notice how he makes connections and then analyzes those connections as he consistently explores the immediate and ultimate effects of being able to stretch life beyond its normal limits through new medical technology:

Along with the many recent startling advancements in medical technology have come a number of complex moral, ethical, and spiritual questions that beg to be answered. We now have the ability to prolong the life of the human body for a very long time. But what rights do patients and their families have to curtail cruel and unusual medical treatment that stretches life beyond its normal limits? This dilemma has produced a ripple effect in society. Is the extension of life an unquestionable goal in itself, regardless of the quality of that life? Modern scientific technology has forced doctors to reevaluate the exact meaning and purpose of their profession. For example, many medical schools and undergraduate university programs now routinely offer classes on medical ethics—an esoteric and infrequently taught subject only a few years ago. Doctors and scholars alike are realizing that medical personnel alone cannot be expected to decide on the exact parameters of life. In like manner, the judicial process must now evaluate the legal complexities of mercy killings and the rights of patients to die with dignity and without unnecessary medical intervention. The insurance business, too, wrestles with the catastrophic effects of new technology on the costs of today's hospital care. In short, medical progress entails more than microscopes, chemicals, and high-tech instruments. If we are to develop as a thoughtful, just, and merciful society, we must consider not only the physical well-being of our nation's patients, but their emotional, spiritual, and financial status as well.

THINKING CRITICALLY BY USING CAUSE/EFFECT

Thinking about causes and effects is one of the most advanced mental activities that we perform. It involves complex operations that we must think through carefully, making sure all connections are reasonable and accurate. Unlike other rhetorical patterns, cause/ effect thinking requires us to see specific relationships between two or more items. To practice this strategy, we need to look for items or events that are causally related—that is, one that has caused the other. Then, we can focus on either the causes (the initial stimulus), the effects (the results), or a combination of the two.

Searching for causes and effects requires a great deal of digging that is not necessary for most of the other modes. Cause/effect necessitates the ultimate in investigative work. The mental exertion associated with this thinking strategy is sometimes exhausting, but it is always worth going through when you discover relationships that you never saw before or when you uncover links in your reasoning that were previously unknown or obscure to you.

If you've ever had the secret desire to be a private eye or an investigator of any sort, practicing cause/effect reasoning can be lots of fun. It forces you to see relationships among multiple items

and then to make sense of those connections. Completing exercises in this skill by itself will once again help you perfect the logistics of cause/effect thinking before you mix and match it with other thinking strategies.

1. In Sam Shere's famous 1937 photo of the Hindenburg bursting into flames, we can see that the maiden voyage of the zeppelin did not go well. Ninety-seven people were aboard when the Hindenberg went down, and none of them expected to die. Think of other examples of technological inventions or changes where the outcome was different from what people expected. Identify the expectations, the actual results, and what can be learned from these results.
2. Choose a major problem you see in our society, and list what you think are the main causes of this problem on one side of a piece of paper and the effects on the other side. Compare the two lists to see how they differ. Then, compare and contrast your list with those written by other students.
3. What "caused" you to become a student? What influences led you to this choice at this point in your life? How has being a student affected your life? List several overall effects.

READING AND WRITING CAUSE/EFFECT ESSAYS

Causal analysis is usually employed for one of three main purposes: (1) to prove a specific point (such as the necessity for stricter gun control), in which case the writer generally deals totally with facts and with conclusions drawn from those facts; (2) to argue against a widely accepted belief (for example, the assertion that cocaine is addictive), in which case the writer relies principally on facts, with perhaps some pertinent opinions; or (3) to speculate on a theory (for instance, why the crime rate is higher in most major cities than it is in rural areas), in which case the writer probably presents hypotheses and opinions along with facts. This section will explore these purposes in cause/effect essays from the standpoint of both reading and writing.

How to Read a Cause/Effect Essay

Preparing to Read.   As you set out to read the essays in this chapter, begin by focusing your attention on the title and the synopsis of the essay you are about to read and by scanning the essay itself: What do you think Stephen King is going to talk about in "Why We Crave Horror Movies"? What does the synopsis in the Rhetorical Table of Contents tell you about Michael Dorris's "The Broken Cord" or about Richard Rodriguez's "The Fear of Losing a Culture"?

Also, at this stage in the reading process, you should try to learn as much as you can about the author of the essay and the reasons he or she wrote it. Ask yourself questions like the following: What is King's intention in "Why We Crave Horror Movies"? Who is Mary Roach's intended audience in "Meet the Bickersons"? And what is Alice Walker's point of view in "Beauty: When the Other Dancer Is the Self"?

Finally, before you begin to read, answer the prereading questions for each essay and then consider the proposed essay topic from a variety of perspectives: For example, concerning Rodriguez's topic, how important to you is your ethnic or national background? Which segments of American society are most aware of cultural differences? Which the least? Do you have a desire to understand relationships better? What do you want to know from Roach about people and arguing?

Reading.   As you read each essay in this chapter for the first time, record your spontaneous reactions to it, drawing as often as possible on the preliminary material you already know: What do you think of horror movies (King)? What is Dorris suggesting about fetal alcohol babies? Have you experienced an addiction of any kind? Why did Roach choose the title she did?

Whenever you can, try to create a context for your reading: What is the tone of Rodriguez's comments about culture? How does this tone help him communicate with his audience? What do you think Walker's purpose is in her essay concerning her childhood accident? How clearly does she get this purpose across to you?

Also, during this reading, note the essay's thesis and check to see if the writer thoroughly explores all possibilities before settling on the primary causes and/or effects of a particular situation; in addition, determine whether the writer clearly states the assertions that naturally evolve from a discussion of the topic. Finally, read the questions following each essay to get a sense of the main issues and strategies in the selection.

Rereading. When you reread these essays, you should focus mainly on the writer's craft. Notice how the authors narrow and focus their material, how they make clear and logical connections between ideas in their essays, how they support their conclusions with concrete examples, how they use other rhetorical modes to accomplish their cause/effect analysis, and how they employ logical transitions to move us smoothly from one point to another. Most important, however, ask yourself if the writer actually discusses the real causes and/or effects of a particular circumstance: What does King say are the primary reasons people crave horror movies? According to Roach, why do many couples have trouble in their marriages? What are the primary causes and effects of Walker's childhood injury?

For a thorough outline of the reading process, consult the checklist on page 20 of the Introduction.

How to Write a Cause/Effect Essay

Preparing to Write. Beginning a cause/effect essay requires—as does any other essay—exploring and limiting your subject, specifying a purpose, and identifying an audience. The Preparing to Write questions before the essay assignments, coupled with the prewriting techniques outlined in the Introduction (pp. 21–23), encourage you to consider specific issues related to your reading. The assignments themselves will then help you limit your topic and determine a particular purpose and audience for your message. For cause/effect essays, determining a purpose is even more important than usual, because your readers can get hopelessly lost unless your analysis is clearly focused.

Writing. For all its conceptual complexity, a cause/effect essay can be organized quite simply. The introduction generally presents the subject(s) and states the purpose of the analysis in a clear thesis. The body of the paper then explores all relevant causes and/or effects, typically progressing either from least to most influential or from most to least influential. Finally, the concluding section summarizes the various cause/effect relationships established in the body of the paper and clearly states the conclusions that can be drawn from those relationships.

The following additional guidelines should assist you in producing an effective cause/effect essay in all academic disciplines:

1. Narrow and focus your material as much as possible.
2. Consider all possibilities before assigning real or ultimate causes or effects.
3. Show connections between ideas by using transitions and key words—such as *because, reasons, results, effects,* and *consequences*—to guide your readers smoothly through your essay.
4. Support all inferences with concrete evidence.
5. Be as objective as possible in your analysis so that you don't distort logic with personal biases.
6. Understand your audience's opinions and convictions so that you know what to emphasize in your essay.
7. Qualify your assertions to avoid overstatement and oversimplification.

These suggestions apply to both cause/effect essay assignments and exam questions.

Rewriting.   As you revise your cause/effect essays, ask yourself the following important questions:

• Is your thesis stated clearly at the outset of your paper?

• Does it include your subject and your purpose?

• Do you accomplish your purpose as effectively as possible for your particular audience?

• Do you use logical reasoning throughout the essay?

• Do you carefully explore all relevant causes and/or effects, searching for the real (as opposed to the immediate) reasons in each case?

• Do you state clearly the conclusions that can be drawn from your paper?

More specific guidelines for writing and revising your essays appear on pages 31–32 of the Introduction.

STUDENT ESSAY: CAUSE/EFFECT AT WORK

In the following essay, the student writer analyzes the effects of contemporary TV soap operas on young people: Notice that she states her subject and purpose at the beginning of the essay and then presents a combination of facts and opinions in her exploration of the topic. Notice also that, in her analysis, the writer is careful to draw clear connections between her perceptions of the issue and various objective details in an attempt to trace the effects of this medium in our society today. At the end of her essay, look at her summary of the logical relationships she establishes in the body of the essay and her statements about the conclusions she draws from these relationships.

Distortions of Reality

Background   Television's contributions to society, positive and negative, have been debated continually since this piece of technology invaded the average American household in the 1950s. Television has brought an unlimited influx of new information, ideas, and cultures into our homes. However, based on my observations of my thirteen-year-old cousin, Katie, and her friends, I think we need to take a closer look at the effects of soap operas on adolescents today. <u>The distortions of reality portrayed on these programs are frighteningly misleading and, in my opinion, can be very confusing to young people.</u>   *Thesis statement*

Transition   <u>During the early 1990s, the lifestyle of the typical soap opera "family" has been radically transformed from comfortable pretentiousness to blatant and unrealistic decadence. The characters neither live nor dress like the majority of their viewers, who are generally middle-class Americans.</u> These television families live in large, majestic homes that are flawlessly decorated. The actors are often adorned in beautiful designer clothing, fur coats, and expensive jewelry, and this opulent lifestyle is sustained by people with no visible means of income. Very few of the characters seem to "work" for a living. When they do, upward mobility—without the benefit of the proper   *First distortion of reality*

Concrete examples

education or suitable training—and a well-planned marriage come quickly.

Transition   From this constant barrage of conspicu-ous consumption, my cousin and her friends *First effect* seem to have a distorted view of everyday economic realities. I see Katie and her group becoming obsessed with the appearance of *Concrete* their clothes and possessions. I frequently *examples* hear them criticize their parents' jobs and modest homes. With noticeable arrogance, these young adolescents seem to view their parents' lives as "failures" when compared to the effortless, luxurious lifestyles por-trayed in the soaps.

Transition   One of the most alluring features of this genre is its masterful use of deception. Con-flicts between characters in soap operas are based on secrecy and misinformation. *Concrete* Failure to tell the truth and to perform hon-*examples* orable deeds further complicates the entan-gled lives and love affairs of the participants. But when the truth finally comes out and all *Second* mistakes and misdeeds become public, the *distortion* culprits and offenders hardly ever suffer for *of reality* their actions. In fact, they appear to leave the scene of the crime guilt-free.

Transition   Regrettably, Katie and her friends consis-tently express alarming indifference to this lack of moral integrity. In their daily view-*Concrete* ing, they shrug off underhanded scenes of *examples* scheming and conniving, and they marvel at how the characters manipulate each other into positions of powerlessness or grapple in distasteful love scenes. I can only conclude that continued exposure to this amoral be-*Second* havior is eroding the fundamental values of *effect* truth and fidelity in these kids.

Transition   Also in the soaps, the powers-that-be *Third* conveniently disregard any sense of respon-*distortion* sibility for wrongdoing. Characters serve jail *of reality*

Concrete examples terms quickly and in relative comfort. Drug or alcohol abuse does not mar anyone's physical appearance or behavior, and poverty is virtually non-existent. Usually, the wrongdoer's position, wealth, and prestige are quickly restored—with little pain and suffering.

Third effect Adolescents are clearly learning that people can act without regard for the harmful effects of their actions on themselves and others when they see this type of behavior go unpunished. Again, I notice the result of this delusion in my cousin. Recently, when a businessman in our community was convicted of embezzling large sums of money Concrete examples from his clients, Katie was outraged because he was sentenced to five years in prison, unlike her daytime TV "heartthrob," who had been given a suspended sentence for a similar crime. With righteous indignation, Katie claimed that the victims, many of whom had lost their entire savings, should have realized that any business investment involves risk and the threat of loss. Logic and common sense evaded Katie's reasoning as she insisted on comparing television justice with real-life jurisprudence.

The writers and producers of soap operas argue that the shows are designed to entertain viewers and are not meant to be reflections of reality. Theoretically, this may be true, but I can actually see how these soap operas are affecting my cousin and her crowd. Although my personal observations are limited, I cannot believe they are unique or unusual. Too many young people think that they can amass wealth and material pos- Ultimate effect sessions without an education, hard work, or careful financial planning; that material goods are the sole measure of a person's success in life; and that honesty and integrity are not necessarily admirable qualities.

Proposed solution   Soap operas should demonstrate a realistic lifestyle and a responsible sense of behavior. The many hours adolescents spend in front of the television can obviously influence their view of the world. As a society, we cannot afford the consequences resulting from the distortions of reality portrayed every day in these shows.

Student Writer's Comments

In general, writing this essay was not as easy as I had anticipated during my prewriting phase. Although I was interested in and familiar with my topic, I had trouble fitting all the pieces together: matching causes with effects, examples with main points, and problems with solutions.

My prewriting activities were a combination of lists and journal entries that gave me loads of ideas and phrasing to work with in my drafts. From this initial thinking exercise, I created an informal outline of the points I wanted to make. I played with the order of these topics for a while and then began to write.

Because I had spent so much time thinking through various causal relationships before I began to write, I generated the first draft with minimal pain. But I was not happy with it. The examples that I had chosen to support various points I wanted to make did not fit as well as they could, and the whole essay was scattered and incoherent. Although all writing requires support and focus, I realized that a cause/effect essay demands special attention to the relationship between specific examples and their ultimate causes and/or effects. As a result, I had to begin again to revise my sprawling first draft.

I spent my first revising session on the very sloppy introduction and conclusion. I felt that if I could tighten up these parts of the essay, I would have a clearer notion of my purpose and focus. I am convinced now that the time I spent on the beginning and ending of my essay really paid off. I rewrote my thesis several times until I finally arrived at the statement in the draft printed here. This final thesis statement gave me a clear sense of direction for revising the rest of my paper.

I then worked through my essay paragraph by paragraph, verifying that the examples and illustrations I cited supported as effectively as possible each of my points. I made sure that the causes and effects were accurately paired, and I reorganized sections of the essay that didn't yet read smoothly. I put the final touches on my conclusion and handed in my paper—with visions of causes, effects, and soap opera characters still dancing around in my head.

SOME FINAL THOUGHTS ON CAUSE/EFFECT

The essays in this chapter deal with both causes and effects in a variety of ways. As you read each essay, try to discover its primary purpose and the ultimate causes and/or effects of the issue under discussion. Note also the clear causal relationships that each author sets forth on solid foundations supported by logical reasoning. Although the subjects of these essays vary dramatically, each essay exhibits the basic elements of effective causal analysis.

CAUSE/EFFECT IN REVIEW

Reading Cause/Effect Essays

Preparing to Read

✓ What assumptions can you make from the essay's title?
✓ Can you guess what the general mood of the essay is?
✓ What is the essay's purpose and audience?
✓ What does the synopsis tell you about the essay?
✓ What can you learn from the author's biography?
✓ Can you guess what the author's point of view toward the subject is?
✓ What are your responses to the "Preparing to Read" questions?

Reading

✓ What is the author's thesis?
✓ What are the primary causes and/or effects in the essay?
✓ Did you preview the questions that follow the essay?

Rereading

✓ How does the writer narrow and focus the essay?
✓ Does the writer make clear and logical connections between the ideas?
✓ What concrete examples support the author's conclusions?
✓ Does the writer discuss the real causes and effects?
✓ What are your responses to the questions after the essay?

Writing Cause/Effect Essays

Preparing to Write

✓ What are your responses to the "Preparing to Write" questions?
✓ What is your purpose?
✓ Who is your audience?

Writing

✓ Do you narrow and focus your material as much as possible?
✓ Do you consider all possibilities before assigning real causes or effects?
✓ Do you show connections by using transitions and key words?
✓ Do you support all inferences with concrete evidence?
✓ Are you as objective as possible in your analysis?
✓ Do you understand your audience's opinions and convictions?
✓ Do you qualify your assertions?

Rewriting

✓ Is your thesis stated clearly at the outset of your paper?
✓ Does it include your subject and your purpose?
✓ Do you accomplish your purpose as effectively as possible?
✓ Do you use logical reasoning throughout the essay?
✓ Do you state clearly your conclusions?

STEPHEN KING   (1947–   )

Why We Crave Horror Movies

"People's appetites for terror seem insatiable," Stephen King once remarked, an insight that may help justify his phenomenal success as a writer of horror fiction since the mid-1970s. His books have sold over one hundred million copies, and the movies made from them have generated more income than the gross domestic product of several small countries. After early jobs as a janitor, a laundry worker, and a high school English teacher in Portland, Maine, King turned to writing full time following the spectacular sales of his first novel, *Carrie* (1974), which focuses on a shy, socially ostracized young girl who takes revenge on her cruel classmates through newly developed telekinetic powers. King's subsequent books have included *The Shining* (1976), *Firestarter* (1980), *Cujo* (1981), *The Dark Tower* (1982), *Christine* (1983), *Pet Sematary* (1983), *Misery* (1987), *The Stand* (1990), *Four Past Midnight* (1990), *The Waste Lands* (1992), *Delores Claiborne* (1993), *Desperation* (1996), *Bag of Bones* (1999), *On Writing: A Memoir of the Craft* (2000), *Dreamcatcher* (2001), and *The Dark Tower V: Wolves of the Calla* (2003). Asked to explain why readers and moviegoers are so attracted to his tales of horror, King explained that most people's lives "are full of fears—that their marriage isn't working, that they aren't going to make it on the job, that society is crumbling all around them. But we're really not supposed to talk about things like that, and so they don't have any outlets for all those scary feelings. But the horror writer can give them a place to put their fears, and it's OK to be afraid then, because nothing is real, and you can blow it all away when it's over." A cheerful though somewhat superstitious person, King, who now lives in Bangor, Maine, admits to doing most of his best writing during the morning hours. "You think I want to write this stuff at night?" he once asked a reviewer.

Preparing to Read

This essay, originally published in *Playboy* magazine, attempts to explain why horror movies satisfy our most basic instincts.

They give us an acceptable way to channel our everyday fears about life in general.

Exploring Experience: As you prepare to read this article, consider your thoughts on America's emotional condition: How emotionally healthy are Americans? Were they more emotionally healthy twenty years ago? A century ago? What makes a society emotionally healthy? Emotionally unhealthy? How can a society maintain good health? What is the relationship between emotional health and a civilized society?

Learning Online: Conduct an Internet search on two recently released horror movies. Use the title of the film as well as the phrase "movie trailer" as your search terms. Find links that allow you to watch the film's preview trailer. How do you feel after watching the trailer? Do you like or dislike this type of film genre?

I think that we're all mentally ill; those of us outside the asylums   1
only hide it a little better—and maybe not all that much better, after all. We've all known people who talk to themselves, people who sometimes squinch their faces into horrible grimaces when they believe no one is watching, people who have some hysterical fear—of snakes, the dark, the tight place, the long drop . . . and, of course, those final worms and grubs that are waiting so patiently underground.

When we pay our four or five bucks and seat ourselves at tenth-   2
row center in a theater showing a horror movie, we are daring the nightmare.

Why? Some of the reasons are simple and obvious. To show   3
that we can, that we are not afraid, that we can ride this roller coaster. Which is not to say that a really good horror movie may not surprise a scream out of us at some point, the way we may scream when the roller coaster twists through a complete 360 or plows through a lake at the bottom of the drop. And horror movies, like roller coasters, have always been the special province of the young; by the time one turns 40 or 50, one's appetite for double twists or 360-degree loops may be considerably depleted.

We also go to reestablish our feelings of essential normality; the   4
horror movie is innately conservative, even reactionary. Freda

Jackson as the horrible melting woman in *Die, Monster, Die!* confirms for us that no matter how far we may be removed from the
beauty of a Robert Redford or a Diana Ross, we are still light-
years from true ugliness.

And we go to have fun.   5

Ah, but this is where the ground starts to slope away, isn't it?   6
Because this is a very peculiar sort of fun, indeed. The fun comes
from seeing others menaced—sometimes killed. One critic has
suggested that if pro football has become the voyeur's version of
combat, then the horror film has become the modern version of
the public lynching.

It is true that the mythic, "fairy-tale" horror film intends to take   7
away the shades of gray. . . . It urges us to put away our more civilized and adult penchant for analysis and to become children
again, seeing things in pure blacks and whites. It may be that horror movies provide psychic relief on this level because this invitation to lapse into simplicity, irrationality, and even outright madness is extended so rarely. We are told we may allow our emotions
a free rein . . . or no rein at all.

If we are all insane, then sanity becomes a matter of degree. If   8
your insanity leads you to carve up women, like Jack the Ripper
or the Cleveland Torso Murderer, we clap you away in the funny
farm (but neither of those two amateur-night surgeons was ever
caught, heh-heh-heh); if, on the other hand, your insanity leads
you only to talk to yourself when you're under stress or to pick
your nose on your morning bus, then you are left alone to go
about your business . . . though it is doubtful that you will ever be
invited to the best parties.

The potential lyncher is in almost all of us (excluding saints, past   9
and present; but then, most saints have been crazy in their own
ways), and every now and then, he has to be let loose to scream
and roll around in the grass. Our emotions and our fears form their
own body, and we recognize that it demands its own exercise to
maintain proper muscle tone. Certain of these emotional muscles
are accepted—even exalted—in civilized society; they are, of
course, the emotions that tend to maintain the status quo of civilization itself. Love, friendship, loyalty, kindness—these are all the
emotions that we applaud, emotions that have been immortalized
in the couplets of Hallmark cards and in the verses (I don't dare
call it poetry) of Leonard Nimoy.

When we exhibit these emotions, society showers us with pos-   10
itive reinforcement; we learn this even before we get out of dia-
pers. When, as children, we hug our rotten little puke of a sister
and give her a kiss, all the aunts and uncles smile and twit and cry,
"Isn't he the sweetest little thing?" Such coveted treats as
chocolate-covered graham crackers often follow. But if we deliberately slam the rotten little puke of a sister's fingers in the door,
sanctions follow—angry remonstrance from parents, aunts, and
uncles; instead of a chocolate-covered graham cracker, a spanking.

But anticivilization emotions don't go away, and they demand   11
periodic exercise. We have such "sick" jokes as, "What's the difference between a truckload of bowling balls and a truckload of
dead babies?" (You can't unload a truckload of bowling balls with
a pitchfork . . . a joke, by the way, that I heard originally from a
ten-year-old.) Such a joke may surprise a laugh or a grin out of us
even as we recoil, a possibility that confirms the thesis: If we share
a brotherhood of man, then we also share an insanity of man.
None of which is intended as a defense of either the sick joke or
insanity but merely as an explanation of why the best horror films,
like the best fairy tales, manage to be reactionary, anarchistic, and
revolutionary all at the same time.

The mythic horror movie, like the sick joke, has a dirty job to   12
do. It deliberately appeals to all that is worst in us. It is morbidity
unchained, our most base instincts let free, our nastiest fantasies
realized . . . , and it all happens, fittingly enough, in the dark. For
those reasons, good liberals often shy away from horror films. For
myself, I like to see the most aggressive of them—*Dawn of the
Dead*, for instance—as lifting a trap door in the civilized forebrain
and throwing a basket of raw meat to the hungry alligators swimming around in that subterranean river beneath.

Why bother? Because it keeps them from getting out, man. It   13
keeps them down there and me up here. It was Lennon and
McCartney who said that all you need is love, and I would agree
with that.

As long as you keep the gators fed.   14

UNDERSTANDING DETAILS

1. Why, in King's opinion, do civilized people enjoy horror
   movies?

2. According to King, in what ways are horror movies like roller coasters?
3. According to King, how are horror films like public lynchings?
4. What is the difference between "emotions that tend to maintain the status quo of civilization" (paragraph 9) and "anticivilization emotions" (paragraph 11)?

ANALYZING MEANING

1. How can horror movies "reestablish our feelings of essential normality" (paragraph 4)?
2. What is "reactionary, anarchistic, and revolutionary" (paragraph 11) about fairy tales? About horror films?
3. Why does the author think we need to exercise our anticivilization emotions? What are some other ways we might confront these emotions?
4. Explain the last line of King's essay: "As long as you keep the gators fed" (paragraph 14).

DISCOVERING RHETORICAL STRATEGIES

1. What is the cause/effect relationship King notes in society between horror movies and sanity?
2. Why does King begin his essay with such a dramatic statement as "I think that we're all mentally ill" (paragraph 1)?
3. Who do you think is the author's intended audience for this essay? Describe them in detail. How did you come to this conclusion?
4. What different rhetorical strategies does King use to support his cause/effect analysis? Give examples of each.

MAKING CONNECTIONS

1. Apply Stephen King's definition of *horror* to such frightening experiences as the preparation of a dead body for its funeral (Jessica Mitford, "Behind the Formaldehyde Curtain") and/or caring for a fetal alcohol syndrome child (Michael Dorris, "The Broken Cord"). In what way is each of these events "horrible"? What are the principal differences between watching a horror movie and living through a real-life horror?

2. In this essay, King gives us important insights into his own writing process, especially into how horror novels and movies affect their audiences. Compare and contrast his revelation of the techniques of his trade with those advanced by Amy Tan ("Mother Tongue"), Linda Formichelli ("Engage in Word Play!"), Roger Rosenblatt ("I am Writing Blindly"), and Rita Mae Brown ("Writing as a Moral Act"), all of whom discuss the writing process. Whose comments are most helpful to you? Explain your answer.

3. Compare King's remarks about "fear" with similar insights into the topic by such other authors as Richard Rodriguez ("The Fear of Losing a Culture") and Alice Walker ("Beauty: When the Other Dancer Is the Self"). How would each of these writers define the term differently? With which author's definition would you most likely agree? Explain your answer.

IDEAS FOR DISCUSSION/WRITING

Preparing to Write

Write freely about how most people maintain a healthy emotional attitude: How would you define emotional well-being? When are people most emotionally healthy? Most emotionally unhealthy? What do your friends and relatives do to maintain a healthy emotional life? What do you do to maintain emotional health? What is the connection between our individual emotional health and the extent to which our society is civilized?

Choosing a Topic

1. Think of a release other than horror films for our most violent emotions. Is it an acceptable release? Write an essay for the general public explaining the relationship between this particular release and our "civilized" society.

2. If you accept King's analysis of horror movies, what role in society do you think other types of movies play (e.g., love stories, science-fiction movies, and comedies)? Choose one type, and explain its role to your college composition class.

3. Your psychology instructor has asked you to explain your opinions on the degree of sanity or insanity in America at present. In what ways are we sane? In what ways are we insane?

Write an essay for your psychology instructor explaining in detail your observations along these lines.

4. King's essay focuses on the benefits of watching horror films. What are other practices we have that on the surface may seem silly or trivial, but actually serve an important purpose? Select one such practice, and write an essay in which you identify its causes and effects. Conduct an Internet search on your topic, and use credible references to support your theories. Try to use relevant, vivid imagery, as King does, to engage your audience.

Before beginning your essay, you might want to consult the checklists on page 454.

MICHAEL DORRIS   (1945–1997)

The Broken Cord

Michael Dorris, a descendant of Modoc American Indians and Irish and French settlers, grew up in Kentucky and Montana. He earned his B.A. at Georgetown University and his Master of Arts degree at Yale and was for many years a professor of anthropology and Native-American Studies at Dartmouth, where he was also head of the Native-American Studies program. His training was quite eclectic. "I came to cultural anthropology," he has explained, "by way of an undergraduate program in English and classics and a Master's Degree in history of the theater." He was also a Guggenheim Fellow (1978), a Rockefeller Fellow (1985), a member of the Smithsonian Institution Council, a National Endowment for the Humanities consultant, a National Public Radio commentator, and a member of the editorial board of the *American Indian Culture and Research Journal* during his distinguished academic career. His many publications included *Native Americans: Five Hundred Years After* (1975); a bestselling novel, *A Yellow Raft in Blue Water* (1987); *The Broken Cord* (1989), a work of nonfiction that won the Heartland Prize, the Christopher Medal, and the National Book Critics Circle Award; *Morning Girl* (1992), a book of short stories; and two more novels, *Working Men* (1993) and *Rooms in the House of Stone* (1993). Dorris also coauthored several books with his wife, Louise Erdrich, including *Route Two and Back* (1991), a collection of travel essays. Prior to his recent death, he advised students using *The Prose Reader* to "work at as many kinds of jobs as possible while they are young and to keep daily journals of their experiences and impressions."

Preparing to Read

The following excerpt from *The Broken Cord* details some of Dorris's frustrations in raising his adopted son, Adam, who suffered from fetal alcohol syndrome until his death in 1991.

Exploring Experience: As you prepare to read this article, take a few moments to think about your own physical and mental growth: What do you know about your birth? How did you develop as a child? Are you reaching your physical and mental potential? How do you know? Are there any barriers between you and this potential? What are they? How can you surmount them? How will you maintain your potential?

Learning Online: Conduct an Internet search on the term *Fetal Alcohol Syndrome* to find facts and photos about the condition described so vividly in Dorris's essay.

A dam's birthdays are, I think, the hardest anniversaries, even though as an adoptive father I was not present to hear Adam's first cry, to feel the aspirated warmth of his body meeting air for the first time. I was not present to count his fingers, to exclaim at the surprise of gender, to be comforted by the hope at the heart of his new existence.

From what I've learned, from the sum of gathered profiles divided by the tragedy of each case, the delivery of my premature son was unlikely to have been a joyous occasion. Most fetal alcohol babies emerge not in a tide, the facsimile of saline, primordial, life-granting sea, but instead enter this world tainted with stale wine. Their amniotic fluid literally reeks of Thunderbird or Ripple, and the whole operating theater stinks like the scene of a three-day party. Delivery room staff who have been witness time and again tell of undernourished babies thrown into delirium tremens when the cord that brought sustenance and poison is severed. Nurses close their eyes at the memory. An infant with the shakes, as cold turkey as a raving derelict deprived of the next fix, is hard to forget.

Compared to the ideal, Adam started far in the hole, differently from the child who began a march through the years without the scars of fetters on his ankles, with eyes and ears that worked, with nothing to carry except what he or she collected along the path.

Adam's birthdays are reminders for me. For each celebration commemorating that he was born, there is the pang, the rage, that he was not born whole. I grieve for what he might have, what he

1

2

3

4

should have been. I magnify and sustain those looks of understanding or compassion or curiosity that fleet across his face, fast as
a breeze, unexpected as the voice of God—the time he said to me
in the car, the words arising from no context I could see, "Kansas
is between Oklahoma and Texas." But when I turned in amazement, agreeing loudly, still ready after all these years to discover a
buried talent or passion for geography, for anything, that possible
person had disappeared.

"What made you say that?" I asked.   5

"Say what?" he answered. "I didn't say anything."   6

The sixteenth birthday, the eighteenth. The milestones. The   7
driver's license, voting, the adult boundary-marker birthdays. The
days I envisioned while watching the mail for the response to my
first adoption application, the days that set forth like distant skyscrapers as I projected ahead through my years of fatherhood. I had
given little specific consideration to what might come between,
but of those outstanding days I had been sure. They were the pillars I followed, the oases of certainty. Alone in the cabin in Alaska
or in the basement apartment near Franconia while I waited for
the definition of the rest of my life to commence, I planned the
elaborate cake decorations for those big birthdays, the significant
presents I would save to buy. Odd as it may seem, the anticipation
of the acts of letting Adam go began before I even knew his name.
I looked forward to the proud days on which the world would
recognize my son as progressively more his own man. Those were
among the strongest hooks that bonded me to him in my imagination.

As each of these anniversaries finally came and went, nothing   8
like I expected them to be, I doubly mourned. First, selfishly, for
me, and second for Adam, because he didn't know what he was
missing, what he had already missed, what he would miss. I
wanted to burst through those birthdays like a speeding train blasts
a weak gate, to get past them and back into the anonymous years
for which I had made no models, where there were no obvious
measurements, no cakes with candles that would never be lit.

It was a coincidence that Adam turned twenty-one as this book   9
neared completion, but it seemed appropriate. On the morning of
his birthday, I rose early and baked him a lemon cake, his favorite,
and left the layers to cool while I drove to Hanover to pick him
up. His gifts were wrapped and on the kitchen table—an electric

shaver, clothes, a Garfield calendar. For his special dinner he had requested tacos, and as always I had reserved a magic candle—the kind that keeps reigniting no matter how often it is blown out—for the center of his cake.

I was greeted at Adam's house by the news that he had just had   10
a seizure, a small one this time, but it had left him groggy. I helped him on with his coat, bent to tie his shoelace, all the while talking about the fun we would have during the day. He looked out the window. Only the week before he had been laid off from his dishwashing job. December had been a bad month for seizures, some due to his body's adjustment to a change in dosage and some occurring because Adam had skipped taking medicine altogether. The bowling alley's insurance carrier was concerned and that, combined with an after-Christmas slump in business, decided the issue. Now he was back at Hartford for a few weeks while Ken Krambert and his associates sought a new work placement. I thought perhaps Adam was depressed about this turn of events, so I tried to cheer him up as we drove south on the familiar road to Cornish.

"So, Adam," I said, making conversation, summoning the con-   11
ventional words, "do you feel any older? What's good about being twenty-one?"

He turned to me and grinned. There *was* something good.   12

"Well," he answered, "now the guys at work say I'm old   13
enough to drink."

His unexpected words kicked me in the stomach. They   14
crowded every thought from my brain.

"Adam, you can't," I protested. "I've told you about your   15
birth-mother, about your other father. Do you remember what happened to them?" I knew he did. I had told him the story several times, and we had gone over it together as he read, or I read to him, parts of this book.

Adam thought for a moment. "They were sick?" he offered   16
finally. "That's why I have seizures?"

"No, they weren't sick. They died, Adam. They died from   17
drinking. If you drank, it could happen to you." My memory played back all the statistics about sons of alcoholic fathers and their particular susceptibility to substance abuse. "It would not mix well with your medicine."

Adam sniffed, turned away, but not before I recognized   18
the amused disbelief in his expression. He did not take death

seriously, never had. It was an abstract concept out of his reach and therefore of no interest to him. Death was less real than Santa Claus—after all, Adam had in his album a photograph of himself seated on Santa Claus's lap. Death was no threat, no good reason to refuse his first drink.

My son will forever travel through a moonless night with only   19
the roar of wind for company. Don't talk to him of mountains, of tropical beaches. Don't ask him to swoon at sunrises or marvel at the filter of light through leaves. He's never had time for such things, and he does not believe in them. He may pass by them close enough to touch on either side, but his hands are stretched forward, grasping for balance instead of pleasure. He doesn't wonder where he came from, where he's going. He doesn't ask who he is, or why. Questions are a luxury, the province of those at a distance from the periodic shock of rain. Gravity presses Adam so hard against reality that he doesn't feel the points at which he touches it. A drowning man is not separated from the lust for air by a bridge of thought—he is one with it—and my son, conceived and grown in an ethanol bath, lives each day in the act of drowning. For him there is no shore.

UNDERSTANDING DETAILS

1. Why are Adam's birthdays difficult for Dorris?
2. What are some of the problems Adam was born with?
3. Why will Adam never reach his full potential?
4. In what ways did Dorris feel Adam's birthdays would be "oases of certainty" (paragraph 7)? How did the actual celebrations differ from these expectations?

ANALYZING MEANING

1. Why does Dorris "doubly" mourn (paragraph 8) his son's birthdays? Explain your answer.
2. In what way was "the definition of the rest of [Dorris's] life" (paragraph 7) connected with his son's birthdays?
3. In what way is death like Santa Claus for Adam? Explain your answer.
4. What does Dorris mean when he says "Questions are a luxury" for his son (paragraph 19)?

DISCOVERING RHETORICAL STRATEGIES

1. At what points in this essay does Dorris either directly or indirectly analyze the causes of Adam's behavior? When does he study its effects (on either himself or his son)? Divide a piece of paper in half. List the causes of Adam's behavior on one side and the effects on the other. Record the paragraph references in each case. Then, discuss the pattern that emerges from your two lists. Does Dorris give more attention to the causes or the effects of Adam's behavior? Why do you think the author develops his essay around this particular emphasis?

2. Dorris uses several comparisons to help his readers understand what raising a fetal alcohol child is like. Look, for example, at paragraph 19, in which he compares Adam's life to "a moonless night" and to "the act of drowning." Find two other vivid comparisons in this essay. What do all these comparisons add to the essay? What effect do they have on the essay as a whole?

3. What tone does Dorris establish in his essay? Describe it in three or four well-chosen words. How does he create this tone? What effect does this particular tone have on you as a reader?

4. What rhetorical strategies does Dorris use to support his cause/effect analysis? Give examples of each.

MAKING CONNECTIONS

1. Contrast Dorris's definition of "addiction" with the definitions in the following essays that discuss other addictive topics: Kimberly Wozencraft's "Notes from the Country Club," Franklin Zimring's "Confessions of an Ex-Smoker," and/or Stephen King's "Why We Crave Horror Movies." What specific substance is addictive in these essays? Which addiction do you think would be most difficult to recover from? Explain your answer.

2. Love and concern for a child is the principal topic of Dorris's essay, as it is in Lewis Sawaquat's "For My Indian Daughter," Russell Baker's "The Saturday Evening Post," Bill Cosby's "The Baffling Question," and Judith Wallerstein and Sandra Blakeslee's "Second Chances for Children of Divorce." If we were able to get all these authors together in a roundtable discussion about parent–child relationships, do you think they would agree on any of the issues? If so, what would these areas of agreement be?

3. Birthdays are milestones in Dorris's essay, just as they are for Malcolm Cowley in "The View from 80." What are the principal differences in the ways each author celebrates these birthdays? Why do these differences exist?

IDEAS FOR DISCUSSION/WRITING

Preparing to Write

Write freely about the process of growing up and reaching your potential: What special problems did you experience while growing up? How did you deal with these problems? How did your parents deal with these problems? Do you feel you are heading toward your full potential, or have you already reached it? How do you plan to reach or maintain your potential? What experiences or people have disappointed you mainly because they were not what you expected? What were their shortcomings? Can these shortcomings be remedied? What effects do such shortcomings have on society as a whole?

Choosing a Topic

1. In a conversation with your mother, father, or another close relative, explain what problems you found most difficult as you were growing up, and speculate about the causes of those problems. In dialogue form, record the conversation as accurately as possible. Add an introduction, a conclusion, and an explanation of your discussion in order to mold the conversation into an essay.

2. In the last paragraph of his essay, Dorris implies that his son is slowly drowning in his birth-mother's alcohol abuse. This essay is Dorris's process of grieving about "what [his son] was missing, what he had already missed, what he would miss" (paragraph 8). In an essay of your own, explain something (a process, a person, an event, a relationship, or an activity) that disappointed you mainly because your expectations weren't met. What were the principal reasons for your disappointment? What were the effects of your disappointment? What could have changed the situation?

3. Many forms of addiction and abuse plague our society at present. In an essay written for your composition class, choose one of these problems and speculate on its primary causes and

effects in society today. As often as possible, give specific examples to support your observations.

4. In his article, Dorris personalizes the effects of alcoholism on unborn children. Conduct an Internet search on other threats to infant and child health. To begin your search, you may want to visit the Centers for Disease Control and Prevention's Web site (http://www.cdc.gov). Choose a topic that interests you, and write an article for your campus's student health Web site. Describe the causes and effects of your chosen topic. Find a way to personalize your essay so that it will strike a nerve with your intended audience.

Before beginning your essay, you might want to consult the checklists on page 454.

RICHARD RODRIGUEZ   (1944–   )

The Fear of Losing a Culture

Richard Rodriguez was raised in Sacramento, California, the son of industrious working-class Mexican immigrant parents. He attended parochial schools there and later continued his education at Stanford University, Columbia University, London's Warburg Institute, and, finally, the University of California at Berkeley, where he earned a Ph.D. in English Renaissance literature. A writer and journalist, he is now associate editor of the Pacific News Service in San Francisco. In 1982, he received wide critical acclaim for the publication of his autobiography, *Hunger of Memory: The Education of Richard Rodriguez*, which detailed his struggle to succeed in a totally alien culture. A regular contributor to the *Los Angeles Times*, he has also published essays in *New Republic, Time, Harper's, American Scholar, Columbia Forum*, and *College English*. His most recent books are *Days of Obligation: An Argument with My Mexican Father* (1992), an autobiographical study of Mexican immigrants in America, and *Brown: The Last Discovery of America* (2002). Asked to provide advice for students using *The Prose Reader*, Rodriguez explained that "there is no 'secret' to becoming a writer. Writing takes time—and patience, more than anything else. If you are willing to rewrite and rewrite and rewrite, you will become a good writer."

Preparing to Read

The following essay, originally published in *Time* magazine (July 11, 1988), discusses the causes and effects of cultural pride.

Exploring Experience: As you prepare to read this essay, take a few moments to think about culture and assimilation: How would you describe America's culture? Does it have a central core of its own? What are the main features of this American culture? To what extent are Americans threatened by the intrusion of other cultures? What can be gained through assimilation with another culture? What can be lost?

Learning Online: How does the Internet preserve culture? Spend a few moments online browsing different sites by using the search term *preservation of culture.* Consider how international cultural preservation issues relate to Rodriguez's concerns.

W hat is culture?   1
The immigrant shrugs. Latin American immigrants   2
come to the United States with only the things they need in mind—not abstractions like culture. Money. They need dollars. They need food. Maybe they need to get out of the way of bullets.

Most of us who concern ourselves with the Hispanic-American   3
culture, as painters, musicians, writers—or as sons and daughters—are the children of immigrants. We have grown up on this side of the border, in the land of Elvis Presley and Thomas Edison; our lives are prescribed by the mall, by the DMV and the Chinese restaurant. Our imaginations yet vascillate between an Edenic Latin America (the blue door)—and the repellent plate glass of a real American city—which has been good to us.

Hispanic-American culture is where the past meets the future.   4
Hispanic-American culture is not an Hispanic milestone only, not simply a celebration at the crossroads. America transforms into pleasure what America cannot avoid. Is it any coincidence that at a time when Americans are troubled by the encroachment of the Mexican desert, Americans discover a chic in cactus, in the decorator colors of the Southwest? In sand?

Hispanic-American culture of the sort that is now showing (the   5
teen movie, the rock song) may exist in an hourglass, may in fact be irrelevant to the epic. The US Border Patrol works through the night to arrest the flow of illegal immigrants over the border, even as Americans wait in line to get into *La Bamba.* Even as Americans vote to declare, once and for all, that English shall be the official language of the United States, Madonna starts recording in Spanish.

But then so is Bill Cosby's show irrelevant to the 10 o'clock   6
news, where families huddle together in fear on porches, pointing at the body of the slain boy bagged in tarpauline—which is not to say that Bill Cosby or Michael Jackson are irrelevant to the future or without neo-Platonic influence. Like players within the play, they prefigure, they resolve. They make black and white audiences aware of a bond that may not yet exist.

Before a national TV audience, Rita Moreno tells Geraldo 7
Rivera that her dream as an actress is to play a character rather like
herself: "I speak English perfectly well . . . I'm not dying from
poverty . . . I want to play *that* kind of Hispanic woman, which is
to say, an American citizen." This is an actress talking, these are
show-biz pieties. But Moreno expresses as well the general
Hispanic-American predicament. Hispanics want to belong to
America without betraying the past.

Hispanics fear losing ground in any negotiation with the 8
American city. We come from an expansive, an intimate culture
that has been judged second-rate by the United States of America.
For reasons of pride, therefore, as much as of affection, we are
reluctant to give up our past. Hispanics often express a fear of "losing" culture. Our fame in the United States has been our resistance
to assimilation.

The symbol of Hispanic culture has been the tongue of flame— 9
Spanish. But the remarkable legacy Hispanics carry from Latin
America is not language—an inflatable skin—but breath itself,
capacity of soul, an inclination to live. The genius of Latin
America is the habit of synthesis.

We assimilate. Just over the border there is the example of 10
Mexico, the country from which the majority of U.S. Hispanics
come. Mexico is mestizo—Indian and Spanish. Within a single
family, Mexicans are light-skinned and dark. It is impossible for
the Mexican to say, in the scheme of things, where the Indian
begins and the Spaniard surrenders.

In culture as in blood, Latin America was formed by a rape that 11
became a marriage. Due to the absorbing generosity of the Indian,
European culture took on new soil. What Latin America knows is
that people create one another as they marry. In the music of Latin
America you will hear the litany of bloodlines—the African drum,
the German accordian, the cry from the minaret.

The United States stands as the opposing New World experi- 12
ment. In North America the Indian and the European stood apace.
Whereas Latin America was formed by a medieval Catholic dream
of one world—of meltdown conversion—the United States was
built up from Protestant individualism. The American melting pot
washes away only embarrassment; it is the necessary initiation into
public life. The American faith is that our national strength derives
from separateness, from "diversity." The glamour of the United

States is a carnival promise: You can lose weight, get rich as Rockefeller, touch up your roots, get a divorce.

Immigrants still come for the promise. But the United States   13 wavers in its faith. As long as there was space enough, sky enough, as long as economic success validated individualism, loneliness was not too high a price to pay (the cabin on the prairie or the Sony Walkman).

At the beginning of the century, two alternative cultures beck-   14 on the American imagination—both highly communal cultures— the Asian and the Latin American. The United States is a literal culture. Americans devour what we might otherwise fear to become. Sushi will make us corporate warriors. Combination Plate #3, smothered in mestizo gravy, will burn a hole in our hearts.

Latin America offers passion. Latin America has a life—I mean   15 *life*—big clouds, unambiguous themes, death, birth, faith, that the United States, for all its quality of life, seems without now. Latin America offers communal riches: an undistressed leisure, a kitchen table, even a full sorrow. Such is the solitude of America; such is the urgency of American need; Americans reach right past a fledg- ling, homegrown Hispanic-American culture for the real thing— the darker bottle of Mexican beer, the denser novel of a Latin American master.

For a long time, Hispanics in the United States withheld from   16 the United States our Latin American gift. We denied the value of assimilation. But as our presence is judged less foreign in America, we will produce a more generous art, less timid, less parochial. Carlos Santana, Luis Valdez, Linda Ronstadt—Hispanic Americans do not have a "pure" Latin American art to offer. Expect bastard themes, expect ironies, comic conclusions. For we live on the side of the border, where Kraft manufactures bricks of "Mexican style" Velveeta and where Jack in the Box serves "Fajita Pita."

The flame-red Chevy floats a song down the Pan American Highway: 17 *From a rolled-down window, the grizzled voice of Willie Nelson rises in disembodied harmony with the voice of Julio Iglesias. Gabby Hayes and Cisco are thus resolved.*

Expect marriage. We will change America even as we will be   18 changed. We will disappear with you into a new miscegenation.

Along the border, real conflicts remain. But the ancient tear   19 separating Europe from itself—the Catholic Mediterranean from the Protestant north—may yet heal itself in the New World. For generations, Latin America has been the place—the bed—of a confluence of so many races and cultures that Protestant North America shuddered to imagine it.

Imagine it.   20

UNDERSTANDING DETAILS

1. In what way is "culture" an abstraction? Explain your answer.
2. What does Rodriguez mean when he says "Hispanic-American culture is where the past meets the future" (paragraph 4)?
3. In what ways are Asian and Latin American cultures "communal" whereas America's is "literal" (paragraph 14)?
4. What does Rodriguez claim is the source of the hostility Hispanics have traditionally felt from other Americans?

ANALYZING MEANING

1. To what extent do you think Hispanics can belong to America "without betraying the past" (paragraph 7)? How might they accomplish this?
2. What is the main difference in philosophy between North America and Latin America? Why is assimilation so difficult under these circumstances?
3. What does Rodriguez mean when he says that "people create one another as they marry" (paragraph 11)? Explain your answer in detail.
4. What do North America and Latin America have to offer each other? What can they learn from each other?

DISCOVERING RHETORICAL STRATEGIES

1. According to Rodriguez, the fact that Hispanics sometimes don't easily assimilate into American culture causes some consequences and is the result of others. List the causes of this action in one column and the effects in another. In what way does the question of assimilation become a focal point for the essay?
2. Why does Rodriguez introduce the Asian culture into this essay? How does this reference help strengthen his argument?

3. Rodriguez ends his essay with a one-sentence paragraph. What effect does this ending have on you? Explain your answer.

4. What other rhetorical strategies besides cause and effect does Rodriguez use to support his essay about Hispanic-American assimilation? Give examples of each.

MAKING CONNECTIONS

1. Rodriguez and Robert Ramirez ("The Barrio") both discuss the complex topic of how immigrants can assimilate into a new culture without "betraying their past." Compare and contrast their opinions on this controversial subject; then give your own views on the issue.

2. Rodriguez's image of an "Edenic" former Latin culture is similar to the pleasant memories John McPhee provides of an unspoiled wilderness area before the intrusions of civilization ("The Pines") and Bruce Catton's depiction of Robert E. Lee's tidewater Virginia aristocratic heritage ("Grant and Lee: A Study in Contrasts"). To what extent do you think each of these memories has been warped and changed by the passage of time? How accurate are your own recollections of pleasant events and places from the past?

3. How many different causes does Rodriguez suggest to explain why some Hispanic-Americans resist assimilation into American culture? Contrast the number of causes Rodriguez mentions with the number introduced by Stephen King ("Why We Crave Horror Movies") and Michael Dorris ("The Broken Cord"). How does the number of causes in a cause/effect essay influence your ability to follow the author's argument?

IDEAS FOR DISCUSSION/WRITING

Preparing to Write

Write freely about culture and assimilation: What makes up a culture? In what ways do merging cultures threaten one another? What does assimilation consist of? Why is assimilation between cultures such an emotional issue? What are the ground rules in the process of assimilation? What major cultural changes is our country experiencing at present? In what way are these changes affecting you personally?

Choosing a Topic

1. We all confront assimilation every day in different situations. We may choose to assimilate into a club we want to join but may refuse to make the necessary changes to fit into a fast-moving party scene. For an article in your campus newspaper demonstrating the constant role of assimilation in our lives, explain the causes and/or effects of one time you chose or refused to assimilate. What were the circumstances leading up to your decision? What were the consequences of your decision?

2. America is currently undergoing some dramatic cultural changes. We are rapidly becoming a multiracial, multicultural society. In an essay written for your local newspaper, analyze the causes and effects of some of these changes, and explain how they are affecting you personally.

3. As a foreign-exchange student, you have just arrived in another country to attend college for one year. Naturally, you realize that you must adapt to many new customs and attitudes; however, you will still cling to many of your country's ways. In an essay, explain which of your national traditions you would find most difficult to give up and why. Do you think assimilating into a new culture and still holding on to your beliefs and customs is possible? Explain your reasoning.

4. Write an e-mail to a grandparent, either living or deceased. Use Rodriguez's title "The Fear of Losing a Culture" and write about the ways in which your family's cultural practices have changed over the years. Consider the ways your grandparent(s) practiced their culture and how your practice differs. Identify the causes and effects of these changes. Try to use Rodriguez's method of employing concrete examples to classify abstract concepts. If you feel that your family does not have a particular cultural practice, consider generational differences in social practices for your topic.

Before beginning your essay, you might want to consult the checklists on page 454.

MARY ROACH   (1959–   )

Meet the Bickersons

A native of Hanover, New Hampshire, Mary Roach received her B.A. in psychology from Wesleyan University, then worked as a copy editor and a public relations consultant for the San Francisco Zoo. Following five years in the business world, she began her career as a freelance writer after deciding that "it was a lot easier to write the stuff in the first place than to clean it up after someone else had written it." She has been a contributor for many years to the "Diversions" section of the *San Francisco Examiner Sunday Magazine*, focusing on such quirky, interesting topics as drive-in movies and old black-and-white photo booths. She is currently a contributing editor for such well-known periodicals as *Health*, *Discover*, *Wired*, *Muse* (the Smithsonian Museum's children's magazine), and *SALON.com* (an online journal). Her most recent book is *Stiff: The Curious Lives of Human Cadavers* (2003). Asked to give advice to students using *The Prose Reader*, she confides that "people think writing is harder than it is. They tie themselves up in knots over it. Good writing is really just talking on paper. If it were difficult to do, I would not be that successful at it." Roach now lives in San Francisco, where her hobbies include bird watching, reading, and traveling.

Preparing to Read

The following humorous essay on arguing, originally published in *Health* magazine, explains different strategies for arguing among couples.

Exploring Experience: Before you read this essay, think for a moment about how important arguing fairly is to you: Do you argue fairly? Do you expect your partner to argue fairly? What are the qualities of a fair argument? Do you argue with other people? Are you able to control your temper? Do you feel better after you argue? Why or why not? When is arguing most worthwhile? When is it never worthwhile? Do you have any special ground rules for arguing with the people you love?

Learning Online: Visit "About.com" (http://about.com), and type "Why do couples fight?" into the search field. Read a short article about why couples fight. Consider the format and content of this article as you read Mary Roach's essay. Why is Roach's presentation more effective?

P sychologists have long said it's possible to predict whether a   1
couple will stay happily married simply by looking at how
they fight. This did not bode well for yours truly, who got
married not too long ago. Pretty much all I'd learned about
spousal arguing came from *The Newlywed Game,* which taught us
1) that the proper form of conflict resolution is to hit your partner
over the head with a large piece of poster board and 2) that most
problems can be resolved with the acquisition of a brand-new
washer and dryer or a gift pack of Turtle Wax.

I've been told I'm defensive—"like a cornered mongoose"   2
were the exact words. I've also been criticized for being sarcastic,
overreacting, and crying too easily. I don't deny these things
(though if you were to accuse me of them in the heat of battle,
you can be sure I would—vehemently, and with pointy little teeth
bared).

I had a boyfriend who tried to change me. He asked me to use   3
a therapy technique called "active listening," a mainstay of many
modern marriage counselors. It's supposed to make you a more
fair, less combative arguer. I (and here's something you couldn't
see coming) objected to this, stating that I was already an active listener. My ex countered that deep sighs, nostril flares, pacing, and
storming from the room did not qualify. Active listening means
focusing care-fully on what your partner is saying, as though there
were going to be a test, because, in fact, there is. You are required
to paraphrase your beloved's misguided rantings—sorry, feelings—
beginning with the phrase "What I hear you saying is . . ."

I agreed to try it. He went first. Minutes passed. Fortunately,   4
we were on the phone at the time, which allowed me to scribble
notes. He finished and fell silent.

"What I hear you saying," I began, "is that you think I'm   5
defensive, and I don't allow you to feel what you're feeling and
that makes you incredibly . . . truncated, wait, flat-footed?"

"Frustrated."   6

"Of course."   7

"You're cheating," he said. "You're writing things down."   8

"Am not."   9

Nothing—not counseling, not even Turtle Wax—was going to   10
save that relationship.

With Ed, I was determined to do things right and asked a friend   11
with a degree in counseling for advice. She encouraged me to use
"I" statements because "you" statements put people on the defensive. For instance, one does not say to one's beloved, "You never
do the dishes, you self-centered pea brain." One says, "I feel angry
and taken advantage of when the people I love leave their dishes
for me, especially when it was those people who dirtied them in
the first place and ate the leftovers they knew darn well I was planning to have for lunch."

Another suggested technique was validation, in which each   12
partner makes an effort to endorse the other's feelings: "I can see
why you'd be upset with my failing to wash one small dish and
eating an eighth of a taco. I would be, too, if I were an oversen-
sitive, petty person who only focuses on the negative."

A while back I put all these techniques to work. We were   13
driving, and I had failed to notice a stop sign, which even the most
vigilant driver will do from time to time, am I right? Ed did not
fail to notice the stop sign, as was evinced by his slamming of the
imaginary brakes on his side of the car. "When you constantly
remark upon my driving irregularities," I began, "I feel scrutinized
and inadequate, and by the way, who was it that nearly got us
killed by turning into traffic outside Costco?"

Ed was unperturbed by the Costco barb. What got him was the   14
I-feel-blah-dee-blah business. "Why don't you just get mad and
call me a back-seat driver, and that'd be that?"

Later that evening I tried to explain what I'd learned about   15
"you" statements and active listening and validating feelings. Ed
listened carefully. Then he took my hand in his. "When you talk
about things like this, I feel, let me see, like throwing up. How
was that?"

Shortly after, Ed left a newspaper clipping on my desk. It   16
described a university study in which 130 newlywed pairs were
videotaped arguing and then tracked for six years. It turns out the
couples who stayed married had seldom used techniques like
active listening and validation. The researcher was "shocked" to

find that the happy couples fought like normal people—getting angry, clearing the air, and making up. (Their spats, however, were tinged with soothing and humor.)

This was one instance in which I was glad to be proved wrong.   17
So thrilled was I at the prospect of never again having to begin a sentence with "What I hear you saying is" that I made a vow on the spot that the next time Ed got mad at me, I would not get defensive.

It happened on a Saturday afternoon. I had thrown away a set   18
of circa-1970 stereo speakers that Ed had wanted to keep because they might come in handy for taking up space in the basement for the next ten years. It didn't go quite the way I'd envisioned. I heard myself lambasting Ed for having gone through the garbage, checking up on what I'd junked. "You're scrutinizing me!"

Ed looked flabbergasted. "You toss things without even   19
asking!"

The bell rang, and we withdrew to our corners. Around din-   20
nertime I appeared in the kitchen with the speakers, dusted and polished. Ed, in turn, promised not to supervise my spring clean-ing. He asked me to let him know when I caught him checking over something I'd done. "I'm not even aware of it. So please tell me." He smiled sweetly. "And then I'll deny it."

UNDERSTANDING DETAILS

1. What is "active listening" (paragraph 3)? What verbal tech-nique did Roach learn as an active listener?
2. Explain the technique of "validation" in your own words.
3. Does Roach think she is too defensive? What animal did some-one compare her defensiveness to?
4. What did a university study learn about the argumentative habits of 130 newlywed couples? How did Roach feel about the findings of this study?

ANALYZING MEANING

1. According to psychologists, how does the way couples fight affect the survival of their marriages?
2. Why was Roach trying different strategies for getting along with her partner?

3. Who is Ed? Why was Roach trying so hard to make her relationship with Ed work?

4. What does Roach mean when she says about the first boyfriend, "Nothing—not counseling, not even Turtle Wax—was going to save that relationship" (paragraph 10)?

DISCOVERING RHETORICAL STRATEGIES

1. List the causes and effects that this essay studies.
2. What is the general mood of Roach's essay?
3. Roach begins her essay with some references to the *Newlywed Game*. What do the poster board, a washer and dryer, and Turtle Wax have to do with that game? Do you think this is an effective way to start her essay? Explain your answer.
4. What other rhetorical strategies support this cause/effect essay? Give examples of each.

MAKING CONNECTIONS

1. Compare and contrast Roach's conclusions about successful communications within a relationship with similar advice provided in Wallerstein and Blakeslee's "Second Chances for Children of Divorce," Judith Viorst's "The Truth About Lying," and Mary Pipher's "Beliefs About Families."
2. Analyze Roach's prescription for dealing with anger in light of the following essays: Lewis Sawaquat's "For My Indian Daughter," Brent Staples's "A Brother's Murder," and Michael Dorris's "The Broken Cord."
3. Compare Roach's use of humor in her essay to similar anecdotes in Russell Baker's "The Saturday Evening Post," Garrison Keillor's "How the Crab Apple Grew," and Bill Cosby's "The Baffling Question."

IDEAS FOR DISCUSSION/WRITING

Preparing to Write

Write freely about your views on arguing: Do you know how to argue? Have you ever been sorry for anything you said while you were arguing? Do you argue with your parents differently than you argue with your friends? With your boyfriends/

girlfriends/spouses? Why do you argue? What do you try to accomplish when you argue? Does arguing usually make you feel better or worse? Is it difficult to make up after you argue? How do you make up?

Choosing a Topic

1. Your college newspaper is accepting essays on your interests in life. Write an essay for the newspaper explaining in detail your most passionate interest. Cover both the causes and effects of this interest. (This interest does not have to be related to school matters.)

2. Your college counselor/adviser wants to know if you consider yourself emotionally healthy. In a detailed essay written for this counselor, who is writing a letter of recommendation for you, explain why you are or are not in good emotional health. What events, attitudes, or activities have played a part in developing your mental health?

3. Americans seem to be obsessed with their health these days. Why do you think this is so? How did this obsession start?

4. What are some other techniques necessary for maintaining healthy relationships? Choose an issue such as compromise, honesty, or communication, and reflect on your experience with this topic. Then write an essay in which you explore the cause and effect of positive—and negative—uses of this technique. Roach supports her personal observations with case studies. Strengthen your essay by using case studies and statistics that you have found online.

Before beginning your essay, you might want to consult the checklists on page 454.

ALICE WALKER   (1944–   )

Beauty: When the Other Dancer Is the Self

Born in Eatonton, Georgia, and educated at Spelman College and Sarah Lawrence College, Alice Walker is best known for her Pulitzer Prize-winning novel *The Color Purple* (1983), which was later made into an immensely popular movie of the same title. The book details a young African-American woman's search for self-identity within a world contaminated by racial prejudice and family crisis. Although many critics have argued that the work "transcends culture and gender," Walker's focus on the racial and ethnic climate of the Deep South is crucial to the novel's success and importance. The author has explained that "the Black woman is one of America's greatest heroes," though she has been denied credit for her accomplishments and "oppressed beyond recognition." Most of Walker's other novels and collections of short stories echo the same theme, and most share the "sense of affirmation" featured in *The Color Purple* that overcomes the anger and social indignity suffered by so many of her characters. The author's many other publications include *In Love and Trouble: Stories of Black Women* (1973), *Meridian* (1976), *You Can't Keep a Good Woman Down* (1981), *In Search of Our Mothers' Gardens* (1983), *Living by the Word* (1988), *To Hell with Dying* (1988), *The Temple of My Familiar* (1989), *Possessing the Secret of Joy* (1992), *Everyday Use* (1994), *Alice Walker Banned* (1996), *By the Light of My Father's Smile* (1998), *The Way Forward Is With a Broken Heart* (2000), and *Absolute Trust in the Goodness of the Earth: New Poems* (2003). Walker has been a professor and writer-in-residence at Wellesley College, the University of Massachusetts, the University of California at Berkeley, and Brandeis University. She is also a member of the board of trustees of Sarah Lawrence College. Walker currently lives in Mendocino, California.

Preparing to Read

The following essay, from *In Search of Our Mothers' Gardens*, focuses on young Alice Walker's reaction to being blinded in one eye as a result of an accident with a BB gun.

Exploring Experience: As you begin to read this essay, take a few minutes to consider the role of physical appearance in our lives: Do you find that you often judge people based on their physical appearance? Do you feel that people judge you based on your appearance? What other characteristics play a part in your judgment of others? How important are good looks to you? Why do they carry this importance for you? What specific people affect the way you feel about yourself? Do you want more control over your own self-esteem? How can you gain this control?

Learning Online: In her essay, Alice Walker describes concerns about her own appearance. Look for pictures of Alice Walker online; use *Alice Walker* as your search term. Consider your opinions of her appearance as you read her essay.

It is a bright summer day in 1947. My father, a fat, funny man   1
with beautiful eyes and a subversive wit, is trying to decide
which of his eight children he will take with him to the county
fair. My mother, of course, will not go. She is knocked out from
getting most of us ready: I hold my neck stiff against the pressure
of her knuckles as she hastily completes the braiding and then
beribboning of my hair.

My father is the driver for the rich old white lady up the road.   2
Her name is Miss Mey. She owns all the land for miles around, as
well as the house in which we live. All I remember about her is
that she once offered to pay my mother thirty-five cents for cleaning her house, raking up piles of her magnolia leaves, and washing
her family's clothes, and that my mother—she of no money, eight
children, and a chronic earache—refused it. But I do not think of
this in 1947. I am two and a half years old. I want to go everywhere my daddy goes. I am excited at the prospect of riding in a
car. Someone has told me fairs are fun. That there is room in the
car for only three of us doesn't faze me at all. Whirling happily in
my starchy frock, showing off my biscuit-polished patent-leather
shoes and lavender socks, tossing my head in a way that makes my
ribbons bounce, I stand, hands on hips, before my father. "Take
me, Daddy," I say with assurance; "I'm the prettiest!"

Later, it does not surprise me to find myself in Miss Mey's shiny   3
black car, sharing the back seat with the other lucky ones. Does not

surprise me that I thoroughly enjoy the fair. At home that night I tell the unlucky ones all I can remember about the merry-go-round, the man who eats live chickens, and the teddy bears, until they say: that's enough, baby Alice. Shut up now, and go to sleep.

It is Easter Sunday, 1950. I am dressed in a green, flocked,   4 scalloped-hem dress (handmade by my adoring sister, Ruth) that has its own smooth satin petticoat and tiny hot-pink roses tucked into each scallop. My shoes, new T-strap patent leather, again highly biscuit-polished. I am six years old and have learned one of the longest Easter speeches to be heard that day, totally unlike the speech I said when I was two: "Easter lilies/pure and white/blossom in/the morning light." When I rise to give my speech I do so on a great wave of love and pride and expectation. People in the church stop rustling their new crinolines. They seem to hold their breath. I can tell they admire my dress, but it is my spirit, bordering on sassiness (womanishness), they secretly applaud.

"That girl's a little *mess*," they whisper to each other, pleased.   5

Naturally I say my speech without stammer or pause, unlike   6 those who stutter, stammer, or, worst of all, forget. This is before the word "beautiful" exists in people's vocabulary, but "Oh, isn't she the *cutest* thing!" frequently floats my way. "And got so much sense!" they gratefully add . . . for which thoughtful addition I thank them to this day.

It was great fun being cute. But then, one day, it ended.   7

I am eight years old and a tomboy. I have a cowboy hat, cow-   8 boy boots, checkered shirt and pants, all red. My playmates are my brothers, two and four years older than I. Their colors are black and green, the only difference in the way we are dressed. On Saturday nights we all go to the picture show, even my mother; Westerns are her favorite kind of movie. Back home, "on the ranch," we pretend we are Tom Mix, Hopalong Cassidy, Lash LaRue (we've even named one of our dogs Lash LaRue); we chase each other for hours rustling cattle, being outlaws, delivering damsels from distress. Then my parents decide to buy my brothers guns. These are not "real" guns. They shoot "BBs," copper pellets my brothers say will kill birds. Because I am a girl, I do not get a gun. Instantly I am relegated to the position of Indian. Now there appears a great distance between us. They shoot and shoot at everything with their new guns. I try to keep up with my bow and arrows.

One day while I am standing on top of our makeshift   9 "garage"—pieces of tin nailed across some poles—holding my bow and arrow and looking out toward the fields, I feel an incredible blow in my right eye. I look down just in time to see my brother lower his gun.

Both brothers rush to my side. My eye stings, and I cover it   10 with my hand. "If you tell," they say, "we will get a whipping. You don't want that to happen, do you?" I do not. "Here is a piece of wire," says the older brother, picking it up from the roof; "say you stepped on one end of it and the other flew up and hit you." The pain is beginning to start. "Yes," I say. "Yes, I will say that is what happened." If I do not say this is what happened, I know my brothers will find ways to make me wish I had. But now I will say anything that gets me to my mother.

Confronted by our parents we stick to the lie agreed upon.   11 They place me on a bench on the porch, and I close my left eye while they examine the right. There is a tree growing from underneath the porch that climbs past the railing to the roof. It is the last thing my right eye sees. I watch as its trunk, its branches, and then its leaves are blotted out by the rising blood.

I am in shock. First there is intense fever, which my father tries   12 to break using lily leaves bound around my head. Then there are chills: my mother tries to get me to eat soup. Eventually, I do not know how, my parents learn what has happened. A week after the "accident" they take me to see a doctor. "Why did you wait so long to come?" he asks, looking into my eye and shaking his head. "Eyes are sympathetic," he says. "If one is blind, the other will likely become blind too."

This comment of the doctor's terrifies me. But it is really how   13 I look that bothers me most. Where the BB pellet struck there is a glob of whitish scar tissue, a hideous cataract, on my eye. Now when I stare at people—a favorite pastime, up to now—they will stare back. Not at the "cute" little girl, but at her scar. For six years I do not stare at anyone, because I do not raise my head.

Years later, in the throes of a mid-life crisis, I ask my mother   14 and sister whether I changed after the "accident." "No," they say, puzzled. "What do you mean?"

What do I mean?   15

I am eight, and, for the first time, doing poorly in school, where   16
I have been something of a whiz since I was four. We have just
moved to the place where the "accident" occurred. We do not
know any of the people around us because this is a different county.
The only time I see the friends I knew is when we go back to our
old church. The new school is the former state penitentiary. It is a
large stone building, cold and drafty, crammed to overflowing with
boisterous, ill-disciplined children. On the third floor there is a
huge circular imprint of some partition that has been torn out.

"What used to be here?" I ask a sullen girl next to me on our   17
way past it to lunch.

"The electric chair," says she.   18

At night I have nightmares about the electric chair and about all   19
the people reputedly "fried" in it. I am afraid of the school, where
all the students seem to be budding criminals.

"What's the matter with your eye?" they ask, critically.   20

When I don't answer (I cannot decide whether it was an "acci-   21
dent" or not), they shove me, insist on a fight.

My brother, the one who created the story about the wire,   22
comes to my rescue. But then brags so much about "protecting"
me, I become sick.

After months of torture at the school, my parents decide to send   23
me back to our old community, to my old school. I live with my
grandparents and the teacher they board. But there is no room for
Phoebe, my cat. By the time my grandparents decide there *is* room,
and I ask for my cat, she cannot be found. Miss Yarborough, the
boarding teacher, takes me under her wing and begins to teach me
to play the piano. But soon she marries an African—a "prince," she
says—and is whisked away to his continent.

At my old school there is at least one teacher who loves me. She   24
is the teacher who "knew me before I was born" and bought my
first baby clothes. It is she who makes life bearable. It is her presence that finally helps me turn on the one child at the school who
continually calls me "one-eyed bitch." One day I simply grab him
by his coat and beat him until I am satisfied. It is my teacher who
tells me my mother is ill.

My mother is lying in bed in the middle of the day, something   25
I have never seen. She is in too much pain to speak. She has an

abscess in her ear. I stand looking down on her, knowing that if she dies, I cannot live. She is being treated with warm oils and hot bricks held against her cheek. Finally a doctor comes. But I must go back to my grandparents' house. The weeks pass but I am hardly aware of it. All I know is that my mother might die, my father is not so jolly, my brothers still have their guns, and I am the one sent away from home.

"You did not change," they say.   26

Did I imagine the anguish of never looking up?   27

I am twelve. When relatives come to visit I hide in my   28
room. My cousin Brenda, just my age, whose father works in the post office and whose mother is a nurse, comes to find me. "Hello," she says. And then she asks, looking at my recent school picture, which I did not want taken, and on which the "glob," as I think of it, is clearly visible, "You still can't see out of that eye?"

"No," I say, and flop back on the bed over my book.   29

That night, as I do almost every night, I abuse my eye. I rant   30
and rave at it, in front of the mirror. I plead with it to clear up before morning. I tell it I hate and despise it. I do not pray for sight. I pray for beauty.

"You did not change," they say.   31

I am fourteen and baby-sitting for my brother Bill, who lives   32
in Boston. He is my favorite brother, and there is a strong bond between us. Understanding my feelings of shame and ugliness he and his wife take me to a local hospital, where the "glob" is removed by a doctor named O. Henry. There is still a small bluish crater where the scar tissue was, but the ugly white stuff is gone. Almost immediately I become a different person from the girl who does not raise her head. Or so I think. Now that I've raised my head I win the boyfriend of my dreams. Now that I've raised my head I have plenty of friends. Now that I've raised my head classwork comes from my lips as faultlessly as Easter speeches did, and I leave high school as valedictorian, most popular student, and *queen*, hardly believing my luck. Ironically, the girl who was voted most beautiful in our class (and was) was later shot twice through the chest by a male companion, using a "real" gun, while she was pregnant. But that's another story in itself. Or is it?

"You did not change," they say. 33

It is now thirty years since the "accident." A beautiful journalist 34
comes to visit and to interview me. She is going to write a cover
story for her magazine that focuses on my latest book. "Decide
how you want to look on the cover," she says. "Glamorous, or
whatever."
Never mind "glamorous," it is the "whatever" that I hear. 35
Suddenly all I can think of is whether I will get enough sleep the
night before the photography session: if I don't, my eye will be
tired and wander, as blind eyes will.
At night in bed with my lover I think up reasons why I should 36
not appear on the cover of a magazine. "My meanest critics will
say I've sold out," I say. "My family will now realize I write scan-
dalous books."
"But what's the real reason you don't want to do this?" he asks. 37
"Because in all probability," I say in a rush, "my eye won't be 38
straight."
"It will be straight enough," he says. Then, "Besides, I thought 39
you'd made your peace with that."
And I suddenly remember that I have. 40
I remember: 41
I am talking to my brother Jimmy, asking if he remembers any- 42
thing unusual about the day I was shot. He does not know I consider that day the last time my father, with his sweet home remedy
of cool lily leaves, chose me, and that I suffered and raged inside
because of this. "Well," he says, "all I remember is standing by the
side of the highway with Daddy, trying to flag down a car. A
white man stopped, but when Daddy said he needed somebody to
take his little girl to the doctor, he drove off."
I remember: 43
I am in the desert for the first time. I fall totally in love with it. I 44
am so overwhelmed by its beauty, I confront for the first time, consciously, the meaning of the doctor's words years ago: "Eyes are sympathetic. If one is blind, the other will likely become blind too." I
realize I have dashed about the world madly, looking at this, looking
at that, storing up images against the fading of the light. *But I might
have missed seeing the desert!* The shock of that possibility—and gratitude for over twenty-five years of sight—sends me literally to my
knees. Poem after poem comes—which is perhaps how poets pray.

ON SIGHT

I am so thankful I have seen
The Desert
And the creatures in the desert
And the desert Itself.
The desert has its own moon
Which I have seen
With my own eye.
There is no flag on it.

Trees of the desert have arms
All of which are always up
That is because the moon is up
The sun is up
Also the sky
The stars
Clouds
None with flags.

If there were flags, I doubt
the trees would point.
Would you?

But mostly, I remember this: 45
    I am twenty-seven, and my baby daughter is almost three.   46
Since her birth I have worried about her discovery that her mother's eyes are different from other people's. Will she be embarrassed? I think. What will she say? Every day she watches a television program called *Big Blue Marble.* It begins with a picture of
the earth as it appears from the moon. It is bluish, a little battered-
looking, but full of light, with whitish clouds swirling around it.
Every time I see it I weep with love, as if it is a picture of
Grandma's house. One day when I am putting Rebecca down for
her nap, she suddenly focuses on my eye. Something inside me
cringes, gets ready to try to protect myself. All children are cruel
about physical differences, I know from experience, and that they
don't always mean to be is another matter. I assume Rebecca will
be the same.
    But no-o-o-o. She studies my face intently as we stand, her   47
inside and me outside her crib. She even holds my face maternally
between her dimpled little hands. Then, looking every bit as serious and lawyerlike as her father, she says, as if it may just possibly
have slipped my attention: "Mommy, there's a *world* in your eye."

(As in, "Don't be alarmed, or do anything crazy.") And then, gently, but with great interest: "Mommy, where did you *get* that world in your eye?"

For the most part, the pain left then. (So what, if my brothers 48 grew up to buy even more powerful pellet guns for their sons and to carry real guns themselves. So what, if a young "Morehouse man" once nearly fell off the steps of Trevor Arnett Library because he thought my eyes were blue.) Crying and laughing I ran to the bathroom, while Rebecca mumbled and sang herself off to sleep. Yes indeed, I realized, looking into the mirror. There *was* a world in my eye. And I saw that it was possible to love it: that in fact, for all it had taught me of shame and anger and inner vision, I *did* love it. Even to see it drifting out of orbit in boredom, or rolling up out of fatigue, not to mention floating back at attention in excitement (bearing witness, a friend has called it), deeply suitable to my personality, and even characteristic of me.

That night I dream I am dancing to Stevie Wonder's song 49 "Always" (the name of the song is really "As," but I hear it as "Always"). As I dance, whirling and joyous, happier than I've ever been in my life, another bright-faced dancer joins me. We dance and kiss each other and hold each other through the night. The other dancer has obviously come through all right, as I have done. She is beautiful, whole and free. And she is also me.

UNDERSTANDING DETAILS

1. What time frame in the author's life does this essay cover?
2. What is the focal point of the essay? What activities lead up to this "accident"? What are the long-term effects of this "accident"?
3. In what ways does Walker think her life changed after she was shot in the eye?
4. Describe the author's relationship with her brothers, before and after the accident.

ANALYZING MEANING

1. Why is Walker devastated by the scar tissue in her eye? Which bothers her more, the scar tissue or the blindness? Explain your answer.

2. Which of the people introduced in the essay (other than her family members) mean the most to her? List them in order of importance. Then explain why each is important in this cause/effect essay.

3. List the changes that Walker mentions in her actions and personality. Then analyze these changes by discussing their causes and effects.

4. Why is Rebecca's declaration "Mommy, there's a *world* in your eye" (paragraph 47) so important to the author? What changes in Walker result from this particular encounter with her daughter?

DISCOVERING RHETORICAL STRATEGIES

1. Why do you think Walker wrote this essay? What was she trying to accomplish by writing it?

2. How does Walker use blank spaces between her paragraphs? In what ways does this spacing contribute to her essay?

3. Why does Walker put the sentences "It was great fun being cute. But then, one day, it ended" (paragraph 7) by themselves in italics?

4. Explain the emotional ups and downs in the essay. How does Walker's language change in each case?

MAKING CONNECTIONS

1. Walker's essay centers on a single momentous event, the blinding of her right eye, that affected her life from the instant it happened. Similarly significant events shape the lives of the principal characters in Ray Bradbury's "Summer Rituals," Sandra Cisneros's "Only daughter," and Michael Dorris's "The Broken Cord." Compare and contrast the extent to which each of these events influences the characters involved.

2. One of Walker's primary themes involves the eventual acceptance of who we are in life. Find the same theme in Malcolm Cowley's "The View from 80," Lewis Sawaquat's "For My Indian Daughter," or Richard Rodriguez's "The Fear of Losing a Culture"; then decide which of these authors seems most content with his or her own self-image. How did you come to this conclusion?

3. The relationship between Walker's original injury and the shyness and insecurity that resulted from it imply a negative cause/effect connection. Find an essay in this chapter of the book that implies a positive connection between a cause and its effect. How are the two essays different? How are they the same?

IDEAS FOR DISCUSSION/WRITING

Preparing to Write

Write freely about your self-esteem and the role of self-esteem in the life of college students: How important is self-esteem to you personally? To your academic performance? What affects your self-esteem most? Why do these events affect you? Do they help or hinder your self-esteem? What elements affect the self-esteem of other students you know? Of friends of yours? Of relatives? What effects have you observed in college students that result from low self-esteem? In friends? In relatives? How do you control your self-esteem? Do you recommend this method to others?

Choosing a Topic

1. Low self-esteem can cause a number of serious problems in different aspects of college students' lives. Conduct a study of the causes and effects of low self-esteem in the lives of several students at your school. Write an essay for the college community explaining these causes and effects.
2. Your campus newspaper is printing a special issue highlighting the psychological health of different generations of college students. Interview some people who represent a generation other than your own. Then characterize the students in this generation for the newspaper. In essay form, introduce the features you have discovered, and then discuss their causes and effects.
3. Some people believe self-esteem is a result of peer groups; others say that it is a result of one's family environment. What do you think? *Time* magazine is soliciting student reactions on this issue and has asked for your opinion. Where do you stand on this question? Give specific examples that support your opinion. Respond in essay form.
4. Despite her concerns about the wound in her eye, photographs of Alice Walker are published in several places on the Internet. How would you feel about having your picture published on

the Internet? Do you have any insecurities about your appearance? Write an essay in which you explore these feelings. With Walker's essay as a model, use vivid description in your analysis of the causes of these insecurities and their effects on other aspects of your life.

Before beginning your essay, you might want to consult the checklists on page 454.

CHAPTER WRITING ASSIGNMENTS

Practicing Cause/Effect

1. Think about a time in your life when you had definite, clear expectations of an event or experience. Where did these expectations come from? Were they high or low? Were they fulfilled or not? If not, what went wrong? Explain the situation surrounding this experience in a coherent essay.

2. Brainstorm about some challenges or difficult times you have faced. Then describe the most important challenge you have overcome. Explain why this experience was so difficult and what helped you face and conquer it.

3. What do you believe are the major causes of violence in American society? Write an essay that explains why the causes you cite are real or valid. Can you propose any possible solutions to the predicament you describe?

Exploring Ideas

1. How does our reading help us perceive the world? Do you think short stories, plays, and poems help us understand people's behavior and feelings? Write an essay responding to these questions.

2. Compare your memory of a particular childhood experience with that of another family member. How accurately do you both seem to remember this same event? What do you think accounts for the differences in what we remember about various events? What do these differences say about us? Write an essay exploring these questions, using the event from your childhood to support your discussion.

3. Television has been blamed for causing violent behavior, shortening attention spans, and exposing young people to sexually explicit images. Should we as a society monitor what appears on television more closely, or should parents be responsible for censoring what their children watch? Write an essay that takes a stand on this issue.

9

ARGUMENT AND PERSUASION
Inciting People to Thought or Action

Almost everything we do or say is an attempt to persuade. Whether we dress up to impress a potential employer or argue openly with a friend about an upcoming election, we are trying to convince various people to see the world our way. However, some aspects of life are particularly dependent upon persuasion. Think, for example, of all the television, magazine, and billboard ads we see urging us to buy certain products or of the many impassioned appeals we read and hear on such controversial issues as school prayer, abortion, gun control, and nuclear energy. Religious leaders devote their professional lives to convincing people to live a certain way and believe in certain religious truths, whereas scientists and mathematicians use rigorous logic and natural law to convince us of various hypotheses. Politicians make their living persuading voters to elect them and then support them throughout their terms of office. In fact, anyone who wants something from another person or agency, ranging from federal money for a research project to a new bicycle for Christmas, must use some form of persuasion to get what he or she desires. The success or failure of this type of communication is easily determined:

If the people being addressed change their actions or attitudes in favor of the writer or speaker, the attempt at persuasion has been successful.

DEFINING ARGUMENT AND PERSUASION

The terms *argument* and *persuasion* are often used interchangeably, but one is actually a subdivision of the other. Persuasion names a purpose for writing. To persuade your readers is to convince them to think, act, or feel a certain way. Much of the writing you have been doing in this book has persuasion as one of its goals: A description of an African tribe might have a "dominant impression" you want your readers to accept; in an essay comparing various ways of celebrating Thanksgiving, you might try to convince your readers to believe that these similarities and differences actually exist; and in writing an essay exam on the causes of the Vietnam War, you are trying to convince your instructor that your reasoning is clear and your conclusions sound. In a sense, some degree of persuasion propels all writing.

More specifically, however, the process of persuasion involves appealing to one or more of the following: to reason, to emotion, or to a sense of ethics. An *argument* is an appeal predominantly to your readers' reason and intellect. You are working in the realm of argument when you deal with complex issues that are debatable; opposing views (either explicit or implicit) are a basic requirement of argumentation. But argument and persuasion are taught together because good writers are constantly blending these three appeals and adjusting them to the purpose and audience of a particular writing task. Although reason and logic are the focus of this chapter, you need to learn to use all three methods of persuasion as skillfully as possible to write effective essays.

An appeal to reason relies on logic and intellect and is usually most effective when you are expecting your readers to disagree with you in some way. This type of appeal can help you change your readers' opinions or influence their future actions through the sheer strength of logical validity. If you want to argue, for example, that pregnant women should refrain from smoking cigarettes, you could cite abundant statistical evidence that babies born to mothers who smoke have lower birth weights, more respiratory problems, and a higher incidence of sudden infant death syndrome than the children of nonsmoking mothers. Because smoking clearly endangers the health of the unborn child, reason dictates that mothers who wish to give birth to the healthiest possible babies should avoid smoking during pregnancy.

Emotional appeals, however, attempt to arouse your readers' feelings, instincts, senses, and biases. Used most profitably when your readers already agree with you, this type of essay generally validates, reinforces, and/or incites in an effort to get your readers to share your feelings or ideas. In order to urge our lawmakers to impose stricter jail sentences for alcohol abuse, you might describe a recent tragic accident involving a local twelve-year-old girl who was killed by a drunk driver as she rode her bicycle to school one morning. By focusing on such poignant visual details as the condition of her mangled bike, the bright red blood stains on her white dress, and the anguish on the faces of parents and friends, you could build a powerfully persuasive essay that would be much more effective than a dull recitation of impersonal facts and nationwide statistics.

An appeal to ethics, the third technique writers often use to encourage readers to agree with them, involves cultivating a sincere, honest tone that will establish your reputation as a reliable, qualified, experienced, well-informed, and knowledgeable person whose opinions on the topic under discussion are believable because they are ethically sound. Such an approach is often used in conjunction with logical or emotional appeals to foster a verbal environment that will result in minimal resistance from its readers. Premier golfer Tiger Woods is a master at creating this ethical, trustworthy persona as he tries to persuade television viewers to buy Nike products. In fact, the old gag question "Would you buy a used car from this man?" is our instinctive response to all forms of attempted persuasion, whether the salesperson is trying to sell us Puppy Chow or gun control, hair spray or school prayer. The more believable we are as human beings, the better chance we will have of convincing our audience.

The following student paragraph is directed primarily toward the audience's logical reasoning ability. Notice that the writer states her assertion and then gives reasons to convince her readers to change their ways. The student writer also brings both emotion and ethics into the argument by choosing her words and examples with great precision.

Have you ever watched a pair of chunky thighs, a jiggling posterior, and an extra-large sweatshirt straining to cover a beer belly and thought, "Thank God I don't look like that! I'm in pretty good shape . . . for someone my age." Well, before you become too smug and self-righteous, consider what kind of shape you're really in. Just because you don't look like Shamu the Whale doesn't mean you're in good condition. What's missing, you ask? Exercise. You can diet all day, wear the latest slim-cut designer jeans, and still be in worse shape than someone twice your age if you don't get a strong physical workout at least three times a week. Exercise is not only good for you, but it can also be fun—especially if you find a sport that makes you happy while you sweat. Your activity need not be expensive: Jogging, walking, basketball, tennis, and handball are not costly, unless you're seduced by the glossy sheen of the latest sporting fashions and accessories. Most of all, however, regular exercise is important for your health. You can just as easily drop dead from a sudden heart attack in the middle of a restaurant when you're slim and trim as when you're a slob. Your heart and lungs need regular workouts to stay healthy. So do yourself a favor, and add some form of exercise to your schedule. You'll feel better and live longer, and your looks will improve, too!

THINKING CRITICALLY BY USING ARGUMENT AND PERSUASION

Argument and persuasion require you to present your views on an issue through logic, emotion, and good character in such a way that you convince an audience of your point of view. This rhetorical mode comes at the end of this book because it is an extremely complex and sophisticated method of reasoning. The more proficient you become in this strategy of thinking and presenting your views, the more you will get what you want out of life (and out of school). Winning arguments means getting the pay raises you need, the refund you deserve, and the grades you've worked so hard for.

In a successful argument, your logic must be flawless. Your conclusions should be based on clear evidence, which must be organized in such a way that it builds to an effective, convincing conclusion. You should constantly have your purpose and audience in mind as you build your case; at the same time, issues of emotion and good character should support the flow of your logic.

Exercising your best logical skills is extremely important to all phases of your daily survival—in and out of the classroom. Following a logical argument in your reading and presenting a logical response to your course work are the hallmarks of a good student. Right now, put your best logic forward and work on your reasoning and persuasive abilities in the following series of exercises. Isolate argument/persuasion from the other rhetorical strategies so that you can practice it and strengthen your ability to argue before you combine it with other methods.

1. Charles Moore uses this photograph to document how the police in Birmingham, Alabama used a dog to harass a peaceful protester in a 1963 civil rights struggle. Identify another social struggle or protest that you believe is important. Brainstorm about the many views people might hold about this issue. Choose one and identify the types of evidence you would need to support this view, the resolutions you might offer, and the concessions you would be willing to make to resolve the issue. Present a five-ten minute presentation arguing your point to your class or within a small group in your class.

2. Bring to class two magazine ads—one ad that tries to sell a product and another that tries to convince the reader that a particular action or product is wrong or bad (unhealthy, misinterpreted, politically incorrect, etc.). How does each ad appeal to the reader's logic? How does the advertiser use emotion and character in his or her appeal?

3. Fill in the following blanks: The best way to _____ is to _____. (For example, "The best way to lose weight is to exercise.") Then list ways you might use to persuade a reader to see your point of view in this statement.

READING AND WRITING PERSUASIVE ESSAYS

Although persuasive writing can be approached essentially in three different ways—logically, emotionally, and/or ethically—our stress in this chapter is on logic and reason, because they are at the heart of most college writing. As a reader, you will see how various forms of reasoning and different methods of organization affect your reaction to an essay. Your stand on a particular issue will control the way you process information in argument and persuasion essays. As you read the essays in this chapter, you will also learn to recognize emotional and ethical appeals and the different effects they create. In your role as a writer, you need to be fully aware of the options available to you as you compose. Although the basis of your writing will be logical argument, you will see that you can learn to control your readers' responses to your essays by choosing your evidence carefully, organizing it wisely, and seasoning it with the right amount of emotion and ethics—depending on your purpose and audience.

How to Read Persuasive Essays

Preparing to Read.   As you prepare to read the essays in this chapter, spend a few minutes browsing through the preliminary material for each selection: What does bell hooks' title, "Justice: Childhood Love Lessons," prepare you for? What can you learn from scanning Robert Heilbroner's essay, "Don't Let Stereotypes Warp Your Judgment," and reading its synopsis in the Rhetorical Table of Contents?

Also, you should bring to your reading as much information as you can from the authors' biographies: What is the source of

Robert Heilbroner's interest in stereotyping ("Don't Let Stereotypes Warp Your Judgment")? Why do you think Dave Grossman writes about violence and the media? Does he have the proper qualifications to teach us about how "We Are Training Our Kids to Kill"? For the essays in this chapter that present two sides of an argument (on media coverage and immigration), what biographical details prepare us for each writer's stand on the issue? Who were the original audiences for these pro and con arguments?

Last, before you read these essays, try to generate some ideas on each topic so that you can take the role of an active reader. In this text, the Preparing to Read questions will help you get ready for this task. Then, you should speculate further on the general subject of the essay: What are the main arguments related to disciplining children? What side do you think hooks is on? Where do you stand on the subject? How do you think stereotyping is affecting American society? What would you change about America's approach to this controversial topic? What would you continue?

Reading.   Be sure to record your spontaneous reactions to the persuasive essays in this chapter as you read them for the first time: What are your opinions on each subject? Why do you hold these opinions? Be especially aware of your responses to the essays representing opposing viewpoints at the end of the chapter; know where you stand in relation to each side of the issues here.

Use the preliminary material before an essay to help you create a framework for your responses to it: Who was hooks' primary audience when her essay was first published? In what ways is the tone of her essay appropriate for that audience? What motivated Heilbroner to publish his arguments on stereotyping? What makes Grossman so knowledgeable about children and TV violence? Which argument on media coverage do you find most convincing? On immigration?

Your main job at this stage of reading is to determine each author's primary assertion or proposition (thesis statement) and to create an inquisitive environment for thinking critically about the essay's ideas. In addition, take a look at the questions after each selection to make sure you are picking up the major points of the essay.

Rereading.   As you reread these persuasive essays, notice how the writers integrate their appeals to logic, to emotion, and to ethics. Also, pay attention to the emphasis the writers place on one or more appeals at certain strategic points in the essays: How does hooks integrate these three appeals in "Justice: Childhood Love Lessons"? Which of these appeals does she rely on to help bring her essay to a close? How persuasive is her final appeal? What combination of appeals does Dave Grossman use in "We Are Training Our Kids to Kill"? In what way does the tone of his writing support what he is saying? How does he establish this tone?

Also, determine what other rhetorical strategies help these writers make their primary points. How do these strategies enable each writer to establish a unified essay with a beginning, a middle, and an end?

Then answer the questions after each reading selection to make certain you understand the essay on the literal, interpretive, and analytical levels in preparation for the discussion/writing assignments that follow.

For a list of guidelines for the entire reading process, see the checklists on page 20 of the Introduction.

How to Write Persuasive Essays

Preparing to Write.   The first stage of writing an essay of this sort involves, as usual, exploring and then limiting your topic. As you prepare to write your persuasive paper, first try to generate as many ideas as possible—regardless of whether they appeal to logic, emotion, or ethics. To do this, review the prewriting techniques in the Introduction and answer the Preparing to Write questions. Then choose a topic. Next, focus on a purpose and a specific audience before you begin to write.

Writing.   Most persuasive essays should begin with an assertion or a proposition stating what you believe about a certain issue. This thesis should generally be phrased as a debatable statement, such as, "If individual states reinstituted the death penalty, Americans would notice an immediate drop in violent crimes." At this point in your essay, you should also justify the significance of the issue you will be discussing: "Such a decline in the crime rate would affect all our lives and make this country a safer place in which to live."

The essay should then support your thesis in a variety of ways. This support may take the form of facts, figures, examples, opinions by recognized authorities, case histories, narratives/anec-dotes, comparisons, contrasts, or cause/effect studies. This evi-dence is most effectively organized from least to most important when you are confronted with a hostile audience (so that you can lead your readers through your reasoning step by step) and from most to least important when you are facing a supportive audience (so that you can build on their loyalty and enthusiam as you advance your thesis). In fact, you will be able to engineer your best support if you know your audience's opinions, feelings, and back-ground before you write your essay, so that your intended "target" is as clear as possible. The body of your essay will undoubtedly consist of a combination of logical, emotional, and ethical appeals—all leading to some final summation or recommendation.

The concluding paragraph of a persuasive essay should restate your main assertion (in terms slightly different from your original statement) and should offer some constructive recommendations about the problem you have been discussing (if you haven't already done so). This section of your paper should clearly bring your argument to a close in one final attempt to move your audi-ence to accept or act on the viewpoint you present. Let's look more closely now at each of the three types of appeals used in such essays: logical, emotional, and ethical.

To construct a *logical* argument, you have two principal patterns available to you: inductive reasoning or deductive reasoning. The first encourages an audience to make what is called an "inductive leap" from several particular examples to a single, useful general-ization. In the case of the death penalty, for instance, you might cite a number of examples, figures, facts, and case studies illustrating the effectiveness of capital punishment in various states, thereby lead-ing up to your firm belief that the death penalty should be reinsti-tuted. Used most often by detectives, scientists, and lawyers, the process of inductive reasoning addresses the audience's ability to think logically by moving them systematically from an assortment of selected evidence to a rational and ordered conclusion.

In contrast, deductive reasoning moves its audience from a broad, general statement to particular examples supporting that statement. In writing such an essay, you would present your the-sis statement about capital punishment first and then offer clear, orderly evidence to support that belief. Although the mental process we go through in creating a deductive argument is quite sophisticated, it is based on a three-step form of reasoning called the *syllogism,* which most logicians believe is the foundation of logical thinking. The traditional syllogism has

A *major premise:* All humans fear death.

A *minor premise:* Criminals are humans.

A *conclusion:* Therefore, criminals fear death.

As you might suspect, this type of reasoning is only as accurate as its original premises, so you need to be sure your premises are true so your argument is valid.

In constructing a logical argument, you should take great care to avoid the two types of fallacies in reasoning found most frequently in lower-division college papers: giving too few examples to support an assertion and citing examples that do not represent the assertion fairly. If you build your argument on true statements and abundant, accurate evidence, your essay will be effective.

Persuading through *emotion* necessitates controlling your readers' instinctive reactions to what you are saying. You can accomplish this goal in two different ways: (1) by choosing your words with even greater care than usual and (2) by using figurative language whenever appropriate. In the first case, you must be especially conscious of using words that have the same general denotative (or dictionary) meaning but bear decidedly favorable or unfavorable connotative (or implicit) meanings. For example, notice the difference between *slender* and *scrawny, patriotic* and *chauvinistic,* or *compliment* and *flattery.* Your careful attention to the choice of such words can help readers form visual images with certain positive or negative associations that subtly encourage them to follow your argument and adopt your opinions. Second, the effective use of figurative language—especially similes and metaphors—makes your writing more vivid, thus triggering your readers' senses and encouraging them to accept your views. Both of these techniques will help you manipulate your readers into the position of agreeing with your ideas.

Ethical appeals, which establish you as a reliable, well-informed person, are accomplished through (1) the tone of your essay and (2) the number and type of examples you cite. Tone is created through deliberate word choice: Careful attention to the mood implied in the words you use can convince your readers that you are serious, friendly, authoritative, jovial, or methodical—depending on your intended purpose. In like manner, the examples you supply to support your assertions can encourage readers to see you as experienced, insightful, relaxed, or intense. In both of these cases, winning favor for yourself will usually also gain approval for your opinions.

Rewriting. To rework your persuasive essays, you should play the role of your readers and impartially evaluate the different appeals you have used to accomplish your purpose:

- Is your thesis statement clear?
- Is the main thrust of your essay argumentative (an appeal to reason)?
- Do the other appeals you use effectively accomplish your purpose with your intended audience?
- Does your conclusion restate your argument, make a recommendation, and bring your essay to a close?

You should also look closely at the way your appeals work together in your essay:

- When you use logic, is that section of your paper arranged through either inductive or deductive reasoning?
- Is that the most effective order to achieve your purpose?
- In appealing to the emotions, have you chosen your words with proper attention to their denotative and connotative effects?
- Have you chosen examples carefully to support your thesis statement?
- Are these examples suitable for your purpose and audience?

Any additional guidance you may need as you write and revise your persuasive essays is furnished on pages 31–32 of the Introduction.

STUDENT ESSAY: ARGUMENT AND PERSUASION AT WORK

The following student essay uses all three appeals to make its point about the power of language in shaping our view of the world. First, the writer sets forth her character references (ethical appeal) in the first paragraph, after which she presents her thesis and its significance in paragraph 2. The support for her thesis is a combination of logical and emotional appeals, heavy on the logical, as the writer moves her paragraphs from general to particular in an effort to convince her readers to adopt her point of view and adjust their language use accordingly.

The Language of Equal Rights

Up front, I admit it. I've been a card-carrying feminist since junior high school. I want to see an Equal Rights Amendment to the U.S. Constitution, equal pay for equal—and comparable—work, and I go dutch on dates. Furthermore, I am quite prickly on the subject of language. I'm one of those people who bristles at terms like *lady doctor* (you know they don't mean a gynecologist), *female policeman* (a paradox), and *mankind* instead of *humanity* (are they really talking about me?).

Many people ask "How important are mere words, anyway? You know what we really mean." A question like this ignores the symbolic and psychological importance of language. What words "mean" can go beyond what a speaker or writer consciously intends, reflecting personal and cultural biases that run so deep that most of the time we aren't even aware they exist. "Mere words" are incredibly important: They are our framework for seeing and understanding the world.

Man, we are told, means woman as well as man, just as *mankind* supposedly stands for all of humanity. In the introduction of a sociology textbook I recently read, the author was anxious to demonstrate his awareness of the controversy over sexist language and to assure his female readers that, despite his use of noninclusive terms, he was

Ethical appeal — Up front, I admit it. I've been a card-carrying feminist since junior high school. I want to see an Equal Rights Amendment to the U.S. Constitution, equal pay for equal—and comparable—work, and I go dutch on dates. Furthermore, I am quite prickly on the subject of language.

Emotional appeal — I'm one of those people who bristles at terms like *lady doctor* (you know they don't mean a gynecologist), *female policeman* (a paradox), and *mankind* instead of *humanity* (are they really talking about me?).

Assertion or thesis statement — What words "mean" can go beyond what a speaker or writer consciously intends, reflecting personal and cultural biases that run so deep that most of the time we aren't even aware they exist.

Significance of assertion — "Mere words" are incredibly important: They are our framework for seeing and understanding the world.

Logical appeal — *Man*, we are told, means woman as well as man, just as *mankind* supposedly stands for all of humanity.

not forgetting the existence or importance of women in society. He was making a conscious decision to continue to use *man* and *mankind* instead of *people, humanity,* etc., for ease of expression and aesthetic reasons. "Man" simply sounds better, he explained. I flipped through the table of contents and found "Man and Society," "Man and Nature," "Man and Technology," and, near the end, "Man and Woman." <u>At what point did *Man* quit meaning *people* and start meaning men again?</u> The writer was obviously unaware of the answer to this question, because it is one he would never think to ask. Having consciously addressed the issue only to dismiss it, he reverted to form.

<u>The very ambiguity of *man* as the generic word for our species ought to be enough to combat any arguments that we keep it because we all "know what it means" or because it is both traditional and sounds better.</u> And does it really sound all that much better, or are we just more used to it, more comfortable? Our own national history proves that we can be comfortable with a host of words and attitudes that strike us as unjust and ugly today. A lot of white folks probably thought that Negroes were getting pretty stuffy and picky when they began to insist on being called *blacks*. <u>After all, weren't there more important things to worry about, like civil rights?</u> But black activists recognized the emotional and symbolic significance of having a name that was parallel to the name that the dominant race used for itself—a name equal in dignity, lacking that vaguely alien, anthropological sound. After all, whites were called *Caucasians* only in police reports, textbooks, and autopsies. *Negro* may have sounded better to people in

Right margin annotations:

Examples organized deductively

Emotional appeal

Logical appeal

Examples organized deductively

Emotional appeal

the bad old days of blatant racial bigotry, but we adjusted to the word *black* and have now moved on to *African American,* and more and more people of each race are adjusting to the wider implications and demands of practical, as well as verbal, labels.

Logical appeal

<u>In a world where *man* and *human* are offered as synonymous terms, I don't think it is a coincidence that women are still vastly underrepresented in positions of money, power, and respect.</u> Children grow up learning a language that makes maleness the norm for anything that isn't explicitly designated as female, giving little girls a very limited corner of the universe to picture themselves in. Indeed, the language that nonfeminists today claim to be inclusive was never intended to cover women in the first place. "One man, one vote" and "All men are created equal" meant just that. Women had to fight for decades to be included even as an afterthought; it took constitutional amendments to convince the government and the courts that women are human too.

Examples organized deductively

Conclusion/ restatement

The message is clear. <u>We have to start speaking about people, not men, if we are going to start thinking in terms of both women and men. A "female man" will never be the equal of her brother.</u>

Student Writer's Comments

The hardest task for me in writing this essay was coming up with a topic! The second hardest job was trying to be effective without getting preachy, strident, or wordy. I wanted to persuade an audience that would no doubt include the bored, the hostile, and the indifferent, and I was worried about losing their attention.

I chose my topic after several prewriting sessions that generated numerous options for me to write about. I stumbled on the idea of sexist language in one of these sessions and then went on to generate new material on this particular topic. Eventually satisfied that I had enough ideas to stay with this topic, I doubled back and labeled them according to each type of appeal.

Even before I had written my thesis, I had a good idea of what I wanted to say in this essay. I began working from an assertion that essentially remained the same as I wrote and revised my essay. It's more polished now, but its basic intention never changed.

To create my first draft, I worked from my notes, labeled by type of appeal. I let the logical arguments guide my writing, strategically introducing emotional and ethical appeals as I sensed they would be effective. I appealed to ethics in the beginning of the essay to establish my credibility, and I appealed to the readers' emotions occasionally to vary my pace and help my argument gain momentum. I was fully aware of what I was doing when I moved from one appeal to another. I wrote from a passionate desire to change people's thinking about language and its ability to control our perceptions of the world.

Next, I revised my entire essay several times, playing the role of different readers with dissimilar biases in each case. Every time I worked through the essay, I made major changes in the introduction and the conclusion as well. At this point, I paid special attention to the denotation, connotation, and tone of my words (especially highly charged language) and to the examples I had chosen to support each point I decided to keep in my argument. Though I moved a lot of examples around and thought of better ones in some cases, I was eventually happy with the final product. I am especially pleased with the balance of appeals in the final draft.

SOME FINAL THOUGHTS ON ARGUMENT AND PERSUASION

As you can tell from the selections that follow, the three different types of persuasive appeals usually complement one another in practice. Most good persuasive essays use a combination of these methods to achieve their purposes. Good persuasive essays also rely on various rhetorical modes we have already studied—such as example, process analysis, division/classification, comparison/contrast, definition, and cause/effect—to advance their arguments. In the following essays, you will see a combination of appeals and a number of different rhetorical modes at work.

ARGUMENT AND PERSUASION IN REVIEW

Reading Argument and Persuasion Essays

Preparing to Read

✓ What assumptions can you make from the essay's title?
✓ Can you guess what the general mood of the essay is?
✓ What is the essay's purpose and audience?
✓ What does the synopsis tell you about the essay?
✓ What can you learn from the author's biography?
✓ Can you guess what the author's point of view toward the subject is?
✓ What are your responses to the "Preparing to Read" questions?

Reading

✓ What is the author's main assertion or thesis?
✓ What are the primary appeals at work in the essay?
✓ Did you preview the questions that follow the essay?

Rereading

✓ How does the writer integrate the appeals in the essay?
✓ What is the tone of the essay? How does the author establish this tone?
✓ What other rhetorical strategies does the author use?
✓ What are your responses to the questions after the essay?

Writing Argument and Persuasion Essays

Preparing to Write

✓ What are your responses to the "Preparing to Write" questions?
✓ Do you narrow and focus your material as much as possible?
✓ What is your purpose?
✓ Do you understand your audience's background?

Writing

✓ Is your thesis a debatable question?
✓ Do you justify the organization of your essay?
✓ Is your essay organized effectively for what you are trying to accomplish?
✓ Does the body of your essay directly support your thesis?

Rewriting

✓ Is your thesis statement clear?
✓ Is the main thrust of your essay an appeal to reason?
✓ Have you used figurative language whenever appropriate?
✓ Have you chosen examples carefully to support your thesis?
✓ Does your conclusion restate your argument, make a recommendation, and bring your essay to a close?

BELL HOOKS   (1952–   )

Justice: Childhood Love Lessons

Writer, professor, and social critic bell hooks was born Gloria
Jean Watkins in Hopkinsville, Kentucky, but has written for
many years under the pseudonym "bell hooks" (all lowercase
letters) in tribute to her great-grandmother, a woman "who
spoke her mind, a woman who was not afraid to talk back."
Following a B.A. at Stanford University, an M.A. at the
University of Wisconsin, and a Ph.D. at the University of
California, Santa Cruz, she embarked on an enviable academic
career, first as an assistant professor of African American Studies
and English Literature at Yale University, followed by positions
in American Literature and Women's Studies at Oberlin College
and in Black Studies at the City College of New York, where she
currently teaches. Her prolific and controversial publications have
included *Ain't I a Woman: Black Women and Feminism* (1981),
Feminist Theory: From Margin to Center (1984), *Talking Back:
Thinking Feminist, Thinking Black* (1989), *Yearning: Race, Gender,
and Cultural Politics* (1990), *Black Looks: Race and Representation*
(1992), and *Killing Rage: Ending Racism* (1995). Her works always
raise important cultural issues, particularly with regard to the
goals of feminism and the place of black women within the
movement.

Preparing to Read

In the following essay, originally published in 2000, bell hooks
logically and persuasively presents her opinions on the relationship between love and punishment for children.

Exploring Experience: As you prepare to read her essay, take a
few moments to focus your own thoughts on the connection
between discipline and expressions of love: In what ways do you
think children should be disciplined? How should parents express
love to their children? Do you believe in hitting children? Why or
why not? How else should children be disciplined? Do you believe
that discipline and love can coexist?

Learning Online: Conduct an Internet search using the phrase "advice for disciplining children." Explore at least two Web sites. What types of advice do the Web sites offer? How does each site argue its case? Consider these varying opinions while reading bell hooks's essay.

Severe separations in early life leave emotional scars on the brain because they assault the essential human connection: The [parent–child] bond which teaches us that we are lovable. The [parent–child] bond which teaches us how to love. We cannot be whole human beings—indeed, we may find it hard to be human—without the sustenance of this first attachment.

—Judith Viorst

We learn about love in childhood. Whether our homes are happy or troubled, our families functional or dysfunctional, it's the original school of love. I cannot remember ever wanting to ask my parents to define love. To my child's mind, love was the good feeling you got when family treated you like you mattered and you treated them like they mattered. Love was always and only about good feeling. In early adolescence when we were whipped and told that these punishments were "for your own good" or "I'm doing this because I love you," my siblings and I were confused. Why was harsh punishment a gesture of love? As children do, we pretended to accept this grown-up logic; but we knew in our hearts it was not right. We knew it was a lie. Just like the lie grown-ups told when they explained after harsh punishment, "It hurts me more than it hurts you." There is nothing that creates more confusion about love in the minds and hearts of children than unkind and/or cruel punishment meted out by the grown-ups they have been taught they should love and respect. Such children learn early on to question the meaning of love, to yearn for love even as they doubt it exists.

On the flip side, there are masses of children who grow up confident love is a good feeling who are never punished, who are allowed to believe that love is only about getting your needs met, your desires satisfied. In their child's minds, love is not about what they have to give, love is mostly something given to them. When children like these are overindulged either materially or by being allowed to act out, this is a form of neglect. These children, though not in any way abused or uncared for, are usually as unclear about love's meaning as their neglected and emotionally abandoned counterparts. Both groups have learned to think about love primarily in relation to good feelings, in the context of reward and punishment. From early childhood on, most of us remember being told we were loved when we did things pleasing to our parents. And we learned to give them affirmations of love when they pleased us. As children grow they associate love more with acts of attention, affection, and caring. They still see parents who attempt to satisfy their desires as giving love.

Children from all classes tell me that they love their parents and are loved by them, even those who are being hurt or abused. When asked to define love, small children pretty much agree that it's a good feeling, "like when you have something to eat that you really like" especially if it's your f-a-v-o-r-i-t-e. They will say, "My mommy loves me 'cause she takes care of me and helps me do everything right." When asked how to love someone, they talk about giving hugs and kisses, being sweet and cuddly. The notion that love is about getting what one wants, whether it's a hug or a new sweater or a trip to Disneyland, is a way of thinking about love that makes it difficult for children to acquire a deeper emotional understanding.

We like to imagine that most children will be born into homes where they will be loved. But love will not be present if the grown-ups who parent do not know how to love. Although lots of children are raised in homes where they are given some degree of care, love may not be sustained or even present. Adults across lines of class, race, and gender indict the family. Their testimony conveys worlds of childhood where love was lacking—where chaos, neglect, abuse, and coercion reigned supreme. In her recent book *Raised in Captivity: Why Does America Fail Its Children?*, Lucia Hodgson documents the reality of lovelessness in the lives of a huge majority of children in the United States. Every day thousands of children in our culture are verbally and physically abused, starved, tortured, and murdered. They are the true victims of intimate terrorism in that they have no collective voice and no rights. They remain the property of parenting adults to do with as they will.

There can be no love without justice. Until we live in a culture that not only respects but also upholds basic civil rights for children, most children will not know love. In our culture the private family dwelling is the one institutionalized sphere of power that can easily be autocratic and fascistic. As absolute rulers, parents can usually decide without any intervention what is best for their children. If children's rights are taken away in any domestic household, they have no legal recourse. Unlike women who can organize to protest sexist domination, demanding both equal rights and justice, children can only rely on well-meaning adults to assist them if they are being exploited and oppressed in the home.

We all know that, irrespective of class or race, other adults 6
rarely intervene to question or challenge what their peers are doing with "their" children.

At a fun party, mostly of educated, well-paid professionals, a 7
multiracial, multi-generational evening, the subject of disciplining kids by hitting was raised. Almost all the guests over thirty spoke about the necessity of using physical punishment. Many of us in the room had been smacked, whipped, or beaten as children. Men spoke the loudest in defense of physical punishment. Women, mostly mothers, talked about hitting as a last resort, but one that they deployed when necessary.

As one man bragged about the aggressive beatings he had 8
received from his mother, sharing that "they had been good for him," I interrupted and suggested that he might not be the misogynist woman-hater he is today if he had not been brutally beaten by a woman as a child. Although it is too simplistic to assume that just because we are hit as kids we will grow up to be people who hit, I wanted the group to acknowledge that being physically hurt or abused by grown-ups when we are children has harmful consequences in our adult life.

A young professional, the mother of a small boy, bragged about 9
the fact that she did not hit, that when her son misbehaved she clamped down on his flesh, pinching him until he got the message. But this, too, is a form of coercive abuse. The other guests supported this young mother and her husband in their methods. I was astounded. I was a lone voice speaking out for the rights of children.

Later, with other people, I suggested that had we all been lis- 10
tening to a man tell us that every time his wife or girlfriend does something he does not like he just clamps down on her flesh, pinching her as hard as he can, everyone would have been

appalled. They would have seen the action as both coercive and abusive. Yet they could not acknowledge that it was wrong for an adult to hurt a child in this way. All the parents in that room claim that they are loving. All the people in that room were college educated. Most call themselves good liberals, supportive of civil rights and feminism. But when it came to the rights of children, they had a different standard.

One of the most important social myths we must debunk if we   11
are to become a more loving culture is the one that teaches parents that abuse and neglect can coexist with love. Abuse and neglect negate love. Care and affirmation, the opposite of abuse and humiliation, are the foundation of love. No one can rightfully claim to be loving when behaving abusively. Yet parents do this all the time in our culture. Children are told they are loved even though they are being abused.

It is a testimony to the failure of loving practice that abuse is   12
happening in the first place.

Many of the men who offer their personal testimony in   13
Boyhood, Growing Up Male tell stories of random violent abuse by parents that inflicted trauma. In his essay "When My Father Hit Me," Bob Shelby describes the pain of repeated beatings by his dad, stating, "From these experiences with my father, I learned about the abuse of power. By physically hitting my mother and me, he effectively stopped us from reacting to his humiliation of us. We ceased to protest his violations of our boundaries and his ignoring our sense of being individuals with needs, demands, and rights of our own." Throughout his essay, Shelby expresses contradictory understandings about the meaning of love. On the one hand, he says, "I have no doubt that my father loved me, but his love became misdirected. He said he wanted to give me what he didn't have as a child." On the other hand, Shelby confesses, "What he most showed me, however, was his difficulty in being loved. All his life he had struggled with feelings of being unloved." When Shelby describes his childhood, it is clear that his dad had affection for him and also gave him care some of the time. However, his dad did not know how to give and receive love. The affection he gave was undermined by the abuse.

Writing from the space of adult recollection, Shelby talks about   14
the impact of physical abuse on his boyhood psyche: "As the intensity of the pain of his hits increased, I felt the hurt in my heart. I

realized what hurt me the most were my feelings of love for this man who was hitting me. I covered my love with a dark cloth of hate." A similar story is told by other men in autobiographical narrative—men of all classes and races. One of the myths about lovelessness is that it exists only among the poor and deprived. Yet lovelessness is not a function of poverty or material lack. In homes where material privileges abound, children suffer emotional neglect and abuse. In order to cope with the pain of wounds inflicted in childhood, most of the men in *Boyhood* sought some form of therapeutic care. To find their way back to love they had to heal.

Many men in our culture never recover from childhood   15 unkindnesses. Studies show that males and females who are violently humiliated and abused repeatedly, with no caring intervention, are likely to be dysfunctional and will be predisposed to abuse others violently. In Jarvis Jay Masters's book *Finding Freedom: Writings from Death Row,* a chapter called "Scars" recounts his recognition that a vast majority of the scars covering the bodies of fellow inmates (not all of whom were on death row) were not, as one might think, the result of violent adult interactions. These men were covered with scars from childhood beatings inflicted by parenting adults. Yet, he reports, none of them saw themselves as the victims of abuse: "Throughout my many years of institutionalization, I, like so many of these men, unconsciously took refuge behind prison walls. Not until I read a series of books for adults who had been abused as children did I become committed to the process of examining my own childhood." Organizing the men for group discussion, Masters writes, "I spoke to them of the pain I had carried through more than a dozen institutions. And I explained how all these events ultimately trapped me in a pattern of lashing out against everything. Like many abused children, male and female, these men were beaten by mothers, fathers, and other parental caregivers."

When Masters's mother dies, he feels grief that he cannot be   16 with her. The other inmates do not understand this longing, since she neglected and abused him. He responds, "She had neglected me, but am I to neglect myself as well by denying that I wished I'd been with her when she died, that I still love her?" Even on death row, Masters's heart remains open. And he can honestly confess to longing to give and receive love. Being hurt by parenting adults rarely alters a child's desire to love and be loved by them. Among grown-ups who were wounded in childhood, the desire to be loved by uncaring parents persists, even when there is a clear acceptance of the reality that this love will never be forthcoming.

Often, children will want to remain with parental caregivers 17 who have hurt them because of their cathected feelings for those adults. They will cling to the misguided assumption that their parents love them even in the face of remembered abuse, usually by denying the abuse and focusing on random acts of care.

In the prologue to *Creating Love,* John Bradshaw calls this con- 18 fusion about love "mystification." He shares, "I was brought up to believe that love is rooted in blood relationships. You naturally loved anyone in your family. Love was not a choice. The love I learned about was bound by duty and obligation. . . . My family taught me our culture's rules and beliefs above love . . . even with the best intentions our parents often confused love with what we would now call abuse." To demystify the meaning of love, the art and practice of loving, we need to use sound definitions of love when talking with children, and we also need to ensure that loving action is never tainted with abuse.

In a society like ours, where children are denied full civil rights, 19 it is absolutely crucial that parenting adults learn how to offer loving discipline. Setting boundaries and teaching children how to set boundaries for themselves prior to misbehavior is an essential part of loving parenting. When parents start out disciplining children by using punishment, this becomes the pattern children respond to. Loving parents work hard to discipline without punishment. This does not mean that they never punish, only that when they do punish, they choose punishments like time-outs or the taking away of privileges. They focus on teaching children how to be self-disciplining and how to take responsibility for their actions. Since the vast majority of us were raised in households where punishment was deemed the primary, if not the only, way to teach discipline, the fact that discipline can be taught without punishment surprises many people. One of the simplest ways children learn discipline is by learning how to be orderly in daily life, to clean up any messes they make. Just teaching a child to take responsibility for placing toys in the appropriate place after playtime is one way to teach responsibility and self-discipline. Learning to clean up the mess made during playtime helps a child learn to be responsible.

And they can learn from this practical act how to cope with emotional mess.

Were there current television shows that actually modeled lov-   20
ing parenting, parents could learn these skills. Television shows oriented toward families often favorably represent children when they are overindulged, are disrespectful, or are acting out. Often they behave in a more adult manner than the parents. What we see on television today actually, at best, models for us inappropriate behavior and in worst-case scenarios, unloving behaviors. A great example of this is a movie like *Home Alone,* which celebrates disobedience and violence. But television can portray caring, loving family interaction. There are whole generations of adults who talk nostalgically about how they wanted their families to be like the fictive portraits of family life portrayed on *Leave It to Beaver* or *My Three Sons.* We desired our families to be like those we saw on the screen because we were witnessing loving parenting, loving households. Expressing to parents our desire to have families like the ones we saw on the screen, we were often told that the families were not realistic. The reality was, however, that parents who come from unloving homes have never learned how to love and cannot create loving home environments or see them as realistic when watching them on television. The reality they are most familiar with and trust is the one they knew intimately.

There was nothing utopian about the way problems were   21
resolved on these shows. Parent and child discussion, critical reflection, and finding a way to make amends was usually the process by which misbehavior was addressed. On both shows, there was never just one parenting figure. Even though the mother was absent on *My Three Sons,* the lovable Uncle Charlie was a second parent. In a loving household where there are several parental caregivers, when a child feels one parent is being unjust, that child can appeal to another adult for mediation, understanding, or support. We live in a society where there are a growing number of single parents, female and male. But the individual parent can always choose a friend to be another parenting figure, however limited their interaction. This is why the categories of godmother and godfather are so crucial. When my best girlhood friend chose to have a child without a father in the household, I became the godmother, a second parenting figure.

My friend's daughter turns to me to intervene if there is a mis-   22
understanding or miscommunication between her and her mom.
Here's one small example. My adult friend had never received an
allowance as a child and did not feel she had the available extra
money to offer an allowance to her daughter. She also believed her
daughter would use all the money to buy sweets. Telling me that
her daughter was angry with her over this issue, she opened up the
space for us to have a dialogue. I shared my belief that allowances
are important ways to teach children discipline, boundaries, and
working through desires versus needs. I knew enough about my
friend's finances to challenge her insistence that she could not
afford to pay a small allowance, while simultaneously encouraging
her not to project the wrongs of her childhood onto the present.
As to whether the daughter would buy candy, I suggested she give
the allowance with a statement of hope that it would not be used
for overindulgence and see what happened.

It all worked out just fine. Happy to have an allowance, the   23
daughter chose to save her money to buy things she thought were
really important. And candy was not on this list. Had there not
been another adult parenting figure involved, it might have taken
these two a longer time to resolve their conflict, and unnecessary
estrangement and wounding might have occurred. Significantly,
love and respectful interaction between two adults exemplified for
the daughter (who was told about the discussion) ways of problem
solving. By revealing her willingness to accept criticism and her
capacity to reflect on her behavior and change, the mother modeled for her daughter, without losing dignity and authority, the
recognition that parents are not always right.

Until we begin to see loving parenting in all walks of life in our   24
culture, many people will continue to believe we can only teach
discipline through punishment and that harsh punishment is an
acceptable way to relate to children. Because children can innately
offer affection or respond to affectionate care by returning it, it is
often assumed that they know how to love and therefore do not
need to learn the art of loving. While the will to love is present in
very young children, they still need guidance in the ways of love.
Grown-ups provide that guidance.

Love is as love does, and it is our responsibility to give children   25
love. When we love children we acknowledge by our every action

that they are not property, that they have rights—that we respect and uphold their rights.

Without justice there can be no love.   26

UNDERSTANDING DETAILS

1. According to hooks, how do we first learn about love?
2. What two types of activities cause confusion about love in the hearts and minds of children?
3. What age group of parents usually insists on physical punishment for their children?
4. How do abused children generally feel about their parents? Why is this true?

ANALYZING MEANING

1. Why are children's civil rights so delicate, according to hooks?
2. Why does hooks think we must challenge the idea that "abuse and neglect can coexist with love" (paragraph 11)?
3. Why do we use different standards for the treatment of children and adults?
4. Explain what hooks means in the last sentence of her essay: "Without justice there can be no love"?

DISCOVERING RHETORICAL STRATEGIES

1. Who do you think is hooks' primary audience? How did you come to this conclusion?
2. Why do you think hooks refers to Bob Shelby's story in her essay? Is this reference effective where she has placed it?
3. Are you convinced by this essay that physical punishment and love cannot coexist in the same household? What details or examples are most persuasive to you?
4. What additional rhetorical strategies does hooks use to develop her argument? Give examples of each.

MAKING CONNECTIONS

1. Imagine that bell hooks, Lewis Sawaquat ("For My Indian Daughter"), Bill Cosby ("The Baffling Question"), Judith

Wallerstein and Sandra Blakeslee ("Second Chances for Children of Divorce"), Mary Pipher ("Beliefs About Families"), and Michael Dorris ("The Broken Cord") were having a discussion about the best ways to discipline children. Which author would you probably agree with most? Explain your answer.

2. To what extent do you think that bell hooks and Brent Staples ("A Brother's Murder") would agree about the need for physical discipline in inner-city neighborhoods? Do you think the discussion would change dramatically if it were expanded to include the treatment of children from all neighborhoods? Why or why not?

3. According to hooks, what is the proper relationship between love and punishment? What kinds of discipline does she favor? Which of the following authors would most likely agree with her: Kimberly Wozencraft ("Notes from the Country Club"), Bill Cosby ("The Baffling Question"), Jimmy Santiago Baca ("Past Present"), and Jill Leslie Rosenbaum and Meda Chesney-Lind ("Appearance and Delinquency: A Research Note")?

IDEAS FOR DISCUSSION/WRITING

Preparing to Write

Write freely about your views on disciplining children: Do you think hitting children is ever justified? In what other ways could children be punished? Do children have rights? How do they differ from the rights that adults have? What is the difference between children and adults in terms of humane treatment? Who should receive more respect—adults or children?

Choosing a Topic

1. Your old high school has asked you to talk to its senior psychology class about the topic of child abuse. What constitutes "abuse" in your opinion? Write a well-developed essay on this issue that will start a spirited discussion in class.

2. hooks claims that "No one can rightfully claim to be loving when behaving abusively" (paragraph 11)? Write a well-developed essay arguing for or against this assertion.

3. In your opinion, what is the relationship between civil rights and mutual respect? To what extent are they companion privileges? Take a stand on this question, and use carefully chosen evidence from bell hook's essay (whenever appropriate) to support your principal points.

4. Do you have an issue about which you feel strongly? Find a credible Web site (ending in ".org," ".gov," or ".edu") that supports your cause. Write an argument that could be published on this Web site. Following bell hooks's example, employ the three types of appeals, and use persuasive evidence to support your claims. Feel free to integrate data and quotes from your chosen Web site.

Before beginning your essay, you might want to consult the checklists on page 511.

ROBERT HEILBRONER   (1919–   )

Don't Let Stereotypes Warp Your Judgment

One of America's premiere economic theorists, Robert Heilbroner was born in New York City and earned his B.A. at Harvard University and his Ph.D. at the New School for Social Research, where he has been Norman Thomas Professor of Economics since 1972. During World War II, he served in Army Intelligence interviewing Japanese prisoners of war. He has written more than twenty books, including his most famous, *The Worldly Philosophers,* which has sold over three million copies since its initial publication in 1953. Over the past 50 years, the book has introduced millions of high school and college students to the economic theories of such prominent authors as Malthus, Ricardo, Marx, Veblen, Keynes, and many others. In his engaging, conversational prose style, Heilbroner not only makes these influential economists come alive on the pages of the book, but he also places each of them within the global context of social, political, historical, and economic theory. Additional publications have included *The Quest for Wealth* (1956), *The Limits of American Capitalism* (1966), *Beyond Boom and Crash* (1978), *The Economic Problem* (1990), and *Twenty-First Century Capitalism* (1993). An avid piano player, he also enjoys painting and bird watching.

Preparing to Read

In the following essay from *Think* magazine (June 1961), Heilbroner argues that stereotypes distort our view of the world and our ability to be unique and intelligent individuals.

Exploring Experience: As you prepare to read this essay, take a few moments to think about your own views on stereotyping: What exactly is stereotyping? How often do you see it take place? In what ways have stereotypes affected you directly? What are the perils connected with stereotyping? How can we avoid making such inaccurate and unfair generalizations?

Learning Online: Visit the "Remember" Web site (http://www.remember.org), and conduct a site search on the term *stereo-*

types. Find an article titled "Stereotypes and Prejudices," and read the first few paragraphs. Consider this perspective of stereotypes as you read Heilbroner's essay.

I s a girl called Gloria apt to be better looking than one called   1
Bertha? Are criminals more likely to be dark than blond? Can
you tell a good deal about someone's personality from hearing
his voice briefly over the phone? Can a person's nationality be
pretty accurately guessed from his photograph? Does the fact that
someone wears glasses imply that he is intelligent?

The answer to all these questions is obviously, "No."   2

Yet, from all the evidence at hand, most of us believe these things.   3
Ask any college boy if he'd rather take his chances with a Gloria or
a Bertha, or ask a college girl if she'd rather blind-date a Richard or
a Cuthbert. In fact, you don't have to ask: College students in ques-
tionnaires have revealed that names conjure up the same images in
their minds as they do in yours—and for as little reason.

Look into the favorite suspects of persons who report "suspi-   4
cious characters," and you will find a large percentage of them to
be "swarthy" or "dark and foreign-looking"—despite the testimony of criminologists that criminals do not tend to be dark, foreign or "wild-eyed." Delve into the main asset of a telephone stock
swindler, and you will find it to be a marvelously confidence-
inspiring telephone "personality." And whereas we all think we
know what an Italian or a Swede looks like, it is the sad fact that
when a group of Nebraska students sought to match faces and
nationalities of 15 European countries, they were scored wrong in
93 percent of their identifications. Finally, for all the fact that
horn-rimmed glasses have now become the standard television
sign of an "intellectual," optometrists know that the main thing
that distinguishes people with glasses is just bad eyes.

Stereotypes are a kind of gossip about the world, a gossip that   5
makes us prejudge people before we ever lay eyes on them. Hence
it is not surprising that stereotypes have something to do with the
dark world of prejudice. Explore most prejudices (note that the
word means *prejudgment*), and you will find a cruel stereotype at
the core of each one.

For it is the extraordinary fact that once we have typecast the   6
world, we tend to see people in terms of our standardized pictures.

In another demonstration of the power of stereotypes to affect our vision, a number of Columbia and Barnard students were shown 30 photographs of pretty but unidentified girls and asked to rate each in terms of "general liking," "intelligence," "beauty," and so on. Two months later, the same group were shown the same photographs, this time with fictitious Irish, Italian, Jewish, and "American" names attached to the pictures. Right away the ratings changed. Faces which were now seen as representing a national group went down in looks and still farther down in likability, while the "American" girls suddenly looked decidedly prettier and nicer.

Why is it that we stereotype the world in such an irrational and   7 harmful fashion? In part, we begin to type-cast people in our childhood years. Early in life, as every parent whose child has watched a TV Western knows, we learn to spot the Good Guys from the Bad Guys. Some years ago, a social psychologist showed very clearly how powerful these stereotypes of childhood vision are. He secretly asked the most popular youngsters in an elementary school to make errors in their morning gym exercises. Afterwards, he asked the class if anyone had noticed any mistakes during gym period. Oh, yes, said the children. But it was the unpopular members of the class—the "bad guys"—they remembered as being out of step.

We not only grow up with standardized pictures forming inside   8 of us, but as grown-ups we are constantly having them thrust upon us. Some of them, like the half-joking, half-serious stereotypes of mothers-in-law, or country yokels, or psychiatrists, are dinned into us by the stock jokes we hear and repeat. In fact, without such stereotypes, there would be a lot fewer jokes. Still other stereotypes are perpetuated by the advertisements we read, the movies we see, the books we read.

And finally, we tend to stereotype because it helps us make   9 sense out of a highly confusing world, a world which William James once described as "one great, blooming, buzzing confusion." It is a curious fact that if we don't know what we're looking at, we are often quite literally unable to see what we're looking at. People who recover their sight after a lifetime of blindness actually cannot at first tell a triangle from a square. A visitor to a factory sees only noisy chaos where the superintendent sees a perfectly synchronized flow of work. As Walter Lippmann has said, "For the most part we do not first see and then define; we define first and then we see."

Stereotypes are one way in which we "define" the world in   10
order to see it. They classify the infinite variety of human beings
into a convenient handful of "types" towards whom we learn to
act in stereotyped fashion. Life would be a weaning process if we
had to start from scratch with each and every human contact.
Stereotypes economize on our mental effort by covering up the
blooming, buzzing confusion with big recognizable cutouts. They
save us the "trouble" of finding out what the world is like—they
give it its accustomed look.

Thus the trouble is that stereotypes make us mentally lazy. As   11
S. I. Hayakawa, the authority on semantics, has written, "The
danger of stereotypes lies not in their existence, but in the fact that
they become for all people some of the time, and for some people
all the time, substitutes for observation." Worse yet, stereotypes
get in the way of our judgment, even when we do observe the
world. Someone who has formed rigid preconceptions of all Latins
as "excitable," or all teenagers as "wild," doesn't alter his point of
view when he meets a calm and deliberate Genoese or a serious-
minded high school student. He brushes them aside as "exceptions
that proved the rule." And, of course, if he meets someone true to
type, he stands triumphantly vindicated. "They're all like that," he
proclaims, having encountered an excited Latin, an ill-behaved
adolescent.

Hence, quite aside from the injustice which stereotypes do to   12
others, they impoverish ourselves. A person who lumps the world
into simple categories, who type-casts all labor leaders as "racke-
teers," all businessmen as "reactionaries," all Harvard men as
"snobs," and all Frenchmen as "sexy" is in danger of becoming a
stereotype himself. He loses his capacity to be himself—which is
to say, to see the world in his own absolutely unique, inimitable
and independent fashion.

Instead, he votes for the man who fits his standardized picture   13
of what a candidate "should" look like or sound like, buys the
goods that someone in his "situation" in life "should" own, lives
the life that others define for him. The mark of the stereotype person is that he never surprises us, that we do indeed have him
"typed." And no one fits this strait-jacket so perfectly as someone
whose opinions about other people are fixed and inflexible.

Nor do we suddenly drop our standardized pictures for a blind-   14
ing vision of the Truth. Sharp swings of ideas about people often

just substitute one stereotype for another. The true process of change is a slow one that adds bits and pieces of reality to the pictures in our heads, until gradually they take on some of the blurriness of life itself. Little by little, we learn not that Jews and Negroes and Catholics and Puerto Ricans are "just like everybody else"—for that, too, is a stereotype—but that each and every one of them is unique, special, different and individual. Often we do not even know that we have let a stereotype lapse until we hear someone saying, "all so-and-so's are like such-and-such," and we hear ourselves saying, "Well—maybe."

Can we speed the process along? Of course we can.   15

First, we can become aware of the standardized pictures in our   16
heads, in other people's heads, in the world around us.

Second, we can become suspicious of all judgments that we   17
allow exceptions to "prove." There is no more chastening thought
than that in the vast intellectual adventure of science, it takes but
one tiny exception to topple a whole edifice of ideas.

Third, we can learn to be chary of generalizations about peo-   18
ple. As F. Scott Fitzgerald once wrote, "Begin with an individual,
and before you know it you have created a type; begin with a
type, and you find you have created—nothing."

Most of the time, when we type-cast the world, we are not in   19
fact generalizing about people at all. We are only revealing the
embarrassing facts about the pictures that hang in the gallery of
stereotypes in our own heads.

UNDERSTANDING DETAILS

1. What are stereotypes?
2. When and how do we learn to stereotype?
3. What is another word for *prejudice* in Heilbroner's essay?
4. What are Heilbroner's three steps for discarding our stereotypical view of the world?

ANALYZING MEANING

1. Why do we stereotype people?
2. How does seeing the world in stereotypes "impoverish" us (paragraph 12), according to Heilbroner?
3. How can we change a stereotypical view of the world? What is the process we must go through to rid ourselves of stereotypes?

4. What do you think Walter Lippmann means when he says, "For the most part we do not first see, and then define; we define first, and then we see" (paragraph 9)? Explain your answer in detail.

DISCOVERING RHETORICAL STRATEGIES

1. To what extent does this essay convince you to look beyond stereotypes and discover the unique traits of individual people? Explain your answer.
2. What is the dominant type of appeal (see pages 504–506 of the chapter introduction) that Heilbroner uses in this essay? What parts of Heilbroner's argument are most persuasive to you? Why do you think they are persuasive?
3. Who do you think is Heilbroner's intended audience? Describe them in detail.
4. Which different rhetorical strategies does Heilbroner use to develop his argument? Give examples of each.

MAKING CONNECTIONS

1. Imagine that Heilbroner, Malcolm Cowley ("The View from 80"), Lewis Sawaquat ("For My Indian Daughter"), Harold Krents ("Darkness at Noon"), and Jill Leslie Rosenbaum and Meda Chesney-Lind ("Appearance and Delinquency: A Research Note") were discussing the peril of using stereotypes. Which particular stereotypes would they find most dangerous? Explain your answer.
2. How do you think Gloria Steinem ("The Politics of Muscle") would respond to Heilbroner's essay? In which principal ways does society stereotype women? Why does this happen so frequently? How damaging are these misconceptions?
3. Find three examples chosen from among the essays in this book in which, in Heilbroner's words, "stereotypes get in the way of . . . judgment" (paragraph 11).

IDEAS FOR DISCUSSION/WRITING

Preparing to Write

Write freely explaining your thoughts about stereotypes: How often do you form opinions of people from first impressions? Do you rely on features like names, looks, race, accent, or tone of voice to make these opinions? Do you find these initial impressions generally right or wrong after you get to know someone? How frequently do you take the time to learn about people as individuals? Are you conscious of stereotypes? Do you generally accept them or fight against them? Have you ever been stereotyped by others? How did it make you feel?

Choosing a Topic

1. Do you agree or disagree with the following claim in the final paragraph of Heilbroner's essay: "Most of the time, when we type-cast the world, we are not in fact generalizing about people at all. We are only revealing the embarrassing facts about the pictures that hang in the gallery of stereotypes in our own heads" (paragraph 19)? Direct an essay to your classmates in which you agree or disagree with this statement. Be sure to explain your reasoning carefully.

2. In your opinion, how serious a problem is stereotyping at your school or at your job? How is it manifested? Who suffers most from this discrimination? In a coherent essay, persuade your friends that stereotyping is or is not a serious social evil at your school or your workplace.

3. In an essay written for a group of employers, present a plan that will help individuals avoid stereotyping in the workplace. Explain the details of its implementation and its projected long-term effects.

4. Most popular television networks have Web sites. Pick a network you frequently watch or one that reflects your interests, and find its Web site. Explore the Web site, and note stereotypes in its text, photos, or advertisements. Write a persuasive argument in which you assert that stereotypes are an unnecessary feature of the Web site. Offer concrete recommendations for change. Following Heilbroner's example, use case studies, quotes, and statistics to support your argument.

Before beginning your essay, you might want to consult the checklists on page 511.

DAVE GROSSMAN   (1956–   )

We Are Training Our Kids to Kill

Lieutenant Colonel Dave Grossman is a retired professor of psychology and military science and a former Army Ranger who has recently founded a new field of scientific study he calls "killology," which investigates how and why people kill each other during wartime, the psychological costs of battle, the root causes of violent crime, and the process of healing that victims of violence must go through (see www.killology.com). Following a B.S. at Columbus College in Georgia (where he was elected to Phi Beta Kappa) and an M.Ed. at the University of Texas, Grossman joined the Army, where he rose quickly through the ranks to lieutenant colonel and served as a professor at both the United States Military Academy at West Point and as chair of the Department of Military Science at Arkansas State University. The author of two books—*On Killing: The Psychological Cost of Learning to Kill in War and Society* (1995) and *Stop Teaching Our Kids to Kill: A Call to Action Against TV, Movie, and Video Game Violence* (with Gloria deGaetano, 1999)—he spends nearly three hundred days on the road each year consulting and giving workshops about combat and violence. He also writes military science fiction and will soon publish a new book entitled *The Two-Space War*. His advice to students using *The Prose Reader* is to avoid a steady diet of violent visual images, which "will lobotomize the brain and make thinking and writing more difficult. If you cleanse your mind (particularly the frontal cortex) with periods of contemplation and reading, you will become a much better writer."

Preparing to Read

The following controversial essay, originally published in the *Saturday Evening Post* in July/August 1999, contains a clear, well-reasoned analysis of the dangers connected with violence on TV and in video games. The author, Dave Grossman, is especially concerned with the way in which these media sources actually train our children to kill.

Exploring Experience: Before you read this essay, think about your views on violence in the media: Do you think watching violence on television and in the movies or playing video games can lead to violent acts? How useful are movie ratings for violence and sex? At what age do you think children should be able to see violence without adult supervision or censorship? Who do you think should control the violence children are exposed to? To what extent should we censor violence in the media? What specific types of violent behavior should be regulated in the media? What should not be censored?

Learning Online: Go to your favorite online news source. How many of the headlines describe violent acts? Consider this while reading Grossman's argument.

I am from Jonesboro, Arkansas. I travel the world training medical, law enforcement, and U.S. military personnel about the realities of warfare. I try to make those who carry deadly force keenly aware of the magnitude of killing. Too many law enforcement and military personnel act like "cowboys," never stopping to think about who they are and what they are called to do. I hope I am able to give them a reality check.

So here I am, a world traveler and an expert in the field of "killology," when the (then) largest school massacre in American history happens in my hometown of Jonesboro, Arkansas. That was the March 24, 1998, schoolyard shooting deaths of four girls and a teacher. Ten others were injured, and two boys, ages 11 and 13, were jailed, charged with murder.

Virus of Violence

To understand the why behind Littleton, Jonesboro, Springfield, Pearl, and Paducah, and all the other outbreaks of this "virus of violence," we need to first understand the magnitude of the problem. The per capita murder rate doubled in this country between 1957—when the FBI started keeping track of the data—and 1992. A fuller picture of the problem, however, is indicated by the rate at which people are attempting to kill one another—the aggravated assault rate. That rate in America has gone from around 60 per 100,000 in 1957 to over 440 per 100,000 in 2002.

As bad as this is, it would be much worse were it not for two major factors.

The first is the increased imprisonment of violent offenders.   4
The prison population in America nearly quintupled between 1975 and 2002. According to criminologist John A. DiIulio, "dozens of credible empirical analyses . . . leave no doubt that the increased use of prisons averted millions of serious crimes." If it were not for our tremendous imprisonment rate (the highest of any industrialized nation), the aggravated assault rate and the murder rate would undoubtedly be even higher.

The second factor keeping the murder rate from being even   5
worse is medical technology. According to the U.S. Army Medical Service Corps, a wound that would have killed nine out of ten soldiers in World War II, nine out of ten could have survived in Vietnam. Thus, by a very conservative estimate, if we still had a 1940-level medical technology today, our murder rate would be ten times higher than it is. The murder rate has been held down by the development of sophisticated lifesaving skills and techniques, such as helicopter medevacs, 911 operators, paramedics, CPR, trauma centers, and medicines.

Today, both our assault rate and murder rate are at phenome-   6
nally high levels. Both are increasing worldwide. In Canada, according to their Center for Justice, per capita assaults increased almost fivefold between 1964 and 2002, attempted murder increased nearly sevenfold, and murders doubled. Similar trends can be seen in other countries in the per capita violent crime rates reported to Interpol between 1977 and 2002. In Australia and New Zealand, the assault rate increased approximately fourfold, and the murder rate nearly doubled in both nations. The assault rate tripled in Sweden and approximately doubled in Belgium, Denmark, England and Wales, France, Hungary, the Netherlands, and Scotland. Meanwhile, all these nations had an associated (but smaller) increase in murder.

This virus of violence is occurring worldwide. The explanation   7
for it has to be some new factor that is occurring in all of these countries. There are many factors involved, and none should be discounted: for example, the prevalence of guns in our society. But violence is rising in many nations with Draconian gun laws. And though we should never downplay child abuse, poverty, or racism, there is only one new variable present in each of these

countries that bears the exact same fruit: media violence presented as entertainment for children.

Killing Is Unnatural

Before retiring from the military, I spent almost a quarter of a 8 century as an army infantry officer and a psychologist, learning and studying how to enable people to kill. Believe me, we are very good at it. But it does not come naturally; you have to be taught to kill. And just as the army is conditioning people to kill, we are indiscriminately doing the same thing to our children, but without the safeguards.

After the Jonesboro killings, the head of the American Academy 9 of Pediatrics Task Force on Juvenile Violence came to town and said that children don't naturally kill. It is a learned skill. And they learn it from abuse and violence in the home and, most pervasively, from violence as entertainment in television, the movies, and interactive video games.

Killing requires training because there is a built-in aversion to 10 killing one's own kind. I can best illustrate this fact by drawing on my own military research into the act of killing.

We all know how hard it is to have a discussion with a fright- 11 ened or angry human being. Vasoconstriction, the narrowing of the blood vessels, has literally closed down the forebrain—that great gob of gray matter that makes one a human being and distinguishes one from a dog. When those neurons close down, the midbrain takes over and your thought processes and reflexes are indistinguishable from your dog's. If you've worked with animals, you have some understanding of what happens to frightened human beings on the battlefield. The battlefield and violent crime are in the realm of midbrain responses.

Within the midbrain, there is a powerful, God-given resistance 12 to killing your own kind. Every species, with a few exceptions, has a hardwired resistance to killing its own kind in territorial and mating battles. When animals with antlers and horns fight one another, they head-butt in a nonfatal fashion. But when they fight any other species, they go to the side to gut and gore. Piranhas will turn their fangs on anything, but they fight one another with flicks of the tail. Rattlesnakes will bite anything, but they wrestle one another. Almost every species has this hard-wired resistance to killing its own kind.

When we human beings are overwhelmed with anger and fear,   13 we slam head-on into that midbrain resistance that generally prevents us from killing. Only sociopaths—who by definition don't have that resistance—lack this innate violence immune system.

Throughout all human history, when humans have fought each   14 other, there has been a lot of posturing. Adversaries make loud noises and puff themselves up, trying to daunt the enemy. There is a lot of fleeing and submission. Ancient battles were nothing more than great shoving matches. It was not until one side turned and ran that most of the killing happened, and most of that was stabbing people in the back. All of the ancient military historians report that the vast majority of killing happened in pursuit when one side was fleeing.

In more modern times, the average firing rate was incredibly   15 low in Civil War battles. British author Paddy Griffith demonstrates in his book *The Battle Tactics of the Civil War* that the killing potential of the average Civil War regiment was anywhere from five hundred to a thousand men per minute. The actual killing rate was only one or two men per minute per regiment. At the Battle of Gettysburg, of the 27,000 muskets picked up from the dead and dying after the battle, 90 percent were loaded. This is an anomaly, because it took 90 percent of their time to load muskets and only 5 percent to fire. But even more amazing, of the thousands of loaded muskets, only half had multiple loads in the barrel—one had 23 loads in the barrel.

In reality, the average man would load his musket and bring it   16 to his shoulder, but he could not bring himself to kill. He would be brave, he would stand shoulder to shoulder, he would do what he was trained to do; but at the moment of truth, he could not bring himself to pull the trigger. And so he lowered the weapon and loaded it again. Of those who did fire, only a tiny percentage fired to hit. The vast majority fired over the enemy's head.

During World War II, U.S. Army Brig. Gen. S. L. A. Marshall   17 had a team of researchers study what soldiers did in battle. For the first time in history, they asked individual soldiers what they did in battle. They discovered that only 15 to 20 percent of the individual riflemen could bring themselves to fire at an exposed enemy soldier.

That is the reality of the battlefield. Only a small percentage of   18
soldiers are able and willing to participate. Men are willing to die.
They are willing to sacrifice themselves for their nation; but they
are not willing to kill. It is a phenomenal insight into human
nature; but when the military became aware of that, they systematically went about the process of trying to fix this "problem."
From the military perspective, a 15 percent firing rate among riflemen is like a 15 percent literacy rate among librarians. And fix it
the military did. By the Korean War, around 55 percent of the soldiers were willing to fire to kill. And by Vietnam, the rate rose to
over 90 percent.

The method in this madness: desensitization.   19

How the military increases the killing rate of soldiers in combat   20
is instructive because our culture today is doing the same thing to
our children. The training methods militaries use are brutalization,
classical conditioning, operant conditioning, and role modeling. I
will explain each of these in the military context and show how
these same factors are contributing to the phenomenal increase of
violence in our culture.

Brutalization and desensitization are what happens at boot   21
camp. From the moment you step off the bus, you are physically
and verbally abused: countless push-ups, endless hours at attention
or running with heavy loads, while carefully trained professionals
take turns screaming at you. Your head is shaved; you are herded
together naked and dressed alike, losing all individuality. This brutalization is designed to break down your existing mores and
norms, and force you to accept a new set of values that embraces
destruction, violence, and death as a way of life. In the end, you
are desensitized to violence and accept it as a normal and essential
survival skill in your brutal new world.

Something very similar to this desensitization toward violence is   22
happening to our children through violence in the media—but
instead of 18-year-olds, it begins at the age of 18 months when a
child is first able to discern what is happening on television. At that
age, a child can watch something happening on television and
mimic that action. But it isn't until children are six or seven years
old that the part of the brain kicks in that lets them understand
where information comes from. Even though young children have
some understanding of what it means to pretend, they are develop-
mentally unable to distinguish clearly between fantasy and reality.

When young children see somebody shot, stabbed, raped, bru- 23
talized, degraded, or murdered on TV, to them it is as though it
were actually happening. To have a child of three, four, or five
watch a "splatter" movie, learning to relate to a character for the
first 90 minutes and then in the last 30 minutes watch helplessly as
that new friend is hunted and brutally murdered, is the moral and
psychological equivalent of introducing your child to a friend, letting her play with that friend, and then butchering that friend in
front of your child's eyes. And this happens to our children hundreds upon hundreds of times.

Sure, they are told, "Hey, it's all for fun. Look, this isn't real; 24
it's just TV." And they nod their little heads and say OK. But they
can't tell the difference. Can you remember a point in your life or
in your children's lives when dreams, reality, and television were
all jumbled together? That's what it is like to be at that level of
psychological development. That's what the media are doing to
them.

The *Journal of the American Medical Association* published the 25
definitive epidemiological study on the impact of TV violence.
The research demonstrated what happened in numerous nations
after television made its appearance as compared to nations and
regions without TV. The two nations or regions being compared
are demographically and ethnically identical; only one variable is
different: the presence of television. In every nation, region, or
city with television, there is an immediate explosion of violence
on the playground, and within 15 years there is a doubling of the
murder rate. Why 15 years? That is how long it takes for the brutalization of a three-to five-year-old to reach the "prime crime
age." That is how long it takes for you to reap what you have
sown when you brutalize and desensitize a three-year-old.

Today the data linking violence in the media to violence in 26
society are superior to those linking cancer and tobacco. Hundreds
of sound scientific studies demonstrate the social impact of brutalization by the media. The *Journal of the American Medical Association* concluded that "the introduction of television in the 1950s
caused a subsequent doubling of the homicide rate, i.e., long-term
childhood exposure to television is a causal factor behind approximately one half of the homicides committed in the United States,
or approximately 10,000 homicides annually." The article went
on to say that ". . . if, hypothetically, television technology had

never been developed, there would today be 10,000 fewer homicides each year in the United States, 70,000 fewer rapes, and 700,000 fewer injurious assaults" (June 10, 1992).

Classical Conditioning

Classical conditioning is like the famous case of Pavlov's dogs   27
they teach in Psychology 101. The dogs learned to associate the ringing of the bell with food, and once conditioned, the dogs could not hear the bell without salivating.

The Japanese were masters at using classical conditioning with   28
their soldiers. Early in World War II, Chinese prisoners were placed in a ditch on their knees with their hands bound behind them. And one by one, a select few Japanese soldiers would go into the ditch and bayonet "their" prisoner to death. This is a horrific way to kill another human being. Up on the bank, countless other young soldiers would cheer them on in their violence. Comparatively few soldiers actually killed in these situations, but by making the others watch and cheer, the Japanese were able to use these kinds of atrocities to classically condition a very large audience to associate pleasure with human death and suffering. Immediately afterwards, the soldiers who had been spectators were treated to sake, the best meal they had in months, and to so-called comfort girls. The result? They learned to associate committing violent acts with pleasure.

The Japanese found these kinds of techniques to be extraordi-   29
narily effective at quickly enabling very large numbers of soldiers to commit atrocities in the years to come. Operant conditioning (which we will look at shortly) teaches you to kill, but classical conditioning is a subtle but powerful mechanism that teaches you to like it.

This technique is so morally reprehensible that there are very   30
few examples of it in modern U.S. military training, but there are some clear-cut examples of it being done by the media to our children. What is happening to our children is the reverse of the aversion therapy portrayed in the movie *A Clockwork Orange.* In *A Clockwork Orange,* a brutal sociopath, a mass murderer, is strapped to a chair and forced to watch violent movies while he is injected with a drug that nauseates him. So he sits and gags and retches as he watches the movies. After hundreds of repetitions of this, he

associates violence with nausea. And it limits his ability to be violent.

We are doing the exact opposite: Our children watch vivid pic-   31
tures of human suffering and death, and they learn to associate it with their favorite soft drink and candy bar, or their girlfriend's perfume.

After the Jonesboro shootings, one of the high-school teachers   32
told me how her students reacted when she told them about the shootings at the middle school. "They laughed," she told me with dismay. A similar reaction happens all the time in movie theaters when there is bloody violence. The young people laugh and cheer and keep right on eating popcorn and drinking pop. We have raised a generation of barbarians who have learned to associate violence with pleasure, like the Romans cheering and snacking as the Christians were slaughtered in the Colosseum.

The result is a phenomenon that functions much like AIDS,   33
a phenomenon I call AVIDS—Acquired Violence Immune Deficiency Syndrome. AIDS has never killed anybody. It destroys your immune system, and then other diseases that shouldn't kill you become fatal. Television violence by itself does not kill you. It destroys your violence immune system and conditions you to derive pleasure from violence. And once you are at close range with another human being and it's time for you to pull that trigger, Acquired Violence Immune Deficiency Syndrome can destroy your midbrain resistance.

Operant Conditioning

The third method the military uses is operant conditioning, a   34
very powerful repetitive procedure of stimulus-response, stimulus-response. A benign example is the use of flight simulators to train pilots. An airline pilot in training sits in front of a flight simulator for endless hours; when a particular warning light goes on, he is taught to react in a certain way. When another warning light goes on, a different reaction is required. Stimulus-response, stimulus-response, stimulus-response. One day the pilot is actually flying a jumbo jet; the plane is going down, and 300 people are screaming behind him. He is wetting his seat cushion, and he is scared out of his wits; but he does the right thing. Why? Because he has been conditioned to respond reflexively to this particular crisis.

When people are frightened or angry, they will do what they   35
have been conditioned to do. In fire drills, children learn to file
out of the school in orderly fashion. One day there is a real fire,
and they are frightened out of their wits; but they do exactly what
they have been conditioned to do, and it saves their lives.

The military and law enforcement community have made   36
killing a conditioned response. This has substantially raised the firing rate on the modern battlefield. Whereas infantry training in
World War II used bull's-eye targets, now soldiers learn to fire at
realistic, man-shaped silhouettes that pop into their field of view.
That is the stimulus. The trainees have only a split second to
engage the target. The conditioned response is to shoot the target,
and then it drops. Stimulus-response, stimulus-response, stimulus-
response—soldiers or police officers experience hundreds of repetitions. Later, when soldiers are on the battlefield or a police officer is walking a beat and somebody pops up with a gun, they will
shoot reflexively and shoot to kill. We know that 75 to 80 percent
of the shooting on the modern battlefield is the result of this kind
of stimulus-response training.

Now, if you're a little troubled by that, how much more should   37
we be troubled by the fact that every time a child plays an interactive point-and-shoot video game, he is learning the exact same
conditioned reflex and motor skills?

I was an expert witness in a murder case in South Carolina   38
offering mitigation for a kid who was facing the death penalty. I
tried to explain to the jury that interactive video games had conditioned him to shoot a gun to kill. He had spent hundreds of dollars on video games learning to point and shoot, point and shoot.
One day he and his buddy decided it would be fun to rob the local
convenience store. They walked in, and he pointed a snub-nosed
.38 pistol at the clerk's head. The clerk turned to look at him, and
the defendant shot reflexively from about six feet. The bullet hit
the clerk right between the eyes—which is a pretty remarkable
shot with that weapon at that range—and killed this father of two.
Afterward, we asked the boy what happened and why he did it. It
clearly was not part of the plan to kill the guy—it was being videotaped from six different directions. He said, "I don't know. It was
a mistake. It wasn't supposed to happen."

In the military and law-enforcement worlds, the right option is   39
often not to shoot. But you never, ever put your money in that

video machine with the intention of not shooting. There is always some stimulus that sets you off. And when he was excited, and his heart rate went up, and vasoconstriction closed his forebrain down, this young man did exactly what he was conditioned to do: he reflexively pulled the trigger, shooting accurately just like all those times he played video games.

This process is extraordinarily powerful and frightening. The   40
result is ever more "homemade" sociopaths who kill reflexively. Our children are learning how to kill and learning to like the idea of killing; and then we have the audacity to say, "Oh my goodness, what's wrong?"

One of the boys involved in the Jonesboro shootings (and they   41
are just boys) had a fair amount of experience shooting real guns. The other one, to the best of our knowledge, had almost no experience shooting. Between them, those two boys fired 27 shots from a range of over 100 yards, and they hit 15 people. That's pretty remarkable shooting. We run into these situations often— kids who have never picked up a gun in their lives pick up a real gun and are incredibly accurate. Why? Video games.

UNDERSTANDING DETAILS

1. According to Grossman, what is the "virus of violence" (paragraph 3)?
2. What evidence does the author use to argue that "killing is unnatural"?
3. What three methods does the military use to train its soldiers to kill?
4. How does Grossman claim we are training our children to kill?

ANALYZING MEANING

1. What two factors does the author believe control the murder rate in the United States? How do these factors affect this rate?
2. How are the techniques used in video games similar to those taught in military training?
3. How did the U.S. military train more soldiers to actually fire their guns?
4. How can we control this epidemic of violence that Grossman outlines?

DISCOVERING RHETORICAL STRATEGIES

1. What do you think Grossman's purpose is in this essay?
2. Who do you think would be most interested in this essay?
3. What effect do you think this essay will have on parents?
4. Describe the writer's point of view in a complete sentence.

MAKING CONNECTIONS

1. To what extent would Grossman, Brent Staples ("A Brother's Murder"), and Barbara Ehrenreich ("The Ecstasy of War") agree that violence is encoded in our human DNA? What outside influences, according to these authors, make us a more violent culture? Which of the three authors makes the most convincing case for his or her point of view? Explain your answer.
2. Imagine a conversation between Grossman, Kimberly Wozencraft ("Notes from the Country Club"), Jimmy Santiago Baca ("Past Present"), and Jill Leslie Rosenbaum and Meda Chesney-Lind ("Appearance and Delinquency: A Research Note") about the relationship between societal pressures and incarceration. Why do you think our jails are so crowded? What can be done about this massive increase in America's prison population?
3. How do you think Bill Cosby ("The Baffling Question"), Robert Ramirez ("The Barrio"), Mary Pipher ("Beliefs About Families"), and bell hooks ("Justice: Childhood Love Lessons") would each respond to Grossman's implication that parents need to be more vigilant in monitoring what their children watch on television? What is your own opinion on this issue?

IDEAS FOR DISCUSSION/WRITING

Preparing to Write

Write freely about your feelings concerning censorship: Should violence on TV be censored in any way? Why or why not? At what age can children safely watch violence in the media? Do you believe a relationship exists between watching violence and acting in a violent manner? Who is most responsible for restricting or editing the violence that children see?

Choosing a Topic

1. *Time* magazine has asked you to respond directly to Grossman's article. Do you think his argument about the relationship between children and video games is reasonable? Give specific examples to support your contention.

2. As an apprentice at a TV station, you have been asked to represent your age group by giving your opinion on the network's inclusion of violence in their programming. What is your opinion concerning TV violence? In what ways do you think your opinion represents the consensus of American society as a whole?

3. Research and describe the censorship practices of another country. Explain specifically how that country's views on censorship are carried out in practice. Give as many examples as possible to support your explanation.

4. What is the most popular current video game? How violent do you think it is? Do you believe that video games, movies, television shows, or popular music influence youth violence? Write an argument in which you take a position regarding this controversial issue. Following Grossman's style, use several different types of examples to support your claims.

Before beginning your essay, you might want to consult the checklists on page 511.

Media Coverage

The next two essays debate the recent habit of "embedding" journalists in combat units. The first article, in favor of embedding, is by David Shaw, a feature writer for the *Los Angeles Times* who has won more than twenty-five major journalism awards from such organizations as the American Bar Association, the Los Angeles Press Club, and the American Political Science Organization. His most prestigious honor, the Pulitzer Prize, was awarded in 1991 for his series on media coverage of the McMartin Pre-School child molestation trial. His most recent books include *Wilt: Just Like Any Other 7-Foot Black Millionaire Who Lives Next Door* (with Wilt Chamberlain, 1973), *Journalism Today* (1977), *Press Watch: A Provocative Look at How Newspapers Report the News* (1984), *The Pleasure Police* (1996), and *The Cheapskate's Guide to Weddings and Honeymoons* (1996). Good reporters, he claims, should never lose touch with the people and events they cover: "Professional detachment often leads to personal detachment—detachment from most readers' everyday concerns. That reinforces the elitist tendencies that come from education and a good income."

Born in Phoenix, Arizona, Justin Ewers, representing the "con" side of the argument, was educated at Stanford University, where he earned a B.A. and an M.A. in history and was a member of the swimming team, specializing in freestyle sprints and the backstroke. After graduation, he worked at *Sunset Magazine* in Los Angeles for a year, then moved to *U.S. News & World Report*, where he has been a feature reporter for the past four years. His assignments in education and twentieth-century history have generated a number of award-winning articles on topics ranging from the Treaty of Versailles and the Faulklands War to war memorial history, which included research on "Jarhead" marines. When he lived in Los Angeles, he enjoyed surfing but had to give up the sport when he moved to his present home in Washington, D.C. His advice to students using *The Prose Reader* is that "good writing takes time and effort." "Several drafts of an article are usually required," he explains, "because ideas generally tumble out in pieces. You'll often have to sleep on an idea for it to come into perfect focus."

Preparing to Read

These two essays, which concentrate in particular on media and the War on Iraq, were written a day apart in the middle of a period of intense combat. Ewing's essay originally appeared in *U.S. News & World Report* on April 7, 2003, while Shaw's article was first published in the *Los Angeles Times* on April 6, 2003. They present opposing perspectives on the custom of embedding journalists in active military units.

Exploring Experience: Before you begin reading these essays, think for a minute about your opinion of the media: Do you believe the press does an accurate job of reporting information to the public? How could it do a better job? What types of reporting does it do best? What are its main flaws? Do you think the press should have total freedom? Why or why not? Do you think it should be limited in any way? If so, how? Do your expectations about news coverage change when we are at war? What war reporting do you expect? Why is this coverage important to you?

Learning Online: Select three online news sources, and briefly review their headlines. Does each source cover different stories? Are the stories presented in unique ways? Consider your observations while reading Shaw's and Ewers's articles.

DAVID SHAW   (1943–   )

Embedded Reporters Make
for Good Journalism

I'm thoroughly baffled by my journalistic colleagues who com- 1
plain about embedding reporters with U.S. combat units in
Iraq.

I've heard essentially two criticisms of embedding. One is that 2
the more than 500 reporters hunkered down with soldiers will
inevitably focus on the small picture, rather than the big picture;
they'll cover the individual battles their units engage in and the
human-interest stories of individual soldiers, instead of giving their
readers and viewers an overall account of the war.

The other complaint is that embedded reporters are not just 3
embedded but—inevitably—in bed with the military, providing
coverage that "translates into victories for the U.S. military in their
concerted propaganda campaign against Iraq, its allies, and its sympathizers," as Jack Shafer wrote recently on Slate.com.

Embedded journalists, according to this argument, become so 4
dependent on their military partners for their stories and their
safety that they come to identify with the soldiers, thus abandoning their professional detachment and allowing themselves to be
co-opted into reporting more favorably—and less skeptically—
than the facts may warrant.

All this may well be true. And there's no question that the 5
confluence of modern technology and a radical change in the
Pentagon's approach to combat access has given embedded journalists an unprecedented opportunity for which they're deeply
grateful.

"What you're seeing is truly historic television and journalism," 6
Walter Rodgers of CNN said, with more than a hint of pride, one
day recently as a tank from "his" unit went rumbling across both
the Iraqi landscape and millions of TV screens.

But how can reporters—any reporters, anywhere—complain 7
about too much access? Access and information are our life's
blood. In Iraq, embedding with front-line units is "a reporter's
dream," as ABC's Ted Koppel puts it. Reporters—and their

editors—just have to decide how best to turn that dream-come-true into useful coverage.

I see nothing wrong—and a great deal right—with real-time 8
television stories and pictures and next-day newspaper accounts of
individual battles and the triumphs, tragedies and daily routine of
individual soldiers. Nor am I terribly concerned with reporters
falling prey to some more or less beneficent version of the
Stockholm syndrome and identifying with the soldiers they're
accompanying.

Much as I hate to agree with Donald Rumsfeld, I think the 9
Secretary of Defense is absolutely right when he said during a
recent Pentagon briefing, "What we're seeing [on television] is not
the war in Iraq. What we're seeing are slices of the war in Iraq."

A slice is all that reporters—no matter how good—can give 10
viewers (or readers) if they're covering a war, or any big, ongoing
story, on a daily basis. What reporters try to do is make that slice
as accurate and fair and responsible as they can. What better way
to do that in a war than by traveling with the troops waging the
war? And what better way to tell their fellow Americans what the
war is like for individual soldiers—who, after all, have the most to
risk (their lives)—than by providing some details on their routine,
their thoughts, their hopes, and their fears?

Again, it's then up to the editors and news directors back home 11
to put all that in context, to provide the necessary balance and big-picture perspective.

I've heard the complaints that the reportage of embedded jour- 12
nalists is so immediate, so dramatic, so unprecedented that it
shoves big-picture journalism out of the picture.

Baloney. 13

The all-news networks waste hours every day broadcasting 14
speculation and journalistic food fights, repeating each develop-ment *ad nauseam* and interviewing former generals whose analyses
and second-guessing are often as laughably misinformed as those
armchair experts who are now predicting the Dodgers will win the
World Series.

There would be plenty of time for the big picture were not TV 15
so enamored of the big mouth.

Meanwhile, the better newspapers are also devoting huge 16
resources to the war—and they do provide the big picture,
every day.

As for the alleged loss of independence and objectivity of the   17
embedded reporter, well, sure, any reporter who spends a lot of
time in close proximity to sources and subjects has to guard against
the tendency to identify with them, to feel competing and conflicting loyalties. It's tempting to overstate their accomplishments
and overlook their shortcomings, either unwittingly or in a conscious desire to curry favor and ensure future access.

Reporters who cover the White House, the police beat, the   18
Lakers, the movie studios, or any other beat have to deal with this
problem daily. Of course, it's more difficult in a combat situation.
Much more difficult.

Wanting to stay in the good graces of sources so they'll return   19
your phone call or let you in the locker room is not remotely as
compelling as wanting to stay in the good graces of sources who
could save your life. But the principle is the same. Editors and
news directors thousands of miles from Iraq, who don't have that
same sense of dependency, have a professional obligation to evaluate and decide when, how, and whether to use the stories and
pictures their embedded reporters and photographers send them.

Moreover, given the traditional skepticism of journalists here   20
and the multiplicity of their outlets, the burgeoning number of
antiwar activists, the ubiquity of the Internet, and the presence of
many reporters in Iraq who are not embedded—"unilaterals," in
the argot of this war—I can't imagine any news outlet except Fox
getting away with gung-ho coverage for very long.

Some second thoughts?   21

In fact, we've already seen so much questioning, critical cover-   22
age of the war—Did the U.S. military underestimate the Iraqis?
Did the invasion start too soon, with too few troops? Was the initial strategy misguided?—that the administration has dispatched all
of its top policy makers and talking heads to make the rounds of
the weekend TV shows to defend their war plans and praise the
progress of the war effort.

I wouldn't be surprised if the Pentagon comes to regret having   23
agreed to the embedding process.

It embedded reporters because it realized, as ABC's John   24
McWethy told me, that "a huge part of winning any war has to
do with the world's perception of how that war is being fought."

The White House was so confident that its mission was just and   25
its victory assured that it wanted independent witnesses on hand to

show the world its righteous triumph—and the heinous acts it was sure the enemy would commit.

Those heinous acts have already begun. But victory hasn't   26 come as quickly or as easily as the White House expected, and I'd be willing to bet that if U.S. casualties mount, if the war drags on for months instead of weeks, and if embedded journalists start providing daily accounts, in living color, of failed missions, civilian casualties, and combat atrocities, they may find themselves unembedded faster than you can say John Wayne.

Just look at the story William Branigin of the *Washington Post*   27 filed last week while being embedded with the Army's 3rd Infantry Division. Soldiers in that division killed seven women and children in a car the troops said failed to stop, despite commands and warning shots.

Branigin's story quoted Capt. Ronny Johnson, who ordered   28 the warning shots, as subsequently telling his platoon leader, "You just . . . killed a family because you didn't fire a warning shot soon enough!"

The Pentagon has ordered an investigation, but I suspect that   29 military brass wasn't happy with Branigin's account—and we should be grateful for it, an account we would not have had if he had not been embedded.

For now, embedding is giving us a rare window on war. The   30 critics should stop carping.

JUSTIN EWERS   (1976–   )

Is the New News Good News?

Before the current war in Iraq began, CBS news anchor Dan   1
Rather voiced the concern of many in the news business
troubled by the idea of "embedding" journalists in active
military units. "There's a pretty fine line," he warned, "between
being embedded and being entombed." A little over a week in,
however, Keith Olbermann on MSNBC had already dubbed the
embedding of journalists a "transcendent thing." Olbermann
praised one of his own network's "embeds" for offering a satellite
phone to an injured marine so the young man could call home.
"Somewhere right now," said the former sportscaster, "a journalism professor is telling a student, 'Don't get involved with the subject of your stories,' and now you know how wrong that really is."

And there, many media experts say, is the rub. Five hundred   2
journalists are currently embedded with American and British military units in Iraq. And with a recent survey indicating that 86 percent of Americans are getting their war news from television, the
TV embeds especially have emerged as the country's primary
source of news on the ground in Iraq. They have wowed viewers
with their high-tech broadcasts and up-to-the-minute reports,
making Pentagon and CentCom briefings seem banal by comparison. But among historians and media experts, their performance
has revived the debate about how much frontline journalists are
able to maintain their objectivity during wartime—and how much
their reporting really tells us about war.

Before Iraq, American journalists had never been "embedded"   3
or assigned exclusively to specific military units (and forbidden to
move around without them). In both world wars, reporters could
join individual groups for days at a time, and they were usually free
to roam across the battlefield as far as their courage would allow.
Reporters were issued uniforms; some even carried weapons. All
bore the weight of heavy censorship, though a few, most notably
Ernie Pyle, found a way around the many restrictions imposed by
the military in World War II. Not allowed to report what was
actually happening on the field, Pyle, a correspondent for the now
defunct *Washington Daily News,* still brought the war home. He

wrote, for example, about how it felt to be a GI in the Pacific, washing your socks in your helmet and complaining about the food, and he asked soldiers for their own thoughts on the war. "Pyle's great gift," says Phillip Knightley, a former correspondent for the *Times* of London and author of *The First Casualty: The War Correspondent as Hero and Myth-Maker From the Crimea to Kosovo,* "was to find the voice of the soldier."

Cold war. By the time of Vietnam, television allowed reporters   4 even more of a chance to bring home the view from the front. But as the war turned sour, so too did reports from the field. And the results put relations between the media and the military into deep-freeze. "To this day," says Knightley, "there are generals in the military who remain absolutely convinced that the media lost the war in Vietnam."

The result—in Grenada, Panama, and the first Gulf War—was   5 a denial of access to the action. The first President George Bush famously said in 1990 that media coverage of the Gulf War would "not be a new Vietnam"—meaning U.S. forces wouldn't face negative broadcasts from the field. Journalists were sequestered in briefing rooms and spoon-fed gun-camera footage and rosy reports of success. As recently as Afghanistan, that was still the rule. But the rise of al Jazeera and other non-American media outlets convinced the military that it could not win the public relations battle if American journalists were to be muzzled. As Secretary of Defense Donald Rumsfeld put it in a memo to top officials, "We need to tell the factual story—good or bad—before others seed the media with disinformation, as they most certainly will."

Enter today's embeds, armed with digital video cameras and   6 satellite phones. Their reports from Umm Qasr early in the war revealed a gritty and chaotic scene, soldiers scrambling to the top of sandy berms and firing mercilessly on Iraqi positions. Then an embed happened to be on hand when a soldier from the 101st Airborne Division attacked his comrades with grenades. "If it weren't for the embedding program," says Robert Wiener, a veteran war correspondent who produced much of CNN's coverage from Baghdad in the Persian Gulf War, "I doubt the American public would have heard about that fragging incident for a long, long time—maybe even years." Indeed, the news was on American television screens only minutes after it occurred—a far cry from the weeks-old newsreels of the world wars. Even in Vietnam, says

Wiener, reels had to be shipped to Tokyo or Bangkok before they could be sent via satellite to the United States.

Today's insta-news has its price, however. Sitting on top of a   7
Bradley fighting vehicle in southern Iraq might tell you a lot about one particular skirmish—but not necessarily anything about the overall state of the war. "The truth is," says Daniel Hallin, a professor of political science at the University of California–San Diego, "all journalists are caught up in a lot of cross-pressures in wartime," to be patriotic and supportive of the troops but at the same time objective. And that's exacerbated on the front lines. "Historically speaking," he says, "I don't think journalists on the ground keep their objectivity very well in wartime."

Point of view. Indeed, a study of the 23 British journalists accom-   8
panying the British Task Force in the Falkland Islands war discovered that the men covering the British troops began, in only a short time, to strongly identify with their units. "They called themselves 'troopy groupies,'" says Howard Tumber, professor of sociology at City University, London, and coauthor of the study. Many of the reporters, Tumber says, look back now on their coverage as "very unjournalistic." "They weren't being knowingly deceitful," he says, "but they sort of colored their copy, wrote more optimistically about things, didn't try to question the direction of the war."

"There's no such thing as objectivity in wartime," says Wiener.   9
"What there is is balance." To be sure, the swarms of pundits and armchair generals filling time on the TV dial can sometimes provide the needed breadth and analysis. But viewers should keep in mind, Wiener says, that the embeds are under a great deal of pressure to conform to the military's view of what's happening on the ground. Says Hallin, "We'd be very naive if we imagined that what we're hearing from these guys is the whole truth." In the meantime, the best of their reporting will continue to provide some truths about war; the full story will take more time to be written.

UNDERSTANDING DETAILS

1. What are the main arguments of Shaw ("Embedded Reporters Make for Good Journalism") and Ewers ("Is the New News Good News?")? Explain the principal disagreement between their two points of view.

2. What specific arguments would you add to both sides of this debate?

3. According to Ewers, what percent of Americans get their news from television broadcasts? How does this important statistic affect the issue of embedding?
4. How does Shaw counter the two main aguments he cites against embedding journalists in military units?

ANALYZING MEANING

1. Which side of this particular argument seems most convincing to you? Which examples or statistics are most persuasive?
2. Ewers implies that the reports we receive from embedded journalists are biased and sometimes even inaccurate. To what does he attribute this assertion?
3. Do you agree with Shaw when he says, "A slice is all that reporters . . . can give viewers (or readers) if they're covering a war, or any big, ongoing story, on a daily basis" (paragraph 10)? Explain your answer.
4. Both articles give us a unique view of embedding from the front lines of a war. Do you think Ewers and Shaw would change their opinions about embedding when the major battles are over? Would they say embedding was effective or ineffective from a journalistic perspective?

DISCOVERING RHETORICAL STRATEGIES

1. Who do you think is the intended audience for each of these essays? Are there any important differences between these audiences in your opinion?
2. Describe the tone or mood of each essay and explain whether you think that particular voice was the most effective for the author's purpose.
3. How does the organization of the two essays differ? What is the general organizing principle in each essay?
4. What other rhetorical strategies does each essay use to make its point? Give examples of each strategy.

MAKING CONNECTIONS

1. Imagine that David Shaw and Justin Ewers were having a round-table conversation about the media with Robert

Heilbroner ("Don't Let Stereotypes Warp Your Judgment"). How strongly do you think each of these authors would argue that the process of embedding journalists during wartime helps counter the spread of military stereotypes?

2. To what extent are William Least Heat-Moon ("Red, White and Blue Highways"), Jessica Mitford ("Behind the Formaldehyde Curtain"), and Sucheng Chan ("You're Short, Besides!") "embedded" in the topics described in their essays? How is their point of view altered by their immersion in the subjects they describe? Has their "professional detachment" (Shaw, paragraph 4) been compromised in any way? If so, how?

3. Compare and contrast the use of examples in the essays written by Shaw and Ewers. Which argument seems most persuasive to you? Explain your answer.

IDEAS FOR DISCUSSION/WRITING

Preparing to Write

Write freely about your opinion of the media: What do you think of the media in general? In your opinion, is any one form of media more accurate, reliable, or interesting than the others? On what do you base this judgment? What do you think the main goals of the press should be in reporting information to the public? What guidelines do you think it follows in reporting the news? What form of media do you rely on most for the news? Why do you prefer this particular media?

Choosing a Topic

1. Your school newspaper has been charged with unethical reporting, and the school administration is considering whether to limit its freedom. The president of the college is soliciting opinions, and you decide to send your suggestions in essay form to the president. Justify your opinions as thoroughly as possible.

2. The media are a vital part of our lives today. In what ways do they affect the morals and values of our society? Of us as individuals? How much freedom should the media be allowed to have? In an essay written for your peers, write a set of guidelines for keeping the media focused and accurate. Explain the details of these guidelines.

3. Choose an important national or international event from the recent past, and analyze the media's coverage of that event. Consider newspapers, TV newscasts, *Time, Newsweek,* and several other sources of information. How did the coverage of these different types of media vary? Now that the event has passed, are you aware that any of these sources was more accurate than the others? More interesting? More ethical? Present a summary of your findings and your conclusions in an essay addressed to your classmates.

4. Shaw and Ewers both address the increased amount of information provided by the daily media. In your opinion, how does the Internet contribute to this increase? Do you believe the Internet can provide too much information? Why or why not? Write an essay in which you argue your position. Use quotes from Shaw's and Ewers's articles, as well as other news articles, case studies, or statistics, to support your claims.

Before beginning your essay, you might want to consult the checklists on page 511.

Immigration

The following essays take opposite views on the question of immigration controls. The first, by Michael Scott, argues in favor of more stringent restraint on immigration into the United States. Scott is a graduate of the UCLA School of Management currently employed as a national sales manager for a high-tech electronics firm. His interest in immigration began twelve years ago when he stumbled upon nearly one hundred illegal aliens hiding in the scrub brush in Newport Beach, California. His advice to students using *The Prose Reader* is to concentrate on topics they feel passionate about: "The first draft of an essay should come straight from the heart or gut. Don't worry about spelling or punctuation at that early stage. Just let it all hang out. Then go back and smooth everything out to create the finished product."

Richard Raynor, who takes the other side of the immigration question, is a British-born journalist and Cambridge graduate who has published six novels, among them *The Elephant* (1992), *The Blue Suit: Memoir of a Crime* (1995), *Los Angeles Without a Map* (1997), and *The Cloud Sketcher* (2001, soon to be made into a movie starring Brad Pitt). His advice for aspiring authors is to "write about the kinds of things you like to read . . . something that will make you want to turn the page. As John Cleese says in a Monty Python sketch, 'it's not just getting the right number of words—it's getting them in the right order.'"

Preparing to Read

The following essays were first published in *The Social Contract* (2000) and *New York Times Magazine* (1996) respectively. They take opposing viewpoints on the many complex issues associated with illegal immigration.

Exploring Experience: Before you begin to read these essays, think about immigration and its effect on society: How do you feel about illegal immigration? Whom should we stop from entering our borders? Whom should we let through? Why is immigration such a major issue in the United States? What do immigrants generally bring to America? What do they take from our country? Do you worry about the expense of illegal aliens? What other issues concern you about this topic?

Learning Online: Visit the U.S. government's Bureau of Citizenship and Immigration Services Web site (http:// www. immigration.gov). Click on the "FAQ" link, and select "Statistics" from its alphabetized list. Read the most recently published statistical report. Pay special attention to the number of illegal immigrants, their regional location, and their average monthly wage. Consider how each writer uses statistics to develop his argument.

MICHAEL SCOTT   (1948–   )

America Must Take Stronger Measures to Halt Illegal Immigration

I n 1991, I accidentally stumbled upon a botched illegal immi-   1
gration operation on a nearby Southern California beach—in
broad daylight. Nearly one-hundred illegal immigrants were
hiding in a few tiny gullies, partially protected by a cadre of look-
outs, presumably waiting for transportation to get them to their
destinations. Neither the local police nor Los Angeles Immigration
and Naturalization Service (INS) showed much concern. This
resulted in my researching the background and realities of illegal
immigration, and the more I learned, the worse it got. We've got
a ticking time bomb on our hands, made worse by legions of government officials who just slumber on or push their heads deeper
into the sand to curry flavor with those who support this relentless
invasion. Just as bad, lots of Americans have been sucker-punched
into inaction by threats of being called "racist," "bigot" and
sundry yada yada.

Then, in 1999, I had a conversation with Arizona rancher   2
Roger Barnett, whose property is under year-round siege by
hordes of illegal aliens. His Chochise County border sector is
overwhelmed by about 475,000 illegal aliens annually. Although
Barnett has apprehended over 1000 illegal aliens on his property
and turned them over to the Border Patrol, he's anything but a
vigilante. Roger has lived in Douglas, Arizona, all of his 50-some
years and is infuriated by the on-going destruction of his property
caused by incessant swarms of illegal immigrants, as well as by the
repeated failures of the INS to stem this relentless flood. Barnett
and his neighbors have had it with an unmerciful stealth migration
that generates mountains of rotting garbage, piles of discarded dia-
pers, food containers and plastic water bottles, and sundry filth
everywhere—exacerbated by the stench of excrement, poisoned
(or throat-slit) pets and livestock, and lots of stolen property that
wasn't tied down.

Of special ire is Barnett's 80-year-old widowed neighbor who   3
lives behind her chain-link fence, with a shotgun and pistol always

near by, and who's afraid to come out at night and challenge the hoards who have ruined her crops and garden and made her a virtual prisoner in her own home. She's afraid to buy more guard dogs since the last two were poisoned, probably by "coyotes."

Costs of Illegal Immigration

One look at the ravages of illegal immigration in California is   4
enough to make most Americans sick. At least 40 percent of the nation's 6 million illegal immigrants are here. From a base of 2.4 million illegal immigrants already present, they just keep coming—120,000 net new illegals each year into California (300,000 nationally), and the horrendous social costs just keep rising. There are 408,000 illegal immigrant K–12 students to educate at a cost to California taxpayers of approximately $2.2 billion annually, for example. Never mind that these students can't work, drive, or vote once they graduate, unless they obtain fraudulent documents.

Taxpayers subsidize 96,000 illegal immigrant births in statewide   5
county hospitals (200,000 nationally) at a yearly cost of $352 million. Then we have annual . . . [welfare] costs for these new citizen children of nearly $552 million. Add another $557 million to incarcerate 23,000 illegal alien felons in California, plus $60 million health care costs for various services, and we're over $3.7 billion annually—out of our pockets, and against our overwhelming opposition to such outrages.

Eliminating this brutal migratory devastation involves two basic   6
actions—enforcing our own immigration laws and accepting the ugly reality that "we've met the enemy and it is us."

Enforcing the Law

Three fundamental law enforcement steps must be taken to   7
break the back of illegal immigration. First, our borders must be sealed. No more baloney about how difficult this might be. The INS instituted a Border Patrol crackdown in 1994 in the El Paso sector and then took it to San Diego a year later. In 1993, 90 percent of all illegal aliens crossed at border cities. Today [in 2000], two-thirds cross in remote areas. In 1994, in the San Diego sector, 42 percent of all illegals surged through a 14-mile corridor near

Imperial Beach. Another 22.6 percent entered in and around El Paso. Both sectors are now almost impregnable, as these flows have become trickles. So today's illegals are going where it's easier to get across, like Douglas, Arizona. The inescapable conclusion is that the crackdown has succeeded where sufficient resources have been applied. This isn't a matter of insufficient resources or wherewithal; it's a matter of insufficient willpower, as well as a writing-off of those individuals and organizations who want illegal immigration to succeed.

The next critical law enforcement step is to prosecute employ-   8
ers who hire illegal aliens. The Justice Department is hardly lifting a finger in this area. If there were no jobs, most illegal aliens would leave, or most wouldn't come in the first place. The fantasy of illegal immigration cheerleaders that the economy would collapse without illegal labor simply doesn't wash. Since when don't we enforce laws (or break them) in accordance with our own standards of right and wrong? I sometimes speed on California interstates, and I'm prepared for the fines if caught. But this doesn't excuse me from punishment nor the California Highway Patrol (CHP) from enforcement.

This baloney about the need for "guest workers" is pure bunk.   9
Both the California Division of Labor and the General Accounting Office (GAO) have confirmed there are currently two farm workers for every agricultural job in California. This glut of farm workers has depressed agricultural wages over the past twenty years, in inflation adjusted terms, by 20 percent and spawned deplorable working conditions.

Job opportunities for low-skilled workers have been declining   10
for three decades. The continued influx of low-skilled, uneducated immigrants has depressed earnings and limited opportunities. Income disparity has widened as a result of too many low-skilled workers pursuing too few jobs.

A University of California (Davis) agricultural economist (and   11
several other noted researchers) published "Poverty Amid Prosperity," a compilation of research findings on "The processes of immigration and its unexamined impacts on cities and towns" (July 1997; The Urban Institute Press). They offered the following analysis (on pp. 89–90) of the impact of farm worker wage increases on both grower expenses and the price of food:

And suppose that the entire cost of higher farm wages is passed on to consumers, so that the annual cost of the farm labor used to produce the fresh fruit consumed by the average American household rises from $8.60 to $13 and the cost of farm labor rises from $10.20 to $15. If these increased farm labor costs were completely passed on to consumers, spending on fresh fruits and vegetables eaten at home for a typical 2.6 person consumer unit would increase by less than $10, from $270 to almost $280.

I'd welcome the opportunity to pay higher consumer prices to   12
rid our land of illegal immigrants. We'd lift an enormous financial albatross from our backs and provide better educational opportunities for thousands of American kids to receive the full attention of teachers in schools crowded with the children of illegal immigrants.

Americans Willing to Work

Finally, to address perhaps the biggest lie of all—that Americans   13
won't do the work that illegals perform—the truth is that uneducated and unskilled Americans won't live in garages with multiple families and endure similar hardships to take on backbreaking work at below minimum wages. Get rid of illegal immigrants, and wages would have to rise to attract those native-born and legal residents who lack the skills and education to do much else.

About deportation. With the exception of illegal alien felons   14
incarcerated in various prisons and those illegals caught by the border patrol (at the border), deportations are virtually nonexistent. Yet there are six million illegal aliens in this country. We could make a huge deportation dent in this stealth population if we only had the commitment and determination to do so. Once again, it's a national administration attempting to curry favor with the wrong people.

About "we've met the enemy and they are us," some conser-   15
vatives and liberals support Cardinal Roger Mahony's statement, "the right to immigrate is more fundamental than that of nations to control their borders"—conservatives because they get their jollies from exploiting cheap labor and liberals because it gives them another opportunity to smother someone with compassion. Added to these afflictions are the wishes of politicians to get reelected by ducking issues and the hidden agendas of opportunists and ideologues to advance their causes. . . .

Proposition 187

Let's look at California's Proposition 187. This was a 1994 bal-   16
lot initiative that barred illegal immigrant access to public social
services, including education and public health care services,
except emergency care. In November of 1994, 59 percent of the
California electorate voted for Proposition 187. Of California's 58
counties, 49 voted yes.

The day after Proposition 187 passed, a federal court in Los   17
Angeles and a state court in San Francisco barred enforcement of
most of its provisions. A federal judge kept this bottled up for
nearly 3½ years before voiding it. Immediately thereafter the State
of California appealed the decision, but because a conniving
governor was soon thereafter elected—a person opposed to
Proposition 187—he saw to it that the initiative never reached the
Supreme Court through the appellate process.

Just before Governor Gray Davis strangled Proposition 187 in   18
April 1999, he said with the most angelic of faces, "If this
(Proposition 187) were a piece of legislation, I would veto it. But
it's not. It's an initiative, passed by nearly 60 percent of the voters
through a process specifically designed to go over the heads of the
legislature and the governor. If officials choose to selectively
enforce only the laws they like, our system of justice will not long
endure." Davis then walked off the press conference stage
and betrayed the people of California by stabbing them in the
back.

Our Own Worst Enemies

Then there's the shameful AFL-CIO [labor union] clamor for   19
amnesty for 6 million illegal aliens, hoping lots of them will
become union members. The AFL-CIO is attempting to line their
pockets with membership dues over the short run, while rolling
the dice with the futures of American workers. All this will do is
end control of our borders and unleash terrible wage depression
pressures on millions of American workers as hordes of foreigners
surge across unprotected borders looking for American jobs.

We've clearly become our own worst enemies and will suffer a   20
terrible fate unless we end this madness. A series of national
administrations have buried their collective heads in the sand and
ignored the acrid odors of the white hot burning fuse attached to

the illegal immigration time bomb. There just aren't enough Roger Barnetts around, and that's what's necessary for us to retake our country. Just remember folks, the only card your opponents hold in their hands is the race-baiting card, the threat of calling you a racist or a bigot. But the collective votes of an ignored and aggrieved articulate voting population are the strongest cards of all, and if you chose to play them, it's a slam-dunk for the good guys.

Illegal immigration is repudiated by our laws, by the facts, and   21
by most Americans. So, one more time folks, let's seal our borders, deport all illegal aliens, prosecute any employer hiring illegals, throw the rascals out who live on the Planet Beltway and kowtow to the illegal immigration lobby, and begin to pay close attention to the calamity that awaits us unless we do all of these things.

RICHARD RAYNOR   (1955–   )

Illegal Immigration Does Not Threaten America

Maria T. bites her nails. At 31, with five children, she's one of the 1.7 million immigrants now estimated to be living in California illegally. She speaks almost no English, even though she has been in America for more than eight years. In her clean and sparsely furnished living room, her kids— Gustavo (11), Mario (7), Maribel (6), Cesar (5) and Joan (4)—are in front of the TV, laughing first at "Home Improvement," then at "The Simpsons."   1

The refrigerator is almost empty; it contains only a gallon of milk, some Kool-Aid, a few tortillas. Her life is frugal, a devotion to the future of her children. Though there are three bedrooms in the apartment, all five sleep with her because she hates to let them out of her sight. Since she has no car and can rarely afford the bus, the family walks everywhere, Maria leading the way like Mother Goose with the kids behind toting Batman and Pocahontas backpacks. On a typical day she walks six miles, shuttling between her apartment and the local school in Van Nuys.   2

For her, as for so many, the decision to make the journey to El Norte was the beginning of an epic. Gustavo was 3 at the time, Mario was 8 months, and she was 5 months pregnant with Maribel. Maria crossed the border with the help of a "coyote," a guide, but when she arrived in San Diego the woman who'd paid for her brothers' crossings didn't have any money this time. Maria was kept a slave in the coyote's house. He beat and raped her until, after three months, her brother raised $300, half the sum agreed for the crossing, and the coyote let her go.   3

She stayed with her brother in Los Angeles, the Pico-Union district, and it was here that Maribel was born. "I'd come out of labor and I was staring at the wall and I said to my sister-in-law, 'Look, she's there.' She said, 'Who?' I said, 'The Virgin Mary.' She said, 'There's nothing there. You're crazy.' But it was true all the same. For eight months the Virgin would appear to me. She made me strong."   4

"At first, I had to beg for food. Sometimes I did day work for 5
Latinos, for $10 a day. I'd take off into the city on the bus, not
really knowing where I was going and get off to beg on the streets.
I'm ashamed of that."

Slowly, she clawed her way up. It is in so many ways a classic 6
immigrant's tale, although she has been the beneficiary not just of
her own drive, but also of something equally important—welfare.
She's here illegally, with fake ID, and she doesn't work. She
receives $723 in cash and $226 in food stamps, and Section 8 takes
care of more than two-thirds of her $1,000 rent (high, because
landlords know illegals won't complain).

It's a myth, however, that anyone can come over the border 7
and start milking the system. Only Medicaid and limited food benefits are available to illegal immigrants, and most don't apply for
these because they fear detection by the Immigration and
Naturalization Service (I.N.S.). Maria T. gets what she does
because of her children who were born here.

Local, state, and federal governments spend about $11.8 billion 8
a year educating legal and illegal immigrant children, according to
the Urban Institute, a nonpartisan research organization, compared
with the $227 billion spent to educate all children. Generally, this
is more than offset by the taxes that legal and illegal immigrant
families pay—$70.3 billion a year, the Urban Institute says—while
receiving $42.9 billion in total services. Illegal immigrants pay
$7 billion in taxes.

Maria T., however, represents the nightmare scenario—an illegal 9
immigrant who's sucking money from the system and putting nothing back. Even so, it's not clear that she's a villain. She hopes one
day to go to work herself. She hopes and believes that her bright
children will become outstanding. She believes in America. . . .

Fears of Strangers

My wife, from Finland, has a green card; I'm English, in the 10
process of applying for one myself; our son was born an American.
When we moved into our house in Venice, Calif., one of our
neighbors, an elderly white woman with whom we're now very
friendly, said, "No Americans live on our block anymore."

Maybe she had the jitters about new neighbors, or maybe there 11
was something else at play. I knew that her father had been born

in Germany and had journeyed to Detroit, where she was born. I wanted to say that logically, therefore, our son is every bit as American as she is. But in any debate about nationality, I know, logic fades fast.

My own father once traced our family tree back to 1066, when 12 one Baron de Rainier sailed from Normandy to help conquer England. Since then, give or take the occasional Irish excursion, my progenitors were all born within a hundred or so miles of one another in the north of England. So, when I came to America and found that nearly everyone was from somewhere else if they stepped back a generation or two, I found myself thrilled and oddly at ease. It explained America's drive, its generosity and up-for-anything energy. As (novelist Herman) Melville wrote, "We are not a nation, so much as a world."

Not everyone sees things this way. Many have drawn a line 13 behind which they stand, true Americans, fearful and angry about the erosion of their identity. With unintended irony they talk of themselves as "natives." On immigration, they argue that enough is enough, that the borders must be secured and a drastic cutback enforced. Those who are allowed in, they say, must be professionals or skilled workers because the others—mobs of unskilled, third-world peasants—drain resources and take jobs. They cost billions and dilute the gene pool. They are mutating the face of America.

California itself, for instance, passed an anti-immigrant measure 14 with scary ease. In 1994's state election nearly 60 percent voted for Proposition 187, the so-called Save-Our-State initiative, which sought to deny public education, nonemergency health care and welfare to illegal immigrants. By linking illegal immigration to joblessness and crime, Pete Wilson revived his flagging gubernatorial campaign and was swept back into office, even though, as an exit poll showed, few who voted for 187 actually thought it was going to work.

Wilson was avid for votes and a reaction and he got both. Many 15 illegal Latinos, fearful of deportation, refused to go near schools and emergency rooms. There was immigrant bashing and hate mail. Since the Republicans took control of the United States House and Senate, moreover, it seems as though all Washington has been grandstanding on the issue. Dozens of immigration-related bills were introduced.

Many of the proposals are mean-spirited and, to a lot of   16
observers, wrongheaded. One would impose a tax on employers
who hire legal aliens. Others would deny citizenship to children
born in this country to illegals or eliminate some categories of family immigration. The anti-immigration forces have done an excellent job of creating an atmosphere of crisis in which the debate has
focused on how to slow the "flood" of immigration, legal and illegal. But illegal immigration should not be folded over to scapegoat
legals as well. The real point is that there isn't any immigration
crisis.

How Many Immigrants?

"The perception is that immigration is out of control," says Joel   17
Kotkin, author of *Tribes* and a fellow at the Pepperdine University
Institute of Public Policy. "It isn't. If you say to most Americans,
'We have 800,000 legal immigrants a year,' they're going to reply,
'Hey, that's not so bad.' And this is the truth of the situation. But
it's somehow been demonized so that people think there are mil-
lions coming across the border."

The Border Patrol logged 1,094,718 apprehensions in 1994.   18
On page 26 of his *Alien Nation,* a leading restrictionist, Peter
Brimelow, writes that legal immigration is "overwhelmed by an
estimated 2 to 3 million illegal entries into the country in every
recent year." He goes on to note, correctly, that many of these
illegal entrants go back home and that some trundle to and fro
across the border every day. By page 33, however, he's writing "a
remarkable 2 to 3 million illegal immigrants may have succeeded
in entering the country in 1993."

Within seven pages illegal entrants have mysteriously become   19
illegal immigrants, attached to that hyperbolic two to three million, a figure vigorously disputed by I.N.S., which regards as pre-
posterous the idea that for every border crosser caught another
three get away. Indeed, throughout the 1970's there were some
eight million border apprehensions and during that time, according to the best estimates of I.N.S., about one million illegals came
to reside—eight apprehensions per illegal immigrant.

So how many illegals are coming in and staying each year now?   20
The Urban Institute says 250,000 to 300,000. The Center for
Immigration Studies, a conservative research group, says 400,000,

while I.N.S. says 300,000. The Census Bureau until recently guessed 200,000 to 400,000; now it agrees with the I.N.S.

The 300,000 figure is considered firm because it was based on 21 the years following 1988, when the I.N.S. started to process the genuinely reliable data it amassed following the 1986 amnesty for illegals. Too much of this and the eyes glaze over, but the gist is, the further you get from 1988, the flakier the statistics become. And the argument over the number of illegal immigrants is nothing compared with the furor over how much they cost.

The fact is, no one knows for sure; there is simply no up-to- 22 date research. "The issue has caught political fire," Papademetriou says. "But serious academics haven't got out into the field yet. They're reluctant to play into the hands of the politicians."

Immigration is in the spotlight not because of money but 23 because it so impinges on issues like race, the role of government, national identity, and change. Name an issue and you can hook it to immigration. One side looks at crime, failing schools, and soaring welfare spending and sees too many immigrants. The other sees America, the greatest nation on earth, built on the backs of immigrants and still benefiting enormously from the brains, energy, and determination (not to speak of low wages) of the next generation of newcomers. Right now the debate is more emotional than informed. It's all temper tantrums and red-hot sound bites.

Fear of Latinos

When people complain about immigration, about the alien 24 "flood," it's Latin Americans they mean, who from their entry points in California and Miami are fanning out through the country. There's concern about the small minority, who are criminals, and the seeming reluctance of these people to learn English. Mixed in with this is the prejudice summarized by D. H. Lawrence in *Mornings in Mexico*. They are other, he concluded; they are dirty; I don't trust them and they stink. There's also the suggestion that Latinos are lazy, though everywhere you look in Los Angeles you see evidence to the contrary.

A Demand for Labor

Historically, immigration has been tolerated, even encouraged 25 during labor shortages. Labor migration has been going on for centuries, and it's hard to see how 300,000 or so illegal immigrants per year will make or break the American economy. Indeed, in Los Angeles they're most likely an asset. The number of illegals in California is thought to be growing by 125,000 a year—hardly an economic catastrophe in a state of 31 million. In Los Angeles, where 80,000 jobs were created last year, it's a definite plus. The city has a thirst for people who will work for $5 or even $3 an hour.

The legal Chinese immigrants who have revitalized the San   26
Gabriel Valley, the Latinos who are opening businesses in depressed areas of South Los Angeles, and the Russians and Iranians who are opening businesses all over are the principal reasons the city is so different from, say, Detroit. Says Joel Kotkin, "The only place where American society is evolving is where the immigrant influx is strong. Cities would have no future without them. But if you're sitting in Idaho, it looks different."

The Race Issue

Pro-immigration forces have tended to keep their focus tight   27
on the economic issues because they sense that Americans don't want to be told they're racist. Nobody does. Yet, one of the problems with the immigration issue is that it does impinge on the race issue and thus appeals temptingly and dangerously to the worst side of all of us.

A central argument of Brimelow's "Alien Nation" is that   28
America has always had an essential nature, an ethnic core, and that it's white. He writes that "the first naturalization law, in 1790, stipulated that an applicant must be a 'free white person.' Blacks became full citizens only after the Civil War."

He goes on, "Maybe America should not have been like this.   29
But it was." And now, "Americans are being tricked out of their own identity."

Reading this, I'm overcome with a weird looking-glass giddi-   30
ness. Someone's trying to change the rules here, to wipe a rag over history. America's identity is precisely that of mutation, its power drawn from an energetic and quite fearless ability to adapt and win. Its national book, after all, is *The Adventures of Huckleberry Finn,* about a beautiful and dangerous river that never stops changing. . . .

An Immigrant Nation

America is an immigrant nation, indeed, a nation of strangers. I   31
like it that way, though the arguments in favor of the idea are not
merely sentimental and historical. Corporate interests value immigration for something that troubles us—keeping wages lower, and
these days not just at the level of busboys and dayworkers.

The American economy is in relatively good shape and has   32
pretty much the legal immigration it needs. The system isn't broken, doesn't need fixing—and certainly not in the ways that are
now being proposed. Illegal immigration is touchier. Listening to
academics makes it easy to forget the racially inflamed brush fire
that is the debate in California.

Recent polls show a surprising sympathy even for illegal immi-   33
grants, provided they otherwise play by the rules: work, get documentation, learn English. Only 20 percent say immigrants take
jobs away from citizens, and 69 percent say they do work that citizens don't necessarily want and that needs to be done. Few say
that the American-born children of illegals should be deprived of
education and welfare, let alone their citizenship. The message
here is a sensible one: beef up the Border Patrol; deport criminals;
don't break up families; target labor-enforcement at bad-guy
sweatshop employers and make an effort to deal with temporary
visa overstays, who surprisingly make up as much as 50 percent of
all illegals; supply Federal assistance to heavily impacted areas such
as Los Angeles; and forget the idea of a national verification system or an identification card.

Ultimately, this is a debate about values, not money. This is   34
about how America feels about itself.

UNDERSTANDING DETAILS

1. What are Scott ("America Must Take Stronger Measures to
   Halt Illegal Immigration") and Raynor ("Illegal Immigration
   Does Not Threaten America") each saying about illegal immigration in these two essays?
2. What arguments can you think of to supplement both of their
   essays?
3. What three basic steps does Scott say must be taken through
   law enforcement to stop illegal immigration? Explain each in
   detail.

4. What does Raynor mean when he says, "Ultimately, this is a debate about values, not money. This is about how America feels about itself"?

ANALYZING MEANING

1. Which stand on this particular argument is most convincing to you? Which examples or statistics seem most persuasive? Explain your reactions to each of these two positions.
2. Would you agree to pay higher prices "to rid our land of illegal immigrants" (Scott, paragraph 12)?
3. What do you think Melville means by the words "We are not a nation, so much as a world" (Raynor, paragragh 12)? Do you agree with this statement?
4. How might the opinions in these two essays be reconciled? Can you make a compromise prediction that combines both these views of the world?

DISCOVERING RHETORICAL STRATEGIES

1. Who do you think is the intended audience for each of these essays? Are there any important differences between these audiences in your opinion?
2. These two authors make their points with slightly different writing voices. Describe the tone or mood of each essay, and explain whether you think that particular voice is most effective for the author's purpose.
3. How does the organization of the two essays differ? What is the general organizing principle in each case?
4. What other rhetorical strategies does each essay use to make its point? Give examples of each strategy.

MAKING CONNECTIONS

1. Compare and contrast the arguments used by Scott and Raynor. Which essay seems most persuasive to you? Which essay comes closest to matching your own personal viewpoint? Could you conceivably find an essay convincing and well-argued even if it conflicts with your own opinion? Why or why not?

2. If Scott and Raynor were having a conversation with Kimberly Wozencraft ("Notes from the Country Club") about the difficulties in enforcing laws against illegal aliens versus those concerning drug abuse, which issue would the authors say receives less attention from our legal system? Would you agree? What does this disparity in justice tell us about laws in the United States? About the power of special interest groups?

3. Imagine that Scott and Raynor were having a round-table discussion about the topic of illegal immigration with Sandra Cisneros ("Only daughter"), Amy Tan ("Mother Tongue"), Sucheng Chan ("You're Short, Besides!"), and Richard Rodriguez ("The Fear of Losing a Culture"). Which of these authors would speak most vigorously in favor of having the United States truly integrated with people from many different countries? What specific skills and abilities do immigrants bring to America? Do you think that the strain on our economy and infrastructure is worth the positive values these immigrants bring to our country? Why or why not?

IDEAS FOR DISCUSSION/WRITING

Preparing to Write

Write freely about your views on the role of immigrants in the United States: What do immigrants offer America? In what ways do immigrants weaken our country? What is your general view of immigrants? Who should be allowed to enter our national borders? What guidelines would you put on immigrants? Why would you establish these guidelines? Explain your answer in as much detail as possible.

Choosing a Topic

1. Whether or not we should pay for the education of illegal aliens has been an issue in politics for quite some time. What is your opinion on this issue. Use facts and statistics from these two essays to support your point of view.

2. Many sociologists and politicians who have studied immigration claim that the issue ultimately centers upon race. Do you agree with this contention? Present your own argument on this statement, supporting your opinion with persuasive examples and facts.

3. Your local library is sponsoring a writing contest with a first place prize of $1000. All contestants must write a 500-word essay on the following topic: "How does understanding other cultures help make us better human beings?" Write an essay on this topic that would win the first place award.
4. Which of the two arguments was presented most effectively? Regardless of your personal feelings about the issue, evaluate which argument presented its case most persuasively. Write an editorial essay for your favorite online news source in which you evaluate both articles and argue that one's presentation is more effective. Be sure to use specific details to support your claims.

Before beginning your essay, you might want to consult the checklists on page 511.

CHAPTER WRITING ASSIGNMENTS

Practicing Argument/Persuasion

1. What is the best method for disciplining a child? What kinds of "discipline" constitute child abuse? What rights should parents have in deciding how to discipline their own children? Write an essay explaining what disciplinary actions you believe are acceptable and arguing why others are not.

2. Many people argue that the media actually run the elections in the United States. What is your opinion on this issue? What should be the role of the media in the political arena? How should we force them to limit themselves to this role? In what ways do the media help us understand certain important issues? In what ways do they hinder our understanding? Write an essay in which you argue for a specific relationship between the media and politics, including elections, referendums, and bond issues. Support your position with concrete details.

3. Look up the term *immigration* in the dictionary. Ask a variety of people about their positive and negative responses to immigration. Write an essay in which you explain your position on immigration, using your interviews as background and support.

Exploring Ideas

1. Do you think people are prone to violence because of inborn qualities or because of learned behavior? Why are some people violent while others are not? Where does this difference come from in your opinion—nature or nurture?

2. Do you think any limits should be put on free speech? If so, what should these limits be? If not, why not? What is the reasoning behind your opinion? Write an essay supporting your position with examples.

3. American society often argues about whether or not voting materials and other government documents should be printed in multiple languages. Does this practice work against the principle of speaking only one language in America? Write an essay that explains your opinion on this issue. Be sure to include specific examples to support your argument.

10

DOCUMENTED ESSAYS
Reading and Writing from Sources

We use sources every day in both informal and formal situations. We explain the source of a phone message, for example, or we refer to an instructor's comments in class. We use someone else's opinion in an essay, or we quote an expert to prove a point. We cite sources both in speaking and in writing through summary, paraphrase, and direct quotation. Most of your college instructors will ask you to write papers using sources so they can see how well you understand the course material. The use of sources in academic papers requires you to understand what you have read and to integrate this reading material with your own opinions and observations—a process that requires a high level of skill in thinking, reading, and writing.

DEFINING DOCUMENTED ESSAYS

Documented essays provide you with the opportunity to perform sophisticated and exciting exercises in critical thinking; they draw on the thinking, reading, and writing abilities you have built up over the course of your academic career, and they often require you to put all the rhetorical modes to work at their most analytical level. Documented essays demonstrate the process of analytical thinking at its best in different disciplines.

In the academic world, documented essays are also called *research papers, library papers,* and *term papers.* Documented essays are generally written for one of three reasons: (1) to **report,** (2) to **interpret,** or (3) to **analyze.**

The most straightforward, uncomplicated type of documented essay **reports** information, as in a survey of problems that children have in preschool. The second type of documented essay both presents and **interprets** its findings. It examines a number of different views on a specific issue and weighs these views as it draws its own conclusions. A topic that falls into this category would be whether children who have attended preschool are more sociable than those who have not. After considering evidence on both sides, the writer would draw his or her own conclusions on this topic. A documented essay that **analyzes** a subject presents a hypothesis, tests the hypothesis, and analyzes or evaluates its conclusions. This type of essay calls for the most advanced form of critical thinking. It might look, for example, at the reasons preschool children are more or less socially flexible than non-preschool children. At its most proficient, this type of writing requires a sophisticated degree of evaluation that forces you to judge your reading, evaluate your sources, and ultimately scrutinize your own reasoning ability as the essay takes shape.

Each of these types of documented essays calls for a higher level of thinking, and each evolves from the previous category. In other words, interpreting requires some reporting, and analyzing draws on both reporting and interpreting.

In the following paragraph, a student reports, interprets, analyzes, and uses sources to document the problem of solid waste in America. Notice how the student writer draws her readers into the essay with a commonly used phrase about America and then questions the validity of its meaning. The student's opinions give shape to the paragraph, while her use of sources helps identify the problem and support her contentions.

"America the Beautiful" is a phrase used to describe the many wonders of nature found throughout our country. America's natural beauty will fade, however, if solutions to our solid waste problems are not discovered soon. America is a rich nation socially, economically, and polit-

ically. But these very elements may be the cause of Americans' waste-fulness. Americans now generate approximately 160 million tons of solid waste a year—3½ pounds per person per day. We live in a consumer society where "convenience," "ready-to-use," and "throwaway" are words that spark the consumer's attention (Cook 60). However, many of the products associated with these words create a large part of our problem with solid waste (Grossman 39). We are running out of space for our garbage. The people of America are beginning to produce responses to this problem. Are we too late? A joint effort between individuals, businesses, government industries, and local, state, and federal governments is necessary to establish policies and procedures to combat this war on waste. The problem requires not one solution, but a combination of solutions involving technologies and people working together to provide a safe and healthy environment for themselves and future generations.

READING AND WRITING DOCUMENTED ESSAYS

Reading and writing documented essays involves the skillful integration of two complex operations: research and writing. Reading documented essays critically means understanding the material and evaluating the sources as you proceed. Writing documented essays includes reading and understanding sources on the topic you have chosen and then combining this reading with your own conclusions. The two skills are essentially mirror images of one another.

How to Read Documented Essays

Preparing to Read. You should approach a documented essay in much the same way that you approach any essay. First, take a few minutes to look at the preliminary material for each selection: What can you learn from scanning Ehrenreich's essay ("The Ecstasy of War") and Rosenbaum and Chesney-Lind's essay ("Appearance and Delinquency: A Research Note") or from reading their synopses in the Rhetorical Table of Contents? What does Barbara Ehrenreich's title, "The Ecstasy of War," prepare you to read? And what questions do you have about the relationship between "appearance and delinquency" before you read Rosenbaum and Chesney-Lind's essay?

Also, you should learn as much as you can from the authors' biographies: What is Ehrenreich's interest in war? What biographical details prepare us for her approach to this topic? What are Rosenbaum's and Chesney-Lind's backgrounds? Do they have the proper qualifications to write about "appearance and delinquency"?

Another important part of preparing to read a documented essay is surveying the sources cited. Turn to the end of the essay and look at the sources. What publications does Ehrenreich draw from? Are these books and magazines well respected? Do you recognize any of the authorities Rosenbaum and Chesney-Lind quote?

Last, before you read these essays, try to generate some ideas on each topic so you can participate as fully as possible in your reading. The Preparing to Read questions will get you ready for this task. Then, try to speculate further on the topic of each essay: What is the connection for Ehrenreich between war and ecstasy? What does this relationship tell us about human nature in general? Why has the relationship between female appearance and delinquency gained so much momentum in the United States? Where will this momentum take us in the future?

Reading.   As you react to the material in this chapter, you should respond to both the research and the writing. Record your responses as you read the essay for the first time: What are your reactions to the information you are reading? Are the sources appropriate? How well do they support the author's main points?

Use the preliminary material before each essay to help you create a framework for your responses to it: What motivated Ehrenreich to publish her essay on war? Do you find it convincing? Who was Rosenbaum and Chesney-Lind's primary audience when their essay was first published? In what ways is the tone of their essay appropriate for that audience?

Your main job at this stage is to determine each essay's primary assertion (thesis statement), note the sources that support this thesis, and begin to ask yourself questions about the essay so you can respond critically to your reading. In addition, take a look at the questions after each selection to make sure you are comprehending the major ideas of the essay.

Rereading.   As you reread these documented essays, take some time to become aware of the difference between fact and opinion, to weigh and evaluate the evidence brought to bear on the arguments, to consider the sources the writers use, to judge the interpretation of the facts cited, to determine what the writers omitted, and to confirm your own views on the issues at hand. All these skills demand the use of critical thinking strategies at their most sophisticated level.

You need to approach this type of argument with an inquiring mind, asking questions and looking for answers as you read the essays. Be especially conscious of the appeals (logical, emotional, and ethical) at work in each essay (see "How to Write Persuasive Essays" in the Introduction of Chapter 9), and take note of other rhetorical strategies that support each author's main argument.

Also, be aware of your own thought processes as you sort facts from opinions. Know where you stand personally in relation to each side of the issues.

For a list of guidelines for the entire reading process, see the checklists on page 20 of the Introduction.

How to Write Documented Essays

Preparing to Write.   Just as with any writing assignment, you should begin the task of writing a documented essay by exploring and limiting your topic. In this case, however, you draw on other sources to help you with this process. You should seek out both primary and secondary sources related to your topic. **Primary sources** are works of literature, historical documents, letters, diaries, speeches, eyewitness accounts, and your own experiments, observations, and conclusions; **secondary sources** explain and analyze information from other sources. Any librarian can help you search for both types of sources related to your topic.

After you have found a few sources on your general topic, you should scan and evaluate what you have discovered so you can limit your topic further. Depending on the required length of your essay, you will want to find a topic broad enough to be researched, established enough to let you discover ample sources on it in the library, and significant enough to demonstrate your abilities to grapple with important ideas and draw meaningful conclusions. The Preparing to Write questions can help you generate and focus your ideas.

Once you have established these limitations, you might try writing a tentative thesis. At this point, asking a question and attempting to find an answer are productive. But you should keep in mind that your thesis is likely to be revised several times as the range of your knowledge changes and your paper takes different turns while you research and write. Then decide on a purpose and audience for your essay.

Once your tentative thesis is formed, you should read your sources for ideas and take detailed notes on your reading. These notes will probably fall into one of four categories: (1) *summary*—a condensed statement of someone else's thoughts or observations; (2) *paraphrase*—a restatement in your own words of someone else's ideas or observations; (3) *direct quotations from sources;* or (4) *a combination of these forms.* Be sure to make a distinction in your notes between actual quotes and paraphrases or summaries. Also, record the sources of all your notes—especially of quoted, summarized, and paraphrased material—which you may need to cite in your essay.

As you gather information, you should consider keeping a "research journal" where you can record your own opinions, interpretations, and analyses in response to your reading. This journal should be separate from your notes on sources and is the place where you can make your own discoveries in relation to your topic by jotting down thoughts and relationships among ideas you are exposed to, by keeping a record of sources you read and others you want to look at, by tracking and developing your own ideas and theories, and by clarifying your thinking on an issue.

Finally, before you begin your first draft, you might want to write an informal working outline for your own information. Such an exercise can help you check the range of your coverage and the order and development of your ideas. With an outline, you can readily see where you need more information, less information, or more solid sources. Try to be flexible, however. This outline may change dramatically as your essay develops.

Writing.   Writing the first draft of a documented essay is your chance to discover new insights and to find important connections between ideas that you may not be aware of yet. This draft is your opportunity to demonstrate that you understand the issue at hand and your sources on three increasingly difficult levels—literal, interpretive, and analytical; that you can organize your material effectively; that you can integrate your sources (in the form of summaries, paraphrases, or quotations) with your opinions; and that you can document (that is, cite) your sources.

To begin this process, look again at your thesis statement and your working outline, and adjust them to represent any new discoveries you have made as you read your sources and wrote in your research journal. Then, organize your research notes and information in some logical fashion.

When you begin to draft your paper, write the sections of the essay that you feel most comfortable about first. Throughout the essay, feature your own point of view and integrate summaries, paraphrases, and quotations from other sources into your own analysis. Each point you make should be a section of your paper consisting of your own conclusion and your support for that conclusion (in the form of facts, examples, summaries, paraphrases, and quotations). Remember that the primary reason for doing such an assignment is to let you demonstrate your ability to synthesize material, draw your own conclusions, and analyze your sources and your own reasoning.

A documented paper usually blends three types of material:

1. *Common knowledge, such as the places and dates of events (even if you have to look them up).*
   EXAMPLE: Neil Armstrong and Edwin Aldrin first walked on the moon on July 20, 1969.
2. *Your own thoughts and observations.*
   EXAMPLE: Armstrong and Aldrin's brief walk on the moon's surface was the beginning of a new era in the U.S. space program.
3. *Someone else's thoughts and observations.*
   EXAMPLE: President Richard Nixon reacted to the moonwalk in a telephone call to the astronauts: "For one priceless moment in the history of man all the people on this earth are truly one—one in their pride in what you have done and one in our prayers that you will return safely to earth."

Of these three types of information, you must document or cite your exact source only for the third type. Negligence in citing your sources, whether purposeful or accidental, is called *plagiarism,* which comes from a Latin word meaning "kidnapper." Among student writers, plagiarism usually takes one of three forms: (1) using words from another source without quotation marks; (2) using someone else's ideas in the form of a summary or paraphrase without citing your source; and (3) using someone else's term paper as your own.

Avoiding plagiarism is quite simple: You just need to remember to acknowledge the sources of ideas or wording that you are using to support your own contentions. Acknowledging your sources also gives you credit for the reading you have done and for the ability you have developed to use sources to support your observations and conclusions.

Documentation styles vary from discipline to discipline. Ask your instructor about the particular documentation style he or she wants you to follow. The most common styles are the Modern Language Association (MLA) style, used in humanities courses, and the American Psychological Association (APA) style, used in behavioral science and science courses. (See any writing handbook for more details on documentation formats.)

The World Wide Web is an exciting new source of information for your research papers. Electronic sources include online journals and magazines, CD-ROMs, software programs, newsletters, discussion groups, bulletin boards, gopher sites, and e-mail. But not all electronic sources are equally accurate and reliable. Based on your topic, you need to exercise your best judgment and get your instructor's help in assessing the most useful online sites for your purposes. If you use electronic sources in any of your papers, remember that you have two goals in any citation: (1) to acknowledge the author and (2) to help the reader locate the material. Then you should check the MLA or APA Home Pages for their current guidelines for online documentation: The URL for the Modern Language Association is http://www. mla.org and for the American Psychological Association, http://www.apa.org.

Even though documentation styles vary somewhat from one discipline to another, the basic concept behind documentation is the same in all disciplines: You must give proper credit to other writers by acknowledging the sources of the summaries, paraphrases, and quotations that you use to support the ideas in your documented paper. Once you grasp this basic concept and accept it, you will have no trouble avoiding plagiarism.

Rewriting. To rewrite your documented essay, you should play the role of your readers and impartially evaluate your argument and the sources you have used as evidence in that argument. To begin with, revise your thesis to represent all the discoveries you made as you wrote your first draft. Then, look for problems in logic throughout the essay; you might even develop an outline at this point to help evaluate your reasoning:

- Are the essay's assertions clear?
- Are they adequately supported?
- Are other points of view recognized and examined?
- Does the organization of your paper further your assertions/ argument?
- Have you removed irrelevant material?

Next, check your documentation style:

- Is your source material (either summarized, paraphrased, or quoted) presented fairly and accurately?
- Have you rechecked the citations for all the sources in your paper?
- Do you introduce the sources in your paper when appropriate?
- Are your sources in the proper format according to your instructor's guidelines (MLA, APA, or another)?

Then, proofread carefully. Finally, prepare your paper to be submitted to your instructor:

- Have you followed your instructor's guidelines for your title page, margins, page numbers, tables, and abstracts?
- Have you prepared an alphabetical list of your sources for the end of your paper?

Any additional guidance you may need as you write and revise your documented essays is furnished on pages 31–32 of the Introduction.

STUDENT ESSAY: DOCUMENTATION AT WORK

The following student essay uses documented sources to support its conclusions and observations about our eating habits today. First, the writer creates a profile of carnivorous species in contrast to human beings. She then goes on to discuss the harsh realities connected with eating meat. After recognizing and refuting some opposing views, this student writer ends her paper with her own evaluation of the situation and a list of some famous vegetarians. Throughout the essay, the student writer carefully supports her principal points with summaries, paraphrases, and quotations from other sources. Notice that she uses the MLA documentation style and closes the paper with an alphabetical list of "Works Cited."

Food for Thought

The next time you sit down to a nice steak dinner, pause for a moment to consider whether you are biologically programmed to

Background information eat meat. Unlike carnivores, such as lions and tigers, with claws and sharp front teeth allowing them to tear and eat raw flesh, humans are omnivores, with fingers that can pluck fruits and grains and flat teeth that can grind these vegetable foods. To digest their *Common knowledge* meals, carnivores have an acidic saliva and a very strong hydrochloric acid digestive fluid. In contrast, we humans have an alkaline saliva, and our digestive fluids are only one-tenth as potent as those of carnivores.

Common knowledge Moreover, carnivores have an intestinal tract barely three times their body length, which allows for faster elimination of rotting flesh; humans have an intestinal tract eight to twelve times our body length, better enabling us to digest plant nutrients. What happens, then, when we eat flesh? <u>The effects of a meat-based diet are far-reaching:</u> *Thesis* <u>massive suffering of the animals killed and eaten, a myriad of diseases in humans, and a devastating effect on world ecology.</u>

Student's first conclusion

<u>The atrocities committed daily to provide meat should be enough to make a meat-based diet completely unconscionable.</u> According to Peter Singer, of People for the Ethical Treatment of Animals (PETA), every year several hundred million cattle, pigs, and sheep and 3 billion chickens are slaughtered to provide food for humans (Singer 92). That is equal to 6,278 animals every minute of every day—and those are just the ones that make it to the slaughterhouse. Over 500,000 animals die in transit each year (150).

Citation (MLA form)

Summary of source

Support for first conclusion

A slaughterhouse is not a pretty sight. Anywhere from 50 to 90 percent of the cattle are slaughtered in a "kosher" manner. "Kosher" sounds innocent enough, but what it actually means is that the animal must be "healthy and moving" at the time of death. This requires the animals to be fully conscious as "a heavy chain is clamped around one of their rear legs; then they are jerked off their feet and hung upside down" for anywhere from two to five minutes, usually twisting in agony with a broken leg, while they are moved down the conveyer belt to be slaughtered (Robbins 140–41).

Paraphrase of source (fact)

Summary of source

Student's opinion

While we would like to assume the animals we eat are healthy at the time of butchering, this is often not the case. Most veal calves, for example, are near death from anemia when sent to the butcher (Diamond and Diamond 238). Inspections have revealed leukosis (cancer) in 90 percent of the chickens (Robbins 67), pneumonia rates of 80 percent and stomach ulcers of 53 percent in pigs (94). Salmonellosis is found in 90 percent of the chickens dressed and ready to be purchased (303).

Examples from sources

<u>Even if we, like the industry leaders, could turn a cold heart to the plight of our fellow creatures, we would still find many reasons to warrant a vegetarian diet, beginning with our own health</u>. Recapping just a few of the hundreds of studies that link diet to disease, we might consider the following:

—A study of nearly 90,000 American women published in the *New England Journal of Medicine* reports that daily pork, lamb, or beef eaters have a 250 percent greater likelihood of developing colon cancer than people who consume these foods once a month or less ("Red Meat Alert").

—Heart specialist Dr. Dean Ornish states, "It's no surprise that half of all Americans develop heart disease because the typical U.S. diet puts everyone at risk" (Marcus 3).

—The *Journal of the American Medical Association* stated that a vegetarian diet could prevent 97 percent of coronary occlusions (Robbins 247).

—Even though officials in Great Britain and other countries deny any connection between BIV, a bovine disease very closely related to the human HIV virus, and HIV, many companies are refusing to handle any meat or dairy products from BIV-infected herds (Clayton 585).

The effects of meat diets go beyond causing human disease and death. <u>Perhaps the most frightening legacy being left by America's dietary ritual is just now being realized, and that is the profound ecological impact factory farming is having on our planet</u>.[1] Every five seconds, one acre of forest is cleared in America, and one estimate is that 87 percent is cleared for either livestock grazing or growing livestock feed (Robbins

Margin notes:
- Student's second conclusion
- Paraphrase of sources (facts)
- Support for second conclusion
- Quotation from source
- Student's third conclusion
- Support for third conclusion

361). Approximately six square yards of jungle must be cleared for every single hamburger made of imported beef. By the late 1970s, nearly two-thirds of all agricultural land was used as pastureland for animals, while countless people living just outside of those same pasturelands were starving to death (Rifkin 99). Says Alan Durning, senior researcher at the Worldwatch Institute in Washington, D.C., "Producing the red meat and poultry eaten each year by a typical American takes energy equal to 50 gallons of gasoline. Supplying vegetarians with nourishment requires one-third less energy on the farm" (4).

Paraphrase of sources (facts)

Quotation from source

Forests are not all that we are sacrificing. Local governments are constantly calling for water conservation, yet over 50 percent of all water used in America goes into grain production for livestock. According to one study, the water required to feed a meat eater for one day is 4,000 gallons, but it is only 1,200 gallons for a lacto-ovo (dairy- and egg-eating) vegetarian and 300 gallons for a vegan (one who consumes no animal-derived products) (Robbins 367). Not only is the vast amount of water wasted through a meat-based diet outrageous, but the added cost of controlling animal waste must also be taken into account. One cow produces sixteen times as much waste as one human, and cattle waste produces ten times the water pollution that human waste does (372–373).

Student's opinion

Paraphrase of sources (facts)

A third loss is even more serious than the losses of forests and water. This year, 60 million people will die of starvation, yet in America, we feed 80 percent of our corn and 95 percent of our oats to farm animals. The feed given to cattle alone, excluding

Student's opinion

pigs and chickens, would feed double the population of humans worldwide. Three and one-quarter acres of farmland are needed to provide meat for one person per year. A lacto-ovo vegetarian can be fed from just one-half of an acre per year; a vegan needs only one-sixth of an acre. This means twenty vegans can eat a healthy diet for the same acreage needed to feed just one meat eater. Cutting our meat habit by only 10 percent would provide enough food for all of the 60 million people worldwide who will starve this year (Robbins 352–353).

Paraphrase of sources (facts)

Student's final remarks

With all the devastation the average American diet is creating, we must begin to take responsibility for the consequences of our actions. Let us follow in the footsteps of such famous vegetarians as Charles Darwin, Leonardo da Vinci, Albert Einstein, Isaac Newton, Plato, Pythagoras, Socrates, and Tolstoy (Parham 185). Every time we sit down to eat, we can choose either to contribute to or to help put an end to this suffering and destruction. Only one move matters, and that is the one we make with our forks.

Notes

[1]For more information on meat and its effects on our health and the environment, see <http://www.envirolink.org/arrs/essays/BB9. html>.

Works Cited

Alphabetical list of sources

Clayton, Julie. "Spectre of AIDS Haunts Reports of Sick Cows." <u>Nature</u> 367 (1994): 585.

Modern Language Association format

Diamond, Harvey, and Marilyn Diamond. Fit for Life II: Living Health. New York: Warner, 1987.

Durning, Alan B. "Fat of the Land." World Watch. July 1992 <http://envirolink.org/arrs/essays/fat.html>.

Marcus, Erik. Vegan: The New Ethics of Eating. Ithaca: McBooks P, 1998.

Parham, Barbara. What's Wrong with Eating Meat? Denver: Ananda Marga, 1981.

"Red Meat Alert." New Scientist 22 Dec. 1990: 9.

Rifkin, Jeremy. "Beyond Beef: The Cattle Industry Threatens the Environment, Human Health, and the World Food Supply." Utne Reader 50 (1992): 96–109.

Robbins, John. Diet for a New America. Walpole: Stillpoint, 1987.

Singer, Peter. Animal Liberation: A New Ethics for Our Treatment of Animals. New York: Hearst, 1975.

Student Writer's Comments

From the moment this essay was assigned, I knew my topic would be vegetarianism, because I felt that the key to a convincing argument was to select a topic I was passionate about. Since I was undertaking the task of speaking out against the time-honored American tradition of eating meat, I knew I needed to approach the topic in as nonthreatening a manner as possible. I wanted to be graphic as I appealed to the emotions, concerns, and ethics of my audience, so that my message would not easily be forgotten, but I had to strike a careful balance, so that I would not alienate my readers by appearing preachy, accusatory, or unduly crude.

I began the process of writing this paper by going to the library every chance I had (between classes, during lunch, and at night before I went home) and collecting information on the horror stories connected with eating meat. (I had been a loyal vegetarian for years and actually wanted some concrete information on some of the choices I had made in my own eating habits.) I found plenty of horror stories, but I also uncovered some counterarguments that I hadn't been aware of. I was fascinated by the information—both facts and opinions—that I was discovering. But the material wasn't taking any shape at all yet; the only common denominator was the general topic and my interest level.

I was taking notes on notecards, so I had filled quite a stack of cards when I stopped to reread all my material to see if I could put it into any coherent categories. Happily, my notes fell quite naturally into three divisions: (1) the overwhelming cruelty to the animals that we kill and eat, (2) the diseases resulting from eating animals, and (3) the effect of this type of slaughter on world ecology. After this exercise, I could see right away that I had enough material on the suffering of the animals killed for human consumption, and my material in this area was from well-known, reputable sources. My notes on world ecology would also be sufficient with a few more library sessions, but I had to do some serious investigation on the topic of human diseases in reference to meat eaters or else drop the topic altogether. I had some stray notes that didn't fit any of these categories, but I decided to worry about those later. I tried my hand at a thesis statement, which I think had been floating around in my head for days. Then I wrote the paper topic by topic over a period of several days. I didn't attempt the introduction and the conclusion until I began to rewrite. As I composed the essay, I was especially aware of the types of material I had to support each of my topics. I had a good distribution of summaries, paraphrases, and quotations and had remembered to keep careful notes on my sources, so I put my source and page numbers into my first draft. I also had several examples for each of my topics and a good blend of facts and opinions.

When I rewrote, I kept in mind that I would be successful in arguing my case only if my words caused the readers to make a change, however small, in their own behavior. I reworked my research paper several times as I played different readers with various biases, paying special attention to word choice and sentence structure.

Overall, writing this paper gave me a great deal of pleasure. I feel even stronger in my determination to be a vegetarian, and now I have some concrete reasons (and their sources!) for my natural instincts.

SOME FINAL THOUGHTS ON DOCUMENTED ESSAYS

The two essays that follow offer vigorous exercises in critical thinking. They also use a combination of the three different types of persuasive appeals we studied in Chapter 9 (logical, emotional, and ethical) and draw on a wealth of rhetorical modes that we have studied throughout the book. In the first essay, Barbara Ehrenreich illustrates the Modern Language Association documentation style as she uses sources to support her thesis that people do not have a natural instinct to kill. The second essay, by Jill Leslie Rosenbaum and Meda Chesney-Lind, explains the connection between female appearance and judgments in criminal cases; its use of sources illustrates the American Psychological Association documentation style. As you read these essays, be aware of the combination of appeals at work, the various rhetorical modes each author uses to further her argument, and the way the authors use sources to support the topics within each essay.

DOCUMENTED ESSAYS IN REVIEW

Reading Documented Essays

Preparing to Read

✓ What assumptions can you make from the essay's title?
✓ Can you guess what the general mood of the essay is?
✓ What is the essay's purpose and audience?
✓ What does the synopsis tell you about the essay?
✓ What can you learn from the author's biography?
✓ What are your responses to the "Preparing to Read" questions?

Reading

✓ What is the author's main assertion or thesis?
✓ What sources does the author cite to support the thesis?
✓ What questions do you have about this topic?
✓ Did you preview the questions that follow the essay?

Rereading

✓ How does the author use facts and opinions in the essay?
✓ Are the sources the writer cites valid and reliable?
✓ Does the author interpret facts accurately?

Writing Documented Essays

Preparing to Write

✓ What are your responses to the "Preparing to Write" questions?
✓ What is your purpose?
✓ Who is your audience?

Writing

✓ Do you have a thesis statement?
✓ Have you organized your material effectively?
✓ Have you avoided plagiarism and cited your sources correctly?
✓ Do you use the appropriate documentation style?

Rewriting

✓ Are the essay's assertions clear? Are they adequately supported?
✓ Are other points of view recognized and examined?
✓ Does the organization of your paper further your argument?
✓ Are your summaries, paraphrases, or quotations presented accurately?
✓ Do you introduce the sources in your paper when appropriate?
✓ Are your sources in the proper format (MLA, APA, or another)?
✓ Have you followed your instructor's guidelines for your title page, margins, page numbers, tables, and abstracts?
✓ Do you have an alphabetical list of sources for the end of your paper?

BARBARA EHRENREICH   (1941–   )

The Ecstasy of War

Barbara Ehrenreich is a respected author, lecturer, and social commentator with opinions on a wide range of topics. After earning a B.A. from Reed College in chemistry and physics and a Ph.D. from Rockefeller University in cell biology, she turned almost immediately to freelance writing, producing a succession of books and pamphlets on a dazzling array of subjects. Early publications examined student uprisings, health care in America, nurses and midwives, poverty, welfare, economic justice for women, and the sexual politics of disease. Her most recent books include *The Hearts of Men: American Dreams and the Flight from Commitment* (1983), *Fear of Falling: The Inner Life of the Middle Class* (1989), *The Worst Years of Our Lives: Irreverent Notes from a Decade of Greed* (1990), *Blood Rites: Origins and History of the Passions of War* (1997), and *Nickel and Dimed* (2001). Ehrenreich is also well known as a frequent guest on television and radio programs, including *The Today Show, Good Morning America, Nightline, Crossfire,* and *The Phil Donohue Show.* Her many articles and reviews have appeared in the *New York Times Magazine, Esquire,* the *Atlantic Monthly,* the *New Republic, Vogue, Harper's,* and the *Wall Street Journal.* She has been an essayist for *Time* since 1990. Ehrenreich, whose favorite hobby is "voracious reading," lives in Syosset, New York.

Preparing to Read

Taken from *Blood Rites: Origins and History of the Passions of War* (1997), the following essay analyzes the psychology of war. Its citations and bibliography illustrate proper MLA (Modern Language Association) documentation form.

Exploring Experience: As you prepare to read this article, take a few minutes to think about aggression in society today: Do you think aggression plays a significant role in American society? In other societies? What do you think is the origin of aggression? In your opinion, what role does aggression play in war? In everyday life? How do you react to aggressive behavior? How do people you associate with react to aggressive behavior?

Learning Online: Review the descriptions of current video games with a war theme. You may visit Web sites for Electronic Arts, Activision, or Take 2 Interactive to peruse their current game lists. Consider the techniques and intents of these games while reading Ehrenreich's essay.

"So elemental is the human need to endow the shedding of blood with some great and even sublime significance that it renders the intellect almost entirely helpless" (Van Creveld 166).

Different wars have led to different theories of why men fight them. The Napoleonic Wars, which bore along with them the rationalist spirit of the French Revolution, inspired the Prussian officer Carl von Clausewitz to propose that war itself is an entirely rational undertaking, unsullied by human emotion. War, in his famous aphorism, is merely a "continuation of policy . . . by other means," with policy itself supposedly resulting from the same kind of clearheaded deliberation one might apply to a game of chess. Nation-states were the leading actors on the stage of history, and war was simply one of the many ways they advanced their interests against those of other nation-states. If you could accept the existence of this new super-person, the nation, a battle was no more disturbing and irrational than, say, a difficult trade negotiation—except perhaps to those who lay dying on the battlefield.

World War I, coming a century after Napoleon's sweep through Europe and northern Africa, led to an opposite assessment of the human impulse to war. World War I was hard to construe as in any way "rational," especially to that generation of European intellectuals, including Sigmund Freud, who survived to ponder the unprecedented harvest of dead bodies. History textbooks tell us that the "Great War" grew out of the conflict between "competing imperialist states," but this Clausewitzian interpretation has little to do with the actual series of accidents, blunders, and miscommunications that impelled the nations of Europe to war in the summer of 1914.[1] At first swept up in the excitement of the war, unable for weeks to work or think of anything else, Freud was eventually led to conclude that there is some dark flaw in the human psyche, a perverse desire to destroy, countering Eros and the will to live (Stromberg 82).

So these are, in crude summary, the theories of war which 3 modern wars have left us with: That war is a means, however risky, by which men seek to advance their collective interests and improve their lives. Or, alternatively, that war stems from subrational drives not unlike those that lead individuals to commit violent crimes. In our own time, most people seem to hold both views at once, avowing that war is a gainful enterprise, intended to meet the material needs of the groups engaged in it, and, at the same time, that it fulfills deep and "irrational" psychological needs. There is no question about the first part of this proposition—that wars are designed, at least ostensibly, to secure necessaries like land or oil or "geopolitical advantage." The mystery lies in the peculiar psychological grip war exerts on us.

In the 1960s and '70s, the debate on the psychology of war centered on the notion of an "aggressive instinct," peculiar to all 4 humans or only to human males. This is not the place to summarize that debate, with its endless examples of animal behavior and clashes over their applicability to human affairs. Here I would simply point out that, whether or not there is an aggressive instinct, there are reasons to reject it as the major wellspring of war.

Although it is true that aggressive impulses, up to and including 5 murderous rage, can easily take over in the heat of actual battle, even this statement must be qualified to take account of different weaponry and modes of fighting. Hand-to-hand combat may indeed call forth and even require the emotions of rage and aggression, if only to mobilize the body for bursts of muscular activity. In the case of action-at-a-distance weapons, however, like guns and bows and arrows, emotionality of any sort can be a distinct disadvantage. Coolness, and the ability to keep aiming and firing steadfastly in the face of enemy fire, prevails. Hence, according to the distinguished American military historian Robert L. O'Connell, the change in the ideal warrior personality wrought by the advent of guns in the fifteenth and sixteenth centuries, from "ferocious aggressiveness" to "passive disdain" (119). So there is no personality type—"hot-tempered," "macho," or whatever— consistently and universally associated with warfare.

Furthermore, fighting itself is only one component of the enter-   6
prise we know as war. Wars are not barroom brawls writ large, or
domestic violence that has been somehow extended to strangers.
In war, fighting takes place within battles—along with much anxious waiting, of course—but wars do not begin with battles and
are often not decided by them either. Most of war consists of
preparation for battle—training, the organization of supplies,
marching and other forms of transport—activities which are hard
to account for by innate promptings of any kind. There is no plau-
sible instinct, for example, that impels a man to leave his home,
cut his hair short, and drill for hours in tight formation. As anthro-
pologists Clifton B. Kroeber and Bernard L. Fontana point out, "It
is a large step from what may be biologically innate leanings
toward individual aggression to ritualized, socially sanctioned,
institutionalized group warfare" (166).

War, in other words, is too complex and collective an activity   7
to be accounted for by a single warlike instinct lurking within the
individual psyche. Instinct may, or may not, inspire a man to bayonet the first enemy he encounters in battle. But instinct does not
mobilize supply lines, manufacture rifles, issue uniforms, or move
an army of thousands from point A on the map to B. These are
"complicated, orchestrated, highly organized" activities, as social
theorist Robin Fox writes, undertaken not by individuals but by
entities on the scale of nations and dynasties (15). "The hypothesis of a killer instinct," according to a commentator summarizing
a recent conference on the anthropology of war, is "not so much
wrong as irrelevant" (Clark McCauley in Haas 2).

In fact, throughout history, individual men have gone to near-   8
suicidal lengths to avoid participating in wars—a fact that proponents of a warlike instinct tend to slight. Men have fled their
homelands, served lengthy prison terms, hacked off limbs, shot off
feet or index fingers, feigned illness or insanity, or, if they could
afford to, paid surrogates to fight in their stead. "Some draw their
teeth, some blind themselves, and others maim themselves, on
their way to us" (Mitchell 42), the governor of Egypt complained
of his peasant recruits in the early nineteenth century. So unreliable was the rank and file of the eighteenth-century Prussian
army that military manuals forbade camping near a woods or
forest: The troops would simply melt away into the trees
(Delbrück 303).

Proponents of a warlike instinct must also reckon with the fact   9
that even when men have been assembled, willingly or unwillingly, for the purpose of war, fighting is not something that seems
to come "naturally" to them. In fact, surprisingly, even in the
thick of battle, few men can bring themselves to shoot directly at
individual enemies.[2] The difference between an ordinary man or
boy and a reliable killer, as any drill sergeant could attest, is profound. A transformation is required: The man or boy leaves his former self behind and becomes something entirely different, perhaps
even taking a new name. In small-scale, traditional societies, the
change was usually accomplished through ritual drumming, dancing, fasting, and sexual abstinence—all of which serve to lift a man
out of his mundane existence and into a new, warriorlike mode of
being, denoted by special body paint, masks, and headdresses.

As if to emphasize the discontinuity between the warrior and   10
the ordinary human being, many cultures require the would-be
fighting man to leave his humanness behind and assume a new
form as an animal.[3] The young Scandinavian had to become a bear
before he could become an elite warrior, going "berserk" (the
word means "dressed in a bear hide"), biting and chasing people.
The Irish hero Cuchulain transformed himself into a monster
in preparation for battle: "He became horrible, many-shaped,
strange, and unrecognizable," with one eye sucked into his skull
and the other popping out of the side of the face (Davidson 84).
Apparently this transformation was a familiar and meaningful one,
because similarly distorted faces turn up frequently in Celtic art.

Often the transformation is helped along with drugs or social   11
pressure of various kinds. Tahitian warriors were browbeaten into
fighting by functionaries called Rauti, or "exhorters," who ran
around the battlefield urging their comrades to mimic "the
devouring wild dog" (Keeley 146). The ancient Greek hoplites
drank enough wine, apparently, to be quite tipsy when they went
into battle (Hanson 126); Aztecs drank pulque; Chinese troops at
the time of Sun Tzu got into the mood by drinking wine and
watching "gyrating sword dancers" perform (Sun Tzu 37). Almost
any drug or intoxicant has served, in one setting or another, to
facilitate the transformation of man into warrior. Yanomamo
Indians of the Amazon ingest a hallucinogen before battle; the
ancient Scythians smoked hemp, while a neighboring tribe drank
something called "hauma," which is believed to have induced a

frenzy of aggression (Rolle 94–95). So if there is a destructive instinct that impels men to war, it is a weak one and often requires a great deal of help.

In seventeenth-century Europe, the transformation of man into soldier took on a new form, more concerted and disciplined, and far less pleasant, than wine. New recruits and even seasoned veterans were endlessly drilled, hour after hour, until each man began to feel himself part of a single, giant fighting machine. The drill was only partially inspired by the technology of firearms. It's easy enough to teach a man to shoot a gun; the problem is to make him willing to get into situations where guns are being shot and to remain there long enough to do some shooting of his own. So modern military training aims at a transformation parallel to that achieved by "primitives" with war drums and paint: In the fanatical routines of boot camp, a man leaves behind his former identity and is reborn as a creature of the military—an automaton and also, ideally, a willing killer of other men.   12

This is not to suggest that killing is foreign to human nature or, more narrowly, to the male personality. Men (and women) have again and again proved themselves capable of killing impulsively and with gusto. But there is a huge difference between a war and an ordinary fight. War not only departs from the normal; it inverts all that is moral and right: In war one *should* kill, *should* steal, *should* burn cities and farms, *should* perhaps even rape matrons and little girls. Whether or not such activities are "natural" or at some level instinctual, most men undertake them only by entering what appears to be an "altered state"—induced by drugs or lengthy drilling, and denoted by face paint or khakis.   13

The point of such transformative rituals is not only to put men "in the mood." Returning warriors may go through equally challenging rituals before they can celebrate victory or reenter the community—covering their heads in apparent shame, for example; vomiting repeatedly; abstaining from sex (Keeley 144). Among the Maori, returning warriors could not participate in the victory celebration until they had gone through a whaka-hoa ritual, designed to make them "common" again: The hearts of slain enemies were roasted, after which offerings were made to the war god Tu, and the rest was eaten by priests, who shouted spells to remove "the blood curse" and enable warriors to reenter their ordinary lives (Sagan 18). Among the Taulipang Indians of South   14

America, victorious warriors "sat on ants, flogged one another with whips, and passed a cord covered with poisonous ants, through their mouth and nose" (Métraux 397). Such painful and shocking postwar rites impress on the warrior that war is much more than a "continuation of policy . . . by other means." In war men enter an alternative realm of human experience, as far removed from daily life as those things which we call "sacred."

Notes

1. See, for example, Stoessinger, *Why Nations Go to War,* 14–20.
2. See Grossman, *On Killing.*
3. In the mythologies of the Indo-European tradition, Dumézil relates, thanks "either to a gift of metamorphosis, or to a monstrous heredity, the eminent warrior possesses a veritable animal nature" (Dumézil 140).

Works Cited

Davidson, Hilda Ellis. *Myths and Symbols in Pagan Europe: Early Scandinavian and Celtic Religions.* Syracuse: Syracuse UP, 1988.

Delbrück, Hans. *The Dawn of Modern Warfare.* Lincoln: U of Nebraska P, 1985.

Dumézil, Georges. *Destiny of the Warrior.* Chicago: U of Chicago P, 1969.

Fox, Robin. "Fatal Attraction: War and Human Nature." *National Interest* Winter 1992/93: 11–20.

Grossman, Lt. Col. Dave. *On Killing: The Psychological Cost of Learning to Kill in War and Society.* Boston: Little, Brown, 1995.

Haas, Jonathan, ed. *The Anthropology of War.* Cambridge: Cambridge UP, 1990.

Hanson, Victor Davis. *The Western Way of War: Infantry Battle in Classical Greece.* New York: Knopf, 1989.

Keeley, Lawrence H. *War Before Civilization: The Myth of the Peaceful Savage.* New York: Oxford UP, 1996.

Kroeber, Clifton B., and Bernard L. Fontana. *Massacre on the Gila: An Account of the Last Major Battle Between American Indians, with Reflections on the Origin of War.* Tucson: U of Arizona P, 1986.

Métraux, Alfred. "Warfare, Cannibalism, and Human Trophies." *Handbook of South American Indians.* Vol. 5. Ed. Julian H. Steward. New York: Cooper Square, 1963.

Mitchell, Timothy. *Colonizing Egypt*. Berkeley: U of California P, 1991.

O'Connell, Robert L. *Of Arms and Men: A History of War, Weapons, and Aggression*. New York: Oxford UP, 1989.

Rolle, Renate. *The World of the Scythians*. Berkeley: U of California P, 1989.

Sagan, Eli. *Cannibalism: Human Aggression and Cultural Form*. New York: Harper and Row, 1974.

Stoessinger, John G. *Why Nations Go to War*. New York: St. Martin's, 1993.

Stromberg, Roland. *Redemption by War: The Intellectuals and 1914*. Lawrence: U of Kansas P, 1982.

Sun Tzu. *The Art of War*. Translated and with an introduction by Samuel B. Griffith. London: Oxford University Press, 1971.

Van Creveld, Martin. *The Transformation of War*. New York: Free Press, 1991.

UNDERSTANDING DETAILS

1. What do you think Ehrenreich's main purpose is in this essay?
2. According to Ehrenreich, what is the difference between hand-to-hand combat and fighting at a distance?
3. What does Ehrenreich say are the various components of what we call "war"?
4. In what ways do some cultures ritualize the transformation from regular citizen to warrior? Give three examples.

ANALYZING MEANING

1. Do you believe that war can ever be emotionless and rational, like "a difficult trade negotiation" (paragraph 1)?
2. What do Kroeber and Fontana mean when they say, "It is a large step from what may be biologically innate leanings toward individual aggression to ritualized, socially sanctioned, institutionalized group warfare" (paragraph 6)?
3. Why is "the hypothesis of a killer instinct" "not so much wrong as irrelevant" to the "anthropology of war" (paragraph 7)?
4. Are you convinced by this essay that "in war men enter an alternative realm of human experience, as far removed from daily life as those things which we call 'sacred'" (paragraph 14)?

DISCOVERING RHETORICAL STRATEGIES

1. Who do you think is Ehrenreich's main audience? How did you come to this conclusion?
2. The author begins her discussion of war with different "theories of why men fight" wars (paragraph 1). Is this an effective beginning for what Ehrenreich is trying to accomplish? Explain your answer.
3. What information in this essay is most persuasive to you? What is least persuasive?
4. What tone does the author establish by citing frequent statistics and referring to other sources in her essay?

MAKING CONNECTIONS

1. Compare and contrast Ehrenreich's insights on the psychology of war with Stephen King's theories on "Why We Crave Horror Movies." How do their ideas support one another? How do they contradict each other?
2. Compare Ehrenreich's use of examples with those of Rosenbaum and Chesney-Lind ("Appearance and Delinquency: A Research Note").
3. In a conversation among Ehrenreich, Brent Staples ("A Brother's Murder"), bell hooks ("Justice: Childhood Love Lessons"), and Dave Grossman ("We Are Training Our Kids to Kill") about the "aggressive instinct" in people, on what points would they agree and disagree? Give examples.

IDEAS FOR DISCUSSION/WRITING

Preparing to Write

Write freely about aggression in general: Why do people fight? Why do countries go to war? What are some ways in which people take out their aggression? Have you ever noticed people fighting just for the sake of fighting? When is aggression acceptable? When is it unacceptable?

Choosing a Topic

1. Ehrenreich claims that "even when men have been assembled, willingly or unwillingly, for the purpose of war, fighting is not something that seems to come 'naturally' to them" (paragraph

9). Do you agree or disagree with this statement? Explain your reaction in a clearly reasoned argumentative essay. Cite Ehrenreich's selection whenever necessary.

2. In the last paragraph of her essay, Ehrenreich suggests that warriors often have to go through rituals to return to their civilizations. Use Ehrenreich's article as one of your sources; then read further on such transformations. Next write a clear, well-documented argument expressing your opinion on a specific transformation. Organize your paper clearly, and present your suggestions logically, using proper documentation (citations and bibliography) to support your position.

3. Use additional sources to study the circumstances of a war you are familiar with. Then, referring to Ehrenreich's explanation of "the anthropology of war" (paragraph 7), write a well-documented argument explaining the causes and effects of the war by discussing or analyzing in depth the consequences you have discovered.

4. Video games simulate war situations involving strategy, combat, and sometimes death. Ehrenreich claims that no personality type has a "single warlike instinct" (paragraph 7). How do her theories apply to video game users? Develop a documented essay in which you test Ehrenreich's theories by applying them to video game users. Be sure to use credible sources to support your claims.

Before beginning your essay, you might want to consult the checklists on page 592.

JILL LESLIE ROSENBAUM   (1955–   )

AND MEDA CHESNEY-LIND   (1947–   )

Appearance and Delinquency: A Research Note

Jill Leslie Rosenbaum, a criminologist specializing in female crime, earned her B.A. in sociology at the University of Michigan, her M.S. in Addiction Studies at the University of Arizona, and her Ph.D. in criminal justice at the State University of New York, Albany. She is currently a professor of criminal justice at California State University, Fullerton, where she has published recent articles in *Crime and Delinquency, Justice Quarterly,* and *Youth and Society.* In her spare time, she enjoys working out at a local gym, reading good novels, and participating in children's theater. She has also done extensive work with the California Office of Criminal Justice Planning on the topic of sexual assault. Her advice to students using *The Prose Reader* is to "spend lots of time writing. Write and rewrite your work until it is perfect!" Her coauthor, Meda Chesney-Lind, earned her B.A. at Whitman College and her M.A. and Ph.D. at the University of Hawaii. She is currently a professor of Women's Studies at the University of Hawaii at Manoa, where she has published three books on women and crime—*Girls, Delinquency, and Juvenile Justice* (1992, with Randall Shelden), *The Female Offender* (1997), and *Female Gangs in America* (1999, with John Hagedorn)—plus over fifty articles on related topics. Her recreational activities include walking and haunting thrift shops. She advises student writers to "practice, practice, practice," explaining that "you have to trust your instincts in order to become a better writer, which also requires patience, discipline, and a healthy sense of humor."

Preparing to Read

Taken from a journal entitled *Crime and Delinquency* (April 1994), the following essay explains that perceived attractiveness of female offenders in particular plays an important part in the criminal justice system. Its citations and bibliography illustrate proper APA (American Psychological Association) documentation form.

Exploring Experience: As you prepare to read this article, take a few minutes to think about the influence appearance has on your view of the world: Do you consciously think about appearance? Do someone's looks influence your professional judgment of that person? Would a defendant's appearance affect your view of his or her guilt? Does appearance play any part in how well you listen to someone or whether or not you agree with a person? How does appearance affect your opinion of a stranger?

Learning Online: To prepare for Rosenbaum and Chesney-Lind's discussion of the treatment of female delinquents, visit the National Criminal Justice Reference Library (http://www.ncjrs. org). Browse the sections to familiarize yourself with terms related to arrests and incarceration.

Women are judged by culturally derived standards of attractiveness. These culturally created standards affect women in all walks of life, including, it appears, the way they are treated by the criminal justice system. Research has shown that perception of physical appearance can have a significant impact on an individual's success in a variety of endeavors. These endeavors include dating opportunities (Crause & Mehrabian, 1977; Stretch & Figley, 1980; Walster, Aronson, Abrahams, & Rottman, 1966), the initiation of relationships (Murstein & Christy, 1976; Price & Vandenberg, 1979; White, 1980), teachers' evaluations of students (Clifford & Walster, 1973; Dion, 1973), and corporate success (Heilman & Stopeck, 1985; Heilman & Sarawatari, 1979).

The role of appearance in judgments of criminal reponsibility and the punishment of such behavior have also been the focus of a variety of psychological studies (Efran, 1974; Sigall and Ostrove, 1975; Stewart, 1980). These studies consistently indicate that physical attractiveness influences judgments of wrongdoing. Dion (1973) found that adult judgments of children's transgressions were affected by the attractiveness of the child. Transgressions, both mild and severe, were perceived to be less undesirable when committed by an attractive child than by an unattractive child.

Furthermore, subjects were less likely to attribute chronic antiso-
cial behavior to attractive than to unattractive children.

The work of Sigall and Ostrove (1975) suggest that the sen-   3
tences given to offenders are often conditioned by the appearance
of the offender. Attractive female offenders, whose offense was not
appearance-related (burglary), received greater leniency than unattractive offenders. However, when the offense was attractiveness-
related (swindle), attractive offenders received harsher sentences
than their unattractive counterparts. These findings are consistent
with those of Efran (1974), whose work has shown that attractive
defendants are much less likely to be found guilty than unattractive defendants. This becomes especially pronounced when males
are judging the culpability of females. Sigall and Ostrove (1975)
and Efran (1974) also indicate that when a female offender is seen
as using her attractiveness to assist in the commission of a crime,
attractive defendants were more likely to be found guilty.

Studies of appearance also demonstrate that society has higher   4
expectations for attractive individuals; some of these expectations
pertain exclusively to women. For instance, attractive women are
assumed to be more feminine and have a more socially desirable
personality, and as a result, they are assumed to have greater overall happiness in their personal, social and professional lives (Dion,
Berscheid, & Walster, 1973). It is also assumed that they are less
likely to remain single, more likely to marry earlier, be better
spouses, and be better sexual partners as well.

Although the lives of attractive women are assumed to be far   5
superior to those of less attractive women, some believe that
attractive women have less integrity, and thus managerial opportunities for them may be hindered. In fact, Heilman and Sarawatari
(1979) concluded that women with more masculine characteristics
are believed to have greater ability than women with feminine
characteristics. Thus, although attractive women are thought to be
more feminine, they are also thought to be less well-suited for
nontraditional female roles.

Finally, Emerson (1969) noted that judges and other juvenile   6
court personnel often expressed considerable interest in the
appearance of girls appearing before the court he observed. He
noted a judge's interest in whether runaway girls were "clean"
after having been away from home for more than a day or two;

the assumption was that if they were clean and/or heavily made up, they might be engaging in prostitution (p. 112).

Since the establishment of the first juvenile court, there has   7 been ongoing interest by judges and other court workers in the sexual activity of girls. In the early days of the court (1899–1920), there was a clear bias against girls deemed sexually active and a harsh official response to their misbehavior. Virtually all of the girls who appeared before the first juvenile courts were charged with immorality or waywardness (Chesney-Lind, 1971; Rafter 1990; Schlossman & Wallach, 1978; Shelden, 1981); and the response of the courts to this noncriminal behavior frequently was incarceration.

In Honolulu during 1929–1930, over half of the girls referred   8 to court were charged with immorality, which meant evidence (or inferences drawn) of sexual intercourse. In addition, another 30% were charged with waywardness. Evidence of immorality was vigorously pursued both by arresting officers and social workers through lengthy questioning of the girl and, if possible, males with whom she was suspected of having sex. Other evidence of exposure was provided by gynecological examinations, which were routinely ordered. Doctors, who understood the purpose of such examinations, would routinely note the condition of the hymen: "admits intercourse-hymen ruptured," "no laceration," and "hymen ruptured" were typical of their notations. Girls during this period were also twice as likely as boys to be detained, and they remained in detention five times as long on the average as their male counterparts. They were also nearly three times more likely to be sentenced to training schools (Chesney-Lind, 1971) where well into the 1950s they continued to be half of those committed in Honolulu (Chesney-Lind, 1973).

National statistics reflect the official enthusiasm for the incarceration of girls during the early part of this century; their share of   9 the population of juvenile correctional facilities increased from 1880 (when girls were 19% of the population) to 1923 (when girls were 28%). By 1950, girls had climbed to 34% of the total, and in 1960 they were still 27% of those in correctional facilities. By 1980, this pattern appeared to be reversed, and girls were again 19% of those in correctional facilities (Calahan, 1986, p. 130), and in 1989, girls accounted for 11.9% of those held in public detention centers and training schools (Allen-Hagen, 1991, p. 4).

The decline in incarceration of juvenile females in public facil-   10
ities run by the juvenile justice system is directly linked to an
intense debate on the issue of the institutionalization of young
people, especially youth charged with noncriminal status offenses
(e.g., running away from home, being incorrigible, truant, or in
danger of leading a lewd and lascivious lifestyle). In particular, the
Juvenile Justice and Delinquency Prevention Act (JJDPA) of 1974
stressed the need to divert and deinstitutionalize youth charged
with status offenses and provided states with a number of incentives to achieve this goal.

Critical to any understanding of the dynamics of gender bias in   11
the juvenile justice system, then, is an appreciation of the gendered
nature of delinquency, and particularly status offenses. It should be
understood that status offenses have also served as "buffer charges"
for the court's historic, but now implicit, interest in monitoring
girls' sexual activities and their obedience to parental authority
(Gold, 1971, p. 571). In essence, modern status offense charges
mask the court's historic interest in girls' propriety and obedience
to parental authority (Chesney-Lind & Shelden, 1992).

Because of the recent but eroding success of the JJDPA of 1974,   12
it is perhaps essential to review the dynamics of sexism within the
juvenile justice system immediately prior to the passage of this act.
The study reported here, although relatively modest, documents
one aspect of the sexism that girls encountered as they entered
institutions in the 1960s: the interest of criminal justice professionals in the physical appearance of girls.

Data and Methods   This analysis is based on the records of   13
159 women who, as juveniles, were committed to the California
Youth Authority (CYA) during the 1960s. Records were requested
on all 240 of the girls who were sentenced to the CYA between
1961 and 1965 from San Francisco and the Sacramento Valley.
There were 59 cases unavailable because the juvenile records had
been purged and another 22 cases could not be located. For the
159 cases where data was available, the records included the complete CYA files containing all comments/reports regarding the
ward and the case by the CYA intake workers, counselors, teachers, living unit personnel, chaplains, social workers, and psychologists (for more information regarding data collection, see Warren
and Rosenbaum, 1986).

The racial composition of these 159 cases was 51% Caucasian,   14
30% African-American, 9% Latino, and the remaining 10% were
Asian or Native American. Two-thirds of the girls had been committed to the CYA for status offenses, and more specifically, 49%
were charged with running away from home, 28% for being
"beyond control," 12% for "being in danger of a lewd and lascivious lifestyle," 7% for truancy, and 4% for curfew. To say that
these girls were committed for status offenses actually understates
the role of status offenses in their delinquency records; this group
of girls committed 698 offenses prior to their commitment to the
CYA. The average number of arrests was six, and over 90% of
these were status offenses. There were no racial differences
observed in the distribution of these offenses.

Each file was examined by two independent coders who coded   15
data on the type of offenses committed prior to CYA commitment, the gender of the social worker who did the evaluation of
the ward, whether mention was made of the ward's appearance,
and if so, the description given of the girl's appearance.[1] Reliability
among the coders was over 96%. Because all of the girls in the
sample were part of an experimental program and were randomly
assigned to treatment programs, the length of their incarceration
was not coded.

Findings   Female case workers did intake evaluations on 29%   16
(46) of the 159 cases, whereas males were responsible for 71%
(113) of them. When female CYA personnel conducted the intake
evaluation, there was no mention of physical appearance in any of
the 46 cases for which they were responsible. This was not the case
when males performed the evaluation; appearance was mentioned
in 63% (75) of the cases.

A variety of physical descriptions was recorded for the 75 wards   17
whose appearance was mentioned in the files. These show male
staff concern with the physical maturity of the girls, as well as some
evidence of racial stereotyping; indeed, of those where evaluative
judgments about appearance were made, 60% were made about
minority group females. Moreover, those viewing these young
women of color adhered to "representations of race" (hooks,
1992) that negate any beauty that does not conform to White standards of appearance, while celebrating those images that mimic
White appearance.

From the descriptions of the girls' appearance, four general cat-   18
egories emerged: attractive, unattractive, plain/wholesome, and
"well-built."[2] Of the wards whose appearance was mentioned,
26% (19) were described as attractive (e.g., "The ward is an attractive, physically mature 13-year-old"), whereas 38% (27) were
described as unattractive (e.g., "Her appearance is rather uninteresting and unattractive"); 19% as plain or wholesome; and 17%
(14) were described as well-built.

Differences emerged when the relationship between the type of   19
offense and the mention of appearance in the intake evaluations
was examined. About 50% (56) of the girls who had been evaluated by a male had at least one immorality charge against them.
When females who had been charged with immorality offenses
(being in danger of leading a lewd and lascivious life and prostitution) were compared with those who had no such charge, differences in the mention of appearance became especially pronounced. For instance, for those charged with one or more counts
of immorality, a physical description was present in 93% (55) of
the cases. However, when no immorality charges were present, a
physical description was included in only 37% (20) of the cases (see
Table 1). Looking at the data from another perspective, in cases
where no description of the girl's appearance was present, 89%
(34) had no charges of immorality. As indicated in Table 1, a significant relationship ($\chi^2 = 37.5$) was found between having at least
one immorality charge and having mention made of the girl's
appearance in her file.

Differences also existed with respect to the type of offenses pres-   20
ent and the description given. All of the girls who were described
as attractive and all of the girls who were described as well-built
had been charged with at least one immorality offense. However,

TABLE 1: Appearance by Presence of Immorality Charges

	Appearance Described	No Description Included	
Immorality charges	93 (55)	7 (4)	100 (59)
No immorality charges	37 (20)	63 (34)	100 (54)

$\chi^2 = 37.4$, 1 *df*, significance = .000.

only 26% of the girls described as plain/wholesome and 34% of those described as unattractive had similar charges against them. Although these numbers are small, the magnitude of the difference is clearly significant.

More Recent Data To assess whether or not appearance   21
remains an issue today, more recent data from the CYA was examined. In the process of collecting data from the CYA files of all girls who were wards of the CYA in 1990, close attention was paid to any mention of the girl's appearance. Similar attention was paid in a separate examination of the case files of all boys and girls who were confined in the Hawaii Youth Correctional Facility in 1989.

Although there were 214 girls who were wards of the CYA in   22
1990, comments regarding appearance were found in only eight files. All, except one who was described as slovenly and unattractive, were simply described as attractive. Five of the eight had arrests for violent crime; the other three had long records for property and drug offenses. Although the vast majority of the girls' arrests during the 1960s were for status offenses, only 4% of their 1990 counterparts' arrests were for status offenses.

Comments found in girls' files in Hawaii concerned when and   23
where they had been arrested for curfew violations. This same research effort noted that no such comments appeared in boys' files and that a third of the girls held in training schools were being held solely for "probation violation," which is a mechanism for continuing to incarcerate status offenders (Saiki, 1990, p. 23). The Hawaii study found that roughly half of the girls incarcerated during spring 1990 were "bootstrapped" status offenders (Costello and Worthington, 1991) and even for those girls who had committed criminal offenses, their offenses were far less serious than the boys and "the bulk of their juvenile offenses consisted of status offenses" (Saiki, 1990, p. 48).

Discussion The emphasis on physical appearance found in   24
this small study and the link between this interest in girls' appearance and their noncriminal delinquent behavior is more important than it might first seem. In essence, these observations provide a window into the worldview of the keepers of young women during the years prior to the passage of the JJDPA of 1974; sadly, they may also reflect a bias that remains in the states that have been

resistant to the deinstitutionalization efforts signaled by the passage of that act. Like earlier studies, which found a large number of girls in institutions subjected to physical examinations to determine if they were virgins (see Chesney-Lind and Shelden, 1992), interest in the physical appearance of girls, and particularly their physical maturity, indicates substantial interest in the sexual behavior of girls and illuminates another important dimension of the sexual policing of girls (Cain, 1989).

Particularly troubling are the comments which indicate a pre-   25
sumed association between "beauty," specifically male Caucasian standards of beauty, and sexual behavior. Certainly the fact that these girls were incarcerated for noncriminal offenses indicates the seriousness with which the criminal justice system viewed their transgressions. In short, these data provide some support for the notion, suggested by Sigall and Ostrove (1975), as well as that by Efran (1974), that judges, social workers, and other criminal justice professionals (particularly if they are male) may look upon attractive girls who engage in sexual "immorality" more harshly. They may also overlook some of the same behaviors in less attractive girls.

Such a fascination with appearance is also at odds with the lit-   26
erature on street prostitutes. These studies indicate that the pace and pressure of this life does not produce "attractive" young women, but instead tends to take a physical toll on the girls engaged in the behavior (Weisberg, 1985, p. 116). Indeed, some descriptions of prostitutes describe them as unattractive, over-weight, with poor complexions and bad teeth (Winick & Kinsie, 1972, p. 35).

The remarks found in the files which were made by male intake   27
workers suggest a fascination with the appearance of the girls who were charged with immorality. Clearly there was considerable concern with their physical maturity and physical attraction. The comments regarding the girls' appearance suggest that status offenses may have functioned as buffer charges for suspected sexual behavior. Although it appears that at least in California, where girls are no longer incarcerated for noncriminal offenses, this no longer seems to be a problem, national data suggest that in some states, like Hawaii, the detention and incarceration of girls for noncriminal status offenses persists; thus the concerns raised by this article may, sadly, not be of simply historic interest.

References

Allen-Hagen, B. (1991). *Children in custody,* 1989. Washington, DC: Bureau of Justice Statistics.

Cain, M. (1989). *Growing up good: Policing the behavior of girls in Europe.* London: Sage.

Calahan, M. W. (1986). *Historical corrections statistics in the United States, 1950–1984.* Washington, DC: U.S. Department of Justice.

Chesney-Lind, M. (1971). *Female juvenile delinquency in Hawaii.* Unpublished master's thesis, University of Hawaii, Manoa.

Chesney-Lind, M. (1973). Judicial enforcement of the female sex role. *Issues in Criminology, 8,* 51–70.

Chesney-Lind, M., & Shelden, R. (1992). *Girls, delinquency, and the juvenile justice system.* Pacific Grove, CA: Brooks/Cole.

Clifford, M., & Walster, E. (1973). The effect of physical attractiveness on teacher expectations. *Sociology of Education, 46,* 248–258.

Costello, J. C., & Worthington, N. L. (1991). Incarcerating status offenders: Attempts to circumvent the Juvenile Justice and Delinquency Prevention Act. *Harvard Civil Rights–Civil Liberties Law Review, 16,* 41–81.

Crause, B. B., & Mehrabian, A. (1977). Affiliation of opposite-sexed strangers. *Journal of Research in Personality, 11,* 38–47.

Dion, K. (1973). Physical attractiveness and evaluation of children's transgressions. *Journal of Personality and Social Psychology, 24,* 207–218.

Dion, K., Berscheid, E., & Walster, E. (1973) What is beautiful is good. *Journal of Personality and Social Psychology, 24, 285–290.*

Efran, M. (1974). The effect of physical appearance on the judgment of guilt, interpersonal attraction, and severity of recommended punishment. *Journal of Experimental Research in Personality, 8,* 45–54.

Emerson, R. (1969). *Judging delinquents.* Chicago: Aldine.

Flanagan, T. J., & McGarrell, E. F. (Eds.). (1986). *Sourcebook of criminal justice statistics, 1985.* Washington, DC: U.S. Department of Justice.

Gold, S. (1971). Equal protection for girls in need of supervision in New York State. *New York Law Forum, 17,* 570–591.

Heilman, M., & Sarawatari, L. (1979). When beauty is beastly: The effects of appearance and sex on evaluations of job applicants for managerial and nonmanagerial jobs. *Organizational Behavior and Human Performance, 23,* 360–372.

Heilman, M., & Stopeck, M. (1985). Attractiveness and corporate success: Different casual attributions for males and females. *Journal of Applied Psychology, 70,* 379–388.

hooks, b. (1992). *Black looks.* Boston: South End Press.

Jamieson, K. M., & Flanagan, T. (Eds.). (1987). *Sourcebook of criminal justice statistics, 1986.* Washington, DC: U.S. Department of Justice.

Murstein, B., & Christy, P. (1976). Physical attractiveness and marriage adjustment in middle-aged couples. *Journal of Personality and Social Psychology, 34,* 537–542.

Price, R., & Vandenberg, S. (1979). Matching for physical attractiveness in married couples. *Personality and Social Psychology Bulletin, 5,* 398–399.

Rafter, N. (1990). *Partial justice: Women, prisons, and social control.* New Brunswick, NJ: Transaction Books.

Saiki, S. (1990). *Girls, double standards and status offenses in Hawaii's juvenile court.* Unpublished paper. University of Hawaii, William Richardson School of Law.

Schlossman, S., & Wallach, S. (1978). The crime of precocious sexuality: Female delinquency in the progressive era. *Harvard Educational Review, 48,* 65–94.

Shelden, R. (1981). Sex discrimination in the juvenile justice system: Memphis, Tennessee, 1900–1971. In M.Q. Warren (Ed.), *Comparing male and female offenders.* Beverly Hills, CA: Sage.

Sigall, H., & Ostrove, N. (1975). Beautiful but dangerous: Effects of offender attractiveness and nature of crime on juridic judgment. *Journal of Personality and Social Psychology, 31,* 410–414.

Stewart, J. (1980). Defendant's attraction as a factor in the outcome of criminal trials: An observational study. *Journal of Applied Social Psychology, 10,* 348–361.

Stretch, R., & Figley, C. (1980). Beauty and the beast: Predictions of interpersonal attraction in a dating experiment. *Psychology, 17,* 34–43.

Walster, E., Aronson, E., Abrahams, D., & Rottman, L. (1966). Importance of physical attractiveness in dating behavior. *Journal of Personality and Social Psychology, 4,* 508–516.

Warren, M. Q., & Rosenbaum, J. (1986). Criminal careers of female offenders. *Criminal Justice and Behavior, 13,* 393–418.

Weisberg, D. K. (1985). *Children of the night: A study of adolescent prostitution.* Lexington, MA: Lexington Books.

White, G. (1980). Physical attractiveness and courtship progress. *Journal of Personality and Social Psychology, 39,* 660–668.

Winick, C., & Kinsie, P. M. (1972). *The lively commerce.* New York: Signet.

Notes

1. Nowhere on any of the CYA forms was there any particular place for a physical description of the ward. Comments were found throughout the narratives by the CYA personnel who became involved with the case. As far as we can tell, the issue of appearance was never discussed with regard to policy. It seemed to be merely an issue for the intake personnel.

2. These categories are broad and somewhat evasive; however, they were the factors that emerged during this analysis. It is important to remember that attractiveness is in the eye of the beholder and we, as researchers, are merely reporting the subjective assessments that we found.

UNDERSTANDING DETAILS

1. What do Rosenbaum and Chesney-Lind mean when they argue that "women are judged by culturally derived standards of attractiveness" (paragraph 1)?
2. How does being attractive usually affect judgments in the criminal justice system?
3. What expectations does society have of attractive people? Which sources do Rosenbaum and Chesney-Lind cite to verify these expectations?
4. What are "status acts"? In what ways did the Juvenile Justice and Delinquency Prevention Act of 1974 affect the court's reaction to status acts?

ANALYZING MEANING

1. Can you explain the relationship the researchers found between appearance and immorality charges in California

Youth Authority females? Why do you think this relationship existed?

2. What effect do the recent data show the Juvenile Justice and Delinquency Prevention Act had on immorality charges since 1990? Can you explain this change?

3. Are males ever unfairly treated because of their appearance? If so, in what situations? Explain your answer in detail.

4. Can you speculate about the future of status and immorality offenses? Do you think they will continue to be connected to descriptions of appearance in female criminal records?

DISCOVERING RHETORICAL STRATEGIES

1. Who do you think is Rosenbaum and Chesney-Lind's main audience? How did you come to this conclusion?

2. The authors begin their essay by citing various professional sources that verify the connections in American society between appearance and success in various aspects of life. Is this an effective beginning for what Rosenbaum and Chesney-Lind are trying to accomplish? Explain your answer.

3. What information in this essay is most persuasive to you? Least persuasive?

4. What tone do the authors establish by citing statistics and referring to other sources in their essay?

MAKING CONNECTIONS

1. If Rosenbaum and Chesney-Lind were having a conversation about sexism with Gloria Steinem ("The Politics of Muscle") and bell hooks ("Justice: Childhood Love Lessons"), what issues would the four writers agree on? What would they disagree on?

2. Compare and contrast the way Rosenbaum and Chesney-Lind present statistics and documentation in their argument with the use of this technique by Barbara Ehrenreich ("The Ecstasy of War"). Which author provides such information most skillfully? Explain your answer.

3. Examine the relationship in Rosenbaum and Chesney-Lind's essay among logical, emotional, and ethical appeals. Then compare and contrast it with the balance in the essays by Robert Heilbroner ("Don't Let Stereotypes Warp Your Judgment")

and Dave Grossman ("We Are Training Our Kids to Kill"). Which author uses the most logic? Who uses emotion most frequently? And whose ethical appeal is strongest? Which author do you find most convincing? Explain your answer.

IDEAS FOR DISCUSSION/WRITING

Preparing to Write

Write freely about your views on the relationship between appearance and delinquency: What role does the notion of appearance play in the justice system? Do you find that you have certain biases regarding people's appearances? What are they? Do you know others who hold biases about attractiveness? Do the biases verge on sexism? Do they involve both males and females? What do these biases say about our society in general?

Choosing a Topic

1. Design a constructive solution to the problem of sexist criminal reports. Then, using Rosenbaum and Chesney-Lind's essay as your main source, write an argumentative essay presenting the problem as you understand it and offering a detailed solution to it.

2. What do you think the role of appearance and behavior should be in America's judicial system? Use Rosenbaum and Chesney-Lind's article as one of your sources; then, read further on the subject. Finally, write a clear, well-documented argument on what part appearance and behavior should play in the court's judgment of criminals.

3. Choose another problem related to the American system of justice, and research it further. Then, write a well-documented argument explaining the problem and offering a solution based on the information you have discovered.

4. What other studies have been conducted on differences in treatment related to appearance? Find a case study online that interests you, and conduct further research on the topic. Write a documented essay that refers to the case study and analyzes it using your other sources.

Before beginning your essay, you might want to consult the checklists on page 592.

CHAPTER WRITING ASSIGNMENTS

Practicing Pro/Con

1. In what ways can the Internet benefit college students? How could the Internet pose problems for students? Research this topic. Then, in an essay, explore the advantages and disadvantages of the Internet for students. Provide examples to illustrate your points.

2. How well do you think national news broadcasts inform the public? Do they focus too much on negative rather than positive events in life? Investigate the role of television news over the last ten years. Then write an essay in which you review its history and discuss the role it should play in American society today.

3. What are the primary advantages and disadvantages of pursuing an online education or degree? After studying this option, write an essay discussing the reasons this type of education may benefit or hinder students and whether it is a worthwhile educational option.

Exploring Ideas

1. While voters often approve measures for funding more prisons, they are just as likely to vote against measures proposing to build new schools. As a society, should we work harder to fund new prisons, to build new schools, or to fund each equally? Research these options, and explain your view in a well-reasoned essay.

2. Most experts agree that young children learn languages easily, while older teens and adults often struggle to learn a new language. Should children be taught more than one language in elementary school so that they can become bilingual early in life? Or does a single language give the students an advantage in the school system? Investigate these options, and write an essay that explains why bilingual education for all children would or would not benefit their education.

3. In what ways is violence natural or unnatural to society? How does society promote or prohibit violence? Look into this issue. Then write an essay presenting your view about the ways violence may or may not be inherent in society.

11

FURTHER THINKING, READING, AND WRITING

In each of the preceding chapters, we have examined a single rhetorical mode to focus attention on how writers use that pattern to organize and present their thoughts. In this final chapter, we consider the topics of thinking, reading, and writing through the interrelated genres of essays, fiction, poetry, and drama which creatively combine the various rhetorical modes we have previously studied.

Our primary purpose in this text has been to show how thinking, reading, and writing work together as fine machinery to help all of us function as intelligent and productive human beings. Our introduction discusses the relationship of thinking, reading, and writing; the text itself illustrates the crucial interdependence of these skills; and this last chapter concludes the book by presenting two essays, two short stories, two poems, and a brief play by some of America's best writers on such topics as why we feel the need to respond to others verbally, the morality of writing, the importance of reading, the secrets of communication, books, poetry, and the teaching of writing.

These different views of thinking, reading, and writing are intended for you to enjoy, letting your mind run freely through the material as you recall in a leisurely way what you have learned throughout this text. They bring together the theoretical framework of this book as they illustrate how thinking, reading, and writing inform each other and work interdependently to make meaning. They also integrate the rhetorical patterns in such a way that each entry in this final chapter is a complex blend of the various rhetorical modes discussed in the preceding chapters—a perfect summary of the topics and strategies you have been learning throughout this text.

ROGER ROSENBLATT   (1940–   )

"I Am Writing Blindly"

Besides the newsworthy revelation of Lieut. Captain Dimitri   1
Kolesnikov's dying message to his wife recovered from the
husk of the sunken submarine *Kursk*—that 23 of the 118
crewmen had survived in an isolated chamber for a while, in
contradiction to claims by Russian officials that all had perished
within minutes of the accident—there was the matter of writing
the message in the first place.

In the first place, in the last place, that is what we people do—   2
write messages to one another. We are a narrative species. We
exist by storytelling—by relating our situations—and the test of
our evolution may lie in getting the story right.

What Kolesnikov did in deciding to describe his position and   3
entrapment, others have also done—in states of repose or terror.
When a JAL airliner went down in 1985, passengers used the long
minutes of its terrible, spiraling descent to write letters to loved
ones. When the last occupants of the Warsaw Ghetto had finally
seen their families and companions die of disease or starvation, or
be carried off in trucks to extermination camps, and there could be
no doubt of their own fate, still they took scraps of paper on which
they wrote poems, thoughts, fragments of lives, rolled them into
tight scrolls, and slipped them into the crevices of the ghetto walls.

Why did they bother? With no countervailing news from the   4
outside world, they assumed the Nazis had inherited the earth; that
if anyone discovered their writings, it would be their killers, who
would snicker and toss them away. They wrote because, like
Kolesnikov, they had to. The impulse was in them, like a biological fact.

So enduring is this storytelling need that it shapes nearly every   5
human endeavor. Businesses depend on the stories told of past failures and successes and on the myth of the mission of the company.
In medicine, doctors increasingly rely on a patient's narrative of
the progress of an ailment, which is inevitably more nuanced and
useful than the data of machines. In law, the same thing. Every
court case is a competition of tales told by the prosecutor and
defense attorney; the jury picks the one it likes best.

All these activities derive from essential places in us. Psy- 6 chologist Jerome Bruner says children acquire language in order to tell the stories that are already in them. We do our learning through storytelling processes. The man who arrives at our door is thought to be a salesman because his predecessor was a salesman. When the patternmaking faculties fail, the brain breaks down. Schizophrenics suffer from a loss of story.

The deep proof of our need to spill, and keep on spilling, lies 7 in reflex, often in desperate circumstances. A number of years ago, Jean-Dominique Bauby, the editor of *Elle* magazine in Paris, was felled by a stroke so destructive that the only part of his body that could move was his left eyelid. Flicking that eyelid, he managed to signal the letters of the alphabet, and proceeded to write his auto-biography, *The Diving Bell and the Butterfly,* with the last grand ges-ture of his life.

All this is of acute and consoling interest to writers, whose odd 8 existences are ordinarily strung between asking why we do it and doing it incessantly. The explanation I've been able to come up with has to do with freedom. You write a sentence, the basic unit of storytelling, and you are never sure where it will lead. The readers will not know where it leads either. Your adventure becomes theirs, eternally recapitulated in tandem—one wild ride together. Even when you come to the end of the sentence, that dot, it is still strangely inconclusive. I sometimes think one writes to find God in every sentence. But God (the ironist) always lives in the next sentence.

It is this freedom of the message sender and receiver that con- 9 nects them—sailor to wife, the dying to the living. Writing has been so important in America, I think, because communication is the soul and engine of democracy. To write is to live according to one's terms. If you ask me to be serious, I will be frivolous. Magnanimous? Petty. Cynical? I will be a brazen believer in all things. Whatever you demand I will not give you—unless it is with the misty hope that what I give you is not what you ask for but what you want.

We use this freedom to break the silence, even of death, even 10 when—in the depths of our darkest loneliness—we have no clear idea of why we reach out to one another with these frail, perish-able chains of words. In the black chamber of the submarine, Kolesnikov noted, "I am writing blindly." Like everyone else.

RITA MAE BROWN   (1944–   )

Writing as a Moral Act

Language is decanted and shared. If only one person is left   1
alive speaking a language—the case with some American
Indian languages—the language is dead. Language takes two
and their multiples.

Speaking is a social contract. You and I agree to exchange   2
sounds whose organized noises represent agreed-upon symbols.
Cat means the same thing to you as it does to me. It doesn't mean
a thing to a Portuguese person. You might think of a sleek tiger
cat, and I might be thinking of a long-haired red cat, but we are
in sync about the species. If you want to get fancy you could say
feline (Latin again) but we're in the same ballpark.

Up to this point we are in agreement. We are cooperating as   3
two individuals conceding to civilization. Literacy, or even simple
speech, is the starting point of civilization. The unspoken truth is
that we are unequal; we are different. If you and I were exactly the
same, a pair of identical strangers, we wouldn't need to speak to
one another or to write. You'd know what I was thinking and
vice versa. All communication rests upon inequality. That's the
sheer excitement of it. I don't know what you think. I can't wait
to find out. Language is the common thread by which we explore
our differences and, if we are both lucky and mature, the thread
that will bring us to a form of agreement or at least understanding.

Therefore it is imperative that people write and speak the truth.   4
There can be no community if a person is not as good as her/his
word. How easy to write that and how hard to put it in practice.
You, my reader, whoever you are, know things that will disturb
others. You must tell. Camus said, "It is immoral not to tell."

Again we can split hairs. A dear friend of mine has put on ten   5
pounds. Do I say, "Gee, Frank, you're fat as a toad" (the truth) or
"Frank, you look wonderful." It may be wonderful to see him, but
he still looks fat. I'll choose to make my friend feel better.

If Frank, involved in a sordid affair with the wife of another   6
friend of mine, asks my opinion, I'll tell him the truth. "Either she
leaves him and goes to you, or you leave her. Don't mess with
married people."

Telling the truth should be simple. Writing the truth should be   7
even easier because you don't have to look your listener/reader in
the eye. Writing the truth is far more treacherous. The act of
putting words down on paper gives them a glamour and permanence not associated with speech. Writing, to most everyone, is a
more serious act than speaking.

Every generation produces those people—writers, composers,   8
plastic artists, and even the re-creative artists—who shatter social
convention and tell the truth. They aren't saying "Here I am."
They are saying "Here you are." The "you" is both individual and
plural. In the case of *Oedipus Rex* or *Crime and Punishment,* this
recognition can be horrifying. In the case of *The Birds* or *School for
Scandal* it can be deliciously funny.

If this is prevented from happening (as in Stalin's Soviet Union,   9
Hitler's Germany, Botha's South Africa) the civilization begins to
die from the inside out. There may be a plethora of books in such
nations but they aren't upsetting. They merely entertain. Art must
both entertain and provoke.

If people refrain from telling what they know, how long before   10
they actively lie? Is there not a subtle and corrosive connection
between withholding the truth and lying? You are as sick as you
are secret.

If you don't believe that words will be followed by deeds, how   11
can you trust anyone? How can you form a community? When
language no longer corresponds to reality, any form of betrayal and
misconduct are to be expected.

Writers are the moral purifiers of the culture. We may not be   12
pure ourselves, but we must tell the truth, which is a purifying act.
Therefore it is impossible for a real fiction writer to be the mouth-
piece for a political cause. A writer should, as should any citizen,
cherish his or her political beliefs but that's not the same as being
a propagandist.

By political beliefs I am not talking about the American two-   13
party system. The Republican party is a study in unlimited van-
dalism, and the Democratic party presides over the cadaver of lib-
eralism. The difference between Republicans and Democrats is
the difference between syphilis and gonorrhea. Political beliefs are
stronger than that. The separation of church and state is a political
belief. Affirming or repudiating capital punishment is a political
belief. The desire for a state-controlled economy is not only a

political belief, in some nations it's a religion. You get the difference. Our political parties skate over the political fashions that are current. Opportunism wears many masks.

Since politicians seek to conceal the truth in order to dupe the   14
public, every writer alive is critical of whatever political system
s/he lives in. Not everyone in politics is bad and politics is a necessary evil, *but* politics is never ever about the truth. Politics seeks
to conceal; Art, to reveal.

The severest blasts in Russia or in our own country are directed   15
at people the state considers expendable. First, writers get it
because they are potentially dangerous. Scientists run into walls
only if they become critical of the uses of science by the government. If they shut up and continue as the hired help, they're okay.
In our country, we are too sophisticated to put writers in jail. It
looks bad. Also, we are very fortunate in that most of our elected
officials are semi-illiterate, and therefore they don't even know
what we're writing. Should a writer happen to become disturbing
and powerful enough to come to the attention of our civic worthies, then the fur flies. A politician will cite the offending author
and make a stink. His acolytes will press to have the subversive
texts banned from the libraries. (Actually, the acolytes control the
politician. S/he usually responds to their pressure.) Loathsome as
it is, such talk does get into the newspapers, and once publicity
attaches itself to a book, the sales shoot upward. Bless the narrowminded! You can survive that. You'll know when you're really in
Dutch when the IRS hounds you. You think a highly placed government official wouldn't stoop that low? You think the IRS is
not a punitive instrument of whatever administration is current?
You also believe in the tooth fairy, don't you?

Communist and fascist nations recognize the power of writers.   16
They imprison them or drive them out of their homeland. The
United States of America, no matter how absurd and contradictory
our various administrations, has drawn the line here. When push
comes to shove, we defend the First Amendment. By defending
the First Amendment we are defending writers. Buried in the marrow of our collective bones is the recognition that we must know
the truth about ourselves. Even the most bigoted American hates
a liar. Despite our economic struggle, far better to be a writer here
than elsewhere.

Morality is involved in issues other than lying or withholding   17
information. What happens when the word is substituted for the
deed? Some act of faith is always involved in the connection
between theory and action. To write and talk and not produce
the action is to destroy faith. Once again, community becomes
impossible.

The best example I can think of for this phenomenon involves   18
the protest movements of the late 1960s and early 1970s. While
the Nazis committed unspeakable acts (I mean unspeakable—they
had no word for what they were doing), the New Left and the
Women's Movement spoke incessantly but committed few acts.
This seems to be a hallmark of leftist politics: the substitution of
the word for the deed. Yes, some things got accomplished, but
compare it to the dedicated raising of money by the New Right
and the intelligent daily application of those funds, and you quickly
grasp the difference.

The New Right has few writers. The New Left was top-heavy   19
with them. From the New Left true fiction writers emerged, leaving behind the restrictions of ideology and moving toward a wider
embrace of human experience but, I hope, imbued with a belief
in justice, equality, and innovation. To date, not one decent fiction writer has emerged from the New Right.

I was one of those people to emerge from the New Left. I recall   20
the early days of the movement. The blind were leading the blind
with great excitement into walls, into ravines, into the waiting
rifles at Jackson and Kent State. These anguished memories are
then supplanted with pride; we did help to end a war which was
ill-conceived. We wrested a few changes from the system for the
nonwhite, and we created the conditions for the removal of a
President who may have committed criminal acts. From this
haunted terrain sprang a generation of scribblers. Perhaps the New
Right will fool me yet and bring forth fiction writers capable of
making us see ourselves as we really are. One thing is certain: That
writer or those writers will get clobbered by their former associates. The Right suffers little dissent.

Some writers maintain that they are apolitical. A worm is apo-   21
litical; a human being is not. If you live in a political system and
do not seek to make it better, you are still a product of that system. Your lack of involvement is a political statement. All Art rests

on a political foundation but it need not concern itself with politics.

Go back to *The Iliad*. Achilles has plopped his butt in his tent   22
and won't fight. Agamemnon took a damsel awarded to Achilles for his battle prowess. Briseis was her name, and Achilles, although in love with Patroclus, a man, wanted the girl. Why not eat your cake and have it too? The Greeks were not as ravaged by sexual definitions as we are. Agamemnon, as head of the armed forces (think of him as Eisenhower during World War II), could take this woman. He had the power but he didn't have the right. Achilles, by our standards, should set aside personal ego and fight for his people. Achilles, by Greek standards, is absolutely right. His first allegiance is to his honor. This conflict between the need of the individual to be sovereign and the need of the community to triumph/survive provides the context for the unfolding drama. *The Iliad* has a political basis but you can read it without giving politics a thought.

Even *Alice's Adventures in Wonderland* rests on a political foun-   23
dation. It can be read as a glorious fantasy, or it can be read as a comment on the powerlessness of a child, of children in society. You don't have to choose—you can read it on many levels, including reading it as a drug trip.

Both *The Iliad* and *Alice in Wonderland* ring true. People read   24
them today with as much pleasure as people derived from them when they were first written. A work lives like that if it is morally true.

You bring to a book your past, your system of beliefs. First, you   25
read a book and answer that book with those beliefs. If you are a student of literature, you will study the environment of the writer, and then you'll read the book again, setting aside your values. When you've finished the second reading you can engage the writer's beliefs with your own. Reading is an active moral and intellectual exchange. If you aren't reading books that challenge you, you're reading the wrong books.

If you aren't writing books that challenge you, keep writing. It   26
takes years to get there. I know the book I wanted to write, the challenging, lyrical work I dreamed about. You know only the book I wrote. I am acutely aware of the gap between desire and performance. Lash me though you might, you'll never hit me as hard as I hit myself, for only I know the full extent of my failure.

Morality shifts. Infanticide was acceptable to the Greeks. It isn't   27
acceptable to us. Your work will reflect your implied faiths and
fears. Without your being necessarily conscious of it, your work
reflects your society. Here's an example. Since *The Iliad,* Western
writers have treated common experience as comic relief. This attitude depends on a clear class structure in which the superior
classes, aristocrats, are assumed better than the inferior classes.
When the middle classes began to assert themselves, this shifted.
Chaucer in *The Canterbury Tales* presents sympathetic middle-class
characters. Some are comic, and some are not, but none of them
is heroic. A great revolution took place on the page. This accelerated over time. Shakespeare used all the classes, to his and our
great profit.

Eventually, middle-class people developed the leisure in which   28
to write, and what did they do? They wrote about themselves. As
the Industrial Revolution wears on, their literature takes over. The
middle-class character is not a king or a landed aristocrat but
a lawyer or a doctor perhaps. Chekhov comes to my mind instantly. The tendency to present ordinary people (an assumption
in itself—are there ordinary people?) as vaguely comic still exists
but it isn't as strict a literary convention as it was for a good two
thousand years.

When you reject inferiority at the lowest level, you topple the   29
whole structure of dominance. The shift in literature, beginning
with Chaucer, reflected real life and, in turn, had an impact upon
real life. No longer were kings and queens so important. They
were replaced with parliaments or by revolutions. They were
replaced on the page. Morally, there's nothing wrong with having
a king for your form of government or for your literary hero, but
as an American I bet you don't write about one.

This struggle for literary representation bubbles over the   30
decades. Today, the lower classes, thanks to programs to get them
into colleges, are producing literature. The class in control of the
arts, the middle class, finds itself besieged from below. Not only
are the lower classes becoming literate, nonwhite and non-
Christians have acquired the skills to create English literature. Stick
around—the show is just beginning!

As Shakespeare arrived at a creative imbalance between the   31
passing medieval world and the coming modern world (Bacon,
Newton, Descartes), so we are at a similar overlap between the

nation–state and global interdependence, between men and women, between whites and nonwhites, between the Christian world and science, the Christian world and the non-Christian world, between spiritual concerns and material ones. Like Shakespeare we find ourselves in a time where the future, so thrilling to the nonrigid, terrifies the rigid. Every action has an equal and opposite reaction. Every cultural/social push forward is followed by people organizing to hold back the hands of time. Those men who were willing to kill you if you thought the earth revolved around the sun instead of believing Ptolemy are still here. Those people, like Elizabeth I, who killed their political enemies are here too. Like Shakespeare, you've got to try to make sense of it. You don't have to explain it. He didn't. You need to use it, use every bit of it. This overlap and straining of divergent world views is a gift. Don't ask to live in tranquil times. Literature doesn't grow there.

RICHARD WRIGHT   (1908–1960)

The Library Card

One morning I arrived early at work and went into the ¹ bank lobby where the Negro porter was mopping. I stood at a counter and picked up the Memphis *Commercial Appeal* and began my free reading of the press. I came finally to the editorial page and saw an article dealing with one H. L. Mencken. I knew by hearsay that he was the editor of the *American Mercury*, but aside from that I knew nothing about him. The article was a furious denunciation of Mencken, concluding with one, hot, short sentence: Mencken is a fool.

I wondered what on earth this Mencken had done to call down ² upon him the scorn of the South. The only people I had ever heard denounced in the South were Negroes, and this man was not a Negro. Then what ideas did Mencken hold that made a newspaper like the *Commercial Appeal* castigate him publicly? Undoubtedly he must be advocating ideas that the South did not like. Were there, then, people other than Negroes who criticized the South? I knew that during the Civil War the South had hated northern whites, but I had not encountered such hate during my life. Knowing no more of Mencken than I did at that moment, I felt a vague sympathy for him. Had not the South, which had assigned me the role of a nonman, cast at him its hardest words?

Now, how could I find out about this Mencken? There was a ³ huge library near the riverfront, but I knew that Negroes were not allowed to patronize its shelves any more than they were the parks and playgrounds of the city. I had gone into the library several times to get books for the white men on the job. Which of them would now help me to get books? And how could I read them without causing concern to the white men with whom I worked? I had so far been successful in hiding my thoughts and feelings from them, but I knew that I would create hostility if I went about the business of reading in a clumsy way.

I weighed the personalities of the men on the job. There was ⁴ Don, a Jew; but I distrusted him. His position was not much better than mine and I knew that he was uneasy and insecure; he had always treated me in an offhand, bantering way that barely concealed his contempt. I was afraid to ask him to help me get books; his frantic desire to demonstrate a racial solidarity with the whites against Negroes might make him betray me.

Then how about the boss? No, he was a Baptist and I had the   5
suspicion that he would not be quite able to comprehend why a black boy would want to read Mencken. There were other white men on the job whose attitudes showed clearly that they were Kluxers or sympathizers, and they were out of the question.

There remained only one man whose attitude did not fit into   6
an anti-Negro category, for I had heard the white men refer to him as a "Pope lover." He was an Irish Catholic and was hated by the white Southerners. I knew that he read books, because I had got him volumes from the library several times. Since he, too, was an object of hatred, I felt that he might refuse me but would hardly betray me. I hesitated, weighing and balancing the imponderable realities.

One morning I paused before the Catholic fellow's desk.   7

"I want to ask you a favor," I whispered to him.   8

"What is it?"   9

"I want to read. I can't get books from the library. I wonder if   10
you'd let me use your card?"

He looked at me suspiciously.   11

"My card is full most of the time," he said.   12

"I see," I said and waited, posing my question silently.   13

"You're not trying to get me into trouble, are you, boy?" He   14
asked, staring at me.

"Oh, no sir."   15

"What book do you want?"   16

"A book by H. L. Mencken."   17

"Which one?"   18

"I don't know. Has he written more than one?"   19

"He has written several."   20

"I didn't know that."   21

"What makes you want to read Mencken?"   22

"Oh, I just saw his name in the newspaper," I said.   23

"It's good of you to want to read," he said. "But you ought to   24
read the right things."

I said nothing. Would he want to supervise my reading?   25

"Let me think," he said. "I'll figure out something."   26

I turned from him and he called me back. He stared at me 27
quizzically.

"Richard, don't mention this to the other white men," he said. 28

"I understand," I said. "I won't say a word." 29

A few days later he called me to him. 30

"I've got a card in my wife's name," he said. "Here's mine." 31

"Thank you, sir." 32

"Do you think you can manage it?" 33

"I'll manage fine," I said. 34

"If they suspect you, you'll get in trouble," he said. 35

"I'll write the same kind of notes to the library that you wrote 36
when you sent me for books," I told him. "I'll sign your name."

He laughed. 37

"Go ahead. Let me see what you get," he said. 38

That afternoon I addressed myself to forging a note. Now, what 39
were the names of books written by H. L. Mencken? I did not
know any of them. I finally wrote what I thought would be a foolproof note: *Dear Madam: Will you please let this nigger boy*—I used
the word "nigger" to make the librarian feel that I could not possibly be the author of the note—*have some books by H. L. Mencken?*
I forged the white man's name.

I entered the library as I had always done when on errands for 40
whites, but I felt that I would somehow slip up and betray myself.
I doffed my hat, stood a respectful distance from the desk, looked
as unbookish as possible, and waited for the white patrons to be
taken care of. When the desk was clear of people, I still waited.
The white librarian looked at me.

"What do you want, boy?" 41

As thought I did not possess the power of speech, I stepped for- 42
ward and simply handed her the forged note, not parting my lips.

"What books by Mencken does he want?" she asked. 43

"I don't know, ma'am," I said, avoiding her eyes. 44

"Who gave you this card?" 45

"Mr. Falk," I said. 46

"Where is he?" 47

"He's at work, at the M——— Optical Company," I said. 48
"I've been in here for him before."

"I remember," the woman said. "But he never wrote notes like 49
this."

Oh, God, she's suspicious. Perhaps she would not let me have   50
the books? If she had turned her back at that moment, I would
have ducked out the door and never gone back. Then I thought
of a bold idea.

"You can call him up, ma'am," I said, my heart pounding.   51

"You're not using these books, are you?" she asked pointedly.   52

"Oh, no, ma'am. I can't read."   53

"I don't know what he wants by Mencken," she said under her   54
breath.

I knew now that I had won; she was thinking of other things   55
and the race question had gone out of her mind. She went to the
shelves. Once or twice she looked over her shoulder at me, as
though she was still doubtful. Finally she came foreward with two
books in her hand.

"I'm sending him two books," she said. "But tell Mr. Falk to   56
come in next time, or send me the names of the books he wants.
I don't know what he wants to read."

I said nothing. She stamped the card and handed me the books.   57
Not daring to glance at them, I went out of the library, fearing that
the woman would call me back for further questioning. A block
away from the library I opened one of the books and read a title:
A Book of Prefaces. I was nearing my nineteenth birthday and I did
not know how to pronounce the word "preface." I thumbed the
pages and saw strange words and strange names. I shook my head,
disappointed. I looked at the other book; it was called *Prejudices.* I
knew what that word meant; I had heard it all my life. And right
off I was on guard against Mencken's books. Why would a man
want to call a book *Prejudices?* The word was so stained with all
my memories of racial hate that I could not conceive of anybody
using it for a title. Perhaps I had made a mistake about Mencken?
A man who had prejudices must be wrong.

When I showed the books to Mr. Falk, he looked at me and   58
frowned.

"That librarian might telephone you," I warned him.   59

"That's all right," he said. "But when you're through reading   60
those books, I want you to tell me what you get out of them."

That night in my rented room, while letting the hot water run   61
over my can of pork and beans in the sink, I opened *A Book of
Prefaces* and began to read. I was jarred and shocked by the style,
the clear, clean, sweeping sentences. Why did he write like that?

And how did one write like that? I pictured the man as a raging demon, slashing with his pen, consumed with hate, denouncing everything American, extolling everything European or German, laughing at the weaknesses of people, mocking God, authority. What was this? I stood up, trying to realize what reality lay behind the meaning of the words . . . Yes, this man was fighting, fighting with words. He was using words as a weapon, using them as one would use a club. Could words be weapons? Well, yes, for here they were. Then, maybe, perhaps, I could use them as a weapon? No. It frightened me. I read on and what amazed me was not what he said, but how on earth anybody had the courage to say it.

Occasionally I glanced up to reassure myself that I was alone in the room. Who were these men about whom Mencken was talking so passionately? Who was Anatole France? Joseph Conrad? Sinclair Lewis, Sherwood Anderson, Dostoevski, George Moore, Gustave Flaubert, Maupassant, Tolstoy, Frank Harris, Mark Twain, Thomas Hardy, Arnold Bennett, Stephen Crane, Zola, Norris, Gorky, Bergson, Ibsen, Balzac, Bernard Shaw, Dumas, Poe, Thomas Mann, O. Henry, Dreiser, H. G. Wells, Gogol, T. S. Eliot, Gide, Baudelaire, Edgar Lee Masters, Stendhal, Turgenev, Huneker, Nietzsche, and scores of others? Were these men real? Did they exist or had they existed? And how did one pronounce their names? 62

I ran across many words whose meanings I did not know, and I either looked them up in a dictionary or, before I had a chance to do that, encountered the word in a context that made its meaning clear. But what strange world was this? I concluded the book with the conviction that I had somehow overlooked something terribly important in life. I had once tried to write, had once reveled in feeling, had let my crude imagination roam, but the impulse to dream had been slowly beaten out of me by experience. Now it surged up again and I hungered for books, new ways of looking and seeing. It was not a matter of believing or disbelieving what I read, but of feeling something new, of being affected by something that made the look of the world different. 63

As dawn broke I ate my pork and beans, feeling dopey, sleepy. I went to work, but the mood of the book would not die; it lingered, coloring everything I saw, heard, did. I now felt that I knew what the white men were feeling. Merely because I had read a 64 book that had spoken of how they lived and thought, I identified myself with that book. I felt vaguely guilty. Would I, filled with bookish notions, act in a manner that would make the whites dislike me?

I forged more notes and my trips to the library became frequent. Reading grew into a passion. My first serious novel was Sinclair Lewis's *Main Street*. It made me see my boss, Mr. Gerald, and identify him as an American type. I would smile when I saw him lugging his golf bags into the office. I had always felt a vast distance separating me from the boss, and now I felt closer to him, though still distant. I felt now that I knew him, that I could feel the very limits of his narrow life. And this had happened because I had read a novel about a mythical man called George F. Babbitt.   65

The plots and stories in the novels did not interest me so much as the point of view revealed. I gave myself over to each novel without reserve, without trying to criticize it; it was enough for me to see and feel something different. And for me, everything was something different. Reading was like a drug, a dope. The novels created moods in which I lived for days. But I could not conquer my sense of guilt, my feeling that the white men around me knew that I was changing, that I had begun to regard them differently.   66

Whenever I brought a book to the job, I wrapped it in newspaper—a habit that was to persist for years in other cities and under other circumstances. But some of the white men pried into my packages when I was absent and they questioned me.   67

"Boy, what are you reading those books for?"   68

"Oh, I don't know, sir."   69

"That's deep stuff you're reading, boy."   70

"I'm just killing time, sir."   71

"You'll addle your brains if you don't watch out."   72

I read Dreiser's *Jennie Gerhardt* and *Sister Carrie* and they revived in me a vivid sense of my mother's suffering; I was overwhelmed. I grew silent, wondering about the life around me. It would have been impossible for me to have told anyone what I derived from these novels, for it was nothing less than a sense of life itself. All my life had shaped me for the realism, the naturalism of the modern novel, and I could not read enough of them.   73

Steeped in new moods and ideas, I bought a ream of paper and tried to write; but nothing would come, or what did come was flat   74 beyond telling. I discovered that more than desire and feeling were necessary to write and I dropped the idea. Yet I still wondered how it was possible to know people sufficiently to write about them? Could I ever learn about life and people? To me, with my vast ignorance, my Jim Crow station in life, it seemed a task impossible of achievement. I now knew what being a Negro meant. I could endure the hunger; I had learned to live with hate. But to feel that there were feelings denied me, that the very breath of life itself was beyond my reach, that more than anything else hurt, wounded me. I had a new hunger.

In buoying me up, reading also cast me down, made me see   75
what was possible, what I had missed. My tension returned, new, terrible, bitter, surging, almost too great to be contained. I no longer *felt* that the world about me was hostile, killing; I *knew* it. A million times I asked myself what I could do to save myself, and there were no answers. I seemed forever condemned, ringed by walls.

I did not discuss my reading with Mr. Falk, who had lent me   76
his library card; it would have meant talking about myself and that would have been too painful. I smiled each day, fighting desperately to maintain my old behavior, to keep my disposition seemingly sunny. But some of the white men discerned that I had begun to brood.

"Wake up there, boy!" Mr. Olin said one day.   77
"Sir!" I answered for the lack of a better word.   78
"You act like you've stolen something," he said.   79
I laughed in the way I knew he expected me to laugh, but I   80
resolved to be more conscious of myself, to watch my every act, to guard and hide the new knowledge that was dawning within me.

If I went north, would it be possible for me to build a new life   81
then? But how could a man build a life upon vague, unformed yearnings? I wanted to write and I did not even know the English language. I bought English grammars and found them dull. I felt that I was getting a better sense of the language from novels than from grammars. I read hard, discarding a writer as soon as I felt that I had grasped his point of view. At night the printed page stood before my eyes in sleep.

Mrs. Moss, my landlady, asked me one Sunday morning: 82
"Son, what is this you keep on reading?"   83

"Oh, nothing. Just novels."   84

"What you get out of 'em?"   85

"I'm just killing time," I said.   86

"I hope you know your own mind," she said in a tone which   87
implied that she doubted if I had a mind.

I knew of no Negroes who read the books I liked and I won-   88
dered if any Negroes ever thought of them. I knew that there
were Negro doctors, lawyers, newspapermen, but I never saw any
of them. When I read a Negro newspaper I never caught the
faintest echo of my pre-occupation in its pages. I felt trapped and
occasionally, for a few days, I would stop reading. But a vague
hunger would come over me for books, books that opened up
new avenues of feeling and seeing, and again I would forge another note to the white librarian. Again I would read and wonder
as only the naïve and unlettered can read and wonder, feeling that
I carried a secret, criminal burden about with me each day.

That winter my mother and brother came and we set up house-   89
keeping, buying furniture on the installment plan, being cheated
and yet knowing no way to avoid it. I began to eat warm food and
to my surprise found that regular meals enabled me to read faster.
I may have lived through many illnesses and survived them, never
suspecting that I was ill. My brother obtained a job and we began
to save toward the trip north, plotting our time, setting tentative
dates for departure. I told none of the white men on the job that
I was planning to go north; I knew that the moment they felt I
was thinking of the North they would change toward me. It
would have made them feel that I did not like the life I was living, and because my life was completely conditioned by what they
said or did, it would have been tantamount to challenging them.

I could calculate my chances for life in the South as a Negro   90
fairly clearly now.

I could fight the southern whites by organizing with other   91
Negroes, as my grandfather had done. But I knew that I could
never win that way; there were many whites and there were but
few blacks. They were strong and we were weak. Outright black
rebellion could never win. If I fought openly I would die and I did
not want to die. News of lynchings were frequent.

I could submit and live the life of a genial slave, but that was   92
impossible. All of my life had shaped me to live by my own feelings, and thoughts. I could make up to Bess and marry her and

inherit the house. But that, too, would be the life of a slave; if I did that, I would crush to death something within me, and I would hate myself as much as I knew the whites already hated those who had submitted. Neither could I ever willingly present myself to be kicked, as Shorty had done. I would rather have died than do that.

I could drain off my restlessness by fighting with Shorty and   93
Harrison. I had seen many Negroes solve the problem of being black by transfering their hatred of themselves to others with a black skin and fighting them. I would have to be cold to do that, and I was not cold and I could never be.

I could, of course, forget what I had read, thrust the whites out   94
of my mind, forget them; and find release from anxiety and long-ing in sex and alcohol. But the memory of how my father had conducted himself made that course repugnant. If I did not want others to violate my life, how could I voluntarily violate it myself?

I had no hope whatever of being a professional man. Not only   95
had I been so conditioned that I did not desire it, but the fulfill-ment of such an ambition was beyond my capabilities. Well-to-do Negroes lived in a world that was almost as alien to me as the world inhabited by whites.

What, then, was there? I held my life in my mind, in my con-   96
sciousness each day, feeling at times that I would stumble and drop it, spill it forever. My reading had created a vast sense of distance between me and the world in which I lived and tried to make a living, and that sense of distance was increasing each day. My days and nights were one long, quiet, continuously contained dream of terror, tension, and anxiety. I wondered how long I could bear it.

JESS ROW   (1975–   )

The Secrets of Bats

A lice Leung has discovered the secrets of bats: how they 1
see without seeing, how they own darkness, as we own
light. She walks the halls with a black headband across
her eyes, keening a high C—*cheat cheat cheat cheat cheat cheat*—
never once veering off course, as if drawn by an invisible thread.
Echolocation, she tells me, it's not as difficult as you might
think. Now she sees a light around objects when she looks at
them, like halos on her retinas from staring at the sun. In her
journal she writes, *I had a dream that was all in blackness. Tell me
how to describe.*

It is January: my fifth month in Hong Kong.   2
In the margin I write, *I wish I knew.*   3

After six, when the custodians leave, the school becomes a perfect 4
acoustic chamber; she wanders from the basement laboratories to
the basketball courts like a trapped bird looking for a window. She
finds my door completely blind, she says, not counting flights or
paces. Twisting her head from side to side like Stevie Wonder, she
announces her progress: another room mapped, a door, a desk, a
globe, detected and identified by its aura.

You'll hurt yourself, I tell her. I've had nightmares: her   5
foot missing the edge of a step, the dry crack of a leg breaking.
Try it without the blindfold, I say. That way you can check
yourself.

Her mouth wrinkles. This not important, she says. This only   6
practice.

Practice for what, I want to ask. All the more reason you have to 7
be careful.

You keep saying, she says, grabbing a piece of chalk. E-x-p-e- 8
r-i-m-e-n-t, she writes on the blackboard, digging it in until it
squeals.

That's right. Sometimes experiments fail.   9

Sometimes, she repeats. She eyes me suspiciously, as if I in- 10
vented the word.

Go home, I tell her. She turns her pager off and leaves it in her 11 locker; sometimes police appear at the school gate, shouting her name. Somebody, it seems, wants her back.

In the doorway she whirls, flipping her hair out of her eyes. 12 Ten days more, she says. You listen. Maybe then you see why.

The name of the school is Po Sing Uk: a five-story concrete block, 13 cracked and eroded by dirty rain, shoulder-to-shoulder with the tenements and garment factories of Cheung Sha Wan. No air conditioning and no heat; in September I shouted to be heard over a giant fan, and now, in January, I teach in a winter jacket. When it rains, mildew spiderwebs across the ceiling of my classroom. Schoolgirls in white jumpers crowd into the room forty at a time, falling asleep over their textbooks, making furtive calls on mobile phones, scribbling notes to each other on pink Hello Kitty paper. If I call on one who hasn't raised her hand, she folds her arms across her chest and stares at the floor, and the room falls silent, as if by a secret signal. There is nothing more terrifying, I've found, than the echo of your own voice: *Who are you?* it answers. *What are you doing here?*

I've come to see my life as a radiating circle of improbabilities that 14 grow from each other, like ripples in water around a dropped stone. That I became a high school English teacher, that I work in another country, that I live in Hong Kong. That a city can be a mirage, hovering above the ground: skyscrapers built on mountainsides, islands swallowed in fog for days. That a language can have no tenses or articles, with seven different ways of saying the same syllable. That my best student stares at the blackboard only when I erase it.

She stayed behind on the first day of class: a tall girl with a narrow 15 face, pinched around the mouth, her cheeks pitted with acne scars. Like most of my sixteen-year-olds, she looked twelve, in a baggy uniform that hung to her knees like a sack. The others streamed past her without looking up, as if she were a boulder in the current; she stared down at my desk with a fierce vacancy, as if looking itself was an act of will.

How do you think about bats? 16

Bats? 17

She joined her hands at the wrist and fluttered them at me. 18

People are afraid of them, I said. I think they're very interesting.   19
Why? she said. Why very interesting?   20
Because they live in the dark, I said. We think of them as being   21
blind, but they aren't blind. They have a way of seeing, with
sound waves—just like we see with light.
Yes, she said. I know this. Her body swayed slightly, in an   22
imaginary breeze.
Are you interested in bats?   23
I am interest, she said. I want to know how—she made a face   24
I'd already come to recognize: *I know how to say it in Chinese*—
when one bat sees the other. The feeling.
You mean how one bat recognizes another?   25
Yes—recognize.   26
That's a good idea, I said. You can keep a journal about what   27
you find. Write something in it every day.
She nodded vehemently, as if she'd already thought of that.   28
There are books on bat behavior that will tell you—   29
Not in books. She covered her eyes with one hand and walked   30
forward until her hip brushed the side of my desk, then turned
away, at a right angle. Like this, she said. There is a sound, she said.
I want to find the sound.

18 September   31
First hit tuning fork. Sing one octave higher: A B C. This is best way.
Drink water or lips get dry.
I must have eyes totally closed. No light!!! So some kind of black—like
cloth—is good.

Start singing. First to the closest wall—sing and listen. Practice ten times,   32
twenty times. IMPORTANT: can not move until I HEAR the wall. Take
step back, one time, two time. Listen again. I have to hear DIFFERENCE
first, then move.
Then take turn, ninety degrees left.
Then turn, one hundred eighty degrees left. Feel position with feet. Feet
very important—they are wings!!!

I don't know what this is, I told her the next day, opening the   33
journal and pushing it across the desk. Can you help me?
I tell you already, she said. She hunched her shoulders so that   34
her head seemed to rest on them, spreading her elbows to either
side. It is like a test.
A test?   35

In the courtyard rain crackled against the asphalt; a warm wind   36
lifted scraps of paper from the desk, somersaulting them through
the air.

The sound, she said impatiently. I told you this.   37

I covered my mouth to hide a smile.   38

Alice, I said, humans can't do that. It isn't a learned behavior.   39
It's something you study.

She pushed up the cover of the composition book and let it fall.   40

I think I can help you, I said. Can you tell me why you want   41
to write this?

Why I want? She stared at me wide-eyed.   42

Why do you want to do this? What is the test for?   43

Her eyes lifted from my face to the blackboard behind me,   44
moved to the right, then the left, as if measuring the dimensions
of the room.

Why you want come to Hong Kong?   45

Many reasons, I said. After college I wanted to go to another   46
country, and there was a special fellowship available here. And
maybe someday I will be a teacher.

You are teacher.   47

I'm just learning, I said. I am trying to be one.   48

Then why you have to leave America?   49

I don't, I said. The two things—I took off my glasses and   50
rubbed my eyes. All at once I was exhausted; the effort seemed
useless, a pointless evasion. When I looked up she was nodding,
slowly, as if I'd just said something profound.

I think I will find the reason for being here only after some   51
time, I said. Do you know what I mean? There could be a purpose I don't know about.

So you don't know for good. Not sure.   52

You could say that.   53

Hai yat yeung, she said. This same. Maybe if you read you can   54
tell me why.

This is what's so strange about her, I thought, studying her red-   55
rimmed eyes, the tiny veins standing out like wires on a circuit
board. She doesn't look down. I am fascinated by her, I thought.
Is that fair?

You're different from the others, I said. You're not afraid of   56
me. Why is that?

Maybe I have other things be afraid of.   57

At first the fifth-floor bathroom was her echo chamber; she sat in   58
one corner, on a stool taken from the physics room, and placed an
object directly opposite her: a basketball, a glass, a feather. Sound
waves triangulate, she told me, corners are best. Passing by at the
end of the day, I stopped, closing my eyes, and listened for the difference. She sang without stopping for five minutes, hardly taking
a breath: almost a mechanical sound, as if someone had forgotten
their mobile phone. Other teachers walked by in groups, talking
loudly. If they noticed me, or the sound, I was never aware of it,
but always, instinctively, I looked at my watch and followed them
down the stairs. As if I too had to rush home to cook for hungry
children or boil medicine for my mother-in-law. I never stayed
long enough to see if anything changed.

Document everything, I told her, and she did; now I have two   59
binders of entries, forty-one in all. *Hallway. Chair. Notebook.* As if
we were scientists writing a grant proposal, as if there were something actual to show at the end of it.

I don't keep a journal or take photographs, and my letters   60
home are factual and sparse. No one in Larchmont would believe
me—not even my parents—if I told them the truth. *It sounds like
quite an experience you're having! Don't get run over by a rickshaw.*
And yet if I died tomorrow—why should I ever think this
way?—these binders would be the record of my days. Those and
Alice herself, who looks out of her window and with her eyes
closed sees ships passing in the harbor, men walking silently in the
streets.

> 26 January   61
> Sound of light bulb—low like bees hum. So hard to listen!

A week ago I dreamed of bodies breaking apart, arms and legs   62
and torsos, fragments of bone, bits of tissue. I woke up flailing in
the sheets, and remembered her immediately; there was too long
a moment before I believed I was awake. *It has to stop,* I thought,
you have to say something. Though I know that I can't.

Perhaps there was a time when I might have told her, *This is*   63
ridiculous, or, *You're sixteen, find some friends. What will people think?*
But this is Hong Kong, of course, and I have no friends, no basis
to judge. I leave the door open, always, and no one ever comes to
check; we walk out of the gates together, late in the afternoon,

past the watchman sleeping in his chair. For me she has a kind of professional courtesy, ignoring my whiteness politely, as if I had horns growing from my head. And she returns, at the end of each day, as a bat flies back to its cave at daybreak. All I have is time; who am I to pack my briefcase and turn away?

There was only once when I slipped up. 64

Pretend I've forgotten, I told her, one Monday in early October. 65
The journal was open in front of us, the pages covered in red; she squinted down at it, as if instead of corrections I'd written hiero-glyphics. I'm an English teacher, I thought, this is what I'm here for. We should start again at the beginning, I said. Tell me what it is that you want to do here. You don't have to tell me about the project—just about the writing. Whom are you writing these for? Whom do you want to read them?

She stretched, catlike, curling her fingers like claws. 66

Because I don't think I understand, I said. I think you might 67
want to find another teacher to help you. There could be some-thing you have in mind in Chinese that doesn't come across.

Not in Chinese, she said, as if I should have known that already. 68
In Chinese cannot say like this.

But it isn't really English, either. 69

I know this. It is like both. 70

I can't teach that way, I said. You have to learn the rules before 71
you can—

You are not teaching me. 72

Then what's the point? 73

She strode across the room to the window and leaned out, plac- 74
ing her hands on the sill and bending at the waist. Come here, she said, look. I stood up and walked over to her.

She ducked her head down, like a gymnast on a bar, and tilted 75
forward, her feet lifting off the floor.

Alice! 76

I grabbed her shoulder and jerked her upright. She stumbled, 77
falling back; I caught her wrist, and she pulled it away, steadying herself. We stood there a moment staring at each other, breathing in short huffs that echoed in the hallway.

Maybe I hear something and forget, she said. You catch me 78
then. Okay?

28 January   79
It is like photo negative, all the colors are the opposite. Black sky, white
trees, this way. But they are still shapes—I can see them.

I read standing at the window, in a last sliver of sunlight. Alice   80
stands on my desk, already well in shadow, turning around slowly
as if trying to dizzy herself for a party game. Her winter uniform
cardigan is three sizes too large; unopened, it falls behind her like
a cape.

This is beautiful.   81

Quiet, she hisses, eyebrows bunched together above her head-   82
band. One second. There—there.

What is it?   83

A man on the stairs.   84

I go out into the hallway and stand at the top of the stairwell,   85
listening. Five floors below, very faintly, I hear sandals skidding on
the concrete, keys jangling on the janitor's ring.

You heard him open the gate, I say. That's cheating.   86

She shakes her head. I hear heartbeat.   87

The next Monday, Principal Ho comes to see me during the lunch   88
hour. He stands at the opposite end of the classroom, as always: a
tall, slightly chubby man in a tailored shirt, gold-rimmed glasses,
and Italian shoes, who blinks as he reads the ESL posters I've
tacked up on the wall. When he asks how my classes are and I tell
him that the girls are unmotivated, disengaged, he nods quickly, as
if to save me the embarrassment. How lucky he was, he tells me,
to go to boarding school in Australia, and then pronounces it with
a flattened *a, Austrahlia,* so I have to laugh.

Principal Ho, I ask, do you know Alice Leung?   89

He turns his head toward me and blinks more rapidly. Leung   90
Ka Yee, he says. Of course. You have problem with her?

No sir. I need something to hold; my hands dart across the desk   91
behind me and find my red marking pen.

How does she perform?   92

She's very gifted. One of the best students in the class. Very   93
creative.

He nods, scratches his nose, and turns away.   94

She likes to work alone, I say. The other girls don't pay much   95
attention to her. I don't think she has many friends.

It is very difficult for her, he says slowly, measuring every word.   96
Her mother is—her mother was a suicide.

In the courtyard, five stories down, someone drops a basketball   97
and lets it bounce against the pavement, little *pings* that trill and
fade into the infinite.

In Yau Ma Tei, Ho says. He makes a little gliding motion with   98
his hand. Nowadays this is not so uncommon in Hong Kong. But
still there are superstitions.

What kind of superstitions?   99

He frowns and shakes his head. Difficult to say in English.   100
Maybe just that she is unlucky girl. Chinese people, you understand—some are still afraid of ghosts.

She isn't a ghost.   101

He gives a high-pitched, nervous laugh. No, no, he says. Not   102
her. He puts his hands into his pockets, searching for something.
Difficult to explain. I'm sorry.

Is there someone she can talk to?   103

He raises his eyebrows. *A counselor,* I am about to say, and explain   104
what it means, when my hand relaxes, and I realize I have been
crushing the pen in my palm. For a moment I am water-skiing again
at Lake Patchogue: releasing the handle, settling against the surface,
enfolded in water. When I look up, Ho glances at his watch.

If you have any problem, you can talk to me.   105

It's nothing, I say. Just curious, that's all.   106

★

She wears the headband all the time now, I've noticed: pulling it   107
over her eyes whenever possible, in the halls between classes, in
the courtyard at lunchtime, sitting by herself. No one shoves her
or calls her names; she passes through the crowds unseen. If possible, I think, she's grown thinner, her skin translucent, blue veins
showing at the wrists. Occasionally I notice the other teachers
shadowing her, frowning, their arms crossed, but if our eyes meet
they stare through me, disinterested, and look away.

I have to talk to you about something.   108

She is sitting in a desk at the far end of the room, reading her   109
chemistry textbook, drinking from a can of soymilk with a straw.
When the straw gurgles she bangs the can down, and we sit silently, the sound reverberating in the hallway.

I give you another journal soon. Two more days.   110

Not about that.   111

She doesn't move: fixed, alert, waiting. I stand up and move   112
down the aisle toward her, sitting two desks away, and as I move
her eyes grow slightly rounder and her cheeks puff out slightly, as
if she's holding her breath.

Alice, I say, can you tell me about your mother?   113

Her hands fall down on the desk, and the can clatters to the   114
floor, white drops spinning in the air.

Mother? Who tell you I have mother?   115

It's all right—   116

I reach over to touch one hand, and she snatches it back.   117

Who tell you?   118

It doesn't matter. You don't have to be angry.   119

You big mistake, she says, wild-eyed, taking long swallows of   120
air and spitting them out. Why you have to come here and mess
everything?

I don't understand, I say. Alice, what did I do?   121

I trust you, she says, and pushes the heel of one palm against her 122
cheek. I write and you read. I *trust* you.

What did you expect? I ask, my jaw trembling. Did you think   123
I would never know?

Believe me. She looks at me pleadingly. Believe *me*.   124

Two days later she leaves her notebook on my desk, with a note   125
stuck to the top. *You keep.*

1 February   126
Now I am finished
It is out there I hear it

I call out to her after class, and she hesitates in the doorway for 127
a moment before turning, pushing her back against the wall.

Tell me what it was like, I say. Was it a voice? Did you hear   128
someone speaking?

Of course no voice. Not so close to me. It was a feeling.   129

How did it feel?   130

She reaches up and slides the headband over her eyes.   131

It is all finish, she says. You not worry about me anymore.   132

Too late, I say. I stand up from my chair and take a tentative   133
step toward her: weak-kneed, as if it were a staircase in the dark.
You chose me, I say. Remember?

Go back to America. Then you forget all about this crazy girl.   134
This is my life too. Did you forget about that?   135
She raises her head and listens, and I know what she hears: a   136
stranger's voice, as surely as if someone else had entered the room.
She nods. *Whom do you see?* I wonder. *What will he do next?* I reach
out, blindly, and my hand misses the door; on the second try I
close it.
I choose this, I say. I'm waiting. Tell me.   137
Her body sinks into a crouch; she hugs her knees and tilts her   138
head back.
Warm. It was warm. It was—it was a body.   139
But not close to you?   140
Not close. Only little feeling, then no more.   141
Did it know you were there?   142
No.   143
How can you be sure?   144
When I look up to repeat the question, shiny tracks of tears   145
have run out from under the blindfold.
I am sorry, she says. She reaches into her backpack and splits   146
open a packet of tissues without looking down, her fingers nim-
ble, almost autonomous. You are my good friend, she says, and
takes off the blindfold, turning her face to the side and dabbing her
eyes. Thank you for help me.
It isn't over, I say. How can it be over?   147
Like you say. Sometimes experiment fails.   148
No, I say, too loudly, startling us both. It isn't that easy. You   149
have to prove it to me.
Prove it you?   150
Show me how it works. I take a deep breath. I believe you.   151
Will you catch me?
Her eyes widen, and she does not look away; the world swims   152
around her irises. Tonight, she says, and writes something on a slip
of paper, not looking down. I see you then.

In a week it will be the New Year: all along the streets the shop   153
fronts are hung with firecrackers, red-and-gold character scrolls,
pictures of grinning cats, and the twin cherubs of good luck.
Mothers lead little boys dressed in red silk pajamas, girls with New
Year's pigtails. The old woman sitting next to me on the bus is
busily stuffing twenty-dollar bills into red *lai see* packets: lucky

money for the year to come. When I turn my head from the window, she holds one out to me, and I take it with both hands, automatically, bowing my head. This will make you rich, she says to me in Cantonese. And lots of children.

Thank you, I say. The same to you.   154

She laughs. Already happened. Jade bangles clink together as she   155
holds up her fingers. Thirteen grandchildren! she says. Six boys. All
fat and good-looking. You should say Live long life to me.

I'm sorry. My Chinese is terrible.   156

No, it's very good, she says. You were born in Hong Kong?   157

Outside, night is just falling, and Nathan Road has become a   158
canyon of light: blazing neon signs, brilliant shop windows, decorations blinking across the fronts of half-finished tower blocks. I
stare at myself a moment in the reflection, three red characters
passing across my forehead, and look away. No, I say. In America.
I've lived here only since August.

Ah. Then what is America like?   159

Forgive me, aunt, I say. I forget.   160

Prosperous Garden no. 4. Tung Kun Street. Yau Ma Tei.   161

A scribble of Chinese characters.   162

Show this to doorman he let you in.   163

The building is on the far edge of Kowloon, next to the recla-   164
mation; a low concrete barrier separates it from an elevated highway that thunders continuously as cars pass. Four identical towers
around a courtyard, long poles draped with laundry jutting from
every window, like spears hung with old rotted flags.

Gong hei fat choi, I say to the doorman through the gate, and he   165
smiles with crooked teeth, but when I pass the note to him all
expression leaves his face; he presses the buzzer and turns away
quickly. Twenty-three A-ah, he calls out to the opposite wall.
You understand?

Thank you.   166

When I step out into the hallway I breathe in boiled chicken,   167
oyster sauce, frying oil, the acrid steam of medicine, dried fish,
Dettol. Two young boys are crouched at the far end, sending a
radio-controlled car zipping past me; someone is arguing loudly
over the telephone; a stereo plays loud Canto-pop from a balcony
somewhere below. All the apartment doors are open, I notice,
walking by, and only the heavy sliding gates in front of them are

closed. Like a honeycomb, I can't help thinking, or an ant farm.
But when I reach 23A the door behind the gate is shut, and no
sound comes from behind it. The bell rings several times before
the locks begin to snap open.

You are early, Alice says, rubbing her eyes, as if she's been   168
sleeping. Behind her the apartment is dark; there is only a faint
blue glow, as if from a TV screen.

I'm sorry. You didn't say when to come. I look at my watch: 169
eight-thirty. I can come back, I say, another time, maybe another
night—

She shakes her head and opens the gate.   170

When she turns on the light I draw a deep breath, involuntar-   171
ily, and hide it with a cough. The walls are covered with stacks of
yellowed paper, file boxes, brown envelopes, and ragged books;
on opposite sides of the room are two desks, each holding a computer with a flickering screen. I peer at the one closest to the door.
At the top of the screen there is a rotating globe and, below it, a
ribbon of letters and numbers, always changing. The other, I see,
is just the same: a head staring at its twin.

Come, Alice says. She has disappeared for a moment and re-   172
emerged dressed in a long dress, silver running shoes, a hooded
sweatshirt.

Are these yours?   173

No. My father's.   174

Why does he need two? They're just the same.   175

Nysee, she says impatiently, pointing. Footsie. New York Stock   176
Exchange. London Stock Exchange.

Sau Yee, a hoarse voice calls from another room. Who is it?   177

It's my English teacher, she says loudly. Giving me a homework   178
assignment.

Gwailo a?   179

Yes, she says. The white one.   180

Then call a taxi for him. He appears in the kitchen doorway: a   181
stooped old man, perhaps' five feet tall, in a dirty white T-shirt,
shorts, and sandals. His face is covered with liver spots, his eyes
shrunken into their sockets. I sorry-ah, he says to me. No speakee
English.

It's all right, I say. There is a numbness growing behind my   182
eyes: I want to speak to him, but the words are all jumbled, and
Alice's eyes burning on my neck. Goodbye, I say, take care.

See later-ah.   183

Alice pulls the hood over her head and opens the door.   184

She leads me to the top of a dark stairwell, in front of a rusting   185
door with light pouring through its cracks. *Tin paang*, she says,
reading the characters stenciled on it in white. Roof. She hands
me a black headband, identical to her own.

Hold on, I say, gripping the railing with both hands. The   186
numbness behind my eyes is still there, and I feel my knees growing weak, as if there were no building below me, only a framework of girders and air. Can you answer me a question?

Maybe one.   187

Has he always been like that?   188

What like?   189

With the computers, I say. Does he do that all the time?   190

Always. Never turn them off.   191

In the darkness I can barely see her face: only the eyes, shining,   192
daring me to speak. *If I were in your place,* I say to myself, and the
phrase dissolves, weightless.

Listen, I say. I'm not sure I'm ready.   193

She laughs. When you be sure?   194

Her fingers fall across my face, and I feel the elastic brushing   195
over my hair, and then the world is black: I open my eyes and
close them, no difference.

We just go for a little walk, she says. You don't worry. Only   196
listen.

I never realized, before, the weight of the air: at every step I feel   197
the great mass of it pressing against my face, saddled on my shoulders. I am breathing huge quantities, as if my lungs were a giant
recirculation machine, and sweat is running down from my forehead and soaking the edge of the headband. Alice takes normal-
sized steps and grips my hand fiercely, so I can't let go. Don't be
afraid, she shouts. We still in the middle. Not near the edge.

What am I supposed to do?   198

Nothing, she says. Only wait. Maybe you see something.   199

I stare fiercely into blackness, into my own eyelids. There is the   200
afterglow of the hallway light, and the computer screens, very
faint; or am I imagining it? What is there on a roof? I wonder, and
try to picture it: television antennas, heating ducts, clotheslines.

Are there guardrails? I've never seen any on a Hong Kong building. She turns, and I brush something metal with my hand. Do
you know where you're going? I shout.

Here, she says, and stops. I stumble into her, and she catches my   201
shoulder. Careful, she says. We wait here.

Wait for what?   202

Just listen, she says. I tell to you. Look to left side: there's a big   203
building there. Very tall white building, higher than us. Small
windows.

All right. I can see that.   204

Right side is highway. Very bright. Many cars and trucks   205
passing.

If I strain to listen I can hear a steady whooshing sound, and   206
then the high whine of a motorcycle, like a mosquito passing my
ear. Okay, I say. Got that.

In the middle is very dark. Small buildings. Only few lights on.   207

Not enough, I say.   208

One window close to us, she says. Two little children there.   209
You see them?

No.   210

Lift your arm, she says, and I do. Put your hand up. See? They   211
wave to you.

My God, I say. How do you do that?   212

She squeezes my hand.   213

You promise me something.   214

Of course. What is it?   215

You don't take it off, she says. No matter nothing. You prom-   216
ise me?

I do. I promise.   217

She lets go of my hand, and I hear running steps, soles skidding   218
on concrete.

Alice! I shout, rooted to the spot; I crouch down, and balance   219
myself with my hands. Alice! You don't—

Mama, she screams, ten feet away, and the sound carries,   220
echoes; I can see it slanting with the wind, bright as daylight, as if
a roman candle had exploded in my face. *Mama mama mama mama
mama mama mama,* she sings, and I am crawling toward her on
hands and knees, feeling in front of me for the edge.

She is there, Alice shouts. You see? She is in the air.   221

I see her. Stay where you are.   222

You watch, she says. I follow her.   223

She doesn't want you, I shout. She doesn't want you there. Let   224
her go.

There is a long silence, and I stay where I am, the damp con-   225
crete soaking through to my knees. My ears are ringing, and the
numbness has blossomed through my head; I feel faintly seasick.

Alice?   226

You can stand up, she says in a small voice, and I do.   227

You are shaking, she says. She puts her arms around me from   228
behind and clasps her chest, pressing her head against my back. I
thank you, she says.

She unties the headband.   229

6 February   230
Man waves white hands at black sky
He says arent you happy be alive
arent you
He kneels and kisses floor

BILLY COLLINS   (1941–   )

Books

From the heart of this dark, evacuated campus   1
I can hear the library humming in the night,
a choir of authors murmuring inside their books
along the unlit, alphabetical shelves,
Giovanni Pontano next to Pope, Dumas next to his son,   5
each one stitched into his own private coat,
together forming a low, gigantic chord of language.

I picture a figure in the act of reading,
shoes on a desk, head tilted into the wind of a book,
a man in two worlds, holding the rope of his tie   10
as the suicide of lovers saturates a page,
or lighting a cigarette in the middle of a theorem.
He moves from paragraph to paragraph
as if touring a house of endless, paneled rooms.

I hear the voice of my mother reading to me   15
from a chair facing the bed, books about horses and dogs,
and inside her voice lie other distant sounds,
the horrors of a stable ablaze in the night,
a bark that is moving toward the brink of speech.

I watch myself building bookshelves in college,   20
walls within walls, as rain soaks New England,
or standing in a bookstore in a trench coat.

I see all of us reading ourselves away from ourselves,

straining in circles of light to find more light
until the line of words becomes a trail of crumbs   25
that we follow across a page of fresh snow;

when evening is shadowing the forest
and small birds flutter down to consume the crumbs,
we have to listen hard to hear the voices
of the boy and his sister receding into the woods.   30

Catch

Two boys uncoached are tossing a poem together,   1
Overhand, underhand, backhand, sleight of hand, every hand,
Teasing with attitudes, latitudes, interludes, altitudes,
High, make him fly off the ground for it, low, make him stoop,
Make him scoop it up, make him as-almost-as-possible miss it,   5
Fast, let him sting from it, now, now, fool him slowly,
Anything, everything tricky, risky, nonchalant,
Anything under the sun to outwit the prosy,
Over the tree and the long sweet cadence down,
Over his head, make him scramble to pick up the meaning,   10
And now, like a posy, a pretty one plump in his hands.

Glass

Words of a poem should be glass   1
But glass so simple-subtle its shape
Is nothing but the shape of what it holds.

A glass spun for itself is empty,
Brittle, at best Venetian trinket.   5
Embossed glass hides the poem or its absence.

Words should be looked through, should be windows.
The best words were invisible.
The poem is the thing the poet thinks.

If the possible were not,   10
And if the glass, only the glass,
Could be removed, the poem would remain.

NEENA BEBER   (1964–   )

Misreadings

(Lights up on SIMONE.) 1

SIMONE. It's important to dress right. I want to look slick. 2
To look sleek. To look like a fresh thing. I've got a message. I'm
the message. Study me, baby, because in ten minutes, I'm outta
here.

(SIMONE lights a cigarette. Lights up on RUTH. A stack of blue exam 3
composition books on her desk.)

RUTH. What are the issues for which you would kill? I like to 4
ask my students this on their first day of class. I assign novels where
the hero or heroine kills, or is killed. I try to bring it home. They
tell me they would kill to defend their family. They'd kill to
defend their friends. I ask them if they would kill for their country . . . for their freedom . . . what would it take?
SIMONE. I'd kill for a pair of Prada velvet platforms in deep 5
plum. *Those* are to die for.
RUTH. Simone. I didn't know what she was doing in my class. 6
Neither did she, apparently. *(To SIMONE.)* Nice segue, Simone;
would we be willing to die for the same things we'd kill for?
(Out.) She usually sat in the back, rarely spoke, wore too much
lipstick and some costume straight out of, what, Vogue. When she
did speak, it was always—disruptive.
SIMONE. I'd die for love except there ain't no Romeos, not 7
that I've seen; I'd take a bullet for my daddy but he's already dead;
I'd die of boredom if it were lethal, but I guess it isn't.
RUTH. If I couldn't inspire her, I wanted her gone. I'd asked 8
her to come to my office hours. I asked her several times. She was
failing, obviously. I would have let her drop the class, but it was
too late for that. She never bothered to come see me. Not until
the day before the final exam. She wanted me to give her a passing grade. *(RUTH turns to SIMONE.)* How can I do that,
Simone? You haven't even read the material. Have you read any
of the material?

SIMONE. I don't find it relevant.   9

RUTH. If you haven't read it, how do you know? You may   10
find yourself surprised. *Anna Karenina* is wonderful.

SIMONE. It's long.   11

RUTH. Why not give it a shot?   12

SIMONE. The books you assign are depressing. I don't want   13
to be depressed. Why read stuff that brings you down? Kafka, Jesus
Christ—I started it, okay? The guy was fucked up.

RUTH. So you were moved at least.   14

SIMONE. Moved to shut the book and find something more   15
interesting to do.

RUTH. That's too bad; you might have found one of these   16
books getting under your skin, if you stuck with it. Haven't you
ever read something that's really moved you?

SIMONE. Nothing moves me, Dr. Ruth.   17

RUTH. I'm going to have to have to ask you to put out that   18
cigarette.

SIMONE. Okay, ask. (*But she puts it out.*) See art or be art. I   19
choose the latter.

RUTH. Somebody must be paying for this education of yours.   20
I imagine they expect a certain return for their money.

SIMONE. How do you know I'm not the one paying for it?   21

RUTH. I don't believe someone who was spending their own   22
money would waste it so flagrantly.

SIMONE. Okay, Dad chips in.   23

RUTH. Would that be the same father you said was dead?   24

SIMONE. That was a joke or a lie, take your pick.   25

RUTH. You're frustrating the hell out of me, Simone.   26

SIMONE. I don't consider it a waste, you know. I like the   27
socialization part.

RUTH. If you fail out of this school, you won't be doing any   28
more "socialization."

SIMONE. You assume that I'm failing the others.   29

RUTH. So it's just this class, then? That you have a problem   30
with?

SIMONE. (*Referring to her grammar.*) Dangling. (*Beat.*) Do you   31
enjoy being a teacher?

RUTH. Yes, I do.   32

SIMONE. So I'm paying for your enjoyment.   33

RUTH. It's not a sin to enjoy one's work, Simone.   34

SIMONE. I just don't think you should charge me, if it's more   35
for your pleasure than for mine.

RUTH. I didn't say that.   36

SIMONE. Did you ever want to teach at a real school, not   37
some second-rate institution like this?

RUTH. I like my job. You're not going to convince me   38
otherwise.

SIMONE. Four-thousand two-hundred and ninety-eight.   39

RUTH. That is—?   40

SIMONE. Dollars. That's a lot of money. Do you think you're   41
worth it? Do you think *this class* is *worth* it? Because I figured it out:
this is a four credit class, I broke it down. Four-thousand two-
hundred and ninety-eight. Big ones. Well, do you think that what
you have to teach me is worth that? Come on, start talking and
we'll amortize for each word.

RUTH. You're clearly a bright girl. You can't expect an edu-   42
cation to be broken down into monetary terms.

SIMONE. You just did. That's a lot of money, right? It's, like,   43
food for a starving family in a fifth-world country for a year at
least. It's a car. Well, a used one, anyway. Minus the insurance.
Suddenly this number doesn't sound so huge. It's a couple of
Armani suits at most. I don't even like Armani. So hey, come on,
can't you even say "Yes, Simone, I am worth two Armani suits. I
have that to offer you . . ."

RUTH. I can't say that, no.   44

SIMONE. No useful skills to be had here.   45

RUTH. The money doesn't go into my pocket, by the way.   46

SIMONE. I think it should. It would be more direct that way;   47
you'd feel more of a responsibility. To me. Personally. Don't you
think, Dr. Ruth?

RUTH. I'd prefer that you not call me that.   48

SIMONE. Wrong kind of doctor, man. All you're interested in   49
is a bunch of books written a hundred years ago, and the books
written about those books; you're probably writing a book about
a book written about a book right now, am I right?

RUTH. If you don't see the connection between books and   50
life, you aren't reading very well. I want you to try. Can you do
that? Books might even show you a way to live.

SIMONE. I'm already living, Dr. Ruth. Are you? Because it   51
looks like you haven't changed your hair style in twenty-five years.

RUTH. You weren't even born then, Simone.   52

SIMONE. Stuck in your best year? Because I see you in a   53
close-cropped, spiky thing.

RUTH. That's enough.   54

SIMONE. P.S.: You might want to do something about the   55
way you dress.

RUTH. Have you been in therapy?   56

SIMONE. Don't think that's an original suggestion.   57

RUTH. I'm not suggesting anything. I simply want to point   58
out that this is not therapy. I am a teacher, not your therapist. You
can't just waltz into my office and say whatever hateful thing you
please.

SIMONE. I don't know how to waltz.   59

RUTH. I'm giving up here, Simone. You don't like my class,   60
you don't like me, you want to fail out, I can't stop you. (*RUTH
goes back to her work. SIMONE doesn't budge.*) What?

SIMONE. Drew Barrymore would move me.   61

RUTH. Who?   62

SIMONE. I think Drew would do it. Getting to meet Drew.   63

RUTH. Who is Drew Barrymore?   64

SIMONE. Damn, you really should know these things. She's   65
extremely famous. She's been famous since she was, like, born. I
saw her on TV yesterday and she was so real. She connected. You
know? You really might relate to your students better if you got a
little more up to date.

RUTH. You might be right. But you might not be so behind   66
in class if you spent a little less time watching television.

SIMONE. Drew is a *film* star, she's in *films.*   67

RUTH. You said you saw her on television.   68

SIMONE. Don't you even go to the movies? Probably only the   69
ones that are totally L-Seven. And I know you don't know what
that means. (*She makes an "L" and a "7" with her fingers.*) Square?
Anyway, Drew was on TV because she was being interviewed.
They have these daytime talk shows nowadays?

RUTH. I've heard of them.   70

SIMONE. And this chick was in the audience and she started   71
to cry. Because she couldn't believe she was there in the same
room with Drew, who's been famous forever, right? She was just,

like, sitting there sobbing. And this chick, she had her bleached blond hair pasted down real flat, and she was wearing a rhinestone barrette just like Drew used to, but that whole look is so old Drew, so ten-minutes-ago Drew. The new Drew is sleek and sophisticated and coiffed and this girl, this girl who wanted to be Drew so bad, she wasn't even *current*.

    RUTH. I don't think we're getting anywhere.   72

    SIMONE. And that is so sad. Because the thing about Drew is,   73
she's always changing. It's a constant thing with her, the change. And that is, like, what you've got to do . . . keep moving or you die. Drew knows that. How to invent yourself again and again so you can keep being someone that you like, the someone that you want to be. And once you're it, you've got to move on. Now where was it you were hoping we'd get to?

    RUTH. The exam is tomorrow morning at 9 AM. If you read   74
the material, any of the material, I might actually be able to give you a passing grade. But right now I don't think we need to waste any more of each other's time.

    SIMONE. (*Starts to go.*) You might have said that I go to the   75
movies the way you read books. I would have pointed that out, Dr. Ruth.

    RUTH. Well, I suspect we don't think very much alike.   76

(*SIMONE turns back.*)   77

    SIMONE. A wall between our souls? (*RUTH looks at her, about*   78
to say something, about to reach out.) I'm sorry if I've been rude. I'm sure a lot of people like your class. Maybe I wasn't raised well. I'm sure somebody's to blame.

(*SIMONE goes.*)   79

    RUTH. The next day she showed up at nine on the dot. I felt   80
a certain pride that I had somehow managed to reach her, that she was finally going to make a real effort, but she handed in her blue book after a matter of minutes. I was rather disgusted and let it sit there, until a pile formed on top of it, a pile of blue books filled with the scrawling, down-to-the-last-second pages of my other more eager, or at least more dutiful, students. Later I began to read them straight through from the top, in the order they were stacked in. I wasn't looking forward to Simone's.

In answering my essay question about how the novel *Anna*   81
Karenina moves inevitably toward Anna's final tragic act, my students were, for the most part, thorough and precise. They cited all
of the events that led to Anna's throwing herself in front of the
train, touching on the many parallel plots and the broader social
context. I was satisfied. I felt I had taught well this last semester.
My students had learned.

In the blue book she had written, "All happy people resemble   82
one another, but each unhappy person is unhappy in their own
way." So I guess she had read *Anna K;* the opening sentence, at
least. My first instinct was to correct the grammar of her little
variation. There was nothing else on the page. I flipped through
the book; she'd written one more line on the last page: "Any
world that I'm welcome to is better than the one that I come
from." I'm told it's a rock lyric. Something from the seventies.
Anna was written in the seventies, too, funnily enough, a century
earlier.

I would have given Simone an F, but I noticed she had already   83
marked down the failing grade herself, on the back of the book.
Or maybe the grade was for me.

By the time I came to it, days had passed. I didn't leap to con-   84
clusions. Come to think of it, Anna's suicide always takes me by
surprise as well, though I've read the novel many times and can
map its inexorable progression.

(*SIMONE, just as before* . . .)   85

SIMONE. That's a lot of money. Do you think you're worth   86
it? Do you think *this class* is *worth* it?

(*RUTH turns to her.*)   87

RUTH. I live in worlds made by words. Worlds where the   88
dead can speak, and conversations can be replayed, altered past the
moment of regret, held over and over until they are bent into new
possibilities.

(*RUTH tries to reach out* . . .)   89

SIMONE. Do you think I'm worth it? Am I? Am I? Am I?   90

RUTH. I live there, where death is as impermanent as an   91
anesthesia, and the moment of obliteration is only . . . a black-out.

(*SIMONE lights a cigarette as lights black out.*)   92

SIMONE. Ten minutes, time's up—told you I'd be gone by   93
now, baby.

(*The flame illuminates her for a moment, darkness again.*)   94

THE END   95

CHAPTER WRITING ASSIGNMENTS

Practicing Thinking, Reading, and Writing

1. In her essay, Rita Mae Brown claims, "Reading is an active moral and intellectual exchange." In what way is reading an "exchange." How does this notion make reading more interesting and worthwhile. Write an essay in which you explain how to engage in different types of reading material that a college student encounters. Anticipate questions that another student might ask.

2. Think about the details of your own writing process, and list all the activities, routines, rituals, and crises you go through to produce a good piece of writing. Then write a humorous essay that makes fun of your own writing process. Through satire, guide students to an understanding of the features of a good, functional writing process.

3. Discuss in an essay the differences between fiction, such as short stories and novels, and non-fiction, such as informational essays and excerpts from your college textbooks. How is each kind of reading important for a college student? What can we learn from each genre?

Exploring Ideas

1. In what ways do you believe television, video games, movies, computers, and other technology have affected reading? In an essay written to other college students, identify the ways technology has improved and/or decreased the reading skills of a particular group of people (for example, college students, children, people on the job).

2. If thought is at least partly language-based, how does our ability to use language influence our ability to think? Can we have a thought that we have no language to express? Write an essay that explores the effect language skills have on our ability to think.

3. Choose a word that has changed over a period of time. Think about what it meant originally and the connotations or meanings it has acquired over time. How do changes in our words reflect changes in our thinking? Write an essay that explores the way changes in language reflect changes in thought, using the initial word you chose as an example.

GLOSSARY OF USEFUL TERMS

Numbers in parentheses indicate pages in the text where the term is defined and/or examples are given. Italicized terms within definitions are also defined in this glossary.

Abstract (158–159) nouns, such as *truth* or *beauty,* are words that are neither specific nor definite in meaning; they refer to general concepts, qualities, and conditions that summarize an entire category of experience. Conversely, *concrete* terms, such as *apple, crabgrass, computer,* and *French horn,* make precise appeals to our senses. The word *abstract* refers to the logical process of abstraction, through which our minds are able to group together and describe similar objects, ideas, or attitudes. Most good writers use *abstract* terms sparingly in their *essays,* preferring instead the vividness and clarity of *concrete* words and phrases.

Allusion is a reference to a well-known person, place, or event from life or literature. In "Summer Rituals," for example, Ray Bradbury alludes to Herman Melville's great novel *Moby Dick* when he describes an old man who walks on his front porch "like Ahab surveying the mild day" (52).

Analogy (323) is an extended *comparison* of two dissimilar objects or ideas.

Analysis (2–3, 16, 17, 208–209, 576) is examining and evaluating a topic by separating it into its basic parts and elements and studying it systematically.

Anecdote (102) is a brief account of a single incident.

Argumentation (496–511) is an appeal predominantly to *logic* and reason. It deals with complex issues that can be debated.

Attitude (106, 108) describes the narrator's personal feelings about a particular subject. In "Past Present," Jimmy Santiago Baca shows his deep disdain for the prison system that kept him incarcerated for five agonizing years. *Attitude* is one component of *point of view.*

Audience (26, 37, 42–44, 214–215, 501–502, 504–506) refers to the person or group of people for whom an *essay* is written.

Cause and effect (440–454) is a form of *analysis* that examines the causes and consequences of events and ideas.

Characterization (109) is the creation of imaginary yet realistic persons in fiction, drama, and *narrative* poetry.

Chronological order (26, 108–109, 165, 214) is a sequence of events arranged in the order in which they occurred. Brent Staples follows this natural time sequence in his *example* essay entitled "A Brother's Murder."

Classification (265–276) is the analytical process of grouping together similar subjects into a single category or class; *division* works in the opposite fashion, breaking down a subject into many different subgroups. In "The Truth About Lying," Judith Viorst classifies lies into several distinct categories.

Clichés are words or expressions that have lost their freshness and originality through continual use. For example, "busy as a bee," "pretty as a picture," and "hotter than hell" have become trite and dull because of overuse. Good writers avoid clichés through vivid and original phrasing.

Climactic order (165) refers to the *organization* of ideas from one extreme to another—for example, from least important to most important, from most destructive to least destructive, or from least promising to most promising.

Cognitive skills (2–4) are mental abilities that help us send and receive verbal messages.

Coherence (165) is the manner in which an essay "holds together" its main ideas. A coherent *theme* will demonstrate such a clear relationship between its *thesis* and its logical structure that readers can easily follow the argument.

Comparison (322–337) is an *expository* writing technique that examines the similarities between objects or ideas, whereas *contrast* focuses on differences.

Conclusions (32, 504) bring *essays* to a natural close by summarizing the argument, restating the *thesis,* calling for some specific action, or explaining the significance of the topic just discussed. If the *introduction* states your thesis in the form of a question to be answered or a problem to be solved, then your *conclusion* will be the final "answer" or "solution" provided in your paper. The *conclusion* should be approximately the same length as your *introduction* and should leave your reader satisfied that you have actually "concluded" your discussion rather than simply run out of ideas to discuss.

Concrete: See *abstract.*

Conflict is the struggle resulting from the opposition of two strong forces in the plot of a play, novel, or short story.

Connotation and Denotation (505–506) are two principal methods of describing the meanings of words. *Connotation* refers to the wide array of positive and negative associations that most words naturally carry with them, whereas *denotation* is the precise, literal *definition* of a word that might be found in a dictionary. See, for example, Amy Tan's description of the terms "broken" or "fractured" English in "Mother Tongue" (193).

Content and Form (30–32) are the two main components of an *essay.* *Content* refers to the subject matter of an *essay,* whereas its *form* consists of the graphic symbols that communicate the subject matter (word choice, spelling, punctuation, paragraphing, etc.).

Contrast: See *comparison.*

Deduction (504–505) is a form of logical reasoning that begins with a *general* assertion and then presents specific details and *examples* in support of that *generalization. Induction* works in reverse by offering a number of *examples* and then concluding with a *general* truth or principle.

Definition (389–400) is a process whereby the meaning of a term is explained. Formal *definitions* require two distinct operations: (1) finding the *general* class to which the object belongs and (2) isolating the object within that class by describing how it differs from other elements in the same category. In "Grandma," for example, Erma Bombeck defines grandmothers as their grandchildren's mothers' mothers (402), and in "Ways to *Ai,*" Wang Ping explains the Chinese symbol for "love" as a drawing of a house enclosing a human heart (429).

Denotation: See *connotation*.

Description (36–50) is a mode of writing or speaking that relates the sights, sounds, tastes, smells, or feelings of a particular experience to its readers or listeners. Good descriptive writers, such as those featured in Chapter 1, are particularly adept at receiving, selecting, and expressing sensory details from the world around them. Along with *persuasion, exposition*, and *narration, description* is one of the four dominant types of writing.

Development (26–29) concerns the manner in which a *paragraph* of an essay expands on its topic.

Dialect is a speech pattern typical of a certain regional location, race, or social group that exhibits itself through unique word choice, pronunciation, and/or grammatical *usage*. See John McPhee's "The Pines," in which Fred and Bill, two residents of a wilderness area in southern New Jersey, speak in a discernible *dialect*.

Dialogue is a conversation between two or more people, particularly within a novel, play, poem, short story, or other literary work.

Diction (26, 505–506) is word choice. If a vocabulary is a list of words available for use, then good *diction* is the careful selection of those words to communicate a particular subject to a specific *audience*. Different types of *diction* include *formal* (scholarly books and articles), *informal* (essays in popular magazines), *colloquial* (conversations between friends, including newly coined words and expressions), *slang* (language shared by certain social groups), *dialect* (language typical of a certain region, race, or social group), *technical* (words that make up the basic vocabulary of a specific area of study, such as medicine or law), and *obsolete* (words no longer in use).

Division: See *classification*.

Documented essay (575–592) is a research or library paper that integrates *paraphrases, summaries,* and *quotations* from secondary sources with the writer's own insights and conclusions. Such *essays* normally include bibliographic references within the paper and, at the end, a list of the books and articles cited.

Dominant impression (40, 41–42, 43) in *descriptive* writing is the principal effect the author wishes to create for the *audience*.

Editing (30–31) is an important part of the *rewriting* process of an *essay* that requires writers to make certain their work observes the conventions of standard written English.

Effect: See *cause and effect.*

Emphasis (103, 503) is the stress given to certain words, phrases, sentences, and/or *paragraphs* within an *essay* by such methods as repeating important ideas; positioning thesis and *topic sentences* effectively; supplying additional details or *examples;* allocating more space to certain sections of an *essay;* choosing words carefully; selecting and arranging details judiciously; and using certain mechanical devices, such as italics, underlining, capitalization, and different colors of ink.

Essay is a relatively short prose composition on a limited topic. Most *essays* are five hundred to one thousand words long and focus on a clearly definable question to be answered or problem to be solved. *Formal essays,* such as bell hooks' "Justice: Childhood Love Lesson," are generally characterized by seriousness of *purpose,* logical organization, and dignity of language; *informal essays,* such as Garrison Keillor's "How the Crab Apple Grew," are generally brief, humorous, and more loosely structured. *Essays* in this textbook have been divided into nine traditional *rhetorical* types, each of which is discussed at length in its chapter introduction.

Etymology (394) is the study of the origin and development of words.

Evidence (497, 501, 503–504, 606) is any material used to help support an *argument,* including details, facts, *examples,* opinions, and expert testimony. Just as a lawyer's case is won or lost in a court of law because of the strength of the *evidence* presented, so, too, does the effectiveness of a writer's essay depend on the evidence offered in support of its *thesis statement.*

Example (158–170) is an illustration of a *general* principle or *thesis statement.* Harold Krents's "Darkness at Noon," for instance, gives several different examples of prejudice against handicapped people.

Exposition is one of the four main *rhetorical* categories of writing (the others are *persuasion, narration,* and *description*). The principal purpose of expository prose is to "expose" ideas to your readers, to explain, define, and interpret information through one or more of the following modes of exposition: *example, process analysis, division/classi-fication, comparison/contrast, definition,* and *cause/effect.*

Figurative language (44, 505) is writing or speaking that purposefully departs from the literal meanings of words to achieve a particularly vivid, expressive, and/or imaginative image. When, for example, Bernard Cooper says that the truth "is never naked, but always wearing some disguise" (97), he is using *figurative language.* Other principal figures of speech include *metaphor, simile, hyperbole, allusion,* and *personification.*

Flashback (109) is a technique used mainly in *narrative* writing that enables the author to present scenes or conversations that took place prior to the beginning of the story.

Focus (24–27) is the concentration of a *topic* on one central point or issue.

Form: See *content.*

Formal essay: See *essay.*

Free association (22) is a process of generating ideas for writing through which one thought leads randomly to another.

General (158–159) words are those that employ expansive categories, such as *animals, sports, occupations,* and *clothing; specific* words are more limiting and restrictive, such as *koala, lacrosse, computer programmer,* and *bow tie.* Whether a word is *general* or *specific* depends at least somewhat on its context: *Bow tie* is more specific than *clothing,* yet less *specific* than "the pink and green striped bow tie Aunt Martha gave me last Christmas." See also *abstract.*

Generalization (158–159, 161, 505) is a broad statement or belief based on a limited number of facts, *examples,* or statistics. A product of inductive reasoning, generalizations should be used carefully and spar-ingly in *essays.*

Hyperbole, the opposite of *understatement,* is a type of *figurative language* that uses deliberate exaggeration for the sake of emphasis or comic effect (e.g., "hungry enough to eat 20 chocolate eclairs").

Hypothesis (445, 576) is a tentative theory that can be proved or dis-proved through further investigation and analysis.

Idiom refers to a grammatical construction unique to a certain people, region, or class that cannot be translated literally into another language.

Illustration (158–159) is the use of *examples* to support an idea or *generalization*.

Imagery (42–44) is *description* that appeals to one or more of our five senses. See, for example, Malcolm Cowley's description in "The View from 80" of one of the pleasures of old age: "simply sitting still, like a snake on a sun-warmed stone, with a delicious feeling of indolence that was seldom attained in earlier years" (88). Imagery is used to help bring clarity and vividness to descriptive writing.

Induction: See *deduction*.

Inference (504–505) is a *deduction* or *conclusion* derived from *specific* information.

Informal essay: See *essay*.

Introduction (32) refers to the beginning of an *essay*. It should identify the subject to be discussed, set the limits of that discussion, and clearly state the *thesis* or general *purpose* of the paper. In a brief (five-*paragraph*) *essay*, your *introduction* should be only one *paragraph;* for longer papers, you may want to provide longer introductory sections. A good *introduction* will generally catch the audience's attention by beginning with a quotation, a provocative statement, a personal *anecdote*, or a stimulating question that somehow involves its readers in the topic under consideration. See also *conclusion*.

Irony (174) is a figure of speech in which the literal, *denotative* meaning is the opposite of what is stated.

Jargon is the special language of a certain group or profession, such as psychological *jargon*, legal *jargon*, or medical *jargon*. When *jargon* is excerpted from its proper subject area, it generally becomes confusing or humorous, as in "I have a latency problem with my backhand" or "I hope we can interface tomorrow night after the dance."

Levels of thought (1–2) is a phrase that describes the three sequential stages at which people think, read, and write: literal, interpretive, and analytical.

Logic (497, 504) is the science of correct reasoning. Based principally on *inductive* or *deductive* processes, *logic* establishes a method by which we can examine *premises* and *conclusions*, construct *syllogisms*, and avoid faulty reasoning.

Logical fallacy (441–443) is an incorrect conclusion derived from faulty reasoning. See also *post hoc, ergo propter hoc,* and *non sequitur.*

Metaphor (44–45, 505–506) is an implied *comparison* that brings together two dissimilar objects, persons, or ideas. Unlike a *simile,* which uses the words *like* or *as,* a *metaphor* directly identifies an obscure or difficult subject with another that is easier to understand. For example, when Bernard Cooper claims that he is "lost in the folds and bones" of his body (97), he is using a metaphor to describe the way in which his middle-aged self seems suddenly alien to him.

Mood (108, 505–506) refers to the atmosphere or *tone* created in a piece of writing. The mood of Jill Leslie Rosenbaum and Meda Chesney-Lind's "Appearance and Delinquency: A Research Note" is serious and scholarly; of Jessica Mitford's "Behind the Formaldehyde Curtain," sarcastic and derisive; and of Mary Roach's "Meet the Bickersons," good-humored and sensible.

Narration (102–116) is storytelling: the recounting of a series of events, arranged in a particular order and delivered by a narrator to a specific *audience* with a clear *purpose* in mind. Along with *persuasion, exposition,* and *description,* it is one of the four principal types of writing.

Non sequitur, from a Latin phrase meaning "it does not follow," refers to a *conclusion* that does not logically derive from its *premises.*

Objective (37, 41) writing is detached, impersonal, and factual; *subjective* writing reveals the author's personal feelings and attitudes. Judith Wallerstein and Sandra Blakeslee's "Second Chances for Children of Divorce" is an *example* of *objective* prose, whereas Amy Tan's "Mother Tongue" is essentially *subjective* in nature. Most good college-level *essays* are a careful mix of both approaches, with lab reports and technical writing toward the *objective* end of the scale and personal *essays* in composition courses at the *subjective* end.

Organization (26, 30–31, 102, 108–109, 164–165, 214–215, 503–506) refers to the order in which a writer chooses to present his or her ideas to the reader. Five main types of *organization* may be used to develop *paragraphs* or *essays:* (1) *deductive* (moving from general to specific), (2) *inductive* (from specific to general), (3) *chronological* (according to time sequence), (4) *spatial* (according to physical relationship in space), and (5) *climactic* (from one extreme to another, such as least important to most important).

Paradox is a seemingly self-contradictory statement that contains an element of truth. In "The View from 80," Malcolm Cowley paradoxically declares that the Ojibwa Indians were "kind to their old people" by killing them when they became decrepit (82).

Paragraphs are groups of interrelated sentences that develop a central topic. Generally governed by a *topic sentence, a paragraph* has its own *unity* and *coherence* and is an integral part of the logical *development* of an *essay.*

Parallelism is a structural arrangement within sentences, *paragraphs,* or entire *essays* through which two or more separate elements are similarly phrased and developed. Look, for example, at William Least Heat-Moon's first childhood experience eating fresh fish in New Orleans: "I was on my way to becoming a citizen of America, for it was there I began a lifetime of conjoining places and cultures, accents and aromas, ice cream sodas and oysters" (179).

Paraphrase (579–580) is a restatement in your own words of someone else's ideas or observations.

Parody is making fun of a person, an event, or a work of literature through exaggerated imitation.

Person (44, 108) is a grammatical distinction identifying the speaker or writer in a particular context: first person (I or we), second person (you), and third person (he, she, it, or they). The *person* of an *essay* refers to the voice of the narrator. See also *point of view.*

Personification is *figurative language* that ascribes human characteristics to an abstraction, animal, idea, or inanimate object. Consider, for example, Robert Ramirez's description in "The Barrio" of the bakery that "sends its sweet messenger aroma down the dimly lit street, announcing the arrival of fresh, hot, sugary *pan dulce*" (411).

Persuasion (496–511) is one of the four chief forms of *rhetoric.* Its main purpose is to convince a reader (or listener) to think, act, or feel a certain way. It involves appealing to reason, to emotion, and/or to a sense of ethics. The other three main *rhetorical* categories are *exposition, narration,* and *description.*

Point of view (44, 108) is the perspective from which a writer tells a story, including *person, vantage point,* and *attitude.* Principal *narrative* voices are first-person, in which the writer relates the story from his or her own vantage point "I've often wondered if I would have been a different person had I not been physically handicapped" (384) from "You're Short, Besides!" (by Sucheng Chan); omniscient, a third-person technique in which the narrator knows everything and can even see into the minds of the various characters; and concealed, a third-person method in which the narrator can see and hear events but cannot look into the minds of the other characters.

Post hoc, ergo propter hoc (442–443), a Latin phrase meaning "after this, therefore because of this," is a *logical fallacy* confusing *cause and effect* with *chronology*. Just because Cheryl wakes up every morning before the sun rises doesn't mean that the sun rises *because* Cheryl wakes up.

Premise (503–506) is a proposition or statement that forms the foundation of an *argument* and helps support a *conclusion*. See also *logic* and *syllogism*.

Prereading (5–8, 20) is thoughtful concentration on a topic before reading an *essay*. Just as athletes warm up their physical muscles before competition, so, too, should students activate their "mental muscles" before reading or writing *essays*.

Prewriting (21–27, 30–31), which is similar to *prereading,* is the initial stage in the composing process during which writers consider their topics, generate ideas, narrow and refine their *thesis statements,* organize their ideas, pursue any necessary research, and identify their *audiences*. Although prewriting occurs principally, as the name suggests, "before" an essay is started, writers usually return to this "invention" stage again and again during the course of the writing process.

Process analysis (208–220), one of the seven primary modes of *exposition,* either gives directions about how to do something (directive) or provides information on how something happened (informative).

Proofreading (32), an essential part of *rewriting,* is a thorough, careful review of the final draft of an *essay* to ensure that all errors have been eliminated.

Purpose (26, 40, 42–43, 501–502, 506) in an *essay* refers to its overall aim or intention: to entertain, inform, or persuade a particular *audience* with reference to a specific topic (to persuade an audience, for example, that violence on television and in video games is psychologically damaging our children in Dave Grossman's "We Are Training Our Kids to Kill"). See also *dominant impression.*

Refutation is the process of discrediting the *arguments* that run counter to your *thesis statement*.

Revision (30–31, 32), meaning "to see again," takes place during the entire writing process as you change words, rewrite sentences, and shift *paragraphs* from one location to another in your *essay*. It plays an especially vital role in the *rewriting* stage of the composing process.

Rewriting (30–31, 32) is a stage of the composing process that includes *revision, editing,* and *proofreading*.

Rhetoric is the art of using language effectively.

Rhetorical questions are intended to provoke thought rather than bring forth an answer. See, for example, Jay Weiner's opening rhetorical question in "Sports Centered": "How far back must we go to remember that sports matter?" (242).

Rhetorical strategy or mode is the plan or method whereby an *essay* is organized. Most writers choose from methods discussed in this book, such as *narration, example, comparison/contrast, definition,* and *cause/effect*.

Sarcasm is a form of *irony* that attacks a person or belief through harsh and bitter remarks that often mean the opposite of what they say. See, for example, Jessica Mitford's sarcastic praise of the funeral director in "Behind the Formaldehyde Curtain": "He has relieved the family of every detail, he has revamped the corpse to look like a living doll, he has arranged for it to nap for a few days in a slumber room, he has put on a well-oiled performance in which the concept of *death* has played no part whatsoever. . . . He has done everything in his power to make the funeral a real pleasure for everybody concerned" (238). See also *satire*.

Satire is a literary technique that attacks foolishness by making fun of it. Most good satires work through a "fiction" that is clearly transparent. Bill Cosby, for example, feigns amazement that anyone would ever want to have children in "The Baffling Question," yet he clearly loves kids and believes the opposite.

Setting refers to the immediate environment of a *narrative* or *descriptive* piece of writing: the place, time, and background established by the author.

Simile (44–45, 505) is a *comparison* between two dissimilar objects that uses the words *like* or *as*. See, for example, Ray Bradbury's description of the women in "Summer Rituals," who appear "like ghosts hovering momentarily behind the door screen" (53). See also *metaphor.*

Slang is casual conversation among friends; as such, it is inappropriate for use in formal and informal writing, unless it is placed in quotation marks and introduced for a specific rhetorical purpose: "Hey dude, what's up?" See also *colloquial expressions.*

Spatial order (103, 165) is a method of *description* that begins at one geographical point and moves onward in an orderly fashion. See, for example, the opening of John McPhee's "The Pines," which first describes the front yard of Fred Brown's house, then moves through the vestibule and into the kitchen, and finally settles on Fred himself, who is seated behind a porcelain-topped table in a room just beyond the kitchen (73).

Specific: See *general.*

Style is the unique, individual way in which each author expresses his or her ideas. Often referred to as the "personality" of an *essay, style* is dependent on a writer's manipulation of *diction,* sentence structure, *figurative language, point of view, characterization, emphasis, mood, purpose, rhetorical strategy,* and all the other variables that govern written material.

Subjective: See *objective.*

Summary (580) is a condensed statement of someone else's thoughts or observations.

Syllogism (505) refers to a three-step *deductive argument* that moves logically from a major and a minor *premise* to a *conclusion.* A traditional example is "All men are mortal. Socrates is a man. Therefore, Socrates is mortal."

Symbol refers to an object or action in literature that metaphorically represents something more important than itself. In Wang Ping's "Ways to *Ai,*" for instance, the Chinese graphic symbol for "love" is representative of an entire series of interrelated emotions.

Synonyms are terms with similar or identical *denotative* meanings, such as *aged, elderly, older person,* and *senior citizen.*

Syntax describes the order in which words are arranged in a sentence and the effect that this arrangement has on the creation of meaning.

Thesis statement or thesis (26) is the principal *focus* of an *essay*. It is usually phrased in the form of a question to be answered, a problem to be solved, or an assertion to be argued. The word *thesis* derives from a Greek term meaning "something set down," and most good writers find that "setting down" their thesis in writing helps them tremendously in defining and clarifying their topic before they begin to write an outline or a rough draft.

Tone (108, 505) is a writer's *attitude* or *point of view* toward his or her subject. See also *mood*.

Topic sentence is the central idea around which a *paragraph* develops. A *topic sentence* controls a *paragraph* in the same way a *thesis statement* unifies and governs an entire essay. See also *induction* and *deduction*.

Transition (109) is the linking together of sequential ideas in sentences, paragraphs, and essays. This linking is accomplished primarily through word repetition, pronouns, parallel constructions, and such transitional words and phrases as *therefore, as a result, consequently, moreover,* and *similarly*.

Understatement, the opposite of *hyperbole,* is a deliberate weakening of the truth for comic or emphatic purpose. Commenting, for example, on the great care funeral directors take to make corpses look lifelike for their funerals, Jessica Mitford explains in "Behind the Formaldehyde Curtain," "This is a rather large order, since few people die in the full bloom of health" (234).

Unity (164–165) exists in an *essay* when all ideas originate from and help support a central *thesis statement*.

Usage (30–31, 32) refers to the customary rules that govern written and spoken language.

Vantage point (44, 108) is the frame of reference of the narrator in a story: close to the action, far from the action, looking back on the past, or reporting on the present. See also *person* and *point of view*.

CREDITS

INDEX OF AUTHORS AND TITLES

"America Must Take Stronger Measures to Halt Illegal Immigration" (Scott), 558–563

Angelou, Maya, 124

"Appearance and Delinquency: A Research Note" (Rosenbaum, Chesney-Lind), 603–616

Baca, Jimmy Santiago, 345

"Baffling Question, The" (Cosby), 171–176

Baker, Russell, 130

"Barrio, The" (Ramirez), 409–416

"Beauty: When the Other Dancer Is the Self" (Walker), 483–494

Beber, Neena, 657

"Behind the Formaldehyde Curtain" (Mitford), 229–240

"Beliefs About Families" (Pipher), 417–425

Blakeslee, Sandra, 295

Bliss, Edwin, 221

Bombeck, Erma, 401

"Books" (Collins), 653–654

Bourland, Julia, 255

Bradbury, Ray, 51

"Broken Cord, The" (Dorris), 462–469

"Brother's Murder, A" (Staples), 200–206

Brown, Rita Mae, 622

"Calculated Risks" (Cole), 283–294

"Catch" (Francis), 655–656

Catton, Bruce, 338

Chan, Sucheng, 376

Chesney-Lind, Meda, 603

Cisneros, Sandra, 141

Cole, K.C., 283

Collins, Billy, 653

"Confessions of an Ex-Smoker" (Zimring), 305–311

Cooper, Bernard, 94

Cosby, Bill, 171

Cowley, Malcolm, 81

"Darkness at Noon" (Krents), 184–189

"Don't Let Stereotypes Warp Your Judgment" (Heilbroner), 524–530

Dorris, Michael, 462

"Ecstasy of War, The" (Ehrenreich), 593–602

Ehrenreich, Barbara, 593

"Embedded Reporters Make for Good Journalism" (Shaw), 546–549

"Engage in Word Play" (Formichelli), 248–254

Ewers, Justin, 550

"Fear of Losing a Culture, The" (Rodriguez), 470–476

"For My Indian Daughter" (Sawaquat), 117–123

Formichelli, Linda, 248

Francis, Robert, 655

"Getting Out of Debt (and Staying Out)" (Bourland), 255–263

"Glass" (Francis), 655

Goodman, Ellen, 433

"Grandma" (Bombeck), 401–408

"Grant and Lee: A Study in Contrasts" (Catton), 338–344

Grossman, Dave, 531

Heat-Moon, William Least, 177
Heilbroner, Robert, 524
hooks, bell, 512
"How the Crab Apple Grew" (Keillor), 148–156

"'I Am Writing Blindly'" (Rosenblatt), 620–621
"Illegal Immigration Does Not Threaten America" (Raynor), 564–573
"Is the New News Good News?" (Ewers), 550–555

"Japanese and American Workers: Two Casts of Mind" (Ouchi), 357–366
"Justice: Childhood Love Lessons" (hooks), 512–523

Keillor, Garrison, 148
King, Stephen, 455
Krents, Harold, 184

"Labyrinthine" (Cooper), 94–100
"Library Card, The" (Wright), 629–637

"Managing Your Time" (Bliss), 221–228
McPhee, John, 72
"Meet the Bickersons" (Roach), 477–482
"Memory: Tips You'll Never Forget" (Schneider), 277–282
"Misreadings" (Beber), 657–663
Mitford, Jessica, 229
"Mother Tongue" (Tan), 190–199

"New Directions" (Angelou), 124–129
"Notes from the Country Club" (Wozencraft), 58–71

"Only daughter" (Cisneros), 141–147
Ouchi, William, 357

"Past Present" (Baca), 345–356
"Pines, The" (McPhee), 72–80

Pipher, Mary, 417
"Politics of Muscle, The" (Steinem), 367–375

Ramirez, Robert, 409
Raynor, Richard, 564
"Red, White and Blue Highways" (Heat-Moon), 177–183
Roach, Mary, 477
Rodriguez, Richard, 470
Rosenbaum, Jill Leslie, 603
Rosenblatt, Roger, 620
Row, Jess, 638

"Saturday Evening Post, The" (Baker), 130–140
Sawaquat, Lewis, 117
Schneider, Phyllis, 277
Scott, Michael, 558
"Second Chances for Children of Divorce" (Wallerstein, Blakeslee), 295–304
"Secrets of Bats, The" (Row), 638–652
Shaw, David, 546
"Sports Centered" (Weiner), 241–247
Staples, Brent, 200
Steinem, Gloria, 367
"Summer Rituals" (Bradbury), 51–57

Tan, Amy, 190
Thomas, Lewis, 11
"To Err Is Human" (Thomas), 11–15
"Truth About Lying, The" (Viorst), 312–320

"View from 80, The" (Cowley), 81–93
Viorst, Judith, 312

Walker, Alice, 483
Wallerstein, Judith, 295
Wang Ping, 426
"Ways to *Ai*" (Wang), 426–432
"We Are Training Our Kids to Kill" (Grossman), 531–543

Weiner, Jay, 241
"Why We Crave Horror Movies"
  (King), 455–461
"Working Community, A"
  (Goodman), 433–438
Wozencraft, Kimberly, 58
Wright, Richard, 629

"Writing as a Moral Act" (Brown),
  622–628

"You're Short, Besides!" (Chan),
  376–387

Zimring, Franklin, 305